CULINARIA
FRANCE

CULINARIA
FRANCE

André Dominé • Editor

Günter Beer • Photography

Peter Feierabend • Art direction

Martina Schlagenhaufer • Language editor

Michael Ditter • Coordination

h.f.**ullmann**

Abbreviations and Quantities

1 oz	= 1 ounce = 28 grams
1 lb	= 1 pound = 16 ounces
1 cup	= 8 ounces = 16 ounces
1 cup	= 8 fluid ounces = 250 milliliters (liquids)
2 cups	= 1 pint (liquids)
8 pints	= 4 quarts = 1 gallon (liquids)
1g	= 1 gram = 1/1000 kilogram
1kg	= 1 kilogram = 1000 grams = 2 ¼ lb
1 l	= 1 liter = 1000 milliliters (ml) = approx 34 fluid ounces
125 milliliters (ml)	= approx. 8 tablespoons
1 tbsp	= 1 level tablespoon = 15–20g (see below) = 15 milliliters (liquids)
1 tsp	= 1 level teaspoon = 3–5g (see below) = 5ml (liquids)

Where measurements of dry ingredients are given in spoons, this always refers to the prepared ingredient as described in the wording immediately following, e.g. 1 tbsp chopped onions BUT: 1 onion, peeled and chopped.

The weight of dry ingredients varies significantly depending on the density factor; e.g. 1 cup flour weighs less than 1 cup butter.
Quantities in recipes have been rounded up or down for convenience, where appropriate. Metric conversions may therefore not correspond exactly. It is important to use either American or metric measurements within a recipe.

Quantities in recipes

Recipes serve 4 people, unless stated otherwise.
Exception: Recipes for drinks (quantities given per person) and recipes for foods to be served at a buffet (for an unspecified number of people, who will serve themselves).

© 2004/2007 Tandem Verlag GmbH
h.f.ullmann is an imprint of Tandem Verlag GmbH

Photography Assistant: Markus Bassler
Maps: Astrid Fisher-Leitl, Munich
Layout: Georg Windheuser, Michael Ditter

Original title: *Französische Spezialitäten*
ISBN 978-3-8331-1048-1

© 2008 for this edition: Tandem Verlag GmbH
h.f.ullmann is an imprint of Tandem Verlag GmbH

Special edition

Translation from German: Mo Croasdale, David Hefford, Michelle McMeekin,
Elaine Richards, Tim Shepard in association with First Edition Translation Ltd,
Cambridge
Edited and typeset in association with First Edition Translation Ltd, Cambridge
Project Coordination: Bettina Kaufmann and Nadja Bremse
Cover design: Peter Feierabend and Claudio Martinez
Front cover photo: © Tandem Verlag GmbH/Ruprecht Stempell
Back cover photo: © Tandem Verlag GmbH/Günther Beer, www.beerfoto.com

Printed in China

ISBN 978-3-8331-4887-3

10 9 8 7 6 5 4 3 2
X IX VIII VII VI V IV III II

www.ullmann-publishing.com

Contents

France, bordered by the Ardennes, Alps, and Pyrenees, the Atlantic, Rhine, and Mediterranean, offers a great variety of both sophisticated and wholesome foods, a superb array of drinks to accompany the food, and an unending selection of mouthwatering sweets and desserts. Even a comprehensive book like this one cannot do justice to them all. So rather than presenting a general picture of French food, we have focused on certain selected products, which will highlight the flair, expertise, and skill of famous and less well-known chefs and cooks who have created such masterpieces. In all regions of the country we have observed many of these craftsmen at work. We have shared some of their experiences, appreciated their benchmarks for quality and discovered how special tastes and flavors are achieved. Against the backdrop of the beautiful and varied French landscape we have also come to understand how nature first creates the right conditions for many foods and drinks, be they butter or biscuits, Camembert or Champagne, lobster or lentils, peppers or pullets. Due to this diversity, in practise it has been difficult to keep to the geographical frontiers we had established on paper. We have therefore redefined the French regions from the culinary point of view. We

have been enthralled by stories about the old traditions and have witnessed the highest standards of cooking. We devised a systematic approach for our research and found a new way of looking at food and drink. Our hosts have been very friendly throughout France and have made us feel at home, eagerly inviting us into their kitchens, homes, and cellars, sharing with us the secrets of the trade. Each visit, each meeting, each photo session has enriched the wealth of information in our book. In time, from the thousands of pieces of our mosaic, a clear picture of the tastes and preferences of a nation of gourmets has emerged. France is a country in which everyday men and women, gardeners and farmers, cooks and caterers, bakers and cakemakers, butchers and cheesemakers, winegrowers and distillers, professionals and amateurs all have a strong awareness of tradition, and fantastic imagination. They are people with great commitment and passion for their chosen profession. The picture conjured up is of a heavenly abundance of high quality food and drink, both highly sophisticated and simple. If our book can convey a true impression of French lifestyle, our thanks should go to those people.

André Dominé

Paris
Île-de-France

Sharon Sutcliffe

In Paris people love eating out in smart restaurants, bustling brasseries, and friendly bistros.

Each year in the fall Parisians celebrate the arrival of the grapes in Montmartre.

The insatiable appetite of its inhabitants and the ingenuity of its cooks have made Paris the undisputed good food capital of the world. Its twenty districts or *arrondissements*, encircling Notre Dame, are home to countless delights: the small traditionally run bakers' shops, offering their crispy baguettes, lavishly stocked cheese shops, and overflowing delicatessens, where truffles, *foie gras*, and caviar are laid out like precious jewels. One should not forget to mention pâtisseries offering mouthwatering pastries which reveal their creators to be artists as well as skilled bakers. Ingredients of all descriptions are on offer, from the overtly exotic to the modestly simple.

In the past, even in hard times of famine, there was always a variety of produce but this was often very expensive. The River Seine brought exquisite products from Champagne, Burgundy, Normandy, and from the Auvergne to Paris along with the limited supplies of fresh produce from the surrounding Ile-de-France. In those days Parisians enthused about peaches from Montreuil, cherries from Montmorency, and asparagus from Argenteuil. And where the Eiffel Tower stands today there were once large vineyards.

Most of the villages, supplying the capital were eventually swallowed up by Paris. All that remains are the fresh mushrooms and game from the forests of Fontainebleau, delicious chickens from Houdan, and the generous rounds of soft Brie from Meaux and Melun. People often say that Paris does not really have a culinary identity of its own but dishes such as *Entrecôte Bercy*, *Hachis Parmentier*, *Navarin d'agneau*, as well as many soups and sauces, prove just the opposite.

Since the first restaurant opened some 200 years ago, the gastronomical spirit of discovery and culinary creativity has flourished. To be precise it was the French Revolution in 1789 that led to the creation of first-class restaurants, after the execution at the guillotine of the rich aristocrats who had previously employed the chefs and kitchen staff.

Eating out as a general leisure activity only began to be a really common event after the Second World War. Today Parisian palates are pampered by chefs from all the regions of the country and from distant parts of the world. Chefs are still constantly discovering new, exciting recipes, which travel the globe and affirm France's outstanding culinary reputation.

Les Halles

In 1969, plagued by traffic jams, mountains of rubbish, vermin and theft, the Paris market was at the center of a highly controversial decision. After 800 years it was relocated to Rungis, near Orly airport, to a site where traffic conditions were much better. The gigantic halls, mockingly referred to as umbrellas, disappeared forever.

The market, moved from the site of the Saint-Lazare leper hospital to the right bank of the Seine, near the Cimetière des Innocents, by King Philippe Auguste in 1183, grew rapidly to a considerable size and attained significant economical importance despite the proximity of the vast cemetery. A wall surrounding the market allowed the authorities to raise duties and taxes but also provided a certain degree of law and order. Dishonest traders and thieves were put in the stocks and criminals guilty of more serious offences were sent to the gallows. Originally serving as a transshipment center for many types of goods in the 17th century, the market was used exclusively to sell fresh produce and in the 19th century, when Baron Haussmann commissioned the building of new, wide avenues through the city center, Napoleon III appointed the architect Victor Baltard to refurbish Les Halles. Its ten steel and glass halls were to become the symbol of the whole district. The backdrop of market stalls with their colorful array of exotic vegetables, mountains of fattened poultry, gleaming fish and whole sides of beef inspired Emile Zola to write his famous novel, *The Belly of Paris*, which became synonymous with the large market.

Before the move in 1969, night after night, thousands of trucks, coming from all the regions of France jammed the neighboring streets. Each street had been specialized in a specific product. There were no cash desks in the shops, no electronic till systems. Business was sealed with a handshake and no-one asked any tiresome questions. Deep into the night the best chefs from the finest Paris restaurants came personally to choose the ingredients they needed for the dishes that made their reputations. If they were unable to carry the provisions they had bought on their own, they could use the services of well-built porters, known as the *forts des Halles*. Porters had been organized in a guild since the 12th century and their rewards were based on set units: a unit was equivalent to a weight of approximately 440 pounds (200 kilograms) carried over a distance of almost 20 feet (6 meters). Gradually the responsibility for ensuring that traders kept to market regulations also fell to the *forts*.

While producers and dealers, shop owners and chefs haggled about the price of lamb or of lemons from Provence, nighthawks would stroll through Les Halles and head for the overcrowded bistros, some of which still survive today. There, alongside the professional visitors to the market, they would refresh themselves with bowls of steaming hot onion soup, browned over with plenty of golden-yellow cheese. The first homemakers would appear around seven in the morning in search of ingredients for the midday and evening meals. As soon as their shopping baskets were full to the brim, the noisy market would fall silent for a few hours. The clear chiming of the bell, *cloche* in French, was the eagerly awaited signal for vagrants from the city and countryside to rush to the stalls to pick up anything that was still edible, all the leftovers of the day. This is why the vagrants were called *clochards*.

In time, with their location right in the middle of the city, the halls became far too large and unmanagable and risked bringing the city to a standstill. In 1971, when President Georges Pompidou ordered the demolition of Baltard's halls (only one hall has been kept as a museum) to make way for the elegant and now extremely successful Forum des Halles shopping mall, it was the end of an era.

Rungis
The new "Belly of Paris"

Sentimentalists will certainly continue to mourn the passing of Les Halles, but Rungis proved long ago that the large modern-day market is infinitely more appropriate here. The largest, most extensive market in the world covers an area of almost 575 acres (232 hectares) of which more than 135 acres is covered. A further 11 acres of warehousing is planned. Just the parking areas alone cover some 145 acres. Rungis supplies 18 million European consumers, of whom 12 million are French. In total there are 1600 companies in Rungis, including 20 banks and 30 restaurants. Together they employ 14,000 people, including 10,500 in the wholesale trade. On each market day lasting from 11 o'clock in the evening to 6 o'clock in the morning, an average of 28,000 vehicles come to Rungis and its 28 giant halls, where 20,500 regular buyers get their supplies. As regards Paris and its neighboring areas, Rungis supplies 60 percent of the sea and freshwater produce, 50 percent of the fruit and vegetables, 45 percent of the meat and 50 percent of the cut flowers and potted plants. All transactions are processed electronically and monitored by the government to the nth degree. Visitors are welcome to visit Rungis but only professionals are allowed to buy there.

Fish
The fish hall turns over 23 percent of the overall volume of sea and freshwater fish, seafood and shellfish consumed in France. It provides annually
Seawater fish: 55,380 tons (50,240 tonnes)
Freshwater fish: 12,500 tons (11,360 tonnes), including 9,750 tons (8,650 tonnes) of salmon
Crustaceans: 10,950 tons (9,940 tonnes), including 1985 tons (1800 tonnes) of scampi 4630 tons (4200 tonnes) of prawns
Shellfish: 21,695 tons (19,680 tonnes), including 12,655 tons (11,480 tonnes) of mussels 4475 tons (4060 tonnes) of oysters

Meat
In total the quantity supplied, including produce in transit, amounts to 485,541 tons (440,480 tonnes).

Beef: 93,880 tons (85,170 tonnes)
Veal: 34,215 tons (31,040 tonnes)
Lamb: 45,670 tons (41,430 tonnes)
Pork: 114,640 tons (104,000 tonnes)
Organ meat: 41,335 tons (37,500 tonnes)
Poultry and game: 87,675 tons (79,540 tonnes)
Horse meat: 1785 tons (1620 tonnes)
In March 1998 the new organ meat hall, which had started operating the year before, was officially opened. It has since processed 31,415 tons (28,500 tonnes) of organ meat, more than a quarter of the French turnover in this sector.

Dairy produce and eggs
This sector amounts to a total of 219,180 tons (198,840 tonnes)
Cheese: 79,685 tons (72,290 tonnes)
Butter: 10,430 tons (9460 tonnes)
Eggs: 44,455 tons (40,330 tonnes)

Fruit and vegetables
26 percent of the national consumption is turned over here, of which only 28.5 percent of the fruit and 67.6 percent of the vegetables are of French origin. In total this is more than 1,350,300 tons (1,225,000 tonnes) of fruit and vegetables. See the following examples:
Bananas: 87,080 tons (79,000 tonnes)
Strawberries: 21,495 tons (19,500 tonnes)
Grapes: 46,970 tons (42,610 tonnes)
Melons: 44,530 tons (40,400 tonnes)
Tropical fruits: 79,365 tons (72,000 tonnes)
Artichokes: 11,575 tons (10,500 tonnes)
Carrots: 48,500 tons (44,000 tonnes)
Asparagus: 4750 tons (4310 tonnes)
Tomatoes: 115,860 tons (105,110 tonnes)

Garden produce
The centuries old tradition of Les Halles also includes flowers and plants. Rungis has proved itself in this field as well. Some 36 percent of the flowers come from France but almost 58 percent come from Holland.
Cut flowers: 460,000 boxes
Pot plants: 18,377,000 units
Christmas trees: 265,000 trees.

Opposite: The sturdy porters of the old market halls of Paris carried over 400 pounds (200 kilograms) on their shoulders.

Until 1971 most of the groceries for Paris were sold in ten halls like this.

A greeting from the world of the market traders: A picture postcard view of Les Halles.

15

Jean-Luc Poujauran in his shop: "The baker's art lies in his touch. He has to know how to handle the dough and what the dough should feel like."

The Baguette

In no other country has a simple loaf of bread become the symbol of an entire nation. The roughly 28-inch (70-centimeter) long crusty baguette, barely 100 years old, is considered typically French by the rest of the world, while the French themselves associate it with Paris. French townspeople were used to depending predominantly on their own immediate country-side for the supply of food. Since Roman times the broad Beauce plain served the town as a granary so Paris itself was rarely without bread. Notre Dame cathedral, begun in 1163, was built as a direct result of this abundance of cereals. Its magnificent stained glass windows were paid for by the local business people. The bakers, with four windows, donated more than any other guild, which underlines their status at the time. Going back to the 15th century, the bakers rolled their dough into balls, *boules* in French, from which the name *boulanger*, baker, was derived. Loaves were large and round, with a thick crust and compact crumb, which stayed unsalted, as salt was expensive. Bread was the staple diet of the population. The dark, coarse wholemeal bread was made from a mixture of different varieties of flour, as several types of cereal were frequently sown in the fields at the same time to lessen the risk of complete harvest failure caused by stem disease. The poorest of the poor, who could not even afford this rustic bread, bought *biscuit* (*bis-cuit* means baked twice), bread from the previous day, which was rebaked to keep it dry and stop it from becoming stale.

The method of removing bran in order to produce white bread was discovered only at the time of the Sun King, Louis XIV, who preferred fine white wheat bread. To produce this, bread yeast was added to the sourdough. The white bread baked from refined flour existed only in the towns, where it became a status symbol, as the nobility quickly discovered that their delicate stomachs were unable to digest anything else. Like all towns, Paris was at the mercy of bad harvests. The government's decree of 1787 to raise the price of cereals, a wretched harvest in the following year, capped by an extraordinarily hard winter were all factors which eventually lead to the Revolution.

The 18th century saw the appearance of the first long, slim loaves, which changed the crust-crumb ratio in favor of the crust, and which immediately became popular among Parisians. Thanks to the addition of yeast the baguette acquired its fine golden crust and its friable crumb texture. Fortunately for the bakers the growth of the popularity of the baguette came about at the same time as the advent of kneading machines, which made their work much easier. While the whole of Paris ate the breadstick with great relish, the country people continued to swear by the traditional wide, round loaves, and it took until well into the 20th century for the baguette to be accepted in the provinces.

The best baguettes are gold and crispy on the outside and the score marks in the dough have become raised features in the crust. Inside, the crumb should be cream-colored, not too white, as well as being supple and springy to the touch, with small holes and a delicate taste of milk and almonds. If the crust flakes away and the interior tastes of cotton wool or cardboard, the baguette is probably made of deep-frozen ready-made dough. Industrial baking methods shorten the kneading and proving times, which creates an insipid, white, large-pored crumb, which dries out quickly. This loss of moisture takes place on the surface, due to evaporation, with a resulting tough crust and harder interior. This is what sometimes happens in the case of supermarket bread, packed in cellophane with a neutral, harmless gas like nitrogen. This gives it a longer shelf life, because it doesn't go moldy, but it never really possesses the crustiness of a freshly baked loaf.

Unfortunately, since the sixties baking terminals have taken over, and the quality of the baguette has suffered so much that French consumers have either drastically reduced the amount of bread they consume or have turned to types of bread such as *pain complet* or *pain de campagne*, which today are considered more nutritious.

It is only thanks to a new generation of excellent bakers that the Parisians have gradually redis-covered what a baguette should really be like. One of them is Jean-Luc Poujauran, who uses rich flour slowly milled between two millstones and allows the dough to rise slowly but continuously in order to develop the taste. Starter dough, consisting of the leftovers of an older quantity of dough, is used to trigger fermentation and gives the dough a nutty taste like fresh yeast. Young bakers offer their customers a large selection of special rolls and loaves of different shapes and sizes, enriched with herbs, spices, nuts or dried fruit.

In France today there are 35,000 bakeries, producing 3.5 million tons (3.2 million tonnes) of bread a year. But each Frenchmen only eats 5 ounces (150 grams) of bread a day compared with 18 ounces (500 grams) in the 19th century. Every third loaf sold is a baguette. It is estimated that 10 million baguettes are sold a day.

Today the roles have changed. Unrefined wholemeal bread is considered healthy and is mainly bought by the well off, while simple folk resort to mass-produced white flour products. However, baguettes are still served with food as a matter of course in the majority of cafés and restaurants.

During baking the thin, approximately. 28-inch (70 centimeters) long baguette acquires that crispy, golden brown crustiness, which makes it so popular.

Lengths of dough are carefully laid out and left to prove, thereby improving both the taste and the crust.

To give the crust its appetizing crispiness, each baguette is carefully scored in advance by hand before they are baked.

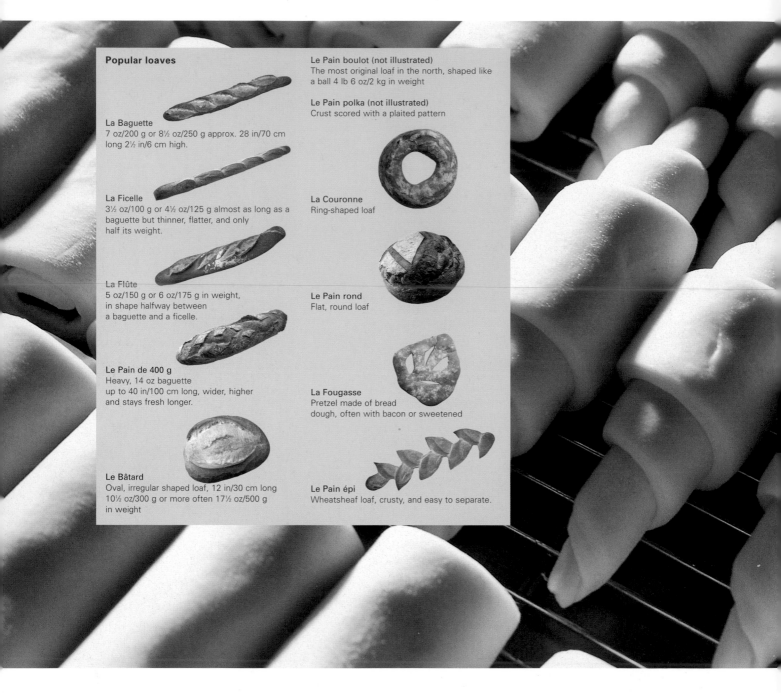

Popular loaves

La Baguette
7 oz/200 g or 8½ oz/250 g approx. 28 in/70 cm long 2½ in/6 cm high.

La Ficelle
3½ oz/100 g or 4½ oz/125 g almost as long as a baguette but thinner, flatter, and only half its weight.

La Flûte
5 oz/150 g or 6 oz/175 g in weight, in shape halfway between a baguette and a ficelle.

Le Pain de 400 g
Heavy, 14 oz baguette up to 40 in/100 cm long, wider, higher and stays fresh longer.

Le Bâtard
Oval, irregular shaped loaf, 12 in/30 cm long 10½ oz/300 g or more often 17½ oz/500 g in weight

Le Pain boulot (not illustrated)
The most original loaf in the north, shaped like a ball 4 lb 6 oz/2 kg in weight

Le Pain polka (not illustrated)
Crust scored with a plaited pattern

La Couronne
Ring-shaped loaf

Le Pain rond
Flat, round loaf

La Fougasse
Pretzel made of bread dough, often with bacon or sweetened

Le Pain épi
Wheatsheaf loaf, crusty, and easy to separate.

Parisian breakfast

For a typical Parisian breakfast, take a piece of baguette or small roll, croissant, brioche or a fruit bun, jam and butter. Sweet pastries are called *viennoiseries*, as it was wrongly assumed that they came from Vienna. They are Parisian inventions, for which puff or choux pastry and great quantities of butter are used. They are bought fresh every day and hardly anyone thinks of baking them themselves.

The most popular however is the croissant. Even if something that seems so essentially French actually originates from Hungary. The name means "crescent moon" and has its own history. At the end of the 17th century the Turks laid siege to the city of Budapest and, in order to subjugate the city, tunneled under the city walls. As the Hungarian bakers practiced their trade in the early hours of the morning, they were able to raise the alarm in time and the enemy failed in their attempt to capture the city. As a symbol of the victory the bakers baked the emblem of the Turkish Empire, the crescent moon, out of puff pastry. It caused a sensation in Vienna as well as in Budapest and it was the Austrian born Marie-Antoinette, Queen of France, who brought it with her to Paris in the 18th century. So as not to be disappointed, ask the baker for *croissants au beurre*, butter croissants.

Types of Parisian Bread

Pain au levain à l'ancienne
Bread made of flour, salt and water, proved with a sourdough starter.

Pain sportif
Made from a mixture of wheat, rye, soya flour, dried fruit, bran, and pumpkin seeds.

Pain de seigle
Rye bread made from a wheat flour starter dough, containing at least two-thirds rye. Eaten with salted butter to accompany seafood and oysters.

Pain au seigle
On paper the difference is slight but this bread has significantly higher wheat content than the previous one.

Pain complet
Yeast bread made of a mixture of various types of flour as well as wholemeal, bran and wheatgerm. Rich in vitamins, minerals and roughage.

Pain à l'ancienne
Made of unrefined, stone-ground flour, rich in bran, vitamins, and minerals and proved with sourdough.

Pain de campagne
Mixed wheat bread with 15 percent rye flour and sourdough. Generally a round, rustic style loaf, weighing about 17½ oz/500 g and with a thick crust often dusted with flour.

Pain au son
An intensive, tasty and especially richly textured wheat bread with a bran content of 20 to 25 percent.

Pain aux noix
Walnut bread, containing at least 15 percent nuts. A specialty from Alsace.

Baguette de campagne
The Parisians are particularly fond of this rich, delicious, and very crusty bread.

Pain de mie
Toast loaf, with added sugar, milk and butter, baked in a tin.

Pain de mie brioché
Its dough contains even more sugar and eggs.

Baguette viennoise
A baguette with a soft, gleaming deeply scored crust, a slightly sweet crumb and rich in milk. Sometimes butter or margarine may be added.

Brioche parisienne
Made of friable yeast dough, prepared with eggs, butter, milk, flour, and sugar, shaped into two balls of dough baked one on top of the other.

Seigle-Apricot & mini pain complet
Rye rolls with dried apricots and unrefined wholemeal rolls.

Seigle-Raisins
Rye rolls with raisins.

Pistolet
Light and crusty rolls mainly eaten on Sundays (originally from Belgium).

Pain campagne aux olives
Wholesome country loaf with black olives.

Pain aux fines herbes & pain à l'ail
Rolls with herbs and garlic bread.

Jockey pavot & sésame
Round wheat loaf with poppy and sesame seeds.

Pain à la confiture d'échalotte
Long bread stick with shallot preserve.

Fougasse aux olives
Round, flat loaf with olives.

Pain de campagne figues et noix
Rustic loaf with figs and walnuts.

Pain de campagne noisette et raisins
Delicious, rustic loaf with hazelnuts and raisins.

Napoléon
Crusty breakfast loaf.

Pavé de campagne
Square country loaf.

Coffee

What would Paris be without coffee and cafés? Most Parisians and the majority of all the French have a large bowl of *café au lait* for breakfast. Just a few prefer a medium-strong black coffee or stave off tiredness with a *petit noir*. As a rule, the small black espresso coffee is taken at the counter. For many it is simply part of their daily routine, dropping in at the café or bistro on the corner, before setting off for work. Many just content themselves with a cup of coffee at breakfast. This makes sense, as caffeine also stimulates conversion of the body's energy reserves, which are stored as fat.

Most coffee beans usually belong to one of two families: Robusta or Arabica. In Paris the landlord of the typical *café-bar-tabac* resorts to the traditional blend, which consists predominantly of Robusta beans, rich in caffeine and extremely bitter in taste. Despite the growing popularity of the more mellow Arabicas, preferred by coffee drinkers in the rest of Europe, the ordinary Robusta enjoys a loyal following in France. This has nothing to do with the much lower price, but rather with the fact that Robusta beans, less demanding when it comes to climate, location and ground conditions, were cultivated in the former French colonies in Africa and Asia. Robusta's caffeine content can be double that of Arabica, which supplies 75 percent of global coffee production. Arabica plants prefer an altitude of 1300 to 4300 feet (400 to 1300 meters) and the flavor of the beans very much depends on the area in which they are cultivated. Coming originally from Ethiopia, where today the finest *moka* beans are still harvested, the best Arabica beans nowadays come from Central and South America where the most favorable growing areas can be found.

The ripening process of the cherry-like fruit of the coffee tree takes eight to twelve months. The flesh of the fruit encloses at most two stones, each containing a seed encased in a thin skin. In order to obtain coffee beans, the flesh of the fruit and the skin of the stone have to be removed, either by drying or washing. In both cases raw green coffee is obtained with beans which still have about a 12 percent moisture content. To release their aroma and produce a good coffee they are then roasted.

Depending on the time and temperature of the roasting process the color and taste change. If they are only roasted for a short time, their color is light, the acidity is stronger but the actual taste of the coffee is weaker. The bitterness is more subtle but the caffeine content is higher. The stronger the roasting, the darker the color, the acidity dissipates and the bitterness is enhanced, with a lower caffeine content. The taste of coffee is at its best somewhere in between the two extremes. It comes from the light, thin coffee oil, which is soluble in water and which is extracted from the core of the beans and brought to their surface during the roasting process. For this reason beans roasted more intensely look more oily. If the heat is too strong the coffee oil evaporates together with its acidity and the caffeine.

In Arab countries, where the use of coffee began to spread in the 15th century, Venetian traders tasted it and introduced it to their home city around 1620. Via Venice, coffee reached central and northern Europe. By 1160 it was widely drunk in Marseille among merchants who traded with the Turkish empire. It was sold to the public through apothecaries. In 1669 the Turkish ambassador in Paris, Soliman Aga, taught Louis XIV to appreciate coffee. The first Parisian café – which still exists today as a restaurant – was opened in 1686 by a Sicilian called Procopio and, with the name *"Procope,"* it fast became the meeting place for literati and philosophers. Soon more cafés opened all over Paris, providing a totally new venue for people to get together and talk. The aroma of coffee accompanied the first intellectual and political exchanges on the development of modern forms of society. Cafés, at the outset unusually smart places, were by no

There are many small coffee shops in Paris, roasting their own coffee and bringing out the flavor of special coffee beans from many different parts of the world.

Elegant coffee makers play their part in the making of good coffee. In the background: *Le petit noir* served in the typically thick porcelain cup. For many Parisians this is how the day begins.

means just restricted to coffee and offered other attractions as well.

The *cafés chantants* or *cafés concerts* provided a stage for musical and variety shows. Many cafés specialized in exquisite ice creams and sorbets; others attracted people with their excellent cuisine. In the 19th century in Paris, the corner café became a local meeting place. Parisians would stop off at any time of day for a *petit noir* or for something a little stronger.

While today coffee multiples promote Arabica bean coffee on the French market with increasing success, French gourmets have discovered the delightfully wide range of exclusive coffees. Small family-run roasteries provide a tempting range of coffees of pure origins or of carefully balanced blends. And there are more and more restaurants which, at the end of the meal, offer their guests a multi-faceted selection of different coffees: from the powerful Moka to the more mellow, slightly bitter Colombian; from the low caffeine Brazilian to the more robust Kenyan; ranging from the original Malabar, the luxurious Blue Mountain of Jamaica or the legendary Maragogype of Mexico or Guatemala.

Coffee chicory

In ancient Egypt wild chicory was already highly regarded for its digestive properties and later was also used as a medicinal plant. In 1690 it was the Dutch who were the first to start the large-scale roasting of chicory. It became fash-

ionable in France just before the Revolution and during the continental blockade imposed by Napoleon on coffee imports. Unlike coffee, it contains no stimulants. In 1858 the Breton Jean Baptiste Alphonse Leroux founded his chicory factory in Orchies near Lille. Leroux today is one of the oldest family companies in France and produces almost 39,000 tons (35,000 tonnes) of roasted chicory per year, accounting for 40 percent of world production.

Chicory is available in three forms:
granulated or ground – added to coffee to mellow its taste
soluble – made of 100 percent chicory, served as a breakfast drink, now available in different flavors too as a general hot drink
liquid – as a liquid extract, suitable for drinking with water added but mainly used in cooking. It is blended with instant coffee.

Closely related to endive, which is very popular in France, whose shoots are prepared as a salad or steamed as a vegetable, coffee chicory also develops magnificent, slightly bitter roots. Through improved cultivation a weight of about 17½ ounces (500 grams) per piece has now been achieved. Its main area of cultivation is the French part of Flanders with its sandy, alluvial land. After harvesting, the roots are washed, thoroughly cleaned and sorted, then thinly sliced and diced. In a rotating, compressed air oven chicory looses 75 percent of its moisture and is dried into *cossettes*, which are stored dry for more than three months. Only then are they roasted. The length of the roasting process depends on the size of the pieces; the temperature ranges between 250 °F (120 °C) and 285 °F (140 °C). Roasting requires certain skills as it involves caramelizing the dried juice without burning it. Only in this way can the chicory keep its full flavor intact. After cooling, the *cossettes* should be hard and brittle enough to be ground. Normally to produce 2 pounds 3 ounces (1 kilogram) of roasted granules, 11 pounds 7 ounces (5.2 kilograms) of fresh roots are needed and no other substances are added to the chicory.

Loaves

Rogalik
Caraway bread
with roast onions
and sesame seed

Pain au cumin
Caraway bread

**Hala aux graines
de pavot**
Plaited loaf with
poppy seed

Hala aux raisins
Plaited loaf with
raisins

**Pain Razowy au seigle
noir**
Russian black rye bread

Jewish bread and other specialties

The Marais, today one of the most beautiful districts of Paris, was by no means always a highly sought-after place to live in. The marshes (*marais*) had been drained as early as the 13th century but up to 17th century members of the nobility never ventured there. When the celebrated writer Madame de Sévigné and other eminent ladies invited philosophers and speakers into their famous salons, the splendid Place des Vosges, the then Place Royale, and with it the entire district enjoyed a golden era. As a consequence of the Revolution the rich had to relinquish their town houses, the *hôtels particuliers*. The well-off moved to the west of the city and the district fell into disrepair. It was not until the 20th century, in the sixties, that the work of renovation began and today the Marais has rediscovered its former splendor.

The lively Jewish Quarter developed in the heart of the Marais. A small Jewish community was already established there in the Middle Ages. However, the largest influx came about at the end of the 19th century, after the arrival of Jewish refugees escaping from the pogroms in eastern Europe and Russia. Then in the sixties of the 20th century Sephardic Jews arrived from Algeria. To this day the Rue des Ecouffes and the Rue des Rosiers are lined with delicatessens and restaurants, offering a fascinating variety of Jewish specialties. The whole year round tra-

Bread, cakes, and pastries enjoy a special place among Jewish specialties and provide a truly cosmopolitan range of delicacies.

ditional Russian, Polish and Hungarian delicacies tempt people into the shops. Pickled herring and pickled gherkins, tasty *goulash* or nourishing *borscht*, salmon pasties or *helzel* (stuffed chicken necks) as well as a rich selection of sweet and savory breads and pastries are on offer. The Algerian Jews have brought their specialties too. The Jewish calendar is the persistent trigger for further culinary activity. At Rosh Hashanah, the Jewish New Year, it is traditional to give people honey cake as a present to start the New Year on a decidedly sweet note. Yom Kippur and other important events are celebrated with stuffed fish and the Festival of Lights, Hanukkah, with golden doughnuts filled with raspberry jelly.

Matzele'h aux graines de pavot
Tasty breadroll with poppy seed

Matzele'h aux graines de sésame et oignons roses
Roll with sesame seed and red onions

Pletzel aux oignons
Onion roll

Latkès
Potato fritter with garlic

Pirojki aux épinards
Pastry roll with spinach filling

Sambos
Beef pasty

Pirojki à la viande
Meat pasty

Gekorte Beigel
A bagel, dipped first in boiling water, then baked

Beigel aux graines de pavot
Bagel with poppy seed

Chausson au fromage blanc
Pastry with quark filling

Houmentach aux noix
Triangle with nut filling for special occasions

Houmentach aux graines de pavot
Pastry triangle with a poppy seed paste filling

Kourabié
Soft almond cake

Roulé aux dattes
Fine dough pastry with date filling

Strudel roumain
Strudel with walnuts, raisins and cinnamon

Apfel strudel aux pommes caramélisés
Apple strudel with caramelized apples

Linzertorte
Sand cake with raspberry jelly, cinnamon, and hazelnuts

Pavé aux noix et raisins
Almond square with hazelnut and raisin filling

Pavé aux pruneaux
Cake slice with plum filling

Pavé noisettes bananes
Cake slice with nut and banana filling

Pavé aux graines de pavot
Cake slice with poppy seed filling

Pavé aux figues
Fig cake slice

Brownie
Chocolate and nut cake

Kraiankis
Colored layered cake

Pianowy
Crumbly quark cheesecake

Vatrouchka
Russian cheesecake

Streuzel
Butter crumble cake

In the center of the Marais you will find the excellent shops of the Jewish Quarter.

Pâtisserie

If France had not been swayed by its weakness for sweet things early on in its history, it would not be renowned as the country of refined taste today. In the 13th century religious host wafer bakers were granted official status and were allowed to bake wafers on holidays too. Then the various trades, concerned with food and drink, were still not clearly defined. So-called doughmakers (*pâtéiers*) made mainly basic cakes and pastries but also highly sought-after doughnuts. The cake business really grew thanks to Catherine de' Medici, who in 1533 married Henry II. Pastry makers and cooks, who made ice cream and invented choux pastry, came to Paris in her retinue. From then on the use of two basic ingredients, sugar and almonds, increased and by 1566 the term *pâtissier* has become recognized as a separate trade.

Puff pastry, *millefeuille* in French, which means "a thousand leaves," was apparently created by a young cook in Paris, who had gotten involved in a foolish wager to bake a cake with a hundred layers. Needless to say he lost, but the result was inspirational and his technique was perfected. So, as early as 1651, *Le Cuisinier français*, the first classical French cookbook, lists a recipe for it. The most popular one is the *Galette des rois*, which is baked to celebrate epiphany. It is filled with almond cream, called *frangipane*, which comes from the name of an Italian perfumer, who lived in Paris in the 17th century.

Parisian *pâtissiers* have always created some of the most popular cakes of the world. In the 19th century the famous Antonin Carême, who in his work *Le Pâtissier royal* laid the foundations of the craft, perfected cream puffs and meringues and created impressive *croquembouches*, shaped like famous buildings. At the beginning of the 20th century this style of baking was perfected as a pyramid made of small cream puffs, held together by caramel icing. Anecdotes about many of these cakes abound. The famous *Saint-Honoré* was devised by the pastry chef Chiboust in 1846 and was named both after the street, where his shop stood, and the patron saint of chefs. Rageneau, creator of the small yet delicious *amandine* cakes, was immortalized by Edmond de Rostand in his famous book *Cyrano de Bergerac*. A cake, as popular now as it was in the past, is the wheel-shaped *Paris-Brest*, created by a baker whose business was situated on the route of the cycling race from Paris to Brest.

The development of freezer and refrigerator machinery for making chocolates and sugar-coated sweets as well as ice cream in the 19th century significantly simplified the practicalities of the trade and imaginative chefs or *pâtissiers* continuously came up with new delicacies. Masters of the trade have to know how to pull out all the stops when it comes to the creation of such mouthwatering delights and are essential to the success of large restaurants. *Pâtisseries* are like jewelry businesses. Their décor is very chic and the choice of fine, sweet cakes, pastries and tarts is a match for any display of precious gems. In the same purposeful way that customers choose exquisite items of jewelry, they select something suitable to crown a meal from the enticing range of highly imaginative cakes, pastries, and sweets – the so-called French gâteaux. The skill of the *pâtissier* determines the final taste on which to end a meal.

Good pâtisseries also offer more substantial fare like savory pastries and quiches alongside cakes, tarts, and ices.

1 La Corne d'abondance
Horn of plenty made of almond nougat filled with various types of ice cream and sorbet and decorated with green marzipan leaves.

2 Croquante aux agrumes
Cake on a macaroon base with vanilla ice cream and a dressing of almond croquant, citrus jelly and oranges.

3 Le Millefeuille
Three-layer puff pastry cake filled with confectioner's cream, decorated with iced almonds and icing sugar.

4 Fraisier
Almond pastry soaked in kirsch with butter cream, fresh strawberries, and strawberry preserve.

3

6

7

10

5 Le Roussillon
Bombe glacée covered with blackcurrant jelly on a sponge and pistachio pastry with peaches and strawberry sorbet, and Cointreau ice cream.

6 Framboisine
Sponge with pistachio paste garnished with vanilla cream, fresh raspberries, pistachio butter and raspberry jelly.

7 Saint-Honoré
Cream puffs arranged in a circle filled with Chiboust's confectioner's cream with added kirsch and eggs, as well as vanilla cream.

8 Régal Chocolat
Bitter chocolate sponge soaked in vanilla syrup with chocolate mousse, served with a strawberry coulis.

9 Paris-Brest
Choux pastry wheel-shaped cake with several layers of cream made of roast almonds and hazelnuts dusted with icing sugar.

10 La Coccinelle
A cool ladybird made of almond sponge with pistachio ice cream, covered with red fruit sorbet and blackcurrant glazing, dotted with chocolate.

Opéra

Cake making too is susceptible to fashion, with new recipes being developed all the time, while outmoded creations go unnoticed and quickly disappear from the displays. Only rarely is one of these creations elevated to the status of a classic recipe, reproduced again and again by many bakers. *Opéra*, a tribute to the Opéra Garnier of Paris, managed to join this exclusive circle. This imposing opera house, today one of the most important ballet stages in the world, was commissioned in 1858 by Napoleon III, who however did not live to enjoy the building designed by Charles Garnier. By the time the Opéra opened in 1875, the emperor had been buried and France had become a Republic.

With its mixture of various types of architecture and styles, the building is reminiscent of the work of a confectioner and because of this was frequently made fun of by the artistically aware Parisians. But as the bastion of music, the Opéra did have its admirers and in time its architecture gained popularity. In 1954 a chef of the famous Pâtisserie Dalloyau created in its honor a square-shaped, multi-layered chocolate cake, which he simply christened *Opéra*. The outward simplicity of this culinary masterpiece conveys an aura of general elegance, in contrast to the ornate Palais Garnier after which it was named. *Opéra* is still made today, in just the same way, at Dalloyau and in other famous *pâtisseries*.

Opposite: The name of the square-shaped chocolate Opéra, just under 1¼ inches (3 centimeters) high, is hand decorated on its surface.

1 *Opéra* starts off with three very soft layers of *biscuit Joconde* made of flour, eggs, butter, beaten egg white, and sugar.
2 The first layer of sponge is spread out flat in a rectangular mold and then soaked in cooled coffee syrup.
3 A light butter cream, colored and flavored with homemade coffee essence and caramel, is spread evenly all over it.
4 Then the second thin sponge layer is carefully laid on top and pressed down hard.

5 The second layer, soaked in coffee, is then spread with a layer of *ganache chocolat*, a bitter chocolate cream, enriched with milk, cream, and creamed butter.
6 The third sponge layer is placed on top of the layer with the *ganache chocolat*, carefully pressed down, and then soaked in coffee.
7 A second, thin layer of coffee butter cream rounds the creation off. The frame is removed and the layered cake is allowed to cool.
8 The icing of the cake is made with a mixture of 2 parts melted bitter chocolate and 1 part melted cocoa butter.

9 After the chocolate icing has hardened, the cake is cut up into standard sizes and then each one is inscribed with liquid icing.

Eating out in Paris

There are many restaurants in Paris where gourmets can eat good food. The French have flocked from all the regions to the capital to try their luck there, followed by landlords and cooks, who satisfied the desires of people from the same regions with specialties and restaurants reminiscent of home. Without leaving Paris, you can sample regional dishes from all over France. Furthermore, since different nationalities settled in Paris and brought their cooking skills with them, the gastronomy of the whole world can be found there.

The natural way in which people go out for a meal today has only developed over the last 200 years. Before that, inns and guesthouses provided basic food for travelers but that was all. Taverns, not frequented by respectable people, first had the right just to provide wine, and then were gradually allowed to offer meat dishes as well. From 1765 a certain Monsieur Boulanger, who provided cooked meals for his customers, became the pioneer of modern catering. The first real restaurant was founded in 1782 in the Rue de Richelieu by Antoine Beauvilliers, a former supply officer to the Count of Provence as well as an experienced chef. Familiar with customs in England, where going out to eat was already socially acceptable, he named it "La Grande Taverne de Londres." In an exclusive atmosphere people chose dishes from a menu. Only a little later Beauvilliers' success was followed by those chefs, whose aristocratic employers had become victims of the Revolution. In 1789 there were less than 50 restaurants in Paris. A hundred years later there were already 150. Today there are more than 5000 restaurants.

The smartest and most exclusive restaurants offer much more than just a meal. The experience is intended to be a celebration of all the senses, as décor, tablecloth and decoration, drinks and service all play their part. Parisians expect an exceptionally high standard of their chefs. The appearance of the dishes should be something for the eyes to feast on, while the composition, texture, and taste of what has been prepared should give lasting pleasure.

Over recent years due to economic recession the trend has been toward good, reasonably priced food. Acknowledged chefs have opened bistros, where people can take advantage of their skill and creativity at a modest price. The *menu-carte* offers a range of dishes at set prices and gives good value for money.

A stylish atmosphere is capable of heightening the experience of an excellent meal.

In the past a visit to a restaurant was not as commonplace as it is today, when in Paris alone there are over 5000 restaurants to choose from.

Great value is generally placed on good service and people are eager to rely on the recommendations of the waiter or wine-waiter.

Places where you can enjoy your favorite food

Restaurant

The classic term for a place to eat out, open only at certain times and where customers select dishes from a menu. Among the 5000 or so restaurants in Paris, alongside the highly praised and expensive shrines to gourmet dining, there are fortunately also many restaurants whose prices

Restaurants are the smart places to eat

are more reasonable and which offer good food. Many specialize in fish, others in meat, but so far only relatively few offer vegetarian dishes. Some provide regional dishes, *cuisine de terroir*, while others have an overtly modern bias. Most of them always offer a set menu that is complete meals for a fixed price.

Bistro(t)

Generally they are smaller and distinctly more informal than restaurants, which is evident from the more modest range of dishes, and menus are chalked up on slates or hand-written. As a rule, they offer a cheap midday meal, *le plat du jour*. Traditional bistros often offer well-established dishes with popular specialties such as *coq au vin* (chicken casserole in red wine), *pot-au-feu* (beef casserole) or *confit de canard* (conserve of duck). *Entrecôte* (entrecote steak) or *bavette* (loin steak) are served almost everywhere, with a generous added helping of local color.

Bistrot à Vin

The special ambience of bistros, cafés or bars owes much to Anglo-Saxon wine bars and at first was not readily accepted by wine lovers. Nevertheless they gained a foothold in Paris long ago in many different guises. While many of the places – reminiscent of former *tavernes* and *cabarets* –

In the *bistrot à vin* wine is as important as the food

are quite content to offer simple, cheap drinks, others have become places of interest for wine enthusiasts, where knowledgable landlords proffer their latest discoveries by the glass to similarly knowledgable customers and frequently offer hundreds of different wines. In some bistros the food is often quite simple and based on a few selected products such as sausages, ham and cheese, while others offer more refined cuisine.

Brasserie

Brasseries, literally breweries, were founded after the war of 1870 by refugees from Alsace-Lorraine, who served various types of beer but mostly

Brasseries serve traditional dishes

wines from Alsace by the carafe or bottle – wines such as Riesling, Sylvaner, and Gewürztraminer. Undisputedly the most popular dish on the menu was and is Sauerkraut, followed closely by seafood served on large serving platters, normally shared by several people. Otherwise menus list more traditional dishes, served throughout the day.

Many brasseries were opened before the turn of the 20th century and furnished and decorated in the then modern *art nouveau* style. They have been popular with artists and politicians for a long time, and even today they are lively and stimulating places to meet, which stay open until late into the night. Some of them have preserved their original interior from the *Belle Époque* with large mirrors, carved wooden paneling, and attractive mosaics which today are especially valued by lovers of this type of décor.

Café

These are by no means as people in other countries might imagine them to be but are primarily places where both coffee and alcoholic drinks are served. The range of foods served throughout the day generally comprises simple dishes and small meals such as *croque monsieur*, salads and, when in season, *moules-frites*, mussels with French fries. Sidewalk terraces are very much part of the large cafés on the Parisian boulevards, with chairs and tables set up outside in the open. The terraces offer the best views of the hustle and bustle of the capital and its inhabitants. Cafés open early in the morning and most shut at the earliest around nine in the evening.

Salon de Thé

This is the form of French eating place which most resembles the cafés of other countries. Tearooms offer a good selection of cakes and *gâteaux* but generally don't serve alcoholic drinks. At lunchtime they frequently offer a basic menu, as well as simple snacks, salads, and sandwiches. The varied, even excellent types of tea and hot chocolate – *chocolat à l'ancienne* – are well worth trying. The best ones also prepare various types of coffee. Tearooms mainly open just before midday for lunch and usually shut in the late afternoon.

Bistros offer simple cooking with atmosphere

Cafés also cater for customers who prefer something alcoholic

Bar

Bars based on the American style, where customers can enjoy a drink, frequently a cocktail or whisky, at the counter, opened originally at the beginning of the 20th century. Very often they stand out because of their individual design and are quite intimate meeting places, which the

Tearooms attract people who enjoy cakes

Parisians particularly enjoy. The best ones have built up their own clientele with common interests in art, music, literature, politics, or sport, which contributes to the special atmosphere. In piano bars musicians provide a discreet musical backdrop. The word "bar" is often placed in front of or after the word "café" to indicate a typical, traditional bar.

In the bar-tabac people meet up when buying cigarettes

From the menu of a brasserie

Huîtres chaudes
Seared oysters

20 oysters
3½ oz/100 g finely diced shallots
1 tbsp/15 g butter
⅔ cup/150 ml crème fraîche
Freshly ground white pepper
½ tsp curry powder
1 tbsp brandy

Open the oysters (preserving the water), leaving them in the lower half of the shell and discarding the other half. Put the shallots with the water from the oysters in a pan, add butter and reduce by half.
Heat the broiler.
Add crème fraîche to the sauce, season with white pepper, curry and brandy and, while stirring, reduce by a third.
Arrange 5 oysters on a plate (bed the half shells on coarse sea salt), arrange some sauce on each shell and brown the oysters quickly under the broiler, until they are golden brown. Serve immediately.

Merlans Bercy
Bercy whiting

Serves 2

2 whiting, each weighing about 12 oz/350 g
½ bunch of parsley
2½ oz/75 g shallots
½ cup/125 g butter
Salt and freshly ground pepper
⅔ cup/150 ml dry white wine
4½ oz/125 g mushrooms
1 bayleaf

Rinse and clean the whiting.
Finely dice the parsley and the peeled shallots.
Mix most of the parsley and shallots with 2½ oz/75 g butter, add salt and pepper and stuff the fish with the mixture.
Preheat the oven to 355 °F/180 °C. Butter an oven-safe dish, spread the remaining shallots and parsley in the dish, place the whiting on top, add salt and pepper and dot with pieces of butter.
Sauté the mushrooms in the remaining butter, then add to the whiting with the wine and bayleaf.
Bake the fish for 15 minutes, basting all the time.
Serve immediately in the dish.

Purée Saint-Germain
Saint-German pea soup

Serves 6

14 oz/400 g dried split peas
2 oz/50 g bacon
4 cups /1 liter light veal stock
I bouquet garni: thyme, bayleaf, celery, leek
Freshly ground pepper
½ cup/120 g butter
24 croûtons

Soak the peas for 2 hours in cold water, then drain and boil in 4 cups/1 liter of salted water, skimming off the foam.
When the peas are ready, drain (keeping the water) and sieve.
Finely dice the bacon and let it cook in a pan. Add the sieved peas, pour on the veal stock and the liquid and add the bouquet garni. Simmer for 15 minutes at very low temperature.
Remove the bouquet garni, pour the pea soup into a preheated tureen, stir in the butter, and add the croûtons separately on serving.

Grand hotels

The larger and better known a restaurant is, the more personnel it needs to cater well for its guests. Whether in the kitchen or in the dining room, it takes a specialized team to ensure that the guests are satisfied. Such a team is strictly structured, rank reflects the level of responsibility, and task areas are clearly defined. Consequently, the kitchen team is made up of many people working hand in hand to deliver perfect meals to the restaurant team, who then provide the highest levels of service to ensure the total satisfaction of the guests.

The Kitchen Team

Chef de cuisine – Kitchen chef

Responsible for the overall operation of the kitchen and for delegating the various activities, the *chef de cuisine* draws up the various menus, is responsible for budgeting and sees also to the purchasing. He or she manages and supervises the preparation of food, checks the presentation of the dishes so that each one conforms to the standards of quality established in advance.

The kitchen chef works together with the manager of the restaurant, with whom he or she discusses and agrees the creation of new recipes and the updating of the menu offered. Both must keep informed about new ideas and trends in gastronomy to be able to bring their own dishes in line with these.

The chef is also responsible for all other matters affecting the kitchen, including hygiene and the training of apprentices, and he represents the kitchen staff with respect to the guest.

Sous-chef de cuisine – Deputy kitchen chef

The *sous-chef de cuisine* receives instructions from the *chef de cuisine* and passes them on to the other cooks. The role of the deputy is to coordinate the interaction of all the personnel in the kitchen. He or she deputizes for the kitchen chef when absent, and frequently takes responsibility for certain tasks such as training. At the same time he or she generally assumes responsibility for an area of the kitchen.

Chef de partie – Senior chef

The *chef de partie* is responsible for a given area of the kitchen, specialized in the preparation of certain ingredients and dishes. If the position is of lesser importance, he or she is referred to as the *demi-chef*.

Cuisinier – Cook

This general description covers quite a distinct position within the kitchen team and enables the holder to work independently. This role can also be described as *cuisinier de partie*.

Commis – Junior cook

A qualified cook, who reports to a chef following his or her instructions, and who prepares one or more components of a menu. The *commis* is also responsible for the maintenance of the kitchen utensils in the area in which he or she works.

Apprenti(e) – Apprentice

Apprentices receive theoretical and practical training at school, work in the hotel, and in the kitchen carry out various preparatory and cleaning jobs.

Plongeur – Dishwasher

Responsible for cleaning and looking after cutlery and cooking implements and at times entrusted with various, simple preparation jobs.

Saucier – Saucemaker

Appointed for the preparation of sauces and warm hors d'oeuvres and, above all, of complete meat dishes and, in smaller kitchen teams, fish dishes too. Of all the positions this is the most important and most respected.

Rôtisseur – Grill-room supervisor

As the name says, the *rôtisseur* is concerned with roasting, broiling, and frying too, including French fries.

Poissonnier – Fish cook

In large restaurants a fish cook deals with the preparation of fish and seafood dishes.

Entremetier – Person in charge of entrées

The *entremetier* concentrates on soups as well other dishes, not involving fish and meat, i.e. dishes with vegetables, cereals, eggs, and cheese, including whole foods.

Garde-manger – Pantry supervisor

The *garde-manger* is responsible for cold food, hors d'oeuvres, and salads and for the composition and preparation of cold buffets as well as the cutting of raw meat and cold storage facilities.

Tournant – Spare hand

The flexible member of the kitchen team, covering any position, where extra help is required.

Pâtissier – Pastry cook

The *pâtissier* produces the desserts as well as all the other sweets, enjoyed at the end of the meal, and frequently all the bread and rolls on the table. Sometimes he or she makes the pasta as well.

Boulanger – Baker

Only hotels with large restaurants have resident bakers, who prepare the daily requirement of fresh bread, cakes and pastries for breakfast, as well as the various breads and rolls served with typically French meals.

Next to these basic job descriptions and task areas, a large kitchen team offers opportunities for further specialization, for instance the *chef de garde*, who outside the kitchen team structure prepares food and organizes the running of the kitchen, the *mise-en-place*, the *potager*, who looks after the preparation of vegetable dishes, while the *légumier* cleans the vegetables. Preparatory or auxiliary work is handled by the *garçon de cuisine* or by the *marmiton*, who is also responsible for the pots and pans. Larger operations occasionally employ a *boucher de cuisine*, a hotel butcher, and perhaps have, alongside the *pâtissier*, a *glacier* for ice cream as well as a *confiseur* for small sweet delicacies.

The Restaurant Team

Directeur de la restauration – Catering manager

This position, with responsibility for the whole area of gastronomy, only exists in leading hotels. The *directeur de la restauration* is responsible for the economic and administrative co-ordination of the various activities, which can include several restaurants, bars, catering and receptions, and other events too.

Directeur de restaurant – Restaurant manager

Responsible for all aspects of the restaurant; from the state of the rooms and their decoration, the cutlery and glasses, to organizational matters such as the delegation and allocation of tasks, the appointment of personnel, and the training of junior staff, as well as business duties. The restaurant manager interacts with the kitchen chef on matters of planning. In larger operations there may be an assistant, who can deputize for him or her.

Maître d'hotel – Maître d'

In the dining room of the restaurant the *maître d'hotel* coordinates the service, welcomes the guests, directs them to their tables and advises them on their choice of menu (if this task is not delegated to a *chef de rang*). He or she supervises the service, ensuring that everything proceeds smoothly, at breakfast, lunch or the evening meal and makes sure that quality is maintained, in line with the standards of the establishment. The maître d'hotel deals with complaints and checks the accuracy of the bills.

Chef de rang

The restaurant is divided into areas, called *rangs*. Each of these is managed by a person who is responsible for that area as well as for supervising and coordinating the service at individual tables. The *chef de rang* also serves at the tables.

Sommelier – Wine waiter

Responsible for drawing up the wine list and for purchasing and stocking the wine cellar as well as for the contents and the condition of the cellar. He advises the guests when choosing wine and ensures it is served appropriately. In larger restaurants the *chef sommelier* or *chef caviste* may also manage a small team of wine waiters.

Serveur de restaurant – Waiter

An experienced waiter who looks after customers on arrival and advises them on their choices. The waiter's main task is to serve at the table. If necessary, he or she can slice meat, fillet fish or flambé dishes at the table. Today this is often carried out by the *chef de rang* or the *maître d'hotel*, and was previously done by a *trancheur*.

Commis – Junior waiter

Commis are employed in the dining room. They have finished their apprenticeship but have only had limited work experience. They are used in various ways: the *commis* assists the *chef de rang* in serving. A *commis de suite* looks after the conveyance of the food from the kitchen to his *rangs* and cleans up if a *commis débarrasseur* is not available.

In large hotels there are further roles such as *barman* or even the *responsable des bars*, who looks after several bars. The services of *voituriers* are also available to park the guests' cars. Cloakroom services are available and the *dame du vestiaire* hands the coats to guests as they leave the restaurant. Previously jobs in the kitchen and restaurant were almost exclusively reserved for men. Now the situation is quite different as more and more women join the team, both in the kitchen and in the dining room.

The complete kitchen and restaurant teams of the Ritz Hotel in Paris

A history of French cuisine

Jean-Anthèlme Brillat-Savarin

Born in 1755, Brillat grew up in Bugey, the rural area between Savoy and Jura, where they know a thing or two about first-class cheese and sausage products as well as good, wholesome cooking. He acquir-

Jean-Anthèlme
Brillat-Savarin

ed the second name from a rich aunt. He studied law in Dijon, became an attorney and quickly made a career for himself first as president of the Court, then as mayor and finally as commander of the National Guard. During the revolution he thought it advisable to escape to Switzerland, and hence to America, where he mainly paid for his keep by teaching French. In France all his property was expropriated, but he was allowed to return in 1796 and four years later was appointed to the Supreme Court. Brillat-Savarin loved to entertain his friends and was also interested in chemistry, physics, archeology and astronomy. A bachelor, he combined his love for gastronomy and for science in his famous work *Physiologie du Goût* (Physiology of Taste), in which he analyzed food and drink in a scientific but also entertaining and literally brilliant way. In 1826, only a few weeks after the anonymous publication of his masterpiece, which left his distinctive mark on French gastronomy, Brillat-Savarin died in Saint-Denis.

Antonin Carême

Carême, christened Marie-Antoine, probably the greatest genius of French culinary art, was born in Paris in 1784 into a very poor family with many children. Shown the door by his father at the age of ten, he came into contact with the cooking trade as a helper at a hot food stall. The famous pâtissier Bailly recognized his talent and, to encourage him, took him on at sixteen as an apprentice. The Duke of Talleyrand, one of Bailly's customers, became aware of Carême and engaged him as a chef. As Napoleon's Foreign Minister, the duke knew how to exploit spectacular dinners for political ends using diplomatic skill in such a way that culinary high points encouraged political success. Carême, who for twelve years created the most refined menus for Talleyrand's famous

Antonin Carême

table, provided such opportunities. Carême became a sort of ambassador for French *haute cuisine*, as he cooked for the English king, George IV, for Czar Alexander I, for the Viennese court, and finally for Baron de Rothschild. With tireless energy Carême created soups and sauces, patés and terrines, fish and meat dishes, and was at the same time an excellent pastry cook. In 1833, when he died aged just 50, he left behind the standard work of French *Haute Cuisine Art De La Cuisine Au XIX. Siècle* (The art of cooking in the 19th century).

Auguste Escoffier

Although Escoffier's career was spent mainly in England, he rose to become one of the most excellent exponents of French cooking of his time. His delicate revision of French cuisine is one of his main legacies. He interpreted many traditional recipes in a new, simpler fashion even though he often adhered to extravagant ways of preparing food. Above all, however, he reorganized and rationalized various tasks in the kitchen. His basic ideas, still valid today, are detailed in his books *Guide Culinaire*, *Livre des menus* and *Ma cuisine*. In 1859, at the age of 13, Escoffier started his apprenticeship

Auguste Escoffier

in Nice in his uncle's restaurant. From there he moved to Paris, Lucerne, and Monte Carlo. Later during a cruise, when he was responsible for providing food to Kaiser Wilhelm II, the latter gave him the name "Emperor of Cooks." Later he moved to London where, in 1892, César Ritz first appointed him to the kitchen of the Savoy, before employing him seven years later at the Carlton. Escoffier managed his kitchen until his retirement in 1921. His best known creation is the *Pêche Melba*, vanilla ice cream with poached peaches and raspberry purée. Escoffier died in 1935 in Monte Carlo.

Right: Noix de veau Brillat-Savarin – veal medallions with morel mushrooms and foie gras

Classic recipes

After the French Revolution the midday meal was gradually established, including up to three hors d'oeuvres and three main courses, but the evening meal continued to be the most important meal of the day. Generally meals were served *à la française* with the first course, kept warm on food heaters, already on the table as the diners came to take their places. Hors d'oeuvres, soups, and fried food were then served, followed by hot and cold meats as well as patés, salads, vegetables, and the first sweet dishes. The meal was finally finished off with desserts, cakes, pastries, and cheeses.

The following three recipes typify the extravagance of the dishes. Ingredients such as béchamel sauce, mixed roasted vegetables, well-skimmed beef stock, or veal gravy are of course included. It becomes more complicated when *quenelles de volaille* are required, dumplings made of flour, suet, eggs, spices, and finely minced meat, which is a recipe in itself. Or *farce mousseline* stuffing for wildfowl or game, served with egg white and well cooled, before being mixed in an ice bath with *crème fraîche*. For some dishes no expense was spared. Nowadays, however, this great tradition is only kept alive in the kitchens of some luxury hotels.

Noix de veau Brillat-Savarin

Veal medallions with morel mushrooms
and foie gras

1 boneless veal joint
3½ oz/100 g dried morel mushrooms
4 shallots
6½ tbsps/100 g butter
¾ cup/200 ml crème fraîche
Béchamel sauce
7 oz/200 g foie gras
Bacon for larding
Bed of roast vegetables
Beef stock
Dry white wine
2 tomatoes, seeded
1 bouquet garni
Salt and freshly ground pepper
Spinach

Beat the veal flat and put it to one side.
Soak the mushrooms for 2 to 3 hours in lukewarm water, pour off and then allow to dry on kitchen paper.
Peel a shallot and dice finely. Sauté slightly in butter with the presoaked mushrooms for 15 minutes. Add the crème fraîche and simmer for 30 minutes.
Peel the remaining shallots and dice finely, bind with a béchamel sauce (or a roux).
Spread the shallot mixture on veal just under ½ inch (1 cm) deep and smooth off.
Sprinkle with the mushrooms and add the foie gras in the center. Roll the veal up and tie in shape with kitchen string. Lard with bacon, and then lightly brown all over in butter.
Place the roast vegetables in a pan, lay the meat on top, at the same time pour on wine and meat stock in equal parts. Add the tomatoes and the bouquet garni, season with salt and pepper. Bring to a boil, reduce the temperature and, keeping it covered, simmer for 2 hours.
Shortly before the end of the cooking time clean and sauté the spinach.
Take the meat from the pot and keep it warm. Reduce the gravy, sieve it, and thicken. Slice the roast and pour on some of the gravy. Put the remaining gravy in a sauceboat.
Serve the sautéed spinach and mushrooms with cream sauce as a side dish.

Chartreuse à la Parisienne Carême style
Chartreuse of river crab and fillets mignons

8 good quality truffles
2 cups/500 ml champagne (according to taste)
100 small river crab tails
Butter
Chicken breast fillets
Quenelles de volaille (chicken dumplings)
Veal sweetbreads (or fillets of game)
12 mushrooms
12 slices fillet mignon (chicken or game)
1 zucchini
1 carrot

Cook the truffles either in the open fire, wrapped in aluminum foil, over hot ashes or otherwise boil in champagne, then allow to cool and slice into long strips.
Lay out the river crab tails around the edge of a round, greased dish and intersperse the truffles among them.
Brown the chicken breast fillets and then place them over the crab tails and truffles. Sprinkle the rest of the truffles in the center of the dish.
Spread the dumplings (made of finely chopped chicken meat, flour, suet, eggs and seasoning) over this, leaving a border. Garnish the center of the dish with the fried pieces of chicken and veal sweetbreads (or game fillets). Even out, fill up and cover with the dumplings. Cover with baking parchment, then steam the *chartreuse* in a *bain marie* at a medium temperature for 1½ hours. Free it carefully from the dish, and arrange on a serving platter. Garnish with fried mushrooms and chicken (or game) fillet mignons, sautéed slices of zucchini, and slices of boiled carrot cut into the shape of flowers.

Poularde Talleyrand Escoffier style
Pullet with macaroni and truffles (illustrated above)

1 pullet
Macaroni
Grated Parmesan cheese
Crème fraîche
5 oz/150 g foie gras
2 oz/50 g truffles, diced
3 oz/80 g truffles, sliced
1½ oz/40 g truffles, cut into strips
Stuffing
Veal gravy

Thoroughly fry the pullet in a pan. Separate the breast meat and dice.
Parboil the same amount of macaroni, cut into small pieces, bind with Parmesan cheese and crème fraîche and mix with the diced breast meat. Mix 5 oz/150 g foie gras with 2 oz/50 g diced truffle. Fill the bird with this mixture. Coat the pullet with a stuffing made of puréed chicken meat or game, beaten egg white, and crème fraîche, following the shape of the pullet, then decorate with slices of truffle and cover with greaseproof paper. Cook at a moderate heat in a preheated oven.
Using the brown veal gravy prepare a sauce, flavoring it with the strips of truffle. Add part to a serving plate. Arrange the pullet on this and generously decorate with strips of truffle. Serve the remaining sauce separately.

Left: *Chartreuse à la Parisienne Carême style*
Chartreuse of river crab and fillets mignons

The caterer

It is the year 1889, and France is celebrating the hundredth anniversary of the Revolution. In Paris the World Exhibition is taking place, at whose opening the Eiffel tower is being unveiled. President Sadi Carnot is hosting a sumptuous dinner in the city hall.

The menu of this memorable evening starts with *Saint-Germain cream* of river crab soup and Lucullus paté. Then there are Conti tartlets, salmon with Indian sauce, turbot with *sauce Normandie*, quarter of wild boar Moscow style, Périgourde pullets, lobster *à la Bordelaise*, cold sautéed sparrow, *Granité Grande Champagne*. All these followed by *Sorbet von Roederer*, truffled peacock, *falaise de foie gras*, Russian salad, asparagus with *sauce mousseline*, *bombe glâcée Tour Eiffel* and Hundred Year ice cream. And for anyone who is capable of eating anything else: waffles, puff pastry, and Neapolitan cakes.

This dinner is organized by Potel & Chabot, a catering company, which in 1900 also organized the Mayor's banquet in the Tuileries garden, the largest banquet ever held in France. Potel & Chabot cooked for 22,000 guests. For the event they called in 6000 helpers, used 95,000 glasses, 66,000 sets of cutlery, 250,000 plates, and 3 miles (5 kilometers) of tablecloths. Among other things the kitchen team prepared 1800 ducklings, 4400 pounds (2000 kilograms) of salmon and 3300 pounds (1500 kilograms) of potatoes. And to finish off the meal all the thoroughly contented guests puffed away at 30,000 cigars. Potel & Chabot still work for the French government and also have branches in the U.S., Russia, and in other parts of the world.

Before the Revolution, at a time when there were hardly any restaurants, people turned to caterers when celebrating weddings or for special occasions. In the modern sense of the word the first caterers were not cooks but gardeners. Prior to the fateful year of 1789 Germain Chevet supplied the queen and court with roses. Forced to pull up his rose bushes and replace them with potatoes by the revolutionary court to "feed the people," Chevet and his wife decided to make small pastries out of the potatoes to enhance their value. In the Palais Royal they opened a business, where soon everyone who was anyone dropped in. Among them was the first food critic, Grimod de la Reynière, who in his almanac of 1812 mentioned the following: "This shop continues to be supplied with all those very good things that appeal to the appetite of a true gourmet, above all game, fish, shellfish, and early vegetables. That does not exclude either pâté or sausage produce from Troyes or Reims, of which the best quality is always found here, as well as an abundance of other items which are no less appetizing."

The concept of being "catered for" with portions of ready-made food is not new. For over 500 years in France there have been *rôtisseurs* and *chair-cuitiers*, who prepare roasts or cook meat. Alongside these there were the *pâtissiers*, who covered everything in pastry. And even today in Paris and all over France people happily fall back on what the caterer has to offer, if they don't have any time, if they don't want to cook or if they want to spoil themselves, their family and guests. *Charcuteries* offer a range of foods to make up complete meals, from tasty appetizers to hors d'oeuvres, to ready-made fish and meat meals, and to cheese and desserts, as well as drinks.

Apart from these every-day culinary services, which in our busy times are more in demand than ever before, caterers have stayed loyal to their historical task of catering for special events, even if their clientele has changed with the passing of time. In the second half of the 19th century, following the success of the Industrial Revolution, the upper classes took the place of the aristocracy. Food was still of a high standard but the caterers were more flexible, and could organize exquisite and intimate dinners for two just as perfectly as luxury banquets for several thousand guests. Nowadays they are entrusted with preparing the menu, the supply of equipment, table linen, porcelain, glasses, cutlery, floral decorations, and lighting.

The role of the caterer is not just that of feeding the guests but also of creating the right atmosphere. So buffets became a celebration for the palate and a feast for the eyes, which required the services of specialists. You don't just need butchers and pastry makers, saucemakers and *rôtisseurs* but also chefs who have a flair for decoration, design, flower arranging, and carving (in ice and butter). In this way caterers adapt their presentation to the theme of the event and provide a grandiose, stunning, bizarre, exotic, or classical backdrop. The success of the banquet, perhaps even of the celebrations, is in their hands and on top of that they turn a meal into a feast of Epicurean proportions. Today caterers are both masters of the improvised, affordable meal, which you can enjoy at home, as well as suppliers of highly specialized party services.

The *Buffet de la Mariée*, which means the bride's buffet, supplied by Potel & Chabot, who took over Chevet's company in 1820.

Croustille d'agneau à la menthe poivrée
Roast potatoes with lamb and peppermint
Thin slices of potato seasoned with mint and crushed tomatoes, topped with a slice of pink roast lamb.

Finguer foie gras
Foie gras finger
Crispy filo pastry fingers filled with foie gras and capped with a raisin.

Marinière de légumes
Marinated vegetables
Sautéed, Italian style, in olive oil with seasonal vegetables sprinkled with Parmesan cheese and basil, served with a balsamic dip.

Oh La La! au crabe et aubergine
Crab and aubergine surprise
Small hollowed roll, garnished with peppermint, crab, and aubergine caviar and garnished with vegetable strips.

Philo de rouget aux tétragones
Red mullet in filo pastry with summer spinach
Filo pastry flavored with basil and olive oil with sautéed red mullet fillet in olive oil, on spinach leaves.

Savarin de sole et saumon
Sole and salmon crown
Sole and salmon garnished with salad and herbs, served with truffle cream and crispy vegetables.

Gambas mille graines
Thousand seed prawns
Prawns tossed in vanilla oil wrapped in an extremely thin slice of apple and then tied with a thin strip of carrot cut lengthwise. ("Seeds" is a reference to vanilla seeds.)

Langoustines au citron
Dublin Bay prawns with lemon
Fried langoustines (scampi) seasoned with lemon, salt, and sugar.

Caille aux poires
Quail with pears
Quail breasts marinated with ginger and deep-fried, then seasoned with honey and vinegar (center) and served with pears and quail sauce.

Roulé de choux au caviar
Cabbage rolls with caviar
Tender, parboiled cabbage leaves wrapped around smoked salmon on lemon quark topped with genuine caviar.

Mangues rôties au jus de passion
Fried mangos with passion fruit juice
Fried mango slices, flambéed with vanilla schnapps, served with passion fruit juice.

Fraises au chocolat
Strawberries in chocolate
Ripe, small flavorful strawberries, dipped in black and white chocolate. Best served chilled.

Sablé pistache et pommes rouges
Pistachio biscuits with red apples
Crispy crumble biscuits made of pistachio dough sandwiching a slice of apple in pomegranate syrup

Macarons
Small almond macaroons, which owe their color and flavor to pistachio, strawberry, and coffee cream

Tulipes au myrtille
Blueberry horns
Rolled almond cornets, filled with kirsch egg cream, and capped with blueberries.

Tartare de saumon au basilic
Smoked salmon with basil
Fresh, chopped, smoked salmon, seasoned with basil oil.

France's stars

Three generations of French gourmets have grown up with the red Michelin guide to hotels and restaurants. Its history began around 1990 and goes hand in hand with the history of the car and of course of Michelin tires. Very few visitors to the 1900 World Exhibition in Paris paid attention to the small, 400-page book, given free of charge to all car owners. On the inside page of its red cover one could read: "This book aims to provide the car driver, traveling through France, with useful information about assistance and repair services for his car and to help him find where to stay, eat, and communicate by post, telegram or telephone."
Bibendum, the Michelin man made of car tires, introduced the guide from the very beginning. His name is derived from the Latin "Nunc est bibendum" (Drink now!). The message of the company meant that their tires "drank the road," or covered a lot of ground quickly. Bibendum symbolizes mobility; the glass full of nails, with which he was originally represented, was used to instill confidence in drivers in times when tires were frequently punctured by horseshoe nails left on the roads by the heavy traffic of countless coaches and horses. The first edition of the Michelin guide contained 50 pages of illustrated instructions on how to deal with car tires. In the early editions an abundance of practical information was offered; they contained street plans, an impressive list of essential spare parts to have in the car and, should the worst happen, the names of the best surgeons in France. The street plans were so reliable that the Allies supplied officers with the 1939 pre-war edition of the Michelin guide before the invasion of Normandy in 1944 to help allied armies find their way more easily during the Liberation of occupied France.
From 1920 Michelin sold copies of the guide to strengthen its credibility, after deciding to ban any form of advertising. Over the years the selection of hotels and restaurants in France grew larger and larger and soon the guide,

Bibendum's head as the new Bib Gourmand symbol

which changed its format twice, covered other countries as well, and introduced local editions enabling travelers in many countries to make use of it.
The star system for the rating of restaurants was developed in 1926. The recognition of one, two or three stars is the greatest acknowledgement of the skills of a chef, guaranteeing him a reputation, prestige, and customers. The powerful and the rich all over the world are willing to wait months for a table in a newly appointed three-star restaurant and everyone in France aspires to eat in one of them at some time. The Michelin guide is a great attraction and encourages custom. Some chefs and their businesses have held the highly regarded three-star rating for decades: Bocuse since 1965, Haeberlin since 1967 and Troisgros since 1968.
All over the world the Michelin guide comes out on the same day. Until then the changes in the ratings are treated like a state secret. The 500 or so restaurants, which display one star in its almost 1500 or so pages, represent just the tip of the iceberg, topped by 21 three-star and 70 two-star restaurants. As for the 3500 remaining restaurants the inspectors have found something worth recom-

The 1998 edition introduced the smiling logo of Bib Gourmand for all good restaurants.

mending and rated them according to their level of comfort and service with one to five of its cutlery symbols, while a glass with a fork beneath a roof symbolizes a basic but good restaurant. The 5800 listed hotels are rated with a similar five-star system. Since 1998 Bib Gourmand has been joined by a new symbol: Bibendum's smiling face, which indicates restaurants offering especially good value for money.
Over a half a million copies of the Michelin guide are sold annually throughout the world. The secret of its success is founded on its reliability, helping travelers to find acceptable accommodation in the remotest of regions, and on the unbiased impartiality of its restaurant critics, who like all other guests order, eat, drink, and pay and then leave the restaurant without making their identity known.

The first edition of the Michelin guide appeared in 1900 at the Paris World Exhibition and was a free gift from the tire company to early car travelers, who were plagued with many fundamental problems.

By necessity the guide was not published during the war years but the detailed town plans from the 1939 edition proved very useful to the allied troops during the Liberation.

Cookery Schools

Apart from the state *écoles hôtelières*, several private schools with excellent reputations have been established, some of which are open to non-professionals. Previous knowledge is not normally required.

Le Cordon Bleu L'Art Culinaire
8, Rue Léon Delhomme, 75015 Paris
In the oldest cookery school in Paris, founded in 1895, students attend the nine-month professional cooking and pâtisserie course and are awarded a diploma. There are also courses for caterers and wine waiters. Courses and workshops are held for amateurs.

Ecole Ritz Escoffier de Gastronomie Française
15, Place Vendôme, 75001 Paris
Since César Ritz opened his hotel in 1898 in the former Hôtel de Gramont, the Ritz has been renowned for its cuisine. Its cookery school was first directed at amateurs and lovers of wine, who were able to expand their culinary abilities and knowledge over a short time. They offer an intensive 30-week diploma course for future professionals in cookery and pâtisserie.

Ecole Lenôtre
40, Rue Pierre Curie, 78735 Plaisir
Among other opportunities it offers a six-month professional course, with hands-on cooker lessons in small classes in Lenôtre's kitchens, restaurants and shops. In certain subjects tuition in basic culinary skills is offered on weekly courses.

Ecole de Paris de Métiers de la Table
17, Rue Jacques Ibert, 75017 Paris
Since 1978 this specialized Paris school has been a training center for young people who want to pursue a career in hotel and restaurant catering, or who want to become pâtissiers or chocolatiers. It offers a one-year supplementary course to would-be wine waiters. Trainees from 14 to 25 years of age are accepted.

Ecole des Arts Culinaires et de l'Hôtellerie d'Ecully
Château du Vivier, 69131 Ecully
The director of this school, housed in a castle in Beaujolais on the outskirts of Lyon, is Paul Bocuse. Here young people employed in the hotel and restaurant trade receive training, and successful students receive a diploma in administration and management equivalent to that of a university. Apart from cookery and hotel management the three-year course also includes training in accounting, marketing, administration, personnel management, and IT.

Ecole Supérieure Internationale de Savignac
24420 Savignac-les-Eglises
This school provides courses exclusively for young women and men already employed in hotels, restaurants, or in tourism. It offers courses in general management structured exactly like those of the top **business schools** but specifically focused on the hotel catering trade.

School meals
Many professional hotel training schools in Paris and elsewhere in France open their restaurants to the public. The following Paris schools are open at lunchtime on weekdays (except Wednesdays): École Hôtellière Jean-Drouant, Lycée Technique Privé Albert-de-Mun, Lycée Hôtelier Jean-Quarre, Institut Vatel Lycée Hôtelier Belliard, and École Ferrandi.

Kitchen Utensils

Sadly, nowadays you cannot tell what country you are in by looking into the kitchen. Informed consumers can obtain typical regional ingredients anywhere in the world, and experienced gourmets are able to discover specialist dishes wherever there is still an appreciation of history and culture. Similarly cookery and kitchen enthusiasts are confronted by an array of knives, ladles, pots, and molds which has become standard and consequently the same in every country. Today the difference lies more in the frequency of use of individual kitchen implements and utensils than in their mere presence in the kitchen. Strictly speaking the earthen or cast-iron pots, in which foods cook slowly on the stove and the shape of which is unique to its French region of origin, are a thing of the past.

Despite its almost universal use throughout the world, a *moulinette* is, in origin, a French device. It is very versatile and is used for sieving the traditional *potage*, thick creamy potato and vegetable soup, for grating carrots and celery for the popular *crudités*, for grating cheese for the many dishes that are topped with cheese, and especially for slicing potatoes for dishes such as *gratin dauphinois*. Another simple but very efficient piece of equipment is the indispensable, hand-operated salad spinner. Knives, cooking spoons, spatulas and ladles are available everywhere in different guises. But the decorative long-handled casseroles look more at home on a French stove than anywhere else. The vast range of ovenproof dishes of different shapes and sizes bears testimony to the fact that the French like cooking food in the oven and have a particulary liking for baked food. So many beautifully shaped porcelain or enameled dishes highlight the fact that France is populated by eaters of pâté and terrines. Molds for *brioches*, *savarins*, and *kougelhopf* are the most common cake molds, while the shell-shaped molds for *madeleines* appear to be the most French looking ones by far. Beautiful copper pans, on a low flame, are still used for the slow setting of preserves in the traditional fashion.

Cocotte en fonte
The cast iron casserole is ideal for slow braising.

Couvercle
This can be used wherever a lid is missing or required.

Casseroles
Thanks to their design the versatile long-handled pans are very practical.

Passoire deux anneaux
A sieve with handles makes straining quicker.

Passoire chinois
A conical strainer used especially for decanting liquids.

Essoreuse
Salad can be dressed more easily when dried in the salad spinner.

Moules à soufflé
Soufflé or ovenproof dishes for small cakes or desserts such as *crème caramel*.

Terrine
In ceramic or pastry dishes ingredients are steamed.

Plat rectangulaire avec support
The oven-safe dish with a built-in stand can be taken directly from the oven to the table.

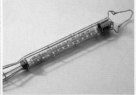

Thermomètre à sucre
A sugar thermometer is indispensable for successful, artistic desserts.

Poche à douille et ses douilles
The piping bag and nozzles are used for decorating and filling.

Moule à madeleine
The liquid dough for madeleines is poured into the molds.

Emporte-pièces
A matching set of pastry cutters is very useful.

Moule savarin
A ring mold for cakes and fish terrines.

Ficelle
Kitchen string is useful for stuffed chicken rolls or steamed beef fillet.

Mixer
A blender is an efficient aid for mixing, whipping and blending.

Véritable mandoline
The universal grater is used for grating and slicing cheese, fruit, and vegetables.

Hachoir
The half moon hachoir finely chops herbs, onions, or garlic cloves.

Background: moulinette
A combined sieve and grater, a quick fix for raw fruit and vegetables, purées, cheese

Kitchen knives (from the left)

Econome office	– Economy peeling knife with adjustable blade for fine peeling of vegetables and potatoes
Bec oiseau	– Paring knife for small to medium-sized fruit and vegetables
Office	– Utility knife for cutting, peeling and dicing all types of vegetables
Eminceur	– Cook's knife with long, wide blade for cutting and flattening thin slices of meat
2 Spatules	– Spatulas, 14 in (35 cm) and 12 in (30 cm), are used for lifting, spreading, and smoothing down icings, fillings, and dough
Tranchelar	– Carving knife for cutting soft meat like salmon into extremely thin slices
Désosser	– Deboning knife with an extremely sharp point
Tranchelar	– Carving or serrated knife for cutting tougher cuts of meat into thin slices
Spatule coudée	– Angled slice for use in skillets

Everyday Parisian fare

It is by no means simply the more elaborate dishes that typify Parisian cuisine. Queuing at lunchtimes and in the evenings to get a place in brasseries and bistros shows that they are patronized by local people. Good, wholesome soups (*potages*), value-for-money fish such as cod or whiting, beef (*entrecôtes* or *bavettes*), ragouts, cooked ham, calf's head, or *andouillettes* (sausages made of organ meat), are all available. The large market and slaughterhouse, Les Halles and La Villette, as well as Bercy, an early center for the wine trade, have had an ongoing influence on these dishes. The world famous French onion soup has its origins in the bars and inns around the market halls, where traders needed to warm themselves up in the early morning. At La Villette on the other hand large pieces of entrecôte or calf's head served with tongue and sweetbreads were dished up. In Bercy a good serving of wine and shallots was part of every typical dish. Parisians have a liking for mayonnaise and especially for their *sauce gribiche*, made with boiled egg yoke, blended and seasoned with vinegar, capers, herbs, pepper and salt, served with calf's head or cold fish. In Paris they also came up with something to satisfy a smaller appetite, known throughout the world as *croque-monsieur*. It supposedly was thought up in 1910 in a café in the Boulevard des Capucines and has remained a classic dish served in cafés and brasseries.

Gratinée des Halles
Onion soup topped with cheese
(illustration bottom left)

14 oz/400 g onions
¼ cup/60 g butter
1 tbsp flour
4 cups/1 l beef stock
Salt and freshly ground pepper
Half a baguette
3 ½ oz/100 g Gruyère cheese, finely grated

Peel the onions and cut them into thin rings. Warm the butter in a pan and lightly sauté the onions in it. Sprinkle on flour and stir, then pour on the hot beef stock. Bring to a boil, lower the temperature and cover. Simmer for 30 minutes. Add salt and pepper to taste. Cut the baguette into thin slices and toast. Pour the soup into oven-safe bowls, cover with slices of baguette and sprinkle with the finely grated Gruyère. Bake over in a preheated oven or broil and serve hot immediately.

Croque Monsieur
Ham and cheese toast
(illustration bottom right)

Per Person

2 slices of bread for toasting
1 tsp butter
Half a slice of cooked ham
2 tbsp/25 g finely grated cheese

Thinly spread the butter onto both slices of bread. Lay the ham on one slice and sprinkle on the finely grated cheese. Cover with the second slice of buttered bread. Preheat the broiler. First broil one side, then the other. When served with a fried egg, it is called *croque madame*.

Potage cressonnière
Cream of cress soup
(no illustration)

14 oz/400 g potatoes
6 cups/1.5 l water
1 bunch of watercress
½ cup/100 ml crème fraîche
Salt and freshly ground pepper

Peel, wash, dice the potatoes and place in salted water. Bring to a boil, lower the temperature, and simmer for 30 minutes. In the meantime finely chop the stalks of the watercress and thoroughly wash the leaves.
Put a few small leaves aside. Add the cress to the potatoes and boil for another 10 to 15 minutes. Liquidize the soup with the blender. Stir in the crème fraîche, add salt and pepper to taste and pour into pre-warmed bowls. Serve garnished with the watercress leaves.

Potage parisien
Parisian potato and leek soup
(no illustration)

3 leeks
¼ cup/60 g butter
6 cups/1.5 l water
14 oz/400 g potatoes
Salt and freshly ground pepper

Clean and wash the leeks and cut into narrow strips. Heat half of the butter in a pan and sauté the leeks. Pour on the boiling and salted water. Peel, wash, and finely dice the potatoes and add to the pan.
Simmer for around 20 minutes at low temperature. Pour into a soup tureen, fold in the remaining butter. Add salt and pepper to taste.

Gratinée des Halles – Onion soup topped with cheese

Croque Monsieur – Ham and cheese toast

Jambon à la Porte Maillot

Porte Maillot cooked ham
(illustration on the right)

Serves 10

1 ham, weighing 5½ lb/2.5 kg
(not too strongly salted)
1 lb 5 oz/600 g carrots
7 oz/200 g onions
2 cloves
2 sprigs of thyme
2 bayleaves
4 basil leaves
1 pinch of cinnamon
1 pinch of ground nutmeg
2 oz/50 g garlic
1 bunch of parsley
2 lettuces
10 oz/300 g scallions
17 oz/500 g peas
17 oz/500 g green beans, blanched
1 bunch of young carrots
3½ tbsps/50 g butter
Pepper

Sauce

2 carrots
2 onions
4 tsps/20 g butter
2 cups/500 ml dry white wine
2 cups/500 ml beef tea
Bayleaf, thyme, parsley

Desalt and pare the ham on the outside, wrap in a muslin cloth and place in a saucepan. Just cover with water and simmer for 4 hours with carrots, onions, seasoning, herbs, and garlic. Carefully remove the ham from the cloth and take out the bone.

For the sauce, sauté carrots and onions in butter, pour on wine and stock and add the herbs. Bring to a boil, then sieve. Pour the sauce over the ham and simmer for another hour.

Shortly before serving, sauté the lettuce, onions, peas, green beans, and carrots in butter. Season the ham with ground pepper and serve with the vegetables.

Entrecôte Villette

Villette entrecote steak
(no illustration)

Per Person

1 entrecote steak, 10 – 12 oz/300-350 g,
approximately ¾ in/15 mm thick
5 shallots
6½ tbsp/100 g butter
Salt and freshly ground pepper
1 tsp finely chopped flat-leaf parsley
Lemon juice
Coarse sea salt

Pepper the meat, cover and allow to rest for 2 hours. Peel and finely chop the shallots. Heat a third of the butter and brown the lightly salted entrecote on each side for a short time. Keep warm. Melt the remaining butter, add the shallots and brown in 2 minutes.

Serve the meat on a warm plate, pour on the shallots and butter, sprinkle with parsley and add a few drops of lemon juice. Then add coarse sea salt and freshly ground pepper to taste. Serve with French fries or roast potatoes.

Cheese

There are more French cheeses than there are days in the year and the French are justly proud of this. You can find and enjoy all of them in Paris. While *crèmeries* are places where cheese is sold, an *affineur* is the artist who structures the raw material of the cheese to his own liking, and applies his skills to perfecting it. A *fromager-affineur*, who takes pride in his work, travels the length and breadth of France in an ongoing search for the very best cheese producers to stock up with fresh cheeses he can mature himself. Only after the long process of *affinage*, when each cheese has fully developed its quite distinct character, is it put on sale.

To practice his trade the *affineur* requires suitable cellars, where constantly low temperatures and high levels of humidity prevail. But to do justice to each type of cheese, several rooms are needed, each kept under certain controlled conditions. A soft cheese with a downy rind like Camembert needs 95 percent humidity, hard cheese 80 percent and goat milk cheese 75 percent. It is not the done thing to store the cheese and leave it to its own devices. On the contrary, each cheese requires special attention to mature well. Some have to be washed in salt solution, beer, or even spirits. Others are dusted with wood ash by the experienced *affineur* or wrapped in leaves or hay. Many are just wiped down with a cloth and turned over. Some are kept in the cool, others in the warm.

The experienced *affineur* can tell at a glance or just a touch what is required. He keeps a Camembert, for example, for three weeks, and a medium-firm Cantal for up to six months. Maturing time is generally dependent on the size of the cheese, but caution is needed as any excessive maturing can have a negative effect on the cheese.

Only scientific care guarantees the right taste, the correct intensity of flavor, the best texture and an attractive appearance. This is what raises the masterpieces of the *affineur* above simple dairy products.

So far 42 cheeses have received the *Appellation d'Origine Contrôlée* stamp of quality. Mass-produced cheeses – the most well known being "La Vache qui rit" – are in a special category of their own. All other cheeses in France, depending on the type of production, are classified as fresh cheese, soft cheese with white or red mold rind, blue vein cheese, goat milk cheese, as well as hard cheese pressed from uncooked and cooked curds. (The different types will be described in detail with examples from the various regions.) Of course a cheese course is an essential part of a good meal, and a trolley with a representative selection of first-rate, matured cheeses is a matter of prestige in any top restaurant.

This trolley displays a rich and carefully selected range of different cheeses.

French cheese at a glance

(The year refers to when the *Appellation d'Origine Contrôlée* was first awarded)

Fromages à croûte fleurie
White mold cheese
Brie de Meaux (1980)
Brie de Melun (1980)
Brillat-Savarin
Camembert de Normandie (1983)
Chaource (1970)
Coulommiers
Neufchâtel (1969)
Saint-Marcellin

Fromages à croûte lavée
Soft cheese with red mold
Epoisses (1991)
Langres (1991)
Livarot (1975)
Maroilles (1955)
Mont d'Or, Vacherin du Haut-Doubs (1981)
Munster, Munster Géromé (1969)
Pont-L'Évêque (1972)

Chèvre – Goat milk cheese
Banon (2003)
Brocciu Corse (1983)
Chabichou du Poitou (1990)
Charolais, Charolles
Chevrotin (2002)
Crottin de Chavignol (1976)
Pélardon (2000)
Rocamadour (1996)
Valençay (1998)

Picodon de l'Ardèche, Picodon de la Drôme (1983)
Pouligny-Saint-Pierre (1972)
Sainte-Maure de Touraine (1990)
Selles-sur-Cher (1975)

Fromages à pâte persillée
Blue mold cheese
Bleu d'Auvergne (1975)
Bleu des Causses (1953)
Bleu du Haut-Jura, Bleu de Gex, Bleu de Septmoncel (1935)
Bleu du Vercors-Sassenage (1998)
Fourme d'Ambert, Fourme de Montbrison (1972)
Roquefort (1921)

Fromages à pâte pressée non cuite
Medium-firm and firm cheese for slicing
Ardi-Gasna
Bethmale
Cantal (1956)
Laguiole (1961)
Mimolette
Morbier (2000)
Ossau-Iraty (1980)
Reblochon (1958)
Saint-Nectaire (1955)
Salers (1961)
Tomme des Bauges (2002)

Fromages à pâte pressée cuite
Hard cheese
Abondance (1990)
Beaufort (1968)
Comté (1952)

In this fascinating shop Roland Barthélémy, president of the Paris Cheese Guild, offers an extensive range of well-matured cheeses.

A cheese chronology

When consuming a selection of cheeses one normally begins with the mildest. The order illustrated below is just an example, as the sequence depends on how mature each cheese is.

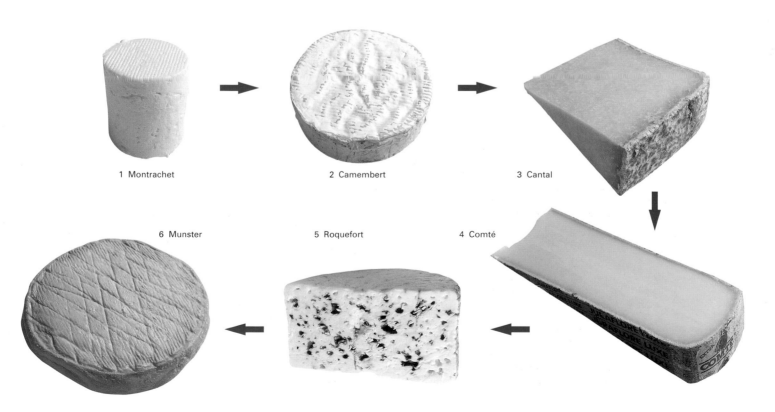

1 Montrachet   2 Camembert   3 Cantal

6 Munster   5 Roquefort   4 Comté

Fromages à croûte fleurie
White mold cheese

Brillat-Savarin
Very mild, slightly sharp, extremely rich cheese with 75 percent fat content from Normandy. The pieces measure almost 5 inches (12 centimeters) in diameter.

Camembert
A famous cheese from Normandy, preferably made of, unpasteurized milk. It matures in at least 21 days and the interior should be slightly supple to the touch.

Neufchâtel
This heart-shaped, square or cylindrical white downy cheese made from unpasteurized or pasteurized milk comes from Seine-Maritime, where it has been recorded since the 11th century. It is only matured for a short time and has a pleasant flavor.

Coulommiers
Brie from the Ile-de-France; the approximately 18-ounce (500-gram) cheeses are produced from both unpasteurized and pasteurized milk.

Brie de Meaux
The most famous of the Bries was held in high regard by Charles the Great. Nowadays mainly mass-produced, the salt content has increased. Flat, mature rounds almost 14 inches (35 centimeters) in diameter and just under 1inch (2.5 centimeters) high exhibit a patchy or striped white downy surface.

The lush grass found in the meadows of Normandy gives the milk its richeness.

Chaource
A cheese known since the Middle Ages from the Champagne area and northern Burgundy; available as a cylinder wrapped in paper, in weights of 15¾ ounces (450 grams) and 7 ounces (200 grams); very creamy, mature with a mushroomy flavor.

Saint-Marcellin
This small cheese from the Isère has most flavor when it is soft and somewhat mis-shapen as illustrated. It used to be produced with goat milk, today cow milk is preferred, be it unpasteurized or pasteurized.

Brie de Melun
The rounds are some 11 inches (28 centimeters) in diameter. After the usual four weeks of maturing (up to ten is possible) the cheese exhibits similar external properties to Brie de Meaux, with a smooth, yellow interior and a nutty taste. Both are produced in Seine-et-Marne and neighboring areas. Not as good in the early part of the year.

Fromages à croûte lavée – Soft cheese with red mold

Epoisses
A specialty of Burgundy, seasoned with marc and/or white wine. The shining smooth or slightly grooved surface is dark orange; it has a striking bouquet, is very creamy and pleasantly spicy.

Livarot
The trademark of this cheese from the Calvados area is the rind, marked by rush strips around its circumference; supple yellow interior.

Maroilles
A famous old favorite, highly regarded since the Middle Ages, square-shaped with approximately 5 inches (13 centimeters) long sides by 2½ inches (6 centimeters) high, with a tile-red, shiny rind. It has a strong aroma, a characteristic taste of its own, and goes well with beer.

Langres
The yellow, cracked, and thin rind of the fresh cheese darkens as it matures. It may be dyed with annatto. The slightly piquant taste of the soft interior is best in the fall.

Munster, Munster Géromé
A flavorful cheese created by monks; made of unpasteurized or pasteurized cow milk from the alpine pastures of the Vosges; available in two different sizes.

Vacherin Mont d'Or
Cheese made in winter from unpasteurized milk, matured on pine boards and keeps its shape with a fir retaining strip.

Pont-l'Évêque
The square-shaped Normandy cheese has been produced since the Middle Ages. It weighs between 12¼ ounces (350 grams) and 14 ounces (400 grams) and is characterized by its smooth yellow interior, which has a distinct, and slightly nutty flavor.

Chèvre – Goat milk cheese

Cabécou
Soft, 1-1½ ounces (30-40 grams) light unpasteurized goat milk cheese from Quercy, Périgord, or Rouergue.

Chabichou du Poitou
The cheese, sold as a high cylinder weighing 5¼ ounces (150 grams), goes back to the time of the Moors.

Charolais, Charolles
Burgundy cheese made from goat and/or cow milk with a natural mold rind in a 7-ounce (200-gram) cylinder.

Crottin de Chavignol
Small 1½-2 inches (4-5 centimeters) in diameter, round cheese, named after a Loire village in the Sancerre wine area.

Montrachet
A very mild, creamy Burgundy cheese, eaten young.

Pélardon
There are many variations of this unpasteurized milk cheese from the Cévennes. Its mild, aromatic flavor requires three weeks to mature.

Picodon de l'Ardèche, or Picodon de la Drôme
The small, flat coin-shaped cheeses have to mature for at least 12 days, but are usually kept for three to four weeks.

Pouligny-Saint-Pierre
This 8¾-ounce (250-gram) cheese pyramid made of full cream goat milk is from the Loire in the center of France. The cheese tastes best when it has a slightly blue mold.

Sainte-Maure
The best known *chèvre* is a hand-made, slightly bluish (or white) 5½-6¼-inch (14-16 centimeter) long roll, which keeps its shape with a piece of straw through its center.

Selles-sur-Cher
From the southern Loire. The slightly tapered cylinders are dusted with a mixture of salt and charcoal and then matured. Delicate nutty flavor.

Fromages à pâte persillée – Blue vein cheese

Roquefort
The most famous blue vein cheese made from unpasteurized sheep milk, matured in the unique limestone caves of Roquefort-sur-Soulzon.

Bleu des Causses
A close relative of Roquefort made only from cow milk matured in the limestone mountain caves of Aveyron in similar conditions. The light, even interior is characterized by a bluish mold.

Fourme d'Ambert, Fourme de Montbrison
The traditional, mild blue mold cheese now made from pasteurized cow milk, probably produced for 2000 years in the mountains of the Auvergne, is shaped into 7½-inch (19 centimeter) high cylinders, then injected with cultures and matured for several months. Molds of various colors often develop on the gray rind. The cheese is usually scooped out with a spoon.

Bleu d'Auvergne
It was first produced by a farmer in the Massif Centrale in the middle of the 19th century. Under the thin, brushed rind there is a firm ivory-colored interior streaked with irregular blue-green veins. The piquant taste makes it very versatile in the kitchen.

Bleu du Haut-Jura, Bleu de Gex, Bleu de Septmoncel
This outsider among the French blue vein cheeses is in 14-inch (36-centimeter) rounds and salted by hand. After at least four weeks' maturing time it develops a beautiful, golden-yellow rind, a cream-colored marbled interior with fine blue-green veins, and has a delicate, nutty flavor. Its best season is from June to October.

Fromages à pâte pressée cuite – Hard cheese

Abondance
Produced by the monks of the Abondance monastery in the Haute-Savoie since the 12th century, with the milk from the breed of cattle of the same name. The cheese curds are heated when drying the cheese and then heated a second time (max. temp. 104 °F/40 °C), wrapped in a cloth and pressed in wooden molds. After three months maturing the rind is bright orange, the interior has few holes and is bright yellow, the taste of the 15½-26½-pound (7-12 kilogram) cheeses is well balanced. It has a particularly fruity flavor in summer.

Comté, Gruyère de Comté
The most popular French hard cheese is from the Franche-Comté, where the cows graze on the alpine pastures of the Jura in summer. For one round of Comté 140 gallons (530 litres) of milk are processed. Traditionally the consistency of the texture is achieved by heating it once to 104 °F (40 °C), after which the curds are pressed in a cloth. The rounds weighing up to 120 pounds (55 kilograms) are salted, rubbed down, and then turned regularly while maturing, for three to six months. The hard rind conceals a yellow interior with a few cherry-sized holes (eyes). The flavor has both fruity and flowery overtones.

Beaufort
Pressed in beechwood ripeners, this cheese measures up to 30 inches (75 centimeters) in diameter with a weight of up to more than 150 pounds (70 kilograms). After maturing for at least six months it develops a hard yellow to brown rind and a nutty flavor. Three types are produced: apart from the simple Beaufort, there is Beaufort *été* (June to October) and Beaufort *d'alpage* (produced on alpine pastures with the milk of a local herd).

Fromages à pâte pressée non cuite
Medium-firm and firm cheese for slicing

Mimolette
This unconventionally shaped cheese made from pasteurized cow milk, also known as Boulle de Lille, is produced by the same process as Dutch Edam. It takes from six weeks to two years to mature.

Ossau-Iraty
The milk for this sheep milk cheese from the valleys and pastures of the western Pyrenees (Ossau is in Béarn, Iraty in the French Basque country) may only be processed 20 days after lambing. After maturing for at least three months the cheeses have a solid rind, smooth interior with few holes, and a delicate, markedly nutty flavor. It is at its best in November and December.

Saint-Nectaire
A well-known medium-firm cheese from the Auvergne, made from unpasteurized milk, which is pressed twice. It matures in damp cellars on rye straw for up to ten weeks and acquires its bright rind, with a fine interior and a mushroomy, nutty flavor.

Morbier
This medium-firm cheese for slicing comes from the Comté region and has a characteristic ash streak in the middle. The Morbier you find on the market is not always the original Morbier, as there are both handcrafted and mass-produced versions.

Ardi-Gasna
Unpasteurized full-cream milk is used for this hard sheep milk cheese (*pur brebis*) from the Basque country, which is traditionally eaten with cherry preserve. After maturing for two to three months the cheese is suitable for consumption, but it can be matured for up to two years.

Bethmale
This mild cow milk cheese from the Pyrenees shares the name of a village in the region. The cheeses weighing approximately 8-13 pounds (3.5-6 kilograms) with a brushed rind mature in two to three months.

Tomme de Savoie
A cheese made from skimmed cow milk originally produced only in Savoy. After maturing for four to six weeks reddish patches form on the gray brown surface.

Cantal
The best known cheese for slicing from the Massif Centrale is available in three sizes and three stages of maturity: fresh (30 days), mild (2 to 6 months) and mature (more than 6 months).

Salers
This Cantal cheese is only produced from unpasteurized full cream milk from Salers cows grazing on the summer pastures. A 12-15½-inch (30-40-centimeter) high cylinder weighs about 75-100 pounds (35-45 kilograms).

Laguiole
A relative of Cantal from the high plateau of Aubrac is handcrafted and matures in four to ten months. It is believed to be a monastery cheese from the 19th century.

Reblochon
The flat, round cheese from the mountains of Savoy sold whole or as a half round is lightly pressed and washed repeatedly. Its rind is orange yellow but coated in white mold. The supple, even, creamy interior has a pleasant taste, faintly reminiscent of hazelnuts. The cheese matures in at least two weeks, but more usually three to four weeks at a temperature below 61 °F (16 °C).

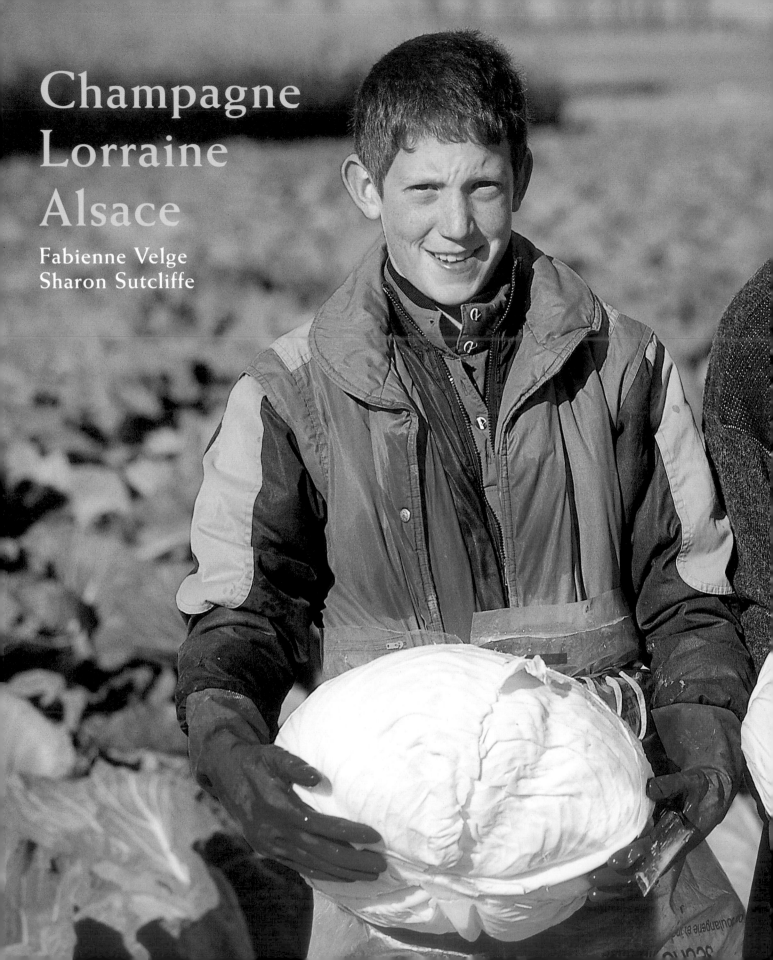

Champagne
Lorraine
Alsace

Fabienne Velge
Sharon Sutcliffe

Champagne

Pig trotters, sausage
 & ham

Hunting

Game dishes from the
 Ardennes

The very best preserves

Quiche Lorraine
 & related dishes

Babas, madeleines,
 & kougelhopf

Alsatian bread, cakes,
 & pastries

Sauerkraut

Alsace beer

Strasbourg goose liver pâté

Wine bars ("Winstub")

Munster cheese

Alsace wines

Eau-de-vie

Choucroute is extremely popular all over France,
but cabbages, sauerkraut and related recipes come
mainly from Alsace.

The Vosges mountains form both the link and the frontier between Alsace and Lorraine.

Calais

Le Havre

Caen

Paris

Brest

Rennes   Orléans

Tours   Champagne
Alsace
Nantes   Lorraine

Dijon

Limoges

Lyon

St-Étienne

Bordeaux   Grenoble

Avignon   Nice

Biarritz

Toulouse   Marseille   Toulon

Perpignan

The northeast of France provides great contrast. Champagne is but a short journey from Paris and when you come across a fascinating landscape of fields stretching into the distance, you know you have arrived. Such a landscape seems to be in conflict with the exclusive reputation the area owes to its world famous wine. In cities like Reims and Epernay this reputation which feeds off the unique image of Champagne can really be felt – especially in the best restaurants. Nevertheless Champagne itself has remained a somewhat provincial area, in which cheeses such as the creamy, mushroomy Chaource, and the orange-colored Langres, with its intense, distinctive flavor, epitomize its reputation for cheese-making. Towards Belgium, the Ardennes, which take its name from a mountain range, has long been renowcd for game and ham, while pork is without doubt the favorite food of the locals, the so-called Champenois. All these specialties link the Champagne region with neighboring Lorraine and, in the north eastern tip of France, with Alsace. The people of Lorraine and Alsace are masters of smoking and pickling, or of preparing pâtés and terrines, and all types of sausage. Apart from its industrial centers, Lorraine is still predominantly a peaceful farming area with quiet villages, where people enjoy eating fresh-water fish and in general prefer good local cooking. The famous *Quiche Lorraine*, meat pastries and also sweet specialties like madeleines, babas, and mirabelle cakes are typical of this region. Despite many of its specialties being common to the whole of the Vosges area, Alsace is conspicuously different, quite picturesque, and has created its own traditions, despite its turbulent history, taking the very best from both French and German cultures. The wines of Alsace pleasantly illustrate this with their own distinct character. While at the same time the extraordinary concentration of restaurants awarded Michelin stars underlines the importance of French cookery and the skill of the cooks in Alsace. This does not change the fact that people enjoy visiting wine bars, whose familiar and convivial atmosphere appeals to them just as much as the attractions of eating at home. Located on the Rhine, this is one of the liveliest, most charming and enjoyable French provinces, where you can drink to someone's health with a *blonde d'Alsace* (*light beer*) as well as enjoy a *sélection de grains nobles* (choice of quality wines).

Champagne

Champagne has enjoyed an aura of luxury from the very beginning. In the 17th century the first to appreciate this sparkling wine were members of London high society; their enthusiasm for this bubbly wine soon spilled over into France. Louis XIV was seduced by his mistresses into drinking this special drink, which is still as important on festive occasions as it was then.

People from all backgrounds celebrate with it (if they can afford it). Champagne turns a special occasion into a party – the opening of the carefully sealed bottles is in itself an experience enjoyed by all. It is easy to forget that champagne is a wine made from grapes cultivated in the northern most part of France. Epernay and Reims, the two main cities of Champagne, are almost 90 miles (140 kilometers) northeast of Paris. Apart from the majestic cathedral of Reims, the towns mainly owe their charm to the houses in the famous borderlands with their impressive cellars, from 30-160 feet (10-50 meters) deep in the limestone rock. This complex of tunnels in the rock reaches an overall length of almost 200 miles (320 kilometers). While the landscape is not particularly impressive, the gentle vine-covered hills and the quiet vine-growing villages, often protected by woods, have their own charm. In this area frost is an ever-present risk that cannot be ignored. In a good year, around 260 million bottles of champagne can be produced; in the worst case, if adverse weather strikes, this figure can be cut by more than two-thirds.

Most of the 80,769 acres (32,700 hectares) of champagne-producing estates are in the *département* of Marne, which is where, together with the Montagne de Reims, the Côte de Blancs, south of Epernay, and a part of the Marne valley, the most famous growing areas are located. A fifth of the champagne comes from vineyards in the areas around Bar-sur-Aube and Bar-sur-Seine, to the east of Troyes. Champagne owes its properties to the mineral rich limestone and the beneficial microclimate of the region, factors which also have a bearing on the price of grapes. Of the 302 municipalities producing champagne only 17 are classified as, and qualify 100 percent as, *grands crus*. A further 41 have been raised to *premiers crus* with awards between 90 and 99 percent, while the majority must be satisfied with 80 to 89 percent. In Champagne there are 14,800 companies harvesting-grapes, many of whom are members of 44 wine producing cooperatives.

Of the 5152 wine producers that sell bottled champagne, only some undertake the expensive manufacturing process themselves. Out in front are the 265 registered trading companies, of which only a few own extensive vineyards, but all of which buy grapes or must, and carry out the champagne making process themselves. Famous brands are in the hands of just a few companies. The holding company, L.V.M.H. (Louis Vuitton Moët Hennessy), which produces Moët et Chandon, Veuve Cliquot, and Mercier, as well as Pommery, Canard-Duchêne, Ruinart, and Henriot, receives a percentage on every fourth bottle of champagne sold.

New champagne corks are cylindrical

Champagne matures at a constant temperature in vaults cut into limestone.

From the vine to the brut

The most popular champagne by far is actually no more than white wine. However, it is by no means an ordinary white wine as up to two thirds of it come from red grapes, from Pinot Noir and Pinot Meunier. The former, a late vintage Burgundy, produces lower yields, but has body and depth. The latter, Pinot Meunier, a black Riesling, is less susceptible to frost, easier to cultivate and with an emerging fruitiness after pressing. The white Chardonnay grape rounds the composition off. At harvest time, towards the end of September, speed is of the essence. Numerous helpers pick the grapes by hand avoiding damage of any kind, as blue skins would color the must. To avoid any tinting, the grapes are pressed immediately. Alcoholic fermentation then takes place with the addition of yeast and at a strictly controlled temperature, generally followed by a second, malolactic, fermentation to biologically break down acidity. The gentle and dry base wine is produced in this way.

At this point the real art of champagne making starts, developed by Dom Pérignon, keeper of the cellars of the Abbey of Hautvilliers at the end of the 17th and the beginning of the 18th century. Wines of different types, from different vineyards and years – as long as they are not vintage champagne – are brought together for the *cuvée* (blending) and bottled. Before it is sealed with a crown cap each bottle receives some *liqueur du tirage*, a mixture of cane sugar ½ ounce/pint (24 grams/liter), old wine and pure yeast culture. Within eight to ten weeks the *prise de mousse*, fermentation in the bottle, is complete. When carbonic gas has turned still wine into sparkling wine, the yeast begins to ferment giving the wine additional flavor and body.

Yeast residues are left in more ordinary champagnes for at least a year, and for up to three times as long in the case of vintage champagnes. Generally vintage champagnes spend longer maturing in the deep limestone cellars of Reims and Epernay before the *remuage* process begins, which encourages the residues to sink into the neck of the upturned bottle. This is followed by the *dégorgement* whereby the deposits are then frozen. The crown cap is then removed by machine and the pressure of the carbonic gas ejects the residues. *Liqueur d'expédition*, expedition liqueur, added for transport, made from a mixture of wine and sugar, is used to top the bottles up. The quantity of sugar determines the type of champagne produced. If only dry wine is added, a *non dosé*, *brut nature*, *ultra brut*, *extra brut* or *brut intégral* is produced. Otherwise the champagne may range from the slightly sweetened *brut* to the *doux*. Non-vintage *brut* is the most popular and the champagne trading houses owe their reputation to its unchanging character and consistent quality.

In the cool, northern climate the vineyards produce Pinot Noir and Chardonnay grapes with a high acidity content, producing a lively champagne.

The yeast residues removed before final bottling are the stamp of traditional bottle fermentation, the *méthode champenoise*.

During *remuage* each bottle is slightly turned every two or three days and at the same time set increasingly at an angle to displace the yeast residues into the neck of the bottle.

Then the champagne is topped up with *liqueur d'expédition*, with wine mixed with sugar, bottled in line with marketing requirements and sealed with the final cork.

Who really bottled your champagne

A champagne label is not too difficult to understand. Apart from the description of origin it gives the name of the brand, the type, depending on its sugar content, *brut* for example, the name of the producer, contents of the bottle, alcohol content by volume, as well as the special blend, if applicable, and the vintage. Often underneath the remaining details there is, in small print, a number prefaced at most by two letters: this identifies who bottled the champagne in question, as every bottler has his own particular code.
NM: négociant-manipulant. This dealing or trading company harvests or buys grapes, musts or base wine and processes them in their cellars into champagne.
RM: récoltant-manipulant – a wine producer, who makes champagne from his own harvest in his own cellars. **RC:** récoltant-coopérateur – this wine producer is a member of a cooperative, from which he takes the wine back to sell it to his own clientele.
CM: coopérative de manipulation – wine producers' cooperative, which presses and matures champagne from the grapes of its members in its own cellars.
SR: société de récoltants – association of independent wine producers, who develop and bottle champagne from the harvest of its members.
ND: négociant distributeur – wine dealer or trading company who buys ready bottled champagne and affixes their own label.
R: récoltant – this wine grower has wine made from his grapes by a négociant-manipulant on an hourly paid basis and receives the bottled champagne back from the latter.
MA: marque auxiliare – literally auxiliary mark, describes commercial marks, produced on behalf of a reseller and supplied with his label.

1	Champagne producer	MOËT et CHANDON
2	Place	Epernay
3	Year of foundation	Founded in 1745
4	Appellation	Champagne
5	Blend	Cuvée Dom Pérignon
6	Alcohol by volume	12,5 %
7	Bottle contents	1.58 pints/750 ml
8	Sugar content	Brut
9	No. and code of bottler	
10	Produced by	élaboré par
11	Company, place, country	MOËT et CHANDON EPERNAY/FRANCE
12	Registered trademark and design	Muselet EPARNIX
13	Vintage	Millésime 1990
(Order and contents may vary)		

Enjoying champagne

Champagne is something special to drink, no daily beverage, but it has to be treated in the right .way to ensure that it fulfills all expectations. The special treatment starts when you buy it. Fundamentally champagne is suitable for all occasions and dishes – but the combination must be right.

First it is important to know which champagne is right for which occasion, as no other wine offers such a wide choice. It is up to each champagne producer to give his *cuvées* their own character by blending grape types, wines from different vineyards and of different vintages, as well as by adding his own particular wine/sugar mixture. There are consequently many different types of champagne – light and full-bodied, fruity and flowery, young and mature, sweet and very dry, new and well-developed. Of course there are bad ones and good ones too, fine and ordinary, harmonious and coarse, expensive and cheap. Even in the case of the most popular type of champagne, the non-vintage *brut*, great differences occur from producer to producer and from company to company. The only source of good advice is a wine waiter, a wine dealer, an informed salesman, a serious wine guide – or one's own acquired experience.

Champagne is a wonderful aperitive; it is lively, fresh, and dry like a large number of non-vintage *bruts* or the young *blancs de blanc*. The latter go extremely well with oysters and other seafood, while a more substantial *brut* should be chosen for caviar and lobster. A *brut* or *blanc de blanc* is an ideal accompaniment for many fish dishes. When the taste and consistency of the food and accompanying sauces have greater substance, the champagne too needs to exhibit more body and complexity, so vintage or rosé wines would be recommended. The rare prestige *cuvées* also need careful preparation. A more robust champagne can be served with cheese, while *sec* and *demi-sec* are usually recommended for subtly sweet desserts.

Once the most suitable champagne has been selected, it has to be served in the right conditions. The correct temperature is between 43 °F and 48 °F (6 °C and 9 °C), and the wine should be gently cooled. This is best done by placing the bottle in an ice bucket filled with ice cubes and water, and returning it to the bucket once opened. Do not serve the champagne in bowl-shaped glasses, as it loses part of its flavor and sparkle. It should be served in clear, slim tulip-shaped crystal glasses with a long stem, which stops body warmth being transmitted via the hand to the bowl of the glass and consequently unbalancing the temperature of the champagne.

Champagne is best cooled in iced water and served at 43-48 °F (6-9 °C).

Cut the metalic wrapper around the neck of the bottle to remove it cleanly.

Then pull off the wrapper, revealing the wire, which is removed by first turning the loop.

Hold the neck of the bottle in the right hand, with the thumb of the same hand securing the cork.

Holding the cork in your right hand, carefully turn the whole bottle with the left.

A true lover of champagne does not let the cork pop: too much carbonic gas and flavor escape.

When serving support the bottle on the fingers, gripping the hollow bottom with the thumb.

Holding the bottle just above the rim of the glass, allow the champagne to trickle into the glass.

A tulip-shaped clear crystal glass sets off the bouquet, the color, and sparkle.

Ayala Brut
Fine bouquet, good sparkle

Taittinger
Fruity, good presence on the palate

Salon
1982, robust, fresh, special class

Philipponat Royal Reserve
Expressive, elegant

Mercier Brut
Pleasant and balanced

Abel Lepitre
Fine sparkle, good harmony

Heidsieck Monopole
Intense bouquet, body

Audoin de Dampierre
Spicy, mature, with character

Henriot Souverain Brut
Clean fine nose, winey

Besserat de Bellefon
Balanced, nicely fresh

De Venoge
Fruity, pleasant as an aperitive

Lanson
Faint lemon overtones, fine acidity

Pommery
Winey, harmonious, and fresh

Veuve Cliquot Ponsardin
Full of flavor, fine fruit

Laurent Perrier
Complex, fruity overtones, spirited

Pol Roger
Harmonious, elegant, varied flavor

Piper Heidsieck
Classically balanced

Jacquart
Complex bouquet and good length

Deutz
Lively and frisky, for seafood

Ruinart
Light, frisky and refreshing

Charles Heidsieck
Smooth, fruity

Perrier-Jouët
Pleasantly harmonious, fine sparkle

Mumm Cordon Rouge
Finesse, lasting on the palate

Bollinger
Complex cuvée, long-lasting flavor

Gosset
Fruity, frisky, good volume

Krug Grande Cuvée
A wine full of finesse

Louis Roederer
Fine fruit, balanced and elegant

Moët & Chandon
Straight and lasting

De Castellane
Flowery bouquet, frisky but balanced

Bricout
Pleasant freshness, good length

Pig trotters, sausage & ham

The Champagne-Ardennes region also has a more down to earth side. Behind the sparkling veneer of champagne there is a rustic way of life, where not everyone is wealthy enough to enjoy a bottle of its famous product. While wine is indeed used for cooking, best of all pike and other fish in white wine, pullets in sparkling wine, and chicken in red wine, the preference of the people of the area between Troyes in the south and Charleville-Mézières in the north is indisputably for pork. Troyes is reputedly one of the main centers producing *andouillettes*, sausages made entirely of pork organ meat: veal intestines would never be put into a sausage as is done in Lyon. *La potée champenoise*, the fortifying stew, which gave the harvesters renewed strength, based on plenty of fatty pork, even if perhaps they would have preferred chicken meat, is another typical dish of the region.

In Reims they insist on using pure pork for pâté, and in preparing the world famous *jambon de Reims*, the slaughterers put their skill and their appreciation of taste to the test. They cook pieces of pork in stock, add finely seasoned jelly, and cover the meat with breadcrumbs to give their creation its typical appearance. The region offers three specialties, regarded as particular culinary highpoints by connoisseurs: pig trotters from Sainte-Menehould, white sausage from Rethel, and ham from the Ardennes.

Pig trotters

In Sainte-Menehould, birthplace of that genial local monk, Dom Pérignon, pig trotters have been considered very special for some time. King Charles VII, who in the 15th century successfully sped to the aid of Joan of Arc, was supposed to have acquired a taste for this incomparable delicacy during a stop in the staging town in 1435 and it is said that from then on pig trotter was added to the menu at court.

It is likely that the tasty dish that met with his approval was similar to our recipe, which is comparatively quick to prepare. The original recipe for pig trotters, eaten in Sainte-Menehould, like so many appetizing specialties, was created by mistake. More than 250 years ago the landlady of the "Soleil d'or" apparently forgot the pan with the pig trotters on the fire, where they cooked slowly through a very long night. In the morning to her surprise they were not overcooked at all. On the contrary, they were tastier than ever, right down to the bone. Once they had hit on the right idea, the people of Sainte-Menehould worked hard to come up with the ideal cooking time.

Today, according to the *Confrérie Gastronomique des Compagnons du Pied d'Or (Gastronomie Brotherhood of the Companions of the Golden Food)*, this is around 40 hours. This is how long the pig trotters are braised in their tasty stock until the small bones melt in the mouth, and the connoisseur can savor the delicious marrow of the larger bones with ease. To further heighten one's enjoyment, in the classical recipe they are breaded and fried until golden in plenty of butter.

White Sausage

The *boudin blanc*, the more delicate version of the substantial blood sausage, the *boudin noir*, can be found in almost every butcher's shop in France. In some areas it had achieved quite an extraordinary status, as in Normandy, in the southwest, mainly in Castres and Mazamet, and in the eastern Pyrenees too, where it benefits from the Catalan (Spain) influence on cooking. However, throughout the country *Boudin blanc à la Richelieu* is the most special, as poultry meat is used, and now and then even truffles. Cardinal Richelieu is indirectly responsible for the birth of France's highly regarded white sausage, from Rethel. As an opponent of the aristocracy, in 1626 Louis XIII's prime minister issued a decree, which made dueling, the favorite pastime of adventurous aristocrats, a severely punishable offence. An aristocrat called Jacques Augustin Chamarande could not resist challenging someone to a duel. He ended up as the victor,

having defended his honor, but out of fear of reprisals by Richelieu, he moved to the small town of Rethel 25 miles (40 kilometers) northeast of Reims, where he set up as a butcher and cooked his way into the history books.

In this area, which is often aptly referred to as *porcien*, only the best, freshest, lightest pork is chosen for making white sausage. To this are added fresh eggs, creamy milk and refined spices the recipe for which is passed on as a family

Les pieds de porc à la Sainte-Menehould Sainte-Menehould pig trotters		
4 pig trotters		
1¾ cups/400 g coarse cooking salt		
1 onion		
2 shallots		
2 garlic cloves		
2 carrots		
Bouquet garni (thyme, bayleaf, parsley)		
1 glass white wine		
2 cloves		
Salt		
2 eggs		
3 cups/200 g breadcrumbs		
6½ tbsps/100 g melted butter		

Flambé the pig trotters over a gas flame, clean and leave in coarse cooking salt for 3 hours. Wrap in strips of cloth, so they keep their shape while cooking.
Add onions, shallots, garlic, carrots, and bouquet garni to a pan, then add pig trotters, white wine, and cloves. Add salt and pour on plenty of water.
Bring to a boil, lower the temperature and let the meat simmer for about 4 hours, until tender. Take the pig trotters out and roll them first in an egg and then in breadcrumbs.
Put in a oven-safe dish, pour on the butter and place in an oven preheated to 390 °F / 200 °C, until they are golden-brown.
Serve on a large plate.
The pig trotters are best accompanied by stewed apples.

Pig trotters are wrapped in strips of cloth to keep their shape during cooking.

After four hours of slow cooking the cloth is removed and the trotters separated.

The pig trotters are allowed to cool before they are divided lengthwise and put into the oven.

The pig trotters are brought to a boil with onions, garlic, carrots, herbs, cloves, and wine.

secret from parent to child. With a skin made of natural pig intestine, the white sausages are parboiled briefly in stock before being rinsed in cold water. Absolutely no preservatives, nor any other ingredients are required. *Boudin blanc* is best eaten warm, simply heated in the oven or gently grilled on a low heat. Before cooking, it is often wrapped in a slice of Ardennes ham. Fried in butter, the sausage skin changes its color to an appetizing amber. Once out of the oven, a tomato or truffle sauce goes well with it too, as served in Périgord. Eaten with mashed or roast potatoes together with finely chopped mushrooms in a *Sauce suprême*, made with a chicken stock base using *crème fraîche*, it makes an excellent lunchtime meal.

Ardennes ham

The Ardennes are partly in Belgium and partly in France but as far as ham is concerned the border makes quite a difference. North of the border it is pickled in brine, smoked, and eaten within a month, while in France it is salted by hand and left to dry for several months. Originally the ham for which the region is famous came from one particular breed of pig. Adapted to the rough environment, the animals had longer legs, were tougher and undemanding. They lived in the woods and fed on acorns, chestnuts, wild fruits, roots, and anything else they could find. The ham they produced probably had little in common with today's, as their meat must have been marbled and quite rich. Ham from the Ardennes was even mentioned by the Greek cartographer Strabon, in his writing, some two thousand years ago.

Today there are two trademarks which identify every ham from the Ardennes: the French hexagon and the region's own emblem, the wild boar. Both guarantee that the ham has satisfied the most rigorous requirements. These start with the pigs themselves, which may only come from the region itself. An animal must be assigned a free range area of approximately 540 square feet (50 square meters). Its fodder must consist of wheat, oats, barley, and forage barley, peas, and

The famous pig trotters of Sainte-Menehould are cooked in these enormous slow cooking pots until they melt in the mouth.

beans. Fattening time may not be less than 16 weeks. Strictly regulated slaughtering must be as free of stress as possible for the animals, which must weigh between 200-265 pounds (90-120 kilograms) to produce hams weighing 17½-22 pounds (8-10 kilograms), when fresh. Over a number of weeks the hams are repeatedly rubbed with salt, then hung to dry for seven to nine months. The longer they dry, the finer the texture and the taste of the ham. Apart from the many different ways of serving it, ham is often used for wrapping around meat ingredients.

Hunting

The huge forests of the Ardennes have an incredible wealth of game birds, fallow deer, and wild boar, although modern forestry has changed the make-up of woodlands. Where once the terrain was varied, with rich undergrowth, tall conifers have taken over and below them any other vegetation dies. As they had insufficient protection and very few sources of food, wild boar, once so common, migrated to the south of the region where they found untouched forests and fields full of corn. Landowners were none too happy with this new interest in their corn, so they came up with the tastiest wild boar recipes and turned to the gun. Today wild boar are quite rare in the Ardennes.

Stags and hinds do not like the extensive forests of conifers either. They are rarely found in the Ardennes west of the Meuse and are attracted to the mixed woodland of Brie. Hunting quotas in the individual reserves are based on the levels of their stock of game and each season an area of forest is designated, where the shooting of animals is permitted. Because it is generally such a well-known hunting area, the area of forests given over to stag hunting is four to eight times greater than in the forests of the southern part of the Champagne-Ardennes region. In contrast stocks of roedeer have increased significantly, as they prosper well in the areas of conifers and almost always find enough food.

Hunting is not only allowed by law but also plays an important role in the life of the inhabitants of the Ardennes. Farmers and foresters, who have their own woodlands, arrange private hunts together or the huntsmen found clubs that hunt in local and state woodlands. In the south of the region they frequently hunt partridge, while pheasant and hare do not figure highly. Unlike pheasant, partridge and hare are not protected game. Hunt organizers generally have to submit reports on the stocks of game on their land. Then the period for the hunt is fixed. If no reports are submitted, forestry officials strictly limit the period of time for the hunt. Drives are organized when hunting red deer and boar. Stalking is less common and is only appropriate for roedeer or stags. Hunters usually share the catch. If they sell their catch to a game reseller, which they have been allowed to do since 1996, the meat is subject to strict inspection. Eating together is an important ritual of the hunt; hunters generally warm themselves up with a good soup, often followed by a main course of pot roast or jugged game, finishing off with cheese and fruitcake.

Sanglier – Wild boar
The most famous game of the Ardennes, which once populated its woods in large herds, but which has since become rare there, is still high on the list from the culinary point of view. Braised meat from young wild boar (*marcassins*) is a delicacy, while the meat of adult animals is mainly prepared in stew or jugged. In various regions wild boar successfully bred in farms can be eaten outside the hunting season.

Chevreuil – roedeer
Deer have adapted to their new living conditions, which have been changed by commercial forestry. As they are afforded the same protection as stags, they have been able to increase their numbers. Their dark red, strongly flavored meat is highly regarded. Filets and cutlets from the young animals are quickly braised in butter, the back and the leg are roasted in the oven. Jugged deer is popular too. Preferred side dishes which make use of the local ingredients mushrooms, sweet chestnuts, cooked pears, and currant jelly.

Lièvre – Hare
The hare is one of the victims of modern agriculture, which has depleted its habitat with its use of chemicals and modern machines and with its greed for new areas of exploitable land. The hare population has been further decimated by disease and by hordes of amateur hunters. Unlike the rabbit the hare has white meat. A *lièvre de l'année* weighing around 5½-6½ pounds (2.5-3 kilograms) is the best. The back, the best part, is prepared with bitter chocolate. Older and heavier animals are marinated in red wine or jugged.

Faisan – Pheasant
Originally from Asia, pheasants reached Europe in the Middle Ages. They like damp conditions and areas close to streams and fallow land, environments which are now difficult to find in the countryside. In the course of time hunting has decimated the stocks of pheasants, which is why today they have to be bred and released into the wild. The meat of the hens is better for cooking. Young birds are simply braised or they are cooked whole or in pieces in white wine or brandy. Older birds are generally used for stew. Mushrooms or cabbage are acceptable side dishes.

Perdreau et Perdrix – Partridge
Partridges are comparatively common. In France there are mainly two types: the red and the gray partridge, of which the latter is more common. The young birds with their tender meat are called *perdreau*, while after October 1, when the partridges are generally over eight months old, they are called *perdrix*. The young birds can be prepared with grapes, the older ones require stronger ingredients such as cabbage or lentils and are often prepared as stews, pâtés, or mousses.

Canard sauvage – Wild duck
A member of the goose family and ancestor of the domestic duck, the wild duck was first domesticated by the Chinese. Thanks to many new artificial lakes its numbers have kept up and there are good stocks but the wild duck is bred as well. The mallard, called *colvert* in French because of its green head feathers, is highly regarded by lovers of duck, who prefer the breast and legs of young birds spit-roasted or roasted in the oven. Otherwise it is used for stew.

Cerf et biche – Stag and hind (large illustration)
The largest animal in the forests of France is rare in the Ardennes today. Traditionally it is used for stew, but the strongly flavored venison of stag calves and of the young hinds makes it good for more exotic recipes. Can be used more or less as deer meat. It is also farmed.

Areas of forest

N

0   20 km

Revin

Lac des Vielles Forges

BELGIUM

Forêt des Ardennes

Rimogne

THIÉRACHE

Rumigny

Charleville-
Mézières

Meuse

Sedan

Carignan

Rocquigny

Mouzon

Le Chesne

Rethel

Canal des Ardennes

A R G O N N E

Asfeld

Vouziers

C H A M P A G N E

FRANCE

Game dishes from the Ardennes

While hunters and country people still relish eating stews and jugged game which have been marinated in wine for a long time and cooked for hours at a low heat, connoisseurs have fundamentally changed their attitude to game.

In today's kitchen more value is placed on the intrinsic taste of the ingredients than on expensive and extravagant preparations, which adversely affect the taste of the meat and cooks value game in a simpler and more direct way than ever before. The long process of hanging or marinating in wine and spices for days on end, which used to be quite normal, is no longer appropriate. The only meat suitable for this new approach is that of younger animals, which is tender enough to be flash fried in a skillet or roasted in the oven and which should remain pink on the inside.

Certain species have now been successfully bred for this purpose and are available to cooks in just the same way as other meats. This applies to fallow deer just as it does to wild boar. Among game birds, pheasants and a cross between a wild duck and the domestic duck have proved particularly successful. Sales of the meat however are limited to the months outside the hunting season. This ensures the availability of genuine game from the beginning of October through to January, for those who prefer the real thing.

Tournedos de chevreuil au jambon de sanglier gratiné à l'oignon
Venison loin steaks with wild boar ham

3 onions
3½ tbsp/50 g butter
Salt and freshly milled pepper
1 medium-sized slice of wild boar ham
2 egg yolks
3½ tbsp/50 ml crème fraîche
8 venison loin steaks, each approx. 2 oz/60 g
1 tbsp breadcrumbs

Peel the onions, slice into thin rings and sauté in 5 tsp/25 g butter. Add salt and pepper. Finely dice the ham. Mix the egg yolks with the crème fraîche, onions, and ham.
Braise the loin steaks in 5 tsp/25 g butter, turning once, season to taste and pour on the ham cream. Sprinkle with breadcrumbs and crust over in a preheated broiler.
Fresh noodles with game sauce go well with this.

Aumônières de biche forestière sauce Champagne
Venison pasties with champagne sauce

12 venison loin steaks, from the hind, each weighing approx. 1½ oz/40 g
3½ tbsp/50 g butter
14 oz/ 400 g mixed mushrooms
1 shallot
1 cup/250 ml Champagne
1 cup/ 250 ml game stock
1 cup/250 ml whipping cream
12 filo pastry leaves, diameter 8 in/20 cm
1 bunch of chervil

Braise the meat in 5 tsp/25 g butter in a pan, so it remains pink on the inside, remove it and allow to rest on a grill.
Clean the mushrooms and finely chop the shallot, then sauté together in the remaining meat fat and juices, remove it and add the champagne.
Pour on the game stock, stir in the cream, season to taste and reduce to the correct consistency.
Preheat the oven to 465 °F/240 °C. Melt the remaining butter and coat the filo pastry leaves with it. Put some of the mushrooms and a loin steak on this, and then fold the leaves together and fasten with chervil.
Bake until golden yellow in the oven. Serve the meat with braised red cabbage.

Tournedos de chevreuil au jambon de sanglier gratiné à l'oignon – Venison loin steaks with wild boar ham

Poêlée minute de cerf au vinaigre de Reims infusée au genièvre – Leg of venison in wine vinegar sauce

Poêlée minute de cerf au vinaigre de Reims infusée au genièvre
Leg of venison in wine vinegar sauce

21 oz/600 g leg of venison (stag or deer)
Thyme
Bayleaf
10 juniper berries
1 tbsp oil
1 tbsp butter
1 shallot
3 tbsp Reims wine vinegar
1 cup/250 ml game stock
1 cup/250 ml whipped cream
Salt and freshly milled pepper

Dice the meat and marinate it with the herbs, berries, and oil overnight.
The next day brown the meat lightly in butter. Lift and keep it warm.
Finely chop the shallot and braise until translucent in the remaining fat and juices.
Add vinegar, pour on the game stock and mix in the herbs of the marinade. Season with salt and pepper and simmer at low heat.
Pass the sauce through a sieve and pour over the meat.
It can be served with a creamed celery.

Rouelles de jarret de marcassin braisées au cassis
Slices of leg of young wild boar in blackcurrant sauce

1 carrot
1 onion
1 bouquet garni
10 juniper berries
3 tbsp red wine vinegar
2 tbsp oil
2 lb 3 oz/1 kg young wild boar leg, in slices each weighing about 9 oz/250 g
4 tbsp red wine
3½ tbsp/50 g butter
Salt and freshly ground pepper
A pinch of sugar
Cornstarch for thickening
3½ oz/100 g blackcurrant pulp

Clean the carrot and onion for the marinade and cut into pieces. Add to the meat with spices, herbs, vinegar and oil, pour over the wine and allow to marinate overnight. Braise the meat in a pan in 5 tsp/25 g butter. Add the vegetables and herbs from the marinade, sauté for 5 minutes, then pour on the marinade. Season with salt, pepper, and sugar and allow to cook for 2 hours. After cooking remove the meat and keep warm. Sieve the sauce into a separate dish and thicken with cornstarch. Add the remaining butter, then stir in the blackcurrant pulp. Put the meat back in the sauce and simmer for a further 10 minutes. Serve with apple quarters sautéed in butter.

Joues de sanglier et poires confites au Bouzy
Wild boar cheeks with red wine pears

1 carrot
1 onion
12 wild boar cheeks
1 bouquet garni
10 juniper berries
3 tbsp oil
3 tbsp wine vinegar
2 cups/500 ml Bouzy wine or another Pinot Noir
3½ tbsp/50 g butter
Salt and freshly milled pepper
4 pears
Cornstarch
A pinch of sugar

Clean the carrot and onion and cut them into pieces. Put them in a dish with the wild boar cheeks, herbs, spices, oil, and vinegar. Pour on the wine and marinate overnight. Brown the meat in a pan in 5 tsp/25 g butter.
Add the vegetables and herbs from the marinade and sauté for 5 minutes. Pour on the marinade, season to taste, bring to a boil and allow to simmer for 2 hours.
Peel and cut the pears into quarters. Remove the meat from the dish, sieve the sauce into a separate dish and thicken with cornstarch. Stir in the remaining butter, then add the pears, sugar and wild boar cheeks and simmer for a further 10 minutes. Serve 3 wild boar cheeks with 4 pieces of pear, add the sauce and serve with polenta.

The very best preserves

Bar-Le-Duc in the west of Lorraine is associated with one specialty, which was first mentioned in a document in 1344: currant preserve.

Cane sugar, and sweet things in general, were still quite rare and consequently a luxury; only the nobility got to enjoy them. For this reason they were very popular as gifts. It was normal in those days for someone who emerged as the winner of a legal dispute to thank the judges by making available to them some boxes of preserve. Yes, boxes. Then jelly was kept in wooden cases, covered in leather. Their fame reached the Court and at the beginning of the 16th century they were also given to guests in small glass receptacles as a token of respect. Old municipal accounts repeatedly list high sums for valuable pots of jelly, which, generously filled, were given to passing travelers of note to try and gain their favors. Even so, in Bar-le-Duc before the Revolution between 40,000 and 50,000 pots were produced annually. They were small glass receptacles, which contained about 4 ounces (110 grams) of preserve.

Currant bushes thrive in the climate of Lorraine. The variety has been continually improved by selection over the centuries, until eventually the optimum variety was achieved. Today this variety, *Groseille de Bar*, a currant bush from Bar-le-Duc, is featured in tree nursery catalogs. The harvest begins at the end of June and can last through the whole of July. Originally picking berries was done by women, who set out early in the morning, before the day had heated up. They knelt down in front of the bushes and picked cluster after cluster, without crushing a single berry. As soon as the picking was finished, the harvest was collected by trucks. At the factories the berries were weighed and then distributed to women who were specially employed to remove the pips. What makes the currant jelly of Bar-le-Duc so special is the way the pips are removed. The red and white currants have the pips removed by hand! Even today the workers carefully take berry after berry between the thumb and index finger of one hand. In the other they hold a pointed angular quill which they use to pierce the fruit at the stem end and then extract the pips, without damaging the fruit any further. The pipless currants are then poached in boiling sugar syrup, which helps keep their flavor and bright color intact.

Rare preserves and jellies

Crameillotte – Dandelion flower jelly
Often called dandelion honey, this preserve is made with dandelion flowers, collected in the spring and blanched in water. The bitter liquid is filtered and boiled with sugar, which reduces the bitterness to a slight aftertaste. This honey-like jelly is eaten on bread, with crêpes, or is used for ice cream.

Confiture de bluets de Vosges – Blueberry jelly from the Vosges
This preserve is protected by an *appellation*. It specifies that the blueberries used may only be cultivated in the heart of the Vosges and may only be enriched with organic fertilizer and spruce bark. The use of pesticides is forbidden. Furthermore the fruit must be picked by hand. It is indeed worth all the effort and work, because the jelly has a very special flavor.

Gelée de sureau – Elderberry jelly
Both black and red elderberries are used. The black ones are sweeter, the red grow in the mountainous areas. The clusters of berries are allowed to burst their skins in water and are boiled for about 10 minutes. The juice is then drained off. Because the small pip is poisonous, it is the juice that is used to make the jelly, rather than the fruit pulp.

Gelée de sorbes – Rowanberry jelly
Rowan trees, which grow to 50 feet (15 meters) form clusters of small red berries, containing a lot of vitamin C and which are also quite bitter. A jelly is made from the juice of the fruit, which also inherits the bitter taste and goes very well with game dishes.

For the most refined of all French preserves most of the small pips are removed by hand before cooking.

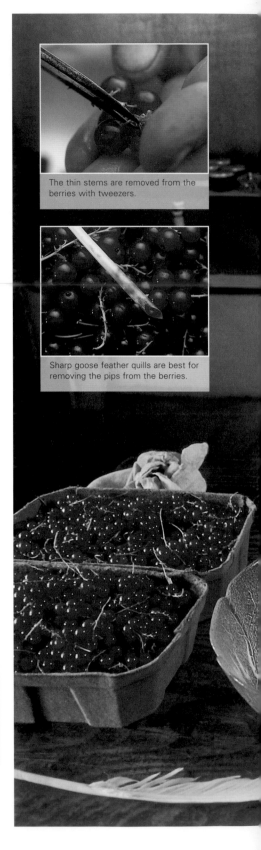

The thin stems are removed from the berries with tweezers.

Sharp goose feather quills are best for removing the pips from the berries.

Red and white currants thrive well in the climate of Lorraine and the bitter hand-picked fruits produce the best preserves.

Quiche Lorraine & related dishes

When food lovers hear the word Lorraine, they think of cream, butter, and eggs, of pork, cakes, and preserves, fruit and fruit-flavored schnapps. The best known and most copied specialty is a delicious pie.

It is said that the *Quiche Lorraine* was discovered by a baker in Nancy in the 16th century. Initially it was prepared with ordinary bread dough and was later refined when short crust (plain) pastry was used for the base. The main ingredient is smoked bacon, another of the province's specialties. Traditionally a cake tin with a 7-inch (18 centimeter) diameter is lined with pastry and the filling is then poured into the lining. It is made of a mixture of cream and eggs, to which small cubes of smoked bacon, are added.

When *Quiche Lorraine* became popular throughout France, grated cheese which originally was not used, somehow tricked its way into the recipe. The original recipe depended solely on the quality of three basic Lorraine products: butter, eggs, and smoked bacon. The bacon owes its quality to hundreds of years of experience.

Since the Middle Ages, when salt was quarried in the salt mines, this valuable and profitable commodity has been used to preserve pork, the preferred meat of Lorraine; it is used for bacon, ham, and various sausages such as *jésu* and *fuseau* which are noteworthy specialties. The first is a large air-dried sausage made by filling the stomach of the pig. The second uses the fatty intestine as a skin.

It is quite difficult to picture the cooking of Lorraine without pork, as this meat forms the basis for the popular and frequently prepared stews. At the same time it plays a large and significant part in two other dishes: the *tourte* and the *pâté* which demonstrate the local people's love of baking, if further proof was needed given the popularity of *Quiche Lorraine*.

Nothing is more popular than a baked hors d'oeuvre, better still when it is encased in a crust. Traditionally, not just pork but also veal or chicken are used to make the tourte. The meat is chopped or cut into narrow strips and often bound with an egg cream seasoned with herbs, bacon, or cheese and sometimes garnished with carrot and onions. The meat is left to marinate in white wine, without adding salt – it is delicately salted just before cooking. Traditionalists prefer short crust (plain) pastry. However, as a compromise, short crust pastry can be used for the base with a top crust made of puff pastry. The more modern approach is to use puff pastry top and bottom.

Quiche Lorraine
Lorraine bacon pie

Serves 2-4

5 oz/150 g wheat flour
Salt, black milled pepper
3 eggs
5 tbsp/75 g butter
5 oz/150 g lean smoked bacon
Grated cheese (to taste)
½ cup /125 g crème fraîche
A pinch of nutmeg

Sieve the flour into a bowl and press out a hollow in the middle. Add a pinch of salt, 1 egg, and butter cut into small pieces. Knead all the ingredients together, shaping the pastry dough into a ball. Press it flat and form a ball again. Place in the refrigerator in plastic wrap and leave for 2 hours.

Roll out the pastry to a thickness of at least about ⅛ in/3 mm. Grease a 7 in/18 cm diameter cake or quiche mold with butter. Line with pastry and trim off the excess. Prick the pastry all over with a fork. Preheat the oven to about 430 °F/220 °C.

Cut the rind from the bacon, remove any gristle, and dice the bacon. Brown lightly in a pan. Beat both remaining eggs, stir in the crème fraîche and season with nutmeg and pepper. Add salt sparingly.

Spread the diced bacon on the pastry (sprinkle with grated cheese to taste) and pour on the mixture of egg and cream. Bake in the oven for 25 minutes. Serve hot.

Tip: The base of the quiche can be baked blind before filling for about 10 minutes or until it is golden brown.

1 Place the egg, butter, and salt on the pastry board. – **2** Knead all the ingredients together and shape the pastry into a ball.
3 Roll the pastry out thin after it has been left to chill in the refrigerator. – **4** Carefully line a well-greased tin.

5 Roll the rolling pin over the rim of the tin to cut off excess pastry cleanly. – **6** Sprinkle grated cheese and bacon onto the base.
7 Beat two eggs with crème fraîche and season. – **8** Spread the mixture of eggs and cream evenly over the base.

Pâté Lorraine
Lorraine meat pie

Serves 8

2 lb 3 oz/1 kg shoulder or neck of pork
2 cups/500 ml white wine
8 shallots
2 bayleaves
1 tbsp chopped parsley
Salt and peppercorns
1½ lb / 700 g puff pastry
1 egg yolk

Cut the meat into pieces, quarter the shallots and leave to marinate overnight with bayleaves, parsley, and pepper in white wine.
Roll the pastry to a thickness of just over ⅛ in/ 4 mm and cut out a long rectangle for the top crust of the pâté.
Preheat the oven to 355 °F/180 °C. Drain the meat and place it in the center of the pastry; cover with the remaining pastry, pressing it down well and brush it with egg yolk.
Make a cylinder from several pieces of aluminum foil and insert it through the center of the pastry covering like a funnel. Bake in the preheated oven for 45 minutes.

La Potée Lorraine
Lorraine stew

Serves 6

1 ham bone
9 oz/250 g lean smoked bacon
17½ oz/500 g pork shoulder
3 smoked sausages
17½ oz/500 g Boston (navy) beans
12 medium-sized potatoes
1 large savoy cabbage
12 carrots
6 turnips
1 onion
Salt and freshly ground pepper

Add the ham bone, bacon, meat, sausages, and beans to a dish with cold water and simmer at a low temperature for 1½ hours.
Then add the vegetables and cook for a further 1½ hours.
Remove the vegetables, drain, and place on a serving dish. Cut the meat, bacon, and sausage into slices and arrange them on top of the vegetables.
Pour the stock through a sieve and serve separately in a tureen. Or serve meat, vegetables, and stock together in a tureen.

Tourte Lorraine
Lorraine pie

Serves 8

9 oz/250 g veal shoulder
1 lb 10 oz/750 g neck of pork
White wine
Thyme, bayleaf, and other herbs to taste
About ½ oz/18 g salt, pepper
1 lb/450 g puff or short crust (plain) pastry
2 eggs
2 cups/500 ml crème fraîche

Cut the meat into narrow strips. Place in a generous amount of white wine with herbs and marinate for 24 hours. Then press out well by hand and add salt.
Preheat the oven to 355 °F/180 °C. Roll the pastry dough to a thickness of just over ⅛ in/4 mm and line a pastry tin. Cut off the excess pastry. Add meat to the tin. Roll the remaining pastry again, this time slightly thinner than before to shape a suitable top crust, and make a hole in the center. Lay the pastry over the meat and press down the edges.
Bake for 40 minutes in a preheated oven and then take the pie out of the oven.
Lightly beat the eggs and cream together, season to taste, and carefully add this through the hole in the pastry.
Bake for a further 30 minutes. Serve it very hot.

A wavy edge makes a *Quiche Lorraine* look more attractive, but it does nothing to enhance the taste.

Rum baba

into a juicy ringcake, which he then dipped in syrup enriched with rum or kirsch. At Court in Nancy, a mixture of sweet Malaga and rum was served with it as well. As the ex-King was an enthusiastic reader of the *Tales of a thousand and one nights*, he gave the cake the name of his favorite hero, Ali Baba. Stohrer, who came to Paris in 1725 with Maria, daughter of Stanislas and consort of Louis XV, opened his *pâtisserie* there in 1730 in Rue Montorgueil, where it still exists today. *Babas* were a success too and there was soon a version, called the *savarin*, made with currants, and filled with fruit, cream, or whipped cream.

The great popularity of *madeleines* is also down to Stanislas. These small shell-shaped cakes are now popular everywhere in France. It transpires that during preparations for a gala dinner the saucemaker and the pastry cook had a quite serious argument and the latter left everyone in the lurch and took to his heels. King Stanislas was dismayed. Could he not offer anything sweet at all to his guests? At this point his butler brought him assistance in the person of one of the chambermaids, who offered to bake some small tasty cakes from her grandmother's recipe. Her cakes met with the great approval of all the guests. When the King summoned her to congratulate her and ask for the name of the cakes, she was unable to supply one. He then asked her for her name and the name of the place where she was born. She told him that her name was Madeleine and that she came from Commercy. "So from now on call your cakes Madeleines de Commercy," replied the King.

Kougloff, kougelhopf or *guglhupf* are the various versions of the name of the famous yeast ring cake. The Alsatians have used this name from time immemorial, but they still do not know how to spell it, although they all agree that the cake is part of a good breakfast or something to eat with afternoon coffee. When a glass of Tokay Pinot Gris or Gewürztraminer is offered, a piece of cake should be offered too. Savory versions with diced bacon instead of currants accompany the aperitive. Its appearance is due to the high-walled wavy mold in which it is baked. Traditional ringcake molds are fired in terracotta and are tile red. The name is derived from German, although it comes from Austria, from where Marie Antoinette brought the recipe to Versailles. An exception is the *kougloff* of Ribeauvillé, where the inhabitants claim that the originator of their ringcake was a former village baker.

Fit for royalty

Babas, madeleines, & kougelhopf

In the world of sweets the region Lorraine is represented by two ambassadors, for which we can thank King Stanislas Leszczynski (1677–1766); Alsace on the other hand is represented by a cake which Queen Marie Antoinette (1755–1793) introduced from Austria. Due to Russian intervention Stanislas had lost his throne to the son of August the Strong, but received as compensation the Dukedom of Lorraine. There he complained to the *pâtissier* Stohrer that he found Polish ringcakes too dry, because they were made from rye flour. The sympathetic cakemaker changed the original recipe, with cream and currants soaked in rum,

Baba au rhum

4½ oz/125 g currants
¾ tbps /200 ml rum
9 oz/250 g wheat flour
½ oz/15 g compressed yeast
3 eggs
1 oz/30 g sugar
Salt
6½ tbsp/100 g butter

Syrup
17½ oz/500 g sugar
4 cups/1l water
1 Pulverized vanilla bean
Peel of an untreated lemon
Peel of an untreated orange
½ cup/125 ml rum

Soak the currants overnight in rum. Mix a starter dough using a third of the flour, the yeast, and some lukewarm water and leave it to prove for 1 hour.
Add the remaining flour, eggs, sugar, and a pinch of salt and knead into a loose dough. Work in the warm butter and currants. Cover and allow to prove for 30 minutes more.
Preheat the oven to 390 °F/200 °C. Fill a greased ring mold of the right size, allow to prove again, and then bake for just 20 minutes.
In the meantime prepare the syrup. Bring to a boil the sugar and water, vanilla, and fruit peel.
Remove from the heat and add the rum.
Dip the babas in the hot syrup. Allow it to soak in, then scoop them out, drain, and serve on deep plates. Pour on some more syrup.
Like savarins, babas are served with fruit and whipped cream, or crème anglaise.

Madeleines

4 eggs
7 oz/200 g sugar
Peel of an untreated lemon
1 Pulverized vanilla bean (according to taste)
7 oz/200 g flour
½ oz/10 g powdered yeast
6½ tbsp/100 g butter

Beat the eggs in a bowl. Add the sugar and grated peel. Stir gently over a pan of simmering water until the sugar has dissolved. Then continue to stir until the mixture has cooled off again.
Gradually add the sieved flour and the dried powdered, stirring all the time and mix well. Melt the butter and add it last.
Preheat the oven to 430 °F/220 °C. Grease each madeleine mold with butter, fill the molds with the mixture and bake in the oven for 10 minutes.
Loosen the cakes from the mold straight away.

Kougelhopf
Fruit and almond ring

2 tbsp/30 ml kirsch	
1 cup /150 g sultanas	
or Malaga currants	
5 cups /700 g flour	
1 oz/30 g compressed yeast	
2 cups/500 ml lukewarm milk	
1 tbsp/10 g salt	
⅔ cup/150 g sugar	
5 eggs	
¾ cup/180 g soft butter	
2 tbsp almond flakes	

Pour the kirsch over the currants, stir, leave covered for a few hours to soak.
To prepare the starter dough sieve 2 cups/ 300 g flour into a bowl, make a hollow in the center, crumble in the yeast, pour on half the lukewarm water and stir.
Lightly knead and leave to prove for 2 hours.
Then add the remaining milk, the remaining flour, salt, sugar, and the eggs to the starter dough, mix all the ingredients well and beat vigorously for at least 10 minutes, which is very important for the texture of the cake. The loose, semi-solid dough should come away from the bowl easily. Mix in the butter and knead the mixture, until it becomes a smooth, supple dough. Now add the currants and work them in until they are evenly distributed in the dough.
Carefully grease two ringcake molds with butter and sprinkle the almond flakes evenly in them. Fill the mold up to halfway with the dough and leave to prove in a draught-free place.
Preheat the oven to 390 °F/200 °C.
Bake the kougelhopf for 20 to 30 minutes, depending on the size of the mold.
When the surface is golden brown, remove the cake from the oven and leave it to cool on a cakestand.

Kougelhopf ingredients: kirsch and currants, flour, butter, yeast, milk, sugar and eggs.

Starter dough made of flour, milk, and yeast is left to prove for 2 hours.

Then milk, flour, eggs, and sugar are added and the dough is beaten for about 10 minutes.

Butter, kirsch, and currants are only added at the end.

The mixture should fill no more than half the greased mold sprinkled with almonds.

Depending on the size of the molds the cakes are baked at 430 °F/220 °C for 20-30 minutes.

Alsatian bread, cakes & pastries

The people of Alsace are intent on preserving the region's individuality. In common with all Frenchmen they have a taste for good food, but what this actually means needs some explanation as the regional differences are quite distinct. While Paris and large parts of the population in other regions rely mainly on the *baguette*, Alsace has always boasted a refreshing variety of breads, cakes, and pastries.

The original bread of this region is undoubtedly the pain de *métier*, the mixed corn bread.

Centuries ago the feudal lord allocated a strip of land to his subjects, which they worked as they wished. Generally a mixture of cereals was grown on this land, normally wheat and rye. By doing this they protected themselves against the injustices of the weather and nature, and ensured that at least some of the grain would be fit to harvest, grind, and bake for their own families. Accordingly the composition of the bread was variable, sometimes wheat, sometimes rye being the main ingredient. When mixed corn bread is made today, however, the cereals are more or less in equal parts.

The *bretzel* or *pretzel* is the emblem of the Alsatian bakers' and millers' guilds. With its knotted shape it was once a lucky charm, and its crossed arms were supposed to offer protection against those evil spirits, intent on ruining cereals, flour,

or bread. It is made from an ordinary flour and water dough, which is then dipped in boiling water and coated with beaten egg. It is then sprinkled with coarse sea salt and dried in the oven. When freshly baked, pretzels have a crusty outside and a soft interior and are a very popular snack.

The *souswerk* or *sübredle* takes its name from the *sou*, the old 5 centimes piece, which is exactly what one used to cost. This reasonably priced bread, which is eaten for breakfast, is made from two balls of dough joined together.

It was assumed that the second ball, known as the *zugob*, had been added by the baker out of

Below: Pretzels made from flour, water, and salt owe their appetizing appearance to an egg glaze.

Daniel Helmstetter and his wife manage one of the best traditional bakeries in Alsace.

Baguette
This super baguette weighs 17½ oz/500 g and is twice as heavy as the normal one.

Berches – Pain au pavot
Jewish bread for the Sabbath with the characteristic plait and the poppy seeds which symbolize manna from heaven.

Couronne
A beautiful crown-shaped mixed wheat loaf, made up of six segments which are easy to separate from one another.

Epi
It is very easy to break off a piece of this loaf, shaped like an ear of corn.

Miche blanche
A 17½ oz/ 500 g pure wheat loaf with its attractive squares dusted with flour.

Pain aux noix
Walnut bread is an Alsatian discovery and its origins can be identified by its attractive dusting with flour.

Pain court
This short 17½ oz/ 500 g wheat loaf is the most popular bread in Alsace.

Pain de méteil
Original mixed corn bread with the initials of the famous Louis Helmstetter bakery in Colmar.

Pain de seigle
This fine dark loaf, made exclusively from rye flour, is unmistakably Alsatian.

Pain Lemaire
The most famous healthfood bread in France. Raoul Lemaire grows the wheat for his own recipe.

Souswek
A traditionally shaped wheatbread roll; the name means that it originally cost only 1 *sou*.

pure generosity. The *berches*, a traditional Jewish bread, is very popular. The wheat dough from which it is made is intentionally more solid and compact, because Jewish families bought the bread on Friday and ate it on Saturday, their Sabbath day. The plait, across the top of the loaf, symbolizes the tribes of Israel, while the poppy seeds represent manna from heaven.

In addition there is an abundance of other specialties, such as the *speckkiechle* rolls seasoned with bacon and caraway seed, or *behrewecka*, a fruit loaf, made with dried pears, figs, prunes, walnuts, and hazelnuts. And as well as the strongly flavored beer bread there is also good, solid pumpernickel made of coarsely ground rye,

more at home the other side of the Rhine.

Of all the many tempting sweets typical of Alsace, the most famous are the great variety of Christmas specialties, which are now available all year round. The most well-known is *bredle* – a type of biscuit, made with almonds, hazelnuts, lemon, aniseed, and cinnamon, in the shape of stars, hearts, or crescents. They are named after their main ingredient – aniseed *bredle*, butter *bredle* or *schowerbredle*, which contain grated almonds. *Schenkele*, the small Christmas cakes, are similar, but with a dash of fruit schnapps.

And of course we must not forget the *lebkueche*. These are derived from the ancient honey loaves, which were known even before the Roman era.

Then when the Crusaders brought spices from the Orient the loaves became spicy. To begin with they were specialties of Christian orders, who baked them for the Saint Nicholas celebrations. At the end of the 16th century they were popular at the Christkindelmärik fairs. In the 18th century lovers gave each other *lebkueche* hearts as gifts. They still do – and a Christmas market without *lebkueche* would lose its familiar charm.

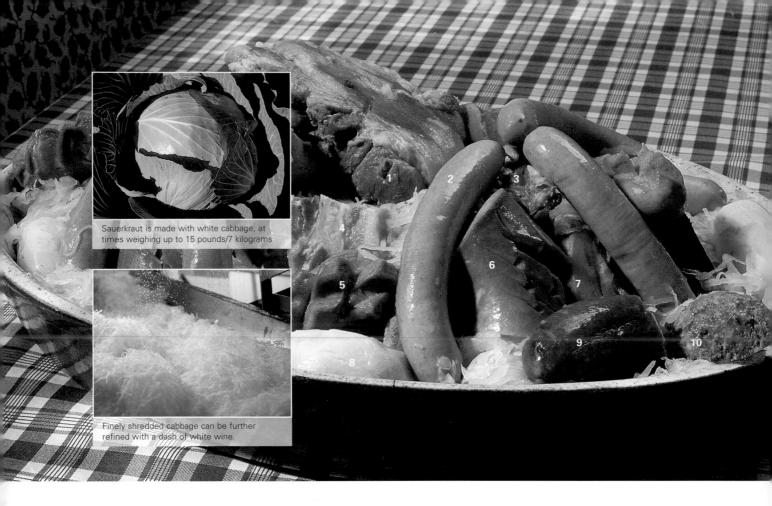

Sauerkraut is made with white cabbage, at times weighing up to 15 pounds/7 kilograms

Finely shredded cabbage can be further refined with a dash of white wine.

Sauerkraut

Every village in Alsace is said to have its own recipe for *choucroute* (Sauerkraut), a delicious meal made with fermented white cabbage which is served under an impressive mountain of mixed sausages, bacon, salted shoulder, smoked ham, and potatoes. Enjoyed with a jug of beer, a glass of Riesling or Sylvaner wine, *choucroute* is synonymous with Alsace.

The pale green white cabbage heads are decidedly larger than normal ones available in the shops. Magnificent examples can reach up to 15 pounds/7 kilograms and are known as *quintals d'Alsace*, Alsatian hundredweights. They are mainly grown in the north of the region in and around Krautergersheim and are harvested between July and November. The outer leaves and the heart are removed. The cabbage is shredded as finely as possible. Today this is generally carried out automatically in a *choucrouterie*.

Years ago there were people who made a living going from door to door offering their services to shred the cabbage, because every family laid down their own supplies for the winter. When the season is in full flow there are still cabbage cutters who demonstrate their skill in the markets and the characteristic smell of freshly cut cabbage fills the air.

To make sauerkraut, alternate layers of cabbage and salt are laid down in tall earthen pots or wooden barrels. If large quantities are to be produced, concrete or plastic tanks are used. Juniper berries often add extra flavor. The layers are pressed together – in domestic use with a wooden lid, with a stone placed on top – and the pots or barrels are sealed and made airtight. The salt draws moisture from the cabbage and forms brine, which protects it. Depending on the temperature, fermentation takes three to eight weeks to transform the cabbage. It loses half of its weight, but the process makes it easy to keep for a longer time. It has also become a healthy and easily digested food, thanks to various trace elements and vitamins.

Before the age of sterilization, deep freezing, and vacuum-packing, sauerkraut guaranteed the population of the countryside adequate supplies of vitamin C in winter. Consequently it provided ideal nourishment for seafarers and protected them from scurvy. It must be crunchy, light-colored, and have a pleasant smell. The local saying too is absolutely right: "Sauerkraut is only good when it has been reheated seven times." Cabbage comes from China. The workers that built the Great Wall were kept in good health by eating fermented cabbage. Mongols and Tartars later introduced it to Europe and in the Balkans fermented vegetables have a long tradition. Alsatians have liked sauerkraut since the Middle Ages and one suspects that they are able to enjoy it so much because there is always so much pork appetizingly served with it: smoked and green bacon, smoked pork shoulder, boiled pork, knuckle of pork and liver dumplings, bratwurst (frying sausage), blutwurst (blood sausage), smoked sausage, knackwurst (little Strasbourg sausages) and fleischwurst (made with finely minced pork). It is just coincidental that new sauerkraut finishes its fermenting process at the same time as local celebrations begin to honor local meat production.

Above: An ideal selection of cooked meats for *Sauerkraut* consists of knuckle of pork (1), knackwurst (Strasbourg sausage) (2), streaky bacon (3), smoked shoulder (4), bratwurst (frying sausage) (5), fleischwurst (made with finely minced pork) (6), kasseler or schiffala (pickled and smoked pork shoulder) (7), potatoes (8), smoked sausage (9) and liver dumplings (10).

Opposite: In factory production it is important to mix the cabbage and the salt thoroughly.

Choucroute à l'ancienne
Traditional sauerkraut

Serves 8

4 lbs 6 oz/2 kg fresh raw sauerkraut
2 bacon rinds
2 carrots
2 onions
½ tsp peppercorns
½ tsp caraway seeds
2 garlic cloves
4 cloves
12 juniper berries
2 bayleaves
1 sprig of thyme
1 knuckle of pork
2 finger thick slices of streaky ham
½ bottle of dry Riesling wine
4 smoked Montbéliard sausages
21 oz/600 g Shiffala smoked pork shoulder
4 pairs knackwurst (little Strasbourg sausages)
1 boiled Morteau sausage

Wash the sauerkraut in a sieve under flowing water, pull it apart and press out the water. Arrange bacon rinds on the bottom of a large cast iron pot. Add half the sauerkraut. Clean the carrots and peel the onions, cut into pieces and spread on the sauerkraut. Sprinkle the peppercorns evenly over it. Tie the remaining spices with thyme in a muslin bag and add to the vegetables. Add the pork knuckle and bacon and cover with the remaining sauerkraut. Pour on the wine and 1 cup/250 ml of water.

Cover the pot well, place in the oven and cook for about 2.5 hours at 355 °F/180 °C.
Place the smoked sausage and smoked pork shoulder in the pot under the sauerkraut. Cook for another 30 minutes. Place the Strasbourg knackwurst and boiled sausage on the sauerkraut and cook again for 20 minutes. Remove the muslin bag. Serve the sauerkraut with meat and sausages. A well-cooled Sylvaner or Riesling wine goes well with this dish.

Alexandre Dumas' Choucroute

"The sauerkraut is preferably kept in barrels, containing vinegar, wine or another fermenting liquid… The cabbage is sliced, by grating it with a sort of plane… The bottom of the barrel is covered with a bed of sea salt and then on this a layer of cabbage cut into strips is placed. Then a handful of juniper berries or caraway seed is sprinkled on it to give flavor. This is repeated, layer after layer until the barrel is full… The last salt layer is covered with large, green cabbage leaves, on top of which a large damp sheet and a rather heavy barrel lid are laid… The cabbage compressed together in this way exudes a foul smelling, sour, dirty liquid, which can be … drawn off through a tap and replaced by a fresh salt solution…, until the strong smell disappears."

Choucroute maison
Homemade sauerkraut

Serves 6-8

1 pickled pork knuckle (*demi-sel*)
2 finger thick slices of streaky bacon
1 tsp peppercorns
1 Cervelat sausage
3-4 pairs of Strasbourg knackwurst sausages
3 lb 5 oz/1.5 kg fresh raw sauerkraut
3 tbsp goose dripping
3 onions
2 bayleaves
10 juniper berries
3 cloves
½ bottle dry Alsace Riesling

Rinse the knuckle and the bacon, place in cold water with peppercorns and simmer at a low temperature for 75 minutes. Add the boiled sausage and knackwurst and simmer for a further 20 minutes.
Wash the sauerkraut in a sieve under flowing water, take it apart, and press out the water. Heat the dripping in a cast iron pot. Peel the onions, finely chop them, and lightly braise. Add the sauerkraut, bayleaves, juniper berries and cloves. Pour on the Riesling and add water until the sauerkraut is completely covered. Cover and cook at a low temperature for 40 minutes.
Pile up the sauerkraut on a large plate. Cut the knuckle and bacon into pieces and the cervelat into slices and surround these with the small sausages. Serve with boiled potatoes. In Alsace they drink beer with it.

Special sauerkraut cooking pots are made of stoneware and have a groove for water.

Pressing is important as sufficient liquid must be separated from the cabbage to completely cover it.

During fermentation the cabbage must be weighted down – in this case with a bottling jar full of water.

The lid is fitted in the groove, which is filled with water to stop air getting into the pot.

Barley is an essential ingredient of beer. In Alsace the best barley comes from the plain of the Ried. After germination the barley is oasted to obtain malt.

Hops are added to the sugary wort extracted from the malt and hot water. Then this mixture is boiled to produce the base wort.

Beer brewing

In Alsace, barley for beer production is still cultivated in the rich Ried river plain. It is soaked to trigger germination, which takes about six days. It is then oasted in a drying oven to obtain malt. The oasted malt is coarsely ground and mixed into a mash in a tank with water at a temperature of 120-165 °F /50-75 °C. Water is an important element of beer production. In the 19th century Schiltigheim became the capital of brewing because the water there has a particular balance of minerals. Other breweries were established in the Vosges mountains because of their excellent springs. The mash is often stirred well for two hours. Then it is given time for the cloudy substances to settle before the wort is drawn off. It is transferred into vats and mixed with hops. The fertile loess area around Kochersberg and Ackerland are famous for hop growing. To make 210 pints (100 liters) of beer takes about 6 ounces (170 grams) of dried hop blossoms – only the female clusters are used. Hops give the beer the bitter taste and a longer life. The brewer lets the wort simmer for 2 to 4 hours. It has to cool off before yeast is added, which triggers fermentation and develops additional flavor. The *Blondes d'Alsace*, lightly fermented beers, related to the well-known Pilsners, are typical of Alsace. They are fermented at 40-50 °F (10-15 °C). At the end of the normally 7 to 9-day-long fermentation the yeast deposits settle on the bottom of the fermenting vats. Now the beer is filtered off and bottled.

Hop blossoms give the beer the bitter taste.

Alsace beer

In Alsace they have been drinking beer since the time of the Gauls. When the Romans introduced wine, beer became the poor man's drink, but the well-to-do did accept a mug of beer as a tolerable replacement for wine – certainly when the grapes had been ruined by bad weather; it was always much better for quenching thirst than water.

In the Middle Ages monasteries were the only places where an exhausted traveler could find accommodation and food. It became increasingly difficult for religious orders to offer wine to all the pilgrims, who sought their hospitality. The monks then began to brew beer in large quantities. The best was reserved for the personal enjoyment of the bishop or abbot, while the most nourishing ones quenched the thirst of the monks after a hard day working and praying. The dregs were sadly kept for the pilgrims.

Before the process of pasteurization was discovered, the only way to keep beer over a long period of time was by keeping it cool. Ice was collected from ponds and from the meadows that had been intentionally flooded for this purpose.

In Alsace people other than the monks were allowed to brew beer, but only in winter. The first person to do this within the city walls of Strasbourg was a certain Arnoldus, who opened his brewery in 1259, behind the cathedral. The Catholic church fundamentally considered beer to be pagan. Gradually brewing was taken over by Protestants.

Martin Luther, son-in-law of a brewer, explained that whoever produced beer served God and the community, if they carried out their trade successfully. He stressed: "Vinum est donatio Dei, cervesia traditio humana" (Wine is a gift of God, beer is a human tradition).

In 1789, the French Revolution put an end to the constraints imposed on brewing which had only been allowed at certain times of the year. Brewers began to open inns *auberges-brasseries* and serve their beer in them. At the end of the 18th century there were already 1774 *auberges* in the Haut-Rhin region and at least 280 in the Bas-Rhin.

Around 1850 a further revolution took place, which had a decisive influence on the brewing of beer: the Industrial Revolution. Pasteurization, developed by Louis Pasteur, modern cooling methods, and the railway had changed many small family run breweries into either simple bars – hence the dual meaning of the expression "brasserie" – or into industrial beer manufacturing companies.

Beer production of the whole of Alsace quadrupled from 2.6 million gallons (100,000 hectoliters) in 1850 to 10.5 million gallons (400,000 hectoliters) in 1869. When Alsace was annexed by Germany at the end of the 19th century, in and around Strasbourg a large number of spacious *brasseries* were built, which emulated the style of the flourishing breweries of Munich. The *stammtisch*, the table reserved for regulars who drank from their own personal beer jugs, became an institution in Alsace too. At the same time the origin of the many *brasseries* in Paris can be attributed to Alsatians, who fled from their homeland to resist the German occupation in 1871. Today there are seven breweries in Alsace, which produce 54 percent of all French beer.

The main center of brewing is the Strasbourg suburb of Schiltigheim. Schutzenberger, the oldest existing brewery founded in 1740, has its home there. It is still a family-run business. Heineken too has been present in Alsace since 1972, as well as the now merged companies of Fischer and Adelshoffen. Kronenbourg, the leading French beer producer, manufactures beer in both Strasbourg-Cronenbourg and Obernai. Right on the border with Lorraine, Saverne, which since 1989 has been under the control of the Karlsberg company from the Saarland, makes use of the excellent water of the Vosges mountains, and Météor in Hochfelden, an independent family-run business which, while employing modern facilities, still brews its beer using traditional methods.

Left: The wort is heated in large copper vats. The fermentation process takes place when it is cool and after yeast has been added.

The Schutzenberger brewery, founded in 1740, was established in 1866 in Schiltigheim, where the water contributes to the high quality of the beer.

1 For the best taste and texture duck and goose livers are manufactured together (the latter are pale pink in color).
2 Arteries and veins must be conscientiously removed, because otherwise the *foie gras* will taste bitter and may develop green patches.
3 All livers are thoroughly cleaned, seasoned with salt and pepper and a small amount of sugar, and sprinkled with port wine.

4 After they have been marinated for a few hours, the pieces are collected together and formed into a slab.
5 The *foie gras* is wrapped tightly in plastic wrap.
6 The temperature of the water is of the greatest importance and should be between 158 and 167 °F (70 and 75 °C). Cooking time is about 30 minutes. Of course *foie gras* can also be cooked the customary way in a lidded terrine.

Strasbourg goose liver pâté

The history of *foie gras* covers some 4500 years and goes back as far as the ancient Egyptians. They probably observed the natural tendency of geese to overeat at the start of the periods of migration to lay down reserves of energy required for the flight. Their distended livers were discovered to be quite delicious and soon became highly regarded in the extreme. In a very short time this may have led to the birds being fattened intentionally and with force so that the sought-after livers were available all year round. The Phoenicians and Romans had some awareness of this special fattening process. It was the latter – and in particular the tyrant Nero – who appears to have been very fond of this delicacy. The Romans used to stuff the animals with figs and soak the livers in milk.

Goose breeding was probably introduced to Alsace by Jews from eastern Europe, who considered roast goose an acceptable alternative to the ubiquitous pork, which was prohibited by their religion. It was Strasbourg's lot to became

the number one town throughout the whole of France famous for *foie gras*.

This breakthrough in cookery is down to Jean-Pierre Clause, a pastry cook by trade. At that time this trade prepared all types of food, dough or pastry-based products – mainly bread, cakes and pastries. Clause often worked for the Maréchal de Contades, the then military governor of Alsace. As a gourmet the Marshall insisted on hosting receptions being famous for the high quality and originality of the food. Clause designed a pastry in the shape of a barrel, which he filled with *foie gras*, and to which he added finely cut ham and chopped veal. He sealed the whole thing off with a pastry crust. This first *pâté de foie gras de Strasbourg* is believed to have been cooked in 1780 and caused great excitement among the guests present. As a result, the Marshall and the pastry maker decided to offer a sample to King Louis XVI who found it delicious and since then *foie gras* has been assured of royal patronage.

Today the goose-breeders remaining in Alsace can easily be counted on the fingers of one hand. The *foie gras* comes either from the southwest or is even imported from Hungary. However *foie gras* is still very much associated with Strasbourg and the region and no good restaurant, *charcutier*, or caterer would exclude it from his range of foods. In Alsace greater value is placed on thoroughly removing arteries and nerve fibers

from the *foie gras*. This is the only way to achieve the neatly proportioned appearance and the uniform, delicate shade of cream of the finished product.

As Alsace was situated on the most important spice route to the Orient, spices were used in a more daring way and *foie gras* was even marinated in madeira. Today port, *eau-de-vie* or brandy is generally used to enhance the flavor, and the use of spices is basically more restrained. It is usual to add freshly ground black pepper and *fleur du sel* (the finest sea salt); in addition *foie gras* and truffle make a delicious combination. Specialties in Alsace are *pain de Colmar* and *millefeuille de foie gras*. For the former a tall, round mold is used, in which *foie gras*, seasoned with 5 percent truffle, is layered and lightly cooked on a very gentle, low heat. For *millefeuille* strips of goose and duck *foie gras* are layered alternately on top of one another in a square mold, in which the finer flavor of the goose liver combines exquisitely with the stronger taste of the duck liver.

Terrine de ris de veau
Terrine of veal sweetbreads

2 lb 10 oz/1.2 kg veal
2 tbsp/22 g salt
A pinch of pepper
About 15 pistachio nuts
1 shallot
2 eggs
10 oz/300 g calf sweetbreads
1 tbsp butter
1⅓ cups/330 ml concentrated veal stock
¾ oz/20 g powdered gelatine
1 tbsp white port wine

Cut the meat into very narrow strips, place in a bowl, add salt and pepper.
Peel and chop the pistachio nuts, peel and finely dice the shallots; add both ingredients to the meat. Whisk the eggs and stir in.
Allow the mixture to marinate overnight in the refrigerator.
The following day thinly slice the calf's sweetbreads, braise both sides in hot butter and lightly brown, then leave to cool.
Preheat the oven to 355 °F/180 °C. Add a layer of strips of meat with some chopped pistachio and onion. Bed the calf's sweetbreads on this and cover all around with strips of meat.
Bake well in a preheated oven for 45 to 50 minutes, then remove and allow to cool.
Soften the gelatine in cold water. Heat the veal stock, add the port wine. Add the gelatine and dissolve it in the stock. Fill the terrine mold with this liquid and allow to cool.

Pâté de volaille en croûte
Chicken pâté in pastry

3 lb 5 oz/1.5 kg chicken (or other poultry)
1½ tbsp/30 g salt
A pinch of pepper
A pinch of pâté spice
A bunch of parsley, finely chopped
2 shallots, finely chopped
6 cloves of garlic, finely chopped
2 eggs
2 glasses of good white wine
17½ oz/500 g short crust (plain) pastry
app. 5 oz/150 g puff pastry
1 egg yolk
¾ oz/20g powdered gelatine
1⅓ cups/330 ml chicken stock
1 tbsp madeira

Cut the meat into fine strips, mix with all the remaining ingredients (except for the pastry) and place in the refrigerator overnight to marinate.
Roll out the short crust (plain) pastry to a thickness of just over ⅛ in/4 mm and completely line a pastry tin. Pour in the meat filling up to the top and close with a top crust made of puff pastry. Coat the crust with egg yolk and cut out two openings in the pastry. Preheat the oven to 390 °F/200 °C and bake the pâté for 50 minutes. After some time lower the temperature to 355 °F/180 °C. Soak the gelatine in a little cold water. Heat the chicken stock, add the madeira, and the gelatine. When the gelatine has completely dissolved, evenly pour the liquid through both openings into the pâté. Allow to cool, take out of the mold and serve sliced.

Tips on foie gras

- When fresh *foie gras* should feel firm, possess a pristine gleam, and preferably be pink. The finer the texture the better the product.
- In terrines the cream-colored liver should have a pinkish inside.
- *Foie gras mi-cuit* (half-cooked) is the best method to bring out the characteristic flavor, as long as it is enjoyed while fresh. The livers are prepared fresh in this way in restaurants and by good caterers, but they also come vacuum-packed in a jar or can.
- *Foie gras entier* is the best type as it is made of whole livers or of one single large liver.
- If it only states *foie gras* on the label, the product consists of several pieces of liver.
- *Bloc de foie gras avec morceaux* (with pieces) describes pressed liver, which combines both large and small pieces.
- *Parfait de foie gras* contains at least 75 percent *foie gras* and a part which is chicken liver.
- At least 50 percent of *foie gras* are for pâtés, mousses, medallions, purées, and galantines.

Pâté de volaille en croûte
Chicken pâté in pastry

Terrine de ris de veau
Veal sweetbreads

Wine bars

Alsatians are sociable people by nature. But they are not the sort to slap shoulders or break into loud singing after a round of drinks. They much prefer to get together round a table and talk. Such occasions used to happen quite often in the courtyards belonging to owners of vineyards who would serve up pitchers of their white wine in convivial surroundings. The name *winstub* slowly came to describe rooms where friends met up to talk and to drink wine in convivial surroundings.

Various factors led to such wine bars gaining a more public status. In the past wine did not travel well, especially the lighter, more ordinary, country wines such as Zwicker or Edelzwicker. Wine producers therefore came to the conclusion that they should try and sell as much of their wine as possible locally. Another consideration was the fact that in the last third of the 19th century Alsace came under German control. The Germans however preferred their own Mosel and Rhine wines and in Strasbourg hordes of German soldiers visited the large *brasseries*, drinking plenty of beer and making noise deep into the night. As a result wine producers began to move their *winstub* into the city to create a place the Alsatians could call their own. The *winstub* was just the opposite of the *brasserie*: a small intimate meeting place, where regional wine from grape varieties such as Sylvaner, Pinot, or Riesling was drunk by the locals. Neither Germans nor beer were to be found there. The food was second rate but it was simple, good, and was mainly based on pork and other meats.

Today menus have become longer – many list the whole range of regional specialties – and here and there Alsatian beer has crept in, but the traditional wine bar has not lost its soul to contemporary décor and still gives the impression of a family bar.

Their exterior promises discretion. The small windows with panes made of bottle bases make sure that the interior of the premises remains unseen by passers-by. Even when opening the door, it is difficult to see inside. A heavy drape separates it from the entrance and keeps the cold out.

Once inside, it is like being part of a family for a few hours. If you come across a collection of kitschy tourist souvenirs it is unlikely to be a genuine wine bar. As in the past, farmers have neither the time nor the money for superfluous decorations so a real tavern is very simply laid out. Nothing distracts the guests from their conversation and from their enjoyment of the wine. Social class and pecking orders have no place here. The most assorted connection of people sit shoulder to shoulder at the wooden tables and all make their contribution to the entertainment. Whereas in the past these wine bars were presided over by the male "head of the household," nowadays a woman is just as likely to be in charge, seeing to the wellbeing of the guests and occasionally calling them to order.

A wine bar should provide a comfortable, familiar atmosphere like this one in Strasbourg.

Flammeküeche
Bacon and onion pie

Serves 8–10

Pastry

¾ oz/20 g compressed yeast
5 cups/750 g flour
1 tbsp salt
2 cups/500 ml water

Filling

2 onions
3 oz/80 g smoked bacon (speck)
3 ½ oz/100 g quark (curd cheese)
Generous ⅓ cup/100 ml crème fraîche
2 tsp flour
1 tsp salt
1 tbsp oil

Crumble the compressed yeast in a small bowl, stir in 2 tbsp lukewarm water and 2 oz/50 g flour. Cover and leave to prove in a draught free place for 1 hour.
Sieve the remaining flour on the work surface, hollow out the center, add the starter dough and the salt. Work the dough gradually from the outside, adding in total 2 cups/500 ml of water. Knead by hand for at least 10 minutes. Shape the dough into a ball, dust with flour and leave to prove in a draught-free place.
In the meantime, peel and chop the onions and dice the bacon. For the filling mix well quark, crème fraîche, flour, salt and oil, until the mixture acquires a creamy consistency.
Preheat the oven to 390 °F/200 °C. Thinly roll out the dough on the work surface and use it to line two fruitcake pans. Evenly spread the quark mixture with a wooden spatula on it. Then sprinkle with onions and bacon cubes.
Allow the dough to prove for a third time. Bake in a preheated oven and serve while still hot.

Flammeküeche – bacon and onion pie

Fleischschnacka de queue de bœuf – Noodle rolls with oxtail filling

Fleischschnacka de queue de bœuf
Noodle rolls with oxtail filling

Serves 10

Pasta Dough

2 lb 3 oz/1 kg flour
12 eggs
Salt

Filling

3 lb 5 oz/1.5 kg ox tail
10 carrots
1 rib of celery
12 cups/3 l red wine
5 carrots
2 onions
2 leeks
2 heads of celeriac
French parsley
Chervil
6–8 garlic cloves
1 bouquet garni
1 tbsp tomato paste

Make the pasta dough from flour, eggs, and salt. Wrap it in plastic wrap and allow to rest for 1 hour. Brown the pieces of oxtail.
Clean and dice the 5 carrots and the celery, add to the meat with some red wine. Pour on the remaining wine. Cover and simmer for 4 to 5 hours at a low temperature. Remove the meat, drain, and free from the bone.
Clean the remaining carrots and the remaining vegetables and dice.
Reduce the sauce to a quarter. Cook the vegetables in it, until soft. Finely chop the herbs and the garlic. Return the meat to the pan with the chopped herbs and garlic, and the tomato paste and cook together for 5 minutes. Allow to cool. Remove the bouquet garni.
Roll out the dough thinly and cut it into long strips. Lift the filling from the pot with a ladle, line the dough with it and roll together. Wrap in plastic wrap and poach in boiling water for 20 minutes. Let the sauce cool.
Allow to rest in the refrigerator for 24 hours. Unwrap, season to taste, pour over the hot Fleischschnacka and serve with frisé lettuce.

Other Winstub Dishes

Baeckoffa or Bäckeoffe
The original version combines three different types of meat – generally pork, lamb, and beef – with layers of potato and onion rings and Riesling. Everything is cooked in the oven in an airtight earthen pot sealed with salt dough. Originally it was the washday meal that women prepared the evening before and were able to leave on its own for hours in the oven the following afternoon.

Beindächla
Pork cutlet wine bar style, cooked in boiling water. The winemaker's version replaces the water with wine.

Bibeleskäs
Quark generously seasoned with finely chopped shallots, garlic, and various herbs, which is served with sautéed potatoes.

Choucroute
This specialty also found outside the taverns is probably one of their original dishes. When it is generously covered with different sausages and pieces of meat, as it should really be, it can hardly be described as a simple meal.

Gfillte Säumawe
A type of sausage filled with potatoes, carrots, leek, onions and any leftover meat, boiled for 2½ hours, cut into slices and served with a sauce made from its own juices. A popular traditional dish which is found in many regional cuisines, known frequently as *Saumagen*.

Grumbeerknepfle
Made from a potato and egg dough, in which uncooked and boiled potatoes are used in a 1:1 ratio. Finger-thick lengths are cut, seared in water, and served sprinkled with lightly browned bacon cubes and croûtons and covered in crème fraîche.

Matelotte de poissons
Fish frequently appears on menus in the wine bars, and the one you are most likely to come across is this freshwater stew, which uses tench, pike, perch, and eel, and is served with sauerkraut.

Presskopf
A classic dish in the wine bar is pig's head brawn.

Salade de Cervelas
The popular Cervelat sausages are skinned, then cut lengthways into strips, seasoned with a vinaigrette, and served with finely chopped onions.

Schiffala
Known as kasseler on the other side of the Rhine, pickled and smoked pork shoulder. While this is an essential component of *Sauerkraut*, it is also eaten on its own with potato salad.

Schwitzerkässalat
Not only does this salad have Gruyère in it, it is itself Swiss in origin. The cheese is cut into narrow sticks, served with a vinaigrette and sprinkled with chopped onion.

Sueri nierli
Originally pig kidneys were pickled in vinegar, but now veal kidneys are used instead.

Munster cheese

Many foods and regional specialties have their own history and that of Munster or Munster-Géromé, a pleasant and tasty cheese from the family of the red mold cheeses called *fromages à croûte lavée* (cheeses with washed rinds), begins with the Irish Benedictine monk Columbanus. He left his homeland around 590 with twelve followers and, as a traveling preacher, made his way across England and Brittany to Burgundy. He settled there, founded several monasteries and introduced cheesemaking. Some 20 years later he moved, not entirely of his own free will, to Bobbio, in Italy, where in 612 he founded one of the most famous Benedictine monasteries. After his death in 615 Italian monks returned to spread their teachings in the Rhine area, where they founded their monastery in the Fecht valley in 660. A village, simply called Munster, quickly grew up around it.

Faithful followers of the order of Saint Benedict, the monks did not eat meat, but consumed mainly dairy products. Cheesemaking was as common an event as preaching – and the villagers benefited from both. While they used the warm, lower slopes for cultivating vineyards, they required rich pastures for the cattle, which from late spring to early fall they found high up in the Vosges mountains.

With the passing of the centuries the inhabitants of Munster traveled even further, crossing the hills of Alsace to graze their animals in parts of Lorraine. They cleared huge areas and created new settlements. In 1285, people from both Alsace and Lorraine founded a new town by a lake, which they called Sancti Gerardi Mare, commonly known as Gérardmer. Their life together did not stay peaceful for long. Alsatian milkers, who spent the summer on the alpine pastures with their cattle and made their cheese there, laid claim to the best pastures. The farmers from Lorraine had quickly emulated their method of cheesemaking and were not happy to stay in second place. They no longer accepted that their Géromé cheese should be forced out of the markets in Munster. The disputes between the herders of the alpine pastures on both sides of the Vosges became increasingly acrimonious, while their cheese acquired even greater fame and was sold even more widely. However, in the Thirty Years' War there were bloody clashes between Protestants and Catholics and at the end of 1648 villages and meadows were depopulated.

The cattle graze in the meadows of the Vosges on lush grass and many herbs, which in summer and early fall help produce pleasant tasting milk and the best cheese.

The comparatively rare Munster *fermier*, cheese produced on the farms, which is either matured locally or by *affineurs*, is of the very best quality.

Almost a century passed before the cheese-making tradition was taken up anew, not just by the locals but by newcomers from Switzerland, the Tyrol, Bavaria, and Denmark. The latter introduced to the Vosges a Scandinavian cattle breed whose casein rich milk was ideal for cheesemaking. These animals with black and white patches are extremely hardy and agile and acquired the appropriate name of Vosgiennes. The best cheese is still made from their milk, which is hardly surprising as in summer and early fall they can be seen grazing on the pastures of the Vosges that provide an unlimited variety of herbs and grasses including chervil, fescue, wood geranium, ranunculus, alpine fennel, forage oats, yarrow, alpine daisies, and mountain cornflower. Cheeses made by the alpine herders and farmers, sold as farmhouse cheeses, now only make up some 600 tons of an annual production of almost 9000 tons (*Appellation d'Origine Contrôlée* since 1978). The rare and justifiably more expensive Munster farmhouse cheeses can only be found at knowlegable suppliers or bought directly from the manufacturers in the Hautes Vosges. The Munster or Munster-Géromé has a smooth, slightly damp, reddish-orange rind. When fresh, the interior is still a little crumbly, with a refreshing, nutty and rich taste. When it matures it has an intense bouquet and the rind is a gleaming red and has a damp sheen. The interior is soft and creamy with a strong taste that is full of character. The smell is never too sharp or too strong. Alsatians eat Munster with jacket potatoes rather than with bread and it goes well with a good, medium-quality, flowery Gewürztraminer.

Birth of a Munster cheese

Munster cheese is made in two ways. either the milk is processed directly after the morning or evening milking, or it is allowed to stand overnight until the cheese is made the following morning. In the latter case the milk must be slightly skimmed, otherwise the cheese will contain the complete fat content of the milk and become creamier.

The milk is heated in vats with a capacity of 22–55 gallons (100–250 liters) to about 94 °F (34 °C). Added lactic bacteria and rennin trigger curdling. Half an hour later when the milk curdles, the curd is broken up using a cheese cutter to assist the draining of the whey, some of which is removed with a copper scoop. Then the cheese mixture is ladled into traditional wooden molds, which have just a few holes. The cheese is left in a gently heated room, and the fermentation process continues. The molds are turned regularly to assist the draining of the whey. After about twenty hours the cheese is sufficiently solid to be taken out of the mold and salted. The maturing process is completed in cellars with a high moisture content at a temperature of around 55 °F (13 °C) and with red mold cultures. Larger Munster or Munster-Géromé cheeses stay there at least 21 days and smaller ones 14 days.

A cheese is turned every two days and washed by hand or using automatic brushes and a salt solution, to prevent the growth of unwanted cultures and at the same time to promote the growth of the red mold, which gives the cheese its color and aroma. The inside becomes creamier over this period and develops its characteristic flavor.

1 After adding the rennin the milk takes just 30 minutes to curdle.
2 The curd is broken up using a cheese cutter to allow the whey to drain off.
3 Fresh cheeses are placed in a cellar with existing cultures and left to mature.

4 In 2 to 3 weeks the red mold bacteria covers the surface of the cheese and give it its characteristic color.
5 To encourage the red mold the cheeses are kept moist with the help of electric brushes.
6 The traditional method is to rub them with salt solution, in hygienic and sterile conditions.

Alsace wines

Although Alsace is at the northeastern tip of France, the climate is good for winegrowing, especially for strongly flavored wines. The mountains of the Vosges protect the vineyards from the Atlantic and its changeable, rainy weather. After cold and frequently snowy winters the summers are long, dry, and very sunny enabling grapes to ripen over a long period and develop their flavor. The often sunny fall provides enough humidity to cause noble rot, which in good years produces late vintage wines. From the geological point of view Alsace is a mosaic of different rocks and soil that created its mountainous features 50 million years ago, with the Vosges in the west and the Black Forest in the east. Starting from the valley of the Rhine there is an abundance of different terrains and soils: sand and pebbles, marl and loess, limestone and clay, slate and granite. Winegrowers take advantage of the variety of soils in different ways, planting different varieties of vine, thus determining the individuality of the wines. Unlike other French wine regions but in common with the German districts of the Rhine valley, in Alsace individual varieties are bottled unblended with their own names on the label.

This only gained acceptance in the 20th century as before that blended wines were more usual in Alsace. Today certain top winegrowers have again introduced *cuvées* in which several types of grape are combined in order to fully express their characteristics. The highest yield of 900 gallons per acre (100 hectoliters per hectare) has since been reduced to the still impressive figure of 700 gallons per acre (80 hectoliters per hectare). The minimum alcohol content by volume must be 8.5 percent. As in Germany, the biological reduction of acidity, which preserves liveliness and intensity of flavor in white wines, is prohibited. Certainly most winemakers in Alsace allow their wines to ferment thoroughly and so acquire more body and dryness, qualities which are enhanced if the wine is left to mature in the bottle for a while.

In Alsace there are three *Appellations d'Origine Contrôlée A.O.C.* This is the highest classification determining the conditions of wine production in France.

A.O.C. Vin d'Alsace on the label indicates one of the more common varieties of grape: Sylvaner, Riesling, Pinot Blanc, Muscat d'Alsace, Tokay Pinot Gris, Gewürztraminer, and the only red variety, Pinot Noir. The term "Edelzwicker" means the wine is blended. Bottling is carried out exclusively in the area and only the typical narrow-bodied bottle, the *flûte*, is used.

The visitor to Alsace can get to know the charming countryside with its romantic villages and typical winegrowers' houses just by following the well-signposted wine routes.

A.O.C. Alsace Grand Cru makes up just 4 percent of the wines produced in Alsace. They consist either of Riesling, Gewürztraminer, Muscat, or Tokay Pinot Gris and must originate from one of the 50 wines classed as *grands crus* (variety and location must be declared.) These relatively small vineyards are selected because of the long-established high quality of their wines. Permitted yields, currently 530 gallons per acre (60 hectoliters per hectare), are lower than the rest of the *appellation*. They also have to produce more natural sugar on the must scales.

A.O.C. Crémant d'Alsace are sparkling wines produced by bottle fermentation and mainly consisting of Riesling, Pinot Blanc, Pinot Gris, and sometimes Chardonnay. Pinot Noir, which gives Blanc de Noir, is also used. If a variety of grape is stated on the label, it can only be Crémant grapes, which are picked earlier than others. As only 10 percent of the Crémant d'Alsace are exported, the lion's share stays in France, where it makes up 30 percent of the overall consumption of sparkling wines.

The 50 Grands Crus of Alsace

Vineyard Name (District Name)	Main Geological Properties	Vineyard Name (District Name)	Main Geological Properties	Vineyard Name (District Name)	Main Geological Properties
Altenberg de Bergbieten	Clayey marl, chalk	Kirchberg de Barr	Limestone marl	Schoenenbourg (Riquewihr, Zellenberg)	Marl with sand and chalk
Altenberg de Bergheim	Limestone marl	Kirchberg de Ribeauvillé	Limestone marl, sandstone	Sommerberg (Niedermorschwihr, Kathenthal)	
Altenberg de Wolxheim	Limestone marl				Granite
Brand (Türckheim)	Granite	Kitterié (Guebwiller)	Volcanic sandstone	Sonnenglanz (Beblenheim)	Limestone marl
Bruderthal (Molsheim)	Limestone marl			Spiegel (Bergholtz, Guebwiller)	Clayey marl, sandstone
Eichberg (Eguisheim)	Limestone marl	Mambourg (Sigolsheim)	Limestone marl		
Engelberg (Dahlenheim, Scharrachbergheim)	Limestone marl	Mandelberg (Mittelwihr, Beblenheim)	Limestone marl	Sporen (Riquewihr)	Limestone marl, stoney
Florimont (Ingersheim, Katzenthal)	Limestone marl	Marckrain (Bennwihr, Sigolsheim)	Limestone marl	Steinert (Pfaffenheim, Westhalten)	Limestone
Frankstein (Dambach-la-Ville)	Granite	Moenchberg (Andlau, Eichhoffen)	Limestone marl, alluvial	Steingrubler (Wettolsheim)	Limestone marl, sandstone
Froehn (Zellenberg)	Clayey marl	Muenchberg (Nothalten)	Volcanic sandstone, stoney	Steinklotz (Marlenheim)	Limestone
Furstentum (Kientzheim, Sigolsheim)	Limestone	Ollwiller (Wuenheim)	Clayey sand	Vorbourg (Rouffach, Westhalten)	Limestone, sandstone
Geisberg (Ribeauvillé)	Limestone marl, sand	Osterberg (Ribeauvillé)	Marl	Wiebelsberg (Andlau)	Quartz, sandstone
Gloeckelberg (Rodern, Saint-Hippolyte)	Granite with clay	Pfersigberg (Egulsheim, Wettolsheim)	Sandstone with limestone	Wineck-Schlossberg (Katzenthal, Ammerschwihr)	
Goldert (Gueberschwihr)	Limestone marl	Pfingstberg (Orschwihr)	Limestone marl, sandstone	Winzenberg (Blienschwiller)	Granite
Hatschbourg	Limestone marl, loess			Zinnkoepflé (Soultzmatt, Westhalten)	Granite
Hengst (Wintzenheim)	Limestone marl, sandstone	Praelatenberg (Kintzheim)	Granite, gneiss	Zotzenberg (Mittelbergheim)	Limestone, sandstone
Kanzlerberg (Bergheim)	Clayey marl, chalk	Rangen (Thann, Vieux-Thann)	Volcanic		Limestone marl
Kastelberg (Andlau)	Slate	Rosacker (Hunawihr)	Dolomitic limestone		
Kessler (Guebwiller)	Clayey sand	Saering (Guebwiller)	Limestone marl, sandstone		
		Schlossberg (Kientzheim)	Granite		

With its delightful landscape, exciting food, and large selection of wines, Alsace is one of the most attractive wine regions of France.

Riesling

Pinot Gris

Pinot Blanc

Pinot Noir

Gewürztraminer

Muscat d'Alsace

Sylvaner

Vendange tardive

Varieties of grape

Riesling

Recognized as one of the finest varieties of grape in the world, the Riesling cultivated in Alsace Riesling produces impressive, bone dry wines, which when fresh have a flowery flavor. They are at times very sharp and many wine producers give them additional residual sweetness. After three of more years of maturing the wine reaches the right balance, acquiring mineral overtones with a more sophisticated bouquet.

Riesling d'Alsace is a wine for connoisseurs. Drier than its German counterpart, it is the perfect accompaniment for sauerkraut. Riesling also delivers late vintage high-quality sweet wines.

How to read an Alsatian wine label

1	Classification	ALSACE GRAND CRU
2	Quality of vintage	VENDAGE TARDIVE
3	Producer's emblem date estate founded	DEPUIS 1658
4	Name of vineyard	HENGST
5	Name of district	WINTZENHEIM
6	Designation of origin and classification	APPELLATION ALSACE GRAND CRU …
7	Alcohol content by volume	14 %
8	Variety of grape	GEWURZTRAMINER
9	Year	1994
10	Bottle contents	750 ml
11	Estate	DOMAINE ZIND HUMBRECHT
12	Winegrower	Léonard et Olivier HUMBRECHT
13	Place, province, country	TÜRCKHEIM (Haut-Rhin) FRANCE
14	Bottling control number	L 37 H

1 ALSACE GRAND CRU

2 VENDANGE TARDIVE
DEPUIS 3 1658

4 Hengst
5 WINTZENHEIM

6 APPELLATION ALSACE GRAND CRU GEWURZTRAMINER CONTRÔLÉE
7 ALC. 14% BY VOL. **8 GEWURZTRAMINER 1994 9** **10** 750 Ml

11 DOMAINE ZIND HUMBRECHT
Léonard et Olivier HUMBRECHT - TURCKHEIM (Haut-Rhin) FRANC
12 **13** **14** L 37

The qualities of traditional varieties of grapes are enriched by the sunny sloping aspect of the vineyards and the poor soil.

Gewürztraminer

If picked late enough, with its unmistakably intense bouquet, this valuable variety of grape produces well-bodied, extremely pleasantly flavored wines. These wines exhibit wonderful fullness and sweetness and offer an astonishing range of flavors, from rosy, spicy, and exotic fruits, among which lychee and mango particularly stand out.

They go well with *foie gras*, complement cheese and are suited to fruity and tangy desserts.

Frequently the ordinary versions do not live up to their promise.

Pinot Gris

Generally called Tokay d'Alsace in Alsace, a name the Hungarians had some success in blocking as it could be confused with the Tokay wines of Hungary: it is none other than gray Burgundy, known in Germany as Ruländer.

It is one of four high quality varieties and produces sumptuous well-textured wines often with a smoky and honey-like character. It quickly develops natural sugar content and is often harvested as a late vintage. It matures well and is served in Alsace with white meat and game.

Muscat d'Alsace

This local variety of muscatel with small grapes – quite different from the muscat of the south of France – produces quite a dry distinct wine that gives you the pleasant feeling that you are really enjoying the grapes themselves. The wine has almost been completely replaced by the more modest Muskat-Ottonel, which is a very light wine normally enjoyed as an aperitive.

Pinot Blanc

The white Burgundy, called Clevner in Alsace, and often blended with Auxerrois, Sylvaner, and Chasselas to produce Edelzwicker, is pleasant and uncomplicated, which is why it is good as a drinking wine or to accompany simple dishes like onion pie or *flammeküeche*. Qualitywise it is inferior to the gray Burgundy and gives higher yields. Some 38 percent of all the Pinot Blanc in Alsace is used for Crémant d'Alsace.

Sylvaner

This variety, widely used on the other side of the Rhine, is losing popularity in Alsace. With little expression of its own and quite high acidity, the Sylvaner produces refreshing, flowery, slightly fruity, and sometimes sharp wines.

Pinot Noir

The only dark grape cultivated in Alsace is often used for red or rosé wines with a fruity taste, reminiscent of cherries. Red wines are generally fortified in oak barrels to give them more body and character. Stronger flavored wines or stunning vintages are not very common.

Chasselas, Auxerrois Blanc etc.

Apart from the varieties of grape mentioned above, of which the first four are considered top quality, there are others which today are of lesser importance. Chasselas or Gutedel play a part in the formulation of Edelzwicker. Another constituent used to be Knipperlé, a red variety, used only for white wine but it has virtually

Vendange tardive

Like the late vintage in Germany the grapes must be gathered when fully mature and consequently have a high natural sugar content for this incredibly strictly controlled category. Depending on the variety, the sugar content must correspond to a potential alcohol content of between 12.9 and 14.3 percent. Consequently fermentation does not always convert all the glucose. So while Vendange tardive always has a good body, both dry and sweet versions are available, although this is not explained on the label. Only the top quality varieties of grape like Riesling, Gewürztraminer, Pinot Gris and Muscat qualify for this wine, but the latter is only rarely picked as late vintage.

Sélection des grains nobles

These top quality selections only occur in exceptional vintages, when the grapes have achieved the highest level of maturity because of favorable weather conditions and when the intensity of noble rot makes the juice in the berries more concentrated to take it to 15.1–16.4 percent potential alcohol content, depending on the type. Together with the straw wine of the Jura this is the highest alcohol level demanded among all the *appellations* in France.

This level of about $4^{1}/_{4}$ ounces/120 grams of sugar per pint ensures that the wines have plenty of body and as a rule essentially higher residual sugar content. Both factors guarantee an excellent potential for maturing. Gewürztraminer in particular gives this excellent level of quality.

Edelzwicker

Meaning "noble blend" this category of wine, whose name always appears so prominently, used to enjoy considerable popularity, which in recent times has somewhat diminished. To produce Edelzwicker, wines are mixed from grapes which are not considered to be top quality, mainly Pinot Blanc, Auxerrois Blanc, and Sylvaner, and also Chasselas and, in the past, Knipperlé. It is a pleasant, drinkable, slightly fruity, and fresh everyday wine.

disappeared. Also used is the widely available Auxerrois Blanc, often compared with Pinot Blanc, but of a lesser quality. Chardonnay, currently more widely used, is frequently included in Crémant.

Klevner de Heiligenstein

This old Traminer with a lighter flavor was introduced to the area of Heiligenstein Barr at the beginnning of the 18th century. Of its two versions, Savagnin Blanc and Rosé, only the latter still exists and is not related to the Savagnin of the Jura. The Traminer has survived in Heiligenstein and its immediate area because of its flavor and body. The A.O.C. status was only awarded in 1997.

Eau-de-vie

In Alsace they say that not only is a lot of wine served up but they drink a lot of it as well! Of all the French provinces, Alsace is number one when it comes to the brewing of beer, and it also rates highly when it comes to wine production. It is cultivated by variety, with the names of the varieties of grape on the label. Alsace is also the only growing region for sweet wines and offers the consumer precise categories such as "Vendange tardive" and "Sélection de grains nobles."

Just like a good meal, the picture of this alcohol-producing province would not be complete if *schnapps* were not considered. As the name *schnapps*, which is common in Alsace, implies, it is closely related to the traditions of *schnapps*-making in Germany. Of course the more sophisticated French name *eau-de-vie* appears on the labels of local brands. This means nothing more than the Latin *aquae vitae*, which was first used by Arnaud de Villeneuve, knight templar, physician, rector of the University of Montpellier, and first master distiller on French soil to describe alcohol. He had become acquainted with the Arab discovery and the principles of distillation while on the Crusades in the East. Soon after his return towards the end of the 13th century he started experimenting himself.

The term "water of life" perfectly encompasses the high esteem in which alcohol was held in those days. This pure liquid was seen as a sort of new wonder elixir, and all possible curative plants were steeped in it to make it into medicine. Based on its enormous medical relevance its production method soon spread. It was only after 1800 that it was generally extracted not just in one distillation but in two and, for pure alcohol, even in three steps.

In Alsace the distillers were able to benefit from local conditions. In the mild climate, which is conducive to wine and hop-growing, fruit trees such as cherries, damsons, mirabelles, plums, or pears also flourish.

The Vosges are very rich in wild fruit too. The sugary wild cherries which helped the most famous *eau-de-vie*, *kirsch*, acquire its fame, are now comparatively rare, but there are still vast amounts of raspberries, wild strawberries, wild blackberries, elderberries, rowanberries, rose hips, or small holly berries. They are all suitable for making *schnapps*, which can be done in two different ways. The more original is mainly based on stone and malaceous fruit. The fruit is mashed and allowed to ferment. Generally, as there is sufficient natural yeast in the skins no further yeast is added. The glucose is converted into alcohol and produces low alcohol fruit wines, which are heated in the stills.

The principle of distillation is simple and is based on the different evaporation temperatures of water and alcohol. While it is well-known that the former becomes steam at 212 °F (100 °C), alcohol evaporates at 174 °F (78 °C). However it is not only the alcohol that behaves in this way, as the various flavorings also react at lower temperatures and rise with the alcohol. They both enter the condenser, where they cool off and become liquid again. With the first stage, 25–30 percent raw distillate is formed, which is then distilled for a second time. Completely clear *eau-de-vie* is collected, which reaches more than 60 percent. As it is not only too strong for the palate but also too rough, it has to be matured, which is where the experience of the distiller comes into play. Many insist that only its freshness keeps the fruity flavor, while others turn up their noses and talk about complexity and finesse. Good quality *eau-de-vie* spends at least three to four years in tanks or glass vats. Better ones mature for seven to ten years and the excellent, but exceptional varieties are only exposed to the noses and palates of connoisseurs after twelve or more years.

There is, however, another method of distilling strongly flavored fruit *schnapps* from particularly delicate fruits, which are slightly damaged or are in too small quantities to be fermented for wine. The fruit is added to alcohol, is allowed to mash for a long time, to release all the flavor, and is then distilled. This process is not only applied to wild strawberries, raspberries or blueberries, elderberries, or rowanberries but it opens up quite new possibilities for the more curious and imaginative distillers.

Jean-Paul Metté was a master of this. He was so fascinated by the world of light, delicate aromas that he created the most incredible distillates from quite varied starting materials like woodruff and mullein, basil and lemongrass, pepper and cinnamon, orange and rhubarb, asparagus and coffee. Not forgetting liqueurs, in all there are something like six dozen types of *schnapps* on top of this.

Mirabelle de Lorraine

The inhabitants of Lorraine share a liking for eau-de-vie with their Alsatian neighbors and are master distillers. Thanks to a long tradition in the cultivation of mirabelle plum trees, a specialty has been developed, which as France's only clear fruit schnapps has, like cognac, armagnac and calvados, an *appellation réglémentée*: mirabelle de Lorraine.
The most well-known variety of mirabelle is mirabelle de Nancy, which blossoms late, is self-pollinating and produces a good yield and rounded, very flavorful fruit, which is good for preserving and distilling. The now less common mirabelle de Metz with its smaller, oval, speckled fruit produces even finer versions. The 45 percent volume, laid down in the past, needs to be attenuated by maturing. For this reason many producers age their high-quality mirabelle schnapps in ash barrels. If mirabelle de Lorraine is adequately matured for several years, it is not just stunningly fruity, but it also has an expressive and varied bouquet and an extraordinarily intense taste.

Right-hand page: To produce the finest distillates the forerun and second run have to be selected at the right times; the degree of alcohol is then measured, as demonstrated here by Philippe Traber, the successor of the legendary Jean-Paul Metté.

Of the Alsatian fruit brandies the most famous schnapps is kirsch, for which various varieties of cherry are fermented into fruit wine. Rare, wild cherries are the best variety.

These relatively small stills are especially good for the production of rare specialties, for which only small amounts of fruits or other raw materials are available.

Alsace is a paradise for clear distillates. The best distilleries frequently offer more than a dozen different eaux-de-vie (schnapps).

Nord – Pas de Calais • Picardie Normandie Bretagne

Sharon Sutcliffe & Fabienne Velge

Fishing

Herring

Sea fish of the north

Genièvre (gin)

Berlingots

Camembert

Andouille de Vire

Lobster

Tripe

Cider

Calvados

Apple desserts

Cauliflower & globe artichokes

Guérande sea salt

Galettes

Crêpes & cakes

Every Frenchman knows that the freshest
and largest variety of fish in France comes
from Brittany.

Gourmets love lamb that has been raised on salt meadows especially those at the foot of the famous Mont-St-Michel.

Nord-Pas de Calais

Picardie

Normandie

Bretagne

Paris

Strasbourg

Orléans

Nantes Tours Dijon

Limoges

Lyon

St-Étienne

Bordeaux Grenoble

Avignon Nice

Biarritz Toulouse

Marseille Toulon

Perpignan

In the area between Flanders and the Loire estuary it is the stretches of coast which lovers of good food first think of: the dunes in the north, the broad beaches of Normandy or the rocky coast of Brittany. They think of trays overspilling with crustaceans, sea bass, monkfish, or herring. Boulogne is, after all, one of the leading European ports for fresh fish.

Normandy supplies the best scallops and sole, while the ports of Brittany are a real paradise for lovers of lobster, crayfish, and mussels. These specialties from the northern seas have only appeared on menus in Brittany in recent times, as in the past people depended largely on produce from the barren interior.

Once the region used to be covered with extensive areas of forestland, which is why the Celts called it *argoat*, meaning the land of forests. After the forests were cleared buckwheat grew in plenty; this was not good for baking but was made into thin pancakes and baked on hot stones.

As recently as fifty years ago Brittany remained a backward region, where small farmers eked out a meager existence. Only in the northwestern coastal region, in the Pays de Léon, were vegetables cultivated. This backwardness was finally brought to an end when progress in the form of industrial farming came to Brittany, rationalizing the cultivation of vegetables, and propagating the mass farming of egg-laying hens, pigs, and milking cows. The latter mainly provide raw materials for butter, while neighboring Normandy is home to famous soft cheeses, above all Camembert.

The description *à la normande* in the name of a dish indicates the use of lavish creamy sauces or a dash of cider. While the wildness of the rough landscape of Brittany is most attractive, Normandy is reminiscent of a large garden with its population of nine million apple trees. Apples provide the must, which is processed into the robust cider and fiery calvados for which the region is renowned. Further north, where winters are unwelcoming and gray, where wheat, sugar beet, and chicory grow in never-ending fields, people keep warm by eating *hochepot*, the tasty, thick stew, or *carbonades*, beef stew cooked in beer. These dishes cannot compete with the exciting specialties, typical of the coast, but when it comes to appetizing cheese, good beers, and sweets, the produce of this area is among the best.

Fishing

Over the centuries, fishing has played an extraordinarily important role for the northern French coastal towns from Dunkirk, Boulogne, and Etaples in Nord–Pas de Calais, to Dieppe, Le Havre, Cherbourg, and Granville in Normandy, and to Saint-Malo, Roscoff, Le Guilvinec, Concarneau, Lorient, and Quiberon in Brittany. This way of life has only responded in the last fifty years to the inevitable pressures of progress and technology.

The more effective the methods of fishing in Europe have become, the more destructive have been their consequences. The survival of independent fishermen became more and more of a challenge, as the sea was virtually emptied by industrial fishing methods with their enormous trawling nets. Healthy, unscathed fish have almost become a rarity. In the past cooking would differentiate between high quality fish like sole, turbot, or sea bass and ordinary fish like pollack or cod. It is a sign of the times that today cooks are willing to fall back on the types of fish which were once considered to be of inferior quality.

An example is herring fishing. Popularized by the Vikings, by the 10th century it had become quite important. Salted herring formed part of the provisions on long sea journeys and could be transported inland with ease. In some places herring was used as currency and, above all, it was

La Criée de Boulogne:
Signed and sealed at the fish auction

It begins at 6 or 7 in the morning, but the harbor has already been busy since midnight, when the large trawling ships begin to unload their catches. The ships of the coastal fishermen are moored and offloaded in the small hours. While in most French ports the auction takes place directly on the quayside, in Boulogne it takes place in a purpose-built hall. Buyers first inspect the goods. In the shed large green boards display the names of the ships, quantities and types of fish, listed by number. The owners of the ships set the starting prices. Five auctioneers lead the procedures and call out the bids of the buyers. These are fish dealers who know the difference between good and bad ships and qualities, and bid on behalf of their customers, mainly wholesalers and large supermarkets. From one day to another price fluctuations can be enormous, and may depend on bad weather, in particular hot weather, on imports, the catches of competing ports, as well as the availability of certain individual types of fish. Individual lots are quickly auctioned off. Only the initiated really understand the proceedings, as during the bidding auctioneers and buyers seem to produce a virtually incomprehensible cacophony of sound. On many days up to 600 tons of fish are auctioned. The most important of the 60 or so different types of fish on offer are pollack, whiting, mackerel, cod, ocean perch, herring and sole.

a staple food in northern Europe, especially during winter months. Over long periods of European history herring was also a significant economic and, consequently, a political factor. Northern countries like Holland, Germany, Scotland, Denmark, and especially Norway played a significant part in herring fishing, and in France too herring used to be very important – mainly for the towns of Le Havre and Dunkirk. The main season extended from the end of October through December. At the beginning of October fishermen started getting the nets and ships ready. The preparation also included a blessing by the priest. Until the sixties at the start of the herring season fishermen organized

religious events, when they were able to attend mass and pray. In November many herring festivals reminiscent of these still take place today. In the past the first herring would appear off the coast when the first cold weather set in, toward the middle of October, after which fishermen would venture out in their ships to cast their nets. The lower the temperature, the greater number of herring would appear. November 25 was known as the *Bouillon de la Sainte-Catherine*. On this day if you dropped a bucket into the sea, it would be full of herring when you hauled it back up. The story was told that on this day you could have put a halberd into the sea and it would have stood upright because of the density of fish in the water. At 3 o'clock in the afternoon driftnets were cast and three hours later at twilight, when the herring would come to the surface, they would be pulled in. The catch was then brought into port. Fishermen used to go out again toward 4 o'clock in the morning, this time to put down ground nets. Around 9 o'clock, when the day was up, the nets were drawn in, which could take up to one and a half hours. Dealers and salters worked around the clock in the ports and employed numerous seasonal workers as well.

With the extraordinary abundance of herrings no one ever thought that fishing would one day get into serious difficulties. But progress took its toll. From 1950 fishermen used nets which "trawled" the bottom of the sea, catching a variety of fish but at the same destroying millions of eggs. Stocks of herring, which had been assumed to be inexhaustible, dropped dramatically and as an emergency measure fishing quotas had to be imposed. Areas of the economy which specialized in herring, were partially destroyed. To cover the requirement, supplies are today obtained from Ireland, Norway, Iceland, and Canada, countries where stocks of herring are still healthy.

The whole catch of Boulogne, once inspected, changes hands in this building. The boards show ships, quantities, and qualities. Five auctioneers call out lot numbers and bids.

Since the fishing industry concentrated on Boulogne-sur-Mer, small ports like Port-en-Bessin have become quiet.

Boulogne-sur-Mer

Boulogne is the largest fishing port in France and is number one for fresh fish in the whole of Europe. It specializes in both fishing and fish processing and its impressive fleet brings home some 64,000 tons per year. A further 300,000 tons are brought to Boulogne from other ports to be processed, sold and distributed by some 150 companies which are based.

Fish wholesaling is the main activity. The catch is presorted into iced boxes on board the ships. Once it is unloaded in the port, there are 118,500 square feet (11,000 square meters) of refrigerated sheds available. The fish, sold or auctioned directly, have their heads removed and are gutted, filleted, sliced, or cut into pieces - depending on what individual dealers have ordered in advance - and packed or loaded whole. In Boulogne 110 refrigerated trucks can be loaded at any one time, which is unique in Europe and makes it possible for fresh fish to be

delivered anywhere on the continent within 24 hours.

What is important is the *salaison-fumaison*, the salting and smoking, which was once intended mainly for herring. Salmon, trout, mackerel, haddock, and other fish are also processed to such an extent that twelve Boulogne companies now supply 65 percent of total French production. The port of Boulogne is excellently equipped with refrigeration facilities. Conventional fish fingers and fillets are produced together with a variety of ready-made dishes. Manufacturers of canned foods are also active in Boulogne and process about 10,000 tons of herring, mackerel, sardines, and other types of fish per year.

Most of the fishing fleet of Boulogne is made up of 80 small, 60-80-foot (18-25-meter) ships, which fish in the traditional way and supply 60 percent of the port's overall catch. Altogether

there are 15 industrial trawlers - the main suppliers of pollack and haddock - which go out for 10-15 days at a time and generally fish north of Scotland, and three refrigerated factory ships. The center for coastal fishing in the region is the small port of Etaples, south of Boulogne, which is connected to the bay of Le Touquet by a canal. Some 70 ships are based in Etaples where hard-working shipowners and crews have come together to form cooperatives. Their ships leave the port on Sunday or Monday and return on Wednesday or Thursday, with their catch of mainly whiting, sole, plaice, and other flat fish. On Fridays the ships are overhauled and Saturdays and Sundays are observed as days of rest.

There are a further six fishing ports in Normandy and twelve in Brittany.

Mackerel belongs to the family of oily fish, is a little larger than herring and ideal for smoking.

Kippers are lightly salted and smoked herrings, gutted from the back, only keep for a short time and must be cooked before eating.

The fine, skinless, subtly salted and smoked herring fillets can be served with a salad as hors d'oeuvres.

Hareng bouffi, cold whole smoked herring keeps for almost a week. Broiled, it is considered a delicacy.

Herring

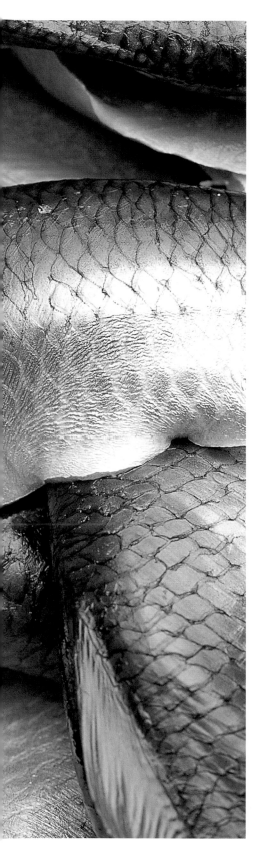

This thin, silvery fish with a bluish-green sheen is found all over the Atlantic. It lives in large schools, which prefer to stay near the coast and avoid depths of over 650 feet (200 meters). Like mackerel, salmon, and tuna, herring is an oily fish, whose meat contains high levels of health-giving fish oils. When fully grown, it reaches a length of up to 10 inches (25 centimeters), and is rarely longer. When searching for food or spawning, schools of herring follow certain movements of the sea and its currents. This is the reason for their predictable appearance near many coastlines, for example, when they reach the northern French coast in the middle of each October.

Two methods are used for conserving herring: salting and smoking. In the past smoking, *saurissage*, was carried out in smoking rooms made of brick, which today have been replaced by modern smoking facilities. First the fish are gutted, cleaned, washed, and placed in salt for exactly twelve days, as Boulogne tradition dictates, until the salt is absorbed and they are *salé à coeur* (salted through). 2½ tons of salt are needed for almost 8 tons of herring. Then the fish are soaked for one, two, or more days, before they are exposed for 12–48 hours to thick smoke, generated by burning beech and ash wood shavings. The temperature is set at 75–82 °F (24–28 °C), as the herring should not be cooked in the smoke. The herring is then stacked in layers, packed and dispatched.

Today, apart from the traditional salted herring, that which is salted on the ships, and canned herring, herring is available in France in the following forms:

Hareng bouffi is a complete whole herring, which still contains spawn and generally has only been salted for a few hours (rarely more than one day). It is then washed, desalted, and smoked for a reasonable length of time. It keeps for four to eight days and, broiled, is considered a special delicacy.

Hareng fumé doux is similarly a complete whole herring, which has its head and tail fins removed and is gutted. Fillets are skinned and washed over grids. After a quick bath in salt solution the herring are cold-smoked for three to eight hours at 64–68 °F (18–20 °C), which gives them their mildness. They are served with a potato salad dressed with oil.

Hareng saur, in its traditional form, was a complete, well-salted and well-smoked fish with quite a distinct taste. Now it is available as a quite discreetly seasoned fillet, salted just for a few days and only lightly smoked. It is eaten like *hareng fumé doux*.

Kippers are herrings which have been gutted, cut open, and flattened. They are fried in a skillet. In England they are part of a typical breakfast menu, and in France they are a mild alternative to *hareng bouffi*.

Rollmops or *filets de hareng marinés au vinaigre* are salted herring fillets complete with the skin, which are rolled around pieces of gherkin and onion, held together with cocktail sticks, and then marinated in a mixture of vinegar, salt, water, and spices. They are eaten raw as an appetizer or with boiled potatoes.

Above: Fillets are sorted and prepared for smoking by hand.

Left: Only carefully cut herring fillets, like these, are selected for smoking.

Sea fish of the north

Carrelet – Plaice
Frequently caught in the north and inexpensive, easily recognized by its orange-colored markings. Its flesh is lean, but a little soft and should not be fried or broiled for too long.

Sole – Sole
One of the most highly valued fish for cooking, it has inspired chefs to create hundreds of recipes. Sole from Normandy is especially good, available early in the year. One of the main fish sold in Boulogne.

Turbot – Turbot
One of the best fish available for eating in the world. The largest of the flatfish, its flesh is particularly flavorful, firm and juicy and consequently produces excellent fillets.

Barbue – Brill
A flatfish like turbot, but smaller. Its firm, lean, low-calorie flesh has a pleasant flavor and is easy to digest. A versatile fish, it is mainly found in markets during the winter months.

Congre – Conger eel
The almost black sea eel, which appears all year round on the coast, can be up to 10 feet (3 meters) long. Because of its bones it is mainly used for soups and sauces. The upper flesh is best.

Saint-Pierre – Peter's fish, John Dory
Rather rare, but has an exceedingly good flavor. According to the legend, Peter wanted to catch it with his hand, and the large, dark patches on each side are the imprints of his thumb and middle finger.

Lotte–Monkfish or Angler
Because of its ugliness, the head is usually removed and the fish is sold as monkfish tails. Its snow-white flesh is very tasty, free of bones, and keeps its firmness during cooking.

Raie – Skate or ray
More common in the English channel and North Sea, there are 18 types of skate. Only the wings are eaten, cooked in their skin, which is then removed, and the fish is then served with *beurre noir* (black butter).

Thon germon – White tuna
The Breton port of Lorient is famous for its white tuna, whose flesh is firm and nutritious, rich in proteins but, contrary to popular belief, low in fat. It is best eaten in summer.

Merlan – Whiting
A fish with white, delicate, and tender flesh, which is still inexpensive, and can be prepared in many different ways. It prefers cold waters and is at its best in the winter months. One of the main fish sold in Boulogne.

Maquereau – Mackerel
A beautiful fish with its greenish-blue sheen, very tasty, but oily. Consequently it is usually broiled and it may be marinated with lemon juice, vinegar or white wine prior to cooking. In spring it is known as *lisette*.

Cabillaud, morue fraîche – Cod
A liking for dried cod has reawakened interest in fresh cod. It lives in the North Atlantic and its firm, flaky flesh makes it easy to prepare. Cod roes are used for taramasalata.

Hareng – Herring
Overfishing has depleted the stocks of herring. Be it fresh or pickled, smoked or salted, it is a much sought-after fish. One of the main fish sold in Boulogne.

Grondin – Gurnard
The firm flesh of the red or gray gurnard has a good flavor, even though it is a little dry. But spiny scales and large, bony heads produce a lot of waste, which is why it is mainly used for soups.

Merlu – Hake
This member of the cod family, often called colin, slightly silver in color and with extremely tasty and tender flesh, which is nice and firm when fresh. Particularly good when broiled or roasted.

Fruits of the sea

Praire clam, mye – Clam
Quahog clams from America, which were introduced to the coasts of northern and southern France. In France they are often eaten raw.

Moule – Mussel
The finest mussels are small ones from the Atlantic coast where they are called *bouchot*; larger mussels are farmed in the Mediterranean; the best time of year for eating them is from July to February.

Amande de mer – Ark shell or dog cockle
It can sometimes be disappointing, as it does not have a particular taste of its own and becomes quite tough quickly; mainly from the Atlantic.

Coque, bucarde – Cockle
Only a small amount of flesh and has to be thoroughly cleaned in fresh saltwater; used uncooked with other seafood; the flavor is better developed when quickly steamed.

Praire – Rough Venus mussel
Easily recognized by the rippled shell, found on almost all the European coastline, particularly popular in the Mediterranean, eaten raw, steamed or broiled.

Clovisse, palourde – Venus mussel or carpet shell
This delicate Venus mussel is eaten raw like oysters or quickly seared; available on the market all year round.

Coquille Saint-Jacques – Scallop
The scallop, which in the Middle Ages was the symbol of the pilgrims visiting Compostela, can measure up to 6 inches (15 centimeters) in length. It has rich, white, mild and firm flesh. The attractive, coral-colored roe sack is edible, while the flesh can become slightly tough. The best recipes use baking or marinating. Scallops are at their best in winter.

Couteau – Razor clam
Long, thin and razor sharp, when in danger the razor clam digs itself into the sand to hide. Its quite insipid tasting flesh is eaten uncooked or boiled.

Pétoncle, peigne – Scallop
Since 1996 this smaller scallop with its bright shell and tender flesh can be sold under the name of its better known relative.

Huître plate et creuse – Oyster
The flat, European oysters, mainly the Belon oysters from Brittany, are higher quality. Decimated by disease, one in ten oysters is of the flat type, while the great majority are made up of the more ordinary rock oysters (*creuses*).

Belon oysters

In the 4th century the Roman poet Ausonius reported on the various places of origin and types of oyster and particularly highlighted the ones from the Armorican sea, the old name for the Breton coastal waters. Of all the oysters farmed in France, the most sought-after are the Belons because of their delicate, nutty taste. Around the middle of the 19th century the stocks of the once rich Cancale oysters decreased dramatically, while the flat oysters reestablished themselves close to the estuary of the river Belon. The laboratory in Concarneau discovered that the mixture of freshwater and seawater, together with the iron bearing springs of the Belon estuary, created excellent farming conditions for oysters. The Solminihac family from Périgord, which had previously farmed oysters in Rieuc-sur-Belon, established the first oyster beds in the vicinity of the estuary. Fifteen years later the secretary of the Collège de France sealed the success of the Belon oysters when he declared that he had "hardly ever seen such wonderfully shaped and excellently tasting oysters that had been artificially farmed."

Today all flat oysters from Brittany may be called Belon, but only the ones with the *Huîtres de la rivière du Belon* label, really come from this unique estuary. Farmers emphasize that oysters there are at their best in March. Like a fine wine, their flavor is enhanced if they are opened an hour before eating.

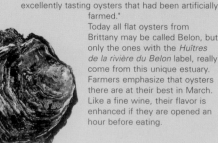

Bulot, buccin – Whelks
They can be up to 4 inches (10 centimeters) long, cooked for a short time in *court-bouillon* (stock) and served with mayonnaise or vinaigrette. The base of the whelk is the best part.

Bigorneau – Periwinkle
Just over an inch (3 centimeters) long, whelks collected on the beach; parboiled or served raw as part of a sea-food salad.

Crevette rose, bouquet
Red shrimp
From the North Atlantic, it can be up to 4 inches (10 centimeters) long. As they are difficult to transport alive, they are available boiled or deep-frozen; popular as hors d'oeuvres.

Crevette grise
North Sea shrimp, prawn
This small shrimp is scarcely 2 inches (5 centimeters) long. Freshly prepared, it has an excellent and distinctive taste. When alive, it is almost transparent, and becomes brown when cooked. Available boiled or deep-frozen.

Araignée de mer – Large spider crab
Much sought after for its very tasty flesh this crab is caught off the coast of Brittany and in the Mediterranean. Uncooked it is an intense red; the smaller females have the best taste.

Grande cigale de mer – Greater slipper lobster
Found in the Atlantic and Mediterranean, but not as common as lobster and crayfish, the tail flesh tastes extremely good; smaller ones are used in fish soups.

Homard – Lobster
Famous, but Breton lobsters of the deep-blue European type are now not so common. Like all types of lobster they turn red when cooked. The flesh is firm, the best coming from the claws. Live lobsters must come from the *viviers* (tanks) where the stress of capture is reduced.

Etrille – Swimming or blue crab
Frequently found on the beaches of the Atlantic, these dark-colored crabs are popular for their excellent flavor. As the flesh is difficult to extract, they are mainly used for soup.

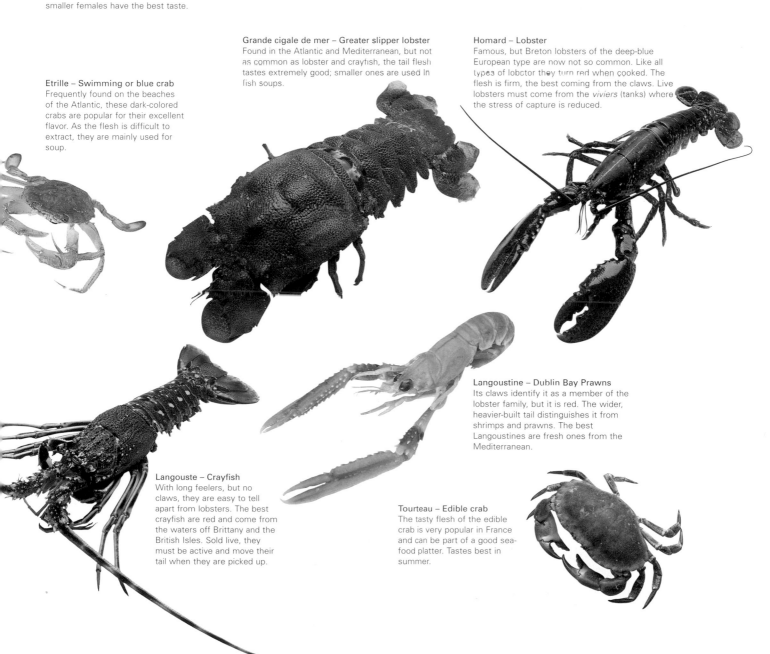

Langouste – Crayfish
With long feelers, but no claws, they are easy to tell apart from lobsters. The best crayfish are red and come from the waters off Brittany and the British Isles. Sold live, they must be active and move their tail when they are picked up.

Langoustine – Dublin Bay Prawns
Its claws identify it as a member of the lobster family, but it is red. The wider, heavier-built tail distinguishes it from shrimps and prawns. The best Langoustines are fresh ones from the Mediterranean.

Tourteau – Edible crab
The tasty flesh of the edible crab is very popular in France and can be part of a good seafood platter. Tastes best in summer.

La Cotriade d'Armor

Fish stew from the Armorican coast
(no illustration)

Serves 8

Soup

About 12 cups/ 3 liters fish stock
1 blue crab weighing approx. 14 oz/400 g
2 small tomatoes
1 apple
1 garlic clove
3 shallots
¼ medium onion
1 medium carrot
¼ medium leek, white part only
½ stalk celery
¼ small red pepper
Scant ½ cup /100 ml olive oil
Butter
3 tbsp brandy
1 heaped tbsp/20 g tomato paste

Solid ingredients

3 fresh fish fillets as preferred, each weighing about 17oz/500 g
14 oz/400 g cockles
14 oz/400 g mussels
24 scallops
32 small broccoli florets, weighing no more than 5½/160 g altogether
4½ oz/130 g smoked bacon, rind removed
1 lb 12 oz/800 g potatoes (Roseval)
1 bouquet garni

Cotriade

Cotriade is to Brittany what *bouillabaisse* is to Marseille, and recipes for this thick, appetizing fish soup are as varied as the Breton coastline itself. The dish was originally prepared by fishermen out at sea. What went into the pot depended on the day's catch. One day it could be mackerel, sardines, John Dory, monkfish, whiting, and mussels, the next perch, eel, sea bream, cod, dragon fish and shrimps. The cooking pot would be filled with seawater, and the fish would simmer in it with a few potatoes and lots of spices to disguise the heavy taste of salt. At the end of a long working day or night the crew would sit down to eat together, each one with his share of the steaming soup in a bowl, accompanied by a slice of bread. Fish and potatoes – sprinkled with vinegar to balance the salt - were eaten separately. In some regions of Brittany, mainly in the area of Cournouaille, the soup was served last to prevent the fish from overcooking.

Today like so many other original regional recipes *cotriade* is celebrating something of a comeback. Modern versions of the stew contain considerably more and varied vegetables, shellfish, or crustaceans. An ordinary *cotriade* could be based on cod, haddock, hake, sardines, and mackerel. The less oily the fish, the better the fish stew. For special occasions lobster, shrimps, and crabs add a touch of luxury.

First prepare fish stock with diced vegetables, fish heads, bones, and skin, add in all cases 1 piece of conger eel and boil everything in white wine, cider and water. Cut the blue crab in half, gut it, and remove the gills. Skin, deseed, and dice the tomatoes, peel the apple and slice very thinly. Chop the garlic. Prepare the onions, carrots, leeks, celery, and pepper and cut into narrow strips. Heat olive oil and butter in a pan, sauté the crabmeat, and flambé with brandy. Add some fish stock and pour into a tureen. Add the prepared vegetables and the tomato paste, then pour on the fish stock, bring to a boil, and simmer for 30 minutes. Blend in the mixer and sieve finely.

Cut the fish fillets into 2 ounce (50g) pieces. Wash the cockles and mussels thoroughly and open. Remove the cockles from their shells, put to one side with the scallops and mussels. Blanch the broccoli florets. Finely dice the bacon, then blanch, drain, and braise in a little butter. Peel the potatoes and cut them into thin slices.

Leave the sieved crab stock to simmer, add the potato slices, then the broccoli, and lastly the pieces of fish fillet, diced bacon, mussels, scallops, and cockles.

Serve immediately in warmed soup bowls.

Rillettes de maquereaux à la Minoise
Mackerel rillettes Pays Minier
(no illustration)

Serves 6

2 lb 3 oz/1 kg mackerel
Salt and freshly milled pepper
3 shallots
6½ tbsps/100 g butter
¾ cup /200 ml white wine
2 cups/500 ml crème fraîche
1 pinch finely chopped thyme
1/8 tsp garlic powder
1 tbsp mustard
Juice of one lemon
½ bunch of chives, chopped

Gut, fillet and cut the mackerel into large cubes, add salt and pepper.
Finely dice the shallots and sauté in 2 tbsp/30 g butter, pour on the wine and leave to simmer until almost all the liquid has evaporated. Then add crème fraîche, diced mackerel, thyme, and garlic powder
Simmer at a very low heat for 30 minutes, so that the ingredients reach the consistency of a stew.
Remove from the heat and mix with the remaining butter, the mustard, lemon juice, and chervil.
Leave to cool and add salt and pepper to taste.
Served well-cooled accompanied by toasted brown rye bread. A muscadet goes well with it.

Soupe d'étrilles
Blue crab soup
(illustration opposite)

3 tbsp/30 g round grain rice
1 carrot
1 leek
1 stalk celery
1 onion
1 tbsp olive oil
1 sprig thyme
1 bayleaf
2 garlic cloves
17½ oz/500 g blue crab
1 tbsp tomato paste
1 cup/250 ml white wine
4 cups/1 liter fish stock
(alternatively 4 cups/1 liter water)
Salt and cayenne pepper
Croûtons

Boil the rice in 1 cup/250 ml of salted water, rinse, drain, and put to one side.
Clean and dice the vegetables. Heat the olive oil in a pot, add thyme, bayleaf, and garlic and braise for 5 minutes.
In the meantime wash the crab under cold flowing water, brush it down, cut it in half widthwise (or if you prefer leave the smaller ones whole).
Sauté the crab with the tomato paste at a high temperature for 3 minutes, stirring all the time.
Add wine and fish stock (or water).
Add the rice and cook for 30 minutes. Then remove the crab pieces with a skimmer, separate from the carcass and blend the meat. Add to the stock again, simmer for 5 minutes, then add salt and pepper to taste.
Pour the soup into a tureen and serve with croûtons.

Ragout de poissons à la bière
Fish stew in beer sauce

4 lb 6 oz/2 kg fish (cod, sole, eel, gurnard)
2 carrots
1 leek
6 shallots
1 bouquet garni
4 cups/1 l dark beer
Flour
Butter
Salt and freshly milled pepper

Gut, fillet and, if necessary, remove any remaining bones.
Thinly slice the carrots, the white part of the leek, and 3 shallots. Add to a pot with the bouquet garni and the fish bones, pour on beer, and simmer for 30 minutes. Sieve the liquid.
Cut the fish fillets into pieces and coat with flour. Finely dice the remaining shallots and sauté in butter in a wide casserole. Braise the fish pieces in it, add the beer stock, and cook for 45 minutes.

Genièvre (gin)

The birth of juniper schnapps came about in the second half of the 16th century, when Holland was fighting for its independence and gradually assuming its importance as a nation. Gin is supposed to have been invented in Schiedam, part of Rotterdam. As the Dutch were more than familiar with French from the longstanding rule of Burgundy, even in Holland this schnapps was named *genièvre*, juniper, which soon became *genever*. Juniper berries only determined the flavor, as in reality the schnapps was distilled from grain mainly barley and rye. In France its production soon spread but it appears to have met with trouble, because of the ban on distillates from grain there toward the end of the 16th century.

This prohibition lasted until 1796 but it wasn't until Napoleon had announced his blockade of England, after 1806, that gin made its comeback. The following year saw the establishment of a large number of distilleries in Nord–Pas de Calais. They soon found their main custom among the mineworkers of the north. With the closing down of the mines, the consumption of gin dropped by 92 percent between 1945 and 1985. Only three distilleries survived, of which the one in Houlle, in existence since 1812, is the most famous due to the high quality of its product.

Gin is based on rye, barley and oats. Only cereals processed in the region are used in Houlle. 70 percent rye is combined with 20 percent barley and 5 percent oats, or they are mixed in equal parts. After mixing, the cereals

This gin is made from several older distillations, combining the strength of the more recent ones with the character and maturity of the older one.

are coarsely ground and soaked in hot water. The starch then turns into sugar and the mash is created. When it has cooled down, yeast is added to trigger alcoholic fermentation, which takes around three days. It results in the 3 percent wort, a cloudy liquid with a marked cereal aroma. It is then distilled three times in a time-honored but almost outmoded way using simple stills, *alambics à feu nu*, which are placed directly over the fire. First 660 gallons (3000 liters) of the wort are heated in the retort, of which only a sixth, the heart, is collected. These 110 gallons (500 liters) have 18 percent alcohol by volume; the remainder is distilled again, right down to the uninteresting *drêche*, the spent mash, which is used as fertilizer. For the second distillation six "hearts" are blended to make up another 660 gallons (3000 liters). This time the distiller obtains 330 gallons (1500 liters), which are 35 percent alcohol. For the third distillation two batches are mixed and juniper berries added.

Now the distillate can be collected at the required strength.

After distilling, the gin is matured in wooden barrels, which may be old or new ones depending on the type required. After several years of maturing *eaux-de-vie* of different ages are blended to combine the strength of the younger ones with the charm of the oldest ones. This is how a dry, mellow *genièvre* is created, with a pleasant typical bouquet.

The distillery of Houlle produces three different types of genièvre: *carte noire* (49 percent volume) matured at least a year in new barrels, *carte dorée* (40 percent volume) fortified in larger tuns, which have always contained gin and do not color or add special taste, *spéciale* (43 percent volume) based on an evenly balanced mixture of cereals and considered a perfect accompaniment for smoked fish. The *brut de fût* are more rare, and in this case a whole single barrel on its own is drawn off into bottles.

Genièvre is suited to many culinary uses, from flavoring goose liver pâté, to marinating salmon, seasoning the famous *potjevlesh* stew, or as a sorbet or as a digestive between courses. It is drunk with ice or in cocktails as an aperitive, with eel and smoked fish, or as an ice-cool digestive. To develop its own flavor as much as possible, it is served slightly cooled in balloon brandy glasses.

Right: In Houlle the *eau-de-vie-de-genièvre* is distilled three times in these old, directly heated stills, producing a particularly fine gin.

Breweries in the north

As is so often the case in matters concerning mankind's wellbeing, French monks were active in beermaking in the French part of Flanders as well as in the area which is now Belgium. The oldest beer of the area, Saint-Landelin, was probably being brewed as early as the 11th century in the monastery of the same name in Crespin, between the Belgian border and Valenciennes. But from the 13th century brewing experienced its first major growth in the north and in its wake more and more breweries were established, reaching the figure of 2000 around 1900. Although most of these no longer exist, the north is the second largest brewing region of France after Alsace. Originally the interest was in strong, top fermented beers but after the Second World War high quality Pils beers and the popular bock beers were produced more intensively. In the north the quality of beer has always been closely related to the cultivation of cereals and, above all, to the region's famous hops.

Gin is based on three types of cereal, rye, barley, and oats (from right to left), and is flavored with juniper berries.

In these new barrels gin is given its subtle flavor and a light coloring over a maturing period of at least a year.

Candy flowers blown like glass.

Bêtises de Cambrai

This famous sweet was created by the Afchain confectionery company around 1850. It is a rectangular white, opaque piece of sugar candy, decorated with a clear amber-colored stripe of caramel and flavored with peppermint. Its components are sugar, glucose, and Mitcham peppermint, which has a rather pleasant menthol taste. What is really special about the candy is its very light, airy texture, which is perfectly suited to the peppermint flavor. It is made by mixing and heating the sugar and glucose; the mixture is, however, beaten to let air into it, before it is drawn and divided into pieces of candy. This unusual procedure is attributed to an act of stupidity (in French *bêtise*) by the owner's son. He is reputed to have confused the proportions of the mixture and beaten the mixture to try and hide his mistake. The confectioner is portrayed in a more complimentary light in another story that links the candy with the cattle market, which used to be held on the 24th day of each month. After business was concluded, many farmers would commit acts of stupidity and candy would appear – probably to prevent even worse ones occurring. The pieces of candy were initially cut in front of the buyers and were known as *bêtises*. For market day Afchain specially created a refined, lighter and more aromatic version, which became the specialty of Cambrai.

Berlingots

Berlingots are classic sugar candy. They are available in various colors and flavors, are clear and opaque and always look like tiny cushions. This characteristic shape is easily achieved by cutting small pieces off the end of a narrow strip of drawn candy mixture.

At the end of the 18th century *berlingots* had already attained an initial stage of perfection, as transparent and opaque strips of sugar mixture were combined and then cut to length. They became fairly well known in the middle of the 19th century thanks to a thrifty confectioner in Carpentras who made them using recycled sugar syrup that he had previously used to make candied fruit, flavoring it with mint from Provence.

The *berlingots* from Berck, a seaside resort on the estuary of the Authie, stem from a 19th century tradition. In those days people used to make their own candy specially for certain festivals in order to give them to members of the family and guests. Progress brought with it mass-produced candy and the custom went into decline. But in the Matifas family they respected the memory of those earlier days and held onto an old family recipe for candy. Madame Michèle was consequently able to exploit the inherited tradition. In her small confectionery business, Le Succès Berckois, *berlingots* are still produced in the old traditional way.

First refined sugar is mixed with just enough water to dissolve it and is gently heated. Once the sugar has dissolved, the mixture is brought to a boil and the temperature is increased until at 320 °F (160 °C) it reaches the state of clear caramel. It is then poured onto a marble surface and evenly spread. At this stage flavoring and coloring can be added and stirred in. Once the mixture has cooled off it is gathered together and hung on a stable hook fixed to the wall. The confectioner can then draw the sugar and obtain the required strips. The strips are cut with scissors into small pieces and the sugar cools off considerably and hardens.

For artificial flowers or other works of art the sugar is moderately heated. At 293–302 °F (145–150 °C) the hot mixture has a consistency that allows it to be blown like glass into the desired shape.

1 Sugar is dissolved in water at a low temperature, then heated at 320 °F (160 °C) until it changes color.
2 Hot caramelized sugar is poured in a thin layer onto a greased marble surface.
3 Flavorings are added.
4 Coloring is also added and mixed well in.
5 When cool, the mixture resembles rather firm dough.
6 It can now be drawn off into a narrow strip and cut into small pieces.

A multi-colored and varied selection

Sugar

Mankind has always had a weakness for sweet things. However, in the past sugar used to be extraordinarily rare. Ancient Indians extracted it from thickened sugar cane, but it took hundreds of years for it to travel via Persia, where extraction was perfected, and reach the Arab countries. The Moors then brought it to Europe for the first time. In the Middle Ages Venice created its wealth by trading in spices and sugar. In those days the first candies were made from boiled cane sugar flavored with spices. But even after the conquest of America when large quantities of sugar were exported from the West Indies to Europe, it remained an expensive and exceedingly profitable commodity. This only changed with the industrial extraction of sugar from sugar beet. The forerunner was the German chemist Franz Carl Achard, who opened the first factory for processing sugar beet in 1801 in Kunern in Silesia.

In France, which had been cut off from the supply of cane sugar because of the continental blockade, Napoleon promoted the cultivation of sugar beet. Benjamin Delessert designed the first French sugar factory, which started production in 1812. Sugar then ceased to be a luxury item, and at the same time the craft of confectioners enjoyed enormous growth. Whereas before they had only worked for the upper classes, they were now able to spoil the whole population. The creation of most traditional candy has its origins in the 19th century.

Sugar, however, did not remain just a treat but became an everyday foodstuff. Cultivation of sugar beet expanded as the demand increased. While in 1900 more than half of the world production of sugar was from beet, today sugar cane provides two-thirds of the raw material. France is the leading country in the European Union and second in the world in sugar beet cultivation. It is the third largest exporting country and, in terms of sugar production, is in seventh place, with over 4.4 million tons which includes the yields of its overseas territories. Sugar beet is cultivated mainly north of the Loire. In total it covers an area of over 1,124,000 acres (455,000 hectares). The beet is planted in May and can be harvested from the end of September to the middle of November.

Sugar does not just enter the home in the form of pure refined sugar; in its pure form it represents only 30 percent of French consumption. The remaining 70 percent gets there indirectly through the food industry and is used in candy and chocolates, fizzy drinks and fruit juices, preserved fruit and jellies, desserts and icecreams, bread and cakes, fruit yogurts and milk-based foods, breakfast cereals and snacks, pickles and sausages, pills and various other products. In France almost 74 lb (33.5 kg) of sugar is consumed per person per year. It is therefore not unusual that a child consumes his own weight or more in sugar a year.

The tendency to eat sweet food has an alarming effect because, in order to process these quantities of pure sugar, the human organism requires an appropriate amount of vitamin B1. Even with other foods insufficient amounts of this vitamin are consumed, leading to metabolic disturbances and consequently nutrition-related disorders such as obesity, diabetes, and gastro-intestinal complaints. Scientists warn that increased sugar consumption can lead to other serious diseases such as cancer, heart disease, and arteriosclerosis, which is why sugar should come with a health warning: "eat in moderation."

Camembert

The most famous representative of the white mold cheese family, *fromages à croûte fleurie*, was neither created in the Middle Ages nor does it originate from a monastery. Camembert is a comparatively recent discovery and has only been in existence for around 200 years. It was discovered by a compassionate farmer, Marie Harel, from the village of Camembert in Normandy. At the height of the terrors during the French Revolution she hid a persecuted priest from the area of Brie on her farm. To show his gratitude he helped her with his knowledge in perfecting the art of cheesemaking. However, the reputation of Camembert only spread after the building of the railroad link between Paris and Alençon in 1862.

Ten years later the Petit family began mass-producing Camembert. In the 1890s, the cheese, which was well-protected during transport in its typical wooden box, began to be so well-known that it became the most imitated soft cheese. In 1983 genuine Camembert from Normandy was awarded the *Apellation d'Origine Contrôlée* and since then it can only be produced in the *départements* of Calvados, Eure, Manche, Orne, and Seine-Maritime. With an output of about 14,500 tons per year it only represents a tenth of all the Camembert produced in France.

A genuine and top-quality Camembert is always made from unpasteurized milk. Each mold is filled by pouring in five portions of curds in the course of an hour using a ladle of a given size, equivalent to just over 4⅖ pints (2.2 liters) of raw milk altogether. Later the product can be labeled as *Fabrication traditionelle au lait cru avec moulage à la louche* (produced by the traditional method using raw milk and with molds individually filled by ladle). When the whey has drained, the cheese is left to settle overnight before it can be taken out of the mold. The formation of the typical downy exterior is today assisted in cheese factories by adding cultures. Only fine dried salt is used for

Once the culture has been added, Camembert needs three weeks to develop its familiar white down.

salting the cheese and in the maturing cellars the rounds are turned every other day. It takes 16 days to obtain an 8¾ ounce (250 grams) Camembert with a white crust, but up to 30 to 35 days for it to fully mature. Under the snow-white exterior speckled with brick red patches, there is a soft, bright yellow interior which almost appears to be liquid and exudes a strong odor. When the crust is pressed, the cheese should flex a little. If its interior is still white the Camembert has not matured long enough. If the markings are too red, it has been left for too long. The best cheeses are produced from early summer through fall.

1 Cheesemaking begins by adding lactic acid bacteria and some rennin to milk which has been heated to just over 93 °F (34 °C).
2 When the milk has curdled, the solids are broken down into granules and the curds scooped out.
3 In the production of Camembert curds are ladled *à la louche* into the small perforated cheese molds.

different shapes: *carré* (square), *bonde* (cylinder), *briquette* (block) or heart-shaped. Young girls are

reputed to have made the heart-shaped cheeses for their English admirers at the time of the Hundred Years' War as a sign of their affection. The best quality is the so-called *fermier* (farmhouse), available in the months between August and November.

Gournay

This is also from the damp Pays de Bray area. It is available as a round weighing 3½ ounces (100

grams) and has a fat content of at least 45 percent. It is only matured for a week, which makes it particularly white, mild, and creamy. It has become the last of a generation of white mold

cheeses, which are produced as *double crème* with more than 60 percent fat or as *triple crème* with over 75 percent fat content in its dry mass.

Livarot

This soft red mold cheese with at least 40

percent fat is only produced in the Pays d'Auge, home of the best camemberts and calvados. It weighs between 12¼ ounces (350 grams) and 17½ ounces (500 grams). It is left to ma-

ture for a month in damp cellars, and is turned and washed several times. It has a yellow, elastic interior, with a strong spicy flavor, which is not at its best in the spring.

Pont-l'Évêque

Known as *Augelot* in the Middle Ages, it adopted the name of this small village in the 17th century

and today is produced throughout Normandy. It weighs up to 14 ounces (400 grams) and is

generally available in small wooden boxes. Even though it develops a red mold, after two weeks of maturing it is milder than Livarot and has a lighter, creamier interior, an orange crust

and tastes of hazelnuts. Best in summer and in the months of fall and winter.

Petit-Suisse

In the second half of the 19th century, a Swiss worker at a cheesemaker's in Pays de Bray

enriched milk for fresh cheese production with cream. The result was a small, unsalted, cylindrical, white cheese, which was first packed in 2 ounce (60 gram) portions and simply

called *Suisse*. When the amount was halved, the Petit-Suisse became a great success.

Maroilles

This cheese was discovered by the Benedictine Monks in the Thiérache area, who a thousand

years ago developed a production process that has virtually remained unchanged to this day. After draining off the whey, the soft white cheese is salted and dried for 10 to 14 days.

Over this period a crust forms with a bluish-white mold. The cheese is brushed down wet and matured for five weeks or, in the case of the larger ones, four months. It is available in four sizes, smaller forms mature a little faster, are milder but still have a strong aroma and taste. Connoisseurs are divided between those who appreciate the outside and those who prefer the inside.

The cheeses of Normandy

Neufchâtel

A white mold cheese like Camembert, but its crust is whiter, its interior lighter and its taste milder, as it is matured for only two weeks. It comes from the large market town of the same name in the Pays de Bray, in the extreme northeast of Normandy, where it has been made since the 10th century. Today it is produced in

4 The ladle holds a specific amount and determines the weight of the cheese, which in the case of Camembert is generally 8¼ ounces (250 grams).
5 When the whey has been completely drained off, the cheese is removed from the molds, salted, and stored in maturing rooms.
6 Once the Camembert has reached the right degree of maturity, red patches appear on the white crust. The inside is yellow and soft.

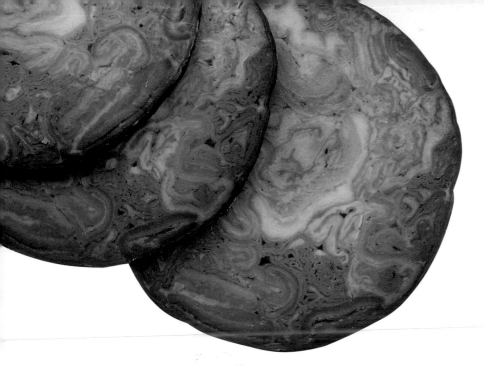

Andouille de Vire

Any butcher in France can make this sausage specialty and sell it under the name of this small Normandy town as it is not protected by any designation of origin. Real gourmets know that it is worth seeking out the genuine article from its original home, particularly when it is produced in the time-honored , intricate way by hand, with its markedly regional character. For genuine *Andouille de Vire* an experienced butcher uses exclusively pig intestine, both the small and large intestine, and the stomach. After it has been thoroughly and carefully cleaned and cut into long, narrow strips, it is made up into bundles, rolled together, and secured with a piece of string, now used in place of the wicker fibers which were used in the past. Meat prepared in this way is marinated in salt and pepper for a week, and then stuffed into an intestine, forming its outer skin. Traditionally this should also be from a pig. *Andouilles* encased in a pig intestine have a typical folded appearance, while cow intestine has a smoother texture. Butchers who want to remain true to the old methods of production that have been handed down from generation to generation, do not use the intestines of domesticated pigs which are too tender, but use more robust sow intestines from the small farms, as they are made tougher through having piglets.

Smoking comes next and can last more than three weeks. It is the decisive stage of manufacture, as it determines the taste and color of the sausage and dries it. As *andouilles* are

smoked at high temperature over an open fire, the smoking process requires a great deal of experience and undivided attention. The choice of wood is also important. The wood from apple trees would be ideal but it is expensive and not widely available. Conifers and oak trees are found around Vire: the former are not suitable because of their pervasive aroma and oakwood has to be stored for at least five years for its tannins to be washed out. Beechwood is therefore used: beech shavings give off light-colored smoke and produce small embers, which stop the temperature rising too much, which would lead to fermentation and an unpleasant sharp taste.

After smoking, the sausages are soaked in water for 24 hours to be desalted, then cooked for six hours at 203 ºF (95 ºC) in well-seasoned stock. In the past the fat given off in this operation was used in soap manufacture. As soon as the sausages are out of the water and come into contact with the air, the color of their skins turns darker. They are hung for a time for the flavor to develop further.   The complete traditional process of making an *andouille* take a whole month, while industrial production takes only three days: only four hours to smoke the sausages, the dark color is obtained by using colored water, and the artificial skins retain the fat so both the quality and its digestibility suffer. The genuine hand-produced Andouille de Vire, made according to the traditional recipe, has a strong taste, and is one of the true regional specialties. It is recognized by its irregular shape and color. It is enjoyed cold, cut into thin slices, or warm, accompanied by creamed potatoes, sautéed apple slices, and a good cider.

The Andouille de Vire shares the reputation as being the best *andouille* of France with the Andouille de Guémene from the village of

Guémene-sur-Scorff in the heart of Brittany, not far from Pontivy. It can be recognized by the pattern of concentric circles visible when first cutting into it. There is no stomach among the ingredients – in its place around 25 good pig intestines are pulled over one another, dried, and then smoked. It is generally served cold with a slice of buttered bread.

Right: The most important step in making *andouilles* is the smoking over an open fire that lasts three weeks. The sausages acquire their taste and dry out at the same time.

Potjevlesh

In the north the *charcuteries* sell *andouilles* and *andouillettes* (above all the famous ones from Cambrai) as well as the *boudin à la flamande*, a sweetened blutwurst, or *Lucullus de Valenciennes*, a terrine in which layers of ox tongue and *foie gras* are alternated. *Potjevlesh*, a rich brawn for which every cook, caterer, or *charcutier* has his or her own recipe, was extolled by Alphonse de Lamartine. At least three different types of meat should be included.

4 chicken legs
4 rabbit backs
8 pieces of neck of veal, each weighing 3 ½ oz/100 g
8 slices of fresh bacon, each weighing 3 ½ oz/100 g
17½ oz/500 g onions
3 sprigs thyme
3 bayleaves
1 tbsp juniper berries
8 cloves
Salt and freshly ground pepper
4 cups/2 liters dry white wine
1¼ cups/300 ml red wine vinegar
2 cups/500 ml meat stock
½ oz/15 g powdered gelatine

Debone the chicken thighs and cut them in half. Cut the rabbit backs into two pieces. Layer alternately all meat pieces in a terrine. Cut the onions into rings and spread all over the meat. Add the spices and add salt and pepper to taste. Pour on the white wine and three quarters of the vinegar. Preheat the oven to 300 °F (150 °C) and bake the terrine for three hours. Then add the remaining vinegar, salt and pepper to taste. Dissolve the gelatine in a little of the stock, over a pan of hot water, pour into the terrine and return to the oven for another 15 minutes. Cool the terrine down to room temperature and place in the refrigerator when cold. Cut into slices and serve cold as a starter with pickled gherkins and pearl onions, toasted brown rye bread and a strong top fermented beer.

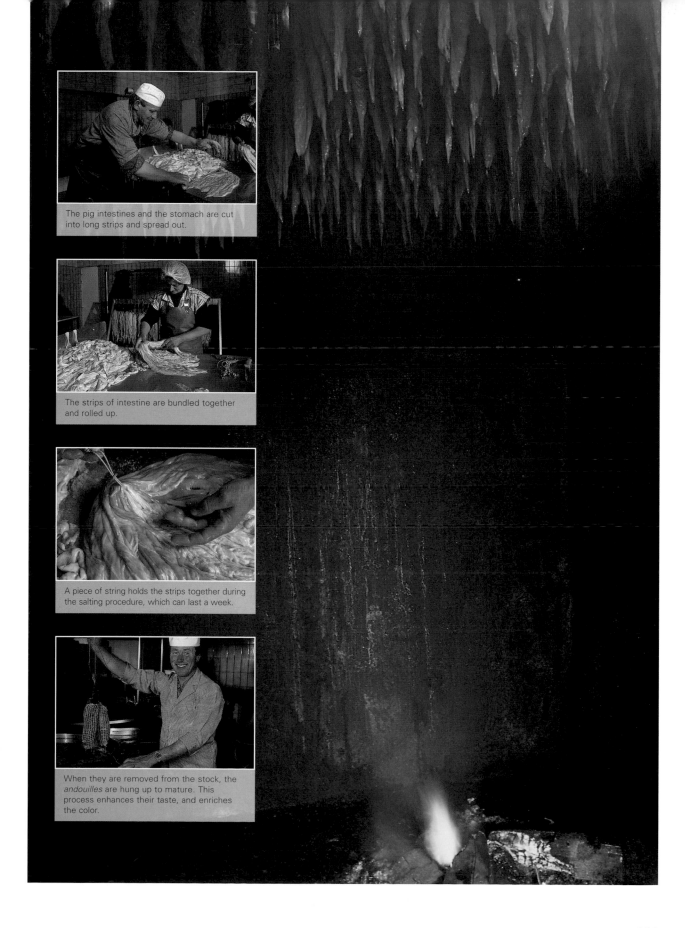

The pig intestines and the stomach are cut into long strips and spread out.

The strips of intestine are bundled together and rolled up.

A piece of string holds the strips together during the salting procedure, which can last a week.

When they are removed from the stock, the *andouilles* are hung up to mature. This process enhances their taste, and enriches the color.

In France lobster is cut in half with a special knife.

The halves are coated with butter and seasoned.

While roasting in the oven they are basted first with stock, then with calvados.

Lobster

Once the king of crustaceans used to be caught in large quantities off the Breton coast and, to a lesser extent, off the Normandy coast. Today it comes mainly from waters off Ireland and Canada. In the 17th century Bretons used to catch lobsters and crabs with hooks from between rocks where they had been trapped by the tide. Inhabitants of the island of Brehat are said to have woven the first lobster baskets and placed them in the sea with small pieces of crabmeat as bait. Historically, from Saint-Malo in the north to Belle Île in the south, lobster baiting has provided fishermen with a good livelihood. The majority of the lobster caught in Brittany would be dispatched to Paris or London, and occasionally the journey took quite a time. In 1767 the *Gazetindu Comestible* advised its Parisian readers "to sell this sea crustacean ready cooked." Nowadays lobsters are mainly caught in the cold waters around Saint-Brieuc and Brest, in the period from the end of May to the beginning of September. At seven years a lobster has a body length of about 12 inches (30 centimeters) and weighs almost two pounds (900 grams). It has strong claws and a thick protective skin. The females spawn only every second year and from the approximately 20,000 eggs, which it carries under the tail, only a few dozen develop into fully-grown animals and reach reproductive maturity themselves. The eggs are also a prized ingredient for sauces to which they give a distinct taste and an intense red color. Lobsters need time to recover from the shock of being caught. If they are cooked straight away their flesh is very tough. Consequently they are allowed to rest for a few days in special cages (*viviers*) immersed in seawater. Their blue-black skin acquires its bright red color only when cooked, which gives the lobster its nickname: "cardinal of the seas."

There are many different lobster recipes but an easy choice would be to prepare it with a sauce

Homard au Calvados
Lobster in calvados

4 small lobsters, each weighing 14 oz/400 g or 2 large lobsters, each weighing 1lb 5 to 1 lb 12 oz/600–800 g
6½ tbsps/100 g butter
Salt and freshly ground pepper
Scant ½ cup /100 ml calvados
1 pinch of sugar

Set the oven at a high temperature.
Cut the lobster in two lengthways, clean the heads, and gut it. Add the halves to a skillet, coat with 3¼ tbsp/50 g butter, add salt and pepper to taste. Cook for 10 to 15 minutes in the oven, continually basting it with the juice. Near the end of the cooking time, carefully add the calvados, as it should not come into direct contact with the lobster meat. Add the remaining butter and the pinch of sugar, and cook the lobster halves in the oven for a further 8 minutes. Serve hot.

Cassolettes de tripes normandes
Normandy tripe cooked in ramekins

17½ oz/500 g cooked tripe Caen style
3½ tbsps/50 g butter
2 oz/50 g flour
1 ⅔ cups/400 ml veal stock
4 tbsp crème fraîche
Salt and freshly ground pepper
1 carrot
1 tbsp finely chopped Horn of Plenty mushrooms
2 tbsp finely chopped chervil
8 oz/250 g puff pastry
2 eggs

Finely dice the precooked tripe. Heat butter in a pan, add the tripe, sprinkle with flour, carefully stir, and brown lightly. Pour on the stock and boil for 4 minutes continually stirring. Lift out the tripe, drain, and put the sauce to one side. Heat the crème fraîche with the tripe, reduce, and taste. Boil the carrots and finely dice them. Divide the tripe between the ramekins, putting 2 tbsp sauce, diced carrot, and mushrooms in each one, and add the chervil.
Preheat the oven to 480 °F/250 °C. Roll out the puff pastry, cut out medallion shapes, brush with egg, and place on top of the contents of the ramekins. Bake in the oven for 5 minutes and serve immediately.

Tripes au goût fumé en écrin de pommes
Tripe with smoked bacon in apple parcels

4 cooking apples
4 thin slices of smoked bacon
Scant ½ cup /100 ml cider
17½ oz/500 g tripe Caen style

Hollow out the apples with a spoon. Wrap each apple in a slice of bacon, and secure it with a cocktail stick.
Preheat the oven to 275 °F/140 °C. Place the apples in a baking tin. Pour the cider into the hollowed-out apples, then fill with the precooked tripe, and pour on the tripe juice.
Bake in a preheated oven for 15 to 20 minutes. When the apples are cooked, serve hot with cider.

Tripe Caen style
Tripe

Scholars attribute the Norman enthusiasm for tripe to William the Conqueror who, so they would have you believe, liked it more than anything else. However, the famous Caen recipe dates from the 16th century, and it is taken as being an absolute certainty that this stew, made from the organ meat of ruminants, was particularly popular with market traders. As soon as they had set up their stalls in one of the many marketplaces of Normandy in the early morning, they would put the tripe on a low heat and let it simmer all day long. Once they had dismantled all their equipment, the meal that awaited them was welcome, nourishing and none too expensive.

Careful cooking over many long hours is one of the secrets of preparing *Tripes à la mode de Caen*. The other is the quality and the variety of the processed tripe. It should be from ruminants and in particular from cows. A good mixture of belly, calf stomach, second stomach, omasum, together with a calf's foot form the basis. The stomachs must have been thoroughly cleaned, before they are cut into 2-inch (5-centimeter) strips.

In Normandy this dish is prepared in a special oven-safe dish, called a *tripière*. The bottom of the dish is covered with Reinette apple quarters, which are covered in turn with generous layers of finely cut onion, followed by a thinner layer of sliced white leek. The most important vegetables in the recipe are carrots, both diced and whole. The meat, seasoned with salt, freshly ground pepper, and a four-spice mixture – pepper, cloves, cinnamon and nutmeg – is bedded on top of the vegetables. Garlic and bouquet garni are added.

Once everything has been covered with a thin layer of beef kidney lard, a liter of cider is poured on and then sufficient water is added to cover the meat. The lid is then sealed with dough to make it airtight and the dish is left in a baker's oven for ten hours. Real enthusiasts swear by a cooking time of twelve hours. Afterwards the stock has to be clarified and the fat removed. The *tripes* can then be served in a bowl washed down with plenty of cider.

If this is all too much work, *Tripes à la mode de Caen* can be bought ready made at a *charcuterie*, *triperie*, or *boucherie* or ordered in a restaurant, where you can wonder at the different ways in which tripe can be prepared.

Lobster and tripe – two contrasting specialties of Normandy representing sea and land, luxury and basic fare.

made of tomatoes, shallots, garlic, and brandy. Bretons call the dish *Homard à l'armoricaine* after Armorica, the old name for Brittany. Others know it as *Homard à l'américaine* and associate it with Pierre Fraisse, a chef from the south of France living in Paris, creating the *homard* it as a reminder of the time he spent studying in Chicago.
In Normandy the *Demoiselles de Cherbourg*, which weigh only about 14 ounces (400 grams) each, are a specialty.

Cider

Normandy was full of apple trees well before the Normans settled there. Today meadows and pastures are full of these tall trees with their projecting branches. Of the hundreds of different types, which have been discovered and developed by botanists, four dozen are classified as suitable for cider and calvados. Most of these varieties have small fruits that seem to have been naturally created for making cider.

Cider is made up of different types of apple that go together perfectly. The three basic elements are: sweet, bitter and sour apples, and two sweet and two bitter apples are used for every sour one. The last provides freshness and bite, the bitter ones body and tannic acids, the sweet ones mildness and alcoholic strength.

Good cider producers appreciate variety, like wine producers they may even swear by the unique properties to be found in certain growing areas. Despite its being a persistently windy area, the plateau of Gonneville near the Seine estuary enjoys a good reputation for cider. Eric Bordelet, former wine waiter and qualified wine producer, insists on the superiority of the slate terrain of Charchigné on the border between Normandy and Brittany, where he ferments very fine, lively, bubbly *sidre* from 20 apple varieties that go well together.

The harvest begins in September and lasts three months. In farms looking for real quality they patiently wait for frost before picking, which prevents fermentation taking place too soon. After growing and sorting the fruit is crushed and layered in the press. Freshly pressed juice is left to its own devices in tuns or steel vats. The coldness of the winter slows the fermenting process, which may last from one to three months.

While large producers filter and pasteurize the juice and bottle it, if necessary, with added carbonic gas, farmers bottle their cider without filtering it. Depending on timing, a given quantity of sugar is left which in the bottle divides into alcohol and carbonic acid, giving the cider its natural effervescence. Once fermented cidre *brut*, dry cider, reaches 4.5 percent alcohol by volume.

Many ciders are left to mature for more than a year for quite a different purpose: to provide the base wine for calvados. While large calvados producers use cider from various regions and in part use fresh apple brandy, smaller farmers and distilleries use cider from their own apples or from their immediate locality.

The press is manually filled with crushed apples which are then pressed hydraulically.

The annual cider production starts after the first frost with the crushing of the apples.

As soon as sufficient pressure is applied to the juicy apples in the press, the must begins to flow.

The press is opened to remove the residue. The must is put into tanks.

The cider is bottled without filtering and without additives. Its effervescence is acquired from fermentation in the bottle.

The quality presentation is completely justified. Eric Bordelet's cider is a pure natural product. As a wine connoisseur he knows how the terrain can influence the taste of the drink.

Calvados

One of the ships of the Armada that Philip II, King of Spain, unleashed again protestant England in 1588 was called *El Salvador*. It had as much luck as the rest of the fleet: it was wrecked on rocks off the coast of Normandy, to the great satisfaction of the locals. Perhaps they even celebrated these easy pickings with apple brandy, which they already distilled in those days from the leftover cider. In any case their drink-befuddled tongues modified the name of the Spanish ship to "Calvados" which became the name of the area and later of the strong local apple based spirit.

The apple schnapps of the time had little in common with today's specialty. It was drunk rough and ready, straight from the still to warm people up in the morning or a shot was added to morning coffee. It wasn't until the beginning of the 20th century that Normans and Bretons took their local drink to Paris, where "calva" soon acquired new friends. In recent times the distilling and maturing processes have become more sophisticated, and since 1942, when calvados was awarded the *Appellation d'Origine Controlée*, it has ranked alongside cognac and armagnac.

The balanced flavor of calvados is down to the 48 varieties of apples from which it can be made. Cider which is to be distilled is also made from 40 percent sweet apples, 40 percent bitter apples, and 20 percent sour apples mixed together. Many of the fruit orchards were planted after the Second World War, and now, after all this years,

most of these trees are reaching their age limit. After many years in which the quantity of schnapps distilled seemed more important than the quality, the old, traditional varieties, which determine the character of the distillate, are being planted once again.

Only 30 percent of the apples picked in Normandy are used for distilling calvados; 50 percent are for cider and 20 percent are for juice. 40 pounds (18 kilograms) of apples are needed to produce just over 2 pints (1 liter) of 70 percent alcohol by volume.

The intense, fruity and aromatic calvados is generally produced in a continuous distilling process in the area from Cherbourg in the north, down almost to Le Mans in the south, and as far as the Seine estuary. There are two other specific regions of origin. Calvados Domfrontais has been recognized for some time. It is distilled from a base wine, containing at least 30 percent pears, which makes it more delicately fruity and gives it a softer texture. The most respected, however, is calvados du Pays d'Auge. All the apples used have to come exclusively from the picturesque countryside around Deauville, also home to two of the most famous cheeses of France, Pont-l'Evêque and Livarot.

Production of their particular calvados involves a double fractional distillation process, similar to that used for cognac. For this reason after the first distillation, a 30 percent rough distillate made from cider, petites eaux, is collected. The second distillation allows the impurities of the two stages to be separated and only the heart is collected. Apple schnapps as clear as water runs out of the cooling coil with 69–72 percent alcohol by volume. The later stages are the same as for the

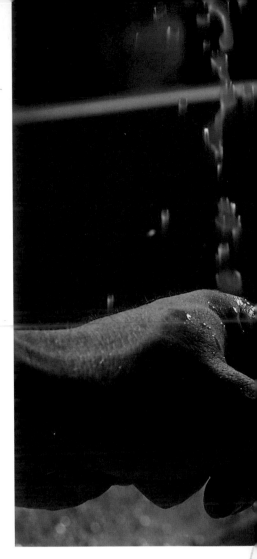

Above: Every calvados producer insists on sampling the bubbling must from the press and testing the sugar and acid content.

other brandies. First kept in new oak barrels, it absorbs some flavor and tannic acids from the wood selected. It is then progressively transferred into much older casks. Every year the careful maturing process refines it to the highest levels. In common with other brandies, calvados ceases to mature after bottling. So, its quality is graded according to the number of years it has spent in the barrel:

- Three stars or apples: two years
- *Vieux* or *Réserve*: three years
- *V.O.* (*Very Old*) or (*Vielle Réserve*): four years
- V.S.O.P. (*Very Special Old Pale*): five years
- Hors d'Age, *Extra* or *Napoléon*: six or more years in the barrel

Every so often cellar masters let a barrel intended for calvados stand for a year filled with cider,

Cheers! With a small glass of calvados...

Apples intended for cider to form the basis of calvados are knocked off the trees with a stick.

Sweet, sour, and bitter varieties of apples are mixed in given proportions for good calvados.

Next the apples are crushed, pressed, and slowly fermented, and finally distilled.

After distilling calvados is sometimes stored for decades in wooden barrels, before bottling and labeling.

before it is filled with calvados. This way the apple brandy absorbs fruity flavors from the barrel. Some of the best producers allow their top quality brandies to stand in former sherry or port barrels and then bottle them as vintage.

Generally, however, calvados is blended from distillations of various ages and origins to offer as large a harmony of taste and durability as possible.

Calvados is generally drunk as a digestive. In Normandy, apart from the abundance of apples there are also excessive amounts of cream. There is generally an unhealthy tendency to indulge in plenty of good food. The stomach requires a little respite between the many courses of a long meal with something that aids digestion. There is nothing better for this than a glass of calvados and so this drink between courses has become a tradition known as *le trou normand*, literally translated "the Norman hole."

Pommeau

Pommeau is another liquid specialty from Normandy, just as old as calvados but hardly known outside the region. It has however experienced a comeback over the last 20 years.
Pommeau is to Normandy what *floc* is to Gascony, what Pineau is to Charente, and what Ratafia is for the south. Freshly pressed must is stopped from fermenting by adding fresh distillate, in this case of course calvados. In this way it maintains its full apple flavor, natural fruity sweetness, and pleasant acidity. To give variety and balance to its bouquet and taste, producers juggle with different combinations of the range of local apple varieties.
Since Pommeau was awarded the *Appellation* in 1991, the choice has been limited to 30 recommended varieties. For Pommeau to acquire harmony and its pleasant taste, it must be allowed to mature for a period of at least 14 months in wooden barrels. It is drunk cool, but not ice-cold, as an aperitive and goes delightfully with apple desserts.

Pommeau is produced by adding young calvados to fresh apple must and arresting fermentation.

Apple desserts

The apples of Normandy were not very suitable for eating but were excellent for cooking and baking, especially when some cider or calvados was added to the recipe to give it some bite. In Normandy they are not impressed by fashionable varieties such as Golden Delicious, Granny Smith, Starking, and Red Delicious, which are popular in other parts of France. They are loyal to the traditional Reine de Reinettes, whose season lasts from August through to the end of October. La Belle de Boskoop, known in short as Boskoop, is also considered a good cooking apple. Despite, or rather because of, the lack of good eating apples, Normandy's apple desserts are second to none.

Douillons aux pommes
Apple in a nightdress

4 apples
7 oz/200 g puff pastry
5 tbsp/50 g icing sugar
3½ tbsp/50 g butter
Cinnamon
1 egg yolk
1 piece of dried apple peel
1 tbsp/25 g cane sugar

Peel and core the apples.
Thinly roll the puff pastry and cut into 4 large squares. Place an apple on each square of pastry. Add some icing sugar and a flake of butter to the apples, dust with a pinch of cinnamon. Fold the edges of the pastry around the apple, moisten with water and press together well. Preheat the oven to 355 °F/180 °C. Coat the apple pockets with egg yolk and bake for 45 minutes. Shortly before serving grate the dried apple peel and mix with cane sugar, sprinkle it on the pastry and caramelize under the broiler for 30 seconds.

Charlotte aux pommes
Apple charlotte

Serves 8

4 lb 6 oz/2 kg Boskoop apples
⅓ cup/80 g butter
⅔ cup/160 g sugar
8 slices of brioche or ringcake
Scant ½ cup /100 ml Calvados

Preheat the oven to 480 °F/250 °C.
Peel, core, cut the apples in half, and place them in a baking tray greased with butter. Sprinkle with sugar and bake for around 30 minutes.
Heat the butter in a pan and sauté the brioche slices until golden-brown. Flambé the baked apples with calvados.
Line a springform pan with greaseproof paper, then alternately layer the slices of brioche and apple. Bake in the oven for 40 to 50 minutes at 425 °F/220 °C.
Leave to cool and place in a refrigerator for 24 hours. Turn out and serve with custard.

Aumônières de pommes au Calvados
Apple pockets with calvados

3 sour apples
(Boskoop or Reinette apples)
1 tbsp butter
2 tsp cane sugar
3 leek leaves (green)
4¼ cups/1 liter sugared water
12 crêpes, flambéed with calvados
(6 in/15 cm diameter)
1 tbsp/20 g sugar
2 tbsp confectioner's cream
flavored with calvados
8 tbsp apple sorbet (according to taste)

Peel and core the apples, cut them into small pieces, and sauté in butter with the sugar. Allow to cool.
In the meantime cut the leek leaves lengthways into four 6-inch (15-centimeter) long strips, glaze for 3 minutes in boiling sugared water, and leave to cool.
Spread out the crêpes and in the center of each one add a blob of confectioner's cream (made of warm milk, egg yolk, vanilla, sugar, and flour) and the same amount of sautéed apple. Then fold the crêpes into small pockets, tie together with the leek strips, and sprinkle with sugar.
Preheat the oven to 300 °F/150 °C and heat the crêpe pockets for 3 to 5 minutes.
Place three crêpe pockets on each plate and serve immediately.
According to taste the dessert can be served with apple ice cream or apple sorbet.

Tarte Tatin
Apple turnover

Pastry
⅔ cup/100 g flour
5 tbsp/70 g butter
1 tbsp/30 g sugar
1 egg
1 pinch of salt

Filling
1 lb 5 oz/600 g sour apples
6½ tbsp/100 g butter
5 tbsp/100 g sugar
1 envelope of vanilla-flavored sugar

Make the short crust (plain) pastry with flour, cold butter, sugar, egg, and salt, cover with plastic wrap and allow to rest in the refrigerator for 1 hour.
Peel and core the apples and cut them into slices. Melt half of the butter in a deep baking pan, sprinkle with half of the sugar and the vanilla sugar. Evenly line the bottom of the pan with apple slices, then layer the remaining apples. Cook for 15 minutes. Remove from the heat.
Preheat the oven to 390 °F/200 °C.
Thinly roll out the pastry into a round shape, place on top of the apple filling, and press well onto the side of the pan. Then bake in the oven for 30 minutes.
Turn the tart carefully out of the pan so that the pastry is on the bottom. Add the flakes of butter to the apples, sprinkle with the remaining sugar and caramelize under the broiler.
The Tarte Tatin is eaten hot. For serving at a dinner party it can be baked in small pans for smaller portions.

Tarte flambée au Calvados
Flambéed apple cake with calvados

Pastry
1 lb 5 oz/600 g flour
¾ cup/180 g sugar
1⅔ cups/400 g butter
5 egg yolks
1 pinch of salt

Filling
2 lb 3 oz/1 kg Reinette apples
3½ tbsp/50 g butter
Grated peel of 1 untreated orange
Juice of 1 lemon
2 tbsp/50 g sugar
Scant ½ cup /100 ml calvados (½ cup/120 ml if Pommeau is used)
⅓ cup/50 g almond flakes

Make the short crust (plain) pastry with the flour, sugar, cold butter, egg yolk, and salt, then cover in plastic wrap, and place in the refrigerator for 1 hour.

In the meantime peel and core the apples, and slice and then sauté them in 3 ½ tbsp/50 g of brown butter.

Thinly roll out the pastry, place in a fruit cake pan greased with butter, and pierce it several times with a fork.

Preheat the oven to 300 °F/150 °C.

Evenly cover the pastry with the apple slices and then bake the tart for 25 minutes in the preheated oven.

Sprinkle with orange peel, sugar, and lemon juice, and then flambé with calvados.

Bake for a further 25 minutes. Sprinkle with the almond flakes and serve lukewarm.

Tarte aux pommes d'hier
Old-fashioned apple cake

Pastry	
2 cups/300 g flour	
13 tbsp/200 g butter	
Salt	

Filling	
8 sour apples	
(Reine de Reinettes or Calville)	
1 tbsp butter	
1 tbsp cane sugar	
Scant ⅓ cup /70 ml calvados	
5 tbsp/100 g sugar	
2 tsp/10 ml crème fraîche	
1 tbsp/25 g ground almonds	
3 egg yolks	

Make the short crust (plain) pastry with the flour, butter, and a pinch of salt, cover with plastic wrap, and place in the refrigerator for 1 hour.

Peel and dice half of the apples and simmer with 1 tbsp butter and 1 tbsp cane sugar until stewed. Cut the remaining unpeeled apples into slithers, pour on calvados, sprinkle with 2½ tbsp/50 g sugar, and leave to soak.

Preheat the oven to 390 °F/200 °C.

Roll out the pastry and place in a cake tin. Pierce the pastry several times with a fork. Spread the stewed apple over the pastry base and top with apple slices. Bake in the preheated oven for 30 minutes.

Mix the crème fraîche, the ground almonds, the remaining sugar, and the egg yolk together and pour over the apples. Bake for a further 15 minutes. Serve lukewarm.

If you like simplicity in the most refined of apple desserts, just wrap puff pastry around pieces of apple caramelized in butter – and stand back and admire the result.

Cauliflower & artichokes

Brittany is the most important region for vegetables in France. The Gulf Stream is responsible for this, as it flows along the coast and warms the air. In its warm water algae also flourish. As a fertilizer, these used to be worked into the soil in coastal areas, before chemicals were employed to enhance production. Breton farmers however took advantage of the sea in other ways: from their voyages their seafaring compatriots brought fruit and vegetable varieties back from distant lands, including cauliflower from Cyprus and Italy. Especially beautiful cauliflower heads were sent to Versailles, as Louis XIV enjoyed eating them with a sauce seasoned with nutmeg. Today 92 percent of French cauliflowers are produced in Brittany. By planting various types it is available virtually all year round but the best varieties are available in fall and winter. Cauliflower is rich in vitamin C, several B vitamins and minerals. It contains 36 calories for every 3½ ounces (100 grams) and is easy to digest, as long as it has not been exposed to too many artificial fertilizers and has not been sprayed too much. It should also be sold with its leaves. To test its freshness, if you break off one of its leaves, the break should be smooth and moist.

Today globe artichokes are one of Brittany's specialties as important as crêpes or calvados, although they were imported from the Mediterranean. Catherine de' Medici introduced them to Paris, when she married Henry II in 1533.

For a long time they were only used for their beneficial medicinal effects on the gallbladder, liver, and stomach. French aristocracy only discovered them as a quality vegetable in the 18th century. They have been systematically cultivated in Brittany since the First World War. Today 95 percent of all French globe artichokes are grown here, mainly the large-headed Camus variety whose leaves have violet-tinged edges. Camus matures between May and October. When buying globe artichokes you should make sure that the stalks are very firm, the heads heavy and compact, and that the leaves are tightly-closed. The fleshy parts of the leaves, the base, and, in the case of the younger plants, the hearts are all edible and are cooked with lemon to prevent discoloring. Depending on the size, cooking time is around 35 minutes (steaming keeps the minerals intact). Fresh globe artichokes can keep for a few days, if they are put in water like cut flowers.

Right: A slice of lemon on each globe artichoke saves adding vinegar or lemon juice to the salted boiling water.

Crème des hortillons aux moules
Mussel and vegetable cream

2 lb 10 oz/1.2 kg mussels
1 onion
¼ bunch of parsley
1¼ cups/300 ml white wine
Salt, pepper
1 cauliflower
4 leeks
1 lettuce
1 stalk of celery
¼ cup/60 g butter
1 tbsp plus 1 tsp/20 ml crème fraîche

Brush and wash the mussels thoroughly. Finely chop the onion and parsley, add these and the mussels to a large pot. Pour on white wine, add salt and pepper to taste, and bring to a boil. As soon as the mussels open, remove the shells and any string attachments. Drain off the liquid and reserve. Keep the mussels warm.
Clean the vegetables: split the cauliflower into florets, cut the leek into thick rings, remove the outer leaves of the lettuce, cut the celery into pieces. Sauté the vegetables with butter in a large pot and pour on 2 cups/500 ml water together with the mussel stock. When the vegetables are cooked, blend the soup in a liquidizer, stir in the crème fraîche, and add the mussels. Pour into warm bowls and serve immediately.

Chou-fleurs et artichauts aux pétoncles et langoustines
Cauliflower and globe artichokes with scallops and Dublin Bay prawns

Serves 6

1 cauliflower
Salt
3 fresh globe artichokes
1 tbsp lemon juice
17½ oz/500 g Dublin Bay prawns/langoustines
2 cups/500 ml court-bouillon
17½ oz/500 g scallops (without shells)
1 bunch of chervil

The globe artichoke is the unopened flower head of a several-year-old thistle-like plant. As it is so highly prized as a vegetable, the bluish or violet-blue bloom is only rarely seen.

To expose the heart and base of a globe artichoke the top part must be ruthlessly trimmed.

Then the hard leaves located around the base of the globe artichoke are removed with a sharp knife.

Sauce

1 cup/250 g butter
1 bunch of tarragon
¾ cup /200 ml white wine
1 tbsp tomato paste
2 tbsp crème fraîche

Let the cauliflower stand for some time in vinegary water, then rinse under running water. Cook in boiling water for about 20 minutes, drain and rinse with cold water.
Cut off the stalk and trim the top of the globe artichokes, cook in boiling salted water with lemon juice for 30 minutes and drain.
Add the Dublin Bay prawns to the boiling, well-salted stock, as soon as this is boiling again.
Drain, then peel the tails and put to one side.
For the sauce sauté the prawn heads in 2 tsp/10 g butter with a sprig of tarragon for 2 minutes.
Then add white wine and reduce by half.
Add the tomato paste, just cover with water and simmer for 30 minutes. Finely sieve and reduce to a third. Stir in 13 tbsp/200 g butter. Stir in some finely chopped tarragon and add the crème fraîche. Keep warm.
Remove the leaves and the stringy "choke" and cut each artichoke heart into eight. Separate the cauliflower into florets.
Quickly sauté the artichokes, florets, Dublin Bay prawns, and the scallops one after the other in butter, seasoning with salt and pepper to taste.
Divide among six warmed earthenware dishes and pour on hot sauce. Garnish with a few chervil leaves and serve immediately.

Les blancs de Saint Pierre en barigoule bretonne
Peter's fish garnished with artichokes

4 large globe artichokes
Lemon juice
4 large carrots
4 large onions
4 tbsp olive oil
Salt and freshly ground pepper
1 cup/250 ml dry white wine
6 cups/1.5 liters white chicken stock
Coriander corns
Thyme
Bayleaf
2 lb 3 oz/1 kg Peter's fish, filleted

Wash the globe artichokes, slit the stalks, remove the leaves, and the stringy choke. Leave the clean globe artichokes standing in lemon water to prevent any discoloring.
Clean and slice the carrots, peel and cut the onions into thin rings.
Heat half of the olive oil in a pan, add the globe artichokes, carrots, and onions, add salt and pepper to taste.
Sauté for 3 minutes, pour on the wine and reduce.
Pour on the chicken stock, until the ingredients are just covered.
Add the coriander corns, thyme and bayleaf to the pan, cover and cook for 35 minutes. Add salt and pepper to taste, if necessary.
Heat the remaining olive oil in a pan and braise the fish fillets. Add salt and pepper, then serve with the globe artichokes.

The stringy choke inside older artichokes has to be scraped out with a teaspoon.

Soufflé de fonds d'artichauts
Artichoke soufflé

6 globe artichokes (Camus, Prince de Bretagne)
Juice of 1 lemon
5 tbsp/70 g butter
1 tbsp flour
1 cup/250 ml milk
Salt, a pinch of nutmeg
4 eggs, separated
2 tbsp grated Gruyère cheese

Boil the globe artichokes for 30 minutes with lemon juice in salted water. Rinse in cold water; take out the fleshy hearts. Make a béchamel sauce with butter, flour, and milk, add salt and nutmeg, and allow to cool. Blend the globe artichokes, mix with the sauce, then add egg yolk and cheese. Preheat the oven at 390 °F/200 °C for 10 minutes. Whisk the egg white until stiff and carefully fold it into the globe artichoke mixture. Grease an oven-safe dish, add the mixture, and bake for 25 minutes. Serve hot.

Guérande sea salt

As long as 2700 years ago, salt was being extracted on the Guérande peninsula, in the southern tip of Brittany, near the Loire estuary. In the distant past clay containers full of saltwater were heated in ovens until salt was produced. The Romans obtained their salt in this way – as three preserved wells prove – and they used it among other things to produce *garum*, their favorite spicy sauce made from salted fish. From at least as early as the 9th century a fundamental change came about in the way salt was extracted. Then it was learned how to exploit the power of evaporation of the sun and wind and the movement of the tides. Following a special pattern, salt basins were created which over the centuries determined the unique ecological features of the Bassin de Guérande and Bassin du Mes.

The oldest salt basins, of which five are still in operation, date back to the Carolingian era. They consist of a series of canals and basins, built into the flat loam terrain. Using an ingenious system, every two weeks at high tide the salt farmer, the *paludier*, allows seawater to run in through the canals to a large collecting reservoir, by opening a sluice gate. Several salt basins are supplied from this 4–16-inch (10–40-centimeter) deep pond, in which the first impurities are deposited. Evaporation then begins in the summer. If one gallon of seawater normally contains 5.4 ounces (34 grams per liter) of common salt, the concentration now rises to 6.4 ounces (40 grams). In the next irregular-shaped basin the salt content is already up to 8 ounces (50 grams), as the water is further treated. From there it transfers through a watercourse to the final, precisely arranged system of evaporation basins, called the *fards*, which are 1½–2 inches (4–5 centimeters) deep. With the warmth of the sun the water temperature rises to 90 ºF (32 ºC). The water is continually flowing but the flow is also restricted by a number of smaller ponds thereby increasing the evaporation rate.

With a salt content of 32 ounces per gallon (200 grams per liter) or 20º Beaumé (specific gravity scale) the water then flows out of the last *fard* into the *adernes*. These ponds contain the daily requirement of salt solution for the *oeillets*, the large (750-square foot/70-square meter), shallow, (0.2–0.4-inch/5–10-millimeter) rectangular-shaped basins where the salt crystalizes. Every day during harvest time, which runs from June to September, salt farmers carefully push the salt to the edge with a long rake and collect it. The main harvest is made up of evenly sized gray crystals.

The salt farmer with his daily harvest

Contents of coarse Guérande sea salt

Humidity	6.75 %
Insoluble materials	0.34 %
Sulfates	1.9 %
Chloride	54.5 %
Potassium	0.2 %
Calcium	0.12 %
Magnesium	0.71 %
Sodium	35.2 %
Copper	0.00025 %
Zinc	0.0005 %
Manganese	0.00068 %
Iron	0.0085 %
Iodine	in traces

From an analysis by the Station Agronomique de Loire-Atlantique

Before this, however, the first fine white crystals are deposited on the surface of the salt solution, the density of which is by now between 40 and 48 ounces per gallon (250–300 grams per liter). This is the best salt, the *fleur du sel*, the ultimate in culinary salts, used exclusively for the refinement of foods after they have been prepared.

Paludiers have the status of farmers and some 200 of them still practice this traditional trade. When fully productive, each one works 60 *oeillets*, each producing about 1.3 tons of salt. The whole year round the salt farmer is busy keeping the basins clean and controlling the movement of water or harvesting the salt.

The salt harvest is very much dependent on the climatic conditions of the summer – the same as for other farmers – and with beneficial weather conditions can easily double. In bad weather it can be reduced by half or more. Sea, sun and wind are the three essential elements of a rich harvest. In this long, airy process all harmful substances are dissipated in a completely natural way. Without further treatment, apart from perhaps the grinding of the salt crystals or mixing it with herbs or algae, the sea salt is packed and put on sale.

The Guérande peninsula supplies 83 percent of sea salt extracted in an exclusively traditional way from the Atlantic. The other salt basins are further south at Noirmoutier, the Ile de Ré, and off the Ile d'Oléron. The main production of sea salt, however, is from the salt-marshes at Aigues Mortes on the Mediterranean coast where the salt is collected with enormous machinery and then refined. Today in France rock salt plays only a minor part in overall salt production.

In addition to salt farmers, mussel and oyster farmers have been active on the Presqu'île de Guérande since the beginning of the 20th century. Both the salt marshes and the basins of the shellfish farmers in the parishes of Guérande, La Turballe, Batz-sur-Mer, Le Poliguen, and Le Croisic are conservation areas. This encompasses both the special architectural legacy of the salt-marshes and their wealth of flora and fauna. As well as protecting rare plants, which have been able to acclimatize to the saltwater, such as *salicornia* whose young shoots are boiled or eaten pickled in vinegar, almost 180 types of bird living there are given protection, of which 72 nest in the area. The protection of wetlands accorded by the convention of Ramsar does not just serve nature, but also safeguards the production of the very best culinary salt.

Left: Collecting the coarse salt
Right: Aerial view of the salt marshes and canals

Dos de saumon grillé au fleur du sel
Broiled salmon steak with sea sal

Serves 1

1 thick salmon steak with skin on
(from a fillet)
1 tbsp duck or goose lard
1 tsp veal stock
1 tbsp lemon juice
1 tbsp salted butter
1 tbsp sherry vinegar
2 tbsp soya sauce
2 tsp cane sugar
1 tsp salt crystals
Freshly ground pepper
1 cup salicornia
Fennel leaves

Preheat the broiler to 390 °F/200 °C. Rinse the salmon steak with cold water and dab it dry.
Braise it on the skin side in duck or goose lard in a pan for 3 minutes.
For the sauce dilute the veal stock in 1 tbsp water, add lemon juice and butter and carefully heat without boiling. Keep warm
Make a marinade from vinegar, soya sauce, and sugar. Coat the fish skin with it and broil for 1 minute. Remove it and immediately sprinkle the crispy skin with salt crystals and pepper.
Heat the salicornia.
Serve the salmon steak on a plate with the crust uppermost. Sprinkle fennel leaves on it, garnish with salicornia, and pour on the sauce. As a side dish fresh tagliatelle are good.

Galettes

The *galette*, a buckwheat pancake, is probably man's oldest food. Called *jalet* in Brittany, its place of origin, it was baked as a substitute for bread on a hot, flat stone.

Buckwheat is really not a cereal but is related to knotgrass. Its original home is Asia, from where it spread toward both Russia and the Orient. It came to France with the Crusaders, and because it was such a dark color it was called *Sarasin* (saracen). Breton farmers accepted it with enthusiasm as it grew to maturity in only four months and even flourished in the barren hinterlands of Brittany. It was almost more important for farmers that buckwheat could not be baked for bread and consequently was not subject to any taxes and duties.

For centuries the low-priced *galettes* made only from flour, salt and water formed the basis of nutrition in Brittany. Breton women were justifiably proud of their skill in baking *galettes*,

and the recipes were handed down from generation to generation. It was customary for a bride to throw the first *galette* baked in her new house onto the cupboard as a tribute to the previous residents of the house, intended to secure protection for her offspring and domestic happiness.

When white wheat was easier to get hold of and cost less, buckwheat fell into oblivion. Nowadays most of the buckwheat ground in Brittany comes from China where it is much cheaper. Very recently the nostalgia for authentic foods from the past has encouraged farmers to sow native varieties of buckwheat once more. They produce a dark, strongly flavored flour that is quite expensive.

Traditionally *galettes* were baked over wood fires, giving them a smoky flavor, but now electric baking plates have taken over. Tasty pancakes filled with ham, a fried egg, sausage, cheese, vegetables, or fish are still very popular outside of Brittany as well.

Pâte à galettes de blé noir
A basic recipe for pancakes made from buckwheat

For 12 *galettes*

2 cups/250 g buckwheat flour
1 egg
2 cups/500 ml water
1 tbsp coarse sea salt
2 tbsp melted lard
Butter or lard for baking

Sieve the flour into a bowl and form a hollow. Whisk the egg in it. Add salt and gradually add water, mixing the ingredients to form a liquid batter. Then beat vigorously with a mixer. Leave to rest for at least 2 hours, or overnight if possible. Whisk again and add some melted lard. Heat the pan and grease well with butter. Add a ladle of dough and shake it so that it is distributed over the whole of the bottom of the pan. Free the browned edges of the pancake from the edge of the pan, turn the pancake over and cook the other side. Breton women grease the iron pan with a mixture of lard and egg yolk (1 egg yolk for approximately 6 1/2–10 tbsp/100–150 g lard). This way the *galette* is freed more easily and the buckwheat flavor develops more effectively.

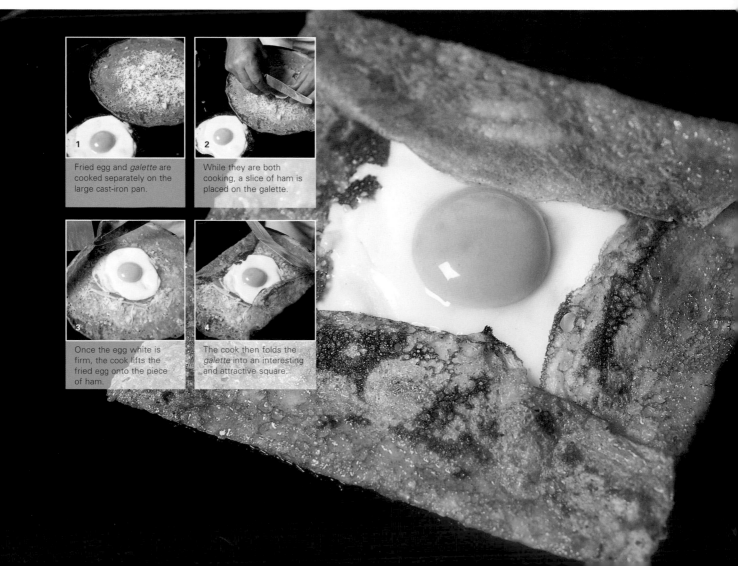

1 Fried egg and *galette* are cooked separately on the large cast-iron pan.

2 While they are both cooking, a slice of ham is placed on the galette.

3 Once the egg white is firm, the cook lifts the fried egg onto the piece of ham.

4 The cook then folds the *galette* into an interesting and attractive square.

Crêpes & cakes

As well as eggs, butter, and milk, good quality *crêpes* require white wheat flour and sugar, both originally luxury items, so it is not surprising that the first *crêpe* recipes were recorded in Paris. When they quickly became a Breton specialty, it was very much down to the centuries of experience gathered in this region, in baking such round flat dough-cakes.

Crêpes came to be one of the region's most popular desserts. From their voyages to distant continents, Breton seafarers brought back rum, orange blossom water, vanilla, and cinnamon, all of which were very useful to *crêpe* bakers. There seemed to be limitless opportunities for sweet, tasty fillings, but pancakes kept their native appeal and simplicity. Long before France was invaded by American fast food chains, *crêperies* had already been established all over the country, providing the most popular form of French fast food. With crêpes it was possible to satisfy your hunger quickly, inexpensively, and appetizingly.

In Brittany there is also another kind of cake, which is decidedly regional in its appeal. The reason for this lies in its essential ingredient: salted butter. *Far*, eaten as a side dish, was transformed into a sweet cake with the addition of eggs and dried fruit. Butter gives *Gâteau breton* its rich, finely crumbed texture. When it is the size of a biscuit, it is called *traou mad* which means something like "good things." The most famous is without doubt the *Kouign Amann*, which literally means "bread and butter." Originally it was only baked in the region of Douarnenez, but now it is available from every Breton baker who takes pride in his or her skills.

Pâte à crêpes
Basic recipe for 12 crepes

2 cups/250 g wheat flour
2 eggs
⅛ tsp salt
2 tbsp sugar
2 tbsp melted butter
2 cups/500 ml lukewarm milk
Butter for baking

Press out a hollow in the sieved flour. Add eggs, salt, sugar, and melted butter. Mix to a liquid batter with lukewarm milk. Leave to rest for 30 minutes.
For baking, heat a small amount of butter in a pan. Add a small amount of the batter and shake the pan to distribute it evenly. Cook until the underside of the crêpe is firm and the edge of the batter is golden yellow, then turn it over and fry the other side.

Kouign Amann
Breton buttercake

Serves 6

1 oz/25 g compressed yeast
4 cups/500 g flour
1 cup/250 g salted butter
1 cup/250 g sugar
1 egg yolk

Dissolve the yeast with a pinch of sugar in ¾ cup/200 ml lukewarm water, sprinkle in the flour, and mix to a smooth dough. Leave to prove for 60 minutes.
Roll out the dough on the work surface, as if you were going to cook a large pancake. Cover with flakes of butter, sprinkle with sugar, and fold to a quarter. Again roll and repeat the process four times as if making puff pastry. Then press the dough into a pan greased with butter and coat with the egg yolk. Preheat the oven to 355 °F/180 °C and bake the cake for 25 minutes until it turns a golden yellow. Serve while warm.

Gâteau breton
Breton cake
(Illustration above)

Serves 10

4 cups/475 g flour
2 cups/475 g sugar
2 cups/500 g salted butter
8 egg yolks
2 tbsp rum
2 tbsp milk

Make a hollow in the sieved flour. Add sugar and soft butter and mix with the flour. Stir in 7 egg yolks, then add rum and work to a smooth dough. Grease a springform pan with butter, dust with flour and press the dough evenly into the pan. Mix the remaining egg yolk with the milk, coat the surface of the dough with it and score a grid pattern with a fork.
Preheat the oven to 390 °F/200 °C and bake the cake for 45 minutes. Leave to cool in the pan.

Far aux pruneaux
Egg plumcake
(Illustration below)

Serves 6

24 prunes
1 generous tbsp/20 ml rum
1 cup/150 g flour
½ cup/150 g sugar
1 pinch salt
6 eggs
4 cups/1 liter milk
1 tbsp salted butter

Soak the prunes in rum.
Mix the sieved flour with sugar and salt, make a hollow, add the eggs and work everything to a smooth dough. Slowly add lukewarm milk and melted butter.
Generously grease a baking pan with butter, spread the prunes on the bottom and pour in the cake dough, which should not be too runny. Bake for 10 minutes at 450 °F/225 °C, then lower the temperature to 340 °F/170 °C. The *far* should remain soft inside. It is served cold or lukewarm with a glass of sweet cider.

Pays de Loire
Centre

Jim Budd & André Dominé

Early vegetables
Champignons
  de Paris
Fish from the Loire
Butcher's specialties
  from Touraine
The wines of the
  Loire Valley
Vinegar from Orléans
Genuine pralines
Crottin de Chavignol

Even today, vinegar is still produced in Orléans
using a process which has been handed down
since the 14th century.

The Château de La Preuille is famous for its
excellent Muscadet wines.

Calais

Le Havre

Caen   Paris

Brest

Rennes   Strasbourg

Pays
de Loire   Centre

Dijon

Limoges   Lyon

St-Étienne

Bordeaux   Grenoble

Avignon   Nice

Biarritz   Toulouse

Marseille   Toulon

Perpignan

rance's longest river is still the stuff of dreams. Even today the far-famed castles along its banks have lost hardly any of their charm. This may have something to do with the fact that their significance is not confined just to their historical prominence or their importance in the history of art. They are also obvious symbols of an artistically refined lifestyle.

The heartland of the Loire Valley, containing the provinces of Anjou and Touraine, is known as the garden of France. This is where the cherries grow for the incomparable Guignolet, a robust liqueur, and the Belle Angevine pears which are so popular when cooked in red wine as a dessert — to say nothing of strawberries, melons, and other kinds of high-quality fruit. There is no lack of vegetables here either. The image of a colorful garden simultaneously suggests a harmonious idyll, and thus describes the cornerstones of a lifestyle in which the idea of balance was just as fundamentally important as the exquisiteness of taste reflected in the buildings it produced. They are constructed from the trass which was quarried out of the galleries that penetrate the slopes above the Loire, extending for several miles. Nowadays, these old quarries not only offer ideal conditions for mushroom growers, but the man-made caves are also among the best wine cellars in the world. The residents of Saumur understood perfectly how to use them to make high-quality sparkling wine. In Vouvray, the caves are used to mature legendary fine sweet wines, and in Bourgueil it is red wines, which after decades develop the refinement that is characteristic of this region. It can even be found reflected in the most substantial specialties, such as *rillettes* or *andouillettes*.

The Loire Valley is still rich in the ingredients without which refined cuisine is inconceivable: the numerous kinds of fish, the wild game birds or animals, lambs, calves, or Charolais cattle, the noble *Géline* fowl, or the goat cheeses, which are among the best in France. The area surrounding Nantes (once the gateway to the colonies) is home to delicate early vegetables, which form the basis of unique soups and garnishes. And when enjoying fish with the exquisite *beurre blanc*, the classic butter sauce, you may well want to accompany it with a rather well-matured Muscadet sur lie, which has fully developed the flavor of its yeast and yet seems to reflect the freshness of the Atlantic into which the Loire finally flows, after a journey of 616 miles (992 kilometers).

Early vegetables

Primeurs are the first vegetables of the season, which manage to trick the calendar by arriving, on the market while the rest of their species are still struggling to survive. Another factor which helps their early appearance on the scene is that the *primeurs* are picked before they are fully grown. They need special conditions to give them a good start.

The Pays Nantais, the area around the port city of Nantes which stretches along the right-hand bank of the Loire, has these conditions: sandy but fertile alluvial soils and a mildly oceanic climate. Vegetable-growing in this area dates from the beginning of the 19ᵗʰ century. As demand grew, the main market for these vegetables was on the other side of the English Channel. Carrots grow particularly well in the sandy soil. Initially, short carrots were cultivated, but then a medium-length type was developed which, from 1864 to the present day, has been well-known as the *carotte nantaise*. When they are grown on open land, they cannot be picked until May, and even then they are very small, not yet as long as a finger. So that the carrots can be picked earlier, the market gardeners give their special breeds particular protection in beds covered with glass. In 1900, one smallholder in the Pays Nantais planted as many as four hundred manure beds with carrots, and a further hundred with other vegetables. That is how it became possible to put early vegetables on the market in March. This proved to be a very good investment, since the consumers, weary of winter vegetables, were happy to pay seven times the normal price for the harbingers of spring.

The Loire created good conditions for market gardening, not only in the area around Nantes but also in the *département* of Maine-et-Loire, and in the region surrounding Orléans. Naturally some growers specialized – in onions or melons, thick red or green beans, asparagus or salsify, but even a hundred years ago or more the region's strong point was its varied produce. Up to a hundred different types of vegetable were grown, many of which have undergone a renaissance in recent years thanks to the Horticultural College in Angers. But vegetable production has changed in the meantime. It has been industrialized and rationalized, which was almost bound to make the growers concentrate on a few types of crop. The most important vegetable grown in the Pays Nantais today is corn salad, which has become much in demand as an export product. Other profitable crops are leeks, turnips, peas, tomatoes, and melons – although the famous carrots can be grown more cost-effectively in the Landes. The most important winter salad vegetable is the chicory. Mazé onions and Sologne asparagus are also still significant.

Tomates — Tomatoes
Although people rightly associate them with the Midi, tomatoes have long been grown in the area around Nantes, where at least 20,392 tons (18,500 tonnes) are produced annually.

Oignons — Onions
The *oignon de Mazé* has held its own so far, and Loiret, with 10 percent of the crop (33,069 tons/ 30,000 tonnes) a year is still one of the most important production areas after Burgundy and Champagne.

Scarole — Chicory
The *cornette d'Anjou* remains one of the most popular specialties of central France for use in winter salads, in terms of the weight of vegetables sold. But the main production areas are on the Mediterranean coast.

Mâche — Corn salad
It has become a specialty and a best-selling export for the Pays Nantais. The highest prices for corn salad can be obtained in January and February, when there is a shortage of other salad greens.

Asperges — Asparagus
Some 23 percent of French asparagus is grown in either the central region or the Loire Valley. The main production area is Gard, and the Landes are also important.

Concombre — Cucumber
The Loire Valley is now the most important cucumber-producing area of France; combined with this area, the central region produces a good third of the crop of around 148,810 tons (135,000 tonnes) a year.

Endive – Chicorée

Originally a Belgian discovery, endive has long had an established place in the range of vegetables available in France. It is used in salads, and is also served steamed or grated. Most of the endive grown in France comes from the French part of Flanders and the neighboring regions. Thus, Nord and Pas-de-Calais alone account for 55 percent of production, and Picardy contributes a further 27 percent to the total harvest, which in a good year may amount to around 264,500 tons (240,000 tonnes) – making France the biggest producer in the world. Only 9 percent of this total is exported. The plants, which take two years to mature, are sown in the open fields in May and June. They initially develop a rosette of leaves and a fleshy root. During the harvest, in September/October, the leaves are removed and the heads are briefly stored below freezing point in cold storage chambers. They are then transferred to a hydroculture system: they go into basins containing only water or a nutrient solution, at a constant 50–64/72 °F (10–18/22 °C) and left to sprout in complete darkness. After three to four weeks, the shoots have formed, and are broken off from the roots. Only rarely is endive still grown in beds with loose earth or sand, where it becomes especially firm and sweet. Endive should be absolutely spotless, and the head should be firm and closed. If the tips of the leaves are green, unpleasant bitter substances may already have spread through the plant.

Poireau – Leek

The *poireau*, particularly *en primeur*, remains a specialty of the Pays Nantais, which leads the market with 17 percent of the annual yield of 237,000 tons (215,000 tonnes).

Carottes – Carrots

Formerly the most important vegetable in the Pays Nantais, they now play almost no role there at all, while the départements of Landes and Gironde account for 27 percent of annual production.

Endives au jambon
Endive with ham

4 endive heads
4 slices cooked ham
¼ cup/60 g butter
5 tbsp/40 g flour
2 cups/500 ml milk
Scant 1 cup/100 g grated Gruyère
Freshly-milled salt and black pepper

Remove the outer leaves of the endives if necessary and cut off the lower ends. Hollow out a conical shape in the heart and wash the roots. Blanch in boiling salted water for 15 minutes. Leave to drain and then wrap a slice of ham around each head.
Preheat the oven to 390 °F/200 °C.
Grease a heat resistant mold with 2 tsp/10 g butter and place the endive heads in it.
For the sauce, lightly brown the flour in the remaining butter and add the milk while stirring continuously; leave to simmer for 5 minutes. Fold in a third of the grated cheese and season with salt and pepper.
Pour the sauce over the endive heads and sprinkle the remaining cheese on top. Bake for about 10 minutes, or until the cheese turns golden brown. Serve immediately, with a Sancerre or a Sauvignon from Touraine.

Navets glacés
Glazed turnips

1¼ lbs/600 g small baby turnips
4 tsp/20 g butter
½ tsp sugar
1¼ cups/300 ml chicken stock

Brush and rinse the baby turnips, then blanch them for 10 minutes.
Melt the butter in a saucepan, add the turnips and sugar and cook briefly. Now pour in the stock, cover and cook for 15 minutes. Then remove the cover and reduce the stock by evaporation.
Toss the turnips in the sauce and serve hot as a side-dish to roasts.

Beets or baby carrots can be cooked in the same way.

Potage printanier
Spring vegetable soup

3 baby carrots
1 small white turnip
3 thin leeks
1 stalk of celery
4 potatoes
2 sprigs of parsley
Generous 3 pints/1.5 liters beef stock
Freshly-milled salt and black pepper
2 tbsp crème fraîche

Clean the vegetables and dice finely. Bring the stock to a boil, add the diced vegetables and parsley, lower the heat and let soup simmer for 1 hour.
Strain the stock through a sieve into a bowl. Purée the vegetables, season with salt and pepper and return to the stock. Then stir in the crème fraîche and serve the soup immediately.

Oyster mushrooms come a rather poor second to mushrooms on the French scale of popularity.
This tree fungus flourishes on a mixture of compost and sawdust, and can be obtained in several different colors: yellow, white and pink.

Champignons de Paris

Although the Loire Valley has long since overtaken the area around Paris as regards growing mushrooms, the popular and historical name is retained. For it was the Parisian gardener Chambry who had the bright idea of using abandoned underground quarries to cultivate meadow mushrooms. This environment conformed to the natural conditions required for growing mushrooms. They did well, the demand in the Parisian market grew, and soon many people were imitating Chambry. And yet it was not until a hundred years later that the mushroom grower Monin was inspired by the trass caves in the Loire Valley and began production there.

Nowadays, specialist growers propagate only the mycelium of different types of mushroom, using sterilized grains of rye or millet as a nutrient medium, and sell it in 4-liter (about 4 quarts) units to the mushroom growers. The latter sow the mycelium in compost. For cultivated mushrooms, such compost consists of a mixture of straw and horse manure, which is piled up into heaps, regularly sprayed with water and turned. This accelerates the decomposition process, so that the compost is ready after only a week, whereas in nature this would take about eight months. The nutrient medium is sterilized by a heat treatment, and has to cool down before the mycelium can be sown and mixed in. The mixture is then put into plastic bags.

The growers lay the bags out in the galleries of the former quarries, where the temperature remains at 54–62°F (12–16°C) all the year round, with an atmospheric humidity of 90 percent.

Above: This variant of the *champignons de Paris* has a brown skin, but is known as *blond*, and is more aromatic than white versions of the same size.

Mushrooms are unable to generate their own nutrients through photosynthesis, as they have no chlorophyll. They are therefore not orientated toward sunlight, but rather toward usable organic materials which the mycelium extracts from the nutrient medium. To promote the growth of the mushrooms, the grower also sprinkles the surface of the bags with mycelium. After an incubation period of 10 to 15 days, in which the mycelium penetrates through the compost, a thin layer of peat and water mixture with ground trass may be added to the surface – *gobetage* – to stop the compost from drying out. The tops of the first mushrooms appear two weeks later. They double in size every 24 hours, and after seven to ten days

Champignons de Paris – not the snowy white ones but the cream-colored variety this time. Once they appear, they double in size each day.

Nowadays mushrooms are frequently cultivated in plastic bags, which are filled with sterile compost, in and on which the mushroom mycelium is deposited.

they are ready for harvesting. Over the next five to eight weeks, five more harvests can take place. All the mushrooms are still picked by hand. A 66–77 pounds (30–35 kilograms) bag of compost yields 13–22 pounds (6–10 kilograms) of mushrooms. By then it is no longer sterile enough, for one of the preconditions for successful mushroom growing is strict hygiene. For this reason, the galleries and all the operating equipment are regularly disinfected. In the area around Saumur, there are about a thousand quarries, the trass stone from which has been used for centuries for building. Nowadays, about 500 miles (800 kilometers) of workings are used for growing mushrooms. After the U.S.A. and China, France is the third largest producer of cultivated mushrooms. They are eaten raw in salads or fried as a side-dish, or baked – and 65 percent of each year's crop now arrives in the kitchen in a can!

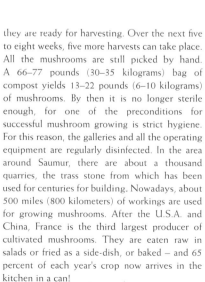

The oldest method of growing mushrooms, which was in use until 1960, was to lay down beds in the galleries, which had to be dismantled and taken away completely after each crop.

The next stage of development in the history of mushroom growing was the use of wooden boxes like this, which were easier to handle and to clean; now the trend is toward containers.

Fish from the Loire

The Loire which, with a length of 616 miles (992 kilometers), is the longest river in France, is still a paradise for many. But for a very long time the river has been under attack by progress. Banks have disintegrated and been reinforced with cement. Weirs, locks and power stations have been established. The river is adorned – and exploited – by Roanne and Orléans, Tours, Angers and Nantes. The commercial fishing industry, which was once so flourishing, is now something which belongs to a fondly remembered past. The salmon, so highly and so rightly prized, which are taken from its waters have become so rare that they are now a protected species. Due to the intensive agriculture carried out along its banks the water often contains excessive levels of nitrate, which delicate tench, fine river perch, and tender shad do not find so easy to tolerate. And

the *civelles*, the elvers so enthusiastically admired by gourmets, which can be found only between January and March in the Loire, find this hard to bear as well. Fortunately, other species are still quite contented, especially the carp and their similarly patient neighbors such as barbel, bream and gudgeon, but also including pike perch, pike and, to a lesser extent, lampreys. Even the little bleak – very popular as a *friture* – is on the increase again. And between Nantes and Saint-Nazaire the fishermen may also find red mullet and salmon trout in their nets. Eels and frogs also form part of the catches. While in Tours they cook eels in red wine to make *matelote*, farther down the river toward its mouth they like to simmer their fish in a *court-bouillon* – a stock seasoned with soup vegetables, herbs, vinegar, pepper and salt, and often served with a white butter sauce. There is no lack at all along the Loire of white wine to accompany the fine fish dishes. People like to show their local patriotism in making their selection. In Nantes, their preference is for a *Muscadet sur lie* at least two or three years old.

Grenouilles sauce poulette
Frog legs in sauce poulette
(illustration below)

2 shallots	
4 mushrooms	
6½ tbsp/100 g butter	
1 lb/500 g fresh frog legs	
1 tbsp flour	
Freshly-milled salt and pepper	
1 cup/250 ml Muscadet wine	
1 cup/250 ml crème fraîche	
2 egg yolks	
Juice of ½ lemon	
2 sprigs of parsley	

Chop the shallots finely. Clean the mushrooms and cut them into slices. Heat 4½ tbsp/70 g butter in a pan until it turns golden. Add the frog's legs and brown them. Then dust them with a little flour. Mix together and add salt and pepper.
Add the shallots, mushrooms and wine and cook for 5 minutes. Take out the frog legs and keep them warm.
Reduce the sauce to three-quarters, then bind with fresh cream and egg yolk. Add the remaining butter and sprinkle with the lemon juice.
Arrange the frog's legs on plates and pour the sauce over them. Chop the parsley finely and sprinkle on top.
A good accompaniment to this dish would be a *Muscadet sur lie* four or five years old.

Anguille de Loire Tartare
Eel with Tartare sauce

1 Loire eel, about 2½ lbs/1.2 kg
Freshly-milled salt and pepper
1 bouquet garni
1 tbsp red wine vinegar
2 tbsp flour
1 egg
2 tbsp oil
Breadcrumbs
1 sprig of parsley
4 tbsp *sauce Tartare*

Skin the eel, gut it and wash it. Coil the eel and tie with kitchen twine. Heat a court-bouillon made with water, salt, pepper, a bouquet garni, and red wine vinegar. Add the eel and let it simmer for 15 minutes. Remove the eel and let it drain; then roll in flour. Beat the egg with the oil and season with salt and pepper. Turn the eel in this mixture and then in breadcrumbs. Brown under the broiler. Garnish with parsley and serve with Tartare sauce made from mayonnaise, fine-chopped parsley, pickled gherkins, capers, and hard-cooked egg.

Anguille de Loire Tartare – Eel with Tartare sauce

Brochet beurre blanc
Pike in butter sauce

1 Loire pike, about 3 lbs/1.5 kg
Freshly-milled salt and pepper
1 bouquet garni
1 tbsp red wine vinegar
2 shallots
3½ tbsp/50 ml white wine vinegar
3½ tbsp/50 ml Muscadet
Scant 1 cup/200 g salted butter
3 sprigs of parsley

Scale the pike, gut it and clean it. Heat a court bouillon made with water, salt, pepper, bouquet garni, and vinegar, and let the fish simmer in it for 10 minutes per pound.
Finely chop the shallots and boil with the vinegar and wine until the liquid has evaporated. Stir in the cold butter little by little in flakes on a low heat; do not let the sauce boil. Season with pepper.
Arrange the pike in a dish on a napkin, remove the top skin and garnish with parsley. Serve with steamed potatoes and butter sauce.

Brochet beurre blanc – Pike in butter sauce

Alose de Loire à l'oseille
Loire shad with sorrel

1 Loire shad, 3–4½ lbs/1.5–2 kg
12 small potatoes
2 shallots
1⅓ cups/320 g butter
2 bunches of sorrel
Scant ½ cup/100 ml Muscadet
Freshly-milled salt and pepper
A few sprigs of parsley

Bake the ready-to-cook shad in a preheated oven at 355 °F/180 °C for 15 minutes per pound. Boil or steam the potatoes. Fine chop the shallots and briefly cook them in butter. Add the fine-chopped sorrel and the wine and cook while stirring until the mixture becomes creamy.
Stir in the remaining butter in flakes without letting the sauce boil, then season.
Serve the shad with the potatoes and garnish with parsley. Serve the sauce separately.

Alose de Loire à l'oseille – Loire shad with sorrel

Butcher's specialties from Touraine

Rillettes and Rillons

In *The Lily of the Valley*, Honoré de Balzac, the insatiable novelist, sang the praises of the substantial specialties of his home town of Tours, *rillettes* and *rillons*. Whereas most respectable people did not want to know about them at the time, he waxed enthusiastic over "these remains of a pig, braised in its lard." He compared *rillons* to cooked truffles, while elevating *rillettes* to the status of brown jams.

Clearly Balzac the hedonist, writing in the 19th century had no problem in declaring his support for the rustic pork products of his native region. Their origins go back centuries and are lost in the details of village life in the dim and distant past. For it seems likely that when the inhabitants of a village slaughtered a pig, they braised pieces of belly, gullet, shoulder, and rind for a long time in lard as a way of making sure it could be kept. By the end of the 15th century, these were already being referred to as *rille* or *rillée*, an expression which goes back to the Old French *reille*, which meant slat, and is derived from the Latin *regula*.

Little has changed since then with regard to the preparation. The quality is determined initially by the quality of the pork, which depends on the way the pig has been reared. The animals must have put on bacon fat really well, and young sows are chosen for preference.

Good *rillettes* are made up of two-thirds belly, shoulder and gullet, and one-third bacon fat and lard. The bacon fat is removed from the rind and finely diced. The lard is heated in a cast-iron pot and the bacon fat is melted while the mixture is stirred. The meat is added, cut up into pieces. It should not include too many bones. The mixture is frequently stirred and the fat begins to bubble. The meat is allowed to brown for about 30 minutes. Then a little water is added and the pot is covered.

The juiciness of the completed *rillettes* depends on the meat being braised only at low temperature. After 5 hours, sea salt is added, with pepper and onions and perhaps a few cloves and herbs, and the pot is left on the stove for another hour. The meat must then be soft enough to disintegrate into fibers.

The contents of the pot are now poured through a large sieve, so that the fat drains out and the meat cools down. This separates out the meat juice, which is removed. The *rillettes* are now tipped out onto large dishes, so that the bones, sinews, and gristle can be removed, which is done by hand. Then they are put back into the pot. The meat juice is added a little at a time and the *rillettes* are heated again while being stirred. Sufficient lard is added to create a balanced mixture. The mixture is seasoned for the last time. Then the *rillettes* can be rapidly cooled in a cold water bath. The mixture must be continuously stirred while this is going on so that the lard, which is still fluid, does not set.

As soon as it starts to become viscous, the *rillettes* are put into jars, pots or molds and kept in cold storage.

Although they are referred to as *rillettes de Tours*, those made by the nearby winemaking center of Vouvray are at least as famous and recently more and more of the connoisseurs are coming to prefer them. When they are served as a first course with lightly toasted farmhouse bread, they really must be accompanied by a dry Vouvray – a white wine full of character, the good acidity of which pleasantly complements the *rillettes*, which are still a little rich.

Rillettes must be easy to spread and creamy. Certainly for that reason, but also because of the taste, they are served at room temperature, not chilled. In addition to *rillettes* from Tours, those from Le Mans are also well-known. They are not so strongly browned initially, and so they remain pale. They are well liked because they still contain whole pieces of lean meat.

Rillettes are not always made entirely from pork. In the southwest, people are fond of adding the remains of fat ducks and geese to them, and rabbit meat is suitable for this too.

Rillons are distinguished mainly by their consistency. They certainly contain larger pieces of meat, but the meat has been preserved in lard in the same way. A generous dash of Vouvray in the pot lends them additional delicacy.

Terrines and pâtés

The central part of France is considered as being the stronghold of pâtés and terrines. The most famous of them is *pâté de Chartres*. Like the magnificent Gothic cathedral, this is an elaborate and complicated work of art, in which the most important element is game. This is initially left to marinate for a relatively long time. It is then mixed with stuffing made from pork and veal, various kinds of liver, truffles and Cognac, and baked in pastry or in a terrine. Gourmets of earlier times greatly prized lark pies. The one they liked the best was *pâté de mauviettes de Pithiviers*, which had made the fortune of the Provenchère family in the 16th century when Charles IX found that their recipe was to his taste. It was the game-rich forests of Beauce and Sologne which supplied the bakers with most of their ingredients. And so they created terrines and pâtés from quails and snipe, partridges, wild ducks and pheasants, rabbits, hares and red deer.

In principle, a distinction is made between *pâtés*, which have a pastry shell and are baked in a metal mold, and *terrines*, which are cooked in porcelain or ceramic molds (often lined with fatty bacon) and which must then be pressed for some time. Nowadays, however, these expressions are used with greater freedom.

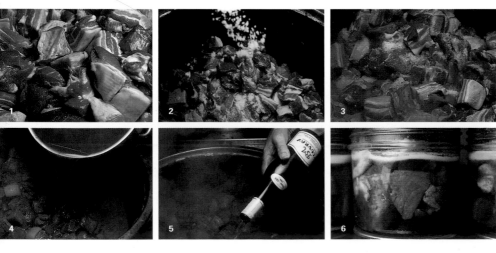

1 For *rillons*, a famous specialty from Touraine, cut pork shoulder and pork belly with fat running through them into large pieces. – 2 Put the meat into a large cast-iron pot, shake 4–5 tsp (20-25 g) of sea salt per 2 pounds (kilogram) over it and let it soak in well. – 3 Now heat the pot, which has previously had lard put into it, and fry the pieces of meat, from all sides. – 4 As soon as they are well browned, add a little caramel and mix it in well to obtain a pleasantly brownish color. – 5 A generous dash of Vouvray toward the end of the preparation adds a special note. – 6 Completed *rillons* in a bottling jar.

Andouillettes

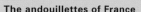

Following the motto *"Tout est bon dans le cochon"* (everything in the pig is edible), French farmers and butchers understood, from back in the Middle Ages, how to make something special out of even the stomach and the intestines. Thus the love the French have for the *andouillette* has developed over centuries, whereas they usually made those of a different nationality turn queasy. For the classic pork version, above all, frequently has a marked, not to say penetrating, odor and taste. Which is why in France these chitterling sausages are considered as one of the greatest achievements of her pork-butchers. Since time immemorial, there have been two factions. The first has its stronghold in Troyes and swears by pork, while the other, centered around Lyon, prefers veal. And those who seek to find the golden mean have chosen Cambrai in the north, not far from Calais, as their capital. But whether pork or veal is used, conscientious, accurate work is required to turn the least noble of ingredients into a sausage which sends gourmets into raptures. After very thorough cleaning, the intestines are cut into long, thin strips and marinated in a well-cooled place for 48 hours in onions, carrots, thyme, bay leaves, white wine and/or vinegar (the marinade is later added to the stock.) For sausages made by hand, the intestines, having been seasoned, are tied up in a bundle with twine, stuffed into skins and tied off. The sausages are cooked in bubbling stock for about 2¹⁄₂ hours. Now the fat is skimmed off and some additional stock is added (for really traditional preparation, the skins are even turned inside out and cleaned and used again). There then follows a second period of cooking which lasts almost as long. When the sausages have cooled down, they are divided into portions 4–6 inches/10–15 centimeters long. *Andouillettes* are thus precooked, which means they can also be served cold with an aperitive or in a salad. However, they should not be stored in the refrigerator for longer than a week. They are preferably eaten hot as an appetizer or a main course – fried, broiled, or baked until the external skin is golden brown and crispy. No fat, or very little fat, is added, and the skin is pricked repeatedly with a fork. Onions or shallots are then fried in the residual fat, with a little white wine added, which is the ideal accompaniment, apart from Beaujolais. In addition, *andouillettes* must conform to a decree which dates from 1912, and the Association Amicale des Amateurs d'Andouillette Authentique (AAAAA) awards diplomas on which the customer can rely.

The andouillettes of France

Andouillette de Cambrai
In this celebrated version from the north, calf's entrails are preferred as the main ingredient, well seasoned with onions, shallots and sometimes with a little gin.

Andouillette de Chablis
These sausages consist of pig's entrails and are comparatively small in diameter, with a distinctive taste. They are also refined by the addition of fresh herbs and snails.

Andouillette de Jargeau
From the village in the *département* of Loiret (with its administrative capital in Orléans) comes a sausage which owes its more delicate character to the addition of lean pork.

Andouillette de Lyon
The best come from Bobosse (René Besson), who makes them entirely from calf's entrails in the Beaujolais region, ties them together with twine and cooks them in well-seasoned stock.

Andouillette du Périgord
In addition to all its other specialties, the gourmet's paradise in the southwest has not neglected to produce its own version of *andouillettes*, which involves processing pork belly.

Andouillette provençale
In Provence, they still use pig's caul and gullet, but they coat them with breadcrumbs. As regards the aroma, the famous herbs come into play, together with garlic.

Andouillette de Rouen
Those who know how to make *andouille* are also good at stuffing *andouillettes*, but here these are a mixture of finely-chopped pig's intestines and calf's entrails.

Andouillette de la Touraine
Calf's and pig's cauls and pluck are used to combine the advantages of both, which gives a satisfactorily balanced taste.

Andouillette de Troyes
Many gourmets consider Troyes to be the stronghold of the pure pork faction of *andouillettes* makers, those who swear by its distinctive and rustic character.

Animelles – Ram's testicles

Bonnet – Reticulum

Caillette – Rennet stomach

Cœurs de veau, agneau et bœuf
Calf's, lamb's and bull's hearts

Joue de bœuf – Bull's cheek

Feuillet – Omasum

Fraise de veau – Calf's caul

Langues de bœuf, agneau et veau – Bull's, lamb's
and calf's tongues

Panse – Paunch

Ris de veau et agneau – Calf's and
lamb's sweetbreads

Rognons de bœuf, agneau et veau – Bull's, lamb's
and calf's kidneys

Tête de veau – Calf's head

Cervelle de veau – Calf's brain

Foies de veau, bœuf et agneau – Calf's, bull's and lamb's livers

Pieds de veau, bœuf et agneau – Calf's, bull's and lamb's trotters

Tête de veau roulée – Rolled calf's head

Gras double – Tripe

Tétine – looked udder

Variety meats

Since the Middle Ages, the *tripiers* have held a special position in the *métiers de bouche* – the occupations connected with food and drink. They specialize in the variety meats, two kinds of which can be distinguished: white and red. The first group covers the various stomachs and intestines, ears, trotters and heads. The second includes organs such as the heart, the liver and the nerves, and even the testicles. But this group also covers the brain, tongue, cheek and tail. Many of these cuts found a use in prehistoric times, when they were eaten in rituals to gain the traits of the animal in question associated with them.

Roman connoisseurs, on the other hand, appreciated the taste and consistency of these extremely varied specialties. In past centuries, most variety meats were scorned by the better off members of society. So they were good value, and were used as an ingredient in many regional specialties. Recently, their gastronomic worth has been rediscovered, especially in France. It is now known that variety meats are comparatively low in calories but rich in vitamins (above all those in group B) and minerals.

Variety meats are not to everybody's taste, although in earlier times they did provide meat for the ordinary person, and still earlier everyone appreciated at least certain parts of them.

The wines of the Loire Valley

The uniqueness of this wine region is predominantly based on the ideal conditions which it offers for three grape varieties. First, there is the versatile Chenin Blanc, from which every conceivable type of wine requiring white grapes can be made, and which does not attain such legendary quality anywhere else. Its sweet wines are practically immortal. Vouvray or Coteaux du Layon wines from 1874 or 1893, for example, are inspiring vintages even today – if you can find a bottle. It is only here on the Loire that the Cabernet Franc on its own can produce such elegant red wine, wine which can be kept for decades. And no-one can appreciate the potential of white Sauvignon until they have tried the best Sancerres and Pouilly-Fumés.

At the same time, the Loire is one of the main areas for French sparkling wine production. This developed mainly around Saumur, Vouvray, and Montlouis, because of the trass caverns, which make ideal cellars. Moreover, sparkling wines provide an attractive option for putting to good use grapes that have failed to ripen due to adverse weather. Saumur, where Jean Ackerman established the first wine cellars in 1811, became the center. Other big companies are Gratien & Meyer, Veuve Amiot, Bouvert-Ladubay, Langlois-Château, and Caves de Grenelle. Over 14 million bottles are filled each year. Less important in terms of quantity is the Crémant de Loire *appellation*, which has existed since 1975, with conditions similar to those for Champagne, but covering the whole of Touraine except Saumur.

Muscadet

Muscadet is well-known as a light, fruity and tangy white wine. The area covers 15,000 hectares (37,065 acres) and, apart from one corner of Coteaux de la Loire, lies to the south of the river and stretches from Pornic almost all the way to the Atlantic. The countryside, broken only by gentle undulations, is permanently exposed to the influence of the ocean, which means the winters are mild and the summers are usually wet. Muscadet is obtained from the grape variety of the same name (Melon de Bourgogne). Its advantage lies in the fact that it is relatively frost-resistant and ripens early. In order to give more complexity to this variety, which has little character, the better Muscadets are not racked off after alcoholic fermentation but are left on the yeast residues until bottling. This also gives them tanginess. They must be bottled in the Muscadet area and are described as *sur lie*. In 1995, the area was restructured to give a general *appellation* and three higher-grade production zones. Muscadet is the overall basic *appellation*, and must not be described as *sur lie*. An exception is made only for wines matured on yeast, which are produced outside the following *appellations*:

- Muscadet des Coteaux du Loire, eastern Pays Nantais, around Ancenis, both sides of the river
- Muscadet de Sèvre-et-Maine, south and east of Nantes, on the Maine and Sèvre rivers
- Muscadet Côtes de Grandlieu, for the low slopes around the Lac de Grandlieu.

Other *appellations* from the Pays Nantais are the white Gros Plant, a good distilling wine, together with Coteaux d'Ancenis and Fiefs Vendéens, which mainly produce fermented red wines from Gamay and Cabernet grapes.

Anjou and Saumur

Upstream, the region around the Loire is bordered by Anjou, a wine area of 14,500 hectares (35,830 acres). It has become known to a wider public through its medium dry rosé, which luckily is fast losing ground. For there are some *appellations* here which can produce not only interesting red wines but also outstanding whites. With Anjou Villages, the *appellation* which was given in 1987 to the best red wine zone, southeast of Angers, Cabernet Franc attains remarkable power and structure. But the real specialties are the white wines obtained from Chenin Blanc. On the north bank of the Loire, almost at the gates of Angers, there are slate slopes facing the sun where the Savennières grape ripens, and where its two best *crus*, Coulée de Serrant and La Roche-aux-Moines, have been promoted to having their own *appellations* – wonderfully dense, complex and long vintages, which place them among the greatest dry white wines in the world. But the Chenin Blanc, or Pineau de la Loire, as it is called here, is best suited to sweet wines.

Four *appellations* are devoted to them in Anjou. Where the Villages wines flourish, Coteaux de l'Aubance is pressed as a sweet or medium sweet wine. The most extensive area is Coteaux du Layon, which extends 31 miles (50 kilometers) to the southeast of Rochefort-sur-Loire and is made up, for the most part, of the slopes along the River Layon. Excellent wines have been created there in recent years, which can easily stand comparison with the two *grands crus* Quarts de Chaume and Bonnezeaux. However sweet these wines may be, the sweetness is balanced out by the characteristic acidity of the Chenin.

The Saumurois has a quite different aspect. Here, white trass stone determines the character of the wines. Although almost as many white wines as reds are produced from the Chenin Blanc variety, the Saumur *appellation* is well-known as the last one that, in its best locations, produces Saumur-Champigny, which is much in demand. The chalky soil gives the Cabernet Franc a bouquet of red fruits, great harmony and captivating elegance.

Touraine

Touraine is the El Dorado of Cabernet Franc. Unlike the later ripening Cabernet Sauvignon, the Franc likes the Loire area. Apart from Saumur, its best locations begin a little upstream in Bourgueil, Saint-Nicolas-de-Bourgueil or Chinon. Here its character varies, depending on the soil. On alluvial soils, it becomes a quaffable, light bistro wine, while on higher locations with argillaceous limestone it has a stronger structure with distinctive tannins, and in locations with lots of sunshine and less soil, it attains real class.

In Montlouis and Vouvray, the Chenin Blanc displays its entire range, from dry through sweet to sparkling, while in the Jasnières area it produces dry wines which reach great heights.

As regards red wines, the predominant variety in terms of quantity is Gamay, well-known from the Beaujolais area. Here too, it is used for *primeurs* and for quaffable reds to be drunk young. For more up-market vintages, it is blended with Cabernet and Cot (Malbec), and is known as *Cuvée Tradition*, or in Touraine Amboise *Cuvée François I*. The leader among the whites of Touraine is Sauvignon, followed by Chenin and a little Chardonnay. The same spectrum of grape varieties can also be found in the Cheverny *appellation*, where the acid-toned Romorantin also grows, and, for the most part, in the *vin délimité de qualité supérieure* (V.D.Q.S.) areas of Coteaux-du-Vendômois, Thouarsais and Valençay, where pleasant light wines are pressed. This is also true of Haut-Poitou, the renaissance of which is based on the quality of its Sauvignon.

Sancerre and Pouilly-Fumé

Sancerre and Pouilly-sur-Loire are the strongholds of Sauvignon. It has recently made the breakthrough in many places because it has become a fashionable variety. But nowhere else can it acquire so much controlled intensity on its own as in the two communes in the central Loire Valley and in the neighboring Menetou-Salon, Quincy and Reuilly. Sancerre is the best-known wine location and the largest production area, with almost 2000 hectares (5000 acres) of vines. Gamay predominated here until the *phylloxera* catastrophe at the end of the 19th century, and above all Pinot Noir, which was sold to the Champagne companies. After the catastrophe,

Châteaugay, in Central France, is known for stylish Gamay wines.

Sauvignon gained preference, and today it accounts for two-thirds of the *appellation*, the remainder being Pinot, which produces a light, fruit-toned red wine. The most powerful wines flourish on the *pierres blanches* made of white marl. Otherwise, chalk and flint predominate, with argillaceous limestone on the high hills near Chavignol and Bué. The *terroirs* are usually blended with one another.

The Pouilly-Fumé vineyards lie on the eastern bank of the Loire a little farther to the south. The hills have gentler shapes here, and the wines are generally somewhat rounder and softer than those from Sancerre – and slightly less aromatic. Some Pouillys are also produced on flint, which gives many of them a note that recalls a match which has just been struck. This is one possible explanation for the description *fumé*, smoky. Except for a few wines fermented in new wooden casks, the Sauvignons should be drunk young. In earlier days, when there were no railroads, Pouilly supplied Paris with eating grapes. So at that time more Chasselas grapes were planted than Sauvignon. There are very few of them left now, and they are used to produce Pouilly-sur-Loire wine, which is rather bland.

To the north of Sancerres lie the Coteaux de Giennois, producing a V.D.Q.S., which is also based on Sauvignon and Pinot Noir (with a little Gamay), but displays less concentration and intensity than its big brother. And Orléans too, at one time an important center for wine, now once again has about 100 hectares (247 acres) of grapes for the *vins de l'Orléanais*.

Other white wines from Central France

Châteaumeillant V.D.Q.S. (about 100 hectares/250 acres): To the northeast of Montluçon, a vigorous *gris* and some perfumed, round red wines are pressed from Gamay. Pinot Noir and Pinot Gris are also grown.

Saint-Pourçain V.D.Q.S. (500 hectares/1235 acres): To the south of Moulins, Gamay and Pinot Noir mature to give pleasant red wines with complex fruitiness, while white wines are represented by Sauvignon, Chardonnay, Aligoté and the old-established Tressalier.

Côte Roannaise V.D.Q.S. (150 hectares/370 acres): Gamay on both sides of the Loire around Roanne. The best red wines come from Renaison, Saint-André-d'Apchon and Villemontais.

Côtes d'Auvergne V.D.Q.S. (500 hectares/1235 acres): On the edge of the Massif Central, north and south of Clermont-Ferrand, Gamay produces dry rosés and fruity reds, which are sometimes very full-bodied, particularly Chanturgue, Châteaugay and Boudès.

Côtes du Forez V.D.Q.S. (200 hectares/495 acres): Northwest of St-Etienne and level with Lyon, the Gamay grows on slopes at the edge of the Loire Valley. In Trelins, the winemakers of Forez produce some satisfying red and rosé wines.

Heavenly nectars

Some of the most magnificent sweet white wines in the world come from the Loire Valley. Although they have been famous since the 15th century, in recent decades most of them have been among the least recognized classic wines. But lately the pendulum of popularity has swung back toward them. This is due to the increasing interest among lovers of wine for sweet wines in general and to a reawakened consciousness among winemakers, who are once again prepared to take on the great risks which are connected with the production of sweet wines. Their basic grape is the Chenin Blanc, which they like to call Pineau de la Loire. This variety bears no relation to the Burgundy Pinot. It is a native of the Loire Valley, and it is known that it was certainly being planted in Anjou as far back as the ninth century. Depending on its degree of ripeness, Chenin can supply a wide spectrum of extremely different wines. In relatively poor years, it sometimes yields just 6 ounces (170 grams) of grape sugar per liter, and thus about 10 percent of alcohol by volume. Then it is suitable only for dry and sparkling wines. But if the weather offers better conditions and the yield is 7–9 ounces (190–260 grams) of sugar, then the winegrowers are already able to use some of that to make medium sweet and sweet wines. But in especially good years, when the sugar content exceeds 7$^{1}/_{2}$ ounces (215 grams), and can even reach 1 pound (500 grams), almost all the wine made is medium sweet or sweet. That means that the potential alcohol content can be up to 30 percent by volume. This applies to the *appellations* which specialize in this type of wine – Vouvray,

Montlouis, Coteaux de l'Aubance and Coteaux du Layon, with the *crus* of Bonnezeaux and Quarts de Chaume. Here the microclimates create suitable conditions, particularly on the slopes above the Loire and those above the valleys of its tributaries. For the grapes attain such an unusual concentration, either through *passerillage* – raisin formation during the hot, dry days of fall – or through *Botrytis cimera*, the noble rot. The former happens on the Loire only with very rare and outstanding vintages, such as 1947 or 1989. The second, in contrast, arises more frequently. It needs morning mists in fall, which are dissipated by the sun during the morning and make way for a warm, clear day which is followed, in the most favorable case, by a cold night. The noble rot is a fungus that penetrates the peel, to extract the water content from the grapes, causing an abundance of sugar to concentrate in the must. Winemakers who are determined to produce sweet wines cut the fast-growing Chenin vines back sharply. In July, they check the way the grapes are hanging on each individual vine and remove any surplus grapes. The harvest takes place in several stages, which are each known as a *tri*, and in each case only the ripe grapes are picked. In many years, therefore, the harvest, which usually begins in the middle of October, can last until the end of November. But the longer the grapes are left on the vine, the higher the risk that they will be spoiled by bad weather. In this way, generally rich wines are obtained from the final selection in years when the vintage is particularly good. While some winemakers use these to make wine separately and bottle the vintage separately, others go for the greatest possible harmony and balance, to

achieve which they mix together the wines brought in at different times. The gently pressed wines usually ferment at low temperatures around 57–59 °F (14–17 °C). In this way, they convert some of the grape sugar into alcohol in slow motion over about two months. To do this, the best winemakers rely exclusively on the natural yeasts of the grapes and their cellar. When the wines reach a state of balance – an example for Vouvrays would be 13 percent alcohol by volume for medium sweet wines and $^{3}/_{8}$–$^{3}/_{4}$ ounce (10–20 grams) of sugar, and 14 percent by volume for sweet wines, with more than 1 ounce (30 grams) of residual sugar, the fermentation process is interrupted by racking off and by the addition of sulfur. Minimal quantities are used nowadays. A characteristic of the Chenin Blanc is its very pronounced acidity. It gives mellow wines an incomparable backbone, however rich in sugar they may be. In the first two years, they display intensive, fresh fruitiness. This is followed by a less attractive phase, during which the wines develop until after at least five to eight years more mature aromas are displayed, especially those of dried apricots and other fruits as well as honey. They are bottled only six or seven months after the harvest, but wine from good vintages can age for decades while continuously developing more variety, depth and harmony. But the temptation to open them much earlier is unfortunately all too seldom resisted.

Le Mont, famous since the 15th century as one of the best locations for Vouvray, is a vineyard on the edge of a hill above the Loire; in 1990 it produced an outstanding wine destined for eternity.

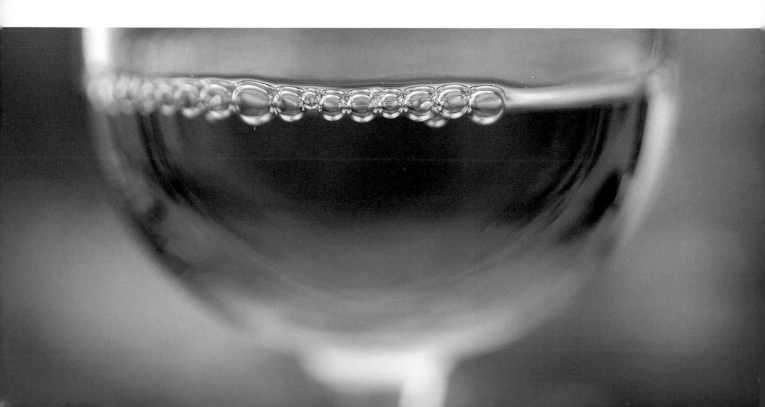

Nature and first-class wines

The Loire Valley is perhaps the area where winemakers have most emphatically declared their support for biological, and above all organic, viticulture. Their spokesman is Nicolas Joly, the owner of the Coulée de Serrant. This vineyard, which is 7 hectares (17.3 acres) in area, in a steeply sloping location above the Loire, was laid out by Cistercian monks in the 12th century. In the course of its 800 year-long history, it has been visited by two French kings and by the Empress Josephine, who greatly appreciated it. Its wine ranks with the greatest and most characterful dry white wines in the world. When Nicolas Joly took over responsibility for it in the 1970, he initially followed the advice of the regional Chamber of Agriculture. Progress moved into the vineyard, which for long had been cultivated on traditional lines, with chemical fertilizers and sprays. After only two years, Nicolas Joly observed a dramatic deterioration in the soil, the flora and the fauna. By chance, he stumbled upon an article on organic farming methods. His first experiments encouraged him, and so in 1984 he turned the entire 12 hectare (30 acre) property over to organic wine production. Little by little, nature awoke once more, and his wines increasingly gained in character and power. He became committed, and since then he has been speaking out in public in favor of organic wine production. In *Le Vin – du ciel à la terre* published in 1997, he has produced an easily comprehensible introduction to the subject, based on his experiences.

The production of sound, high-quality wine can be based only on living soil, with all its microorganisms. But the organic approach goes still further: it also includes the idea of an interchange between the cosmos and the earth. This is based on various observations that have been in existence for some centuries, but which were brought together and explained by Rudolf Steiner, the founder of anthroposophy. Organic farming distinguishes between four states which are related to parts of the plants: mineral and roots, liquid and leaf, light and blossom, heat and fruit. Thus in vegetal life a polarity can be found – namely, that between gravity, which exerts a downward pull, and levity, which exerts an upward pull. The winemaker who knows how to interpret the behavior of plants correctly can observe an amazing effect of gravity in a vine, which is able to drive its roots down dozens of feet deep, but makes futile attempts to climb up into the air. Another point about the vines is that they blossom for only a short time, holding themselves in check until the efficient summer sunshine arrives, so that later they will be able to direct all their power into the fruit.

By taking climate and location into account, organic farming has been able to foster the life of the vine, but it also reinforces its characteristics.

Gaston Huet, the doyen of organic winemaking and the producer of magnificent Vouvray.

The ravages of time gnaw away the corks, but perfect the wines.

White Chenin wines have an unbelievable aging potential.

Organic production differs from the usual methods in the careful way the soil is cultivated, as can be recognized, for example, from the earth in this vineyard.

"An organic wine need not be fundamentally good, but it is always genuine," says Joly. Organic farming develops a subtle way of handling all the parameters which are of use to the vine and its natural environment. This makes it possible to understand a view of the *terroir* which presupposes an authentic approach to the location, whereas nowadays the criteria are more and more diluted – and so are the wines. For when artificial manure and weed-killers are used in the vineyard, when artificial yeasts are used, and even when cellars are sterilized, the very things that make up an *appellation* must fall by the wayside.

In contrast to this, organic viticulture uses various natural preparations, which are usually homeopathically reinforced, to promote or maintain the health of the vines and to recreate a natural equilibrium in the vineyard. Taking into account the movements of the moon and the main planets, whose effects on plants have been investigated by Maria Thun, it is possible to optimize cultivation. In this way, the wine finally becomes a living essence of its *terroir*, and thus a drink which is rich in vital substances and stimulating in the best sense. The exemplary wines from the Coulée de Serrant, the Vouvrays from the Domaine Huet, the Pouilly-Fumés from Didier Dagueneau, the Burgundies from the Domaine Leroy, or those from the Domaine Kreydenweiß in Alsace (to mention only the best-known examples here) have such a distinctive personality, totally independent of fashion, that recently more and more French winemakers are beginning to adopt a more open-minded attitude to the arguments in favor of organic production methods.

Vinegar from Orléans

From the Middle Ages onward, little boats traveled up the Loire to moor in Orléans and unload their cargos there. Everything which was produced along the river's banks and in its hinterland came to the old cathedral city. From here, goods were taken by land right across the Beauce region and all the way to Paris. Alternatively, they were taken on by boat to Nantes, which later rose to be an important port for overseas trade, sending exotic spices and other captivating products from the distant colonies up the Loire. But above all, the little boats brought wine casks to Orléans from Anjou and Touraine, which were primarily intended for Paris. But the leisurely journey by boat sometimes had unfortunate effects on the liquid cargo. Sometimes it had already turned sour when it arrived at what was then an important inland port. So it was an obvious move for some dealers and, above all, caskmakers, to specialize in this product – to buy up this sour wine, the *vin aigre*, develop it into fully fermented vinegar and then to market it. The trades of *vinaigriers*, *buffetiers* and *moutardiers*

first began to flourish in the 13th century. The vinegar-makers' guild was given official recognition by King Charles VI on October 8, 1394, while Henri III confirmed the rights of the Communauté des Maîtres Vinaigriers d'Orléans in 1580. Orléans had become the capital of French vinegar. By the end of the 18th century, more than three hundred vinegar-makers had established their companies there. But of all these only a single firm has survived to the present day – Martin Pouret, which was founded in 1797. This family firm, which is run by a direct descendant of the founder, still produces vinegar via the traditional Orléans process.

Vinegar production begins with the selection of the wine. No process, however ingenious, can make good vinegar from bad wine. Most of the wines used are light and dry. If the vinegar is to maintain a constant character, blending is also important. The chosen wine is pumped into *vaisseaux*, casks with a capacity of 240 liters (63.4 gallons.) They contain a certain amount of old vinegar and, above all, the "mother of vinegar" - a compressed, gelatinous mass of vinegar bacteria. They should be filled up to only two-thirds of their capacity, or at the most three-quarters, to guarantee sufficient contact with the air. The casks are stored in dark cellars at a constant temperature of 28 °C (82 °F). Under these conditions, it takes around three weeks for

the alcohol contained in the wine to be converted to acetic acid by the bacteria. This happens naturally, without the acceleration processes which enable modern industrial installations to produce around 30,000 liters (7925 gallons) in 48 hours. When young, the vinegar is still too sharp and has very little harmony. Like good wine, it too needs time to improve. For the maturation period, it is drained into old wooden vats or casks, many of which have already been in use for 80 years, and left to age for six months. This not only makes it less harsh, but it recreates the wine aromas. The length of the storage period represents a compromise. Further aging gives the vinegar complex aromas, but spoils its fresh color. Various grape varieties produce vinegars with different characters, which is why the company also manufactures varietal vinegars made from Pinot Noir and Cabernet Franc, or from Chardonnay and Sauvignon Blanc. They also aromatize vinegar with tarragon, shallots, and lemon juice, or else with herbs from Provence, with mint, or with raspberries.

Glancing into the cask to observe the vinegar mold skin, a veil which forms on the surface of the wine and contains the vinegar bacteria which oxidize alcohol into acetic acid.

In the casks, which contain a little old vinegar and "mother of vinegar," the wine is converted into the indispensable seasoning and conservation agent.

The vinegar culture develops on the surface of the wine. Its development is regularly checked on this narrow rod, which is inserted into the casks.

Types of vinegar

Vinaigre de Vin Vieille Réserve
The traditional vinegar made according to the Orléans procedure can be used as seasoning for all purposes.

Vinaigre de Vin à l'Estragon
Red wine vinegar with tarragon for salads and sour sauces and, in small doses, to be added to chicken dishes.

Vinaigre de Vin à l'Echalote
Red wine vinegar with shallots, very suitable for deglazing meat juices, but also for salads.

Vinaigre de Vin au Jus de Citron
The captivating combination of vinegar and lemon juice, mainly for fish and Hollandaise sauce.

Vinaigre de Cidre
Cider vinegar has a milder acidity, and is well suited to green salads, but also to fish and crustaceans.

Vinaigre de Vin Jus de Framboise
The fruity vinegar, which particularly well suited mixed (fruit) salads and meat.

Cuvée de Bicentenaire
This particularly fine vinegar, aged for three years in wooden casks, was bottled for the 200th anniversary celebrations in 1997.

Vinaigre de Vin Vieille Réserve
As a comparison, here is the standard vinegar once again – more intensively colored and less mature in quality.

Vinaigre de Cidre au Miel
Honey lends this cider vinegar a sweet note, making it suitable for poultry or sweet and sour desserts.

Vinaigre de Vin à l'Echalote emincée
White wine vinegar with finely chopped shallots, suitable for marinating and pickling fish.

Vinaigre de Vin à l'Estragon frais
Finely aromatic vinegar, seasons herb sauces, deglazes fish dishes.

The right approach to vinegar

Vinegar belongs in the hands of the wise, states an old kitchen maxim. For the right amount can enhance the exquisite taste of a dish, whereas too much can ruin everything. With aromatized vinegars, some precise calculations must be carried out to discover whether their bouquets will be superimposed on the ingredients' own tastes. Anyone using pure, naturally fermented, non-aromatized vinegars would be well advised to become acquainted with their aromas and to find out by initial testing how strong these are and how acid the vinegar is, so as to be able to use them optimally. Vinegars are indispensable as subtle seasoning for fine cuisine. Their use is virtually unlimited:

- In vinaigrette with cold-pressed oil for salads
- For deglazing meat juices
- In drops, to be added to sauces and soups
- To be added to dishes made from pulses
- To protect vegetables such as mushrooms or artichokes from oxidation
- In cold marinades with oil and seasonings for vegetables, meat or fish
- With oil to mix fresh cheeses
- In drops, to be added to fresh fruit salads
- In juices or water, as a refreshing drink
- For preservation

Genuine pralines

Genuine pralines have been sold in this shop in Montargis since 1630. It has been in Benoît Digeon's family since 1902.

As befitted his station, César, Duke of Choiseul, Count of Plessis-Praslin, Marshal and Minister under Louis XIII and Louis XIV, had his *officier de bouche*, Clément Jaluzot. This man not only looked after the Duke's physical wellbeing on a daily basis, but was also responsible for the frequent princely banquets. At one of these feasts he sprang a special surprise. He combined two delicacies which were extremely rare and correspondingly expensive in the 17th century, namely almonds and sugar, and roasted them in a pan over a fire. This caramelized the sugar and surrounded the almonds with a hard, brownish, sugary sweet shell. These burnt almonds were given an enthusiastic welcome, not only around the Duke's table but also at court, where the Duke passed them round, and people soon began to call them simply *praslines*. Clément Jaluzot left his master's service in 1630 and settled down in Montargis, a little town 62 miles (100 kilometers) to the south of Paris. He opened an elegant shop in the central Place Mirabeau, in which he sold his tempting pralines and thus sweetened his retirement. But their overnight fame diminished markedly in the centuries that followed and, like the Sleeping Beauty, the real pralines fell into a deep slumber. Luckily, the very man to awaken them to life again came on the scene, in the shape of Léon Mazet, a

confectioner, and the grandfather of the present owner. He bought the house and the business in 1902. During the renovation of the dusty old shop, he discovered the original recipe for praline candies, and used it to make burnt almonds once again, just like those which had formerly aroused the enthusiasm of the Count de Plessis-Praslin and his contemporaries. Although a good three hundred years had passed since then, the recipe still proved attractive to those with a sweet tooth. For now Montargis lay on the famous Route Bleu which – in the days before the *autoroutes* – linked Paris with the blue expanses of the Mediterranean. Many people considered it worth breaking their journey for the original praline candies, which restored their former reputation very nicely. Since then, "Au Duc de Praslin" has managed to keep their fame alive and to spread it further, thanks to a modern boutique in Paris and a commitment to export. The recipe has changed little since the days of its inventor. The most important thing is to use attractive, well-shaped almonds, which are roasted and mixed with sugar or sugar syrup, which is allowed to caramelize. Several layers of tender caramel surround the almonds completely, and at the last moment Mazet de Montargis add in a little vanilla. Finally a touch of gum arabic, which is obtained from an African variety of acacia, provides the appetizing gloss which makes praline candies so tempting.

Forestines

In 1879 Georges Forest, a pastrycook in Bourges, invented the filled candy – a thin, crispy, satiny sugar shell, which he filled with a delicate, creamy praline chocolate. His *Forestines*, have since 1884 had their home in a magnificent Haussmann-style building and are still produced with unchanged high quality today.

Le Cotignac

This clear, amber-colored quince paste is a specialty of the city of Orléans. It was already being made there in the 15th century, and was presented as a gift to all high-ranking persons visiting the city. It is traditionally packed in little wooden boxes, each containing 1 ounce (25 grams) of paste, and is just eaten from the box.

Le Négus

To honor the Negus, the Emperor of Ethiopia, who visited France in 1901, the confectioner Grelier created a soft chocolate caramel, surrounded by clear, hard caramel. The candy, which was reminiscent of amber and of Menelik's skin color, is still manufactured by the same company (run by the Lyron family since 1909) to the old recipe.

Nougatines

In Nevers in the 1850s, Louis-Jules Bourumeau created the famous *nougatine*, a colorful candy with a white sugar shell and a filling of chopped almonds and sugar. The Empress Eugénie thought they were delicious when she visited the city in 1862. *Nougatines* are still being produced today at the same address in Nevers.

Praline and Ganache

Chocolate candies, which in many countries are known as pralines, can essentially be divided into two categories: *praliné* and *ganache*. The praline or *pralin* is a paste, which consists of a mixture of sugar and almonds or hazelnuts which have been caramelized and then ground. Ganache is a truffle paste which is made from fresh cream, to which chocolate is added. The mixture may also include coffee extract, flavorings or various alcohols.
Both praline and ganache are used in cakes, tarts, desserts or ice creams, as well as candies.

Chavignol
goat cheese

Goats are undemanding animals, which live quite contentedly in rough, mountainous and dry regions, in environments that are not exactly overflowing with good things to eat. Even the domesticated goat loves to climb, and has retained the tastes of its fellows. Many regions of France offer favorable conditions for goats. Most of them have established their territory in barren land where there are only a few people. Chavignol, which is near the famous wine center of Sancerre, provides an eloquent example of this. It is well known that especially good wine can be produced in places where the vines have to suffer – i.e. on stony soils in which not much else would grow. And so, like those in many wine regions in earlier times, the winegrowing families in Berry also kept goats. Apart from the fact that they provided milk and meat for the winegrowers' own kitchen, the goats also supplied cheese, which could improve the family's income from viticulture – this was by no means enormous and was also subject to big risks. When the *phylloxera* plague was raging in the vineyards of Berry around 1870, the farmers in Chavignol and in other villages of the region began to expand their goat-rearing activities as a substitute for making wine. Their cheeses were sold to dealers to be sent off to Auxerre, Orléans, and Paris, where they soon had many loyal customers. *Crottin de Chavignol* became a name which meant something. True, the wine business made a comeback in the best locations, and the local wine obtained a fame it had never had earlier. But the goat cheese too was given the distinction of an *appellation*, and has remained in demand as a specialty to this day. Moreover, both the aromatic Sauvignon and the light, fruity Pinot Noir go splendidly well with goat cheese, provided its consistency is medium hard and its aroma, while full of character, is still mild.

The preparation

Once the nanny goat has dropped her kid, she produces the milk known as colostrum for the first five days which is not suitable for human consumption. Then the milk production increases rapidly, to reach its high point after a month. From then on, the quantity of milk continuously diminishes. After nine months, before the nanny goat is covered again, the milk period ends. On average, a nanny goat gives $8^1/_2$ pints (4 liters) of milk a day, and up to 210 gallons (800 liters) a year. The fat content of the goat's milk remains relatively constant over the nine

months. In spring (from April to the beginning of July) when grasses and leaves are particularly rich, it increases slightly. Only in the last month does it rise markedly. Goat's milk contains 3.5–4.5 percent of fat. Its fat content is thus rather higher than that of cow's milk, but lower than the figure for ewe's milk, which exceeds 6 percent. The most important precondition for a high fat content in milk is healthy nourishment, such as the goats can find on meadows, pastures, and mountain slopes, or on wild heathland. At the same time, the aroma of the plants is carried over into the milk, and also gives the cheese a pronounced taste. On average, 26 gallons (100 liters) of milk gives 24 pounds (11 kilograms) of goat cheese. High-quality cheeses are obtained only from unpasteurized milk, fresh from the goat. Not only is it unpasteurized, it is not processed in any other way nor is it stored for long periods. The typical French procedure for making goat cheese begins with the filtering of the milk through cheesecloth. To make it coagulate, most cheese-makers rely on the natural bacteria which can be found in the air.

The milk is heated to about 91 °F (33 °C) in a boiler. Rennet is added to accelerate the coagulation process. After a good half-hour, the milk begins to coagulate, and the casein is converted into the gelatinous mass, which is carefully broken up with a steel frame, the cheese harp. The so-called curd sinks downward, so that part of the whey, which is on top, can be sucked off. The curd is then poured into molds with perforated bases, using a ladle, so that the rest of the whey can drain away. For goat cheeses produced manually, the small format is the most popular, based on around 2 pints (1 liter) of milk. When the whey has drained off, the cheese is removed from the mold, salted, and air-dried for one to three days. Fresh from the mold, it is soft, white and very creamy, and has little taste. So this stage is followed by the *affinage*, the maturing of the cheese in a cool, damp cellar. After a week, when its volume has already diminished considerably thanks to the drying process, it gradually develops its typical aroma. After two weeks, the mixture has become firmer. It has developed a soft, yellowish, sometimes light blue crust, and gives off a distinct but mild aroma. After 20–30 days, it has already become considerably drier. Now there are cracks in its crust, and often there are brownish flecks of piquant mold. The longer it ages, the harder, drier and more pungent it becomes. Its actual taste depends on the environment in which the goats live. So their season extends from spring to fall, but they are at their best in May and June.

During the *affinage*, the maturation in the moist cellar, a semi-solid crust forms, on which the first flecks of blue mold often appear.

This mottled breed of mountain goat is the one most frequently encountered in France, since these animals are healthy and hardy.

RÉSERVÉ AUX MOINES

Bourgogne
Franche-Comté

André Dominé & Fabienne Velge

History, culture, wine, cheese – without the Cistercians
Burgundy would not be what it is today.

The Clos de Vougeot is considered the cradle of Burgundy's viticulture. Nowadays it is planted exclusively with Pinot Noir.

Calais

Le Havre

Caen

Brest

Rennes

Paris

Strasbourg

Nantes

Tours

Bourgogne Franche-Comté

Limoges

Lyon

St-Étienne

Bordeaux

Grenoble

Avignon

Nice

Biarritz

Toulouse

Marseille

Toulon

Perpignan

For the gourmet, Burgundy really is the land of milk and honey. The former territory of the famous dukes, it now comprises the *départements* of Yonne, Nièvre, Côte d'Or and Saône-et-Loire, and can boast of a wealth of specialty products and a long culinary tradition which the inhabitants are able to put to very good use. The best ambassador Burgundy possesses, and its finest product, is the wine. No other winegrowing area in the world has such an ingenious system that takes account of even the finest variations in the soils, the climate, the orientation of the vineyard and the skill of the winegrower – in short, the *terroir*. Started by the Cistercian monks, the system still demonstrates its validity today, thus expressing a trait in the Burgundian character, which finds new adepts from generation to generation: the search for refinement. This should not be understood as some rather elitist appreciation of quality far removed from day-to-day reality, but rather as an honest search for the best that can be obtained from the region and its landscapes – a wide-stretching, many-sided and often harsh farming area. The famous Hôtel-Dieu of the hospices in Beaune demonstrates this characteristic of the Burgundian culture and way of life. The solid exterior of the building, rooted in the soil, appears simple and powerful, and yet the interior and the roofs display architectural refinement. There is also an emphasis on well-being, so a well-stocked table and high-quality furniture have an important place. This creates a mood which can make it even more of a pleasure to enjoy cheese puffs or ham in aspic, pike perch or river crabs, snails or poultry from Bresse, Charolais beef or game, redcurrants, blackcurrants or honey cake, or Chaource or Epoisses cheese.

The four regions of Burgundy in the east – Haute-Saône, Jura, Doubs and Territoire de Belfort – border the Franche-Comté. What all the varieties of landscape have in common is an aura of great tranquility. More than half of the area is forested, although there are also innumerable rivers and lakes. From the gastronomical point of view, the mountains and high plateaus of the Jura have guaranteed unique traditions. On the farms and in small farmers' cooperatives, magnificent smoked products are created now as they were centuries ago, together with mountain cheese and the mysterious *vin jaune*, the symbol of an unspoilt and unadulterated character.

Anis de Flavigny

One of the best-known ambassadors for French *gourmandise* is a tiny, egg-shaped, pure white candy known as *anis de Flavigny*. The fact that it appears in the French version of Trivial Pursuit is probably the clearest indication of how well-known it is. Its origins can be traced back to 1591, when Semur, a town near Flavigny, offered such candies as presents to high-ranking guests. This means that the sugary miniature has the honor of being France's oldest commercial product of any kind. The runner-up for the title is Leroux's chicory, which first appeared in 1828 – a stripling by comparison. The history of Flavigny as a community goes all the way back to Julius Caesar, who set up his camp there before besieging Alesia (only 2 1/2 miles/4 kilometers away) and defeating Vercingetorix. Flavinius, one of his followers, stayed behind and had a villa built (a fact authenticated by a mosaic which has survived). It was from him that Flavigny took its name.

Widerad, Prince of the Burgundians, was a Christian and founded a monastery run by Benedictines in 719. When Pope John VIII came to Flavigny in 878 and consecrated the abbey church there, the monks presented him with 3 pounds (1.4 kilograms) of aniseed.

The ancient Romans used to dip almonds in honey and so created the precursor of the dragées. Then, in the Middle Ages, French pharmacists created tasty medication using aniseed and other medicinal seeds surrounded by honey. Originally, aniseed was undoubtedly thought of as a medicine rather than a snack. The Ursuline nuns, on the other hand, whose order established a convent in Flavigny in 1632, had other ideas. They surrounded green aniseed with a sugar shell, which was scented with rosewater or orange blossom water. Production is still based on these techniques today. Only the proprietors have changed, for at the time of the French Revolution the convent was dissolved and the convent church destroyed. However, the inhabitants of the village continued to produce aniseed candies in the old ruins. The Troubat family have been continuing this tradition since 1923 until today .

Manufacturing the tiny aniseed dragées used to be a time-consuming procedure. The seed had first to be rolled in sugar syrup until it was completely enveloped in it. Next, the syrup had to dry out completely before the next layer of sugar could be applied. This took up to six months, until the candy had attained the desired size, which made it rare and expensive. In the middle of the 19th century, beet sugar came into use to make manufacture cheaper, while the development of a dragée machine accelerated production. The beautiful old boilers in which the aniseed rotates – making an ear-splitting noise – still exist, but now steam power has been replaced by electric motors. In this process, the aniseed is rolled to and fro in sugar syrup while the water evaporates and the sugar sticks to the seeds. Like a snowball expanding as it is rolled in the snow, the candy grows until it has attained the standard size, as big as a pea. Even with the assistance of turbines, the growth process of an aniseed candy still takes two weeks. 250 tonnes (275 tons) of aniseed candies are produced in Flavigny each year, each of them weighing exactly a gram (0.04 ounce).

There are always almost a million aniseed dragées rolling to and fro in the turbines. (To be very precise, there are 958,904.) The average production is about one ton a day. *Anis de Flavigny* can thank this process, unchanged for generations, for its uniformly high quality. The Troubat family have no plans to rationalize (and thereby endanger the jobs of 20 villagers). The fact that *anis de Flavigny* has become an institution, however, can be traced back to a revolutionary idea from Grandfather Troubat. He replaced the standard cardboard boxes with small metal cans and had them installed in the Paris Metro in some of the earliest automatic vending machines. Nowadays, *anis de Flavigny* comes in 14 exquisite flavors: aniseed, violet, mint, licorice, coffee, cinnamon, vanilla, jasmin, rose, orange blossom, lemon, orange, mandarine and raspberry.

It all begins with the aniseed, which gradually acquires a sugary coating.

In addition to aniseed, there are candies containing vanilla, cinnamon, licorice, mint, coffee and eight other flavors.

The aniseed is given its sugar coating by being rolled in these venerable dragée machines.

The candies are in the turbines for two weeks before their diameter reaches ⅓ inch (1 centimeter).

In Flavigny, modernization has been consciously rejected, in order to employ as many people as possible.

The little candies shine pure white in their boxes and cans, which can be found all over France.

Honey cake from Dijon

Burgundy's capital is known for three specialties – mustard, blackcurrant liqueur and honey cake. In the old days, honey was the most widely available sweetener. The ancient Greeks and Romans dipped their cookies or dried fruit in it. Subsequently the mounted hordes of Genghis Khan used honey cake as their iron rations. Originally from the Orient, the sweet and fortifying substance first conquered southeast Europe and penetrated farther and farther north until it had reached Flanders.

When Philip the Bold, Duke of Burgundy, married Marguérite of Flanders in 1369, he must inevitably have come across the *boichet*, a cake baked from wheat flour and honey, which was the Duchess's favorite. But it was still some time before Dijon became the capital of honey cake. First, a guild of *pain d'épiciers* was formed in Rheims, obtaining recognition in the 16th century.

In the 18th century, honey cake began to become popular in Dijon; above all, at Christmas time. Brottier, a *pain d'épicier* from Champagne, settled in Dijon in 1796, and created a stir with the great variety of shapes and flavors in the honey cake and gingerbread he offered for sale. In 1838, the Mulot family took over his company, which later amalgamated with the Petitjeans through marriage, and which is now the only surviving honey cake factory in Dijon. Once the railroad arrived in 1852, and perishable goods could be transported, the Dijon honey cake bakers were able to take advantage and grow into real entrepreneurs. Somewhere around 1900, when about a dozen companies were turning out a daily total of 3 tonnes (3.3 tons) a day, Dijon overtook Rheims as the honey cake capital.

In many regions rye flour is used to make honey cakes or gingerbread, which are then referred to as *couque*. By contrast, the people of Dijon have remained faithful to wheat. The basic mixture is made from wheat flour, sugar and honey, and kneaded for only 12 minutes. It is then either processed further in its pure form or mixed with dough which has been kept in a cool place for a week or two. In earlier times, it might even have been kept for years. The mixture is kneaded again to aerate it further, a process described as *braquage*. At this stage raising agents, eggs, milk, spices and candied fruit are worked into the mixture. In Dijon, aniseed is also added as a traditional spice, although orange and lemon peel, or ginger and cinnamon, are also appreciated as flavorings.

Félix Kir, the mayor of Dijon, became so popular that a drink was named after him.

Crème de cassis, another Burgundian specialty, flows viscously into bottles via a circuitous route.

Kir & Crème de Cassis

Crème de Cassis, a liqueur made from blackcurrants, would hardly be as familiar to us had it not been for Canon Félix Kir. Born in 1878, the priest became famous as an opponent of the Nazis who helped thousands of Resistance fighters to escape during World War II.

He was already over 60 when he was elected mayor of Dijon. And when the local liqueur distillers were fighting for survival after the war, he made a point of offering all the guests who visited Burgundy's capital a *blanc-cassis*: a dry white wine with a fresh acidity mixed with *crème de cassis*. During the four years of occupation, the cafés which had formerly been the second home of the French became desolate places, simply because uninhibited conversations now carried risks. Many famous aperitives, including *blanc cassis*, were on the verge of being forgotten. Mayor Kir's successful attempt at resurrection led to his receiving a very rare honor in France – a drink was named after him and still bears his name today. *Blanc cassis* was originally brought to Dijon by two businessmen. They had acquired a taste for

it in Neuilly, and in 1841 they began to produce it in their home town. There was only one problem: hardly anyone planted blackcurrants. But the great success attained by the fruit liqueur changed all that. By 1914, 80 liqueur companies had been established. Indeed, the demand encouraged vine producers' wives to plant currant bushes around the edges of the vineyards to supplement their housekeeping money.

Burgundy still supplies blackcurrants – along with areas in the valleys of the Loire and the Rhône – but farmers have been specializing in cultivating them as a main crop for a long time now. If it is to produce abundant buds, a currant bush must have ten weeks of temperatures below freezing point in the winter. The ripe berries keep their optimal flavor for only one day, which is why the crop is picked rapidly using mechanical means. The high vitamin C content makes processing difficult, as the berries oxidize quickly. The most modern methods used to retain the flavors and the black-violet color involve flash-freezing to a temperature of -22 °F (-30 °C). This means that the fruit can also be subjected to further processing if necessary. For this purpose, it is heated up again to a temperature of 23 °F (-5 °C) and sprayed with alcohol. This acts as a solvent for the color and the flavors, and simultaneously prevents fermentation. For five weeks, the fruit is macerated in rotation tanks in a mixture of

Flash-frozen blackcurrants, picked when at their ripest, retain their taste as well as their fresh color and high vitamin C content.

alcohol and water. Skilled producers keep the fruit in pure alcohol for up to three months. The juice at the top, which is of the finest quality, is extracted first and set apart. The remainder is then pressed, and finally sugar is added. Fruit liqueurs described as *crèmes* are obtained through maceration alone. So that the berries' acid content will not dominate the character of the liqueur, it must be optimally balanced by sugar and alcohol. At 20 percent by volume, the liqueur has absorbed the maximum fruit fraction, and the saturation point for sugar is just over 18 ounces (520 grams). The alcohol content is therefore an index of quality, since a cream containing 16 percent by volume has only half as much fruit but a mere 2 ounces (60 grams) of sugar less. In earlier times, *crème de cassis* was placed on the tables in cafés as free seasoning; no-one in France would ever have thought of drinking it neat. But as well as flavoring non-sparkling wine or champagne, vermouth or mineral water, it can also be used to add flavor to cakes or ice cream, or in cooking, particularly with duck or pork dishes. Once opened, a bottle should be kept in the refrigerator and used within three months.

Kir Royal

Pour ⅓–¾ cup (100–200 milliliters) *crème de cassis* into a champagne flute and top up with either well-cooled *champagne brut* or *champagne brut nature,* or with a suitable *crémant de Bourgogne.*

Communard

Pour ¾ cup (200 milliliters) of *crème de cassis* into a bulbous wineglass and top up with well-cooled Burgundy Passe-Tout-Grain or alternatively with another dry and fruity red wine.

Good blackcurrant liqueurs contain more than 18 ounces (500 grams) of berries.

Kir

Pour ¾ cup (200 milliliters) of *crème de cassis* into a bulbous wineglass and top up with well-cooled *aligoté* Burgundy or with another dry, tangy white wine.

A *crème de cassis* with 20 percent alcohol by volume contains twice as much fruit as one with 16 percent by volume, but only one-eighth more sugar. It is thus considerably fruitier and can be used much more economically.

Traditional recipes of Burgundy

Tarte à l'Epoisses et aux pommes
Epoisses cheese and apple tart

Serves 6–8

Pastry
2 cups/250 g flour
1 tsp salt
1 egg yolk
1 cup/125 g butter
3½ tbsp water

Filling
3 eggs
3½ tbsp crème fraîche
1 fully matured Epoisses cheese (9 oz/250 g)
2 – 3 eating apples
3½ oz/100 g cooked ham
Salt, pepper, grated nutmeg

Make a hollow in the sifted flour. Mix in the salt, egg yolk and butter in flakes. Add the water and work into a dough with the flour. Chill in the refrigerator. Whisk the eggs for the filling while adding the crème fraîche. Dice the cheese, apples and ham and fold into the egg mixture. Season with salt, pepper and nutmeg.
Pre-heat the oven to 390 °F/200 °C. Roll the dough out thinly. Butter a spring-form pan (about 10 in/26 cm diameter) and line with the dough. Fill with the cheese mixture and bake for 5 minutes, then reduce the oven temperature to 355 °F/180 °C and bake for another 30 minutes. Serve hot.

Tarte à l'Epoisses et aux pommes – Epoisses cheese and apple tart

Les escargots de Bourgogne en coquille
Snails in herb butter

Serves 8

8 dozen live snails
1 lb/500 g coarse cooking salt
2 cups/500 ml wine vinegar
1 bottle white Burgundy
1 onion, spiced with 1 clove
2 carrots
1 bouquet garni with thyme, bay leaf, parsley
1 stalk celery
4 cloves garlic
Freshly-milled salt and pepper

Herb butter
3 cups/750 g butter
1⅓ cups/80 g parsley
3 shallots
4–6 cloves of garlic
Freshly-milled salt and pepper
5 tbsp breadcrumbs (or as liked)

In Burgundy, the snails are prepared as follows. First leave them to fast for 24 hours, then clean them under running water and remove the chalky plug. Steep them in the salt and vinegar for 10 hours to detach the slime. Then clean them for a second time and put them into boiling water for 30 minutes. They can then be eased out of their shells. Remove the black intestines and wash the snails for a third time. In Germany, the snails are also left to fast, but they are then killed in boiling water before the thorough cleaning continues. Clean the snails using three times as much water. Add them to the wine, onion, carrots, bouquet garni, celery, and garlic cloves. Season with salt and pepper, cover and simmer for 3 hours. Meanwhile, boil the snail shells in plenty of water for 30 minutes. Let them cool and then remove all impurities.

For the herb butter, bring the butter to room temperature. Finely chop the parsley, shallots and garlic and mix with the soft butter. Add salt and pepper and breadcrumbs as liked.
Coat the inside of each snail shell with a fleck of butter. Then lightly press a snail into each shell and seal with the herb butter.
Cook in a pre-heated oven at 320 °F/160 °C on baking sheets until the butter has melted and is beginning to brown.

Quenelles de brochet à la crème d'oseille
Pike dumplings in sorrel sauce

Serves 6–8

Panada
⅔ cup/150 ml milk
8 tsp/40 g butter
1 tsp salt
Freshly-milled white pepper
A pinch of grated nutmeg
⅔ cup/80 g flour

From left: *Les escargots de Bourgogne en coquille* (Snails in herb butter) – *Quenelles de brochet à la crème d'oseille* (Pike dumplings in sorrel sauce) – *Pain d'épice, poires au vin et sorbet au cassis* (Honey cake, pears in wine, blackcurrant sherbet).

Stuffing

1 lb/500 g pike meat or 1 pike (2 lbs/1 kg)	
⅔ cup/150 ml crème fraîche	
6½ tbsp/100 g soft butter	
4 tsp Dijon mustard	
⅓ cup/60 g chopped shallots	
1 tbsp chopped parsley	
Salt, white and cayenne pepper	
4 eggs	

Sauce

4 tsp/20 g butter	
¼ cup/50 g chopped shallots	
7 oz/200 g sorrel	
1¼ cups/300 ml white wine (*aligoté*)	
1⅔ cup/400 ml light cream	
Freshly-milled salt and white pepper	
6½ tbsp/100 g grated Gruyère or Comté cheese	

For the panada, boil the milk up with the butter, salt, pepper and nutmeg. Sprinkle in flour and stir for 2 to 3 minutes with a wooden spoon on a low heat, until the mixture leaves the sides of the saucepan. Chill in the refrigerator. For the stuffing, fillet the pike, bone it and remove the skin. Then chop and purée it. Take the panada out of the refrigerator and work to a smooth mass with the fish meat. Then mix with the crème fraîche, soft butter, mustard, shallots and parsley. Season with salt and pepper. Now fold the eggs under individually. Put to one side.

For the sauce, sauté first the shallots and then the finely chopped sorrel in butter. Add the wine and reduce by boiling. Add the light cream and purée the sauce in a blender. Season.

Form the pike stuffing into dumplings with a table-spoon. Poach these in boiling water for 10 minutes, then strain and drain. Put the pike dumplings into a heat-resistant dish, cover with sauce and sprinkle the cheese on top. Put in a preheated oven at 375 °F (190 °C) until lightly browned.

Pain d'épice, poires au vin et sorbet au cassis
Honey cake, pears in wine and blackcurrant sherbet

Honey cake

½ tsp aniseed	
2 tbsp ground cinnamon	
4 tsp grated nutmeg	
4 cloves	
6 juniper berries	
Peel of 4 oranges	
⅔ cup/200 g honey	
1 cup/200 g sugar	
Generous ¾ cup/190 g butter	
1¼ cups/300 ml water	
1½ cups/220 g corn meal	
1⅔ cups/220 g wheat flour	
2 packages/14 g dried yeast	
6 tbsp/80 g cane sugar	

Pears in wine

6 William pears	
1 bottle red Burgundy	
1 stick cinnamon	
1 orange	
1 lemon	
2 cups/400 g sugar	
2 cups/500 ml water	

Sherbet

1 lb/500 g blackcurrants	
1 cup/200 g sugar	
2 cups/250 ml water	
¾ cup/200 ml *crème de cassis* (blackcurrant liqueur)	

Gougères
Cheese puffs

Serves 6–8

1 cup/250 ml milk	
6½ tbsp/100 g butter	
1 tsp salt	
1¼ cups/150 g flour	
4 eggs	
2 oz/50 g Gruyère or Comté	

Bring the milk to a boil in a saucepan with the butter and salt (1).

Add the flour (2) and stir mixture for 4–5 minutes on a low heat until it leaves the sides of the saucepan.

Leave to cool, then fold the eggs in individually with a wooden spatula (3).

Cut the cheese into small cubes (about ¼ in/5 mm) (4) and work evenly into the mixture (5). Form little balls with a tablespoon and place on a greased baking sheet (6).

Preheat the oven to 340 °F/170 °C. Brush the little balls with egg yolk and sprinkle with grated cheese. Bake for 20–25 minutes.

These little *gougères* are served with an aperitive (kir, crément or white wine.)

For the honey cake, grate the aniseed, cinnamon, nutmeg, cloves and the juniper berries very finely. Chop the orange peel very finely. Put everything into a saucepan with the honey, sugar, water and 10 tbsp/150 g butter, and bring to a boil. Leave to cool a little, then stir in the flour, corn meal, and yeast. Leave for 4 hours in a cold place. Preheat the oven to 340 °F/170 °C. Melt the remaining butter and grease a square baking pan with it (4 x 4 x 8 in/10 x 10 x 20 cm). Sprinkle the pan with cane sugar (so that the cake becomes slightly crunchy). Fill with the cake mixture and bake for 45 minutes.

Peel the pears, leaving the stalks attached. Pour the wine into a saucepan with the cinnamon stick, orange, lemon and sugar. Bring to a boil.
Add the water and pears and boil until the pears are cooked. Then put to one side.
Meanwhile, cook the blackcurrants and sugar in the water for 5 minutes. Pass through a sieve, then mix with the blackcurrant liqueur, place in an ice cream machine and freeze.
Put the pears onto a serving dish or a dessert plate with a slice of honey cake, and add a scoop of blackcurrant sherbet.

Charolais

The Charolais is the star among France's beef cattle. Its ancestors came from the Jura and grazed in Saône-et-Loire. They feasted on rich meadows and were known as being fast-growing, heavy and completely reliable draft animals. The Charolais has come down to us white, though it is sometimes an elegant shade of cream. Its forehead is high, its horns are white and round, its cheeks are pronounced, its muzzle is wide and the neck is short. It has a deep barrel chest. Its muscular back stretches out as taut as a rope. Its loins and the haunches are massive, the limbs are very powerful. A full-grown bull carries around 2650 pounds/1200 kilograms live weight. The Charolais developed as a breed raised purely for meat in the 1920s, when technology moved into agriculture and made cattle superfluous as draft animals. If calves are kept with their mothers for rearing, the Charolais do extremely well. In southwest Burgundy, where the hills of the Brionnais advance into the classic Charolais region, mother animals and their calves live on the pastures from the beginning of April onward. Luxuriant grass, available right through until the summer, results in amazing increases in weight.

It's rush hour all day long on Thursdays in the small village of Saint-Christophe-en-Brionnais (population 700). As long ago as 1488, Jean de Tenay received letters from King Charles VIII giving him the right to hold three annual markets. His descendant, Laurent de Tenay, obtained approval from Louis XIII in 1627 for a weekly market and a fourth annual market. In earlier centuries, deals were made in the open air. The stockbreeders from the surrounding area simply grouped their animals together on the main road which runs through the middle of the village and is 40 feet (12 meters) wide. But since 1866 the cattle market has taken place on an extensive area near the Town Hall. If at first the cattle markets were held only a few times a year, the increasing fame of the Charolais beef cattle led to the intervals becoming shorter and shorter, until in 1961 the decision was taken to move the markets onto a weekly basis.

As many as 100,000 beef cattle are sold here every year. From here they begin their journeys, not only to every corner of France but also – as has been the case for a long time now – into every country in Europe. The market covers an area of 7½ acres (3 hectares), on which up to 4000 cattle can be offered for sale at any one time. There are 120 holding pens and a loading ramp big enough for 50 trucks. Today Saint-Christophe is one of the few important markets where the purchase price continues to be settled on the spot – usually by check. The *mur d'argent*, the money wall, encloses the market and in earlier times all deals had to be done on or over it.

The most famous beef cattle in France come from Burgundy, where they can enjoy the lushest meadows in Saône-et-Loire.

However, it has now been replaced by a modern hall in which buyers and sellers take their places in comfort at long tables.

In the fall in particular, when the young animals intended for fattening change hands, the area is thronged with people. Throughout the night, cattle transporters of every size roar through the narrow country lanes connecting the village with the outside world, on their way to the market. The magnificent animals are unloaded and led to the areas permanently reserved for their categories. Things are already livening up by 5 a.m. in the village's four bars. Breeders and dealers gulp down a *café au lait* or take an early breakfast. In the market area, which has been under cover for 20 years now, the buyers begin to examine the cattle. The farmers spruce their animals up once more. People exchange greetings, but no trading is allowed at this stage – a rule that is strictly enforced. At 6.15 a.m., the loudspeakers announce that the first animals may now be offered for sale – bullocks at least one year old which are intended for fattening; a process which will last until they are 15 to 17 months old. Now is the time for haggling, discussion and striking a bargain. Some dealers are already beginning to use clippers to cut their identification marks into the hair on the animals' buttocks while others mark their purchases with colored lithographic chalk. Three-quarters of an hour later (at 7 a.m.) it's the turn of the *broutards*.

MARCHE DU
OVINS DE VIANDE 500
OVINS D'EMBOUCHE 20
BROUTARDS 734
EUNES BOVINS 157
PETITS VEAUX
TOTAL

This board in the market in Saint-Christophe shows how many beasts of each type are available for purchase.

The meat dealers, known as *chevillards*, inspect the cattle very thoroughly before the market is opened.

These are calves and feeders which were born earlier in the year and have been kept on the pastures with their mothers. They are intended for further rearing and later for fattening. At 8 a.m. it's time for the big meat cattle that are intended for slaughter – this includes cows, heifers and oxen, usually between 24 and 36 months old. The beasts offered for sale are driven by the breeders into pens which the buyers have reserved. All that remains now is the walk to the payment hall to settle the purchase price. Meanwhile, the village's bars are thronged with people. More and more farmers and dealers have concluded their business and now sit down to a hearty meal together. Naturally, they consume *entrecôtes* as big as their plates and thick steaks which are cut from first-class Charolais beef cattle.

Charolais Terroir

With about 1.4 million animals, the Charolais is the most important meat breed in France, and nowadays can be found all over the world. The meat is very tasty and low in fat. However, the decisive factors in establishing its quality and flavor are the conditions in which the animals are reared and the way the meat is processed. Since 1983, Charolais cattle which come from the breed's original home can be awarded a "Red Label" and be described as "Charolais Terroir." This acts as a guarantee of high quality and is based on several preconditions which are strictly monitored:

- The cattle must come from the Charolais region of Burgundy, as defined by strict boundaries.
- They must graze on the wide natural pastures of the Charolais region.

- The only other fodder they may consume must be traditional elements such as grass, hay, corn, oilcake and so on.
- Transport and slaughter must be carried out with particular care.
- The origin of the meat must be unambiguously identifiable at any time until it is sold.
- The quality of the meat is conscientiously checked following slaughter.
- All areas and surfaces with which the beef comes into contact on its way to the consumer are subject to especially strict hygienic and sanitary inspections.
- *Charolais Terroir Label Rouge* may be offered for sale only if unambiguously identified. It must not be mixed with meat of any other origin.

The best meat breeds

Aubrac
Southern Massif Central; very robust and undemanding animals which live outside all the year round; widely-spaced horns. Bull weight: 1875–2425 pounds (850–1100 kilograms). Often crossed with Charolais bulls. Good quality meat.

Bazardaise
Northern Landes and Bazardais hills; rustic, adaptable breed with attractive gray hairy coat. Bull weight: 1985–2425 pounds (900–1100 kilograms). Produces very tasty veal.

Blonde d'Aquitaine
Southwestern hills; blend of Garonnais, Quercy and Blond des Pyrénées breeds; elongated, muscular animals which put on weight rapidly; especially suitable for producing veal. Bull weight: 2200–2870 pounds (1000–1300 kilograms).

Charolais
Saône-et-Loire and Nevers; very robust and adaptable (now found in over seventy countries), puts on weight rapidly, lean tasty meat. Bull weight: 2200–3085 pounds (1000–1400 kilograms). Most important herd book, with 100,000 cows.

Gasconne
Central Pyrénées; adapted for rough, difficult terrain and heights, extremely robust animal, ideal for rearing on mountain pastures, with decidedly impressive horns. Flavorful meat. Bull weight: 1760–2100 pounds (800–950 kilograms).

Limousin
Western Massif Central; medium-sized, undemanding animals with reddish hide; ideal breeding cows (now found in 53 countries); very tender, delicate, tasty meat. Bull weight: 2200–2870 pounds (1000–1300 kilograms).

Maine-Anjou
Maine-Anjou; cross between indigenous Mancelle and Shorthorn meat breed at turn of 20th century; red-white cattle which rapidly put on weight. Dark, marbled meat. Bull weight: 2425–3200 pounds (1100–1450 kilograms).

Normande
Normandy; black and white speckled cross-breed, good for long-term rearing; rich milk and remarkable meat yield; bull weight: 2200–2650 pounds (1000–1200 kilograms).

Parthenaise
Brittany to Charente; originally supplied the milk for the famous butter; predominantly medium-brown animals; fertile cows; high-quality meat; bull weight: 2100–2650 pounds (950–1200 kilograms).

Salers
Auvergne; bright reddish brown, very robust animals with widely spaced horns; good milk (cheese production) and dark, marbled, flavorful meat. Bull weight: 2200–2650 pounds (1000–1200 kilograms).

French cuts of beef

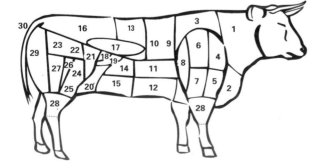

1	Collier	– Neck
2	Gras bout de poitrine	– Fat end of brisket
3	Basses côtes	– Top rib
4	Macreuse à pot-au-feu	– Stewing shoulder
5	Jumeau à pot-au-feu	– Stewing clod
6	Paleron	– Chuck
7	Jumeau à bifteck	– Clod steak
8	Macreuse-à-bifteck	– Shoulder steak
9	Côte	– Rib, beef cutlet
10	Entrecôte	– Entrecôte steak
11	Plat-de-côtes	– Middle or best rib
12	Tendron	– Tendron
13	Faux-filet	– Sirloin
14	Bavette de flanchet	– Flank
15	Flanchet	– Flank undercut
16	Rumsteck	– Rump steak
17	Filet	– Fillet steak
18	Hampe	– Thin flank
19	Onglet	– Prime cut
20	Bavette d'aloyau	– Top sirloin
21	Aiguillette Baronne	– Thick flank
22	Merlan	– Front topside cut
23	Poire	– Cross cut
24	Rond de tranche	– Round of beef
25	Mouvant	– Front bottom round
26	Araignée	– Middle haunch
27	Gîte à la noix	– Top round
28	Gîte et jarret	– Shin
29	Rond de gîte	– Bottom round
30	Queue	– Tail

Côte de bœuf

Côte de bœuf, rib of beef, which on average should weigh about 1¼ pounds (800 grams), is a favorite dish for two people, and is often on the menu in bistros and brasseries.

It is best cooked, initially for 1 minute on each side, in a mixture of 1 tablespoon of butter and 1 tablespoon of oil, which should be allowed to become very hot. When turning the meat over, sprinkle *fleur du sel* on the side facing upward – the finest sea salt the Guérande can offer. Then roast the piece of meat for another 7 minutes on each side, so that it is warm through and through, but remains *saignant* (rare) in the middle.

Only then should it be peppered, and if you wish you can put a little regular butter or herb butter on top. Take the rib out of the pan and cut it diagonally into strips. Serve on warmed plates.

A rib of beef goes well with potatoes *au gratin*. Such a fine piece of meat also merits a good red wine. The best choice from a selection of local wines would be a Moulin-à-Vent.

Dijon mustard

Yellow seeds give delicate flavors, red-brown ones add pungency. Slightly crushed and soaked in advance, they develop their characteristics during grinding.

The mustard needs to mature in wooden casks for a few hours after grinding to lose its initial bitterness and attain its true pungency.

It is as if Rabelais, that restless mocker of the 16th century, had foreseen how different foods can affect the human system. Does he not make his giant Gargantua add shovelfuls of mustard to the dozens of hams, oxtongues, blood puddings, and liver sausages which the glutton puts away? For mustard has a stimulating effect on the stomach and digestive juices. Back in the days of ancient Alexandria, people had already appreciated the spicy burn of the mustard seeds, and crushed them like cloves or coriander. Columella, a Roman farmer and writer, who described the agriculture and stock farming of his time around AD 60 in twelve volumes entitled *De re rustica*, noted in AD 42 the first recipe which has been handed down for edible mustard – it was known as *mustum ardens*, burning juice. After Charlemagne advised his farmers to plant mustard in *capitulare de villis*, it sprang up everywhere where the Franks had once ruled. There were ten *moutardiers* working in Paris around 1300. By 1650, there were already 600. The Dukes of Burgundy, who had their residence in Dijon, considered it advisable, at the end of the 14th century, to guarantee the quality of their city's mustard through a decree. It prescribed "good seeds, dipped in authorized vinegar." In spite of its sound reputation, Dijon mustard did not overtake the products of other regions until 1752, when Jean Naigeon replaced vinegar by the must from unripe grapes, the *verjus*. That gave it more acidity. *Moutarde de Dijon* now became the epitome of best-quality mustard. Since 1937, the description has guaranteed that the mustard is manufactured in a particular way, which means that the mustard must have at least 28 percent dry extract and must not contain more than 2 percent of husks. Biologically, mustard belongs to the Cruciferae family which includes red radishes, wild radishes or cress. It has two varieties in the natural state, which can be mixed during manufacture to obtain the desired degree of pungency. The milder

The creamy *moutarde de Dijon* and the grainy *moutarde à l'ancienne* are the two most popular types of mustard.

Types of mustard

Moutarde de Champagne
Champagne mustard
Coarse-grained mustard, to which the Champagne lends a specially mild character. Ideal for use with roasts or grills, or for salad dressings.

Moutarde à l'ancienne – Traditional-style mustard
Coarse-grained mustard from which the husks have not been removed. For marinating or for a vinaigrette. Can be used with hot or cold meat.

Moutarde à l'estragon – Tarragon mustard
Popular for fish sauces and vinaigrette.

Moutarde au poivre vert – Green pepper mustard
Green pepper mustard is best suited to seasoning grilled dishes.

Moutarde de Dijon – Dijon mustard
Classic delicate mustard, particularly suitable for cooking. For use in sauces of all kinds. Can be rubbed into roasts and quick-fried dishes.

Mustard should always be kept in a properly closed container in the refrigerator, as it can deteriorate through light, heat or contact with the air. In order to retain the pungency and the character of the mustard, it should not be added to a dish until the last few moments of cooking.

Dijon, the capital of Burgundy, is rich in architectural treasures, like Saint-Michel, seen here.

Dijon mustard adds that certain something to many sauces, and is served with all kinds of meat dishes, so restaurants purchase it in bulk.

yellowish *Sinapsis alba* produces delicate flavors, the red-brown *Brassica nigra* lends pungency. Nowadays Canada, which produces more mustard seed than any other country in the world, satisfies almost all the demand from France. Often slightly crushed, in order to split the husks, the seeds are treated with brandy vinegar, water and salt for several hours. They are then weighed and mixed with spices and ground. First, the albumen-like enzyme myrosin and water, work together to generate mustard oil. Delicate and allylic, this oil produces the pungency which then disappears, to a great extent, when hot industrial grinding mills drive it out at 3000 revolutions a minute. Mustard cannot stand heat and its aroma is highly volatile. Horseradish has to be added to replace the lost pungency.

France's most respected mustard millers grind their wares in Beaune. The firm of Edmond Faillot supplies most of France's three-star chefs. The young mustard-maker Marc Desarmeniens proudly shows off the old stone mills where the husks and the paste are separated in the centrifuge. Only in *moutarde à l'ancienne* are the husks retained. Finally, turmeric is added for the yellow color, plus citric acid and an antioxidant. In France mustard is served with both hot and cold meat, but its true realm is the kitchen where it tends to work away unnoticed in the background. Mustard intensifies all tastes in general, but especially those of salad dressings and meat and fish sauces. A good cook always uses it with sensitivity.

Exquisite cooking oils

The first high-quality cooking oils were developed way back in antiquity. Even then people understood the advantages of cold pressing and recognized the distinctive character that an oil can have. And so olive oil began its triumphal progress, which continues to this day, and which has also kindled people's interest in other oils.

In France, oil was already being obtained from walnuts in the Middle Ages. The trees, which can reach a height of up to 98 feet (30 meters) high, are native to many of the *départements* of southern France. Drôme and Isère in the east and the Dordogne in the west are particularly well-known for cultivating this crop. But these trees flourish in southern Burgundy as well. The local people also used to cultivate rape for its oil-bearing seeds. In almost all the larger communities there were oil mills in which the farmers had their walnut and rape harvest pressed for their own use. The oil was used for cooking and also in lamps. With increasing nectarization, the little manually operated oil mills became more and more unprofitable, and eventually ceased to function. Now only a few remain.

One, which survives to this day is the Huilerie Leblanc in Iguérande, a village at the western limit of the *département* of Saône-et-Loire. It was founded in 1878 by the grandfather of the present owner, and is now operated by his son, the fourth generation. It has withstood the ravages of time, and has been operating with the same equipment since it opened, using the same manual methods.

The nuts, delivered without shells, are crushed beneath heavy granite stones for 10 minutes to form a dense paste. The nuts are then transferred to a cast-iron pan, in which they are briefly roasted on a stove. The oil miller carefully monitors the color and odor. Only a few minutes too few or too many can make a decisive change to the flavor. The roast note gives the nuts a delicate chocolate candy taste. The paste is then put under the hydraulic press and the oil is extracted in a single cold pressing at a pressure of 220 bar (3300 pounds per square inch). The pressing takes 10 minutes, so that a uniform operating rhythm is established: as one load is crushed, one is roasted and one pressed.

Depending on the fruit, the oil yield averages 30–50 percent of the original weight. For walnuts and hazelnuts it is 50 percent, for pistachios and almonds 30 percent. After the pressing, the oil is poured into tanks, in which it stands for a week enabling the particles it contains to precipitate on the bottom of the tank. The oil is then poured through a simple

To make sure the aromatic strength of the oil is not diminished, it is allowed time to clarify naturally. It is then drained off into the bottle through a simple paper filter.

The oil miller spreads the nuts out evenly before they are crushed between granite stones to form a homogenous paste in only 10 minutes.

The harvested selection comprises oils made from walnuts, hazelnuts and peanuts, almonds, pine nuts and pistachios, as well as olives and rapeseed.

paper filter into a bottle. In this way, it keeps the full force of its flavor. The pressing residues also find a use, as fish bait or animal fodder.

As well as the intensity of their flavors, the oils obtained through these gentle manual techniques have other characteristics. They are extremely high-quality and healthy foods, for they are extraordinarily rich in fatty acids, enzymes, hormones, and vital substances. It is no accident that chefs from many first-class restaurants are among their many customers. The Huilerie Leblanc produces eight different oils. Apart from peanut oil and olive oil, which are very suitable for heating, rapeseed oil is also used for cooking, but only at low temperatures. The other oils, namely walnut, hazelnut, almond, pistachio, and pine nut, can be used only for cold dishes – in sauces and vinaigrette dressings as well as for seasoning vegetables, fish or meat dishes, and cheese. Their popularity is steadyly increasing.

Standard cooking oils

The French use as much oil for cooking as they do butter and margarine put together, namely around 24 pounds (11 kilogram) or 24 pints (11 liters). People have grown accustomed to the neutral flavor of cheap, industrially produced oils. To make them, seeds and fruits containing oils are subjected to numerous chemical and physical processes, which include a steam treatment to produce a neutral taste before filtration. The comparison becomes particularly marked if a refined sunflower oil is contrasted with a cold-pressed sunflower oil manufactured by biological means. The first has practically no flavors left, whereas the second has an extremely intense aroma and taste, with a pronounced nut note, for which reason it also has a narrower range of uses. The most widespread cooking oils are listed below in the order of their importance, judged by frequency of use:

1. Sunflower seed oil
This is by far the most popular of the oils used in France, since it can be used for everything from salad dressings to deep-frying at temperatures of 340 °F (170 °C).

2. Peanut oil
The runner-up among the oils, this is very easy to heat, and gives excellent frying results at all temperatures up to 410 °F (210 °C).

3. Olive oil
Although it is increasing in public estimation in connection with the trend toward Mediterranean cuisine, the amount used is still only a tenth of the quantity of sunflower seed oil used. It is very aromatic and is used mainly for salad dressings and for frying at up to 375 °F (190 °C).

4. Corn seed oil
It is extremely neutral and does not influence the taste of the actual ingredients. It is the right choice for salads and for all dishes up to a temperature of 340 °F (170 °C).

5. Rapeseed oil (Canola)
A light, neutral oil for salads, or for frying at up to 320 °F (160 °C).

6. Soya oil
This is not used much in France, but is widely used in the rest of the world. Its main application is in salad dressings.

All other oils, even the grapeseed oil that is famous, in particular, in the South of France, account for only small quantities. None of the oils obtained from nuts are used for anything other than seasoning.

Innovative Burgundian cuisine

With its wines and its cuisine, Burgundy is gastronomically an elite region. An area with large snails and river crabs, the finest poultry and the most flavorful beef, as well as a host of other prime ingredients, it cannot but have a high-quality cuisine. Many chefs preserve the traditional recipes and keep the same classic dishes on their menus year in, year out. But the cuisine of a province is kept alive only if it is continually producing interpreters who have their roots deep in the regional tradition, yet still have the courage and the imagination to express it in a surprising and unusual manner.

One such innovator has been at work for some years now in Beaune, the capital of the Burgundian wine industry. At the Hostellerie de l'Ecusson, Jean-Pierre Senelet is constantly finding new combinations of Burgundian ingredients. His creations are often an exquisite surprise. At the same time they provide evidence of the uninterrupted vitality of a great culinary tradition.

Escargots en os à moelle aux pétales d'ail et sel gros

Snails in marrowbones with garlic and coarse salt (illustration right)

12 marrowbones, each about 2½ in/6 cm long
Generous 1 lb/500 g shallots
1 bulb of garlic
1 bottle red Burgundy
Freshly-milled salt and pepper
8 tsp/40 g butter
4 dozen snails
Coarse sea salt
Flat-leaf parsley

Soak the marrowbones in cold water for 3 hours to remove the bloody parts. Press out the marrow with your fingers, then put to one side in a little water with a dash of vinegar.
Slice the shallots and the garlic finely. Put them into a saucepan with the red wine, and season with salt and pepper. Leave to simmer for 1½ hours. Purée the ingredients, then fold in the butter and season.
Preheat the oven to 465 °F/240 °C.
Put three bones on each of four heat-resistant plates.
First fill each bone with the wine and shallot purée. Then place 4 snails on top and cover with a thick slice of marrow. Sprinkle with coarse sea salt and season with freshly-milled pepper. Put into the hot oven for about 10 minutes.
Garnish with parsley leaves and serve immediately.

Coq au vin de Bourgogne, macaronis et truffes d'ici

Coq au vin with macaroni and local truffles (illustration right, top)

Serves 8

1 chicken, weighing about 7¾ lbs/3.5 kg
1 lb/500 g carrots
5 onions
1 bulb of garlic
Thyme
Bay leaf
Cloves
Scant ½ cup/100 ml Marc de Bourgogne
2 bottles strong red Burgundy
Freshly-milled salt and pepper
¾ cup/200 ml olive oil
½ cup/75 g flour
1 tbsp unsweetened cocoa powder
11 oz/300 g macaroni
2 gray Burgundy truffles

Divide the chicken so that each person has at least two pieces.
Clean the carrots and peel the onions and garlic. Cut the carrots into pieces and halve the onions. Put both into a large bowl with the garlic and the chicken pieces. Add the herbs and pour in the *marc* and wine. Add a little salt and pepper and leave to marinate for at least 48 hours.
Remove the chicken pieces from the marinade and let them drain dry. Roll each chicken piece in the flour. Heat the olive oil in a large heat-resistant pot, then brown the chicken pieces in the oil for at least 12 minutes. Take out the chicken and let it drain dry.
Scoop the vegetables out of the marinade and likewise let them drain dry. Bring the marinade to a boil and pass through a fine sieve. Put the vegetables into the pot and brown them in the remaining oil. Dust with the cocoa powder and mix well. Place the pieces of chicken on top and pour marinade over them. Bring to a boil, and cook for 2 to 3 hours. Then transfer to a preheated oven at 320 °/160 °C. Remove the pieces of chicken and keep them warm. Pour the sauce through a fine sieve and season.
Cook the macaroni until it is *al dente*. Dice the truffles finely. Arrange the macaroni and the chicken portions on the plates. Sprinkle the diced truffles over them and pour the sauce on top.

Galette de bœuf bourguignon à la chapelure d'oignons

Boeuf bourguignon galette with onion and breadcrumbs (illustration far right)

Serves 8

3 lbs/1.5 kg shoulder of beef
Olive oil
¾ cup/100 g flour
3 carrots
3 onions
4 cups/1 liter red Burgundy (Pinot Noir)
4 cups/1 liter poultry stock
6 cloves of garlic
Thyme, bay leaf
Freshly-milled salt and pepper
2 eggs
1 cup/100 g powdered onion
3 cups/150 g fresh breadcrumbs

Cut the meat into pieces and dust with a little flour. Put into a pot with some hot oil and brown. Scoop out and leave them to drain.
Clean the carrots and onions, then cut into pieces or quarters. Brown in the remaining fat, then scoop out and leave them to drain in a sieve.
Heat the pot thoroughly, then pour in the wine and stock and bring to a boil. Add the vegetables, meat, garlic, thyme and bay leaf, a little salt and pepper. Cover and cook in a preheated oven at 390 °F/200 °C for at least 4 hours.
The meat is cooked when it can be easily mashed with a fork. Mash all the ingredients and season. Fill the mixture into rings about 5 in (12 cm) in diameter and ¾ in (15 mm) high. Leave them to become firm in the refrigerator.
Preheat the oven to 390 °F/200 °C.
Turn the rings upside down to remove the galettes. Roll the galettes in the remaining flour, then dip in the beaten eggs and turn in the mixture of powdered onion and breadcrumbs. Pour some olive oil into an oven-safe dish and roast the galette in the oven for 5 minutes on each side until golden yellow.
This dish goes well with young salad leaves and carrot juice seasoned with mustard, served separately in a sauceboat.

Ris de veau à la poudre de cassis

Calves' sweetbreads with powdered blackcurrants
(illustration above)

1½ lb/750 g calf's sweetbreads
2 shallots
3½ tbsp/50 ml white Burgundy
⅔ cup/150 ml brown meat juices
5 tsp/25 g butter
Freshly-milled salt and pepper
3½ tbsp/50 ml olive oil
1 tbsp powdered blackcurrants

Remove the nerves and skin from the calf
sweetbreads, then cut them into pieces ¾ in
(2 cm) square. Steam the finely chopped shallots
with the wine until the fluid has evaporated. Add
the meat juices and reduce to a third. Melt the
butter while swivelling the pan, then season and
keep warm.

Brown the sweetbreads thoroughly in hot olive oil,
then cook for 3 minutes on a low heat. Put them
into a sieve and leave to drip dry, then put back
into the pan. Add salt and pepper to season, then
dust with powdered blackcurrants, but do not let
them become too hot. Mix well and serve
immediately with mashed potatoes, over which a
little hot sauce has been poured.

Sandre en meunière de gaude, gros gnocchis au lard paysan

Pike perch meunière, large dumplings
and farmhouse bacon
(no illustration)

1 pike perch, weighing about 3 lbs/1.5 kg
⅔ cup/150 ml red Burgundy
1¼ cups/300 ml vegetable stock
2½ tbsp/40 ml olive oil
1 cup/100 g roasted corn meal
Freshly-milled salt and pepper
3½ tbsp/50 g butter
Lovage leaves for garnish

Bacon dumplings
5 oz/120 g smoked bacon
1 cup/250 ml milk
8 tsp/40 g butter
Freshly-milled salt and pepper
⅔ cup/70 g flour
2 eggs
Scant 1 cup/75 g chopped flat-leaf parsley
1 tbsp grated Parmesan

For the dumplings, blanch the bacon in boiling
water. Leave it to cool, then dice it finely. Bring
the milk to a boil with the butter and a pinch of

salt and pepper. Take it off the stove, then
sprinkle in the flour, working it in well. Boil for
another 3 minutes, then place in a bowl and leave
to cool.

Add the eggs to the flour mixture one by one and
fold them in, then mix in the chopped parsley,
diced bacon and grated parmesan. Scoop out
large dumplings from the mixture using two
tablespoons. Poach in very hot, but not boiling
water for 25 minutes. Take out of the water with
a skimmer and leave to drain on a napkin.

Scale the pike perch, then cut it in half lengthwise
and divide each fillet into two portions. Set aside
in a cool place.

Boil the wine down well, then add the stock and
reduce to a fifth.

Preheat the oven to 435 °F/225 °C. Heat the oil in
a heavy pan. Roll the pike perch fillets in roasted
corn meal (a Burgundian specialty) and put into
the pan with the dumplings. Add salt and pepper
and cook in the oven for 5 minutes. Finish the
sauce by stirring in the butter.

Turn the fish fillets and leave them to cook in the
oven for another 2 minutes. Leave the pike perch
and dumplings to drain on paper towels, then
serve on preheated plates. Pour the sauce over
each plate with a large spoon and garnish with
lovage leaves.

Monks' cheese

The first monastery of the famous and once extremely powerful order of the Cistercians was refounded after 800 years on the same site where Robert de Molesme first established it in 1098. Since that time, monks have again been working and praying in Saône-Ebene, not far from Nuits Saint-Georges. The abbey of Citeaux owns nearly 495 acres (200 hectares) of land, of which about 370 acres (150 hectares) are cultivated. Other than grain, all that is grown here nowadays is fodder for 60 cows, which are also able to roam across extensive pasture meadows. In the 1920s, the monks started manufacturing cheese, at first for their own consumption only. But by 1935 production had grown markedly and it has increased further since then. So in the 1950s, the monks carried out a breeding process in their Montbéliarde herd. Although the number of cows has not changed over the last 40 years, the monks today produce over 50 percent more cheese. The high-fat milk is extraordinarily well suited to cheese. The cows are often grazing on the meadows from the beginning of April onward, though they are always brought into the shelter of the cow barn to be milked. By July it is often too dry in Burgundy for good grass, so they have to be given fodder. And from the end of October the animals are in purpose-built loose-housing sheds all the time.

"Our aim is not to achieve maximum production," says Brother Cyril, the monastery's cheese-master, "but rather to make as much as we need to be able to make a living from it." By "we," the monk

means the present total of 40 monks, who receive 70 percent of their income from the dairy. Production currently stands at 66 tons (60 tonnes) of cheese a year. The monks have organized the cheese production to run in the most efficient way possible, not only to let the monks attend to the cheeses but also to give them as much time as possible for their meditation. So they have no hesitation in introducing modern technology to keep the proportion of purely manual work as low as possible.

They make cheese twice a week, on Tuesdays and Fridays. Immediately after milking, the milk is cooled down to 39 °F (4 °C). While they pasteurize milk obtained from earlier milkings at 140 °F (60 °C), they always process the milk

from the most recent milking unpasteurized. The milk is heated to a good 89 °F (32 °C) and sufficient rennet is added to make it curdle within 40 minutes. The cheese curd is broken up mechanically, and then stirred for 20 minutes so that the majority of the whey drains away. While this is happening, the monks make sure that the core of the cheese mixture remains sufficiently firm. The mixture travels along a short conveyor belt into a hopper, and from there into four pipes. Inside these it slides forward under its own weight and portions are cut off it as the monks fill the molds by hand. Four, six or nine molds, as the case may be, stand on a permeable cloth on special steel plates, which are pushed under the presses. The cheese stays there for 20 minutes. It is then taken out of the molds and placed in a salt bath for 90 minutes while the monks give all the equipment a very thorough clean.

The monastery has four conditioning cellars in which the cheese spends between 15 and 21 days. In summer, the maturing period is shorter, because demand is high. Every two days, the cheese is washed with brine. The cellar temperature is normally 55 °F (13 °C). But in order to slow the maturing process down or accelerate it, the monks vary it between 50°F (10 °C) and 59°F (15 °C) as required. The atmospheric humidity is 95 percent. After two weeks, the cheese is wrapped and undergoes a further week of maturing.

The cheese from the abbey of Citeaux, which is akin to Reblochon, is at its best in summer, when it is mature after a month. It then has a flexible, yellow-red rind, a soft, pliable consistency, and a particularly fine flavor. Unfortunately, it is often cut into when it is too young. The demand for the monks' cheese is so high in Burgundy that it is only rarely found else-where.

1 Checking whether the milk has already curdled.
2 If it has, the equipment is put into operation which mechanically crumbles the gelatinous mass to break it up.

3 The mixture drops through a hopper into the molds.
4 The pressed cheeses are taken out of the mold and enter the salt bath.
  Right: Fresh Citeaux in its mold.

Burgundy cheeses

Epoisses
The best-known Burgundy cheese, which obtained its *appellation* in 1991, is originally from Auxois, but it is now produced as far afield as Dijon or the Côte d'Or. It is first washed with brine and then with *marc de Bourgogne*, and it has to be matured for at least four weeks. It has an intense bouquet, and a moist, red-brown rind, but the cheese itself is soft and almost white. It measures about 4 inches (10 cm) in diameter and is about 2 inches (4–6 cm) high.

Ami du Chambertin
This cousin of Epoisses was not launched until after World War II. It is milder, since it is not matured for so long, but it is also washed with *marc*.
Other varieties of Burgundy red spreading cheese include the very mild Petit Bourgogne and the small Trou du Cru.

Aisy Cendré
A red spreading cheese that is a neighbor of Epoisses, which it resembles. It comes in disks with a diameter of 4–4½ inches (10–12 cm) and weighs between 9 and 21 ounces (250 and 600 grams). It is also washed with *marc*, but is preserved in grape ash and matured for eight weeks.

Pierre-qui-vire
A milder, red spreading cheese in the shape of a flat disk, weighing only 7 ounces (200 grams) and washed only with brine and presented on straw. It is made by the monks of the abbey of Pierre-qui-vire in the Morvan. The monks also make round cheeses that they season with aromatic herbs, and which are marketed under the name Boulette de la Pierre-qui-vire.

Saint-Florentin
In the Auxerrois, where a Chaource is made, as in nearby Champagne, this cheese is sold in "valleys" about 4½ inches (12–13 centimeters) in diameter weighing about 1 pound/450–500 grams). It is matured for up to eight weeks and is then characterized by its distinctive taste.

Soumaintrain
This very mild, almost white, cow's milk cheese, washed only once with brine, has a pleasantly sour taste. It is produced by ten farms and a dairy in the area surrounding the village of the same name in Yonne, which is the most northerly *département* of Burgundy. It matures for only 6–8 weeks.

Bouton de culotte
Also known as Chèvreton de Mâcon or simply Mâconnais, this comes from the south of Burgundy. It is a small, cone-shaped cheese, often made entirely from goat's milk, and weighs about 2½ ounces (60 grams). But there are also cheeses which are made either with 50 percent cow's milk, or entirely from cow's milk. It is commonly sold with a slight amount of blue mold on the rind.

Charolais
This cheese is made entirely from goat's milk or with 50 percent cow's milk. It has a naturally blue or white mold rind, which is shaped into cylinders about 3 inches (8 cm) high and is sold at various stages in its 2–6 weeks maturing process. As far as the cheese itself goes, it is white and firm, and often dry as well, and develops a distinctive taste.

Montrachet
An example of a cheese made entirely from goat's milk, which is also produced in various other places in Burgundy. The tall cylinder, which can weigh up to 3½ ounces (100 grams), matures for only a week and is often wrapped in vine leaves. It is creamy and markedly mild in taste.

The wines of Burgundy

If some of the finest wines in the world flourish in Burgundy, this is not only due to the climate, the soil and the grape varieties, but also to a thousand years of experience in cultivation and cellarage. Burgundy has a Central European continental climate. This means that there are marked differences between the individual seasons: the winters are often cold, but the summers are hot and dry. The vineyards – at least those with the high-quality *appellations* – are situated on slopes with good drainage. They face away from the prevailing west wind, which brings rain, and toward the sun, which ensures that the grapes get enough light and heat.

The soils are outstandingly suitable for viticulture, since they are barren and stony, which forces the vine roots to go down deep. They consist mainly of chalk, clay and silica, and their composition influences the nature and the aromatic character of the wines. Chalk brings out the flavors, the delicacy and fullness; clay brings out the dark color and contributes distinctive structure and tannins; and silica adds lightness and quaffability. Various minerals contribute to the bouquet and the finish.

The climate and soil express their character in two predominant grape varieties which are native to Burgundy – the white Chardonnay and the dark Pinot Noir. Chardonnay buds early,

which makes it susceptible to frost, but it also matures early and produces grapes that are especially rich in sugar. It is not a very aromatic variety, but it does reflect the location it comes from in terms of, acidity and strength. It is best made into wine in small oak casks, where it ages well and often develops elegant roast and honey notes. Pinot Noir, the late Burgundy or blue Burgundy, is sensitive and capricious. Only if its yields are kept low and the small grapes can ripen does it have an exquisite berry character, even when young. Aging then gives it a very complex bouquet, with an incomparable delicacy. Any change in the composition of the soil can influence the aromatic spectrum of the wine, provided the winemakers understand their art.

And it is an old art. In Burgundy, grapes have been cultivated since ancient times and the best locations were first used by the Romans. Indeed winemaking has been carried on without interruption since the early Middle Ages by monks and winegrowers. For centuries past, the vineyards have been maintained in a natural way, allowing the soil fauna to develop, which made the minerals accessible to the roots of the vines. Methods of viticulture handed down from generation to generation are today combined with modern knowledge and technology to make the best possible use of the grapes.

Burgundy offers a host of *appellations*. Arranged in the shape of a pyramid, the regional *appellations* form the base making up more than half of all Burgundy wines. One-third is accounted for by the *appellations* relating to individual communes, the *Villages*. A good tenth of Burgundy is ranked as *premier cru*, while only the top 1.7 percent qualifies as *grand cru*.

The regional Burgundy appellations

In addition to 299 communes in various parts of the three Burgundian *départements* of Yonne, Côte d'Or and Saône-et-Loire, the production area for Burgundy also includes the Beaujolais, with 85 communes which form part of the Rhône-Alpes region. Under certain conditions, the regional *appellations* can apply to wines from the entire area. The number of hectares or acres refers to the area in production.

A.O.C. Bourgogne: About 3000 hectares (7413 acres); for red wine made from Pinot Noir or Gamay, insofar as it originates from the Beaujolais *crus* (as far as Régnié), or from Pinot variations and César; for white wines made from Chardonnay only. Red varieties are also made into wine as rosé and are marketed as Burgundy rosé or Burgundy claret.
A.O.C. Bourgogne Passe-Tout-Grains: About 1200 hectares (2965 acres); red and rosé wines only, with at least one-third being made from Pinot and a maximum of two-thirds from Gamay.

A.O.C. Bourgogne (Grand) Ordinaire: About 192 hectares (474 acres); predominantly red wine, some rosé, but also white, all red and white grape varieties being permissible.
A.O.C. Bourgogne Aligoté: About 1400 hectares (3458 acres); white wines made only from Aligoté, which is widespread on the Côte Chalonnaise and in the Mâconnais, and is practically non-existent in Beaujolais.
A.O.C. Hautes-Côtes de Nuits: Just 570 hectares (1408 acres); 19 communes in the hilly area above Côtes de Nuits; only Pinot Noir and Chardonnay (one-sixth); also rosé or claret.
A.O.C. Hautes-Côtes de Beaune: About 640 hectares (1581 acres); 22 communes on the Côte d'Or and 7 in Saône-et-Loire; here too, one-sixth of the product is white wine, the rest being red or rosé wine made from Pinot Noir.
A.O.C. Bourgogne Côte Chalonnaise: 428 hectares (1057 acres) in Saône-et-Loire, of which a good 100 hectares (247 acres) produce Chardonnay wine, all the rest being Pinot Noir.
A.O.C. Bourgogne Côtes d'Auxerre: About 600 hectares (1482 acres); mainly southeast of Auxerre; Chardonnay and Pinot Noir only.
A.O.C. Bourgogne Irancy: About 367 hectares (906 acres); red wine from the Auxerrois, based on Pinot and César, occasionally on Tressot. The villages of Chitry, Coulanges-la-Vineuse, and Epineuil may also market both red and rosé wines and white wines as Burgundies. Tonnerre and Vezelay are to follow.
A.O.C. Bourgogne Côte Saint-Jacques: Some locations in Joigny, to the north of Auxerre, have also obtained the right to appear as Burgundies. These include Montrecul in Dijon, Le Châpitre in Chenôve, and La Chapelle Notre-Dame in Ladoix-Serrigny.
A.O.C. Crémant de Bourgogne: About 600 hectares (1482 acres), which are scattered over the Burgundy production area. In the first category Pinot and Chardonnay are permissible; in the second category these can be supplemented with Aligoté (virtually only Melon and Sacy nowadays) and up to 20 percent Gamay. The centers of Crémant production are Bailly, near Auxerre, Nuits-Saint-Georges, and Rully; in the Mâconnais these are Lugny, Viré, or Igé. The sparkling Burgundy, pressed exclusively from red grapes, is nowadays rarely encountered.
A.O.C. Mâcon, Mâcon Supérieur: About 880 hectares (2174 acres); red wine made from Pinot and Gamay over the entire production area (43 communes); 200 hectares (494 acres) white wine made from Chardonnay; permitted alcohol 1 percent below Mâcon-Villages. White wines can be declared as Pinot Chardonnay Mâcon.
Mâcon-Villages: About 3048 hectares (7529 acres) in the 43 communes of the region; exclusively white wine made from Chardonnay grapes.

Opposite: Clos de Vougeot in the fall.

The village appellations

The total area given below refers to the areas planted with vines. For *premiers crus*, the classified area is named.

In the Burgundy Villages *appellations*:

- Pinot Noir and/or Chardonnay are the only grape varieties permitted;
- The maximum production for Villages and *premiers crus* amounts to 40 hectoliters/hectare (about 2 tons/acre) for red wines and 45 hectoliters/hectare (about 2.6 tons/acre) for white wines;
- For Villages, Pinot must yield at least 10.5 percent alcohol by volume, and Chardonnay at least 11 percent, and for *premiers crus* each of these figures is increased by 0.5 percent;
- The maximum alcohol content for red Villages is set at 13.5 percent, and for white wines it is 14 percent, with a further 0.5 percent allowed for *premiers crus*;

Unless otherwise stated, all vineyards lie within the area referred to by the Villages *appellation*. Those for the Saône-et-Loire *département* are listed below. Those for other regions of Burgundy are listed on the following pages, together with the *grands crus*.

Côte Chalonnaise

Rully: 450 hectares (1112 acres), including 105,2 hectares (260 acres) of Pinot and a good 205.1 hectares (507 acres) of Chardonnay – a total of 110 hectares (272 acres) classified as *premier cru*, with 23 *climats*, 35 hectares (868 acres) being in the village of Chagny, with 13 hectares (32 acres) of *premier cru*.

Mercurey: About 739 hectares (1825 acres), of which 583.8 hectares (1442 acres) yield red wine and just 64.9 hectares (160 acres) white wine. 142 hectares (351 acres) are classified as *premier cru*, with 30 *climats* in Mercurey. In Saint-Martin-sous-Montaigou, 108 hectares (267 acres) have the A.O.C., of which 16 hectares (40 acres) are *premier cru*.

Givry: A good 219 hectares (541 acres), 186.2 hectares (460 acres) being Pinot Noir and 33 hectares (81.5 acres) Chardonnay. 78 hectares (193 acres) are classified as *premier cru*, with 16 *climats*. 15 hectares (37 acres) belong to the commune of Jambles, and 6 hectares (15 acres) to Dracy-le-Fort, where they are considered *premier cru*.

Montagny: 437 hectares (1079.3 acres) are classified in all, including 276 hectares (682 acres) of *premier cru*, with 53 *climats*. The vineyard locations are distributed between Montagny, Buxy, Saint-Vallerin and Jully-lès-Buxy. Chardonnay only.

Bouzeron: About 61 hectares (151 acres), classified in 1997. Great exception among the *appellations*, since it produces white wine made only from Aligoté.

Mâconnais

Pouilly-Fuissé: 850 hectares (2100 acres) in the communes of Fuissé, Solutré-Pouilly, Vergisson and Chaintré. No *premier cru*, but some recognized *climats*. Chardonnay only.

Pouilly-Vinzelles: 50 hectares (123.5 acres) in Vinzelles and Loché.

Pouilly-Loché: 29 hectares (71.6 acres) in Loché.

Saint-Véran: 558 hectares (1378.2 acres) in the communes of Prissé, Davayé, Chasselas, Leynes, Chânes, Saint-Vérand and Solutré-Pouilly. Chardonnay only.

The entrance to the medieval cellar of Château de Clos de Vougeot.

Chablis

Chablis, the most famous and most imitated white wine in the world, has a long history, during which it has had to overcome various hurdles to attain its fame. In the early Middle Ages, Cistercians promoted viticulture in Chablis and the surrounding area. In 1128, they established the Petit Pontigny estate, the cellar of which could contain 2000 hectoliters (5283 gallons) of wine. (Nowadays, it is the headquarters of the Wine Association.) It was thanks to the monks that the wine pressed from Chardonnay first gained a reputation. The proximity of Paris, which could be reached from nearby Auxerre via the Yonne and Seine rivers, very soon brought about an increase in business and guaranteed recognition. At the beginning of the 16th century, there were almost 1000 hectares (2471 acres) of vines in production. A good 100 years later, the English began to take an interest in the dry white wine. A quantity of Chablis was the first lot of white Burgundy to be sold by Christie's auction house in 1770. The 19th century brought success, when Chablis wines were exported not just to the countries of northern Europe, but also to Russia and the United States. At that time, there were 70 communes producing Chablis. The production area in the *département* of Yonne simultaneously expanded disproportionately, until it eventually covered 43,000 hectares (106,254 acres). However, the *phylloxera* catastrophe which began in 1893 brought a drastic end to this escalating mass production. Wars, economic crises, and the flight from the countryside then did the rest. By 1945, there were just 500 hectares (1235 acres) in the Chablis area still producing wine.

It was hard to begin again. The vines were often hit by frosts in April or May which destroyed entire harvests and discouraged the winegrowers. Only at the end of the 1950s were protective measures taken. Initially, petrol-fired heaters were set up in the vineyards. Irrigation was later introduced as a more ecologically acceptable alternative. Sprayers now go into action as soon as the thermometer falls to freezing point. The fine artificial rain freezes, forming a protective layer of ice round the buds which safeguards them from any serious damage. The more frost protection and modern mechanized working methods improved, the more the local population's interest in viticulture grew. In 1970 the entire area planted with vines constituted 750 hectares (1853 acres); this doubled in the following decade. The cultivated area has grown continuously during the 1980s and 1990s, and by 1998 was approximately 4000 hectares (9884 acres).

Chablis was granted an *Appellation d'Origine Contrôlée* in 1938, which covered locations in 20 communes. One of the pre-conditions was that

The Chablis town gate.

Old half-timbered house in Chablis with wine merchant.

the soils should consist of Kimmeridge, the fossiliferous clay which is typical of the Chablis area, and takes its name from the bay in the south of England where this composition was discovered for the first time. In 1943, Petit Chablis recorded locations with soils of a different composition. Advances in the technology of viticulture made an important contribution to the development of modern Chablis. They did away with the old wooden gyle-tuns used for fermentation. These were replaced by cellars equipped with hygienic steel tanks. Controlled fermentation temperatures and reduced maturing periods in which all oxidation is avoided have resulted in wines of reliable quality and have also emphasized their fresh, fruity and mineral character. It is this which has brought Chablis its worldwide success, guaran-

teeing it a place as both an elegant aperitive and the ideal accompaniment to seafood and fish dishes. However, wine is also cultivated in little oak casks, *pièces*, in Chablis, as in the Côte de Beaune region – particularly in the *premier cru* areas, or in the *climats* where the *grand cru* comes from. These wines need longer to mature and to develop their complex flavors.

There is only one *grand cru* in the Chablis region, but its production is spread over seven different *climats*. This stretch of land extends along the right-hand bank of the little River Serein and over the slope that lies opposite the little town of Chablis. It faces south-southwest, which guarantees the Chardonnay grapes maximum sunshine, and thus ensures they always ripen better and contain more sugar than those in any other vineyard in the region. In addition, the

The little town of Chablis.

The vineyards which are the home of Fourchaume Premier Cru.

Domaine Sainte-Anne in Préhy, with the old church and the futuristic vineyard buildings.

Above: Chardonnay grapes on the vine and the typical limestone soil

Kimmeridge, which is made up of extremely tiny oyster shells, gives the wine its characteristic mineral note. A Chablis *grand cru* is usually reserved when young. It is essential for it to mature for several years in the bottle to reveal its inherent quality and its character. As it ages, a unique range of aromas emerge in addition to the thoroughly delightful honey note. Depending on the year, these veer more toward mushrooms, undergrowth and toast, or dried fruit and wax, while the mineral accent can be retained for a very long time. Chablis *grand crus* are wines for special occasions and for accompanying fine dishes of equal intensity and power.

Locations and communes

Chablis Grand Cru: 98 hectares (242 acres); only one *grand cru*, but divided into 7 *climats*; from west to east, these are Bougros, Preuses, Vaudésir, Grenouilles, Valmur, Les Clos, and Blanchot.

Chablis Premier Cru: About 749 hectares (1850 acres) with 17 main locations.
On the right bank of the Serein: Fourchaume, Montée de Tonnerre, Mont de Milieu, Vaucoupin, Les Fourneaux, Côte de Vaubarousse, and Berdiot. On the left bank of the Serein: Beauroy, Vau-Ligneau, Vau de Vey, Côte de Lechet, Vaillons, Montmains, Chaume de Talvat, Côte de Jouan, Beauregards, and Vosgros.

Chablis: About 3300 hectares (8151 acres) in 19 communes (Beine, Béru, Chablis-Fyé, Milly,

Poinchy, La Chapelle-Vaupelteigne, Chemilly-sur-Serein, Chichée, Collan, Courgis, Fleys, Fontenay, Lignorelles, Ligny-le-Châtel, Maligny, Poilly-sur-Serein, Préhy, Villy, and Viviers).

Petit Chablis: 475 hectares (1174 acres) in 9 communes (Beine, Béru, Chablis, La Chapelle-Vaupelteigne, Lignorelles, Maligny, Poilly-sur-Serein, Préhy and Villy).

The only other communal *appellation* in Yonne:

Sauvignon de Saint-Bris: 100 hectares (247 acres) in 7 communes (Saint-Bris-le-Vineux, Chitry, Cravant, Irancy, Quenne, Saint-Cy-les-Colons, and Vincelottes.) Sauvignon only, in the form of Vin Délimité de Qualité Supérieure [V.D.Q.S.]).

Pinot Noir

More than two-thirds of all the vineyards of the famous Côte d'Or are planted with Pinot Noir, a variety that is as delicate as its quality is high. It is considered to be one of the oldest of all cultivated grapes. Even when the Romans were moving up the Rhône in the first century BC, they are said to have come across a grape akin to the Pinot. There are references to viticulture in Burgundy 400 years later. A further 500 years after that, it had reached Lake Constance. The earliest reference to it by name dates back to the Burgundian Duke Philip the Bold, who had wine made from "*pinot vermeil*" sent ahead of him to Bruges in 1375. Some 20 years later he banned the planting of the "notorious *Gamay*" in Burgundy, which produces higher yields, and therefore less satisfying wines.

The Pinot grape is small and cone-shaped. The dark blue, slightly oval, thick-skinned grapes are bunched up very close together, which explains why they are very susceptible to rot. The juice is colorless, which has made the Pinot the predominant variety in Champagne, where it grows extremely well on the chalky soils. In order to make great red wines, its production must be considerably reduced.

After the removal of all rotten or unripe grapes by hand the grapes are crushed, partially or completely, and the stalks are removed. They are then put into fermentation tanks or gyle-tuns. In order to extract as many colorants and flavors as possible from the peel, they are usually left to ferment in cold must for several days. Fermentation either sets in naturally or is triggered by an increase in temperature, and, possibly, by the addition of pure culture yeasts. There are two ways to guarantee uniform fermentation and continued extraction of the colorants, flavors and tannins. The first is *remontage*, in which the must is drawn off at the bottom of the tank and pumped over the grape layer above; the second is *pigeage*, in which the grape layer is either trodden using the feet and a special rammer, or mechanically, and pushed down into the fermenting must. Following this phase of rapid fermentation the wine is left to ferment for a few days longer for additional extraction. It is then racked off, with the grape residue remaining behind in the tank to be pressed. Some or all of this *vin de presse* is added to the *vin de goutte*. The growers now either leave the wine in the tank until malolactic fermentation takes place or immediately drain it into small-capacity oak casks which normally hold 228 liters (60 gallons). Great red Burgundies are left in the cask for 18 months to two years before they are drained off into bottles. Depending on how good a year it is and on the location, Pinot wines may mature for years, or even for decades.

View of Vosne-Romanée.

Pinot Noir during the *veraison*, the season when the grapes change color.

In the vineyards of the Côte d'Or, which are often planted with up to 10,000 vines, the grapes are picked by hand. When the cutters have filled their pails, they empty them into the carrier's *hod*.

Communal appellations of the Côte d'Or

Côte de Nuits

Marsannay: Just on 188 hectares (464 acres), one-sixth of which produces white wine, in Marsannay, Couchey, Chenôve; no *premier cru*, but has the only Côte d'Or AOC for rosé wine: Marsannay Rosé.

Fixin: 97 hectares (240 acres), including 16.5 hectares (40.7 acres) *premier cru*, 0.5 hectares (1.24 acres) Chardonnay (villages of Fixin and Brochon).

Gevrey-Chambertin: 388 hectares (958.4 acres), including 74.6 hectares (184.3 acres) of *premier cru* with 25 *climats*; 51 hectares (126 acres) classified in Brochon; red wine only.

Morey-Saint-Denis: 90 hectares (222 acres), including 40 hectares (98.8 acres) of *premier cru* with 18 *climats*; 1.2 hectares (2.9 acres) Chardonnay.

Chambolle-Musigny: 153 hectares (378 acres), including 61 hectares (150.7 acres) of *premier cru* with 23 *climats*, Pinot only.

Vougeot: 18 hectares (44.5 acres), including 11.7 hectares (28.9 acres) of *premier cru* with 4 *climats* and a good 3 hectares (7.4 acres) Chardonnay.

Vosne-Romanée: 149 hectares (368 acres), including 57.5 hectares (142 acres) of *premier cru* with 15 *climats* and 25 hectares (62 acres) classified in Flagey-Echezeaux; Pinot only.

Nuits Saint-Georges, Nuits: 293 hectares (724 acres), including 143 hectares (353 acres) of *premier cru* with 41 *climats*; 3.4 hectares (8.4 acres) Chardonnay; 54 hectares (133 acres) classified in Premeaux village, including 42 hectares (104 acres) *premier cru*.

Côte de Nuits-Villages: 161 hectares (398 acres), including a good 3 hectares (7.4 acres) Chardonnay (villages of Fixin, Brochon, Premeaux, Comblanchien, Corgolin).

Côte de Beaune

Ladoix: A good 89 hectares (220 acres), including 14 hectares (34.6 acres) Chardonnay; only in villages of Ladoix-Serrigny, Ladoix Côtes de Beaune (22.7 hectares/56 acres).

Pernand-Vergelesses: 103 hectares (254 acres), including 42 hectares (104 acres) of *premier cru* with 6 *climats*; 35 hectares (86 acres) for white wine. Pernand Côtes de Beaune: 13 hectares (32 acres).

Aloxe-Corton: 127 hectares (313.7 acres), including 37 hectares (91.4 acres) of *premier cru* with 12 *climats*; 8.5 hectares (21 acres) of *premier cru* in the Ladoix-Serrigny region; 0.5 hectares (1.24 acres) Chardonnay.

Savigny-lès-Beaune, Savigny: Just on 350 hectares (865 acres), including 144 hectares (356 acres) of *premier cru* with 22 *climats*, 32 hectares (79 acres) Chardonnay. Savigny Côtes de Beaune: 0.17 hectares (0.42 acres).

Chorey-lès-Beaune or **Chorey:** Approximately 60 hectares (148 acres), no *premier cru*, 3.3 hectares (8.15 acres) Chardonnay. Chorey Côtes de Beaune: 73 hectares (180 acres).

Beaune: 414 hectares (1023 acres), including 322 hectares (795 acres) of *premier cru* with 42 *climats*; just 28 hectares (69 acres) for white wine.

Côte de Beaune: About 25 hectares (62 acres); no *premier cru*; 10.5 hectares (25.9 acres) Chardonnay.

Pommard: About 313 hectares (773 acres), including 125 hectares (309 acres) of *premier cru* with 32 *climats*; red wine only.

Volnay: A good 226 hectares (558 acres), including 144 hectares (356 acres) of *premier cru* with 35 *climats*, of which 29 hectares (72 acres) Volnay-Santenots, in commune of Meursault; Pinot only.

Monthélie: 120 hectares (296 acres), including 31 hectares (77 acres) of *premier cru* with 9 *climats*; just on 7.5 hectares (18.5 acres) Chardonnay. Monthélie Côtes de Beaune: 3.2 hectares (7.9 acres).

Saint-Romain: About 83 hectares (205 acres), including 41 hectares (101 acres) Chardonnay; no *premier cru*. Saint-Romain Côtes de Beaune: 3.2 hectares (7.9 acres).

Auxey-Duresses: Just on 135 hectares (333 acres), including 32 hectares (79 acres) of *premier cru* with 10 *climats*; about 35 hectares (86 acres) Chardonnay. Auxey-Duresses Côtes de Beaune: 42.6 hectares (105.2 acres).

Meursault: 364 hectares (899 acres), including 100 hectares (247 acres) of *premier cru* with 17 *climats*; a good 16 hectares (40 acres) for red wine. Meursault Côtes-de-Beaune: 2.5 hectares (6.17 acres).

Blagny: 18.5 acres (7.4 hectares); red wine only; the entire area of Blagny, which is usually included under Meursault and Puligny-Montrachet, covers 54 hectares (133 acres), of which 44 hectares (109 acres) *premier cru* with 7 *climats*; the white wines can be marketed under the names of the better-known communes.

Puligny-Montrachet: 208 hectares (514 acres), including 100 hectares (247 acres) of *premier cru* with 18 *climats*; 1.7 hectares (4.2 acres) Pinot. Puligny Côtes de Beaune: 0.5 hectares (1.2 acres).

Chassagne-Montrachet: 305 hectares (753 acres), including 159 hectares (393 acres) of *premier cru* with 29 *climats*; 7 hectares (17 acres) fall under the commune of Remigny, 111 hectares (274 acres) are planted with Pinot vines. Chassagne Côte de Beaune: 31 hectares (77 acres).

Saint-Aubin: About 145 hectares (358 acres), including 97.5 hectares (241 acres) of *premier cru* with 16 *climats*; about 75 hectares (185 acres) Chardonnay. Saint-Aubin Côte de Beaune: 16.5 hectares (40.7 acres).

Santenay: About 325 hectares (803 acres), including about 124 hectares (306 acres) of *premier cru* with 13 *climats*; 13 hectares (32 acres) lie within the area of Remigny; a good 28 hectares (69 acres) white wine. Santenay Côte de Beaune: 1.6 hectares (3.9 acres).

Maranges: Just on 180 hectares (445 acres); 100 hectares (247 acres) of *premier cru* with 9 *climats*; the vineyard locations are divided between the villages of Cheilly, Dezize and Sampigny in the *département* of Saône-et-Loire; they are given the suffix "lès-Maranges;" 4 hectares (10 acres) Chardonnay. The red wines can also be labeled as "Maranges Côte de Beaune."

Côte-de-Beaune-Villages: Pinot only; this A.O.C. can replace 14 Côte de Beaune *appellations*, and this is increasingly taking place.

The area measurements given relate to the vineyards in production and are always lower than the classified areas.

Pigeage is used to extract the color and the tannins from Pinot Noir. This is the process of breaking up the grape layer on top and re-immersing the peel in the must.

Côte de Beaune

Corton: 99.5 hectares (245.8 acres); the largest *grand cru* area in Burgundy takes in the communes of Aloxe-Corton, Ladoix-Serrigny, and Pernand-Vergelesses; its 25 *climats* can be named on the label; the most famous are Le Clos du Roi (6.72 hectares/16.6 acres), Le Corton (3.76 hectares/9.3 acres), Les Perrières (8.27 hectares/20.4 acres), Les Bressandes (13.98 hectares/34.5 acres), Clos des Cortons Faiveley (2.98 hectares/7.3 acres); just 2 hectares (4.9 acres) are planted with Chardonnay vines; a few plots can grow Pinot or Chardonnay and their white wine has the *appellation* Corton-Charlemagne.

Corton-Charlemagne: A good 49 hectares (121 acres) in the communes of Aloxe-Corton, Ladoix-Serrigny, and Pernand-Vergelesses. Of the 72 hectares (178 acres) classified, 63 hectares (156 acres) are covered by the *appellation* Charlemagne, which has fallen out of use, and only 0.26 hectares (0.64 acres) of this area is still declared as Le Charlemagne. Chardonnay only; a few vineyards also produce Pinot for red wine with the *appellation* Corton.

Montrachet: 7.96 hectares (19.6 acres), which are evenly divided between the communes of Puligny-Montrachet and Chassagne-Montrachet.

Chevalier-Montrachet: 7.15 hectares (17.6 acres); entirely within the Puligny area.

Bâtard-Montrachet: 11.98 hectares (29.6 acres); it is also divided almost equally between the two communes.

Bienvenues-Bâtard-Montrachet: 3.49 hectares (8.6 acres); entirely within the Puligny area.

Criots-Bâtard-Montrachet: 1.55 hectares (3.8 acres); entirely within the Chassagne area.

Except for Corton, these *grands crus* are white wines which are obtained from Chardonnay grapes. The areas given above relate to those under production and not to the classified areas, which are markedly greater for Corton and Corton-Charlemagne.

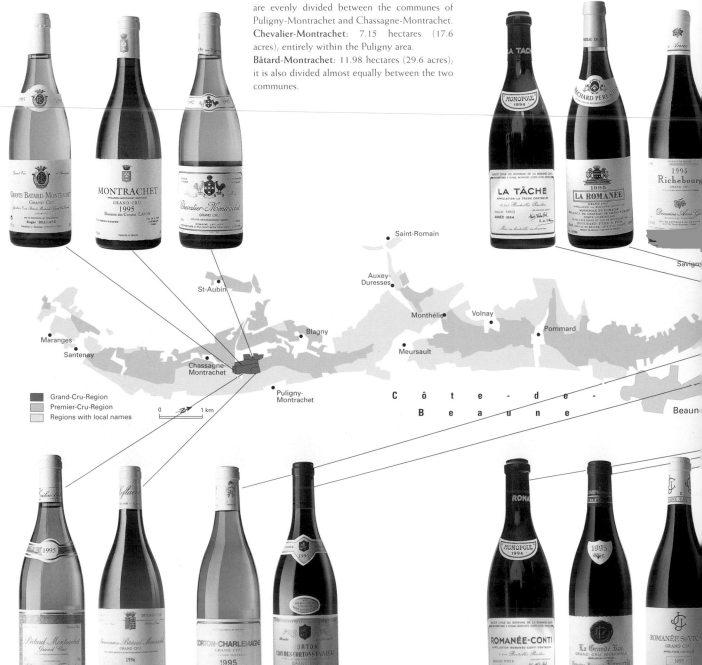

Côte de Nuits

All *grands crus* from the Côte de Nuits are red wines, which are pressed exclusively from Pinot grapes, with the exception of a small area in Musigny.

Chambertin: 13.21 hectares (32.64 acres)
Chambertin-Clos de Bèze: 14.54 ha (35.82 acres)
Chapelle-Chambertin: 5.26 ha (12.99 acres)
Charmes-Chambertin: 30.17 ha (74.55 acres)
Mazoyères Chambertin: 0.28 ha (0.69 acres)
Griottes-Chambertin: 2.7 ha (6.67 acres)
Latricières-Chambertin: 7.15 ha (17.66 acres)

Mazis-Chambertin: 8.42 ha (20.80 acres)
Ruchottes-Chambertin: 3.3 ha (8.15 acres)

Clos Saint-Denis: 6.17 ha (15.24 acres)
Clos de la Roche: 15.98 ha (39.48 acres)
Clos des Lambrays: 8.2 ha (20.26 acres)
Clos de Tart: 7.53 ha (18.60 acres)

Musigny: 8.93 ha (22.06 acres) Pinot and 0.63 ha (1.55 acres) Chardonnay
Bonnes Mares: 14.83 ha (36.64 acres)

Clos de Vougeot: 49.23 ha (121.64 acres)

Echézeaux: 33.18 ha (81.98 acres)
Grand Echézeaux: 8.63 ha (21.32 acres)

La Romanée: 0.75 ha (1.85 acres)
Romanée-Conti: 1.62 ha (4 acres)
Romanée-Saint-Vivant: 9.26 ha (22.88 acres)
Richebourg: 7.17 ha (17.71 acres)
La Grande Rue: 1.65 ha (4.07 acres)
La Tâche: 5.68 ha (14.03 acres)

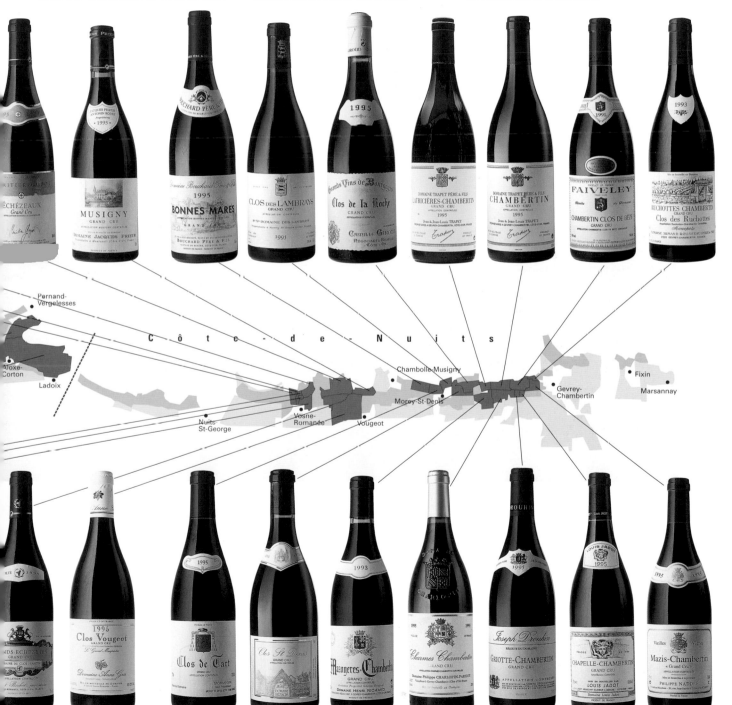

The most expensive red wine in France comes from Vosne.

The adjacent vineyard yields probably the richest *grand cru.*

Grands crus of the Côte de Nuits

On the Côte d'Or there are locations where the conditions are excellent, due to their orientation and the composition of their soils. The Romans, and after them the monks, already knew how to recognize and treasure these locations. The homes of the 32 classified *grands crus* stretch out along the *côte,* and are always situated above the villages and the areas covered by the village *appellations.* They are therefore higher up the slope, where the soils are poorer and better drained, and where the sun's rays touch the vines at an angle that is almost ideal.

Year on year, the wines pressed from the grapes in this area have displayed – and continue to display – a markedly higher quality than those from all other locations. This, at any rate, has remained true as long as the viticulture – and indeed the management of the land in general – has followed the precepts handed down from olden times. Indeed, the fame of the *grands crus* has been growing for centuries, culminating in the second half of the 19th century, with the villages proudly beginning to add the names of

their best wines as an adornment to their own names. Gevrey became Gevrey-Chambertin, Aloxe became Aloxe-Corton and Puligny became Puligny-Montrachet, to give only three examples. But take care! A Montrachet remains a *grands cru,* while a Puligny-Montrachet, in terms of its quality, belongs more on the level of the village *appellations.* With the advances in viticulture and in its technology, the winegrowers have been presented with more extensive options. It must therefore be explicitly emphasized that the exceptional conditions of the *grands crus* really only lead to exceptional wines if both the vineyard and the grapes are looked after extremely conscientiously. Where this is the case, the Burgundy *grands crus* represent extraordinarily complex and almost legendary wines, with an unusually large potential for maturing. Legislators have recognized this, and have created a solid basis for it, by restricting the maximum production to 2 or 2.1 tons per acre (35 or 37 hectoliters per hectare). The red wines must be at least 11.5 percent alcohol by volume, with a maximum of 14.5 percent by volume.

The red wines from the Côte de Nuits in general, and their 24 *grands crus* in particular, are famous for the magnificent and complex character of the Pinot which reflects the different vinyard locations. These are grouped in a narrow strip, which begins in Gevrey-Chambertin, south of

Clos Saint-Jacques, Cazetiers and Champeaux are famous *premier cru* locations in the Gevrey-Chambertin area and stretch out above the village.

Combe Lavaux, and ends with La Tâche. When they are young, the wines pressed here are a dark shining red. Their bouquet is marked by intensely fruity aromas which recall the black, and sometimes red, grapes. The *grands crus* fascinate the palate with a silky fullness, which skillfully conceals their rather robust structure. This is based, firstly, on delicate tannins, and secondly, as a rule, on a very finely balanced amount of pleasant acidity. Such a combination guarantees the high aging potential for the wines. Their young fruit, together with a finely tuned cask maturation, means they are frequently outstandingly delicate and surprisingly stable, and can indeed remain so for at least four years after bottling. After a reserved and unattractive intermediate phase, they begin to develop their own character and their true greatness over many years as they mature in the bottle. The bouquet increasingly takes on an incomparable complexity, in which notes of over-ripe grapes are mixed with flavors of game, fur, truffles and various spices. The blended wine leaves a velvety impression on the palate, that is delicate but also has a long finish.

Grands crus of the Côte de Beaune

The *grands crus* of the Côte de Beaune are completely different from those of the Côte de Nuits. Firstly, there are two markedly distinct areas, Corton and Montrachet, which are quite a long way apart. Secondly, this new area produces only white wines (with one exception). To the north of Beaune is the Montagne de Corton, just 1300 feet (400 meters) high, with a forested summit. On its slopes lie the most extensive *grands cru* areas for red and white Burgundies, Corton and Corton-Charlemagne. The latter did once belong to Charlemagne, who had a special predilection for white wines. On the higher slopes, the predominant soils have a high lime content. From soils like these comes Chardonnay with an extremely powerful character. In 775, Charlemagne transferred ownership of most of these vineyards to the abbey of Saulieu – though he kept some of the best locations for his own requirements. Corton-Charlemagne does not reveal its true nature at once. It keeps its secrets for at least five years, and its longevity is legendary.

The grapes for the Corton red based on late Burgundy flourish on slopes facing east and south, and in soils that contain iron and are rich in clay. This gives the wine strength, fullness and distinctive tannins, and like the *grands crus* of the Côte de Nuits, it needs years to develop.

As the area is so large and the composition of the soil varies, it is normal for the Corton producers to put the names of their properties on their labels – particularly if they own one of the more famous vineyards such as Clos du Roi, Perrières, Vergennes, Bressandes, Maréchaudes or Renardes, and Le Corton. A small part of the region is planted with Chardonnay vines for Corton Blanc and the even rarer Corton Les Vergennes Blanc.

However, it is Montrachet which represents the unequalled peak of dry white wines. The vineyard slopes face south and southeast, above the village of Puligny, which was founded when the Romans were still occupying Gaul. They receive optimal sunshine because the gradient is so slight. This ensures that the grapes have a naturally high degree of maturity and a corresponding degree of sugar. Le Montrachet, the central zone which is a good 800 feet (250 meters) high, consists of brownish limestone. Chardonnay attains a unique quality here. Its admirers must be patient for at least eight to ten years before the wine reveals itself. And wine from the really great vintages can continue to grow in delicacy and complexity for 30 years or more. The higher and somewhat steeper slopes of the Chevalier-Montrachet area, where the soil is particularly poor and rich in magnesium, produce even more elegant wine, though it does not have the same strength. The other three *grands crus* areas of the mountain lie on flatter land where the soil is rather deeper. Their wines often have great fullness of taste and body, and are accessible earlier.

Many *premiers crus* from the Côte de Beaune are particularly highly regarded, such as Meursault Les Perrières and Pommard Les Rugiens. They regularly outstrip other *premiers crus* in terms of demand and price level.

Montrachet, the vineyard belonging to the Bouchards, father and son, is the land of their dreams for lovers of dry white wine. This is where the conditions for Chardonnay are at their best.

Winegrowers' hut near Pommard.

Hospices de Beaune: The most famous wine auction in the world.

The Hospices in Beaune, the Burgundian capital of wine, is one of the most beautiful structural examples of French medieval artistry. Work on this building began in 1443, on the orders of Nicolas Rolin, the Chancellor of Philip the Good. From 1452 onward, the poor and the sick of the city were looked after in the Hôtel-Dieu as part of the building is known. In 1471, vineyards in the Côte d'Or region were donated to the Hôtel-Dieu. The wines from these vineyards were used as tonics or medication, but were also so highly regarded that they were given as presents to important people and benefactors in order to gain their favor.

Over the centuries, the vineyards owned by the Hospices de Beaune expanded, thanks to donations and transfers of ownership, until they became a significant property. Today, this comprises 61 hectares (151 acres) – predominantly *premiers crus* and *grands crus* – and production is now managed using techniques in harmony with nature. All the wines begin maturing in small new oak casks. And on the third Sunday in November, in lots comprising several casks of the same *appellation*, they come under the hammer in the biggest charity auction in the world. This has been held ever since 1859, originally in the Hôtel-Dieu but now in the covered market in Beaune. The proceeds go toward the financing of the Hospices, which was transferred to a modern building as recently as 1971. Only wine merchants accredited in Beaune can make bids. They have two main functions – first, to represent the numerous interested parties, often from abroad, and second, to take responsibility for the further maturing and the bottling of the wine. The Hospices itself does not sell any bottled wine. The auction is still considered an important indicator of how prices are developing in the Côte d'Or region. Since 1872, there has been a general Burgundy wine fair in Beaune over the same weekend. The entrance fee buys a splendid opportunity to taste about 3000 different wines from all the *appellations* in Burgundy.

Right: The wines are auctioned traditionally *à la bougie*, and for this the auctioneer uses a kind of over-sized lighter. When the triple flame goes out, the lot is knocked down to the last bidder.

Marc de Bourgogne

Every year in late fall and winter strange monsters appear in the villages of Burgundy, spewing out smoke and vapor – the mobile distilleries. The master distillers usually settle down on the edge of a village for weeks, or even months, with their trailer-mounted appliances, which are often decades old. The season for the *bouilleurs du cru*, as they are officially known, begins precisely when the winegrowers finish preparing the wine. Their basic material is what the French call the *marc* – the residue that is left over from the grapes when they are pressed. These solid residual grape fragments – predominantly peel and seeds – are referred to as *gène*. For white wines which are directly pressed, these are generated before fermentation, and the must contained in them and adhering to them has first to be fermented before it can be distilled. This does happen automatically, provided the marc is protected from rain and from too much contact with the air. With grape residue from red wines which are created by vat fermentation, the *gènes* already contain a certain proportion of wine, and thus of alcohol.

The distillers prefer the *gènes* to have a high moisture content – meaning that they have not been pressed too forcefully – and have been carefully stored. Winegrowers who bring the distillation master the *gène* from a very average table wine cannot expect to obtain good *marc* as its quality always bears a relation to that of the wine from which the residue was obtained. This means that the vintage is also of importance, as is the winemaking method. Only if the stalks have been removed from the grapes will the *marc* be freed from the astringency, the acidity, and the bitter taste of the stalks. This is why *marc égrappé* – grape spirit without stalks – has been accepted as being of superior quality. Another factor which has a decisive role is how well the *gène* has been preserved. It can certainly be stored without any problems at the beginning of the season. But if it is not distilled until months after pressing, its quality cannot always be guaranteed. The residue can easily become rotten and will then give false tones when distilled. Even a *grand cru* will produce a disappointing *marc* if the residue has not been stored under optimal conditions.

The standard distilling devices known as *alambics* have at least three pot stills. This allows the distiller to work without interruption. While one still is being drained and refilled, the other two are in operation. The grape residue filling the still is steam-heated: the steam rises between the grape solids, separating the alcohol from them

and removing it. The evaporated alcohol is then fed into two cooling vessels. But first it must pass through a rectifier, which allows the master distiller to eliminate "heads" and "tails" which are too weak in alcohol and high in toxins. They can be separated off, because good and poor vapors condense at different rates. The poor or toxic vapors, mainly methanol, are the first to condense and they are returned to the still. Part of the master distiller's skill lies in regulating the cooling temperature in such a way that this process runs smoothly. The good-quality vapors are taken on into the cooling pipes where they condense. They form the "heart" of the distillation (50–75 percent of the total). If some "tails" have slipped through thus reducing the alcohol content, they will give off unpleasant aromas and are eliminated at this stage.

The winegrowers either bring their grape residue so that they can age their own *marc* and market it themselves, or alternatively, they sell it to a firm of liqueur and spirit distillers, or to industry. The well-versed master distiller can decide what the alcohol is later to become, based on the quality of the raw materials, and will not permit any poor *gènes* to be turned into *marc de Bourgogne*. The so-called *fine*, which is known in all wine-producing regions, is distilled, like Cognac or Armagnac, from wine, or from wine plus yeast residues.

The aging of the *marc* is the responsibility of the winegrower or the *liquoriste*, the liqueur-maker. They will both store the *marc* in casks for several years in order to round off its taste and refine it. Although many producers of *marc* nowadays increasingly use new casks for this, traditionalists prefer to swear by old casks and wooden vats which have already served as the cradle for many generations of *marc*. A good *marc* will always have a strong grape aroma and will not belie its character – definitely rooted in the soil – in spite of spices, roundness and the delicacy of long years of maturation.

A wooden conveyor transports the grape residue to the chute which sends it into the stills.

Using several pot stills allows the master distiller to work without interruptions.

The areometer is used to monitor the alcohol content of the grape residue spirit flowing out.

The distillation process completed, the master distiller drains the macerated grape residue from the still.

When the beautifully situated farms of the Jura are cut off from the surrounding world by snow in the winter months, the smoked sausages and hams preserved earlier mean basic nourishment is available.

Smoked products from the Jura

The Jura mountains rise from the broad plain of the Saône, the eastern part of which lies in Burgundy. The Jura region has left its mark on the sausage and ham specialties of Franche Comté. In its mountains, where the farms used to be cut off from the world by winters lasting up to six months, the farmers had to lay in sufficient supplies. And so, in the middle of the gigantic farmhouses, which offered protection to both people and animals under their overhanging roofs, there was a large fireplace (*tuyé*) with an area measuring up to 18 feet square (6 meters square), with a wooden chimney. An ingenious system of bars holds sausages, bacon and ham in the smoke. The *tuyé* itself also included a stove and a bread oven, and was used as a heating system and a washroom. Even cheeses were made here in former times. The *fermes à tuyé* can be found mainly in the Haut-Doubs region near the Swiss border. They are centred around the town of Morteau, which has given its name to the best-known sausage specialty of the region. It is made to a recipe which has not changed since the middle of the 19th century. It consists exclusively of meat from Franche-Comté pigs (80–85 percent lean ham or shoulder meat plus 10–15 percent fatty bacon). Both types of meat are coarsely chopped, mixed with salt and marinated for up to 24 hours. The only other ingredients permitted are sugar, saltpeter and pepper as desired. The sausage is wrapped in pig's intestines and smoked for at least 48 hours over spruce, pine, and juniper chips. If it comes from the Morteau region, was made according to the recipe which has been handed down, and has been smoked in the *tuyé* of a farm over 1970 feet (600 meters) up, then a small wooden peg can be attached at one end and the sausage can be identified by the Morteau logo recognized since 1977. Like its little sister, the *saucisse de Montbéliard*, the Morteau sausage must be cooked. It is put into cold water (without being pricked) and the water is brought to a boil. The sausage is then cooked in boiling water for 30–45 minutes. It forms an indispensable part of the *potée comtoise*, the typical stew of the region, for which it is heated up with vegetables and other smoked meats. White wine from the Jura is frequently added as well. In addition to sauerkraut and curly kale, this kind of sausage goes well with white beans, lentils, fried potatoes, *raclette* (slices of fried cheese) and green salad. It is also good baked in *brioche* dough.

Ham, bacon and sausages are smoked over conifer chips in the enormous chimneys of the typical farmhouses of the Jura.

Smoked specialties of Franche-Comté

Saucisse de Morteau
Morteau boiling sausage
This is the star among the smoked sausage products of Franche-Comté. It is not authentic unless it has the seal and wooden peg.

Jésus de Morteau
Large boiling sausage
Weighing 1–2 pounds (500–1000 grams), this is considerably heavier and is always irregular in shape. It was originally intended for the Christmas season.

Petite Saucisse – Small boiling sausage
The Morteau seal vouches for the origin of this miniature edition of the famous boiling sausage.

Palette fumée – Smoked shoulder of pork
Many parts of the pig were preserved on the farms by salting and smoking; the shoulders were among the favorite cuts.

Saucisse de Montbéliard
Montbéliard boiling sausage
Smaller sausage seasoned and smoked, with garlic and a regional type of caraway seed. It has to be cooked for 20 minutes.

Brési
Smoked beef
The meat must not be too lean for the long, dried French variation on the Swiss *bündnerfleisch*.

Jambon fumé à l'os
Smoked ribs
The ribs are treasured as one of the ingredients which go to make up the *potée comtoise*, the popular and substantial stew of the Jura.

Langue de bœuf fumée
Smoked ham on the bone
Smoked ham at least nine months old is marketed with a seal of origin as *jambon fumé du Haut-Doubs*.

Noix de porc fumée
Smoked oxtongue
Old dairy cattle of the Montbéliard breed provide the Jura with its finest smoked specialties, like the rare smoked tongue.

Jambon cuit à l'os – Cooked ham on the bone
This country ham, cooked on the bone and then smoked, is a rare, fine-flavored delicacy.

Poitrine fumée – Smoked eye of pork
The finest cut from the haunch is also salted and smoked on its own when the rest goes into sausages.

Hams from Luxeuil-les-Bains

Since ancient times, Luxeuil has been known for the beneficial effects of its famous hot springs. But the picturesque town can also delight its visitors' palates as well as look after their good health. Its hams have been making their name since the beginning of the 19th century, and now they may be produced over an area covering 22 communes. The genuine Luxeuil ham comes exclusively from local pigs. Its special feature is that it is initially marinated for four weeks in red Jura wine, together with a special mixture of herbs and spices. Only then is it salted by hand. After this it goes into a refrigeration chamber for a further four weeks. It is then washed down and smoked either over conifer wood, or frequently over wild cherry wood. Finally it matures for five to eight months in drying chambers – for the Haute-Saône region is well known for its cold and dry microclimate. The ham must be at least nine months old to be recognized as genuine Luxeuil ham. By now it has a light brown rind, very tender meat, and a discreet smokey-spicey taste which is only slightly salty.

Some of the ingredients for ham brawn, in which a shoulder replaces the haunch to keep the quantities of managable size.

When enough salt has been removed from the salted shoulder, it is blanched with the pig trotters.

The blanched meat is plunged into cold water and rinsed under flowing water before the actual cooking process begins.

Shoulder of pork and pig trotters, vegetables and seasoning are put into a large cooking pot together.

A bottle of white Burgundy is poured over the meat, vegetables and seasoning, and topped up with cold water.

The meat must simmer for at least 3 hours on a low heat, to become tender and to stay juicy.

The meat is then taken out, boned and cut into small pieces, and the stock is passed through a sieve.

For the stock, finely diced shallots and garlic are braised until they are waxy in a little melted fat.

A generous dash of white Burgundy is added to the lightly braised shallots and garlic cloves.

The gelatine is first soaked in cold water, and then added to the stock and mixed in well.

The crème fraîche is now added, together with 3 cups (750 ml) of the strained meat stock, and the mixture is thoroughly stirred.

The brawn is started with a layer of the stock, which is put into the bottom of the glass bowl with a ladle.

Jambon persillé
tradition bourguignonne
Burgundian ham brawn with parsley

1 salted shoulder of pork	
2 pig trotters	
3 carrots	
1 leek	
2 onions	
1 celery stalk	
Thyme	
Bay leaf	
Cloves	
Coarse sea salt, peppercorns	
1 bottle Aligoté Burgundy	
6 cups/350 g flat-leaf parsley	

Stock	
5 shallots	
5 cloves of garlic	
1 tbsp butter or oil	
1 glass Aligoté Burgundy	
½ oz/10 g gelatin	
½ cup/125 ml crème fraîche	
3 cups/750 ml meat stock	
Freshly-milled salt and pepper	

Leave the pork in cold water for 36 hours, to remove the salt. During this time change the water frequently. Clean the trotters, then blanch them with the pork and plunge them into cold water. Clean the vegetables. Put the pork, trotters, vegetables and seasoning into a saucepan. Pour wine and cold water over them until the meat is just covered. Add a little salt and simmer until done, for about 3 hours. Pour off the liquid and strain it then reduce it slightly. Loosen the meat from the bones and cut it up finely. For the stock, chop the shallots and garlic cloves up finely and braise them lightly in the butter or oil. Add the white wine and let the liquid boil away. Soften the gelatin in cold water for 10 minutes, then add to the stock and fold in. Pour in the crème fraîche and the meat stock. Stir well and season. Chop the parsley up finely. Place a ladleful of stock into a tureen or a glass bowl and sprinkle parsley over it. Arrange small pieces of meat uniformly on top to form another layer. Pour on another layer of stock and sprinkle parsley over it. Repeat this process until the ingredients have been used up. Leave to cool and then let it set for at least 12 hours in the refrigerator. Before serving, turn the mold upside down to release the brawn. Cut it into slices.

The finished ham brawn is considered one of the favorite appetizers in Burgundy.

One of over 200 *fruitières* in the Jura – the small cooperative organizations where skilled craftsmen produce Comté.

King of the mountain cheeses

Comté cheese

As with the excellent smoked hams and sausages, it was the long winters, during which the snow cut off the farms completely from the outside world, that forced the mountain farmers of the Jura to develop a method for storing the milk from their cows. And so they developed a hard cheese, which they compressed into great wheels. Not only could it be stored for one winter without losing anything of its pleasant texture or its fruity taste, but it could even last through the following winter as well – and actually improve in quality. But, since 132 gallons (500 liters) of milk were usually required for a single cheese, even as far back as the

Middle Ages the farmers were already joining together to form little cooperative associations. Each farmer brought the milk from his cows to the *fructerie*, so that it could "bring forth fruit" (*fructifier*). These cooperative cheesemaking plants – nowadays known as *fruitières* – continue to this day. There are over 200 of them making Comté cheese in the Jura. It is closely related to the Swiss Gruyère, and is also known as Gruyère de Comté. This name goes back to the forest wardens of olden days, the *agents gruyères*. Since large amounts of firewood were needed to heat up the milk, the farmers had to provide cheese in exchange as barter. The hazelnut-sized holes usually found in the cheese mixture reminded them of the portion they had to give away, so they soon started to call them *gruyères*. Eventually this became the name of the entire cheese.

The long tradition associated with Comté cheese, which goes back far beyond our own era,

meant that it was one of the first of all cheeses to get an *Appellation d'Origine Contrôlée*, in 1952. Its quality can be attributed to several factors. The Montbéliarde breed of cattle is particularly important. Like the less widespread Pis Rouge de l'Est, the cows provide milk which is especially rich in fat and casein, and which is outstandingly suitable for cheesemaking.

The aroma of the cheese is mainly due to the grasses and herbs eaten by the cows. The specialized flora of the Jura is responsible for the fine taste of the Comté. There are even noticeable variations, which reflect the location of the pastures. But the main difference in the bouquet depends on whether the cows have been fed on grass or hay.

Comté cheese must be made in accordance with all kinds of different regulations. These include a ban on feeding the cows on silage, the use of colorants or other additives. Moreover only

Opposite: A Gruyère de Comté, which normally weighs about 77 pounds (35 kilograms), can be divided into wedges of reasonable size with this special knife.

natural calf's rennet and enzymes from the mountain pastures' flora may be used.

Comté is based exclusively on unpasteurized milk. The farmers deliver the milk to the *fruitière* each day, where it is poured into big copper boilers. It is heated to 89 °F (32 °C) and enzymes and rennet are then added. After about a half hour it has coagulated into a jelly-like mass, which is fragmented into pieces the size of a grain of wheat. The cheese curd is heated to a temperature of 131 °F (55 °C) and stirred constantly, to help the whey to drain off With the help of a linen cloth, the cheesemaster now lifts the curd out of the boiler and transfers it into perforated vessels to separate off the whey. It then goes into the actual mold, a beechwood hoop on a base made of spruce, and is put under the press for 24 hours. After a short period in a cool cellar, which makes the mold stronger and prevents bacterial attacks, the Comté is transferred to a rather warmer cellar for maturation. There it is regularly rubbed down with *morge*, a saturated brine, which forms its natural rind. Its maturing period lasts for at least 90 days, but it can extend to 18 or 24 months. The longer it is matured, the finer and the more pronounced is its fruity aroma, which is reminiscent of hazelnuts.

A Comté has impressive dimensions. Its diameter is 20–28 inches (50–70 centimeters) and its weight is between 66 and 120 pounds (between 30 and 55 kilograms). It cannot be marketed until it has been passed by an inspection committee, which tests and evaluates every cheese. Only when it can meet the high specifications and pass the tests with distinction does it have a green ribbon placed around it and receive the Comté logo with the little green bell. If it is graded only average to good, it receives only a brown ribbon. If it does not even come up to this standard, it loses the right to the Comté *appellation*. It also loses this right if it is to be marketed as grated cheese.

A Comté is displayed to best advantage when it is eaten on its own, particularly if it has a quality obtained by a long period of maturing. The best thing to drink with it is a glass of *vin jaune* from the Jura. This really is one of the most exquisite combinations of wine and cheese. However, younger Comtés have proved their worth in cooking. One famous dish is *ballotine de volaille au Comté* – a thin slice of chicken breast, which is wrapped round with Comté and smoked ham and then cooked in the oven, and served with a cream sauce *au vin blanc du Jura*. But this cheese is very well suited to any kind of dish cooked in the oven or under the broiler, especially quiches. It is also served in small cubes with an aperitive, and makes a good salad ingredient too.

Specialty cheeses from the Jura

Vacherin Mont d'Or
Franche-Comté soft cheese made from unpasteurized milk, which is matured for at least three weeks in boxes made from spruce wood (diameter 5–12 inches/12–30 centimeters). This very creamy cheese -available only from September until March – is also consumed as a fondue. A spoon is used to make a hole in the middle of the cheese. The hole is then filled with Jura wine. After 20 minutes in a hot oven, the melted cheese, which has a strong aroma, is served with potatoes and assorted cooked meats from the Jura. N.B. When wrapped in plastic, this cheese often develops an unpleasant mold.

La Cancoillotte
The mountain farmers make this specialty, also known as *fromagère* from skim milk left over after butter-making. The milk is allowed to coagulate and the whey is drained off, to obtain the *metton*. This is a block which is crumbled and then allowed to ferment until its grains, the size of hazelnuts, become yellowish and give off a strong aroma. It is mixed with brine and butter, in order to obtain the *cancoillotte* – a pleasant, fruity paste, seasoned with white wine, and often with garlic and caraway seeds. As a cheese, it is either eaten hot with potatoes or as an ingredient in scrambled eggs.

Bleu de Gex
A cheese from the Pays de Gex in the Haut-Jura, famous even in the Middle Ages. The only blue mold cheese from the Jura. Made from unpasteurized milk, with a pronounced, slightly piquant, somewhat bitter taste. It is sold, after 2 to 3 months of maturation, in cylinders about 3½ inches (9 centimeters) high, with a diameter of 12 inches (30 centimeters), weighing a good 11 pounds (5 kilograms). Best in summer.

Morbier
Named after a village in the Jura, this mild, hard slicing cheese is made from unpasteurized milk which is merely compressed, but not boiled. The black horizontal stripe running through the cheese halfway up is characteristic. This was originally caused by ash, with which the farmer covered the cheese made from that morning's milk. The ash was washed off in the evening, when the mold was filled up completely with the evening's milk.

Emmental Grand Cru
Produced only from milk from Franche-Comté, the Vosges and Savoy. In contrast to French Emmental, which in general can also be made from sterilized milk, Grand Cru is based on unpasteurized milk and is aged for considerably longer – a minimum of 10 weeks.

1 The milk is heated in big copper boilers and rennet is added to make it coagulate. Then the gelatinous mass is reduced in size and the cheese curd is stirred.
2 With the help of a linen cloth which is pulled under the curd, the cheese mixture is bundled up and the whey is squeezed out.
3 The cloth is tied together so that the cheese mixture can be lifted out of the boiler.

4 The mixture is first put into perforated containers lined with cloths so that any residual whey can run out.
5 The Comté must mature in damp cellars for at least 90 days, but the maturation process frequently takes considerably longer.
6 As part of the process, the cheese has to be regularly turned and rubbed down with brine, which makes the rind form.

The Jura was the home of the notorious absinthe, and Pontarlier was its capital. Nowadays only its aniseed schnapps, which is so clear and green before being diluted with water, recalls the past.

Below: Wormwood (Artemisia absinthum) provided the basic ingredient for absinthe, which is now banned.

Absinthe

Wormwood has been known since the days of antiquity as a medicinal herb used to treat maladies of the stomach and the intestines or loss of appetite. At the end of the 18th century, Dr. Pierre Ordinaire, who came from Franche-Comté, became well-known in what is now the Swiss canton of Neuenburg. He produced a tonic from absinthe, which was not without positive effects. After Ordinaire's death, the Henriod sisters, from the little town of Couvet, purchased the recipe. The two maiden ladies took matters further, and began to distil absinthe and other wild herbs, and to combine them in a *liqueur d'absinthe*. This they sold as a household remedy, with a modest amount of success. It seems the inhabitants of the Jura did not appreciate it for purely medicinal reasons. At all events, Major Dubied enjoyed greater commercial success when he obtained the recipe, and in 1798 he opened a distillery in the little town. He marketed his *extrait d'absinthe* as a spirit. On the other side of the border, in the French Jura, sales were handled by his son-in-law, Henri-Louis Pernod. He was soon selling more bottles of the powerful and highly alcoholic herbal spirit than were bought in Switzerland. However, the Customs duties imposed by Napoleon began to make his schnapps so much more expensive that Pernod was practically compelled to transfer production to France. He opened his own absinthe distillery in Pontarlier, near the frontier, in 1805, producing 4¼ gallons (16 liters) a day. A hundred years later, it was 5285 gallons (20,000 liters) a day. But development was hesitant at first. Pernod's son had already had the monopoly for two decades before absinthe slowly began to make a commercial breakthrough, even if its success was still based on the medicinal effect of the herb. This led to the establishment of three more distilleries in Pontarlier in the period around 1826.

Twenty-five years later, it had become the custom in Paris and in other big French cities to meet in cafés in the late afternoon or early evening and drink absinthe. The Swiss emblem, the cross, still stood resplendent on the label – a promise of purity. The schnapps distilled from *Artemisia absinthium* (wormwood), aniseed, and fennel was not drunk neat. Unsweetened, and with an alcohol content of 65–72 percent by volume, it had to have water and sugar added. Very soon, this was to develop into a ritual with its own rules. First, some absinthe was poured into the glass. Then a special perforated spoon containing the sugar lumps was balanced on the edge. A fine jet of cold water was trickled over this, tipping off some of the sugar. This sweetened and diluted the absinthe, took on a milky green coloration.

Because of this color, people were soon talking of "the green hour" or calling the drink "the green fairy." Its devotees included poets such as Apollinaire and Baudelaire, Rimbaud and Verlaine, as well as large numbers of the middle classes, not to mention military officers. It was considered fashionable to drink absinthe, and it was a relatively inexpensive pleasure.

But the habit slowly became less exclusive until, by the last quarter of the 19th century, absinthe had become a mass-consumption beverage. In the *fin de siècle* era, to be a person of leisure was the ideal. There was an army of people who had taken early retirement – former officials, military officers and business people, who spent their time in cafés and selected absinthe as their usual tipple. At the same time, the price became cheaper and cheaper, and the quality worse and worse. Soon manual workers and clerks were also acquiring the habit of popping into a café after work and indulging in what usually turned out to be several glasses of absinthe before going home.

But there was a price to be paid for these pleasures. Many absinthe drinkers began to show symptoms of physical and mental deterioration. Thujone – an ingredient of absinthe which, if exposed to oxygen, can oxidize and produce the toxic substance thujol – was held to be responsible. (It is probable that the reduction in the quality of the alcohol was the real cause.) Meanwhile, business was booming (there were 22 distilleries in Pontarlier when consumption of absinthe was at its height) and warnings from doctors fell on deaf ears. The Government refused to take responsibility, while the highly esteemed and highly taxed spirit filled up its coffers very nicely. The outbreak of World War I led to the confiscation of alcohol and the sale of absinthe was forbidden by a law passed in 1915.

This was a death sentence for most of the distilleries in Pontarlier. But some survived the "Prohibition era" and tried to find substitute products. It was discovered that aniseed, which was confirmed as harmless by a Government decree of 1922, was particularly suitable. However, there were detailed conditions appended, which insisted on a high sugar content, so that this liqueur-type beverage could not replace the bitter absinthe as an aperitive. It was not until 1932 that a suitable recipe was approved by the French Government. Pontarlier heaved a sigh of relief. Pernod, the former market leaders, were able to build immediately on earlier successes, and remained faithful to the manufacturing principles of herb distillation. The new aperitive was based on green aniseed and was already sweetened. But it still had to be diluted with water like absinthe. As for other distilleries competing in the market, *pastis*, the product from the Provencal distillers Ricard, came out on top. "Anis de Pontarlier" is now no longer heard of outside the Jura region, where people still like to order a "Pon" even today.

This aperitive is distilled only from green aniseed, and takes on its typical milky coloration when water is added.

Here at Pontarlier-Anis, they understand the absinthe ritual. To sweeten the drink, a perforated spoon containing sugar lumps was laid across the glass, and spring water was trickled carefully over it.

Franche-Comté kirsch

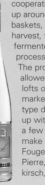

The Haut-Saône region, in the north of Franche-Comté, which borders on the Burgundian Côte d'Or, the Vosges of Lorraine and the Haut-Rhin area of Alsace, is considered the cradle of kirsch. In Fougerolles, where extremely aromatic cherries have long been cultivated, an 18th-century monk had the idea of distilling schnapps from them. He had the compressed fruit fermented, and from the cherry wine he distilled *eau-de-vie de cérise*. Many people were ready to follow his example. The farmers tended and picked their pit fruit and did their own distillation, or else formed themselves into cooperatives. An entire branch of industry sprang up around the distillation process, supplying baskets, casks and bottles. Following the harvest, the cherries were mashed and fermented for several weeks. The distillation process went on from September to March. The products of the highest quality were allowed to mature for three to five years in the lofts of the farms before they were put on the market. In the 20th century, the small artisan-type distilleries had a hard time trying to keep up with their industrial-scale competitors. But a few well-organized firms, which now also make spirits from other fruit, have survived in Fougerolles and in nearby Mouthier-Haute-Pierre, and they continue to market their kirsch, with its exquisite bouquet.

The wines of the Jura

These are not given the recognition they deserve. The wide range of varied wines extends from highly concentrated sweet varieties to extremely dry white wines, from sparkling wines to liqueur wines, from quaffable rosés to long-aging reds. They include simple everyday wines at low prices, but also some of the most original and the rarest wines in France.

Wine has been made in the Jura since the days of antiquity. But the region and its wines attracted special attention in 1860, when Louis Pasteur, the father of modern enology, provided a scientific explanation for the phenomenon of fermentation. This was when wine making in the Jura was at its height and more than 20,000 hectares (49,420 acres) were planted with vines. Then, at the turn of the 20th century, came the *phylloxera* catastrophe.

Nowadays, the area planted with vines is about 1850 hectares (4571 acres). It extends over a strip measuring almost 63 miles (100 kilometers) between Salins-les-Bains and Saint-Amour de Franche-Comté. To the east, the vinegrowing area is bounded by the massif of the Jura, rising to over 5500 feet (1700 meters). To the west, the area stretches to the plain of Bresse. Its height varies from 820 feet (250 meters) to 1575 feet (480 meters). The locations face west, southwest and sometimes south. The soils consist mainly of blue and black marl, and sometimes in the north of chalk rubble or slate as well. This is very suitable for the white varieties, while the reds do well on red marl. The climate is one of hard winters and hot summers, followed by falls which are usually very sunny. However good these preconditions are for grapes, the winegrowers are terrified of spring frosts.

Vin jaune

Vin de paille (straw wine), or *vin jaune* (yellow wine) – these are probably the most unusual Jura wines. *Vin jaune* is produced only here, and only from the Savagnin grape, and its stronghold is Château-Chalon – an *appellation* which is reserved for this wine alone. It prefers soils of blue and black marl or slate, on which layers of chalk rubble or flint pebbles have been deposited. Its locations are steep, to ensure that it receives optimal sunlight. The grapes are not picked until October. It is fermented, like any other white wine, so that no residual sugar remains behind. It

Below: Arbois is the center of the largest production area, and is known, not just for the superb *vin jaune*, but also for fine, full-bodied red wines.

Louis Pasteur, the famous French chemist, discovered the secrets of fermentation in the Jura, where he was born. The grapes from his vineyard are still separately fermented.

is then drained off into 228-liter (60-gallon) wooden casks, which are not filled right to the top. After maturing for six years, only 63 centiliters (about 2¾ cups) remain from every liter (quart) of wine, thanks to evaporation. This is precisely the capacity of the *clavelin*, the special bottle used for *vin jaune*. Contact with the air in the cellar leads to the development of a special yeast occuring in the Jura (*saccharomyces oviformis*), which forms a veil on the surface of the wine. It thus protects the wine, preventing it from turning into vinegar through contact with the air, and slowing down oxidation. This gives the wine the *goût de jaune*, the typical taste, which recalls a dry sherry. And yet, depending on the soil and the grower, it also calls to mind walnuts, hazelnuts, undergrowth, spices, and numerous other scents. The taste remains just as distinctive from one day to the next, and yet the notes in the bouquet have now altered. *Vin jaune* can be drunk at cellar temperature, but it is better when not too cold. It should be decanted so that it can develop fully. *Vin de paille*, which is not found anywhere in abundance, is made from grapes of the Savagnin, Chardonnay, and Poulsard varieties which are allowed to shrivel on the vine. They are individually picked and are bedded on straw to dry. They are then suspended in wooden frames, or stored in perforated cases. The first ten days are the trickiest. Two months later, the raisins are pressed. The sugar content of the must is enormous, and its consistency is like syrup. Low-temperature fermentation takes months. When it is complete, the wine is poured into oak casks. The result is an extremely rich, powerful and sweet nectar. It is drunk, slightly cooled, with desserts, or with *foie gras*.

The *clavelin*, the *vin jaune* bottle, holds 63 centiliters – exactly the quantity left over from 1 liter after six years of maturing.

The green and blue grapes hanging down from the kitchen ceiling are being dried for *vin de paille*.

The grape varieties

Chardonnay: Sometimes also called Melon d'Arbois, this widely distributed white Burgundy strain has been native to the Jura for a long time, and accounts for half the area planted with vines. Chardonnay pleases by its fruitiness and roundness. When blended with Savagnin, it provides the more accessible accent in the subtle, and yet initially confusing taste of the Jura wines. However, even all on its own it displays the unmistakable Jura character.

Savagnin: The king of the Jura grape varieties and the basis of *vin jaune* and *vin de paille*, this also accounts for one-fifth of the production area for fresh white wines. The origin of this white, late-harvested variety is still a mystery, and the long-assumed kinship with the Traminer grape is not confirmed. It is typified by its nut notes and by the great complexity of its flavors, which it develops through aging.

Pinot Noir: Like the Chardonnay, the late Burgundian grape arrived in the Jura in the 14th century, and is now grown in one-tenth of the vineyards. Here it rarely attains sufficient quality on its own, and is added to the other two red varieties because of its beautiful fruit.

Poulsard: Originally called Plousard, it is a genuine child of the Jura, above all of the northern part of the region, and accounts for a fifth of the vines. It produces a delicately fruited and quaffable red wine, which is not infrequently more like a rosé in color, and is therefore known as *vin gris* (gray wine). It grows mainly in Pupillin and Arbois, and sometimes ages well. In L'Etoile it is made into white wine.

Trousseau: Known as Bastardo in Portugal and not highly regarded, this variety reached the Jura by an unknown route. In its hard climate, it shows unexpected character, provided production remains limited. It then produces powerful, well-structured and long-aging wines. Part of the 5 percent of the vine stocks represented by Trousseau is blended with Poulsard to produce red wine which has a character of its own.

The appellations

Arbois: Just 850 hectares (2100 acres) of vines, distributed over 12 communes, of which only Pupillin, which is known mainly for its good Poulsard, is entitled to precede the word "Arbois" on the label. Nowadays, the *appellation* covers equal amounts of red and white wines.

Château-Chalon: About 50 hectares (124 acres) in 4 communes, which are dedicated exclusively to *vin jaune*. The growers have come together to form a committee that tests the grapes for maturity and health before they are picked. In poor years the right to use the *appellation* is withheld.

L'Etoile: 80 hectares (198 acres) in 3 communes; white wine only, but in any form: dry white wine, Crémant, *vin jaune*, *vin de paille* or Macvin. The marl soils are interspersed with tiny star-shaped fossils which have given the commune and the *appellation* their names.

Côtes du Jura: 620 hectares (1531 acres) in 60 communes; the best-known are Poligny, Voiteur, Arlay, Le Vernois, Gevingey, Rotarlier, and Beauffort. Every kind of wine is recognized as Côtes du Jura, whether it be white, red, rosé or the *vin de paille*, yellow sparkling wine, Macvin, or even Marc du Jura.

Crémant du Jura: Sparkling wine can also boast of a tradition going back over 200 years in the Jura. As with Champagne, a second fermentation takes place in the bottle.

Macvin: This has been known for at least 200 years. Produced from fresh-pressed must and *marc*, which prevents fermentation, it stores a great deal of grape sugar, and is drunk as an aperitive or with desserts.

Lyon
Rhône-Alpes

Sharon Sutcliffe
André Dominé

Poultry breeder with a Bresse fowl.

The specific microclimate of the north Rhône assists the maturing of rare wines, as in the St. Joseph appellation

Calais

Le Havre

Caen

Brest

Rennes

Paris

Strasbourg

Orléans

Nantes

Tours

Dijon

Limoges

Lyon
Rhône-Alpes

Bordeaux

Avignon

Nice

Biarritz

Toulouse

Marseille

Toulon

Perpignan

Rhône-Alpes, with its capital in Lyon, is about as big as Switzerland, and is no less rich in contrasts. Stretching from the Alpine peaks to the forests, from the lush farmlands of the Ain to the gorges of the Ardèche, it contains everything to make a gourmet's heart beat faster. The markets of Lyon or Saint-Etienne, Grenoble or Valence are almost overflowing with an abundance of fruit and early vegetables from the Rhône valley, with the fantastic poultry of Bresse and the guinea fowls of the Drôme, and with tasty fish from the Dombes lakes or from mountain streams.

Lyon and Savoy are famous for their sausages, but at the same time the Alpine regions supply outstanding cheeses such as the impressive Abondance, the creamy Reblochon, the robust Tommes, and the delicate Vacherins, which often provide the finishing touch on a Christmas menu. The well-balanced variety of this cheese-board is supplemented by the popular goat's milk cheeses from the hilly area around Lyon.

The city lies at the intersection of important trade routes established since ancient times. From the days of the Romans, it was a meeting point where different civilizations could discover each other's foods and recipes. From the 16th century, silk merchants began bringing back exotic spices and culinary techniques to the Rhône from distant lands. Later it was the well-to-do middle classes who were always eager for new and unusual dishes. As the 19th century drew to an end, many cooks were deprived of their employment, so some set up on their own and stamped their mark on the gastronomy of the city. They were known as the *mères lyonnaises* and, depending on their customers' tastes, their cuisine could be expensive and elaborate or simple and low-budget, but always tasty and nourishing. They also drew inspiration from the butchers' skills to create good food at low prices. An informed knowledge of the excellent fresh products of the region fostered the genius of some of the greatest and most influential French cooks: Fernand Point, Paul Bocuse, the Troisgros brothers and Alain Chapel. Nor was there ever any lack of good wine. For, according to an old saying, there is a third river which flows through the city in addition to the Saône and the Rhône – the Beaujolais. Experienced palates appreciate the wide range available. They can choose between the tangy wines of Savoy, the Burgundies from an adjacent region and, of course, the equally magnificent and rare wines from the northern Rhône.

Lyon: Bistrot & bouchon

It was no accident that Maurice Edmond Saillard, the famous writer on food and drink known as Curnonsky (1872–1956), referred to Lyon as the capital of gastronomy, considering the city's optimal strategic position, from the culinary point of view. Within easy reach are the celebrated poultry of Bresse, the superb meat from Charolais cattle, the outstanding fish of the Dombes, game and fungi from the nearby forests, and fine cheeses from the hills of the Lyonnais and Beaujolais, as well as the exquisite fruit and young vegetables of the Rhône valley. Before the northern gates of the city, grow the grapes which are used to make the very drinkable Beaujolais wine, and to the south lie the lands of the magnificent northern Rhône wines such as Côte-Rôtie and Hermitage.

Many well-to-do gourmets have lived in Lyon during the course of its history, whether they be Romans, medieval princes of the church, bankers, merchants or silk manufacturers. Their cooks created exquisite dishes from the rich variety of ingredients on offer. After the French Revolution and during the Second Empire, the pleasures of the table were held in high esteem in the houses of the bourgeoisie and the textile magnates, and people began to develop their tastes. Families who were well-off often had country estates, from which they obtained not only the best ingredients but also the cooks to do them justice. But then came the Franco-Prussian War of 1870–71, with the collapse of the Empire, and eventually World War I. Many of Lyon's cooks lost their jobs in these periods of crisis. Some were bold enough to open their own restaurants, where they prepared exactly the same dishes which they had previously set before their employers. In doing this, *les mères*, as they were collectively known, kept to familiar ingredients and to what were often no more than a handful of tried and trusted recipes.

A much larger and hungrier clientele was made up of the blue-collar workers, *les canuts*, who earned their bread in the textile industry and as packers in the warehouses. They found *mères* of their own, who cooked for them with the same dedication, but with less costly ingredients, and for less money. They used the meat the fine folk disdained, such as the entrails and the tougher undercuts of beef and veal. But above all, they used a lot of pork, as well as fish such as carp, and eels, which they combined with onions, butter, cream and generous amounts of wine. This was the beginning of the cuisine of the *bistros, bouchons et porte-pots*, which became typical of Lyon. These establishments were initially open primarily between six and nine o'clock in the morning,

The *pot du Beaujolais* holds 46 centiliters (about 1 pint) – the right amount to satisfy the thirst of a mature and experienced man, so the saying goes.

when industrial workers on the night and early morning shifts, crews from the boats on the Rhône and employees from the covered markets needed to fortify themselves. They could choose from hot boiled sausages, chitterling sausages, smoked bacon, or the famous tripe *gras-double*, or the version covered in breadcrumbs, *tablier de sapeur* (fireman's apron), braised calf's trotters or stuffed pig's trotters. The finishing touch was contributed by Saint-Marcellin or *Cervelle de canut*

(literally, workman's brain), a low-fat curd cheese prepared with garlic and herbs. This was washed down with Beaujolais or Côtes du Rhône, which was poured out from the *pot* – a heavy carafe holding 46 centiliters (about 1 pint). These simple cafés and their cuisine proved irresistible, not just to the workers but to their supervisors and managers. Everyone sat down side by side here and ate the same substantial dishes. This kind of breakfast, referred to as a *mâchon*, has

The "Bistrot de Lyon" became the eating place that sparked off the renaissance of the old Rue Mercière, which runs between the Rhône and the Saône.

Linen napkins, good cutlery, proper wine glasses: they know how to treat their faithful customers.

In Lyon, people are knowledgeable about food. They like the relaxed atmosphere of the *bistros et bouchons*, which offer substantial, high-quality country cooking at reasonable prices.

largely fallen victim to changing ways of living and working. But the Lyonnais have retained their love of food. They are still fond of dishes rooted in the tradition of the farmhouse kitchen, and of the relaxed atmosphere of the *bistros et bouchons*, of which the city has many. One which became famous was the "Bistrot de Lyon," which Jean-Paul Lacombe opened in the Rue Mercière, two years after he had succeeded his father at the "Léon de Lyon." By following the pattern of the traditional

The clientele is critical and reserved at first. But once they're won over, they remain loyal. The people of Lyon love eating out, and many guests are regular visitors.

bouchon, he and his restaurant were at the forefront of the renaissance of this old shopping street, which had fallen into disrepute. At the same time Lacombe, as a gastronomic leader, set an example which sparked off a movement.

Lyon bistro cuisine

Le Grand Dessert de la "Vogue" de la Croix Rousse
The "Vogue" is the name of a traditional festival in the Croix Rousse area of the town This dessert combines the sweet-tasting ingredients typical of this occasion: candied apple, strips of marshmallow and a roast almond tart which was originally a dish from Saint-Genix.

Rouget barbet aux épices
An entire red mullet has various spices rubbed into it and is pan-fried. It is served with a saffron and vegetable butter and a small mangold tart wrapped in leaves.

Saint-Cochon au Bistrot
The constituent parts of Saint Pig, in the bistro tradition, are a *sabodet*, a bacon and pig's head sausage, a grilled pig's head brushed with mustard, blood sausage, apple and onion sauce.

Choux farci au lapin de garenne, braisé au serpolet
Cauliflower, stuffed with wild rabbit, bread, diced apple, spices, walnuts and celery, is braised in the oven with wild thyme (*serpolet* in French).

Paleron de bœuf lardé
Larded shoulder of beef is slowly braised over a long period of time. To this are added wild mushrooms in season, diced calf's trotters and potatoes. Shoulder meat – which is also larded with bacon – is ideal for this slow-braised dish.

Andouillette en rouelles
Slices of chitterling sausage, which in Lyon is prepared from calf's intestine and herbs, are served with Lyonnais potatoes, fried in goose fat with onions, and a cream sauce with coarse-grained mustard.

Œufs à la neige
Floating islands are a classic dessert, consisting of beaten egg white and sugar, which is poached in the oven, decorated with roasted almonds and served with a vanilla sauce, *sauce anglaise*.

Salade Lyonnaise
Lyonnais salad is made from curly endive and other kinds of lettuce, which are mixed with fresh herbs. It is seasoned with an olive oil and mustard vinaigrette, scattered with garlic croutons and garnished with a poached egg.

Remoulade de pieds de mouton
Sheep's trotters in a remoulade are made to a traditional recipe from Jean Vignard. They are boned and are served with hard-cooked eggs, slices of potato and a fine herb mayonnaise.

Saucissonaille
A Lyonnais sausage dish which is based on the two most important types of dried sausage from the city – the dry, coarse-grained *rosette* and the finely ground *saucisson*. To these are added bread, butter, pickled gherkins and pickled onions.

Fondant de foies de volaille aux avocats et concassée de tomates
Chicken liver fondant with avocados and tomatoes is a refreshing summer recipe, seasoned with southern herbs. It is spread on little slices of freshly baked olive bread.

Médaillons de tartare de truite et saumon fumé
Trout tartare and smoked salmon medallions, which consist of raw ground trout, seasoned with lemon, olive oil and fresh herbs and wrapped in thin slices of home-cured salmon. They are served with lemon cream sauce and slices of toast.

Soupe blanche de poisson et flan de choux fleur
White fish soup with cauliflower flan appears on the menu at the beginning of the winter. It is prepared from sea fish, and the mild-flavored cauliflower makes it a well-balanced entrée, to which the croutons add the bistro flair.

Quenelle de brochet "Nandron"
Pike dumplings from the recipe of Gérard Nandron, who has obtained two Michelin stars for his restaurant, "Johannès," and who serves this classic Lyonnais dish with a crustacean-based *sauce américaine* and river crab butter.

Sausage specialties from Lyon

Lyon is one of the great centers of the butcher's art. It is the respect paid to the less glamorous parts of the animal, such as the head, trotters and chitterlings, which has formed the basis of Lyon's tradition of high-quality cuisine at reasonable prices. It lies at the origins of, for example, the regional version of *andouillettes* and of *saboudet*, made from pig's head and bacon rind. Anyone who can turn even entrails into tasty sausages must be able to create masterpieces from more noble ingredients. And thus *saucisson de Lyon*, *rosette* and *cervelas* are accepted as among the gastronomic symbols of the city. *Saucisson* and *rosette* fall into the category of dry, salami-type sausages, which were formerly air-dried in the nearby hills of the Lyonnais. *Cervelas* is an exquisitely spiced boiling sausage.

Saucisson de Lyon

The pre-condition for a high-class *saucisson sec* is the right meat, from mature pigs, which has a low water content, is firm and red, and which has to be very fresh. For the best quality, the cuts selected are the hams and the shoulders. The meat is boned, with the veins, tendons, nerves, skin, etc. being removed, and it is then cut into relatively large cubes. The maximum proportion of fat laid down for *rosette* and *saucisson de Lyon* is 25 percent. The diced bacon in the meat is cut from fresh bacon which has been in cold storage for two days. The bacon is mechanically ground together with the other meat. This is deliberately done slowly, so that the mixture

The Reynon brothers are famous for their first-class *cervelas* and *saucissons*, and the next generation shows every sign of promise.

does not heat up. The seasonings – mainly sea salt and pepper – are added to and thoroughly integrated with the mixture. For manual preparation, the meat mixture is then spread out on a stainless steel table and beaten as hard as possible by hand, to expel the air and to give the mixture the desired consistency. The butcher shapes it into large balls and stores it in the cold room overnight. The next day, the mixture is stuffed into natural skins. The sausages are now placed in the drying oven, in which they are first pre-dried, at a temperature of about 75 °F/24 °C, until they have lost about 10 percent of their moisture content. They are now either wrapped in yarn to give them a uniform shape, or else the heavier ones are put into a net, so that they can be suspended without damaging the skins. The drying, which nowadays usually takes place in temperature-controlled and ventilated chambers, lasts a good month and a half for *saucisson de Lyon*, at about 55 °F/12 °C, during which the sausage loses one-third of its original weight. The only difference between *saucisson de Lyon*, *rosette* and *Jésus* is the size of the skin used. The filling is identical. But the sausage's drying time is dependent on its diameter. This is what influences the taste. A *Jésus* is thus dried longer and develops a more pronounced taste.

Cervelas de Lyon

In the 16th century, when Italian silk merchants and bankers were setting the fashion in Lyon, the secrets of Italian gastronomy also crossed the banks of the Rhône and the Saône. They must have included the recipe for *cervelas*, since it is thought to have originated in Florence. Its ingredients originally included brains (*cervelle*), which is where its name comes from. Nowadays, it consists of lean shoulder meat, mixed together with belly meat and bacon in a ratio of 3:1. The meat is seasoned with salt, pepper, nutmeg and sugar, and is then cooled for two days before it is put through the grinder. The flavorings added to the mixture include port, madeira or cognac, but above all finely chopped truffles and/or pistachios, and frequently morels as well. The meat is then stuffed straight into skins, which are tied off to give the desired length. These are then left to dry overnight at 85 °F/30 °C, which gives them a fine color. It is a fresh meat product and must be kept in cold storage.

Truffles (*cervelas truffé* must have a truffle content of at least 3 percent) give the meat an incomparable flavor. But they also make it more expensive, which is why this type of sausage tends to be reserved for important occasions. Those trying not to spend too much money on their cooking choose a simple *saucisson à cuire*. These boiling sausages are cooked without being pricked, in hot water at 195 °F/90 °C for 30–40 minutes per pound (500 grams).

1 Saucisson sec
2 Jésus
3 Saucisson à cuire
4 Rosette
5 Saucisson de Lyon
6 Cervelas aux pistaches
7 Cervelas truffé et pistaché
8 Saucisson à cuire
9 Cervelas aux morilles et aux pistaches
10 Saucisson à cuire

Lean meat and bacon are diced with a knife and then put through the grinder.

It may sound quite surprising, but salt and pepper are the two most important seasonings in a dry sausage.

The butcher takes the meat, formed into balls, out of the machine to prepare it on a stainless steel table.

He tosses and beats the meat mixture as vigorously as he can, for the air must penetrate so that the mixture becomes firmer.

Chocolate in Lyon

Around the year 1900 Lyon, which was already famous for its cuisine, established itself as the capital of the *chocolatiers*, the chocolate makers. All those who wished to devote themselves conscientiously to this art selected and mixed their own cocoa beans. They then roast and ground them to refine the mixture further, and thus obtained a coverture all of their own, which was the pride of every master of the art and the point of origin for every exquisite creation. That's all in the past now. There is only one company left in Lyon which still makes its own chocolate: Bernachon. "What the great lovers of chocolate are looking for is the taste of cocoa," says Maurice Bernachon.

This taste has come a long way. Cocoa beans were first cultivated by the Mayas and later by the Aztecs, who considered them sacred and expensive. The beans were not only used in the preparation of a fortifying drink but also served as a means of payment. Columbus, who landed on the island of Guanaja in 1502, was the first European to taste cocoa, and Hernán Cortés brought it to Spain. From the 17th century onward, cocoa conquered France, and the first chocolate factory, the Chocolaterie Royale, opened in Bayonne in 1776. With the 19th century begins the history of chocolate as a mass consumption product, a fact testified to by Van Houten in the Netherlands, Meunier in France, Suchard, Nestlé and Lindt in Switzerland and Fry, Rowntree and Cadbury in England. Rotterdam became the trade center for cocoa beans, although it was in Bordeaux that the experts were to be found.

As with wine, there are also high-quality and less valuable types of cocoa. There are prime locations and mediocre growing areas. A distinction is made between the robust *forasteros* and the delicate *criollos*. The *trinitarios* are a cross between the first two types, yielding a great deal of cocoa butter, and nowadays accounting for about 20 percent of the world harvest. The fine, aromatic *criollos* scarcely account for 10 percent, while the *forasteros*, with their bitter, slightly acidic taste, are the market leaders with 70 percent.

Cocoa trees are not easy to cultivate. They like it warm, humid and shady – conditions which they can find only in the tropical belt between 20° north and 20° south. And they call for patience. They do not produce their first real crop for ten years, and although after that they may yield up to 100,000 blossoms per year per tree, only about 200 of them will bear fruit. Each of the cucumber-like fruits which ripens will have 20–50 seeds growing inside it – the cocoa beans. They are removed, along with some remains of the flesh of the fruit, and tipped into aerated wooden boxes to ferment. They break down bitter substances and build up aromatic substances in the heat of the fermentation process. They are then dried, and finally they go on their travels. In the consumer country, the raw material for chocolate is roasted in order to release the flavors. Depending on the type of cocoa, this happens at 355–390 °F (180–200 °C), after about 20 minutes.

The *chocolatiers* at Bernachon now put together mixtures of beans, which are balanced by type, and these are then ground. Cocoa butter is added in order to obtain a paste. In the next step, sugar and vanilla beans are rolled into the mixture. In order to eradicate bitterness and acidity and make the chocolate malleable, it must be agitated in a vertical turning mill for between one and three days – part of the time under vacuum. The coverture is then ready, and is poured out to form large tablets which have a cocoa content of 63–70 percent. Anything else which goes into the chocolate, whether it be cinnamon, tea or coffee, ginger, licorice or pepper, nuts or dried fruit, is left to the creativity of the maestro. And this work of art is worth its price. It needs to be carefully looked after, being stored at 70 °F (20 °C) for no longer than three weeks. As if anybody could!

Cocoa beans of various origins are mixed together for a first-class coverture.

At Bernachon, an unerring sense of smell and taste is one of the artisan's indispensable tools.

The ingredients are the decisive factor for the quality of the coverture; the color and consistency are also influenced by the temperature.

Hazelnut chocolate made from the finest, best-quality nuts in a homemade chocolate coverture.

When every nut is in place, a final layer of chocolate is spread over them.

Hérisson – chocolate hedgehog – is a Lyon classic and forms part of the repertoire of every confectioner.

The icing bag, with its many different tips, is an indispensable tool in pastrywork and confectionery. Here chocolate candy molds are being filled.

Artistry with pureé sauces

From time immemorial, there has been a visual aspect to the enjoyment of food. Even in earlier times, this impelled chefs and pastrycooks to create works of art. The most famous of these were the creations of Antonin Carème, the king of chefs, which were unbelievably lavish from a modern point of view. At the beginning of the 19th century, he responded with genius to high society's penchant for beautiful exteriors. His brilliance showed in his exquisite recipes as much as in his polished patisserie, which reached its high point in reproductions of famous buildings and in allegorical tableaux, which were constructed from sponge and from every conceivable type of confectionery.

Following in this great tradition, today's desserts naturally call for a finishing touch which is at least as attractive, but not quite so expensively lavish. Purée sauces are the ideal answer. The sauces are prepared from sugar mixed with berries which are raw or only lightly cooked. Their bright colors depend on the fruit which is used, or stem from nuts or covertures. The sauces can be transformed, with the help of a simple knife-blade – but with a great deal of taste and artistic talent – into amazing patterns (and even into complete pictures), which have only a single disadvantage, that of being very ephemeral. But they have one undeniable advantage, which is that they are pleasing to more than the eye alone. When we look over the shoulder of those using sauces to create such images, it is clear that they

Conjured up on the plate using nothing but a knife, intricate designs provide a touch of class to sherbets.

Ornamental decorations like these are classics. The colors must never run together under any circumstances.

The impromptu artist may also be inspired to create purée landscapes: beautiful, colorful and extremely ephemeral.

are essentially using age-old skills to interweave the various colors of the sauce. These skills were originally used to manufacture special colored papers for book bindings. Now, as then, the consistency of the liquids is the deciding factor, and it must be able to prevent any premature and uncontrolled spreading of the colors. A picture of this kind is destroyed the moment the sauces mix together or react adversely to each other. Thus, for example, any attempt to experiment with kiwi purée sauce and cream must be abandoned – the cream is bound to run.

Left: An older maître d'hôtel taught Jean-Philippe Monot the art of creating intricate designs in purée sauces of different colors.

Mousse au chocolat
Chocolate mousse

10½ oz/300 g best semisweet chocolate
4 egg yolks
⅔ cup/130 g sugar
3½ tbsp/50 ml cream
8 egg whites

Melt the chocolate in a double boiler.
Whisk the egg yolks with 4 teaspoons of sugar until frothy (1). Then stir in the cream (2). Draw the chocolate under the egg yolk and sugar mixture (3). Whisk the egg white with the remaining sugar until stiff (4) and fold under the chocolate mixture (5/6). Fill glasses or small molds with the mousse and serve cold.

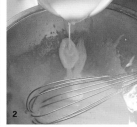

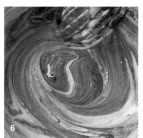

Beaujolais

Let's get one thing out of the way right at the start. The Beaujolais region has never belonged to Burgundy, even if it is part of *Bourgogne viticole*, the Greater Burgundy winemaking area, and its northern tip does form part of the Burgundian *département* of Saône-et-Loire. The Saône forms the eastern boundary of the Beaujolais area. The slopes which face it are covered with vineyards, while above and behind them rise the forested Monts du Beaujolais. In the north, the Beaujolais hills reach almost as far as the famous cliff of Solutré, and in the south they merge, without a break, into the Monts du Lyonnais. In the west the slopes become more gradual as the neighboring *département* of the Loire begins.

No other French red wine is as world-famous as Beaujolais. This is the kingdom of the Gamay, a prolific strain of red grape. In the 14th century, it had even conquered the best sites in the Côte d'Or, which aroused the wrath of Philip the Bold, Duke of Burgundy and a lover of the great Pinot grape. In 1395, without further ado, he ordered that the "infamous" Gamay should be rooted out. The Gamay variety continued to hold its own in the Mâconnais, although in that region it produces completely different red wines, more reserved and stronger. It finds its finest expression on the crystalline soils of the northern Beaujolais, in the *crus*. Nine of the ten *crus* (the exception is the most recently selected, Régnié) have also obtained the right to label their Gamay as Burgundy. The only other varieties which are entitled to the Burgundy *appellation* in the Beaujolais are Chardonnay and Pinot Noir, which are rarely planted there, so such wines are few and far between.

With a few exceptions, the gastronomy of Beaujolais is good rather than great. One can consume eggs in red wine sauce, pike perches with sorrel, *coq au vin* or *boeuf bourguignon* with enjoyment and with pleasure. A special mention should go to the *cochonailles*, the sausages and *pâtés*. The most famous of the outstanding butchers of Beaujolais is René Besson, known as Bobosse. He has his fine *andouillette* in particular to thank for that. *Cochonailles* play an important part in the *mâchon*. Just as the workers of Lyon fortified themselves early in the morning with this substantial breakfast, so the vine-growing Beaujolais region developed its own form of the *mâchon* for the winegrowers and vineyard workers. In earlier times, especially when the grapes were being harvested, this was a match for the version from Lyon. Gradually it has become less ample, and now serves as a snack for the winegrowers, who begin their work in the vineyards while the dew is still rising. So the basket will contain dried sausages and smoked bacon, good farm-baked bread, a bottle of Beaujolais and, last but not least, a few cheeses from the Monts du Beaujolais.

These little cheeses, made by the farmers on their farms from goat's milk and/or cow's milk, are specialties which are so prized in Beaujolais and in Lyon that you hardly ever find them outside the region. If ever there is a leftover *pur chèvre*, a *mi-chèvre* (over 50 percent goat's milk), a *fermier* (composition unspecified) or a *vache* left over, then it is turned into *fromage fort*. The cheese is grated with gruyère and a little sour cheese mixture is added. This mixture is then continuously stirred while a stock made from leeks and a little dry white wine is poured over it, until a soft, but not liquid, paste is obtained. This is spread on bread and is preferably lightly toasted. It is then served with a young, fruity and well-structured Beaujolais.

The color of the masonry in a typical vineyard in the southern Beaujolais is reminiscent of fresh-baked bread, although the region is known as the *Pays des Pierres Dorées*, the land of the golden stones.

Left: In the Beaujolais the *mâchon* is a proper breakfast, which the winegrowers eat in the vineyard, where they have already been working since daybreak or earlier.

It consists, above all, of *cochonailles*, various kinds of sausage, bacon and *pâtés*, as well as the small cheeses which are typical of the Beaujolais hills, good solid farm-baked bread and, naturally, a red, or occasionally a white, Beaujolais.

Working in the vineyard makes them hungry, so the winegrowers like to have a proper breakfast in the course of the morning, which naturally would not be the same without a fruity Beaujolais.

Le Beaujolais nouveau est arrivé

"The Beaujolais nouveau has arrived," the landlords of the *bistros et bouchons* of Lyon used to chalk up on the window shutters in years gone by. The news received a hearty welcome from their ever-thirsty customers. After all, every day they had to rinse down all the new dust they had breathed in at the silk and textile mills. In addition, it should be remembered that the bistro-owners themselves used to stock up once a year with their requirement of wine barrels from Beaujolais and then sell the wine on draft. In an age in which modern scientific approaches to wine and to cellar technology were still unknown, the quality of the house wine suffered very considerably during the course of the year, and the fruity-fresh aromas which had earlier been so exquisite had become a distant memory by the time the new wine arrived. This also explains why its arrival was celebrated with such enthusiasm.

The *primeur* achieved its great breakthrough in 1968 in Paris. From there, it began, little by little, to conquer the entire world. For years, wine merchants and hoteliers engaged in bitter rivalry to be the first to offer their customers the Beaujolais nouveau. But it is now laid down by law that it may not be sold at all until the third Thursday in November. This also applies to its competitors among the French *appellations* most in demand. In contrast to this, the *primeurs vins de pays* can be delivered exactly one month earlier.

The success of the Beaujolais nouveau has been due, firstly, to a handful of winegrowers and wine connoisseurs, who put their heads and their hearts into it. Also important are the great advances made in wine production and cellar equipment. Stored at controlled temperatures, and protected by a controlled biological breakdown of its acidic elements, Beaujolais nouveau guards its clean fruity notes and is easily digestible – which wasn't always so back in the year dot. Although the winegrowers producing Beaujolais and Beaujolais Villages are on the fast track to making money thanks to the *primeur* (which nowadays accounts for two-fifths of all the 173 million bottles of Beaujolais produced), there is also a drawback to this welcome success. Recently, many consumers have convinced themselves that Beaujolais should generally be drunk quickly, before the end of the year. In deciding this, they seem to have forgotten completely that the fully fledged Beaujolais wines – but most of all the *crus* – need to mature in the bottle for one or more years to become wine of a higher quality, for which higher prices are justified.

The wines of Beaujolais

With a good 22,000 hectares (54,360 acres), Beaujolais is the most significant Gamay region in France and indeed the world. The cultivated region extends from Lyon to Mâcon, being about 34 miles (55 kilometers) long and 7–9 miles (12 – 15 kilometers) wide. The grape areas cover the lower slopes of the Monts de Beaujolais, rising out of the flatlands of the Saône, but they attain a height of only 1475 feet (450 meters). In the south, the soils are made up predominantly of marl and of calcareous soils from the Mesozoic period. Toward the Saône, the eastern sites have alluvial soils from more recent periods in the Earth's history. The best soils, to the north of Villefranche, date from the Paleozoic era, and are of a crystalline nature, consisting of granite and slate. This last type of soil, when it decomposes, releases mineral ores which have an effect on the aroma of the wine.

Cultivation and winemaking

The Gamay is an early-ripening and prolific strain, which one has to know how to handle. To start with, there has to be a high planting density,

which in Beaujolais means that there are 9000 – 13,000 vines per hectare (3650 – 4800 vines per acre) – one of the highest planting densities in the world. Moreover, production should be reduced by pruning. For *villages* and *crus*, the vines must be trained in the shape of a goblet (*gobelet*). Three to five shoots are allowed to form, each of which can be allowed to bear a maximum of 12 buds. For the Beaujolais *appellation*, the fan-shaped *guyot* cut is also permitted. Each individual vine is then attached to a stake and trained up on a wire frame.

Manual picking usually starts in mid-September and lasts for three weeks. To avoid damaging the grapes, crates which can take no more than 80 kilograms (175 pounds) of grapes are used to transport them. The grapes are tipped into tanks or old wooden tubs, so that some of the grapes burst. As a result, must gathers at the bottom and begins to ferment, whereupon carbon dioxide develops and saturates the atmosphere. Without oxygen, the remaining grapes are forced into intracellular fermentation, a process during which the must absorbs a particularly large number of flavors from the peel.

The must is extracted after a period of between three and ten days, depending on the character which the maker intends the wine to have. The residue is pressed and, following the blending in of *jus de coule* and *jus de presse*, the fermentation process is completed. The briefer the fermentation period, the fewer tannins the wine absorbs. This certainly means that the wine can

be drunk earlier, but it also has a lighter structure and its aging potential is shorter. The temperature is significant throughout the fermentation process. The fruitiness and freshness of the *vin nouveau* are more likely to be obtained at around 70 °F (20 °C), while the structure and fullness of a *cru* require 85 °F (30 °C). But like all red wines, Beaujolais must also undergo biological acid breakdown to reduce the acid content and stabilize the wine.

Although in summer the climate in Beaujolais is frequently hot and dry, this is an area in which the must can be enriched by a maximum of only 2° of alcohol by adding sugar or concentrate. In addition, Gamay is one of those varieties which forms little natural grape sugar, and this is reduced still further when yields are high. So

The most famous and the best-aging of the ten Crus de Beaujolais, the Moulin-à-Vent with its flowery bouquet, owes its name to this old windmill, which is nowadays surrounded by vines.

Beaujolais grows on the slopes facing the Saône flatlands to the north of Lyon. Each vine is tied to its own stake. In spring, the winegrowers spread fertilizer over the vineyards.

Beaujolais is almost always enriched, except by a few winegrowers who use biological methods or have old vines bearing few grapes.

The particular charm of Beaujolais lies in its intense, captivating aromas. They cover a whole spectrum of flowers such as violets, roses (the bouquet of Moulin-à-Vent is famous), mallow and lily of the valley, as well as fruits, including cherries, raspberries, redcurrants, strawberries and blueberries, and even apricots, kirsch and cherry pits. Although these fresh aromas are expressed at their purest in the young wines, many wines from the region – and not merely the ten *crus* – have sufficient structure to be able to age for a few years. Those most famed for their potential over a number of years are Morgon, Chénas and Moulin-à-Vent. The two last-named *crus*, in particular,

come more and more to resemble Burgundies in bouquet and taste as the years go by.

The younger and fruitier a Beaujolais is, the cooler it should be when drunk (up to 55 °F/13 °C). Similarly, it is easier to savor, as it goes with all simple foods, cold or hot, in a refreshing and pleasant way. This applies not just in the wintry *primeur* period, but also, and particularly, in summer. However, if you have delicate *crus* which have undergone more blending, such as an extraordinary Chiroubles or a Saint-Amour, you should choose finer fare to go with them, perhaps a Bresse fowl or grilled fish. The well-structured *crus* – and also the particularly powerful *villages* varieties or the exceptional Beaujolais vintages – go with either a beautiful piece of Charolais beef or a flavorful game dish.

Above: The cherry blossom heralds the new year in the Beaujolais vineyards. The buds will soon be breaking on the Gamay vines.

Coteaux du Lyonnais

In the 16th century, winemaking flourished in the hills adjacent to the Beaujolais region, lying to the west of Lyon and extending to the beginning of the northern Rhône locations. But after the vine pest crisis, and due to the increasing expansion of Lyon, its renaissance has remained modest. Only something over 350 hectares (865 acres) are planted, and they produce, almost exclusively, fruity-toned, red Gamay-based wines. The wine is bottled by a dozen independent winegrowers and also by the cooperative cellars of Sain-Bel.

Carp and pike from Dombes

The Dombes plateau, not far to the north of Lyon, owes its origins to the last ice age. It has fish breeding ponds which date back to the 12th century, and which nowadays cover an area of about 24,700 acres (10,000 hectares). The catch of fish is significant. From October until February, the total amounts to 60–65 percent carp, 15–20 percent tench, 10–20 percent roach and redeyes and 3–5 percent pike. With a catch amounting to 2200 tons (2000 tonnes) per year, the Dombes takes pride of place among French freshwater fish farms. Divided off by dikes, the ponds are usually arranged in a chain and are connected by a type of little sluice called a *thou*. The gradient is minimal, but sufficient to allow the higher ponds to be drained into the lower ones. The ponds, fed by rainwater and seepage loss water, are used according to a tried and tested cycle. Fish are taken from a pond for three years. Then it is dried out and grain or maize is sown for one year. Any fish roe revealed as the waters drain is tipped into other stretches of water in France or in the countries nearby.

It's an experience to watch a pond being emptied in the Dombes. A good two weeks in advance, a start is made on draining the water away, so that it collects at the end of the pond in front of the sluice, but still extends over about 330 feet (100 meters) of the pond's length. In spite of the low level of water, no fish can be seen as yet. But trucks are waiting on the bank with fresh water tanks to take the catch away alive.

The fishermen stretch out a long net and hook each end onto a tractor. The tractors now slowly move the net toward the ends of the pond, while two dozen fishermen hold its edges on the surface. After that it's muscle power alone as the men pull with all their might to draw the net into a circle. One fisherman sits in a boat where the water is deepest and holds the net up. Nearer the banks the men, in their rubber clothes, are up to their thighs in water, and are pulling and squeezing the net nearer and nearer to the bank. Three of them are inside the circle. They have to go deeper and deeper into the water, which is soon higher than their stomachs. Now the fish can be seen wriggling on the surface. The men then ram rods into the bottom of the pond and stretch the net over the forked top ends. Next, they move a trough into the water to sort out the fish they have caught. Pike and carp are put into separate keep nets – *filochons* – and smaller fish are thrown back into the water. Each keep net is now weighed. The pike are weighed first. They may tip the scale at 24–42 pounds (12–21 kilograms). They are outshone by the mirror carp, every one of which weighs 3 pounds (1.3 kilograms) or more. The tanks on the trucks quickly fill up with fish, which are driven straight off on the first part of their journey to the consumer – who could be in Lyon, Paris, Geneva or Frankfurt. However, one part of the catch is handled in the Dombes region itself: the bones and skins are removed and the fish are turned into fresh or smoked fillets.

In the gray light of dawn, two tractors pull the wide net over onto the far bank of the pond, which has already almost dried out.

The men heave with all their might to pull the net nearer the bank, while standing up to their waists in water.

The circle has grown tighter, and now there are more fish in the net than there is water. It's a catch worth having.

The mirror carp which have been caught are a magnificent size. They always weigh over 3 pounds (1.3 kilograms) and are in peak condition.

Left: Such a fine specimen of a pike brings a satisfied smile even to the face of an experienced fisherman.

The keep nets are suspended from simple scales. The weight registered is carefully recorded by the pond's owner and the representative of the fishing cooperative.

213

Poultry from Bresse

France's most noble poultry (*volaille*) makes its entrance in the national colors. The Bresse fowl walk around on blue feet, sporting a dazzlingly white plumage and a fiery red crest. And they have it pretty good: they can strut proudly over lush green meadows and peck away to their heart's content. When they are one day old, the chicks move to one of the 600 farms on which they are reared. After a maximum of 35 days, the hen-house doors are opened for them, and out they go onto the green grass. The law decrees that each of them has a claim to 10 square meters (12 square yards)

of this grass. In addition to this, every plot of land where they are reared must have a minimal area amounting to 5000 square meters (5980 square yards) in which no more than 500 birds of the same species may enjoy their freedom.

The Bresse region stretches from the foothills of the Jura in the east all the way to the Saône in the west. Anyone passing through it in the warm part of the year feels like a visitor to some picture-book idyll, where ancient trees still stand in the meadows, the hedges and bushes are flourishing, and magnificent plants are in blossom. Flowers grow around wells and picturesque old half-timbered houses, which are often slightly tumbledown. And the Bresse poultry are a part of this rural paradise. At any rate, the French parliament decided in 1957 that they should be the only kind of poultry to be honored by an *Appellation d'Origine Contrôlée*, which is otherwise

restricted to wines, cheeses, and a few other delicacies. It is only recently that they have had to share this honor with the rare Houdan fowls from the Ile de France. The legislation governs their wellbeing from their first day to their last, to ensure that they are reared in accordance with time-honoured custom.

Poultry from Bresse are a breed apart, protected with scientific precision. They are reared mainly on dairy farms. Milk comes in useful for the poultry, since their fodder consists largely of corn soaked in milk. Bresse can also boast of its pigeons, ducks and turkeys, but only the fowl have the highest distinction. A *poulet* will have been permitted nine weeks of freedom, a *poularde*

Below: Every Bresse fowl enjoys the advantage of being able to claim 10 square meters (12 square yards) of meadow.

This proud Bresse cockerel can be recognized by the national colors of France – red, white and blue.

eleven, and a castrated *chapon* – a capon – as long as 23 weeks.

These fine birds are not dispatched to the tables of the most sophisticated clientele in the world without further preparation. For the finishing touch, they are put into small cages. There they continue to receive the best of nourishment, without being able to do much running about or scratching. As a result, they put on an additional thoroughly desirable layer of fat. This is expected, in particular, of capons and *poulards*, which will be the highlight of the festive menus at the end of the year. The capons are treated like princes, and great care must be taken. They are painstakingly plucked and bathed in milk, and then sewn into canvas. What was once a conservation measure is nowadays a matter of decoration. When their robes fall after two days, the birds' bodies, now uniformly shaped, are ready for their grand entrance. Shortly before Christmas, in Bourg-en-Bresse, Montrevel, Veaux-le-Pont and Louhans, hundreds of fine birds are lined up on display tables. Since 1862, severe judges have eyed up the waxy bodies and bestowed passionately sought after prizes on the best. Next it's the hour of the chefs and the dealers when the breeders are rewarded in cash for their labors. The top birds can fetch up to $95.

Anyone taking a Bresse bird home should treat it with appropriate respect. Its fame is based on its tender, tasty meat. The outstanding aroma pervades the fat which covers it. This can be used to best advantage if the bird is simply roasted in the oven. Baste it frequently with its own juices, and do not let it dry out under any circumstances. *Volaille à la crème* is famous. The bird is divided into pieces, browned in butter, then cooked in cream.

Bresse is known, not just for poultry, but also for its beautiful old farmhouses.

The poultry are fed on milk and corn, which makes them as fit as a fiddle.

The birds are given V.I.P. treatment on their way to the consumer. The precious poultry are packaged like chocolates.

Fine fowls

France exports more chickens than any other country in the world. Just under half a million tons of chicken meat is dispatched, fresh or frozen, to foreign customers, and the same amount is eaten in France. As pork and mutton are becoming less popular, the taste for poultry is on the increase. Turkey meat is now the second most popular in terms of mass consumption and exports, and its sales have shown considerable growth (deep-frozen portions in particular). Alongside this purely industrial production, in which the living conditions of the animals do not exactly meet the standards of organic farming, there has been a seal of quality since 1965, the red label. This not only guarantees a more pleasant existence for the bird, but also guarantees the consumer meat of a decidedly higher quality. All kinds of poultry, including turkeys or guinea fowl, which are reared under the strict and detailed conditions required, have a claim to this particular quality mark. Chickens, however, lead the way in this high-class sector of the market.

In order to obtain the red label, the chickens must have been reared on farms, which earns them the description of *poulet fermier*, and they must also fulfil five criteria:

1. Origin: A selective breeding line, scientifically tested for the quality of the meat and for slow growth, which often takes regional breeds into account.
2. Rearing: The henhouse must not exceed an area of 400 square meters (478 square yards). It must be lit by daylight and must give access to a natural run. The description *élevé en plein air* guarantees the chicken at least 2 square meters (just over 2 square yards) of free range, while *élevé en liberté* means it has been guaranteed unlimited space to run about.
3. Feed: This must be at least 75 percent grain, and must contain no added animal fats or meal.
4. Age: They are assured of a minimum of 81 days, while the maximum lifespan for chickens has been set at 110 days.
5. End product: They fall into *classe A* quality category and so must weigh between 1.2 kilograms (2 pounds 10 ounces) and 1.7 kilograms (3 pounds 10 ounces) when oven-ready.

The packaging carries the advice that they should be consumed within nine days of the date of slaughter marked. Almost 100 regions have a recognized red label for their chickens. Their labels provide information on their place of origin, rearing, feed and lifespan, together with details from which each animal can be traced back to the breeder. It is the red label which France has to thank for its high level of quality in poultry rearing.

Canard – Duck
This splendid specimen from the area around Rouen is a cross between a wild duck and a domesticated duck, from the Ferme du Canardier, which also supplied the famous "Tour d'Argent" in Paris with its numbered luxury poultry. Prepared duck dishes such as *magret* and *confit* are highly esteemed, to say nothing of the *foie gras de canard*.

Chapon – Capon
Capon – a castrated cockerel – the life of which is calculated in such a way that it has accumulated enough meat, fat, and fine flavor just in time for the Christmas festivities. It weighs 5-8 pounds (2.4-4 kilograms) and is best spit-roasted.

Dinde – Turkey
The turkey, the gastronomic superbird from America, has won its place as a convenient, lean, problem-free sliced meat. It has recently become more popular as a roast for special occasions.

Coq – Cockerel

Cockerel appear on many menus – mainly, of course, as *Coq au vin*. This is usually not a real cockerel, but is just as likely to be a hen. The genuine sexually mature young cock from a poultry farm brings more vigor, taste, and – weighing 4 or 6 pounds (2 or 3 kilograms) more meat onto the plate.

Poularde – Fatted chicken
A young fatted chicken, which is only a few weeks older than a *poulet*, but has been given preferential treatment, weighs in at 2.5 kilograms (5½ pounds) on the scales. Its very tender and delicate meat accounts for its being consumed as a roast on special occasions.

Poulet Bio – Biochicken
Chickens and pullets reared by organic farming methods have more space to run about, and are reared exclusively on biologically cultivated grain and additives. This has an unmistakable effect, producing aromatic meat.

Poulet – Chicken
Chickens provide the cheapest and most abundant poultry meat, but the consumer buying free-range poultry with the red label is guaranteed high quality, thanks to strict conditions and checks.
Best quality: Bresse, Houdan, Challans.
Good quality: Gers, Janzé, Landes, Loué, among others.

Pintade – Guinea fowl
The guinea fowl, which originally came from Africa, has been reared in France for centuries and is greatly enjoyed because of its gamey character. It is usually prepared either larded with bacon fat or wrapped in strips of bacon, since the meat is somewhat dry.

Caille – Quail
Quail, with its white, very tasty meat, is enjoying great popularity and, since farmers have begun to rear them, can be bought in oven-ready condition at reasonable prices. They are traditionally wrapped in a vine leaf to be roasted. Often stuffed by grocers and caterers.

Pigeon – Pigeon
Reared in the Landes, Gers, Bresse, and Brittany, pigeons or squabs are the gastronomic social climbers of France. Since it is so tricky to prepare them to taste really good, they are eaten almost exclusively in restaurants.

Lapin – Rabbit
In France, rabbit is classed with poultry, and is displayed on the counter next to, or among, the poultry. It is rare for the entire rabbit to be stuffed and prepared for eating. It usually comes to the table braised in a stew with bacon and white wine, or in mustard sauce.

Suprême de poulet de Bresse farci à la julienne de légumes sauce au Gamay du Bugey
Breast of Bresse chicken, stuffed with julienne of vegetables and in red wine sauce

Serves 2

½ leek
1 carrot
1 stalk of celery
4 tbsp/60 g butter
Freshly-milled salt and pepper
2 chicken wings with breast
2 glasses of Gamay wine (preferably from Bugey)

Clean the leek, the carrot and the celery. Cut into narrow strips and steam for 5 minutes until soft in 4 tsp/20 g butter in a braising saucepan. Add salt and pepper.
Cut into the chicken breast lengthwise with a sharp knife and fill the resulting pouches with 1 tablespoonful of vegetables. Melt 4 tsp/20 g butter in a braising saucepan and brown the wing fillets well all around. Add the wine and cook for 10 minutes at a low temperature. Remove the meat and keep it warm. Reduce the sauce, add the remaining butter and whisk.
Place each chicken wing on a plate and pour the red wine sauce over it. Fresh tagliatelle is a good side-dish.

Fricassée de poulet de Bresse à la crème
Bresse chicken fricassee in cream sauce

1 oven-ready Bresse fatted chicken (about 4 lbs/1.8 kg)
4 tbsp/60 g butter
Freshly-milled salt and pepper
1 cup/250 ml Chardonnay white wine
3½ oz/100 g small onions
9 oz/250 g mushrooms
2 tsp/10 g sugar
2 cups/500 ml crème fraîche

Divide the chicken into eight pieces. In a braising saucepan, brown lightly all round in 2 tbsp/30 g butter. Add salt and pepper, pour in the wine and add 2 cups/500 ml of water. Then cover and braise for 20 minutes.
Meanwhile, peel the small onions and clean the mushrooms, cutting off the stalks to use in another recipe. Toss the onions and mushrooms on a low heat in a braising saucepan, using remaining butter. Five minutes before serving, sprinkle the sugar on top, glaze and add salt to taste.
Remove the chicken pieces from the saucepan and put them aside. Reduce the liquid to half, then pour in the crème fraîche. Reduce again, then pour over meat.
Use the glazed onions and mushrooms as a garnish. Spinach and Basmati rice are served as a side-dish.

Suprême de poulet de Bresse farci à la julienne de légumes sauce au Gamay du Bugey – Breast of Bresse chicken, stuffed with julienne of vegetables and in red wine sauce

The perfect way to carve a noble fowl

The oven-roasted Bresse fowl comes onto the table with a *gratin dauphinois* and broccoli florets. Carefully lay the bird on its side so that the first slice can be cut from its body (1). Using a knife, cut through the leg joint, twisting it away from the body (2). Arrange the leg on the plate, pour a little gravy over. Serve with broccoli and potatoes au gratin (3). Now turn the bird over, using a fork and a spoon, so that the second leg is on top (4).

Carefully cut the leg off and then garnish in the same way with sauce, broccoli and potatoes au gratin (5). Turn the body so that it is lying on its back, and stick the fork into a section of breast (6). Use the knife to cut accurately along one side of the breastbone, and thus carefully detach the fillet (7). Then push down the breast section with the wing in such a way that the lower part can be cut off (8).

Place the wing on the plate with the breast fillet and add the garnishes (9). Hold the second section of breast with the fork and use the knife to follow the breastbone again (10). Then move the fork inward, to separate the carcass from the base of the wing completely (11). Then pour a little gravy over the wing, and serve with potatoes au gratin and broccoli (12).

Fricassée de poulet de Bresse à la crème – Bresse chicken fricassee in cream sauce.

Gratin dauphinois
Potatoes au gratin

Serves 4

2 lb/1 kg potatoes, preferably Bintie	
1 clove of garlic	
3 eggs	
1 cup/250 ml crème fraîche	
1 cup/250 ml milk	
Freshly-milled salt and pepper	
A pinch of muscat	

Peel the potatoes, wash them and slice them into thin slices with a slicer. Peel the garlic, halve it and use to rub the inside of an oven-safe baking pan.
Layer the potato slices inside so they overlap. Beat the eggs, then stir them together with the crème fraîche and milk. Season with salt, pepper and muscat, then pour the mixture over the potato slices and bake in a pre-heated oven at 375 °F/190 °C for 1 to 1½ hours. *Gratin dauphinois* is a very popular side-dish, particularly for poultry and lamb.

Bintie, the strain of potato recommended for the *gratin dauphinois*, is one of the oldest varieties grown in the Netherlands. It is bright yellow, oval in shape, neutral in taste and normally has no deep eyes. What is special about it is the way it cooks. It remains mealy and solid when cooked, and is thus outstandingly appropriate for gratins.

Saint-Marcellin

Left: A Lyonnais cheese dish, which combines a small goat milk cheese from the Mâconnais (front), a Dombes sheep milk cheese and a softer Saint-Marcellin made from cow milk (top left).
Right: In the restaurants of the Rhône, the customers are given the choice between the cheeseboard and the *fromage blanc à la crème*, the fresh, top-quality soft curd cheese served with lashings of cream.

This small cheese, which weighs only 2¾ ounces (80 grams) measures 2¾ inches (7 centimeters) in diameter and stands ¾ inch (2 centimeters) high, dates back to the 15th century. The little town from which it takes its name is in the Dauphiné, a region in Isère where the Dauphin, the heir to the throne, used to live while he waited more or less patiently for his position at the court to become vacant. The future Louis XI took up residence there in 1445, and often whiled away the time by hunting.

One day, while on a hunt, he got lost in thick undergrowth. Suddenly a mighty bear reared up in front of him, and the prince thought his last moment had come. In his hour of need, he called on the Virgin Mary for help, swearing that if he survived he would set up a religious order in the nearby village. His cries for help brought two woodcutters to the scene, who courageously drove the bear away. They then took the prince (half-dead with fright) into their hut, where they set before him some refreshments – bread and cheese from the nearby settlement of Saint-Marcellin. Safely back in his castle, Louis declared that from now on the excellent cheese from Saint-Marcellin should be served in the Louvre. It appears in the court accounts for the first time in 1461. The men who had saved Louis's life, Richau and Bouillane, were elevated to the nobility, but they saw not one sou of the promised reward.

Saint-Marcellin cheese, originally known simply as *tomme*, was at first produced exclusively in the farms of Isère from goat milk, and was consumed on the farms themselves. In 1870 a group of farmers decided to collect the cheese and take it on donkeys to the markets in Grenoble, Avignon, Saint-Etienne and Lyon, which is where most Saint-Marcellin is sold to this day. At that time, the cheeses were wrapped in vine leaves and were packed three layers deep in wicker baskets. With the coming of the railroad, the cheese soon reached northern France as well. Increasing demand meant that, from 1876 onward, the cheese was made from a mixture of cow milk and goat milk. The cheese collectors provided the farmers with *faisselles* – small perforated clay pots, which were the optimal vessels into which the whey could drain. A century later, the transition was completed to produce Saint-Marcellin exclusively from cow milk.

There are 580 dairy farms in the *départements* of Isère, Drôme and Rhône today, producing 31.7 million gallons (120 million liters) of milk a year. Half of this goes to the cheese industry. Ten small industrial dairies and 15 farm cheese-making plants produce Saint-Marcellin, a process in which 6.6 million gallons (25 million

Initially, the cream-colored Saint-Marcellin displays a light bluish sheen. As it matures, it takes on a reddish hue and grows softer and softer in its consistency, until eventually it has to be served with a spoon.

La Mère Richard, shown here, is the daughter of the original *mère*. Both have made a valuable contribution to spreading the fame of Saint-Marcellin from their stall in the Part-Dieu market in Lyon. Their cheeses are matured to perfection in the cellars beneath the abbey of Collonges.

liters) of milk are used. To the slightly soured milk, which is left full-cream or half-cream, a little rennet is added, which helps to make the milk coagulate. On the following day, the jelly is ladled into perforated molds and the whey which drips off is collected. Three hours later, the fresh cheese can be salted and turned. After another two days, the cheese is taken out of the mold and salted from the other side. The cheese is now laid on straw mats and deposited in drying ovens at 60 to 70 °F (15 to 20 °C) for up to ten days. The cheese is turned each day. The Saint-Marcellins are matured in cool, damp cellars, where they spend at least a further ten days. During this time, their soft bright rind takes on a bluish sheen. Five or six weeks of further maturing are needed to give the cheese a reddish color and to give the mixture that runny consistency which is so popular in Lyon (where the cheese is sold in little plastic bowls and eaten with a spoon). Incidentally, the wines which go best with it are a fruity Mondeuse from Savoy or the powerful white Condrieu.

Cervelle de canut, a specialty of the Lyonnais cuisine, is made from soft curd cheese, shallots, garlic, fresh herbs, a hint of vinegar and a few drops of olive oil, which are beaten up well together.

A menu from Drôme

The *département* of Drôme is a strange mixture. The southern part of it really forms part of Provence, but the northern and eastern areas border what was once the Dauphiné and even contain the foothills of the Alps. So it has warm, completely Mediterranean regions and also some mountainous areas which are difficult to reach and are bitterly cold in winter. The Rhône forms its western boundary and gives not only fertile orchards and vegetable gardens, but also, in the shape of Hermitage, one of the most characterful wines in all France. From the gastronomical point of view, it is a difficult task to respect the boundaries of the Drôme as laid down by bureaucrats and politicians. For this reason its olives (which flourish in Nyons) and the full, sun-blessed vintages which mature in its southern part (the southern Côtes du Rhône areas) will be found in the chapter on Provence.

The menu assembled here reflects the many baffling facets and contrasts which make the Drôme one of the richest of provinces from the point of view of gastronomy. The entrées are represented by saddle of rabbit, which owes its flavor to olive oil and to the famous olive paste, the *tapenade*, that is entirely a product of the region's hot and dry south. But the main course is just as clearly a product of its northern area. This is demonstrated by the presence of both butter and fresh cream, but also by the famous ravioli, which have been recognized with an *Appellation d'Origine Contrôlée* since 1989, and bear the name of *Ravioles du Dauphiné*. The main centers of Drôme are Romans – the capital of the shoe industry – and the Royans villages, especially Saint-Jean-en-Royans. Its

territory actually takes in a few parishes on either side of the boundary between Drôme and Isère – formed by the Isère river – as well as part of the Vercors. This has played its part in the region's history, for the art of making ravioli was introduced by men from Piedmont. Almost 500 years ago, Piedmontese woodcutters penetrated into the Vercors area and floated their logs down the Isère. They were accomodated in farms where they made their beloved pasta. As they could rarely afford any meat, they originally created the filling from the available goat cheese and herbs from the surrounding area. The locals soon acquired a taste for the tiny ravioli (there are always 48 in a sheet). They incorporated the dish into all of their banquets, but it was not until 1873 that a cook in Romans had the idea of selling ravioli. As Mère Maury, she made culinary history and changed the fortunes of her family. Nowadays, the ravioli are made from wheat flour, and their filling consists of grated Emmental or Comté, soft curd cheese, eggs, butter, parsley and salt. A plateful weighs only about 2 ounces (60 grams) and they are especially delicious if cooked in chicken broth.

Whether or not the guinea fowl really arrived in Drôme with Hannibal's baggage train, as many breeders maintain, is a mystery. Found wild in the African savannas, this pheasant-like bird was sacred to the Egyptians and

considered a much sought-after delicacy by the Romans, and it found an ideal habitat in the southern Rhône region. France is now the world's leading supplier of guinea fowl. The best poultry farms apply the "red label" conditions and rear the noisy birds with their beautiful plumage under free-range conditions, feeding them on grain. The vast majority of guinea fowl are slaughtered when they are only eight weeks old, and are then called *pintadeau*, but high-quality birds are granted a lifespan of 14 weeks. The taste of their delicate meat recalls that of game. The dessert for this menu finally brings together the southern and northern parts of the delightful *département*: Mediterranean figs, accompanied by amber-colored caramel, bring out the taste of the nuts and contrast with Muscat grapes from Die – which is rightly famous for its unmistakable sparkling wine, which the people of the area know how to press from the grapes in question.

Râble de lapereau en gelée d'olive et quenelle de tapenade

Saddle of rabbit in olive jelly
with tapenade dumplings
(illustration far left)

½ cup/125 ml Nyons olive oil
2 saddles of rabbit, drawn
3½ oz/100 g tapenade
Freshly-milled salt and pepper
4 aluminum foil squares (8 x 8 in/20 x 20 cm)
4 cups/1 liter poultry stock
4 sprigs of rosemary

Put the olive oil into the refrigerator. Halve the saddles of rabbit lengthwise and lay the parts down on a working surface. Coat the inner sides with some *tapenade*, season with salt and pepper and then wrap two strips together in each of two aluminum foil packages. Poach them in boiling poultry stock for 20 minutes. In the meantime, shape the rest of the *tapenade* into 4 little dumplings (2 tablespoons each) and put them to one side. Remove the packages of meat from the stock and leave to cool thoroughly.

Unwrap the packages, then cut the meat into thin slices. Sprinkle with the cool olive oil and serve on 4 plates. Garnish with the *tapenade* dumplings, the rosemary sprigs and, if desired, with mixed salad.

Suprême de pintade et ravioles aux poireaux

Breast of guinea fowl
with ravioli and leek
(illustration centre)

1 lb/500 g fresh Romans ravioli
1 leek
4 guinea fowl breasts
3½ tbsp/50 g butter
Freshly-milled salt and pepper
1 cup/250 ml crème fraîche
4 cups/1 liter chicken stock

Put the ravioli into the refrigerator – the sheets will separate better after cooking. Clean the leek and use only the white of it. Cut this into thin strips and blanch them, then rinse them in ice-cold water and leave them to drip dry thoroughly.

Fry the guinea fowl breasts until golden brown in 4 tsp/20 g of the butter. Season with salt and pepper, then remove them from the pan and keep warm. Add a little water to the dregs, together with a little chicken stock. Add the crème fraîche while stirring, then add 4 tsp/20 g of the butter and stir well.

Put the ravioli into weak, boiling stock. Remove with a skimmer after 1–2 minutes and let them drip dry. Then add them to the sauce.

Briefly braise the leek lightly in the remaining butter and place on 4 preheated plates. Cut the guinea fowl breasts into thin slices and place them on top of the leek. Add the ravioli and pour the sauce over the top.

Figues rôties aux mendiants et au caramel épicé

Figs in spiced caramel sauce
(illustration below)

Serves 2

3 figs
Scant ½ cup/100 g sugar
1 tsp saffron
½ tsp 4-spice mixture
½ tsp ground cinnamon
Scant 1 cup/100 g mixed raisins, hazelnuts, almonds and walnuts
10 white Muscatel grapes

Wash and quarter the figs. Roast them lightly in a pan, then remove the figs and keep them warm. Add the sugar to the pan, with a little water, and caramelize. Then add the spices and stir, and finally fold in the nut and raisin mixture.

Place six fig quarters in the center of each of two plates and pour the spiced caramel sauce over them. Put the grapes into the pan and heat them, but only briefly. Then arrange 5 grapes in a circle around the figs on each plate. Serve immediately.

Fruits of the Rhône Valley

The Rhône valley is an extensive orchard, which stretches from Lyon in the north all the way to the Mediterranean in the south. Though statistically Provence produces more fruit than Rhône-Alpes (and, indeed, all of the other French regions) still it is the areas on both sides of the mighty river Rhône where fruit-growing is concentrated. There the heat and the long periods of sunshine, together with the rich alluvial soils and adequate supplies of water, provide the most favorable conditions. Vaucluse and Bouches du Rhône, which border on the Rhône, are the biggest suppliers of apples and pears, though Drôme beats all the other *départements* when it comes to apricots and peaches. From higher and cooler areas, especially in the foothills of the Alps, come particular specialties: walnuts from Grenoble in Isère, sweet chestnuts from Ardèche, exceedingly good apples, pears and cherries from Savoy, and the best of raspberries from the Alpine slopes of Haute Savoie. Nor is this all that the fruit bowl provides, as the next double-page spread demonstrates. It is clear from the "hit list" of the types of fruit grown in the country that the most popular fruit in French households are apples, closely followed by peaches. Included among the peaches are nectarines which are now more popular than yellow peaches and have far outstripped white peaches. Equal third are pears and dessert grapes, with strawberries and melons fighting it out for fourth position. Finally there are apricots, kiwi fruit and cherries, all of which are widely appreciated and consumed in great numbers. All other types of fruit are bought only in small quantities. Every French citizen consumes more than 7 pounds (over 3 kilograms) of peaches a year, and already eats almost 3 pounds (1.3 kilograms) of kiwi fruit. The fondness for fruit, incidentally, varies with age. Studies have shown that consumers aged 35 or above like fruit more than the young.

Right: Ripe fruit, which is particularly sensitive to bruising, is picked and placed directly into boxes for dispatch.

Once placed in boxes, the apricots are manually sorted to make sure that only undamaged fruit is dispatched to be consumed fresh.

These peaches from the northern Rhône valley were organically grown and can offer the best quality of fruit and the healthiest eating.

From the Rhône valley orchard

Pit fruit

Abricot – Apricot
The most commonly grown variety is Bergeron. Since it is sensitive to damage in transit, it is often picked too early and therefore disappoints. When ripe, it is juicy, with a pleasant balance of sweetness and acidity. Eaten raw, or used in salads, for ice-cream and cakes, purées and jams.

Cérise – Cherry
These come mainly from the departments of Vaucluse, Ardèche, Drôme and Rhône. The season is from May until the beginning of July. The early-ripening Bigarreau (Burlat) variety, popular with growers, has big, dark cherries with sweet juice. In Saint-Hilaire-du-Rosier in Isère, they make ratafia cherries into fruit schnapps and liqueurs.

Pêche – Peach
Season – from May until the end of September. Early varieties are white, juicy and delicate, with firmly anchored pits. Most peaches have yellow flesh. They are eaten raw, boiled, in syrup or wine as a dessert, and are sometimes baked with poultry. They are easy to preserve.

Nectarine and brugnon – Nectarine and brugnole
These appear to have developed from accidental crosses between peaches and plums, which were then selectively improved. Their often intense peach aroma and firm, juicy fruit flesh are much appreciated, and they account for 44 percent of all peach-type trees in France. *Brugnon* pits can be removed only with great difficulty.

Prune – Plum
Among the numerous varieties of plum, the *prune d'ente* grown in southwest France is unique, as it is intended to be dried. Other varieties such as Zwetsche and Mirabelle, which flourish mainly in Alsace and Lorraine, are mainly used in distillation. Plums grown along the Rhône, and in particular in Drôme, are intended to be eaten raw. Greengages are the most widely distributed fruit of this kind.

Soft fruit

Fraise – Strawberry
France is the third biggest producer of strawberries in the world (after Spain and Italy). The most important area for this crop is the southwest, followed by the Rhône valley, where the preferred varieties are Valeta and Elsanta, with a scarlet color and conical shape. When picked, strawberries should be a shiny red color all over, since they do not continue to ripen once they are separated from the plant. They should not be stored or served too cold, as this makes them lose too much of their taste.

Framboise – Raspberry
Wild raspberries have a particularly intense flavor, but the semi-bush varieties grown in high locations in Isère, Savoy and Haute Savoie also supply best-quality fruit. They are hand-picked, and go straight into their packs. Once they are ripe and come away easily from the cone-shaped stalks, they should be eaten quickly, and preferably without any washing, to avoid watering down their flavor. They are also very popular in purée form, and they freeze well.

Myrtille – Blueberry
In the woods and on the mountain pastures of Savoy, Haute Savoie and Isère, the wild blueberries find the acid soils which suit them. Picking the ripe little blueberries is a labor-intensive job, and they are harvested with combs by professional gatherers. Cultivated bushes have also been planted recently, which produce berries which are bigger but less flavorful. Blueberries are popular as a filling for fruit pies, or for sherbets. Their juice can be drunk on its own, or used to make syrups or liqueurs, but their most popular use is in jams or jelly.

Cassis – Blackcurrant
Haute Savoie and its Alps provide favorable conditions for this bush, otherwise mainly grown in Burgundy, since it fruits abundantly only if it has been through a frosty winter. The black, full-flavored berries, which are extremely rich in vitamin C, are rarely eaten raw. They are widely used in cakemaking, or for desserts, sherbets and jelly. Blackcurrant juice and syrup are also popular. But their main use is as the base for the very popular *crème de cassis*, a fruit liqueur which is mixed with white wine to make the aperitive kir.

Groseille – Redcurrant
Like their black relations, redcurrants also prefer cooler positions. Because of their high acid content, they are only rarely eaten raw. But they are popular as a filling for pies or cakes. They are made into juices and syrups, but above all into jelly. The latter plays an important part in cake-making, where it is used in numerous recipes for cookies, cakes and pies, as a base, a filling or a topping.

Raisin de table – Dessert grape
Vaucluse is the clear leader among the dessert grape regions, followed by Tarn-et-Garonne (where they specialize in Chasselas grapes). White grape varieties are generally more popular than red. The high flyer among them is the very flavorful Alexandrine Muscat, followed by the Chasselas, while the first place among the black varieties is taken by Alphonse Lavallée. Imports of dessert grapes exceed domestic production, but demand has been falling for some years.

Fruit with cores and pips

Poire – Pear
Summer pears, such as Williams pears and Jules Guyot, are the most popular. Provence grows the most pears, followed by Rhône-Alpes. They are popular raw, but can also be turned into dishes such as stewed fruit, cakes, creams, soufflés or ice cream. They can also be cooked in syrup or wine, or eaten as *poire Hélène* with vanilla ice cream and chocolate sauce. Also used for excellent fruit brandy.

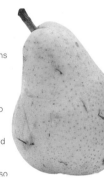

Pomme – Golden Delicious apple
Apples account for 25 percent of French fruit consumption. They top the production and export lists, and in good years they earn big profits. Still unbeaten at the top of the list, with 48 percent, is the Golden Delicious variety. Apples can be used as the basis for doughnuts, turnovers, apple tarts or *tartes Tatin*. They can be stewed or used for making apple juice, syrup, cider and Calvados. They can also be dried.

Coing – Quince
Conditions in the Rhône valley are good for quinces, and yet the hard-skinned fruit of the *cognassiers*, which belong to the rosewood family and are up to 20 feet (6 meters) high, is rarely cultivated commercially. Nonetheless, quinces can be found at the weekly markets in the fall. They are used to make exquisite jelly, and people also like to make pastes from them as a typical Christmas candy.

Exotics

Kiwi fruit

The French production figures are one more indication of the extent to which the kiwi or Chinese gooseberry – which emerged from New Zealand to conquer the world – has now become naturalized in Europe. French production makes up 20 percent of the European kiwi crop and totals 81,500 tons (74,000 tonnes). The medium brown, hairy fruit with green flesh – which contains a great deal of vitamin C – is peeled or halved and spooned out; it is also used for cakes and jams.

Figue – Fig

The fig tree, which originally came from the Orient, has long been established in the southern Rhône region and in Provence. In spring, the trees produce a first generation of embryos which do not mature. The next generation yields the main crop. The color range of the soft shining fruit extends from yellow to green and from red to violet. In the south of France, where they ripen in late summer and fall, figs are cultivated mainly to be eaten raw, as a seasonal dessert or for jams.

Kaki – Persimmon

Originally from the Far East, the sharon fruit trees, known as *plaqueminiers*, prosper well in Mediterranean climates. Their smooth, tomato-like fruits ripen late and their bright orange color has a particularly decorative effect in gardens. It is only when they are fully ripe that they develop their discreet aroma and pleasantly sweet taste. They also contain an extraordinary quantity of carotene. They add richness to the range of fruit available in winter. They are spooned out and used in fruit salads or for jams.

Nuts

Amande douce – Sweet almond

Almond trees were brought to the Rhône in the 16th century by the famous agronomist Olivier de Serres. The pit fruit, a relative of the peach, has an outer shell which is rough and furry and bursts open when it reaches maturity. The almond supplies what is probably the most important basic ingredient for traditional confectionery such as pralines, nougat or marzipan, and is also of prime importance in cake-making. It is cultivated all over the south of France, but production lags far behind demand.

Noisette – Hazelnut

Found everywhere in Europe, the fruit of the hazelnut bush, protected by a hard shell, is one of the oldest of all foods. Demand is certainly markedly higher than domestic production, but French hazelnuts, in particular the Segorbe and Fertile de Contard varieties, are also in demand for export. They are planted mainly in the southwest, but also in Isère and Drôme. Apart from their use in candies, chocolate, cakes and biscuits, their cold-pressed oil is also remarkable.

Melon – Melon

Related to the pumpkin, melons are really a type of vegetable, but with their sweetness and juiciness they claim a place among the fruit. The per capita French consumption is more than 7 pounds (over 3 kilograms) a year. They need fertile soils, a mild climate and a lot of water. Tarn-et-Garonne is the main growing area here, but Vaucluse is close behind. That's where the Charentais is grown – a flavorful Cantaloupe melon, which is also known as the Cavaillon melon, after the main center where it is found. Melons are the ideal fruit for hot days, as their taste and aroma come out especially well when they are cooled. They can be halved and the seeds can be removed (about 20 percent of the fruit's weight consists of waste). The soft flesh of the fruit can be spooned out of the skin, or can be mixed with other fruit such as raspberries. However, there are also classic entrées which combine the sweetness of melons with the strong taste of ham or crustaceans.

Châtaigne – Sweet chestnut

The most extensive sweet chestnut woods are in Ardèche, with trees which are between 50 and 150 years old. The Comballe is the most highly prized of the numerous old varieties. The smallest sweet chestnuts are chosen for dried and ground flour which is used to make bread and cakes. The medium-sized ones are earmarked for *crème de marrons vanillée*, chestnut cream, a popular sweet spread eaten on bread. The largest fruit are sent directly to be sold for roasting, or are cooked as side-dishes. The chestnuts used in *marrons glacés*, candied chestnuts, come from Italy.

Noix – Walnut

Isère possesses the most extensive walnut tree groves in France. The nuts from this region are marketed as *noix de Grenoble*. From the middle of September, fresh nuts are available, and should be consumed rapidly. One month later, they are followed by the new crop of dried walnuts, which are in great demand as ingredients or garnishing for cakes and candies. But they can also be found in salads and sauces, and can be served with poultry or other types of meat. Their cold-pressed oil is used in particular to improve salads.

Great wines of the north Rhône
Côte Rôtie, Condrieu, Hermitage & Co.

Syrah is a fruity variety which buds early. So the fruiting is a very tricky phase, as the weather can often change suddenly, and Syrah grapes have a tendency to drop off the vine. On the other hand, the crop can also be harvested early. In the northern Rhône region in particular, this can be a decisive advantage.

Between Valence in the south and the little town of Vienne in the north (founded by the Romans) lies one of the oldest wine-producing areas of France. It is believed that vines were planted here as far back as the 4th century B.C. At all events the Romans, arriving around 100 B.C., recognized the region's potential. The vineyards extend along the well-protected slopes on the right bank of the Rhône, which are often very steep and face south or southeast. The climate is continental. Granite is the dominant geological element, with only thin layers of soil on top to provide nourishment for the vines. The plots of land, which are mainly arranged in terraces, are very difficult to work, and the yields are decidely low, which is clearly reflected in the high quality of the wines. The only red variety is Syrah, a native of these parts, which produces dark red, tannin-rich wines. These are long-lived and very full-bodied, and frequently carry bouquets of berries or wild herbs.

As for Côte Rôtie, in earlier times it was the custom to add up to 20 percent of the white Viognier to it, thereby emphasizing the elegance of this red wine. In its own right, Viognier lends an outstanding character to the Condrieu and Château Grillet white wines which fascinates connoisseurs and drives prices upward. It has to be fully mature to develop its distinctive floral and fruity bouquet.

The other two white varieties from the northern Rhône are Marsanne and Rousanne. The first is a strong-growing, high-yield variety, and produces powerful, heavy wines. Until recently, the Rousanne variety, which is very difficult to cultivate, was trailing far behind. But it makes the perfect wine for blending – it is refined, spirited, and has a good acidity. It is increasingly used for the best white Hermitage. A better-known wine is the dark red Hermitage. Made from Syrah grapes, sometimes with a little Marsanne blended in, it is a wine which ages very well. Until far into the 19th century, high-quality Bordeaux was often fortified with Hermitage, the result of the process being referred to as *hermitagé*. In recent years, the great varieties of grape from the northern Rhône have begun a triumphal procession around the world. The Syrah grape now allows the wine growers in the south of France to produce red wine of a previously unheard-of quality. The white varieties, on the other hand, present greater difficulties.

Côte Rôtie
The most northern *cru* of the Rhône region – 200 hectares (490 acres), at least 80 percent Syrah (nowadays usually 95–100 percent), enriched with white Viognier. Approximately 1 million bottles a year. Grows on very steep slopes with granite subsoil – on the Côte de Blonde with pebbly loam, on the Côte de Brune with clay soils containing iron oxide. Much in demand since the 1970s, this is a noble red wine with an intense bouquet of raspberries, violets and vanilla, resulting from the new oak casks used for the maturing process. It can age extremely well and, in addition to fruity notes, it also contains smoky aromas and hints of truffles.

Condrieu
Once a sought-after sweet wine, this is nowadays usually a dry white wine. 97 hectares (240 acres), average production 380,000 bottles. Made exclusively from Viognier grapes. This is their classic growing area, on the steep granite terraces above a former river port of the same name, where the vines can be tended only by hand. Pale golden color, with an intense bouquet in which, apart from flowery notes, the predominant factors are apricots and pears, with a silky, sometimes slightly oily, structure. Best drunk at 55 °F (12 °C) as an aperitive and within three years of bottling.

Marsanne grapes

Roussanne grapes

Syrah grapes

Viognier grapes

Château Grillet

The central area of this *appellation* takes up only 3.5 hectares (8.6 acres) within the property of the same name and dates back to before the time of the Romans. The growing area consists of stony, steep terraces, with coarse granite sand. The very meticulously organised terraces were extended lower in the mid-eighties. The Viognier grapes, which were formerly often picked early, are now matured in oak barrels for two years. Approximately 13,500 bottles a year.

Saint-Joseph

This almost 900 hectare (2223-acre) strip extends for over 30 miles (50 kilometers) along the right bank of the Rhône between the Condrieu and Cornas regions. Although the soil structures are many and various, granite and gneiss form the common denominator. Dedicated winegrowers have been able to improve the quality of the wines a great deal in recent times. The Syrah-based reds are grapey and harmonious, with a fine aroma and a medium structure. The whites, pressed from Marsanne and Roussanne, are characterized by floral aromas and elegance. 3.8 million bottles.

Cornas

Behind the first terraces, with their old alluvial soils, the heart of this red wine *appellation* takes the form of an area rising as high as 1475 feet (450 meters). With sandy granite slopes facing the morning and midday sun, it covers 92 hectares (225 acres), and is reserved exclusively for Syrah. Since the 10th century, Cornas has been known for robust, dark red wines. The grapes are usually picked when fully ripe and the stalks are removed. It needs another five years to develop to its full complexity, which combines hints of over-ripe black grapes and cherries with licorice, spice, cocoa and truffle notes. Average production, 415,000 bottles.

Saint-Péray

The most southerly *appellation* area of the northern Rhône region is the coolest, but also the most uniform, from the point of view of the soils. Lying opposite Valance, the greater part of this 60 hectare (148-acre) area consists of steep slopes, with a narrow valley. Entirely dedicated to the white Marsanne and Rousanne varieties, this region has been mainly devoted to producing sparkling wine since 1829. The traditional technique of fermentation in the bottle is used to produce the characteristic intense floral bouquet. The region's non-sparkling dry wines have freshness and style, thanks to the Rousanne grape. 300,000 bottles in all.

Crozes-Hermitage

The largest *appellation* area in the north Rhône area (1200 hectares/2964 acres) surrounds the famous Hermitage. It extends over granite slopes to the north, but in the south consists overwhelmingly of terraces with glacial and fluvial deposits, together with loess. The mistral cools the grapes and the Syrah wines are frequently distinguished by delicate fresh fruit aromas, harmony and delicate tannins; they are often ready for drinking after two or three years. The whites obtained from Marsanne (and occasionally from Roussanne) grapes are initially floral, but then develop notes of honey and dried fruits. A good 6 million bottles.

Hermitage

Like the Crozes on the left bank, but occupying 134 hectares (331 acres) of protected slopes facing south, above the little town of Tain-l'Hermitage. While the highest terraces consist of granite, covered with mica shales and gneiss, the lower layers were formed by deposits. The red wines are made from Syrah grapes with up to 15 percent white grapes. When left to age for long periods – 20 years or more – they develop hints of smoke, leather and candied grapes. The full white wines, tasting of hazelnuts and almonds, are made from Marsanne and Rousanne grapes and age almost as well. 560,000 bottles.

The wines of Savoy

In this extremely fascinating region, with eternal glaciers towering above, the white wines of Savoy flourish. They are fruity and brilliant, dry and refreshing. They are best drunk with fish from the clean lakes and streams.

Vines take root in the low rock rubble slopes of its mountains which face toward the sun. Somewhere around 1500 hectares (3700 acres) betwen Lake Geneva and Albertville are stocked with the 20 white varieties grouped under its four *appellations*, which correspond to its departments, Savoie, Haute Savoie, Isère and Ain.

The most important are Jacquère, Rousette, Chardonnay and Chasselas. One of the finest whites, Chignin-Bergeron, has a bouquet of peaches, and is based on the Rousanne variety (here referred to as Bergeron). Sixteen *crus* have the Savoie A.O.C., which can be coupled with their own names. Four communes are well-known for Rousette, a highly aromatic white wine: Frangy, Marestel, Monterminod and Monthoux. This wine is also known as Altesse. Red and rosé wine also flourish in the soils of Arbin, Chautagne, Chignin,

Cruet, Jongieux, Montmélian and Saint-Jean-de-la-Porte. Here the old-established Mondeuse, with its elegant, slightly sour wines, sets the tone, rather than the Gamay variety.

The fruit-flavored wines of Savoy go splendidly with the local sausage and cheese specialties.

Chartreuse

At one time, every monastery produced its own elixir, but Chartreuse is the only French liqueur which is still manufactured by the monks to this day. Only three of the Carthusian monks know the recipe, with ingredients derived from a total of 130 plants, and the proportions in which they are mixed. The elixir on which the liqueurs are based is still used as a medicine, and is sold in small bottles which are protected against the effects of light by wooden display cases. The liqueurs themselves, which are naturally green or yellow due to the herbs they contain, are known all over the world, and have earned their place on the best drinks trolleys.

The fascinating history of Grande Chartreuse began with Saint Bruno, who came into this world in Cologne in 1030. Later he became one

of the scholastics at the University of Rheims, but the search for matters eternal lay closer to his heart than any desire for fleeting earthly success. So in 1084 he set out for Grenoble to visit his friend Saint Hugo. Hugo had had a dream about an inhospitable place known as the wastes of Chartreuse, where they built a chapel and some wooden cells, helped by the first monks. Saint Bruno, who was called to Rome six years later, later founded a new monastery in Calabria, where he died in 1101. When the original buildings were destroyed by an avalanche in 1132, the Carthusians built a new monastery nearby, on the present site. This rose to be the Grande Chartreuse and the headquarters of the order. But it was not spared further catastrophes, and the present imposing cloister building dates from the 17th century.

In 1605, Marshal d'Estrées gave the Carthusians a manuscript containing the recipe for the herbal elixir. It is not known who actually discovered

Destroyed several times in its history, the headquarters of the Carthusian order has been rebuilt each time in a grander version.

this recipe. But at that time the brothers were so busy mining ore from the mountains and smelting iron that it was not until 1735 that a monk called Jerôme Maubec devoted some serious attention to it. Using the recipe as a basis, this monastic chemist developed a practical way of manufacturing the elixir. His successor, Brother Antoine, perfected it in 1764. Since then, the Grande Chartreuse herbal elixir has always been manufactured in the same way. Its reputation as a stimulant is based on its medicinal properties. Its fame spread far and wide, and the monks distributed it without charge to the poor of the region. Soon they began to use it as the basis for distilling a medicinal liqueur containing 55 percent alcohol by volume.

In Voiron, in the valley far below the Grande Chartreuse, the monks of today distil the elixir which lies at the heart of their liqueur.

The French Revolution drove the monks out and scattered them. A copy of the valuable manuscript was made in 1793 as a precaution, and it was preserved by the only monk who was allowed to stay in the monastery. The original was in the hands of a monk who had been elevated to the priesthood, and he always kept it in his habit. When he was arrested, he managed to slip the manuscript to a monk who had found shelter near the Grande Chartreuse. But this man had lost any belief that his order would be restored, and he gave the recipe to the pharmacist Liotard of Grenoble. In 1810, the Emperor Napoleon issued a decree ordering that all medicines with "secret ingredients" should be submitted to the Ministry of the Interior to be examined. Liotard dutifully submitted the recipe, but it was sent back to him bearing the comment "rejected." After his death, the document was returned to the Grande Chartreuse and distillation was resumed.

From 1838 onward, Brother Bruno Jacquet also used the original elixir to make a sweeter and gentler liqueur containing 40 percent alcohol by volume. He added plants to give it a yellow color, and it proved especially popular with the ladies. Until 1869, the elixir and the green and yellow varieties of Chartreuse were manufactured in the monastery's pharmacy. Production was then transferred to a distillery at Fourvoirie, which was not as high up as the monastery. In 1935, this building was destroyed by a landslide.

When the Carthusians were expelled from France in 1903, the three brothers who had the secret recipe settled in Tarragona, in Spain, and founded their own distillery. Production was actually resumed in France as well, but it did not really get under way until the Carthusians had been given back their original monastery in 1940. Then it was carried on in new buildings in Voiron.

The liqueurs manufactured by the Carthusians are completely natural and are free from chemical additives. The herbs they gather are dried and stored in wooden baskets in the monastery, where the purchased ingredients are added. There the initiated fathers grind and mix the 130 constituents and fill up the bags which are taken to Voiron, to the secular Chartreuse company, which deals with production and sales. The herbs are first macerated in selected alcohol and then distilled to obtain the elixir. To produce the liqueurs, honey must be added, among some other ingredients, and the mixture must then be aged before being drained off into large containers. It has to mature for eight years in the largest liqueur cellars in the world (164 meters/ 538 feet long), and is then bottled and marked V.E.P – *Vieillissement Exceptionellement Prolongé* (Exceptionally Long Ageing). The liqueur is drunk as a digestive, neat with ice cubes, or as a long drink mixed with juice or tonic in a very worldly way. But there are still only three monks who know the recipe, which long ago became a valuable trade secret.

Liqueurs

Flowers, berries, fruit, herbs and, depending on the plant, leaves, stems, roots, shells, bark or seeds, are suitable for the manufacture of liqueurs. The pioneer in this field was none other than Arnau de Villanova, the dean of the medical faculty at the University of Montpellier (at that time in Catalonia), who is also considered as being the father of naturally sweet wines and aperitives. He brought the secrets of distillation home from a crusade in the Orient, and was using alcohol for medicinal purposes in the last quarter of the 13th century. He macerated the most varied medicinal plants in it, and added honey to these elixirs as the finishing touch, to give them a pleasanter taste. Maceration is still one of the two basic techniques for producing liqueurs. The details vary depending on the plant, but basically a pure and neutral-tasting alcohol is used, which is diluted to the desired strength with distilled water. After this plants or fruits are placed in it, individually or in mixtures. This maceration can take anything from a few hours to some weeks. Water swells the plant sections up so that alcohol can penetrate them, which releases flavors. In most cases, this process is followed by distillation. This gives rise to alcohol vapors and essential oils, which then condense. A second distillation process, rectification, refines the flavors. Before or after distillation, the chief distiller brings the components of the liqueur together. This produces the alcoholate, the aromatic principle. Mixed with sugar, alcohol and water and then filtered, this becomes the liqueur. Many recipes are more expensive and complicated, and require natural ingredients which do not yield clean and pleasant flavors when distilled. For this reason, certain fruits and – for example – nutshells may only be macerated. These aromatic solutions are then added to the alcoholate in a process of assemblage.

For a long time these elixirs, which were predominantly used as medicaments and tonics, remained the preserve of monasteries and pharmacies. There was, however, no reason why ladies and gentlemen who could afford it should not drink them simply for pleasure, and as early as the 14th century recipes appeared which put greater emphasis on the potential for enjoyment. This then led to the appearance of genuine liqueurs. The availability of cane sugar and spices from distant lands meant they could be refined. But it was not until after the French Revolution that the entire nation developed a taste for such sweet comforts. Every little town soon had its own liqueur distiller. Or, indeed, several. They macerated, distilled and mixed; combined flavors; juggled with essences; and brewed up dozens of different nips and tipples. Their customers lived in the neighborhood, or at any rate in the same area. Nationally known brands did not as yet exist. It was not until the closing years of the 19th century that better opportunities finally presented themselves for liqueur manufacturers. At this time whatever came from the Orient was very much the height of fashion – from novels to furniture, from celebrations to flavors. Oranges, for instance, became very popular, as did the liqueur Dutch Curaçao, made from bitter oranges – the original oranges were the size of nuts. However it was dark, heavy and overloaded with flavors. Then Edouard Cointreau, a liqueur manufacturer of Angers, devised a simple alternative as transparent as water, which was not so sweet. This was a decisive breakthrough. As a consequence, the great brands were able to establish themselves and gain worldwide recognition. Although they have recently been used as mixers to add modern flair to long drinks or cocktails, they still show their true quality best as a digestive.

Benedictine

The recipe created in 1510 by Dom Bernardo Vincelli, a Benedictine monk, fell into the hands of a dealer in spirits in 1860. He created the "Bénédictine" brand from it, the original recipe for which contains 27 plants and spices, most of which come from abroad. The full-bodied digestive owes its color to an infusion of saffron.

Chartreuse V.E.P.

The eight years it spends maturing in wooden casks provide added complexity and smoothness to the famous green or yellow liqueur from the Carthusian

Bénédictine   Grand Chartreuse Élixir Végétal   Chartreuse V.E.P.   Cointreau   Génépy des Alpes

monastery in Dauphiné. Nowadays it is distilled in Voiron, where it ages in the largest liqueur cellar in the world. The recipe is only ever known at any one time by three silent brothers. It involves 130 different plants.

Cointreau
The transparent liqueur, as clear as water, was created by Edouard Cointreau. With its intense bouquet of oranges, it won a gold medal in Chicago way back in 1893. Its outstanding flavor, which makes it best suited for use as a mixer, is based on a mixture of the peels from bitter and sweet oranges, the essence of which is obtained in a distillation process which lasts eight hours.

Génépy des Alpes
Génépy de Barcelonnette Le Grand Rubren is based on a special kind of mugwort which is gathered in the Provençal Alps. Manufactured according to a recipe from the Ubaye Valley and using the old artisan method of maceration, it was the first liqueur to be awarded the *Provenance Montagne* label ("mountain made"). The fine aromatic liqueur can also be enjoyed with ice.

Grand Marnier
During the siege of Paris in 1870, the distillery owner Lapostolle fled to Charente, where he dealt in first-class cognacs. When the family returned to Paris, his son-in-law Marnier succeeded in distilling a bitter orange essence, which he blended with cognac to produce a fine liqueur. Since 1920, the family has owned its own cognac distillery.

Izarra
The star (which is what the name means in Basque), dates back to a very complex recipe of 1835, which the pharmacist Joseph Grattau used for his full-bodied liqueur. The essence, made up of 30 distilled herbs and spices, is mixed with three macerations of almonds, walnut shells and baked plums, as well as Armagnac and sugar syrup. The liqueur has to mature for six months in the cask before it can be bottled.

Marie Brizard
Around the year 1730, the nurse from a poor family in Bordeaux saved the life of a West Indian sailor. As a reward, he made over to her the recipe for an aniseed liqueur. It was so successful that in 1755 Marie Brizard and her nephew set up a company, which exists to this day. In addition to green aniseed, twelve other plants combine to give the liqueur its fresh taste.

Prunelle
This Burgundian sloe liqueur, for which the wild fruit are picked after a frost and have all their fruit flesh removed, is something of a rarity. The cleaned pits alone are macerated for at least six months in pure alcohol, which takes on their unusual flavor

and which is then distilled. Not only does it make an original digestive, but it is also an agreeable added ingredient of *café bourguignon*, an alcoholic coffee which usually contains *marc de Bourgogne*.

Suprême Denoix
For this exquisite nut liqueur from Brive, the juice of green walnuts from Corrèze, picked before Midsummer's Eve and then ground and mixed with alcohol, matures for five long years in oak casks. By then it has lost its bitterness and has a fine wooden note. Bas-Armagnac, cognac and syrup boiled over a wood fire are added to produce a specialty which is best enjoyed chilled or with ice.

Verveine du Velay
It was in 1859 that the herbalist Rumillet Charretier first put a liqueur on sale in which lemon verbena is the dominant ingredient. To make this product, leaves gathered and dried in the fall were macerated in alcohol for up to nine months, while juniper berries were macerated separately at the same time. He mixed the two with 30 other plants, distilled the result and rounded off the refined taste with honey, sugar and cognac.

Grand Marnier   Izarra   Marie Brizard   Prunelle   Suprême Denoix   Verveine de Velay

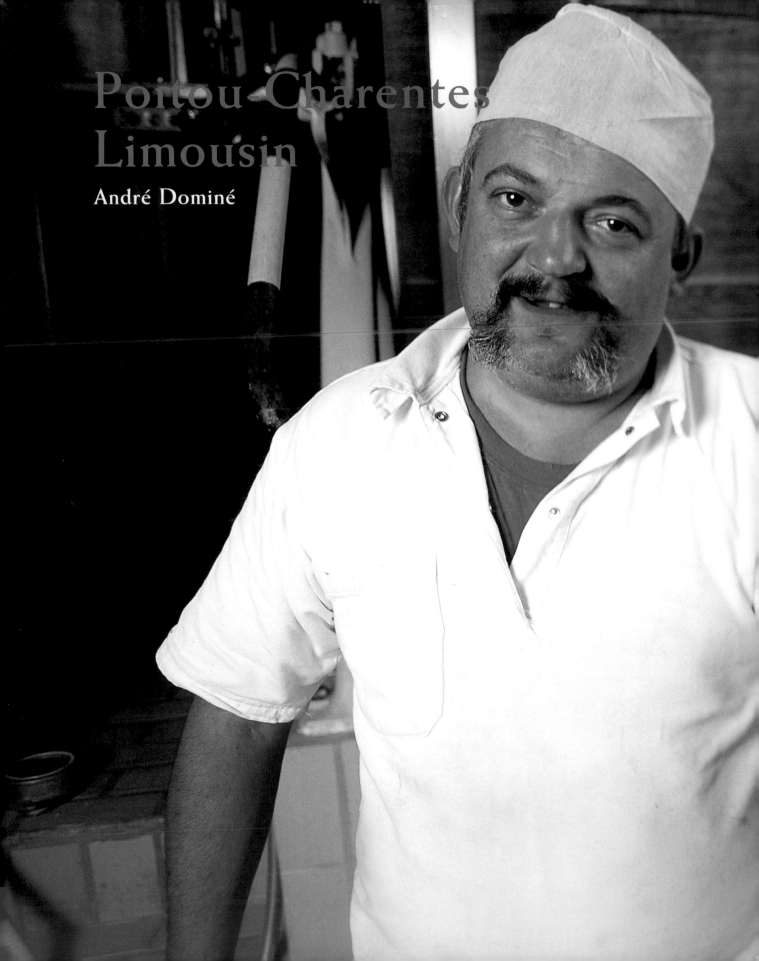

Poitou-Charentes
Limousin

André Dominé

Oysters
Treasures from the coast
France's premium butter
Heavenly allure –
 Angélique de Niort
Limousin cattle
The king of rabbits
Self-sufficiency in the
 kitchen
Cognac
Oak casks & barrels

Standing in front of a butter churn,
the dairyman proudly presents his product –
Echiré butter in the typical wooden basket

In La Tremblade, on the west bank of the 865 foot (800 meter) wide Seudre estuary, as in its counterpart Marennes, everything focuses on the running of the oyster parks, which extend far inland.

Calais

Le Havre

Caen

Paris

Brest

Rennes

Strasbourg

Orléans

Nantes

Tours

Dijon

Poitou-
Charentes

Limousin

Lyon

St-Étienne

Grenoble

Bordeaux

Avignon

Nice

Biarritz

Toulouse

Marseille

Toulon

Perpignan

Each morning as the small cutters unload their catch in the fortified Vieux Port, La Rochelle once more puts to the test its claim not only to be the town with the greatest culinary wealth on the coasts of the Vendée and Charente-Maritime, but also the triumphant victor over rivals in the Poitou and Charente. The offshore Ile de Ré, whose salt once contributed to the wealth of the picturesque port, today supplies such delicacies as top-quality oysters from the nearby Oléron-Marennes basin and delicious *moules de bouchot* from the neighbouring Bay of Aiguillon. But La Rochelle also obtains fresh produce from its hinterland, to which it is connected by the Charente, flowing into the sea only a short distance to the south, and by the Sèvre Niortaise.

The Sèvre Niortaise leads to the Marais Poitevin, the former Gulf of Poitou which has now silted up. In the middle ages, monks began to lay out water courses there and build dikes enabling them to take advantage of the fertile, silt-enriched soil. Today, the Marais is divided up into the drained, intensively cultivated part and the romantic Marais, crossed by innumerable waterways, with its gardens which can be reached by punt. Further inland, the Poitou exhibits barren planes where the most important product is the goat cheese, while in the area around Parthenay the Vendée boasts luscious meadows in which Parthenaise cattle graze. Nearer to the coast, particularly around Challans, top-grade poultry is reared. The most luxuriant meadows of the Poitou and both Charentes produce the best butter and fresh cream in France. However, the most famous commodity of the entire region remains its cognac. The enormous cellars and large stores stand along the banks of the slow-flowing Charente in the town of the same name and in sleepy Jarnac.

To the east, stretching beyond Angoulême, are gently undulating meadows and fields, broken up by numerous small woods, which lead to the Limousin. Here, the wide pasture becomes increasingly hilly, rising to the 2600 feet (800 meters) high Plateau de Millevaches. This area is home to large flocks of sheep, as well as the contented Limousin cattle, whose meat is so highly rated among many connoisseurs. The extensive woodlands have an abundance of game and are a true paradise for mushroom pickers. In the south, around Brive, the cooking is characterized by influences drawn from Perigord and the Auvergne combined with a basic robustness.

Oysters

Oyster farmers are regarded as the farmers of the sea and their work actually has many features in common with conventional farming, even though they are dependent on the tides and must always wait for the ebb before they can "cultivate" their fields, which are referred to as parks in oyster farming. The French oyster parks are situated along the coast of Brittany, at Marennes and Arcachon and also on the Mediterranean at Bouzigues in the Thau lagoon.

The parks in the Marennes area cover some 8600 acres (3500 hectares). They extend to the sand banks between the mouths of the rivers Seudre and Charente and along the east side of the offshore Ile d'Oléron. Here the oysters find a suitable mix of salt and fresh water and water temperatures of over 72 °F (22 °C) in summer, which they need to thrive. The native flat European oyster was seriously decimated by an epidemic in 1922. Fortunately, there was a suitable replacement at hand, since in 1868 a ship in distress had been forced to abandon to the sea its cargo of Portuguese oysters. They flourished on the coast of Marennes until falling

victim to an epidemic. A remedy was provided by the deep-shelled Japanese rock oyster *Crassostrea gigas*, which has since dominated the coastal areas and restaurants of France.

The oysters breed in July on naturally formed but rigorously protected banks. The invertebrate mollusks belonging to the mussel family reproduce by means of millions of larvae which are free-swimming to begin with, but then seek out a firm hold. This is where the *ostréiculteur*, the oyster farmer, has his opportunity. He installs bricks, weatherboards or the now commonly used corrugated plastic pipes at favorable strategic points. The larvae cling to them and immediately

Ostrea edulis, huître plate, European Oyster
Named according to their breeding areas as Belons, Marennes or Gravettes d'Arcachon. This relatively uncommon oyster has a delicately mineral flavor.

Crassostrea angulata, huître creuse, Portuguese or rock oyster
A cupped oyster, particularly farmed in Marennes-Oléron, where its flavor is refined in *claires* or fattening pools; its importance is diminishing.

Crassostrea gigas, huître creuse du Pacifique Pacific rock oyster or Japanese oyster
Referred to as *gigas* or *japonaise* in France. This is the largest and most resilient type and has been gaining significance over recent years.

The oyster farmers use motor boats to gather the harvest from the banks and transfer it to the fattening pools (*claires*) by lorry.

Oysters freshly removed from the *claires* can endure three to four days in transit without any adverse effects; on the contrary, this makes the salt water flavor less pronounced.

Types of oyster

Belons
A flat oyster from Brittany with a very delicate, nutty flavor.

Bouzigues
From the large lagoon of Thau on the Mediterranean coast between Sète and Agde.

Gravette d'Arcachon
Usually referred to simply as "Arcachons"; flat oysters from the Atlantic coast around Bordeaux.

Marennes
Rock oysters from the area between the Charente coast and the Ile d'Oléron are fattened and refined in natural pools or *claires*.
- *Claires* have been briefly refined in fattening pools.
- *Fines de claires* have spent four weeks in the fattening pool with 20 oysters per square yard and are no less than 6 percent meat.
- *Spéciales de claires* have spent eight weeks in the *claires* with 10 oysters per square yard and are at least 9 percent

Hold the oyster firmly with the left hand so that the flatter side is uppermost.

Take a strong short knife and insert the point in the adductor or "hinge."

start to develop their shell. At two months they have already grown to the size of a pea. Only a dozen offspring per oyster will successfully run the gantlet of their first stage of life.

When spring arrives, the breeders from La Tremblade, for instance, move the pipe colonies bearing the young *gigas*, which from now on require the more substantial nourishment for accelerated growth that can only be provided by sea water. They are therefore placed on iron racks in the bay of Ronce-les-Bains. Even in their second year, the dangers to which the young oysters are exposed are still present and they are at risk from fish, snails, starfish mussels – even storms can spell disaster for them and their breeders. The breeders strip the surviving oysters from the pipes, grade them according to size and determine their subsequent use. Some continue their growth in *poches*, black plastic nets on iron frames anchored to the sea bed. Others are sown to maintain the beds and oysters which are too small are given a twelve month season.

Each breeder has leased different parcels from the State. Some of these provide plenty of food, others less so. The oysters will grow quickly in one parcel, while their growth is stunted in another. The breeder takes advantage of these natural conditions to control the development of his oysters.

After three years the oysters could actually be

Left: Whether a pigpen or a palace, each oyster has its home address, where it is kept fresh in its original packing or *bourriches*.

The adductor is severed by moving the blade horizontally, after which the knife is used to prize the shell.

The shells are levered open by twisting the blade.

After removing the top shell, the oyster is either swallowed or served on ice.

fished out and consumed. But not in Marennes-Oléron. Shallow basins used in the past for salt production extend across the coastal marshes and 12 miles (20 kilometers) up the Seudre valley. It was the Romans, themselves great oyster-lovers, who discovered their unique advantage. The *claires*, which receive a fresh supply of seawater with each tide, thanks to an ingenious network of channels, provide an ideal resting place for the oysters where they stop growing but their shells harden, making them less perishable. They feed on single-celled algae, the blue Navicula, which means they not only gain weight and flavor, but at the same time take on a surprisingly green hue. In addition, they develop a large amount of glycogen, a carbohydrate, and are rich in mineral salts and vitamins.

Kept in their original packing, the *bourriche*, at temperatures of 40–60 °F (5–15 °C), *fines de claires* and *spéciales de claires* will stay fresh for eight to ten days, even in summer. This is when the smaller, firmer specimens taste best. True connoisseurs never eat oysters straight out of the water, but give them at least four days to settle. And in the Charente the gourmet pours away the juice from the shell and would never consider drinking it. Apart from this, the wise oyster-lover considers the size of his mouth when selecting oysters because, as everybody knows, it should not be over-full, particularly when eating from the shell.

Most important for the fish stew found on the Atlantic coast is that the ingredients from the sea are supremely fresh.

Prepare a stock using vegetables, bouquet garni, butter and white wine and cook red barbel, skate, Norway lobster and eel in this.

Add pieces of octopus which have been precooked for 45 minutes to the other ingredients and warm through.

After cooking the fish for 5–10 minutes, depending on its texture, arrange it on warmed plates.

Sieve the stock, beat in the remaining butter and adjust the seasoning.

Pour the hot sauce carefully over the fish and garnish each plate with fresh herbs.

Treasures from the coast

Along the coast of the Vendée and Charente-Maritime, the fish and shellfish are of high quality. After all, *chalutiers* and *sardiniers*, trawlers and sardine boats, as well as other fishing boats, set sail from the ports of Royan, La Cotinière, La Rochelle, Les Sables-d'Olonne and Croix-de-Vie. The boats based in the Vendée sail as far as Irish waters, but for ships from the Charente, the coastal waters and the Bay of Biscay are the most important fishing grounds. The best fish auction for interest, if not importance, can be visited in La Rochelle.

Although catches include turbot, monkfish, sole, red barbel, skate, sea bass or white tuna and fresh lobster, crabs, cockles and Venus-shells are to be found on market stalls and in fish shops, local customers set particular store by three categories of regional specialties. The first of these includes *céteau, casseron,* shrimps and crayfish. They are so keen on the sandy coastal and offshore waters that they can be caught there in large quantities. The second category is that of oysters and mussels, for which the river estuaries provide ideal breeding conditions with their mix of salt and fresh water. Elvers and eels also occupy a special position. Eels are caught in equal quantities in both salt and fresh water, while elvers are harvested from the river estuaries.

The *céteau,* a flat fish easily mistaken for young *soles* and often also referred to as *solette* is highly rated. It migrates to the coast in spring and

summer, where it falls prey to the fishermen's nets. Usually only about 6–8 inches (15–20 centimeters) long and with a very delicate flavor, it is preferred roasted or used in the *chaudrée,* the typical fisherman's stew. The *casseron,* as young octopus is referred to here on the Atlantic, is also found in this dish. It is born in the coastal waters and should preferably be eaten when around six months old. The highly rated *crevette rose,* which is nearly 4 inches (10 centimeters) long and takes on an appetizingly bright pink color when cooked, is found along the west coast of the Ile d'Oléron. Its season stretches from September to March. The smaller *crevette grise* only turns slightly pink when cooked, but is available the whole year round. They are both caught using hoop nets.

In order to catch *langoustines,* the boats have to sail further out into the Bay of Biscay. This small

The *chaudrée*, a fish stew found along the entire Atlantic coast, used to be prepared using fish that had not been sold. Today it is the equivalent of the Provençal *bouillabaisse*.

relative of the lobster (a relationship evident from the claws), also referred to as crayfish or scampi, loves the muddy sea bed, which it leaves at night in search of prey. This is when it can be caught using particularly fine-meshed trawling nets, which scour the sea bed (causing ecological damage).

Eels are for the most part the preferred catch of the recreational fishermen who pursue their pastime on the numerous inlets of the Poitevin marshlands, this impressive water garden between Niort and the mouth of the Sèvre. However, they are also fished by boat along the coast and particularly in the river estuaries. Here, and also a short way up the rivers where they are swept by the tide, *piballes* or *civelles*, which are at least 2½ inches (6 centimeters) long, and transparent elvers are fished. They are caught either from boats or by standing in the shallow water at the river edge, using baskets or landing nets. The main season begins in mid-October, when the elvers are born in the Sargasso Sea, swim with the Gulf Stream and reach the Atlantic coast of France.

Although the mild-tasting eel fry are regarded as great delicacies in the Charente, Libournais and Bordeaux regions, many fishermen are unable to resist the premium prices that the Spaniards and, in particular, the Japanese are willing to pay for these. Oysters from Marennes-Oléron and mussels are more abundant and better value for money.

Moules de bouchot

Mussels have been bred in the Bay of Aiguillon since the middle ages. On the one hand, it is sheltered by the offshore Ile de Ré and, on the other, the Sèvre Niortaise which flows into it reduces the salt content, creating natural conditions ideal for mussels.

As elsewhere along the coast of the Vendée and Charente at the mouths of rivers, where attempts had been made to retain the fish using permanent barriers and to catch them in this comparatively simple way, so they tried using stakes in the village of Charron, with its soft, muddy ground. It soon emerged that mussels were attaching themselves to these stakes and quickly growing – the principle of mussel breeding had been devised. Rows of yard-long oak stakes are still planted close together along the sea bed. A *bouchot* always comprises 84 of these. However, ropes and nets are now used as an additional aid, to make it easier for the mussels to settle. Harvesting is no longer done by hand, as in the past, and the mussels are stripped from the poles mechanically.

Mussel breeding, which had undergone an unexpected boom in the 18th and 19th centuries, spread not only on the Ile de Ré but also between the Ile d'Oléron and Brouage, the one-time fortified salt capital marking the point where the oyster parks end.

The comparatively small *moules de bouchot* are juicy and fleshy with an excellent flavor. They are usually used to prepare *mouclade* in the Charente, served in a cream sauce. A summer delight with a long-standing tradition is the *éclade*. This involves the mussels being spread on a board and covered with a thick layer of pine needles. The needles are lit, so that the mussels are broiled and take on a mildly smoked flavor.

A julienne of finely chopped garden vegetables in cream, so frequently used in Poitou-Charentes, garnishes the oysters which have been warmed through in the oven.

In Charente, the most popular way of eating the mussels bred along the coast is in the form of a *mouclade* in a creamy sauce made from the mussel cooking liquid, egg yolk and crème fraîche.

Potatoes from the Ile de Ré and oysters from the Ile d'Oléron are used to make this galette, a tasty combination with a distinctly regional flavor.

Shaped by hand, wrapped in golden, metallic paper and packed in the typical *bourriche* or basket, so beurre Echiré reaches its customers.

France's premium butter

Echiré

Nowadays, butter is so natural a part of our table as to suggest that it has been around for centuries. However, in reality, "good butter" only came to be known scarcely a hundred years ago, in family kitchens at least. It had made an appearance in the kitchens of castles and palaces far earlier, in the 16th century, and has probably been around for thousands of years, but has been a rare product due to the speed with which it spoils.

In both Charentes, an insect – *phylloxera* – prepared the ground for butter. It destroyed vines, leaving many ruined vinegrowers with no option other than to turn to the dairy industry. The first cooperative was established in 1888 and with the introduction of pasteurization and the selective breeding of dairy cattle business flourished, particularly since the Atlantic coast's damp, temperate climate was ideally suited to the growth of lush grass.

In Echiré, a village to the north-east of Niort, where the pasture is girded by the Sèvre Niortaise, the benefits of nature have been exploited to the full and the cooperative founded in 1894 sees to the well-being of its members and their cattle. The milk is collected each day by the cooperative's own trucks, so that it is as fresh as possible when processed.

Once the cream has been separated by centrifuge, 1–2 percent milk ferment is added

Left: The rapid beating of the cream bursts the membranes of the fat globules, the butter fat is released and starts to form the butter grain.

Crème fraîche

It may be either sweet or sour, but this label is generally taken to mean *crème fraîche épaisse*. This is also obtained by separating the cream from milk, after which milk ferments are added to produce a slight acidification. With a 35–40 percent fat content, it has a very creamy structure and is ideal for binding sauces. The most famous is the Isigny Ste Mère *crème fraîche* produced in Calvados, which has its own Appellation d'Origine Contrôlée, although almost every major dairy produces a similar product, including Echiré.

and the cream is left to mature biologically for 16 to 18 hours at 57 °F (14 °C). It is then beaten again in the large, hard-wearing, teak churn. The constant beating breaks down the membrane of the fat globules, so that the butter fat is released and coagulates into ever larger lumps, the butter grains. Once they have grown to the size of peas, the virtually fat-free buttermilk is drained off and the buttermilk residue rinsed with spring water, to prevent it from producing a cheesy flavor. The butter is then kneaded so that the grains finally produce a uniform mass with a 16 percent moisture content. The finished, fresh *beurre Echiré*, wrapped in gold foil in its small basket, has a perfect consistency and its fine, nutty aroma raises it above its numerous rivals from the Charentes-Poitou, Normandy and other regions in northern France.

Once the butter has reached the correct consistency, the workers empty the strong teak churn.

Heavenly allure

Angélique de Niort

It is said that in the middle ages the archangel Gabriel himself revealed to a devout monk the secret of this umbelliferous plant, known as angelica and by its Latin name *Angelica archangelica*, which was launched into a rapidly rising career as a medicinal remedy. It is not only said to have worked wonders with all sorts of chest complaints, stomach and intestinal trouble, bites and rheumatism, but was above all regarded as a heavenly weapon for combating plague and other epidemics. Modern scientists believe that it was not so much angels as charlatans who glorified angelica, as they have been unable to find any medicinally beneficial substances, either in the plant's roots, or its stem or seeds, apart from essential oils. However, this does not alter the fact that angelica made its appearance in Niort in 1603 when plague was devastating the town on the edge of the Poitevin marshland. Leaving aside the therapeutic successes of angelica, one thing is certain: the Niortais enjoyed its taste. In any event, there is a long tradition among the *confiseurs* of this peaceful town, built between two hillsides beside the Sèvre Niortaise and maintaining close links with the surrounding countryside, of candying the angelica stems. As early as the late 18th century, the bright green stems were famous as candy, referred to as *confiture d'angélique*, because they had been preserved in sugar (French: *confire*). Angelica was probably already being planted at the start of the 17th century in the area around Niort, close to the Sèvre where conditions were ideal. This plant, which can grow to heights of up to eight feet (two-and-a-half meters), loves damp, preferably loamy soils, but also sun and a mild climate. Cultivation only spread in the 19th century. A symbolic start was made by a notary from the town. When the castle was pulled down in 1826, with only the twin-towered keep surviving, he sowed angelica in the castle moat, which reawakened the Niortais' love of the plant. Nowadays, 50 tons of angelica a year are harvested in the Deux-Sèvres.

Angelica is a biennial which only develops leaves in the first year. Only in its second year does it

The double keep, symbol of Niort, is the opulent relict of a castle completed by Richard Lionheart. The connecting residential quarters were added in the 15th century.

Angelica has for centuries been the specialty of this quaint town on the edge of the Marais where it is routinely crystallized by all the local *confiseurs*, but only Bernard Albert uses it for modeling.

The much sought-after candied sticks of angelica are produced from the young stems of this medicinal plant from the marshlands which can grow to heights of up to eight feet (two-and-a-half meters).

produce the thick, bed, hollow stems from which the umbels branch. Although the leaves and seeds are used, the stems are the most valuable part. They are cut close to the ground and are either used fresh or preserved in the traditional manner in brine, where they will keep for up to a year without losing any of their natural greenness. They must then be rinsed under running water for half a day to remove the salt before being used. To prepare the stems for candying, the confectioner first blanches them, allows them to cool and then peels them. They are then repeatedly dipped in increasingly strong concentrations of hot syrup over a period of six to ten days. Finally, they are drained and later sprinkled with sugar to be sold in pieces or molded into shapes.

Bernard Albert, one of the town's confectioners, uses his artistic inclination and skill to cut fun shapes from the green mass. Then there is Pierre Thonnard, who himself cultivates angelica and creates a wide variety of products – from liqueur to coulis. As a candied fruit with a predominant sweetness but also a clear hint of fresh acidity, angelica is found in many cakes and tortes, where it is easily recognized by its distinctive clear green color.

Angelica and the frog – the fairy tale memory that turned into a piece of candy has its roots in the Marais itself, where the one cannot be without the other and her green coat is an improvement on her own.

This "sweet" cow – both literally and figuratively – is an angelica tribute to the creature responsible for giving Poitou-Charentes one of its most famous products – butter.

This individual interpretation of a marsh marigold has the undeniable advantage that it is a pleasure to the eyes and the taste buds – but what a shame to eat it!

There are far more of the green-necked wild ducks or *colverts* to be found in the Marais than there are examples of this protected angelica bird which embodies two of Niort's specialties.

Limousin cattle

In Lascaux prehistoric artists immortalized immensely beautiful, russet-colored cows on the cave walls – ancestors of the Limousin cattle. Even today, when thousands upon thousands of these animals populate the wonderfully green regions of the Haute-Vienne, Creuse and Corrèze, their lustrous, evenly colored hide is still striking. But these cattle have had to come a long way since the days of the cave paintings at Lascaux, some 17,000 years ago.

The aurochs, which at the time roamed wild around this part of France, began their slow transformation when man succeeded in domesticating them in the New Stone Age. The natural conditions shaped the evolution of the breed. On the high plateaus, reaching heights of 2600 feet (800 meters), the granite soil is poor and acid and contains few minerals. Here, the natural pasture which is interrupted by woods and large areas of bracken offers no rich grazing for cattle, only unbalanced sustenance. There is no doubt that this nutritional factor has influenced one typical characteristic of the Limousin breed – its slender bone structure. On the other hand, it has the climate of its native region and the associated extremities to thank for its great resilience and adaptability. Hard and often long winters when temperatures can drop to 60 °F (15 °C) contrast with summers of scorching heat and violent storms. There is an abundant rainfall throughout the year.

The cattle, renowned today for their excellent, lean meat, were primarily used by farmers as draft animals in the early centuries. They were harnessed to plows to work the barren land. They could not afford to keep several cows. It was a sad lot for farmer and cattle alike. Only

those with connections among the nobility and clergy occasionally had sizable herds and enjoyed milk, cheese and well-stocked cooking pots. It was only members of the bourgeoisie, which was gradually developing in larger towns in the 17th and 18th centuries, who could even consider the quality of meat. The rural population was so impoverished by taxes that all their energies were consumed with the daily battle for survival.

It was only after the Revolution that living conditions began to improve. This was accompanied by the growth of industry and commerce, with the porcelain and textile trade in the Limousin. The towns prospered. Railways and an extended road network produced greater movement between the regions. The demand for meat rose sharply and with it so did prices. Thus, the scene had been set for the development of the Limousin breed. Moreover, the landscape had been transformed. Larger areas were now being farmed, with greater cultivation of fodder crops. Farmers began breeding cattle because they could see prospects for it – the improvement of meat quality. So in 1886 the Limousin Herd Book came into being and Limousin became established as a pedigree cattle breed in the first third of the 20th century.

Thanks to its adaptability and resilience, its high pregnancy rate and problem-free calving, the high proportion of superior cuts on the carcasses and the quality of their taste, the Limousin breed has spread to over 60 countries, making it the most frequently exported meat breed. It is available in different forms:

Veau de lait fermier du Limousin: The suckling calf comes from small and medium-sized farms. It feeds only by suckling and is slaughtered at four months, weighing 374–440 pounds (170–200 kilograms). Its meat is ivory-colored with a pale pink hue and is particularly tender and tasty.

Veau de Saint-Etienne: The youngest cattle, usually heifers, they have been reared as suckling calves after which they are fed on grass and high-energy fodder until they are sold at 8–10 months, weighing 770–990 pounds (350–450 kilograms). The young, tender meat is pale in color.

Veau de Lyon: The butcher used to ask for them at 10–15 months weighing 880–110 pounds (400–500 kilograms). Nowadays, these young cattle are left to fatten up, usually for a further five months, producing a 20–30 percent weight increase, and sold as older beef.

La vache de réforme: Young cows over two years old with a carcass weight of 660–790 pounds (300–360 kilograms) (or more) produce the tastiest meat, fine-grained, tender and juicy. Well-cared for cattle will produce this quality up to the age of ten, which is why it comes predominantly from rejected animals.

Paupiettes de bœuf
Beef olives
(illustration opposite, bottom)

7 oz/200 g streaky bacon
4 thin slices of beef, approximately 6¼ oz/180 g each (cut from the shoulder)
Salt and freshly ground pepper
1 tbsp goose, duck or pork fat
1 carrot
1 onion
1¼ cups/300 ml beef stock
1 clove garlic, crushed
1 bouquet garni
1 plate dried ceps
1 cup/150 g pickled capers

Remove the rind from the bacon and cut it into 4 pieces to match the width of the beef. Place the bacon and rind in a pan of cold water and bring it to the boil, simmer for 10 minutes then pour off the water and drain. Season the slices of beef with pepper and roll each one around a piece of bacon. Tie with fine string and season lightly with salt and pepper.

Heat the fat in a casserole, add the beef olives and brown all over. Peel the carrot and onion and cut into quarters. Add to the meat and cook over a low heat until soft then pour over the stock. Add the garlic, bouquet garni and ceps. Season lightly with

A dignified Limousin bull, contented and sturdy.

(illustration above, right)

The suckling calf of Brive

Brive-la-Gaillarde has built up its gastronomic reputation over the centuries. Early vegetables and fruit from the flat, open countryside, poultry and truffles on the winter markets, black-topped ceps and orange-colored chanterelles create the impression that we have arrived in a land of milk and honey. Since time immemorial there has been a firmly established tradition on the farms of the lower Limousin, apart from the breeding of the Limousin cattle as working animals and for milk and meat. The cow with the rust-red hide gives of its best when producing suckling calves. There are scarcely more than two pampered and cosseted calves per stall and no contact with grass, just the mother's udder and that of the "aunt" if the calf becomes too hungry and, occasionally, the odd fresh egg to supplement the diet. The result is an ivory-colored meat with a pale pink hue which has an excellent, nutty flavor, exceptional cooking proportions, a juice of outstanding finesse and a tasty consommé, which perfectly justify the reputation earned through this traditional *savoir faire*.

salt and pepper then cover the casserole and simmer for 1 hour. Make sure there is sufficient cooking liquid remaining about 1 inch (at least 2 cm). Add more stock if necessary. Finely chop the bacon rind and add to the meat with the capers. Simmer for a further 20 minutes then serve immediately.
An ideal accompaniment for this dish is a celery purée.

Fraise de veau poulette
Calf's pluck in "poulette" sauce
(illustration above, right)

Serves 6

4 cloves garlic
1 carrot
1 rib celery
1 onion
1 bouquet garni
2 cups/500 ml dry white wine
1 clove
10 black peppercorns
1 tbsp flour
Coarse sea salt
2 lb 10 oz/1.2 kg calf's pluck cut into 1½ in/4 cm pieces
1 bunch flat-leafed parsley, finely chopped

Sauce
1 tbsp goose or duck fat
1 tbsp flour
16 cups/4 l tripe stock
⅔ cup/150 ml crème fraîche
2 egg yolks
Juice of ½ lemon
A pinch of grated nutmeg

Peel and crush the garlic. Clean the vegetables and cut the carrot and celery into slices and the onion into rings. Place them in a large pan along with the herbs and spices, the wine and 16 cups/4 litres of water. Sieve in the flour and whisk. Bring to the boil and add salt. Add the calf's pluck and leave to cook on a medium heat for 1 hour. Partially cover the pan with the lid during this cooking time.
Make a roux and allow it to cook until it starts to brown then cool slightly. Return it to the stove and gradually add 12–16 cups/3–4 litres of stock, stirring continuously. Bring to the boil and simmer on a low heat for 20 minutes, whisking occasionally.
Mix together the crème fraîche, egg yolk, lemon juice and nutmeg in a small bowl. Remove the stock from the stove and immediately thicken with the cream mixture.
Drain the meat through a colander, add it to the sauce and sprinkle with parsley. Serve immediately.

Rôti de veau de lait fermier en croûte de sel
Roast suckling calf in a salt crust
(illustration above, left)

Serves 4–5

2 lb 10 oz/1.2 kg veal (shoulder or leg)
2 tbsp goose or duck fat
Freshly-milled pepper
1 carrot, sliced
1 onion, cut into rings
4 tbsp flour
6 tbsp coarse sea salt
4 egg whites

Season the meat with pepper. Heat the fat in a skillet. Add the meat and quickly brown on all sides then remove. Place the carrot and onion in a roasting pan, lay the meat on top and roast it for 10 minutes in a preheated oven at 465 °F/240 °C. Add the remaining fat, flour, sea salt and egg white to the fat remaining in the cool skillet and combine to produce a smooth mixture. Spread this over the meat to produce a crust and return it to the oven for a further 25 minutes. Remove the roast and let it stand for 30 minutes. Then open up the salt crust, slice the meat and arrange it on a serving plate with the vegetables. This dish can be accompanied by black salsify cooked in the meat juices or chanterelles sautéed in butter.

A pictorial atlas of French cuts for beef

The individual cuts are numbered from top to bottom, starting with the fore section of the carcass. This numbering system relates to the diagram shown on page 162.

1 **Collier** – Neck or shoulder, good, firm meat which develops plenty of flavor if cooked for a long time.
2 **Gras bout de poitrine** – Fatty brisket from the neck end, suitable both for boiling and pot-roasting.
3 **Basses côtes** – Upper rib, well streaked with fat, produces an excellent roast.
4 **Macreuse à pot-au-feu** – Blade or upper shoulder with a high gelatin content, best pot-roasted.
5 **Jumeau à pot-au-feu** – Unterer vorderer Schulterteil, der einen ausgezeichneten Rindfleischeintopf ergibt.
6 **Paleron** – Top blade, the uppermost mid-shoulder cut, especially popular for ragouts.
7 **Jumeau à bifteck** – Lower mid-shoulder cut, the meat is quite tender and cooked as steak.
8 **Macreuse-à-bifteck** – Blade steak, more tender than the front cut and suitable for cooking quickly.
9 **Côte** – Upper rib, rib roast, held in the highest regard in France, whether broiled or roasted.
10 **Entrecôte** – Front rib steak streaked with a certain amount of fat, for broiling or roasting.
11 **Plat-de-côtes** – Short rib cut from above the breast, it requires long cooking at a low temperature.
12 **Tendron** – Flank or skirt, cut from between the front legs and belly, very moist if cooked long and slow.
13 **Faux-filet** – Sirloin, a tasty loin cut lying between the rump and entrecôte and in parts above the fillet, it can be cooked quickly or served as roast beef.
14 **Bavette de flanchet** – Thin slices are cut from the top flank and predominantly used for moist roulades.
15 **Flanchet** – Belly or bottom flank, a particularly streaky cut which is especially recommended for boiling.
16 **Rumsteck** – Rump steak comes from the rump, the top hind part of the back, and is regarded as the best steak.
17 **Filet** – Fillet, the finest cut of beef, small, thick tournedos are cut from the head end.
18 **Hampe** – The belly part or midriff, a muscle next to the leg, which is appreciated as a particularly flavorsome beef steak.
19 **Onglet** – Lower part of the rib cage, sitting below the fillet, with fibrous meat rich in flavor, it can be quickly roasted and is ideal served with shallots.
20 **Bavette d'aloyau** – Sirloin, hind flank cut with particularly tender, flavorsome meat suitable for broiling or quick-roasting.
21 **Aiguillette Baronne** – A narrow strip from the top end of the leg which is good roasted whole.
22 **Merlan** – A lean cut from the front top round of the leg which is particularly good broiled.
23 **Poire** – A pear-shaped, particularly fine, tender cut from the middle of the top round. It can be used raw for fondues or pot-roasted.
24 **Rond de tranche** – Thick flank, also called *tranche grasse*, tender meat for medallions and leg steaks.
25 **Mouvant** – The lowest, foremost round; it is so lean that it is larded and roasted.
26 **Araignée** – (Literally: spider) The mouse, a well-streaked central leg cut which the butcher likes to keep for himself.
27 **Gîte à la noix** – Top round, the central and best leg cut which can be roasted or stewed.
28 **Gîte et jarret** – Shank and shin or a slice from the leg (fore or hind) with marrowbone, mainly used for stock and stews.
29 **Rond de gîte** – Rearmost pure top round cut which is excellent eaten as carpaccio, for example.
30 **Queue** – Oxtail, which is often divided up into pieces and then tied together in a bundle; it is delicious stewed slowly.

1 *Collier*

6 *Paleron*

2 *Gras bout de poitrine*

7 *Jumeau à bifteck*

3 *Basses côtes*

8 *Macreuse-à-bifteck*

4 *Macreuse à pot-au-feu*

9 *Côte*

5 *Jumeau à pot-au-feu*

10 *Entrecôte*

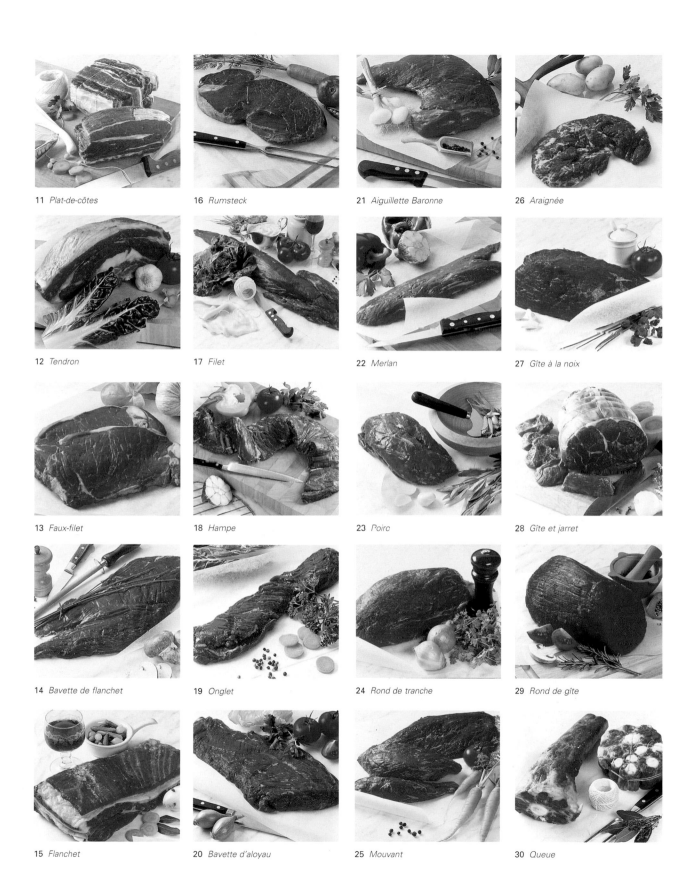

11 *Plat-de-côtes*

16 *Rumsteck*

21 *Aiguillette Baronne*

26 *Araignée*

12 *Tendron*

17 *Filet*

22 *Merlan*

27 *Gîte à la noix*

13 *Faux-filet*

18 *Hampe*

23 *Poirc*

28 *Gîte et jarret*

14 *Bavette de flanchet*

19 *Onglet*

24 *Rond de tranche*

29 *Rond de gîte*

15 *Flanchet*

20 *Bavette d'aloyau*

25 *Mouvant*

30 *Queue*

The king of rabbits

Due to their rich diets, rabbits from the area around Angers enjoy an excellent reputation. Burgundy, Provence, Périgord and Limousin exhibit expertise in their preparation. For some time now, rabbits have also been bred in the area around La Rochelle, in the Pays d'Aunis, resulting in the development of a local breed known among experts as "Rex du Magneraud." This breed has been further developed focusing particular attention on taste and in 1993 twelve or so breeders in the Poitou-Charentes region joined forces to supply particularly high-grade rabbits of guaranteed origin under the name "Rex de Poitou." The animals are kept in comparatively small groups of no more than 150 brood animals, enabling the breeds to be kept far purer than with industrial rearing methods. They are fed on alfalfa and other grain feed with a cereal supplement. This means that they grow more slowly and live longer than is otherwise customary. At the age of 18 weeks, weighing barely five pounds, they meet their fate. At this age they produce finely-structured, moist, mature, flavorsome meat which holds together well. It is suitable for any cooking method, such as braising, roasting or marinating for a ragout.

Choux farcis – Stuffed cabbage

Self-sufficiency in the kitchen

In Brive-la-Gaillarde, capital of the lower Limousin, the eloquent chef, Charlou Reynal, defends the culinary wealth of this center. In so doing, he not only argues in favor of dishes using Limousin beef, rabbit and violet mustard, but advocates authentic dishes and ingredients with passion and authority. He propagates self-sufficiency in the kitchen, retaining the traditional methods of food preparation from the everyday and festive fare of the rural population of the Limousin and its neighboring regions. Not so long ago people were only able to use those ingredients available on the farm for their dishes. For Reynal, stuffed cabbage containing no fresh meat has become the symbol of self-sufficient cookery. Bacon came from the salting tub, lard from the clay pot, vegetables from the garden, bread from the farm's own oven, milk from the cow shed, eggs from the hens. And the fact that people did not go out buying food for recipes, but tailored their recipes to suit the food available, explains the infinite variations on these dishes.

Even the *mique* or *farce dure* is included among these authentic dishes which cannot be found in any old cookbooks, because this method of using up leftovers practiced by rural folk was not fine enough for the bourgeoisie. The preparation involved plenty of eggs and, if possible, a knob of butter – once again all home-produced ingredients. And while one variation has the mixture solidifying in a greased pot, another has it cooking in a stock made from carrot, leek, cabbage, yellow or white turnip and potato, flavored using an onion spiked with cloves and a bouquet garni of bay, thyme and celery. The meat accompaniment was salted pork ribs and organ meat sausage.

Choux farcis
Stuffed cabbage

1 green cabbage, weighing 2 lb 10 oz–3 lb 4 oz/ 1.2–1.5 kg
1 carrot, thinly sliced
1 onion, thinly sliced
½ bay leaf
1 sprig of thyme
Filling
1¾ cups/200 g farmhouse bread crumbs
¾ cup/200 ml milk
6 shallots
2 garlic cloves
1 tbsp goose, duck or pork fat
10½ oz/300 g fatty bacon
1 handful of fresh sorrel
1 bunch of flat-leafed parsley
2 beet leaves
1 egg
freshly-milled pepper and salt

Clean the cabbage, add cold water and salt and bring it to the boil. Blanch it for 10 minutes. Refresh the cabbage under cold, running water and drain. Remove any hard stems. Soak the bread crumbs in milk. Cut the shallots and garlic in half and soften

them both in the fat. Remove and roughly chop with the bacon, bread, fresh sorrel, parsley and beet leaves, season with salt and pepper and bind with the egg. Spread out the green cabbage leaves and cover each one with a white leaf, then spoon on some of the stuffing. Fold the leaves around the filling and secure with fine cooking thread. Preheat the oven to 390 °F/200 °C. Soften the carrot and onion in the remaining fat, pour on 4 cups/1 litre of water, add the herbs and season lightly with salt and pepper. Add the cabbage parcels, cover and simmer in the oven for 45 minutes.

The filling ingredients can be made into *farce dure*: Add an additional cup/100 g of both breadcrumbs and bacon, 2 more beet leaves and 3 further eggs and bake the mixture in a pastry mold in the oven at 425 °F/220 °C for 20 minutes with and 20 minutes without a lid. Turn it out and serve either warm or cold.

Lapereau à la moutarde violette
Rabbit in mustard sauce
(Illustrated right)

Serves 2

1 saddle of rabbit (with the first 2 ribs) or 2 rabbit legs (tied together)
freshly ground pepper and salt
2 tbsp Echiré butter
1 onion
¾ cup/200 g Brive-la-Gaillarde violet mustard
2 rashers of streaky bacon, each weighing about 1¼ oz/40 g
¾ cup/200 ml of "Mille et une pierre" red wine from Corrèze
1 sprig of thyme

Season the rabbit with salt and pepper and lightly brown it in hot fat in a flameproof casserole. Remove it and set to one side. Cut the onions into rings, soften them in the cooking fat and season with salt and pepper. Spread the meat with mustard (keep back 2 tbsps), return it to the casserole, cover with bacon and roast uncovered in the oven at 425 °F/220 °C for 30 minutes. Remove the meat and onion separately. Pour off the roasting fat and place the casserole on the cooker top. Add the red wine and thyme and reduce by half. Stir in the remaining mustard. Assemble the onion, rabbit and bacon on a plate and warm it in the oven for 30 seconds then serve immediately with the sauce.

Bas rond de lapin à la gaillarde
Braised rabbit Brive style

Serves 3–4

1 tbsp goose, duck or pork fat
Leg and saddle (in a piece) of 1 large rabbit
freshly ground pepper and salt
4 large tomatoes from Marmande
10 shallots
2 garlic cloves
1 sprig of thyme
1 lb/500 g ceps, cleaned

Heat the fat in a cast iron pan. Season the rabbit with salt and pepper and brown it all over in the fat. Skin the tomatoes, remove the seeds and cut into eight. Add to the meat with the remaining ingredients. Taste and leave to simmer slowly for 30 to 40 minutes. Ideal served with macaroni cheese.

Bas rond de lapin à la gaillarde – Braised rabbit Brive style.

Violet mustard

It combines sweetness and sharpness, is deep violet in color and adds a bold, spicy flavor to roast duck breast, flash-cooked cuts of Limousin beef or veal, blood sausages and other pork products. Pope Clement VI, native of the Corrèze, who stayed at the court of Avignon in the 14th century, appears to have been unable to tolerate the absence of violet mustard. So he summoned from his native region Messire Jaubertie, who prepared the beloved condiment for him personally. This worked so perfectly that the Holy Father appointed him Grand Moutardier du Pape. Then in the 19th century violet mustard grew to be the widely renowned specialty of Brives. It threatened to sink into complete obscurity when its production ceased at the end of the fifties. But in 1986 the last producer, the liqueur house of Denoix founded in 1839, resumed its operation. The mustard is based on selected red grapes which are seeded and boiled and then finally put through a sieve. Only the natural grape content gives the must its intense sweetness. Ground mustard seeds, vinegar and spices are mixed into it. The creamy mustard is also ideal for seasoning meat before it is cooked or for enriching sauces.

The star among brandies

Cognac

Elongated warehouse buildings throng the banks of the Charente. A fruity aroma fills the air. Black fungus covers the walls like a layer of wadding: *Torula cognaciensis*. It thrives on alcohol fumes and in the darkness of the high, airy, *chais* or stores lie thousands of full barrels. A perceptible dampness creeps up from the river. Its proximity promotes natural reduction and gentle aging. Little by little, what began as a 70 percent spirit turns into the finest brandy in the world.

From the very early days, the area around La Rochelle and the Gironde estuary attracted traders. The Hanseatic League, in particular, sent its ships specifically for the salt which was extracted along the coast. But the cogs also sailed up the Charente and loaded up with wine from the small town of Cognac. This did not survive every journey by any means, as a result of which the Dutch came up with the idea of distilling it. Not only did this stabilize the grape juice but also reduced its volume. Once the destination had been reached, the distillate could be further diluted by the purchasers and flavored to suit their tastes. However, the 17th century saw the outbreak of various disturbances and with them crises in sales. In Cognac the barrels piled up. The distillate began to age and was refined into the spirit which was later to win renown under the town's name.

Today the Cognac area has expanded. It takes in large parts of the *départements* of Charente and Charente-Maritime and is bounded by the Atlantic to the west. Even the islands of Ré and Oléron are classified. Yet of its six cultivation zones, only four produce brandy of the finest quality. The Borderies produce soft wines with a fine bouquet, while the distillates from the Fins Bois age more quickly. The most distinguished cognacs are the Petite and, in particular, the Grande Champagne from the area between Cognac, Jarnac and Segonzac. The reason for their quality is the chalky soil, hence the high label champagne. It is this, ultimately, that gives the cognac its finesse. A Fine Champagne is more than half Grande and the remainder Petite Champagne.

The Ugni Blanc, referred to here as Saint-Emilion, is the grape variety used predominantly in the production of the basic wine. It is a weak, sour, neutral white wine which is distilled in two fractions using the Charentais alembic. First, the wine heater or *bouilleur du cru*, as the independent winegrowers and distillers are called, collect the *brouillis*, a liquid containing about 28 percent alcohol. This is returned to the still for the *bonne chauffe*. Drawing off impurities from the headings and tailings enables only the so-called "heart" to be extracted, the correspondingly fine, 70 percent, water-clear distillate. The crucial aging process begins immediately. Decanted into new barrels made from Tronçais or Limousin oak, the cognac in the *chai* begins to absorb tannins and aromatic substances from the wood and increasingly to harmonize and develop its flavor through oxidation and evaporation. By transferring the cognac to older barrels, the cellarman is able to regulate this process.

The brandy has ahead of it up to 50 years of refining, after which it will have reached its peak. Because it would break down if stored any longer in wood, it is decanted into demijohns, glass bottles in wickerwork capable of holding about 13 gallons (50 liters), if it is not bottled immediately. The Cognac region is so ideally suited to aging brandies because of the high moisture content of the air. This ensures that the evaporation is restrained, occurring to some extent in slow motion, guaranteeing the cognac its finesse.

While smaller producers occasionally supply unreduced, unblended cognacs, the great houses of world repute pride themselves on the reliability of their *cuvées*. It requires great experience to combine brandies of different ages and origins and dilute their strength to reproduce the house's typical style time after time. This applies at every age level. In reality, all quality grades are improved by what are in some cases significantly older cognacs. In addition, there are luxury bottled wines taken from the producer's own collections. It is only after decades of maturing that cognacs develop variety and length, in addition to a subtle roasted flavor and hint of spiciness, floral or fruity bouquets, as well as that unique hint of rancidness, reminiscent of young walnuts, which is the sign of the vintage and proof of their class.

Categories of cognac
- Three-star: matured in wood for over two years
- V.S.O.P. (very superior old pale), V.O, Réserve: finished in wood for over four years
- Napoléon, Extra, XO or Vieille Réserve: over six years in the barrel.

This typical Charentais alembic is a pot still designed for fractional distillation, which produces fine brandy in two cycles.

The secret of cognacs is the way they are matured in oak barrels. Colorless to begin with, they take on an increasingly dark hue and acquire ever more complex bouquets over the years and decades.

Such a selection of cognacs, some of which are very old and grandiose and decanted into luxurious bottles, is only to be found in the capital of the Cognac region, in the famous Cognathèque, which boasts one of the largest collections of cognac in the world.

Only decades of aging gives a cognac this enchantingly inviting color. The connoisseur is able to assess it accurately, prolonging the pleasure of his anticipation – he knows that he is about to savor perfection. And a cognac which has reached the optimum age earns itself a genuine crystal bottle.

Pineau des Charentes

It is said that an absent-minded cognac distiller accidentally ran some freshly pressed must into a barrel which was already a quarter full of cognac. Furious over his mistake, he rolled the barrel into a corner of the cellar. Upon sampling the contents some years later, he found a golden, shimmering nectar with a fruitiness and fine sweetness which left him captivated – or so the story goes. Even if it was the result of an invention, it still provides the basic formula for Pineau. One-year-old cognac with at least 60 percent alcohol is blended with grape must from the cultivation region in the two Charentes and kept in barrels for at least a year. If white varieties, particularly Ugni Blanc, are used, the Pineau has a golden hue with a depth of color depending on its age. Red rather than white grapes are used for the Pineau Rosé. Cabernet, Merlot or Malbec give it a bouquet of red berries. Drunk very cold, Pineau is a pleasant aperitif or light after-dinner drink. It is also a good accompaniment to foie gras or fruity desserts. The origin and production method follow an old tradition and are legally regulated, since the Pineau has an Appellation d'Origine Contrôlée classification.

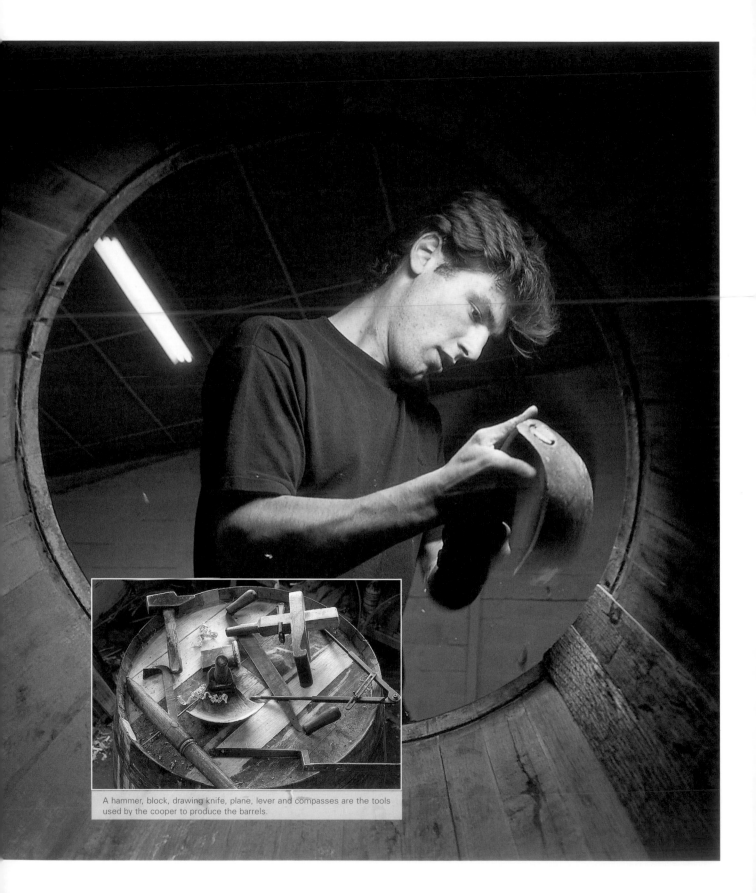

A hammer, block, drawing knife, plane, lever and compasses are the tools used by the cooper to produce the barrels.

Oak casks and barrels

Since the seventies when Californian winegrowers began to take an interest in new barrels to improve their wines, the cooper's craft, which had almost disappeared, has undergone a renaissance. The last bastions of the cooper's art had held out in the area around Cognac and Armagnac, because good brandies are inconceivable without new oak barrels. As a result, several *tonnelleries* were set up in the Charentes and large cognac houses employ their own coopers to satisfy their needs. A special position among barrels (*fût*) is occupied by the smaller *barriques* which only hold 60 gallons (225 liters).

Winegrowers may love to argue about which oak is best for their wines, but the choice was made long ago in the case of cognac. The only oak used comes from the nearby forests of the Limousin or the Tronçais in Allier, to the north of Clermont-Ferrand. In Gascony they still swear by their own black oak from Monlezun. Only trees from high forests regenerated by seedlings are suitable, where the trunks have been growing for up to 250 years wherever possible, so that they have a diameter of 16–24 inches (40–60 centimeters) when felled. *Merrain* is the name given to this sort of wood, from which 3½ feet (1.10 meters) of knot-free lengths suitable for splitting can be cut. The decisive factors are the wood's porosity, grain, the oak and quality of its tannic acid. The grain depends on the speed at which the tree has grown and its regularity. The slower and more even the growth, the closer together the annual rings and the finer the grain. Allier oaks are renowned for their fineness and particularly elegant tannins. Limousin oaks are more porous and produce stronger tannic acids in greater quantities.

Only when the wood has been stored for a sufficient time out in the open can it be worked. The staves for wine barrels are stored for at least two years and in the case of cognac barrels for three or more years. During this time, the rain and heat remove any acid sap and bitter substances. In order to bend the staves, the cooper tips the barrel upside down over a fire. He roasts the insides of the staves which are constantly dampened from the outside. This is crucial in determining the flavor imparted by the barrel. As a result, a severe *chauffe* will produce a noticeable hint of coffee. The quality of the oak, length of storage, precision of the roasting and perfection of the craftsmanship determine the quality of a barrel and therefore that of the cognac.

Left: The cooper painstakingly polishes the entire rim of the barrel, so that no leaks occur here when the barrel is full.

1 The raw material for the barrels comes from oak trees from forests in the Tronçais and Limousin regions, which are usually around 200 years old.
2 The blocks of wood from the trunk are first split. Thankfully, modern technology provides the power for this today.
3 The split wood is fed through the band saw, to ensure the staves are of a uniform length and width from the very start.

4 For brandies, the split wood must be stored outdoors for at least three years, so that it loses any green, bitter taste.
5 The cooper begins to join together the tapered staves using a metal ring, which holds them in place.
6 Once the circle of the barrel is complete, the cooper slips a second and then a third hoop over to secure it.

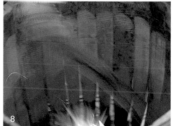
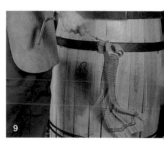

7 The staves are still splayed out at the other end of the barrel and must be made flexible by the heat of the fire so that they can be bent.
8 The severity with which the barrel is heated has a crucial effect on the flavors later imparted to the brandy or wine.
9 A metal hoop is placed around the barrel and the cooper levers it on as far as he can, so that the staves come together.

10 Finally, the staves produce a perfect circle at the other end too, and they are secured with a hoop.
11 The barrel still has no side opening and the cooper drills a bunghole in the wood, which he mills out to the prescribed size.
12 Although the lids still have to be put on, the outside of the barrel is given a final polish at this stage.

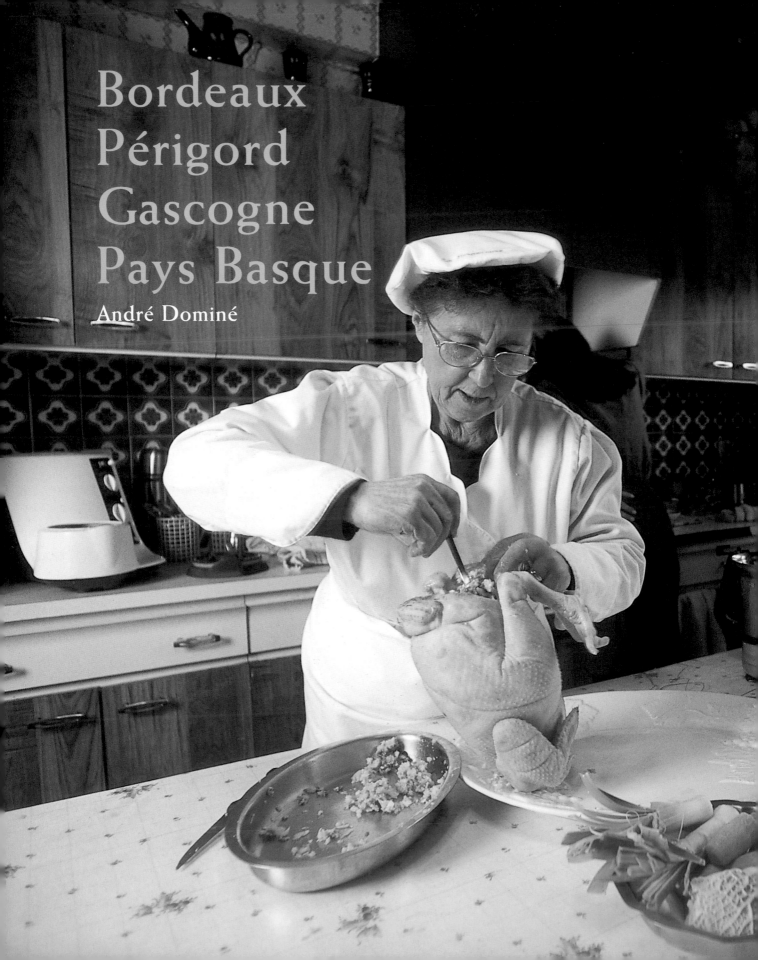

Bordeaux
Périgord
Gascogne
Pays Basque

André Dominé

The appellations of
  Bordeaux
Fishing on the Gironde
Lamb from Pauillac
Basque fishing
Basque through
  and through
Sheep cheese from the
  Pyrenees – Brebis
Pear brandy from Branas
Basque wine: Irouléguy
Paradise on
  earth: Jurançon
Madiran
Poule au pot
Glorious geese
Marché au gras
Ducks on course
Prunes from Agen
Armagnac

Poule au pot, chicken cooked in a pot, has been a classic French dish since the times of Henry IV.

A wide variety of gastronomic specialties has developed around the Pyrenees, and still remains unchanged today..

Calais

Le Havre

Brest
Caen
Paris
Rennes
Strasbourg

Orléans
Nantes
Tours
Dijon

Limoges

Lyon

St-Étienne
Bordeaux
Grenoble
Périgord
Gascogne
Avignon
Pays
Toulouse
Nice
Basque

Perpignan
Marseille
Toulon

Bordeaux is famous throughout the world for its wine, and the history of this wine is bound to that of its natural harbor and its political links with England, dating back to the 12th century. The Dordogne and Garonne rivers, together with the Lot tributary, were the main routes for traffic and trade in the southwest until the railways were constructed. Bordeaux, the gateway to the world, turned out to be the eye of the needle for many products.

But the city's strategic position as an export harbor led to the decline of many products from the hinterland because the locals were entitled to export their own wines first, before any was moved from the hinterland. However, wine is an important feature all over the southwest, not just in Bordeaux. A number of small regions contain remarkable specialties, often produced from indigenous grape varieties.

The Atlantic coast and rivers are still vital to traders today, but that is not their only function. The region is also well known for its fishing industry, which is seen here in many guises: the deep-sea fishing of the Basques, who follow cod far out into the North Sea; fishing with landing nets and traps in the Garonne; the countless anglers who enjoy their sport in the crystal-clear mountain streams of the Pyrenees.

The best firm sheep cheese and first-class lambs come from the mountain pastures of the Pyrenees, while "Agneau de Pauillac" is a sign of quality for suckling lambs in the rest of Gascony.

If you consider the valuable local breeds of cattle, such as Blonde d'Aquitaine, Boeuf de Challose, Bazardaise and Garonnaise, or the region's unusual poultry, including free-range chickens, turkeys, pigeon and capons, not forgetting goose and duck, the entire southwest is a veritable paradise for lovers of good meat and poultry. And Gascony is just as famous for its patés, terrines, *confits* or *magrets* as Périgord is. However, it is not just the specialties that cross the boundaries between regions, the everyday cooking in each province of the generous southwest is firmly rooted in common farming traditions. A wide variety of foodstuffs was both produced and prepared on the farmsteads, and the same is true today. So dishes are often unceremoniously hearty, but no one minds in an area that knows how to deal with Armagnacs as well as prunes from Agen.

The appellations of Bordeaux

Bordeaux owes its importance as a winegrowing region largely to its position at the mouth of the Gironde river. In former times, ships could safely be loaded under the protection of the developing town before taking their goods across the Atlantic to Holland, England or further north. Wine was in great demand as a trading commodity, so it made sense to plant vineyards close to the harbor, especially as little else would thrive on the region's predominantly gravelly soils.

The relationship between England and France increased in importance in the Middle Ages when Eleanor of Aquitaine married Henry of Anjou, who later became Henry II. However, it was not until La Rochelle submitted to the French in 1224 that Bordeaux became the main supplier of wine to the British Isles, and this in turn boosted the area's own viniculture, which had been neglected for centuries.

The next major push came from the Dutch, the leading commercial force of the 17th century. Unlike the British, who preferred the light reds, or clarets, the Dutch preferred darker red and heavy, sweet white wines; they also took large quantities of spirits. Not only did demand increase, but suddenly a much wider range of wines was required that were classified according to quality. A grading system gradually evolved, which culminated in a method of product classification. However, the Dutch were not satisfied with merely ordering the wine. As they wanted to make sure that the goods they received met their expectations and requirements, they wanted to have a certain amount of say in the actual production. Their vast experience on the subject of soil drainage was as much help in promoting viniculture in Bordeaux as their knowledge and experience in sulfurating wine to increase its "shelf life." Once Arnaud de Pontac had supplied the first example of a high-class red wine in Haut-Brion, others soon followed. The culture of quality wines began to evolve, culminating in the appellation system still in use today.

With around 275,000 acres (111,000 hectares) of vineyards, Bordeaux is the world leader in the production of quality wines. Equidistant from the North Pole and the Equator, the region has a particularly mild climate. Its proximity to the Atlantic with the Gulf Stream and vast river courses guarantees mildness and prevents extremes of temperature. The vast pine forests of the Aquitaine coast protect it from sea storms. The autumn often brings sunny days that help the grapes to reach optimum maturity, a prerequisite for a good vintage. The Dordogne and Garonne rivers, which merge in the wide Gironde to the north of the town, divide it into three zones that produce wines of greatly varying characters.

• On the left bank of the Garonne is an 8–12 mile (5–20 kilometer) wide strip of vinegrowing land around Bordeaux and along the left bank of the Gironde, as far as its mouth. This is where you find the world-famous Graves, with Haut-Médoc and Médoc to the north of the town. The soil here benefits from the filtering effects of gravel, with deep chalk layers in some areas, sand and river gravel in others. Sweet golden white wines, of which Sauternes is the most famous and the most popular, develop highly complex aromas here. The Graves produce the best dry white wines of the Bordeaux region. The legendary red wines of the Cabernet Sauvignon grape, whether Graves, Margaux, Saint-Julien, or Pauillac, have an elegant character, which is often closed at first, but subsequently becomes more distinguished and multilayered.

• The region of Entre-Deux-Mers lies between the Garonne and Dordogne rivers, on the right bank of the Garonne, and surrounded by the Premières Côtes de Bordeaux. Here, the soil is predominantly lime on a chalky base. Entre-Deux-Mers is an appellation for dry white wines; the Sauvignon dominates, providing a fruity-aromatic aroma. The Premières Côtes, on the other hand, produce mainly heavy red wines.

• There are also some excellent locations on the right bank of the Dordogne (wines are turned round at Libourne), with gravel on a chalky base, for example in Pomerol and some parts of Saint-Emilion. The prevailing variety here is the Merlot grape, which produces particularly smooth, harmonious red wines. Heavier soils with a large proportion of clay predominate in the surrounding appellations and satellites, and these usually produce good, crisp red wines. The heterogeneous soils of Bourg and Blaye to the north west of Libourne produce fruity red and dry white wines, often with a floral bouquet.

The wines of Bordeaux are available from almost 7000 estates, known as *châteaux* (although only a few actually are castles), and around 400 dealers. Red wines are clearly the more popular, and they are grown on four-fifths of the vineyards. The last fifth consists mainly of dry white wines. By comparison, the mellow, sweeter wines are a rare specialty. Other wines that are produced here are *clairet*, a traditional, light, easy-to drink red wine, *rosé*, and the sparkling *mousseux* and *crémant*. Overall, the Bordeaux classification, or Bordeaux supérieur if the wine is more than 12 percent proof, consists of another 57 *Appellations d'Origine Contrôlée*, which in turn are divided into six wine families.

The six wine families

1 Médoc
A.O.C.: Médoc, Haut-Médoc, Saint-Estèphe, Pauillac, Saint-Julien, Moulis-en-Médoc, Listrac-Médoc, Margaux. Only red wines, grown mainly on the famous *croupes*, slight inclines that consist of sand, gravel, and pebblestones. These barren, well-drained soils (those around Listrac and Moulis also contain argillaceous lime-stone) grow the 60 *crus classés*, which provide 23 percent of the entire volume; the 400 *crus bourgeois*, of which almost every other bottle is a Médoc; the 300 *crus artisans* and *crus paysans*, which provide 11 percent of the production. The remaining 17 percent come from the 13 cooperatives.

2 Graves
A.O.C.: Graves, Pessac-Léognan, Graves Supérieures. This superior region, which adjoins the town to the west and south, contains large amounts of river gravel and was awarded its own *appellation* in 1986: Pessac-Léognan, which includes all 15 of the estates (with the exception of Haut-Brion) that were not classified until 1959. The aromatic, finely constructed reds and the best dry whites, based largely on Sémillon, of the Bordeaux region grow here, as do the *supérieures*, delightful sweet wines that border on Cérons, Barsac, and Sauternes.

3 Blayais and Bourgeais
A.O.C.: Premières Côtes de Blaye, Côtes de Blaye, Côtes de Bourg. The gently undulating vineyards of the Côtes de Bourg extend along the right bank of the Dordogne and the Gironde, where the soil is predominantly argillaceous and produces fruity, well-structured, durable reds. Like the Côtes de Blaye, the whites are pleasantly dry. The Premières Côtes de Blaye, where the soil also contains sand and gravel, provide smooth, frequently strong reds, for which Malbec is a popular choice, and slightly livelier, perfumed white wines.

4 Libournais
A.O.C.: Fronsac, Canon-Fronsac, Lalande-de-Pomerol, Pomerol, Saint-Emilion, Montagne-Saint-Emilion, Lussac-Saint-Emilion, Saint-Georges-Saint-Emilion, Puisseguin-Saint-Emilion, Côtes de Castillon, Côtes de Francs. A broad, heterogeneous red wine area extends around Libourne on the right bank, noted for its Merlot and Cabernet Franc varieties. The gravel soils of Pomerol produce a fruity yet smooth wine. Argillaceous limestone dominates on the well-appointed inclines to the north-west in the Fronsadais. Saint-Emilion varies considerably with respect to both soil and quality. Since 1955, 69 estates have been classified as *grand cru*, ten as *premier cru* and two as *premier grand cru A*. Merlot is often at the forefront because of its fast-maturing

The most important grape types of Bordeaux

Bordeaux produces a wide range of wines. Although red wines dominate, the region also offers dry, medium and very sweet white wines, rosés, and even sparkling wines. They range from light "drinking" wines to world-famous Châteaux-bottled vintage wines. However, Bordeaux wines are always blended from several different types of grape (*assemblage*), which ensures that the wines are always smooth and well-balanced.

Reds
Cabernet Sauvignon
The native "star" that adds distinction to the great wines of the Médoc and is now found throughout the world. These strong, dark-colored wines smell of blackcurrant and cedar. The pronounced tannins need to be allowed to age. The wine will smell unpleasantly of green peppers when immature or if the yield has been too high.

Cabernet Franc or Bouchet
Close relative, early shooting, one of the traditional mixers used in Bordeaux wines. Strong presence in Saint-Emilion and on the Loire, otherwise most frequently grown in Italy. The wine is identified by complex berry fruits, lots of flavor, slim-bodied, less pronounced tannins, slow maturing.

Merlot
Early maturing, usually good yields; important component in Bordeaux, especially in Pomerol and Saint-Emilion; otherwise found primarily in the Midi, Tessin, Italy, eastern Europe, and also in the U.S.A. The wine is fruity, velvety, has lots of body; smooth tannins mean it matures quickly.

Petit Verdot
Very late maturing, so problematic and irregular. Very sparse, but to be found throughout Médoc. A very dark wine with lots of flavor, considerable volume and distinctive tannins. An excellent mixer.

Malbec, Auxerrois, Cot, Pressac
Susceptible to frost; main variety around Cahors; rare in the Médoc and Saint-Emilion regions, more common in Bourg and Blaye, otherwise to be found in the southwest, Hungary, and Argentina. The wine is dark to black with very strong tannins and ages well; plenty of character.

Whites
Sémillon
Prone to infestation with noble rot, then used as the base for Sauternes and other smooth white wines; combined with Sauvignon in dry Bordeaux wines; important in Australia. The wine develops fascinatingly complex aromas of honey, candied fruit, and chocolate when overripe or mature.

Sauvignon
The base for dry white Bordeaux; highly productive; grown predominantly on the Loire, but found all over the world. The wine smells strongly (occasionally too much so) of blackcurrant; very fruity presence of acidity.

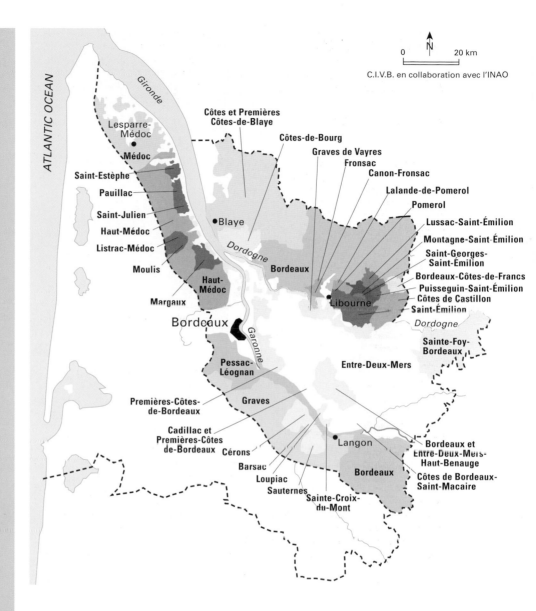

C.I.V.B. en collaboration avec l'INAO

roperties in higher locations; this is also true of the wines from the adjoining slopes of the Côtes de Castillon and Côtes de Francs.

5 Entre-Deux-Mers
A.O.C.: Entre-Deux-Mers, Graves de Vayres, Premières Côtes de Bordeaux, Entre-Deux-Mers-Haut-Benauge, Sainte-Foy-Bordeaux, Côtes de Bordeaux-Saint-Macaire. With its tip pointing towards the Gironde, this region, which is the largest in Bordeaux, is situated between the Garonne and the Dordogne. The greatest quantities of Bordeaux and Bordeaux *supérieur* (and thus also of *rosé* and *crémant*) are produced here. Depending on the particular soil and position, the spectrum ranges from aromatic, lively whites (such as Sainte-Foy, Haut-Benauge, Graves de Vayres) to sweeter

(such as Graves de Vayres, Premières Côtes de Bordeaux) and on to full-bodied red wines, whose tone is usually set by Merlot.

6 Sweet wines
A.O.C.: Cérons, Barsac and Sauternes, Premières Côtes de Bordeaux, Cadillac, Loupiac, Sainte-Croix-du-Mont, Côtes de Bordeaux-Saint-Macaire. Autumn mists promote the growth of *Botrytis cinerea* (noble rot), which concentrates the juice in the grape to an extraordinary intensity of sweetness and flavor. Sauternes and Barsac are the most elegant and can be left to age for long periods of time. On the right bank, the sweeter vines of Sainte-Croix-du-Mont, Loupiac, and Cadillac grow to amazing heights. The base is formed by Sémillon, to which Sauvignon, and the slightly less usual Muscadelles are added..

Crus classés

At the time of the World Exhibition in Paris in 1855, Emperor Napoleon III instructed the chamber of commerce in Bordeaux to set up a classification system for the most famous wine estates. The chamber of commerce delegated this task to the syndicate of wine merchants, who had already been working (albeit unofficially) with a classification consisting of three to five categories based on the award it was hoped a specific wine would achieve. However, apart from Haut-Brion in the Graves district, these grades referred to Médoc, which had made a name for itself as a producer of great red wines, and to outstanding sweet wines from Sauternes and Barsac. Wines from the right bank, such as Pomerol and Saint-Emilion, were not included because their place of transshipment was Libourne and therefore not in the jurisdiction of the merchants of the Quai des Chartrons. Four main *châteaux* had long since established themselves at the top of the classification of red Médoc wines, in fact they had been at the top from the beginning and have maintained this position until today. Since early times, the most important market for Bordeaux wines, and especially for the best and most expensive ones, had been England, thanks to Arnaud de Pontac, the president of parliament. Dissatisfied with the prices that Dutch merchants were prepared to pay for wine in the second half of the 17th century, he was the first person to offer the wines from his Haut-Brion estate for sale on the London market. Haut-Brion became the most sought-after and expensive wine of the time. Wine had always been an important trading commodity for the Bordelaise aristocracy, and they were well aware that the best ones thrived on barren, gravelly soils. They turned their attention to the regions that offered these conditions when the Dutch specialists began to drain Médoc, noting the flat undulations at Margaux, Latour, Lafite, and others. The de Lestonac family had created an estate in Margaux for themselves which, as the result of an inheritance, was combined with Haut-Brion and which, since 1705, had been making a name for itself in London as the second most important Bordeaux estate, followed in 1707 by Lafite and Latour. The latter had been founded over 100 years before by the de Mullet family. Other wine *châteaux* were established during the 18th century. A detailed, three-tier classification system existed as long ago as 1740, divided into parishes. Each agent and dealer set up his own hierarchy, which he continued to develop. A well-informed president of the U.S.A., Thomas Jefferson, also drew up a list of his own preferences when he visited Bordeaux in 1797 during his time as ambassador to France. Other lists followed, always based on the market value

Château Haut-Brion, Pessac-Léognan

Château Lafite-Rothschild, Pauillac

Top: Château Latour, Pauillac.
Left: Château Margaux was raised to premier cru in 1855, together with the other three châteaux seen here.

of the wines, but the 1855 list was the one that received official recognition.

Lafite, Margaux, Latour, and Haut-Brion were classified as *premiers crus*. Mouton was at the top of the 12 *seconds crus*, Kirwan of the 14 *troisièmes crus*. 11 *quatrièmes* and 17 *cinquièmes crus* were also recognized. The 61 *crus classés* of today were brought about by further divisions and amalgamations. The only change in the existing classification system occurred in 1973, when Baron Philippe de Rothschild managed to raise his Mouton from the second to the first grade.

This classification differed from, say, that of Burgundy, where clearly defined characteristics were rated, in that the award recognized the estates that had been able to gain a particular foothold on the market at the time, rather than the quality of the vineyards which were not assessed. Much has changed since then. Many estates now possess more or other vineyards than they did in 1855, and this has not influenced their classification at all. The owners also leave their mark on the quality of the estate. For example, the *crus classés* all have a different history. At the moment some of them deserve a higher, others a lower grade, and some *crus bourgeois* deserve to be included. Once again, as before 1855, non-official valuations are doing the rounds, based on quality and on prices. However, an official revaluation would appear to be unlikely, and so the classification of 1855 remains valid – if only as a piece of history.

Premiers Crus

Deuxièmes Crus

By agreement with the owners,
the label of deuxième cru,
Léoville-Las Cases, does not appear here.

Troisièmes Crus

In 1973, thanks to the excellent quality of his wines, Baron Philippe saw Château Mouton-Rothschild become a premier cru; this is the only time a classification has been amended.

Quatrièmes Crus

Cinquièmes Crus

Château Lafite-Rothschild was the banking family's first premier cru.

Médoc, Graves and Cabernet Sauvignon

The reputation of the Bordeaux region originated just outside the town gates. Graves, the district that was named for the excellent quality of its soil, stretches from the western edge of the town in an arch towards the south as far as the banks of the Garonne, along the river to Langon and Saint-Loubert. The soil is in fact detritus, which was created when the Pyrenees rose up and was transported amazing distances from the mountains by the rivers. During transportation, the water ground the tiny stones (mainly quartz), mixed them with sand as well as other soils that were more or less rich in lime, and deposited them on the river banks in terraces and flat, dune-like hills, with larger river gravel distributed over the surface. Whilst being extraordinarily well drained, these soils are so poor that nothing will thrive on them apart from vines.

When the Romans began cultivating grapevines on the gravelly soil of Burdigala, as it was called at the time, they imported the rootstock. It is generally thought that these first varieties came from what is now Albania, which the natives called "Biturica". The word "Biturica" subsequently changed into "Vidure," which means nothing more than *vigne dure*, hard vine, and is a name still used in Graves for Cabernet Sauvignon rootstock. Graves remained the preferred winegrowing area when there was an upturn in the fortunes of Bordelaise viniculture in the 13th century. It was to be another 400 years before it gave way to Médoc, where the drainage was gradually improved over time.

Due to the width of the Gironde, the Médoc district is virtually a peninsula. The area used to be marshy and could only be reached by boat. In the 17th century, the Bordelaise aristocracy increasingly took advantage of the flat, gravelly layers of soil, and Haut-Médoc between Margaux and Saint-Estèphe, the area closest to the town of Bordeaux, quickly became the core region. The castles and mansions constructed there during the 18th and 19th centuries not only testified to the wealth of their owners, but also to the high regard in which these wines were held, especially by England, Holland, as well as northern Germany.

This situation has not changed, except that the area is now held in esteem by the whole world. With the exception of Haut-Brion and the châteaux of the latest *appellation* Pessac-Léognan, which were classified in 1959, it even outshone

products from Graves. There and in Haut-Médoc, the Cabernet Sauvignon grape achieves its finest expression and gives distinction to the red wines of Bordeaux. This area on the left bank is considered its actual home, and it is thanks to the way in which it is expressed in the great wines of these two wine districts that it is so widely distributed today.

The roots of the late-maturing Cabernet Sauvignon, which easily adapts to almost all soil types and climates, dig deep into gravelly soils, and in good years it produces the most amazing aromas that bring to mind blackcurrants, violets and cedar. If not mature, it is characterized by a distinctive but ordinary smell of green pepper. If it has too much sun, it quickly becomes plump, heavy, and plain. This generally robust variety (apart from its susceptibility to vine mildew) grows cylindrical grapes with small, thick-skinned, dark-colored fruit with a comparatively high proportion of seeds. This constitution produces highly tannic wines that require special balancing, especially if the vintage proves to be a more difficult one. It is therefore a tradition in the Bordeaux region that wines are not produced strictly according to type, but are instead composed of three of four different varieties of grape: Merlot, Cabernet Franc, Malbec, and Petit Verdot are all available.

Cabernet Sauvignon is an old variety from Médoc, which matures late and is low yielding. Its popularity is receding, although its breed and flavor are practically legendary. It is the most prevalent variety at the Châteaux Palmer, Léoville-Barton, and Lascombes. A number of the leading producers add 2–5 percent to their *assemblage*. Cabernet Sauvignon is generally most prevalent in Pauillac wines, where it amounts to 70–80 percent or more. It is followed by the Saint-Estèphes, then the Saint-Juliens with 60–75 percent.

In the remaining *appellations* on the left bank, the mixtures vary dramatically from estate to estate, but as a general rule the proportion remains above 50 or 60 percent. However, in Graves it is frequently replaced by Merlot. The greater the presence of Cabernet Sauvignon in high-quality products from Haut-Médoc and Pessac-Léognan, both of which produce lower yields, the longer the wines should be left to mature in the cellar, always depending on their vintage. The utmost drinking pleasure is the reward for such patience.

Ducru Beaucaillou, deuxième cru classé Saint-Julien, seen from the side that faces the river.

Wines from Château Palmer, troisième cru, frequently reach the highest possible level.

Pichon-Longueville-Baron, deuxième cru, has reaffirmed its excellent position since 1986.

Left: Château Palmer's new vinification cellar.
Right: The entrance to the Pichon Baron vinification cellar.

The dry wines of Médoc and Graves

Médoc
37 million bottles, 62 *crus bourgeois*, 113 *crus artisans*, 5 cooperatives
A broad spectrum of red wines, some of which are lighter in character and therefore more accessible, whilst others are rounder and destined to continue maturing in the bottle. Merlot often achieves a certain softness and harmony.

Haut-Médoc
30 million bottles, 5 *crus classés*, 82 *crus bourgeois*, 116 *crus artisans* and other *crus*, 5 cooperatives
Includes the famous *crus*, and its wines often demonstrate power and solidity with distinctive Cabernet Sauvignon, usually intense aromas. Acquires a complex bouquet and balance when left to mature for several years.

Saint Estèphe
8.3 million bottles, 5 *crus classés*, 36 *crus bourgeois*, 25 *crus artisans* and others, 1 cooperative
They are known for their pronounced and classy tannins, which combine with the acidity that is often present and guarantee that the wines will mature for a long time. They are then earthy and full of character.

Pauillac
8.1 million bottles, 18 *crus classés*, 16 *crus bourgeois*, 7 *crus artisans* and others, 1 cooperative
Especially rich, complex wines with extensive acidity that like to be left to mature in their own time, when they will develop an amazing "classiness." When young, they bring to mind the aroma of blackberries or floral accents.

Saint-Julien
6 million bottles, 11 *crus classés*, 6 *crus bourgeois*, 11 *crus artisans* and others
Much harmony and finesse, both in the bouquet and on the palate. Solid tannins and a good structure that often gives considerable potential.

Listrac-Médoc
4.8 million bottles, 20 *crus bourgeois*, 12 *crus artisans* and others, 1 cooperative
These wines, often quite reserved when young, are robust and full of tannin, but the comparatively high proportion of Merlot gives the mature wines a full-bodied, velvety character.

Moulis-en-Médoc
4 million bottles, 14 *crus bourgeois*, 13 *crus artisans* and others
The wines from Moulis are as varied as the soil types on which they grow. The broad spectrum ranges from the soft and gentle to full-bodied growths with plenty of tannin that peak after about a decade.

Margaux
9 million bottles, 21 *crus classés*, 20 *crus bourgeois*, 38 *crus artisans* and others
Elegance is the watchword for Margaux wines, which combine with a delightful fruitiness when young.
The fine tannins hold their own through a long period of maturing, with the best offering an amazing finesse.

Pessac-Léognan
8 million bottles, 15 *crus classés*: 6 for red and white wines, 7 only for red wines, 2 only for white wines; 41 châteaux
Four-fifths red wines with an elegant character, intense, slightly floral aromas, and often with a distinct hint of smokiness, meaty, well-structured and long-lasting. One-fifth are dry, highly aromatic white wines that keep extremely well and are characterized mainly by an extraordinary roundness and depth.

Graves
About 24 million bottles, 400 producers
The red wines smell pleasantly of ripe red berries, have a good depth and juiciness and achieve finesse and harmony after maturing. The strongly aromatic whites account for about an eighth of the production. They are characterized by a restlessness or edginess, but also by a typical roundness. They improve with bottle ageing.

The great sweet wines from the Gironde

In the 18th and 19th centuries, the medium-sweet wines were the true stars of the Bordeaux region. In the Sauternes district 25 miles (40 kilometers) south of the town, the early morning autumn mists that occur at the point where the Ciron and the Garonne converge and the sunny afternoons encourage *Butrytis cinerea* (noble rot). This microscopically tiny fungus consumes water and around 40 percent of the grapes' natural sugar, but it also "roasts" the grapes, increasing the concentration in them. This helps the wrinkled berries to achieve an exceptionally high sugar content of 350g per liter (about 12 ounces per quart) and more, a figure that is considerably higher than the now legal minimum. If nature is kind, they go on to produce deep golden wines with a high residual sweetness that are destined to last for ever. These wines have always been indestructible, even at times when the best red wines were likely to end up as vinegar and had to be consumed early. The early Dutch dealers on the Quai des Chartrons had a marked preference for them – and a solid client base in all northern European Hanseatic towns.

From the start the Château d'Yquem, a medieval castle in the heart of Sauternes, was considered to be the leading estate. Thomas Jefferson is known to have been partial to these wines. When the classification of Bordeaux wines was introduced in 1855, the wine dealers graded the sweet Sauternes and Barsac higher than the red wines of Médoc because, as a *premier cru supérieur*, they raised Yquem above all others, and classified nine as *premiers crus* – as opposed to four in Médoc and eleven others to *deuxièmes crus*. Sauternes and Barsac became the elixir of emperors and kings and of the blue-blooded and financial aristocracy, all of whom favored an unbelievably wasteful lifestyle.

Once world wars and October revolutions and the ensuing democratization of pleasure and enjoyment had revealed how things were going to be, these major sweet wines entered into a state of crisis that was to last for several decades. It was not until the advent of a new, broader spectrum of wine enthusiast, combined with modern economic development and, last but by no means least, the series of good vintages dating from 86, 88, 89 and 90, that interest in these marvelous wines was rekindled. If we include the wines from other Bordelaise *appellations*, where mellow and medium-sweet wines are produced, production currently amounts to 18 million

Sauvignon grapes

Sémillon grapes

bottles, one third of which are Sauternes and Barsac. There, on almost 5000 acres (2000 hectares), the Sémillon variety enjoys the conditions it likes best: gravelly soils on an argillaceous base, combined with a warm, moist climate which promotes the growth of noble rot. This gives the wine its extraordinary volume, whilst the highly aromatic Sauvignon as well as the more delicate Muscadelle grapes give additional complexity.

In order to harvest a truly great sweet wine,

however, the producers are obliged to rule their vineyards with an iron rod, especially where yields are concerned. An expected yield of one glass, at the most two glasses of wine per vine will ensure the overripeness without which there would be no noble rot. But all the effort is wasted if the weather fails to cooperate for the harvest, when the grapes are picked in several sessions during October and November. Since 1968 Château d'Yquem, at 280 feet (86 meters) the highest point of the *appellation*, has demonstrated

unfailingly under Count Alexandre de Lur Saluce what is needed to achieve and to guarantee legendary quality. Fifty people work in around 260 acres (105 hectares) of vineyards where pesticides are unheard of and horse manure may be used every three or four years. Instead, the workers hoe and heap up the soil, prune the vines extremely short, and remove the leaves from the grapes from the end of August. When it is time to harvest, 120 people turn up for 20–25 days, and in up to ten sessions will pick only the grapes with noble rot. This yields a little over 175 gallons (8 hectoliters) for every 2.5 acres (1 hectare). The must is pressed for five hours before being poured into new oak barrels. It is then left to develop for a maximum of 3½ years, sampled every three months, and finally bottled without filtering. Every year 95,000 bottles are available from ten dealers. In poor years when the desired quality is not achieved (which last happened in 1992), there is no Yquem. The reward for these efforts is a truly legendary

Château d'Yquem Sauternes was awarded a special status in the classification of 1855.

nectar of unbelievably intense, multilayered aromas, some of which are honey, nut, raisins, apricots, candied orange peel, and cedar, of dramatic body, sweetness and flavor combined with an elegant acidity, enormous power and endurance. And despite this delightful interplay, it does not reveal its mystery, but rather keeps a promise of wonderful surprises yet to come.

Saint-Emilion, Pomerol and Merlot

For a lover of good wines, there is no holier place than Saint-Emilion. Situated 25 miles (40 kilometers) to the east of Bordeaux, this little town nestles against an incline in the Dordogne valley. Tiny, narrow alleyways wind around aged houses built from natural stone, reaching up the steep hillside to the plateau with the imposing old church that overlooks the town below. From here, the eye can see over the rooftops to the famous sites and beyond, as far as the expanse of vines.

Wine growing began here in the 3rd century, when Roman legions cleared the woodlands on the elevated plains of Saint-Emilion and neighboring Pomerol. Ausonius, the famous 3rd century poet and consul, had his villa built on the edge of the town – just where the vineyards of the Château Ausonne are today. In the 8th century, the Bretonne recluse Emilion made his home in a cave nearby. This holy man, through example and the miracles he performed, drew numerous people to the area even after his death. From the 9th to the 11th centuries, believers converted the existing caves to a monolithic church whose size and atmosphere are still impressive today. The village retained his name out of respect. The villagers used the local limestone rock which was so easy to handle, to build their houses, and in doing so dug out vast cellars which offered excellent storage facilities for the wine.

Like Pomerol, Saint-Emilion is situated on one of the paths to Santiago de Compostela, and for the constant flow of pilgrims in the middle ages these wines were a welcome refreshment. In 1199 John Lackland gave the residents of Saint-Emilion the chartered right to make their own laws and elect their own parishes: the *Jurade*. In 1289 the English king Edward I extended this right to cover nine parishes, the area of which now includes the appellations of Saint-Emilion and Saint-Emilion *grand cru*. The *Jurade* exercised a controlling function over the wine, as it marked those barrels whose contents it deemed fit with a brand known as the *marque du vinetier*. Any wines that did not receive this quality brand had to be destroyed.

Up to the time of the Revolution, the *Jurade* were issuing certificates authorizing transportation for wines that were shipped or sold. The success of this action is evident from the esteem in which wine from Saint-Emilion was held. It was enjoyed at the royal courts of England and France, where Louis XIV himself praised it as the "nectar of the gods."

As long ago as 1884, a wine syndicate was established, and in 1936 Saint-Emilion was awarded the *Appellation d'Origine Contrôlée*. The *Jurade* was re-established shortly after the second world war, now as a wine fraternity that started to execute quality control in 1951. This resulted – 100 years later – in its own classification which is checked and revised every ten years, most recently in 1996. This classification is headed by the two *premiers grands crus classés A* (Château Ausone and Château Cheval Blanc), with Angélus, Beauséjour, Beau-Séjour-Bécot, Belair, Canon, Clos Fourtet, Figeac, La Gaffalière, Magdelaine, Pavie, and Trottevieille being the other eleven additional *premiers grands crus*. At present, 56 other *châteaux* are also recognized as *grands crus classés*.

Although Saint Emilion has a long and distinguished past, there are considerable soil differences on the 13,500 acres (5400 hectares) that produce 38.5 million bottles every year. Two *terroirs* shine above the others. One is the argillaceous plateau on the edge of which the little town of Saint Emilion itself is situated and on which most of the *premiers grands crus classés* are found, the best of which being Château Ausone. The layer of soil, which is frequently very thin here, contains clay.

The other *terroir* adjoins Pomerol, and the core of this area shows the same gravelly undulations with a loamy base as Pomerol itself does. This area contains the 90 acres (36 hectares) of Château Cheval Blanc and Château Figeac with its 100 acres (40 hectares) of vineyards. Marshy alluvial soils are increasingly evident towards the Dordogne, and these produce wines of less character.

The difference between the individual *châteaux* is based not only on the vast geological diversity, but also on the composition of the grape varieties. Cabernet Sauvignon, which dominates in Médoc, has the greatest requirement for warmth in Saint-Emilion and Pomerol, as

Entrance to the wine cellars of Château Ausone, Grand Cru Classé A

Château Ausone 1993

Château Cheval Blanc, Grand Cru Classé A

Château Cheval Blanc 1994

The Merlot vine and one of the exemplary vineyards of Château Pétrus.

Château Pétrus: The world-famous estate consists of a modest manor house, but the vineyards occupy the prime position in Pomerol.

otherwise it will not ripen without problems. That is why the first Merlot contained 55–60 percent and Cabernet Franc 30–35 percent, whilst the Merlot proportion is even higher in the second. The secret of success in later *assemblages* starts in the vineyard, when the vintner chooses the variety that is best suited to the particular soil and location. Cheval Blanc is the best known example, whose grandiose wines consist of two thirds Cabernet Franc, which gives excellent results on gravel and sand, and one third Merlot. Generally, however, the Merlot sets the tone, as this finds the predominantly loamy soils it needs. It gives Saint-Emilion wines their familiar charm with the soft, round, very fruity character. In the *chais*, however, the cellar halls of the *châteaux*, the different varieties are vinified separately.

Climate plays an extremely important role in the Bordelaise, and the differences between one year and another can be considerable. *Assemblage* gives the cellarman the chance to react to nature's flights of fancy when he is composing the estate's main wine. So, in difficult years he can increase the amount of early harvested Merlot, and in a very warm autumn that of the later ripening Cabernets. However he decides to act, Saint-Emilions and Pomerols generally open out later than Médoc wines, but have a surprisingly long shelf life (especially the better vintages) of two, three, or even more decades.

Merlot fares even better in Pomerol. The famous Château Pétrus, for example, has only 1.2 acres (5000 square meters) of Cabernet Franc (also known as Bouchet) on just under 30 acres (11.5 hectares), and it is not often integrated. Most of the other excellent estates contains 80 percent Merlot and more.

Pomerol is actually gaining in importance amongst the better known red wines of the Bordeaux. Despite a wine growing history that goes back as far as the Romans, the breakthrough only occurred in recent decades. That is why there is no official classification, although Château Pétrus is well able to hold its own amongst the greats and is less expensive. All this, despite the fact that the estate, like most of the 170 estates that share the 1950 acres (785 hectares) of the *appellation*, is neither particularly large nor impressive. However, its vineyards are situated in the northern angle of the area adjoining Saint-Emilion (Cheval Blanc is not far) and on the highest hill in that region where the top layer consists of clay soil.

The rest of the plateau of Pomerol consists of gravel and sand, and the base soil contains argillaceous lime and iron oxides, both of which have a marked effect on the taste of the wine. The well-drained soils are cool, which restrains the early Merlot (normally prone to hasty development) and imparts a noticeable finesse. Pomerols are deep, dark, velvety, voluminous, solid wines. In their youth they are defined by thick blackberry fruit as well as lots of flavor; they are fairly easy to access, but when they mature they develop great harmony and complexity as well as a characteristically delightful hint of truffles.

Merlot in flower

Merlot grapes just starting to form

273

Château de Monbazillac, built around 1550, reaches up from the edge of the wine region's chalk plateau, where the town of Bergerac dominates the valley of the Dordogne.

Château Bélingard is situated on what was once a site holy to the Druids, who were turning wild wine grapes into magic potions long before the Romans did.

The wines of the southwest

The wine regions that adjoin the Bordeaux to the west and continue upriver on the banks of the Dordogne and the Garonne share the same strong climatic influences of the Atlantic. In many *appellations* of the Dordogne, Lot-et-Garonne and Tarn-et-Garonne *départements*, the Bordelaise varieties – Sémillon, Sauvignon and Muscadelle – always play a leading role, if not the main part in white wines, and Cabernet Sauvignon, Cabernet Franc, and Merlot in reds and rosés. And there is another link to Bordeaux that may not be as close, but the effects of which are still apparent today. Since Roman times, wines from this region have been shipped from Bordeaux. The only way the Romans could get their barrels to the coast prior to sending them on to customers in northern countries was via the

two rivers. However, Bordeaux frequently proved to be more of an obstacle than a gateway to the world: its burghers knew well how to get various kings to grant them the right to ship their own wines first, ahead of wines from other regions. Often, the wines from other regions had to wait until the spring before the producers had the chance to pass them on, by which time it was not unheard of for several of the wines from the *Haut-Pays*, as the hinterland was known, to have turned to vinegar.

Still, these *crus* had all gained a certain reputation. Many of them could trace their "parentage" back to the Romans, by whom they were highly prized. In the Middle Ages, vine growing was developed in the monasteries. The Dutch controlled the market in the 17th century, and they wanted two kinds of wine: thin distilled wines, and sweet wines that they liked to have as highly concentrated as possible. Growers in the Bergerac area set about meeting this requirement, and this turned out to be the base for Monbazillac, and for the high esteem in which it

The vineyards of Château Bélingard overlook the Dordogne valley and, depending on the yield and vinification, produce pleasant or more distinctive white and red wines.

would be held a century later.

Although there are no longer any trading restrictions, Bordeaux wines still have such a good reputation all over the world that all the others, and especially those in neighboring regions, are automatically considered to be inferior to them. Although there were successful pioneers who began to extend their vineyards at the end of the 40s and make a name for themselves, such as the Vignerons de Buzet, only in recent times have a few vintners in *appellations* close to Bordeaux been able to achieve growths good enough to attract the attention of the international wine experts. At the moment, however, the *appellations* of the southwest are still a rich source of good wines at keen prices.

Wines from the Dordogne

Bergerac

Regional *appellation* that covers all of the 32,000 acres (13,000 hectares) of vineyards spread over 93 parishes. It applies to the same types of white, rosé and red wines as those produced in the Gironde, even though they may originate from the more closely controlled special *appellations*. The spectrum of the wines is correspondingly broad. In the main it covers pleasant, easily drinkable, frequently quite aromatic wines, but also some of the most concentrated, highly promising red wines and a series of excellent whites that are allowed to mature in oak barrels.

Côtes de Bergerac

Also a regional *appellation*. Its wines require a minimum of 11 percent rather than 10 percent, and its whites are the smooth and mellow (*moelleux*). Ideally, the latter are elegant, finely balanced wines with an intensive fruit flavor and good liveliness; best as an aperitif.

Pécharmant

The *grand cru* of red Dordogne wines is situated to the northeast of the town of Bergerac on 740 acres (300 hectares) of sunny inclines, whose gravelly, loamy soils contain large amounts of iron, which is what gives the wines their solid character. The best *cuvées* are left to improve in barrels and need to mature in bottles for several years before their pronounced tannins have dissipated sufficiently and a complex, elegant bouquet has been allowed to develop.

Rosette

A neighbor of the Pécharmant, but reserved solely for mellow white wines. The loamy gravel vineyards of this tiny *appellation* rise to the north of the town of Bergerac.

Monbazillac

After a long crisis, one of France's oldest and most highly regarded sweet white wines is slowly regaining its former position. Like its cousin, the Sauternes, it has to be harvested by hand and in several sessions. Early autumn mists bring the necessary noble rot to its site south of Bergerac overlooking the Dordogne valley. Today's wines, which come from a designated area covering 6200 acres (2500 hectares), tend to be a little heavy, but this actually increases their elegance.

Saussignac

Once a close relative of Monbazillac and now its nearest rival, this area to the west of it produces gentle, mellow wines that are bottled as *moelleux* under the regional *appellation* of Côtes de Bergerac. However, the vintners of the five permitted parishes reserve their medium-sweet specialties for their own *cru*, which is not yet widely known but is gaining in popularity.

Montravel

The area to the south of the Dordogne. 3200 acres (1300 hectares) of vines are grown here, between Sainte-Foy-la-Grande and Castillon-la-Bataille where the Bordeaux region begins, and stretching out to the north across gentle hills and valleys. Sauvignon sets the tone for this *appellation*, under which dry, fresh, highly aromatic wines are bottled.

Côtes de Montravel

This *appellation*, part of the same growing region, describes mellow wines, Sémillon in particular.

Haut-Montravel

This eastern part of the Montravel region is classified separately. Its calcium-rich soils help the Sémillon grape to achieve a greater concentration, but none the less the wines are still remarkably well balanced thanks to an elegant acidity.

Wines from the Garonne

Côtes de Duras

A close relative of the neighboring Entre-Deux-Mers, thanks to the geographical conditions, in which white wines used to dominate and mainly smooth, Sémillon-based wines were pressed. Now, however, the aromatic Sauvignon has asserted itself as a dry white wine, whilst the reds are based on the two Cabernets, Merlot, and some Cot. Frequently left to develop as pure varieties, the spectrum ranges from light "quaffing" wines to strong, tannic, barrel-matured wines.

Côtes du Marmandais

Adjoining the Entre-Deux-Mers and Côtes de Duras, those vineyards extend over some 4500 acres (1800 hectares) on both sides of the Garonne. The vintners and the two leading co-operatives often use Bordelaise grapes for these pleasant, frequently exotic white wines, whilst Gamay, Syrah, Cot, Fer, and the native Abouriou are also used for the reds and rosés. The reds are usually well balanced and contain lots of flavor.

Buzet

The 4500 acres (1800 hectares) devoted to this wine, whose *appellation* was recognized in 1973, spread from the left bank of the Garonne, between Agen and Marmande, along slopes and old terraces to the edge of the region's woodlands. The two Cabernets and small amounts of Cot, from which the Vignerons de Buzet cooperative vinifies a wide range of red wines and leaves them to develop in oak barrels, grow on loamy, partly gravelly soils. The best *cuvées* are well structured, with plenty of roundness and depth. The area also produces small amounts of rosé and white wines.

Côtes du Brulhois

A vine-growing area to the west of Agen that, like "Sleeping Beauty," fell into a deep slumber around 1930, from which it was roused by a cooperative in 1965. Now just less than 500 acres (200 hectares) of terraces and loamy slopes are cultivated with Tannat, the Cabernets, Merlot, and also with Cot and Fer Servadou. The rosés are fruity, the reds often bring to mind blackberries and can be drunk at an early age.

Lavilledieu

Historic wine region at the confluence of the Tarn and Garonne; now just under 350 acres (140 hectares) of vines on poor, chalky marshy ground, of which Cabernet Franc, Gamay, and Syrah each have a quarter, while the rest is devoted to Negrette and Tannat. Wines produced from these grapes seek an early harmony with an emphasis on fruit, and should be drunk slightly chilled at 12–14 °C. V.D.Q.S. since 1947.

Côtes du Frontonnais

Red Bordelaise and other types grow on three old terraces on the banks of the Tarn with very poor soils in this region between Toulouse and Montauban. The native Negrette lends rosé, and especially the delicate and aromatic red wines, an unusual note that brings to mind violets, liquorice, and blackcurrants. Also increasingly complex, flavorsome *cuvées* that keep well.

The vineyards of the sweet Monbazillac wines reach across the valley of the Dordogne. The autumn mists bring the noble rot which is essential to these grapes.

Lamproie à la bordelaise
Lamprey ragout with red wine
(cook a day ahead)

Serves 8

1 large lamprey
3 bottles good quality red wine
salt and freshly ground pepper
A pinch of ground nutmeg
1 lb/500 g carrots
½ lb/250 g onions
2 lb/1 kg leeks
10 oz/300 g veal bone
½ lb/250 g Bayonne bacon
10 tbsp/150 g butter or goose fat
2 tbsp flour

Place the live lamprey in boiling water for 1 to 2 minutes and remove immediately. Place in cold water and remove the outer membrane with the back of a knife.

Suspend by the head so that the blood can flow from the tail, and then remove the entrails. Pour the blood into a container, mix with some red wine to prevent coagulation, and place on one side.

Carefully cut the lamprey into 1–1½ in/3–4 cm pieces. Put the fish pieces in a large saucepan.

Season, and add a pinch of nutmeg. Cover the fish with red wine.

Bring to the boil. Leave for a few moments, and then remove from the hob. Leave to cool and drain. Keep the cooking liquid.

Peel and finely dice the carrots and onions. Wash the leeks. Cut the white parts into large chunks (discard the green parts).

Braise in a casserole with the veal bone and the bacon. Dust with flour and add the red wine cooking liquid.

Leave to simmer at a low temperature for one hour. Add the pieces of fish and simmer at very low heat for a further 40 minutes.

To serve: Remove the fish and leeks with a ladle and place in a warm dish.

Remove the bones.

Add the drained blood to the sauce and stir well; do not reheat.

Pour the sauce over the fish and leeks and serve immediately.

Fishing on the Gironde

The Gironde is the largest estuary in Europe. Fishermen and seafarers have known since ancient times just how much protection this funnel of water offers against the inclemency of the Atlantic Ocean. It also attracts fish, and especially those varieties that spawn in fresh water. In the past, salmon and sturgeon swam up the Gironde and then the Dordogne or Garonne until man's insatiable appetite for them had decimated stocks to such an extent that they were placed under protection early in the 1980s. However, eel and lamprey remained faithful to the Gironde, much to the delight of fishermen, and are regarded as typical specialties of the region's cooking. The former are grilled, ideally over wine branches, and served with sorrel, whilst the latter are cooked in red wine. Although most

The fishermen's huts on the banks of the Gironde swing their *carrelet*, as their nets are known, out to the river when the tide – and fish – come in.

of the fishing is done from boats, the numerous huts on the coasts add to the attraction of the Gironde. Balanced high on stilts, they protrude into the river. Their capacious, wing-like nets, known locally as *carrelets*, are suspended from long poles over the water and are cast when the tide comes in. The regional delicacies include shrimp, eel (which are caught in baskets), and in late autumn, *pibales*, (elvers).

Gironde caviar

In former times, large amounts of sturgeon were caught in the Gironde estuary, in the Dordogne, and in the Garonne. However, the fishermen had no idea of what to do with the roe. In the early 1920s the Parisian restaurateur Emile Prunier opened a caviar factory in the tiny harbor of Saint-Seurin d'Uzet on the right bank of the Gironde and sent a Russian émigré there to start up production. The factory produced up to 3 tons of caviar a year. Eventually the sturgeon failed to appear, and the business had to close in 1963. Now two breeders in the Arcachon Basin are having some success with breeding sturgeon. Although this is a different member of the sturgeon family, it provides an excellent caviar that is perfectly capable of holding its own against its Russian and Iranian competitors.

Le pressé d'anguilles de Gironde aux girolles
Eel terrine with chanterelles

Serves 20

11 lb/5 kg eel
5 bay leaves
vinegar
2 lb 3 oz/1 kg fresh chanterelles
oil
salt and freshly ground pepper
chervil
toasted sesame seeds

Vinaigrette
1 cup/250 ml hazelnut oil
2 cups/500 ml soybean oil
1 cup/250 ml sherry vinegar
salt and freshly ground pepper

Skin the eels, clean them and remove the bones. (To skin, cut around the body behind the head and pectoral fins and tie a thin piece of string around the cut area to hang the eel up. Using a towel, grasp the skin with one hand and pull it down whilst holding the eel firmly with the other hand.) Cook for about ten minutes in plenty of boiling water to which the bay leaves and vinegar have been added. Remove and drain.
Wash the chanterelles, rinse, and dry with kitchen paper. Heat the oil in a pan and cook the mushrooms for 5 minutes. Season to taste.
Line a terrine with the eels and place the chanterelles down the center. Cover with eels.
Place a well-fitting board over the top, weight with a heavy object, and place in the fridge overnight.
Make a vinaigrette from the hazelnut oil, soybean oil, and sherry vinegar, and season to taste. Serve with the terrine. Chervil and toasted sesame seeds are an excellent garnish.

Flan d'huîtres battu au cresson
Oyster flans with cress butter

Serves 6

12 oysters
1 clove garlic
1 tbsp butter
1 tbsp flour
3½ oz/100 g duck liver
9 oz/250 g white fish fillet
4 eggs
1 shallot
9 tbsp/90 g cornstarch
2 cups/500 ml crème fraîche
salt and freshly ground pepper
1 small bunch chervil, chopped

Sauce
1 tbsp crème fraîche
½ punnet cress
2 tbsp butter

Open the oysters and save the oyster juice. Peel the garlic and pre-cook in water. Make a white sauce with the butter, flour and half the oyster juices. Coarsely chop 6 oysters and finely dice the duck liver.
Chop the fish fillet in a blender, add the eggs, then the sauce, garlic and shallot; blend well. Place everything in a bowl and dust with cornstarch. Add the chopped oysters, duck liver, and crème fraîche, and mix well. Season to taste and divide into 6 buttered ramekins. Pre-heat the oven to 350 °F/180 °C and bake the ramekins for 40 minutes. To make the sauce, use the rest of the oyster juices with the crème fraîche and cress. Heat, and then poach the 6 remaining oysters in this sauce. Place an oyster on each flan. Flake the butter and add to the sauce; pour over the flans. Garnish with chervil.

Le dos de brochet à l'échalote
Saddle of pike with shallots

1 pike (approx. 4 lb/2 kg), dressed
4 oz/120 g shallots
2 oz/60 g garlic
⅓ cup/80 g butter
4 sprigs fresh thyme
½ cup/100 ml white wine
½ cup/100 ml chicken stock
flat-leafed parsley, chopped

Pre-heat the oven to 430 °F/220 °C. Cut the pike into large chunks. Chop the shallots and garlic and braise in butter in a flameproof dish. Add the chunks of pike and thyme, simmer for a short while and then place in the oven. Add the wine and stock after 10 minutes and return to the oven for a further 10 minutes. Arrange the chunks of pike on a bed of creamed potato, pour over the sauce and garnish with parsley.

Flan d'huîtres battu au cresson – Oyster flans with cress butter.

Tuna is a specialty of the Basque seaport town. Here is a white one, which may weigh up to 22 pounds (10 kilograms).

Basque fishing

The Basques' reputation as seafarers is legendary. Having no choice other than to live with the harsh conditions in their homeland, they turned to the sea as a source of food many centuries ago. In about 700 A.D. they met the challenges posed by whale fishing. At that time, whales came regularly and in great numbers to spend the winter in the warm waters of the Gulf of Gascony, known to sailors and fishers as the Bay of Biscay. These gigantic creatures were a vast haul (in both senses of the term), and the Basques specialized in catching them.

Whaling started in Saint-Jean-de-Luz and in Ciboure on the other side of the mouth of the Nivelle, the best harbor of the Pays Basque. It provided a comfortable and respectable way of life from as early as the 11th century. Whales remained faithful to the Bay of Biscay until the 15th century, when their numbers started to decline, and finally they stayed away altogether. The Basques were then forced to go and seek out the whales around Canada and Greenland, and in Arctic waters. Here, however, they were competing increasingly against Dutch and

English whalers, who initially stopped the Basques from landing on the North Sea coast, where they had been processing the blubber obtained from the whales to make concentrated whale oil. As is so often the case, necessity was the mother of invention, and a Captain Sopite from Saint-Jean-de-Luz invented an oven that could be used to make the oil on board ship.

In 1713, England was given Newfoundland, which had formerly belonged to the French, and the effects of the loss of the excellent natural harbors and wealth of fishing grounds were devastating to the Basques of Saint-Jean-de-Luz and Hendaye. Not only had they used these grounds for catching whales, but latterly also for cod fishing, which as stockfish, or dried cod, had become one of their country's national dishes. Many fishermen were forced to emigrate.

Those who stayed behind managed to survive – often lucratively – as pirates, or eked out a living from fishing anchovies and hake in the Bay of Biscay.

Saint-Jean-du-Luz reached a new pinnacle at the middle of the 20th century, when it became the leading port for sardine and shortly afterwards also for tuna. These fish were caught in special ships in waters off the west African coast.

The port of Saint-Jean-de-Luz: nets, fishing smacks and the foothills of the Pyrenees.

However, the charming harbor at the foot of the Pyrenees did not remain unscathed by the European fishing crisis, and its proud fleet was severely decimated. Still, the harbor remained active, and today the connoisseur will find fish of unbeatable quality.

Quantity-wise, anchovies are the major catch at approximately 2300 tons, whilst sardines are no longer so important. Other varieties caught are *chipirones* (small squid), hake, sea-wolf, John Dory, and occasionally turbot – not forgetting tuna, of course. The main catch is red tuna, by far the largest member of the tuna fish family, which can reach a weight of more than 550 pounds (250 kilograms). It has remained a specialty of Saint-Jean despite the fact that no more than 300 tons are caught every year. It is caught between May and September with baited lines, and is best eaten fresh, either marinated, broiled, or as a ragout with paprika, potatoes, garlic, and a good pinch of local red pepper.

Pavé de turbot à l'Auberge Kaïku
Kaïku style turbot steaks

1 turbot, weighing 4½–5½ lb/2.2–2.5 kg
2 aubergines (eggplant)
olive oil
1 onion
1 green pepper
1 tomato
salt and freshly ground pepper
5 cloves garlic
cod heads and bones

Prepare the turbot for cooking, rinse with cold water, pat dry with kitchen paper, and fillet.

Bake the aubergines (eggplant) whole in the oven until the skins turn brown and start to blister. Halve the cooked vegetables and remove the flesh with a wooden spoon. Peel the onion and cut into thin slices. Wash the red pepper and cut into thin slices. Skin the tomato, remove the seeds, and pulp.
Braise the vegetables in the olive oil. Add the cooked aubergine (eggplant) and simmer gently for 5 minutes, stirring continuously. Season to taste. Wash the garlic cloves and simmer gently, covered, in olive oil. Remove, keeping the oil.
To make the fish stock, cover the fish bones with cold water, bring to the boil and reduce until the water becomes creamy.

Grill both sides of the fish fillets for a few minutes so they are crispy on the outside but still soft on the inside. Season to taste.
Place 1 tbsp aubergine (eggplant) mix in the center of each of four plates and place the fish fillets on top. Beat the garlic oil into the fish stock and drizzle over the fillets.
Garnish with fried leeks and a salsa made of red and green peppers.

The "Kaïku" is a well-known fish restaurant located in an old stone building that dates back to the 16th century, in the heyday of the harbor.

Alpine cheese under threat

The idea of moving up into the mountains for up to four months at a time, with only a flock of several hundred ewes and maybe a few cows for company; of milking them by hand every morning (which can take up to three hours) for at least half of that time; of making cheese from the milk, tending to any sick animals, and looking after oneself as well, while living in a draughty hut, possibly without seeing another human being for the duration, is not one that would appeal to many people these days.

And yet they do still exist, the shepherds and cowherds who uphold this ancient tradition in the Pyrenees, the Alps and other European mountain ranges; a tradition that was a way of life long before our so-called modern civilization had even been thought of. It existed, because the pure mountain air encouraged a variety of grasses and herbs to thrive, they in turn providing healthy nourishment for the animals and adding the most wonderful aromas to their milk and cheese. Although the simplest methods are used for making cheese in the mountain huts, herdsmen, farmers, cheesemakers, dealers and cooks are all agreed that the quality and flavor they offer are unrivaled. And if any kind of contamination were to occur, then our eyes and nose would soon notice it. For centuries now, this pure alpine cheese has been considered to be the absolute peak of the cheesemaker's art.

These herdsmen have survived local and national quarrels and differences of opinion, wars, and various other catastrophes, but now their very livelihood is being threatened by something far more insidious – and fatal: European Union bureaucracy. The bureaucrats appear to find the idea of making cheese anywhere other than in sterile, completely tiled, air-conditioned, over-automated units, where the workers are clad from head to toe in plastic, utterly abhorrent, but that is what they want to see in these mountain pastures. It appears that the bureaucrats consider the loss of yet another way of life, which is already under threat, and the destruction of one of our most precious foods, not too high a price to pay for exaggerated and unnecessary standards of hygiene.

Sheep cheese from the Pyrenees

Brebis

Ossau-Iraty is a firm sheep cheese from the western Pyrenees, one which is based on age-old traditions but has only been known to cheese connoisseurs outside the region for a few years. Ossau and Iraty are the two boundaries to its kingdom, which extends from the Ossau valley and the peaks of the imposing Pic du Midi d'Ossau 9465 feet (2884 meters) south of Pau, to the woods at Iraty and the mountains of Saint-Jean-Pied-des-Port in lower Navarre, the central province of the Pays Basque. This region, with its extensive meadows, and the abundance of water in its valleys, is home to two breeds of sheep: the Basco-béarnaise, and the more frequently seen Manech, both excellent milking breeds. Herdsmen have been making use of the meadows since time immemorial, and each one has his own specific area, the boundaries of which he must observe.

Depending on the altitude, the ascent commences in April or, if the pastures are at 5250 feet (1600 meters) or higher, as late as June. The life of the shepherds of lower Navarre, who drive their animals up to the Iraty, is relatively comfortable. Since the development of the access routes, it has been easy for them to ascend to the pastures at 3280 feet (1000 meters) and descend at the end of the season. The younger shepherds and shepherdesses are particularly efficient at organizing themselves. However, the situation is different in Soule, the Pyrenean region of the Béarn, and in the upper Pyrenees. Despite the accoutrements of modern-day life, such as mobile phones, solar power and four-wheel-drive vehicles, providing more reliable links to the outside world at the foot of the mountains, the herdsmen still spend their four months in isolation.

The ascent into the mountains is the most arduous part of the journey. The ewes still have fairly large amounts of milk, and the young animals need to adapt to being milked by hand. At the beginning of the journey, there is enough milk for two 13–pound (6–kilogram) cheeses, one in the morning and one in the evening. By the middle of June, two or three days' milk is required for the same amount of cheese. August is the most pleasant time. As most of the ewes have been serviced by now, the shepherds stop milking to preserve the ewes' strength for lambing. That is the only way the shepherd can ensure the health of the newborn lambs and regular cheese production. As is so often the case, the key to success is in moderation. In June and July, the shepherd's day begins with the milking at 6 a.m.

With 400 animals to milk, this can take a good three hours. The shepherd then takes the milk back to his hut, where he pours it into a large kettle and lights the flame beneath it. This is the beginning of the cheesemaking process. When the milk has reached a temperature of around 86 °F (30 °C), he adds rennet, and 10 minutes later the milk suddenly curdles. The herdsman leaves the milk for another ½ hour to 1 hour whilst he goes to check on his animals. Then, using a wire fork, known as a cheese harp, he cuts the mass again and again. The herdsman heats the milk again for half-an-hour, stirring continuously, to 104 °F (40 °C), before draining off the whey. The remaining mixture is then shaped into a ball, wrapped in muslin, pressed into the round perforated mold (capacity: 11 pints/6 liters), and weighted. Now it is time to lead the animals to the edge of the grazing ground – a round trip that can take up to three hours. When the herdsman returns to his hut, he turns the cheese, putting the weight back on it until the evening. He then removes the cloth and leaves the cheese in the mold for another day. Hand-made cheese is then rubbed with coarse salt for four days, after which it is left in the cellar (where the temperature must be lower than 54 °F/12 °C) for at least three or four months. The cheese is then ivory-colored, with a juicy, nutty flavor. Basques, however, prefer to leave it for nine months, until it is hard and dry and has a more pronounced flavor. Towards the evening, the sheep find their own way back to the hut, and the whole process of milking and cheese-making begins again. Most herdsmen take their flocks back to the valley around September 20. Those with no, or very little land of their own on the lower slopes remain in the mountains until October. In a good season, a shepherd with 400 sheep will bring home 200 top quality Ossau-Iraty Bebis-Pyrénées cheeses.

Left: The best sheep's cheese is made by hand from unpasteurized raw milk by herdsmen whose flocks graze in the Iraty.

Below: Well ripened sheep cheese is accompanied by a little dish of cherry preserve.

Pear brandy from the place of pilgrimage

Branas

The Basque country used to be famous not for its brandy, but for its cider and wine. It is thanks to Etienne Brana that we now also associate Saint-Jean-Pied-de-Port with spirits. Because his pear brandy was named the best in the land in Gault Millau in 1980, it is now offered as a digestive in even the most exclusive restaurants.

In 1897, the Brana family set up as wine merchants in the former capital of the lower Navarre. Although his fine "nose" and good "feeling" for wine helped Etienne and his wife to success, Etienne would rather have grown the vines himself. Their children, Jean and Martine, were still too small to help. Then, when he inherited his grandmother's estate in the middle of rural lower Navarre, Etienne had an idea: he would plant pear trees and distill brandy from the fruit of these trees. On a southern slope of Haxaharria – every house has a name in the Basque country – he planted a magnificent orchard that consisted solely of espaliered Williams Christ pear trees. Together with a distiller from the Charente and an unquenchable desire for quality, he set about his task.

The syrupy base wine of 5–7 percent proof is made by keeping the yield from the orchard low and carefully calculating the date for picking (this guarantees that the fruit has the best possible aroma), leaving the picked fruit to continue to mature so that the starch turns into sugar without the texture of the pears becoming floury, and then distilling it at carefully controlled temperatures. Etienne, who died in 1992, passed his knowledge and his tricks of the trade, which make so much difference, on to his daughter Martine, who has been in charge of the copper still ever since. In the still, the syrupy pear mash is steam-heated to 212 °F/100 °C. The first distillation takes seven hours, and produces the *brouillis*, which is 25–30 percent proof. This liquid is then distilled for another nine to ten hours, a process which is called *bonne chauffe*. The next stage demands a high level of expertise. First, the distiller must draw off the head, as it is too strong and its aroma too aggressive. Then the "heart," which slowly reduces from 69 to 60 percent, flows from the still, and this she collects. Finally, she cuts off the "tail," whose aromas are too heavy. Experience alone will tell you when to switch off the bad ester. Martine Brana usually spends from the middle of September until the middle of January distilling the pear harvest. She stores the *eau-de-vie* in high-grade steel tanks, reducing it gently through a series of passes to 44 percent volume. She then assembles one- and two-year-old brandies in order to achieve definite aromas as well as a

certain smoothness, a task which she achieves with a delightful finesse. Eau-de-vie-de-Poire-Williams is best drunk after a good meal, chilled to 41 °F/5 °C, as a digestive. Or choose the equally excellent Vieille Prune, made from plums, the highly aromatic Framboise, which is made from raspberries, or Marc d'Irouléguy, which is made from marc. And do not fail to try the wines – yes, Etienne Brana's dream has now become reality. The most wonderful vineyards of the district of Irouléguy, where Jean Brana produces his delightful wines, are situated on the breathtaking slopes around the village of Ispoure.

Centenary brews: a Williams pear, trapped in a bottle and floating in the pear distillate, and unreduced plum brandy, grown and produced with particular finesse.

Basque wine

Irouléguy

Irouléguy wine has the famous monastery of Roncesvalles to thank for its existence. The monastery, where the legendary French hero Roland lost his life in 788, was established close to the town. Vines fared badly in the direct vicinity of the monastery, which, situated at a height of almost 3280 feet (1000 meters) and surrounded by woodland, lies on one of the most important ancient routes across the Pyrenees. So the monks in Irouléguy and Anhaux established two sites in the foothills, which were protected by the mountains, and commenced production of the wine they used in their services and for their own wellbeing, as well as that of the pilgrims, for whom they set up a hostel in Saint-Jean-Pied-de-Port. Successive generations of monks enjoyed these wines for centuries, until they were forbidden access to the vineyards by the Pyrenean agreement of 1659. The Basque farmers then took over the clerical vineyards, an area of approximately 1235 acres (500 hectares) in the 19th century. But then came *phylloxera*, wars, and rural exodus, and the wine was almost forgotten. In 1945, however, the farmers, who also possessed a vine garden, established a society for the protection of Irouléguy, which was recognized as a *V.D.Q.S. (Vin Délimité de Qualité Supérieure)* in 1952. In 1954 the farmers formed a winegrowers' cooperative and set up the wine cellars of Baigorri, which remained the only producer for 36 years. Irouléguy is a red wine, made from Cabernet Franc, Cabernet Sauvignon and Tannat, and a highly deserving rosé is also made from the same grapes. It gained its *Appellation d'Origine Contrôlée* in 1970. A new era dawned when, in 1986, Etienne Brana set about fulfilling his dream of having his own vineyards and, copying a Swiss model, had narrow terraces cut in a steep red sandstone slope of the Arradoy above Ispoure. The slope is one of the criteria for the *appellation*. The minimum incline is 15 percent, but it can go up to 70 percent. The vineyards must be situated at least 98 feet (30 meters) above the bottom of the valley, and may not exceed a height of 1410 feet (430 meters). North-facing slopes are not used. More white wine is again being produced today, for which Gros, Petit Courbu, and Petit Manseng are permitted, producing fruity, well-rounded, slightly excitable wines. The red wines are marked by balance, fine fruitiness, and a delicate spiciness.

Cabernet Franc, which plays a highly important role in Bordeaux, the Loire valley and in the whole of the southwest, gives finer tannins in the mountainous microclimate of Irouléguy than Tannat and its cousin, Sauvignon.

This variety, which is a native of the Pyrenees, is called Petit Corbu. It gives the Madiran white wines a crispy character and adds a suggestion of flint, especially to Irouléguy and Pacherenc du Vic-Bilh.

Jurançon

Unlike most other winegrowers, those who tend the vines at the foot of the western Pyrenees are usually farmers as well. Only the south-facing slopes get enough sunshine and warmth for the grapes to ripen. Because there is often a night frost in the valleys in spring, the first rows of vines are a respectful distance from the bottom of the valley. So, even in areas where viticulture has been part of the agriculture for centuries, it is rare for a grower's land to be used solely for wine-growing purposes. In fact, the areas that can and must be used for other purposes are usually considerably larger.

It is not that long since the wines from these small regions were enjoying the benefits of their long-standing reputation. However, after the *phylloxera* catastrophe and the years of war and hardship, many old winegrowing families had neither the strength nor the means to revive their old businesses. Dozens of unique vine varieties from the Pyrenees and surrounding areas fell victim to this situation, and now they are gone for ever. A few winegrowers retained some hybrid vines of a lesser quality, which they continued to grow for their own consumption. When it became apparent after the Second World War that the vineyards at the foot of the Pyrenees could be lost forever, there was a resurgence of interest in them, which resulted in a program of replanting in the 1950s. Fortunately for the new winegrowers at the time, they were first and foremost corn farmers and cattle breeders. This meant that they were not solely dependent on the success of the vineyards, and so could set up their cellars with care and deliberation if they chose not to "go with the flow" and join the newly-established *caves coopératives*.

Despite the onslaught of industrialization, there were still strong links to the old farming ideas and traditions, and self-sufficiency was always the main objective. It was no coincidence that a large vegetable garden decorated the entrance to the famous Madiron-Domaine Bouscassé estate – long before its delightful park was created – and that corn grew on the lowest parts of the grounds. Corngrowing spread quickly around the southwest after its introduction in the 16th century. Corn is ideal for fattening poultry, which is why the southwest also gained a reputation for its stuffed goose liver. The more mountainous the terrain, the smaller the farms, but the more varied their products. This way of life was undoubtedly most common in the Jurançon. On the shadier slopes, which were used mainly for cattle, it was not unusual for a farming family to produce everything, from milk

and butter, ham, bacon and sausages, stuffed liver, pâtés and preserved duck and goose pieces, pork and veal, vegetables and fruit, to dry and medium-sweet wines. And although there is no longer a need for self-sufficiency today, a new awareness of the quality of life and food has reawakened these pleasurable traditions.

The wine of kings

On the day Henry, the future King of France, was born, his grandfather, Henri d'Albret, ruler of Navarre, wet his grandson's lips with Jurançon wine before rubbing them with garlic. This was considered to be the best protection against infection. In view, however, of the somewhat

pleasure-loving nature of Henry IV, the little ceremony could also be seen as a kind of initiation into the gastronomic wealth of his homeland, Béarn. At the same time, it was an ennoblement of this wine from the foothills of the Pyrenees, outside the gates to Pau, an award it may not always have deserved, but it undoubtedly benefited from the district's prevailing conditions.

The vines grow only on south-facing slopes at a height of 1000–1300 feet (300–400 meters). Although the spring is often cold and wet, the region does have the benefit of a long and sunny fall, when the south wind brings warm air over the Pyrenees. With conditions such as these, the winegrowers need not rush the harvest, but can give themselves until the end of November, even

Petit Manseng, the high-quality native grape which ripens slowly and is harvested late after being left to partly-dry on the vine, in November or December. The wine can be left to mature for decades.

waiting until December. Then their Petit Manseng shows itself in all its grandeur.

The grapes grow in light, airy clusters, turning ever darker, and their skins becoming increasingly wrinkled. Warm days and cold nights encourage *passerillage*, a degree of extreme ripeness after which the grapes start to shrivel on the vine. Noble rot, which is encouraged in the Sauternes grape, is rare here, much to the delight of the winegrowers, who are none too keen on this phenomenon.

The most fantastic medium-sweet wines are made from the concentrated must of these grapes. Not only do they contain a pronounced aroma and high volume, but they also have a fine acidity, which gives them an unusual degree of balance and class. The delightful and historical

Jurançon was awarded its *appellation* in 1936. However, such quality can only be guaranteed with low yields, but that is something the winegrowers cannot live on in times of poor economy. That is why they preferred to grow the Gros Manseng, the big brother of Petit Manseng, whose berries are somewhat larger and which brings greater yields, and the rounder Courbu.

Difficulties arose if the weather in a particular year failed to meet expectations. The grapes were unable to produce the natural sugar needed for sweeter wines, and this had a considerable effect on the quality of Jurançon. Fortunately, a solution was found, and in 1975 the *Appellation Jurançon Sec* was awarded. Vinified as a dry wine, Gros Manseng provides highly intense, exotic

Clos Lapeyre, the most beautiful position in the Jurançon, consists of semi-circular wine terraces on which the Manseng vines are trained to a height of up to 6½ feet (2 meters) as protection against frost.

fruit aromas, such as guava or litchi, and at the same time has a strong, round structure with a good freshness. It quickly became popular with head/wine waiters and wine lovers. As a result, winegrowers old and young have taken advantage of the fantastic potential offered by their Petit Manseng, and make the most of good years to produce superlative wines that are perfectly capable of holding their own against the most famous medium-sweet vintages.

Henry IV would have been delighted.

Madiran

It would be easy to drive through Madiran without seeing a single vineyard. That is because this gently undulating farmland is a mosaic of cornfields, meadows, crops, and small woods. Vines can be spotted here and there, perhaps where a slope conveniently faces the sun. And yet it was the Romans who started cultivating vines here. From the 12th century, when Aquitaine belonged to the English crown, more effort was put into viticulture, and the local wines were shipped via Adour and Rayonne to northern Europe. In the 19th century, the vine-growing region in the tiny area to the north of Pau and Tarbes totaled 3460 acres (1400 hectares), and the wine was much appreciated. For example, at a gala held in Versailles on December 23, 1891, Château Montus 1865 and 1870 were on offer, as well as Corton 1874 and Roederer champagne. By 1950, however, the vineyards had been reduced to 123 acres (50 hectares), although Madiran was awarded the A.O.C. in 1948.

Then there was a renaissance, though, and the corn and cereal farmers, who had the necessary land, decided to grow vines once more. New estates developed, and produced good wines. In the 1960s, several pioneers dared to bottle them, so that the clientele in restaurants could experience for themselves just how well these regional wines went with local duck and goose dishes. A handful of wine estates and the Cave de Crouseilles made a good name for themselves. However, when the state experts limited the proportion of Tannat, the robust local red wine variety which required a long maturing period, to 40–60 percent, recommending instead the more agreeable Cabernets and fruity Fer Servadou, this appeared to threaten the individuality of Madiran. Fortunately, some winegrowers came to its aid.

The uprising was announced when the deteriorating Château Montus was taken over by the young winegrower's son, Alain Brumont, who replanted the excellent, highly chalky slopes with four-fifths Tannat. Brumont knew what he wanted and how to get it. By reducing yields, introducing a three-week mash fermentation and frequent tapping, he approached Tannat with respect, commitment, and trust. And when Brumont broke all regulations and made the 1985 vintage as a pure variety for the first time, presenting it to the experts two short years later, a new star had risen in the wine skies. In blind tastings, Château Montus Prestige beat the best Bordeaux and opened up new horizons for Madiran wines. Since then, a new generation of winegrowers has been delighting wine lovers with superb red wines of an entirely unique character, and new estates are constantly being

Left: Winegrower Alain Brumont's imposing tower at Château Bouscasse is a tribute, as modern as it is traditional, to the renaissance of Madiran.
Right: The cellars at Bouscassé, made from reclaimed local stone, compare favorably with the architectural equivalents of the best Bordeaux Châteaux.

The first, and in many respects most important task in the vineyard is pruning the vines, as that is what determines the ration between concentration and yield.

added to the lists of the leading producers. The white Pacherenc du Vic-Bilh, the "Sleeping Beauty" of the Madirans, was also able to benefit from this boost. It possesses a wide range of varieties, including both Mansengs, Courbu, Sauvignon and Sémillon, and the earthy Arrufiac is the cherry on the cake. Aromatic dry whites are composed of these, but the great Tannat winegrowers bravely delay the harvest for as long as they dare, to produce delightful medium-sweets between October and New Year's Eve that do not pale in the face of competition from Jurançon and Sauternais – on the contrary: they glow with the most wonderful shade of gold.

Pyrenean wines

Madiran
Gentle, rolling hills at Pau, now back up to almost 3460 acres (1400 hectares) again, where Tannat has proved its strength. It is still toned down with Cabernets and Fer Servadou. Good maturable reds, with lots of character.

Pacherenc du Vic-Bilh
Comes from the same district as Madiran. An increasingly popular, rare white with two aspects to it. One side has crisp, highly aromatic dry cuvées, and the other grandiose medium-sweets, the most unusual of which are ready in time for the New Year, or later.

Côtes de Saint-Mont
In 1981, the extended Madiran region at Saint-Mont, Riscle, and on the northern side of the River Adour was awarded a V.D.Q.S. for its quality, thanks to the wine cooperatives of the two parishes. Very pleasant rosés, interesting whites and, above all, well rounded, strong, and highly spicy reds are made from the same red and white varieties as those used in the Madirans.

Tursan
A hilly region to the south of Mont-de-Marsan and the Adour, where an old wine-growing tradition is maintained on a generous 2470 acres (1000 hectares). Since the *phylloxera* disaster has been based on the robust Baroque, a white, highly alcoholic, dry variety now gaining in freshness and complexity with the Mansengs and Sauvignon. Also rosés and reds from the Cabernets, of which the latter develop a remarkable structure and density thanks to Tannat.

Jurançon
Grows only on south-facing slopes and over approx. 1730 acres (700 hectares) to the south-west of Pau. Available in two versions: the highly aromatic, dry and lively Jurançon Sec is based on Gros Manseng and Courbu, whilst the sweeter Jurançon *moelleux* is well ripe when harvested and is used in an *assemblage* with Petit Manseng, or pure using the highest qualities.

Béarn and Béarn-Bellocq
Nine-tenths of these 395 acres (160 hectares), which were awarded the A.O.C. in 1990, cover the protected slopes and hills of the parish of Bellocq. The rosés and reds of Béarn are marked by the strong Tannat, and the lighter Béarn-Bellocq by Cabernet Franc. The fruity white wines of Manseng obtain their originality from the native Raffiat de Moncade.

Irouléguy
A tiny region of only 494 acres (200 hectares) in the Pays Basque, predominantly occupying the sunny slopes of the Cize valley and the Arradoy near Saint-Jean-Pied-de-Port. Medium-strong, frequently elegant red wines produced from Cabernet Franc, Sauvignon, and Tannat. Also fruity, excitable rosés and rare whites.

Every three months, the red Madirans are tapped to let the wine breathe. This helps the wines to develop and tones down the more noticeable tannins.

Using a pipette, the oenologist regularly takes samples from the barrels to check that the wine is developing as desired.

The taster glass is the most important instrument for a wine maker, and the nose is the infallible test organ: the smell tells the maker what the next course of action should be.

Sunday chicken for everyone

Poule au pot

Henry IV, king of Navarre and France, wanted every one of his subjects to have a fat, juicy chicken for the pot on Sundays. This was a dish that His Majesty himself enjoyed tremendously, and furthermore one which was virtually a complete meal in itself. It consisted of the nourishing broth in which the well-stuffed chicken was cooked, served as a starter, followed by the chicken and vegetables, the latter including the heart of a cabbage, a delicacy in Béarn and not to be omitted. Compared with the familiar broiled or fried chicken which has invaded our modern-day lives, *poule au pot* is a juicy reminder of bygone, tastier days. The free-range chicken was cooked as in the following recipe, which comes from one of the wine estates of Madiran, and was enjoyed by the winegrower, his wife and the workers from the vineyard and cellars – always accompanied by the appropriate wines, not just on Sundays.

Poule au pot

2 slices ham
1 onion
2 cloves garlic
1 chicken liver
Duck rillettes (optional)
7 oz/200 g white breadcrumbs
1 egg
1 large free-range boiling chicken
4 carrots
1 onion
4 leeks
4 potatoes
1 savoy cabbage

Sauce
Gherkins
1 shallot
1 hard-cooked egg
Oil and vinegar
Sea salt
Freshly milled pepper

Finely chop the ham, onion, garlic, and chicken liver, and mix well with the *rillettes* (optional), breadcrumbs, and egg. Use this mixture to stuff the prepared chicken, and close the orifice with kitchen twine. Peel the vegetables and cut into equal-sized pieces. Place the chicken in a large pot of boiling water, add the vegetables, and leave everything to bubble gently for about three hours (depending on the age of the chicken).
Meanwhile, prepare the sauce. Finely chop the gherkins, shallot, and egg, and add the oil and vinegar, stirring well. Season to taste.
Cut the chicken into pieces and arrange on a serving plate. Serve with the vegetables and the sauce.

Right: Chicken in a pot may be somewhat time-consuming to prepare, but it is full of flavor.

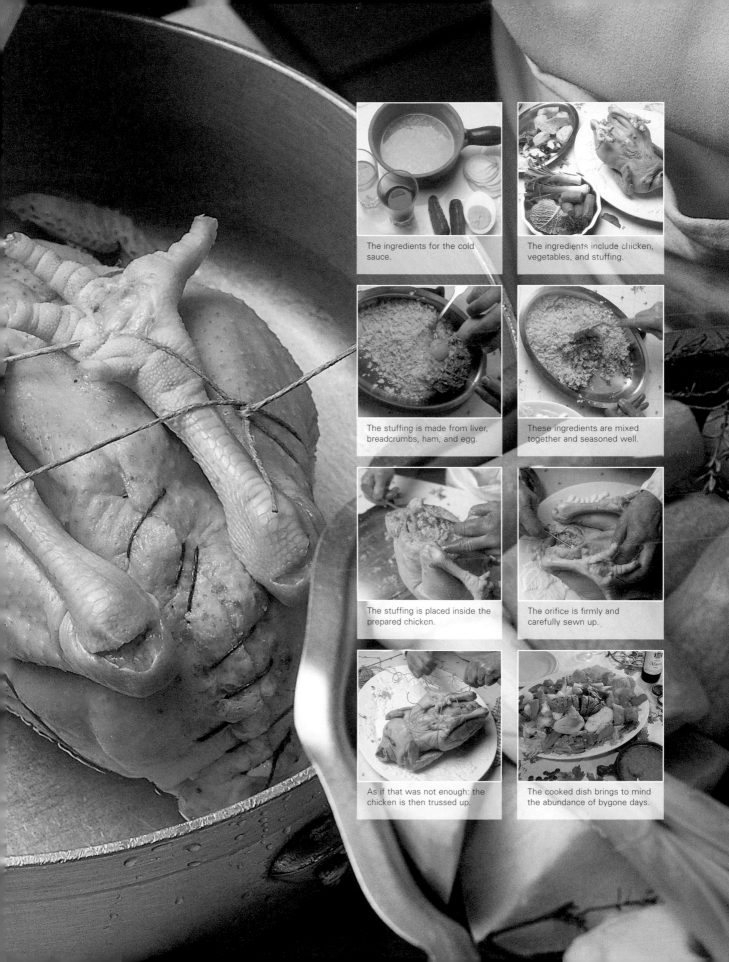

The ingredients for the cold sauce.

The ingredients include chicken, vegetables, and stuffing.

The stuffing is made from liver, breadcrumbs, ham, and egg.

These ingredients are mixed together and seasoned well.

The stuffing is placed inside the prepared chicken.

The orifice is firmly and carefully sewn up.

As if that was not enough: the chicken is then trussed up.

The cooked dish brings to mind the abundance of bygone days.

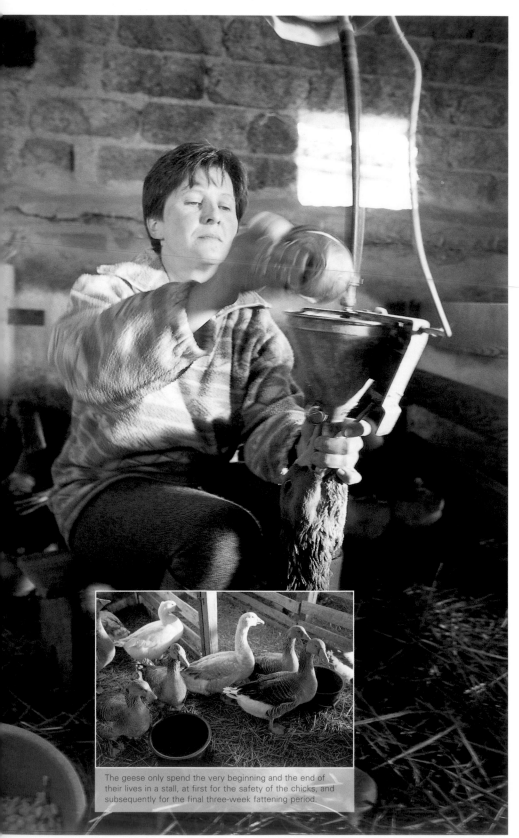

The geese only spend the very beginning and the end of their lives in a stall, at first for the safety of the chicks, and subsequently for the final three-week fattening period.

Glorious Geese

Anyone faced with choosing a heraldic animal to represent the southwest would do well to choose the goose. Ducks may play a more important part today from an economic point of view, representing as they do the most common type of fattening poultry, but the goose is still the queen of farmstead and table, not for its luxurious fattened liver or even the opulent festive roasts it provides, but basically for its naturally thick layer of fat. Cut up and salted for a day or two, then gently cooked in its own fat before being put into stone jars and covered with the same fat, the meat keeps for up to a year. This was a huge advantage in the days before deep-freezers. Add to that the fact that the preserved legs, wings, breasts, stomachs, and other parts still tasted every bit as good at the end of that time, and that any accompaniments cooked in the delicious fat would benefit from the extra flavor, it is hardly surprising that *confit d'oie* soon became the favorite dish of all Gascony and its surrounds. It contributed greatly to the flavor and content of a whole range of dishes, some of which were eaten almost every day, such as the nourishing vegetable soup, *garbure*, and others, such as *cassoulet*, only slightly less frequently. These gray-feathered birds soon spread throughout the whole southwest. They were given different names in different regions or municipalities, and sometimes even at different markets. Today, even the experts are unable to distinguish between the different types, and the birds are now generally referred to as "Toulouse geese." Farmers used to breed their own flocks to suit their taste, and some still continue to do so today.

There is little doubt that the fine liver was appreciated in the past, especially if it was quite fatty, but this was usually determined by the goose's own appetite, fed as it was on plenty of grain and figs. It was some time before tales of the aristocratic goose liver pâté, or *foie gras*, from Strasbourg (and of the stuffing funnel) reached Gascony. There is also little doubt that quite a few 18th century farmers' wives treated their families to the first liver pâtés. However, it wasn't until the 19th century that a demand for this luxury item arose in Paris and other large cities, and that is when full-scale production commenced. Although small concerns that specialized in the purchase and processing of fattened livers sprang up from Dordogne to Gers, the rearing of geese for *foie gras* continued to provide a welcome extra income to

Left: The practice of stuffing geese goes back as far as the ancient Egyptians, although it is no longer done by hand today. An electric machine forces the overdose of corn down the throat.

A picture of a goose's ideal life in Gers and the rest of the southwest – geese need meadows and grassland.

the farmsteads until around 1960. It was only when there was an upturn in the economy and the market for this delicacy grew that the production began to assume industrial proportions – much to the disgust of the geese.

Unlike ducks, these stiff-necked creatures defend their right to graze, a social event which they enjoy to the full, waddling in great numbers through meadows and fields. Even when they are just a few days old, shortly after hatching in the spring, the goslings have a desire for fresh air and open skies – at least during the daytime. Soon, the geese spend all their time outdoors, enjoying the summer until it is time for fattening. The birds, whose liver is quite literally in the right spot (something an experienced goose farmer can tell just by touching the bird's side), are then prepared for their extravagant finale with two daily meals of gigantic proportions, which causes the liver to swell quite considerably. The actual fattening period usually lasts three, occasionally four weeks, and during this time the geese are forced to consume something in the region of 55 pounds (25 kilograms) of food. This forced feeding causes over-expansion of the liver. By carefully increasing and coordinating the amount of food the birds receive in a day, the farmers are able to determine the subsequent size and quality of the liver. Towards the end the liver has become so big (up to 21–32 ounces/600–900 grams in geese, and 10½–17½ ounces/300–500 grams in ducks) that the birds are hardly able to move. Geese can reach a weight of 13–17½ pounds (6–8 kilograms), ganders even 17½–22 pounds

(8–10 kilograms). The best breeders put their geese on a diet just before the end, which helps to clear out the gallbladder.

This unpleasant process is decidedly more costly, both in terms of time and money, for geese, which are more difficult to keep anyway than ducks, which is why their market share is decreasing. It is reckoned today that ducks outnumber geese by at least 25 to 1. It is mainly the traditional farmsteads who have remained faithful to their geese. During the winter, almost one-third of their production is sold on the *marchés au gras*, the special markets for fattened poultry, or directly from the farms, either fresh or preserved. However, every eighth goose is consumed by the farmers. What better recommendation could you ask for?

Toulouse geese are everywhere: those large, majestic, gray-feathered birds, to whom farmers have remained faithful for centuries.

Marché au gras

Plump geese and ducks and their stuffed livers were, until a few years ago, a purely seasonal business. They had to be ready for Christmas and New Year, and the farmers knew well what had to be done to meet this deadline. The dealers and manufacturers of preserves would have contacted their suppliers in plenty of time, but in the strongholds of goose and duck fattening, the last few market days before the holidays at the end of a year became veritable trade fairs for the elegant poultry. Some, such as Samatan, Gimont, Aire-sur-Adour, Périgueux, and Brive even made a name for themselves beyond their provincial boundaries. Even today, when *foie gras* is available throughout the year, these *marchés au gras* (specialized markets) are no less important.

In Gascony, almost a quarter of the total goose trade and an eighth of the duck trade takes place on markets, and the clientele is by no means restricted to locals. For some cooks and

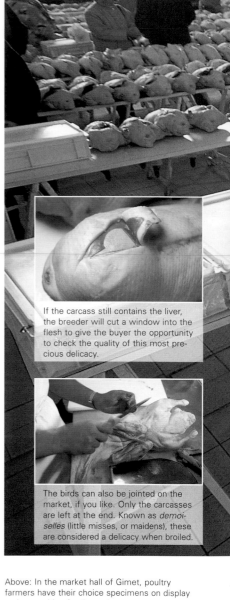

If the carcass still contains the liver, the breeder will cut a window into the flesh to give the buyer the opportunity to check the quality of this most precious delicacy.

The birds can also be jointed on the market, if you like. Only the carcasses are left at the end. Known as *demoiselles* (little misses, or maidens), these are considered a delicacy when broiled.

Criteria for classification			
Quality class	Weight	Appearance	Texture
Fattened goose liver			
Extra	14–32 oz/ 400–900 g	Light in color, with no flaws such as green marks from intestine or bile.	Firm, but gives to the touch.
1st class	17½–41 oz/ 500–1150 g	Does not meet the criteria for "extra"; may contain some blood marks, but no green; some of the liver wing may have been removed.	Firm, but gives to the touch.
Large liver	Over 41 oz/ 1150 g	May contain some blood, but no green; part of the liver may have been removed.	All textures.
2nd class	Over 14 oz/ 400 g	Does not meet the criteria for 1st quality; may contain traces of blood, marks, and red spots provided these do not affect use.	All textures.
3rd class (purée)	Over 14 oz/ 400 g	All other fattened livers that are suitable for human consumption: red livers, fibrous or grainy cut.	All textures.
Fattened duck liver			
Extra R (Restaurants)	14–25 oz/ 400–700 g	Light in color, with no flaws such as blood or green marks from the intestine, or bile.	
Extra F (processing)	10.5–16 oz/ 300–450 g	Light in color, with no flaws such as blood or green marks from the intestine, or bile.	Yields to the touch
2nd class	Over 10½ oz/ 300 g	Does not meet the criteria for R or F; may contain pink marks, traces of blood, or slight marks where the gallbladder was, but no green marks from the intestine.	
Purée	Over 10½ oz/ 300 g	All other fattened livers that are suitable for human consumption.	

connoisseurs, no path is too long if genuine quality awaits them at the end. Some may decide to treat themselves to a bird for a special occasion, but anyone who wants to stock up for the winter to feed a family will need several specimens for the exercise to be worthwhile. So December may be the main season, as it were, but these specialized markets take place from November to April.

Rows and rows of neatly laid out ducks and geese, ready for use, await the potential buyer in the large halls. The birds are available either with or without the liver, or with the liver sold separately.

Left: Buying a goose or duck is a matter of confidence and trust. The market provides an opportunity to meet the farmer and/or his wife who bred and fattened the bird of your choice.

Above: In the market hall of Gimet, poultry farmers have their choice specimens on display and are waiting for the rush.

And if you lack the confidence (or perhaps the expertise) to joint your chosen bird, there are plenty of experts on hand to provide you with advice and encouragement. Some experts even have a sharp knife at the ready, and will joint ducks and geese with a flick of the hand. That's not to say that you won't still have enough work to do at home, but the results will provide you with gastronomic delight throughout the year – and memories of the unique atmosphere at the *marché au gras*.

Ducking the issue

The popularity of duck increased dramatically in the 1960s. This was thanks in no small part to cooks everywhere, and in particular to those in Gascony. They loved to serve *foie gras* as a starter, not just as pâté, but also freshly cooked in a skillet, as *magret de canard*, duck breast, which André Daguin "discovered" as a flash-fried delicacy in Auch, the capital of Gers. Soon, too, French families throughout the country started to feel that the prospect of Christmas without *foie gras* was even worse to contemplate than Christmas without a Christmas tree, and this attitude did a lot to increase demand.

The duck's days were numbered, especially for the *mulard*, a cross between a Barbary Erpel (an American variety) and a common domestic duck. *Mulards* are very resilient birds, but infertile, and the females have a highly vascular liver, which is therefore not suitable for fattening. The male's liver, however, is ideal for that purpose. This cross, which has been known for centuries, finally exceeded the popularity of other gastronomically renowned geese when the demand for *foie gras* declined as the result of their highly obstinate nature. Today, the *mulards* have left all geese, Toulouse and others, far behind them. Although they (and their livers) fail to reach the sizes of their stiff-necked competitors, the ducks are more willing to swallow. This has made them the darlings of the breeders who want mass production. The duck's life is now divided into two stages and farmers and breeders specialize accordingly. One group concentrates on caring for the ducklings for the first 3 to 3½ months of their lives, during which time they enjoy a controlled, yet less complicated, highly nutritious diet. The other group takes care of the fattening. The animals are force fed yellow corn, which has been softened or cooked in hot water, through a funnel. This is usually done by a machine that provides electronically measured quantities. During the short period of time that is given over to fattening, ducks are fed more than 33 pounds (15 kilograms) of corn. Nor are the ducks given much room during this accelerated processing period. The race for greater production and better prices also leads to softer, lower quality livers. Consumers should therefore look for the official quality class (see opposite page) for guidance.

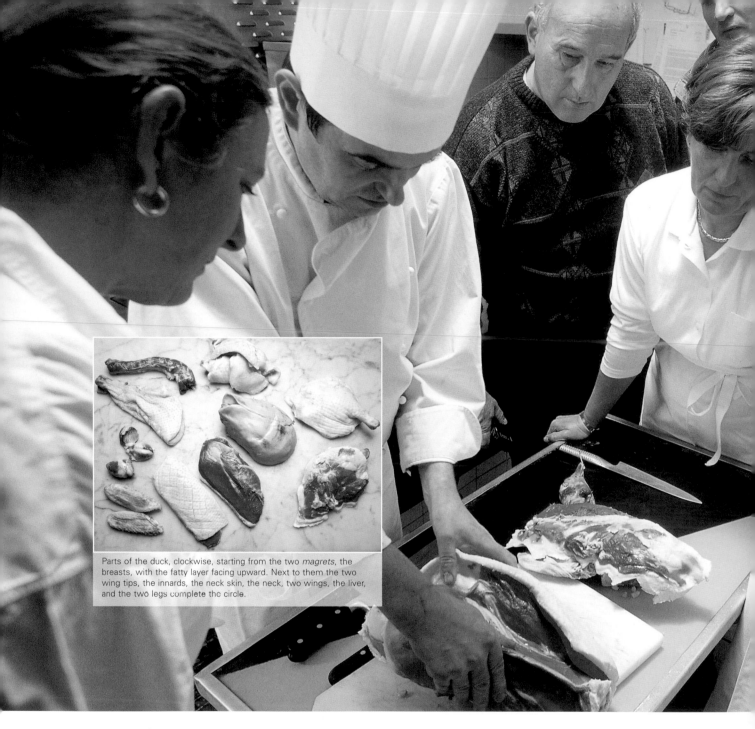

Parts of the duck, clockwise, starting from the two *magrets*, the breasts, with the fatty layer facing upward. Next to them the two wing tips, the innards, the neck skin, the neck, two wings, the liver, and the two legs complete the circle.

Duck on course

The idea of stockpiling *foie gras* is very appealing. Although cookery courses are available all over France, those in the southwest are particularly sought after. After all, not only will you meet more than one (more or less) great chef, several (more or less) pleasant people with the same interests, and learn a few recipes. You will also have something substantial to take home with you, apart from a few memories and

handwritten notes: a variety of jars with bits of preserved duck, something delicious to serve your guests on high days and holidays.

Foie gras is the stuff of legends. It is also expensive, especially when it is ready for consumption and of the best quality. Anyone who is unable to resist its pleasures will have a pecuniary interest in finding out its secrets. With just a little skill, it is possible to halve the cost of this luxurious starter, to say nothing of the peace of mind you have when you know more about just what it is you have. This takes

us on to *confit*. Once you have understood the principles, preserved legs, (*magrets*), and the upper wings are simply delicious, easy to make, ideal for storing, and they keep extremely well. As far as quality is concerned, it is important that the poultry has been reared as naturally as possible, and fed on high-quality grain and corn. Patience is the most important factor in the preparation. First of all, the pieces of duck or goose must be rubbed with a mixture of salt and pepper. As a general rule, ½ ounce (15 grams) sea salt and a pinch of black pepper are used for

These trainee chefs watch closely to see just how to handle a duck before wielding the knife themselves.

each 2 pounds 3 ounces (1kilogram) of meat. The meat is then left in a cool place or in the refrigerator for a day or two, left to drain, and the salt wiped off with kitchen paper. It is then placed in a wide, uncovered pot on a low heat until the fat starts to run. Cook over a low heat until no more blood is to be seen and the layer of fat on the thighs has reduced to about 0.2 inch (5 mm). The more gently the meat is cooked, the juicier it will be. The meat is then either placed in stone containers, which are left in a cool place, or layered in preserving jars. Whichever method you choose, the items are then covered with fat from the birds (it may be necessary to buy some additional duck or goose fat). The jars are sterilized for 20 minutes at 194 °F (90 °C). In the first case the *confit* will keep for up to a year, in the second for several years. Anyone who puts a vast amount of effort into turning a duck or goose into *confit* will find great pleasure in stuffing the neck. For the *cou farci*, the skin is carefully removed from the neck and turned. The organ meat and leftover meat from the ribs are finely chopped, seasoned, mixed with a chopped onion, egg, and bread that has been soaked in milk. Add some finely chopped liver and, if desired and available, a small truffle. Mix the stuffing well, place it inside the skin and sew the neck up. Cook slowly in hot goose or duck fat. This original specialty can be served cold, sliced, as a starter, or warm as a main course. The purist will not even countenance the idea of a stuffing to which pork has been added. Needless to say, a cookery course is about much more than learning and preserving. A look behind the scenes, and you will appreciate the obligatory farewell banquet in a completely different way.

First remove the wings and neck before drawing a sharp knife down the breastbone.

Then draw the knife deeper down the bone to remove the left breast and the leg.

Now to the other side. Remove the leg first, cutting it off completely.

Then cut off the second *magret* from the carcass, thus removing the last meat part.

The organs are now exposed. Remove the liver first, then the stomach, and lastly the heart.

The next task is to tidy up the *magret* and legs, cutting them into a clean, definite shape.

Prunes from Agen

Two out of every three prunes produced in France are a staple in two out of every three French larders, and two out of every three of these prunes are nibbled straight from the package. The third prune is used by farmers and traders, bakers, confectioners, and chefs in all sorts of wonderful and delicious ways. They are turned into creams, pastes, and preserves; juices, syrups and liqueurs; preserved in Armagnac or other types of alcohol; filled or used as a filling; served with duck, rabbit, pork or lamb, and in numerous puddings and desserts.

Plum trees were originally brought from their home in the Near East to the Garonne by the Crusaders, and the monasteries subsequently took over the planting and care of them. The health-giving preserves were loaded onto barges and shipped down the Garonne to Bordeaux, before being forwarded to Paris, London, Rotterdam and the New World. They are now found primarily in Lot-et-Garonne, a plum-growing region that extends as far as Bergerac. There are around 2.9 million plum trees in the southwest, producing something in the region of 77,000 tons (70,000 tonnes) of fruit. In terms of both the quantity and quality of its prunes, France is second only to California.

Today, the growers concentrate their efforts on just one variety that is ideal for drying, and so this type has gradually replaced all the others. The purple *prune d'Ente*, a reddish-pinkish fruit, only comes into its own when it has been dried. The outside is then almost shiny black, the inside amber-colored, soft, and highly aromatic. A true child of the south, it loves sunny slopes, does not tolerate late frosts, and is sensitive to wind. It prefers deep argillaceous and chalky soils; nothing too moist or sandy, and so it cannot cope well with long rainy or dry periods. The trees, which grow to a height of 13–16½ feet (4–5 meters), are set in well-prepared soil, usually about 23 feet (7 meters) apart. The way the trees are trained is of utmost importance, and they are usually left with a trunk height of about 3½ feet (1.10 meters). For the first five years, until the trees begin to bear fruit, the grower prunes them carefully, shaping the top into a pyramid. This shape ensures that the tree obtains maximum ventilation, and it also has a marked effect on the health of the tree and quality of fruit, essential since *prune d'Ente* is susceptible to pests and disease. Still, anyone who wants to enjoy this health-giving fruit, which is simply packed with vitamins, minerals, and fiber, would do well to opt for fruit that has been grown organically.

The degree of ripeness is crucial when preparing the fresh fruit for drying, and timing the harvest exactly right is the key to success. The foliage should be healthy and abundant, and the yield reduced by timely thinning. There are several signs of ripeness: sugar starts to accumulate in the flesh; the acid content reduces; the color of the outer skin deepens; the flesh starts to soften, and ripe fruit drop from the trees, leaving their stalks behind.

The harvest begins during the second half of August, and continues into October. While large companies use special "shakers" to shake the fruit from the trees, small and organic companies tend to work in the time-honored way. However, even in this case, the fruit is not picked by hand, but is beaten from individual branches by experienced laborers wielding wooden poles – the traditional method. Because the ripe fruit falls freely, and without the stalk, this process does not affect the tree. Furthermore, unripe fruit remains on the tree, which helps to maintain quality. In former times, laborers would spread straw over the ground to gather up the fallen fruit; today they spread nets.

The fresh plums are washed and spread, in single layers, over frames so that air can circulate around them. Formerly, they were left in the sun or placed in bread ovens to dry; today, the frames are stacked onto carts and moved into vast drying chambers, or tunnels, where hot air is blown in and the moist air sucked out. From the preliminary drying session at 140 °F (60 °C) to *finition*, which requires 167 °F (75 °C), is between 18 and 24 hours. The objective is to reduce the moisture content of the plums to 21–23 percent while retaining the aroma, and possibly increasing it in the initial stages of fermentation. The trick is to avoid caramelization, as this would both have a negative effect on the flavor and turn the plums an unattractive shade of brown. The temperature inside the fruit should therefore not exceed 167 °F (75 °C).

Depending on the degree of ripeness and the size of the fruit, between 5½ and 7½ pounds (2½ and 3½ kilograms) of ripe fruit is required for 2¼ pounds (1 kilogram) of prunes. Once they have been dried, which should be done as soon as the fruit has been harvested, the prunes are stored in wooden boxes in cool, dark rooms. Before they are sent to market, Pruneaux d'Agen, these delicious prunes from Agen, are briefly dipped in hot water to increase their moisture content to around 30 percent. This gives them an appetizing color and soft consistency – and it means that the consumer can tuck into them straight away.

Right: The traditional frames, on which the plums are placed before being dried in ovens, allow the optimum circulation of hot air.

It is said that crusaders from Syria brought the first plum trees back to Agen. Today, there are 2.9 million plum trees in the southwest.

These glazed plums are filled, by hand, with a delicate plum cream, flavored with Armagnac and vanilla.

Of all the possible ways of using (and enjoying) prunes, this has to be the most exquisite.

The dessert trolley

Amuse-bouche, the appetizer, and one or two main dishes have been served and enjoyed; plates and cutlery have been removed, and then the waiter or waitress appears again and really "clears the decks." Using a napkin, a knife, a special little scoop or other elegant implement, he or she rids the table of crumbs (a procedure known in French as *desservir*), the highlight and conclusion of the table-clearing process. It is almost as if the act which is to follow had nothing at all to do with the visual and culinary play that went before, as if the curtain were about to go up on a completely new production. Indeed, the diner will even feel different; already somewhat sated, delightfully relaxed, and, thanks to the accompanying wine, in a lighter frame of mind. Any initial stiffness and formality is now forgotten, and the final course is awaited with a degree of excitement and anticipation. While many modern chefs like to serve veritable works of art that need to be ordered at the beginning of the meal, others prefer the good old dessert trolley. Which is no bad thing. When it rolls into view, it is as though we are seeing the Promised Land for the first time. We feast our eyes on the delicacies on display. We are seduced by them, we are allowed – expected – to imagine what they will be like; we can quite literally design the last act to suit our own taste, crowning the delights we have already enjoyed with one last – and widely varied – gastronomic bonanza. The attentive staff will, however, tactfully and discreetly restrict servings to a sensible level, something for which the guest will be exceedingly grateful once he has returned to his senses.

Pastis, tourtière and croustade

What *pastis* is to the Gersois, and the *tourtière* to the Landais, the *croustade* is to many other inhabitants of Gascony – namely, a light and airy, rather labor-intensive work of art. There is a world of difference between handmade and commercial puff pastry, but this difference is no greater than that between *pastis gascon* and *pastis landais*, the latter being, of course, a brioche

Pastis gascon

2 cakes, each serving 6 people

3 eggs
1 cup/250 ml cold water
A pinch of salt
9 cups/1 kg flour
1 cup/250 g butter, melted
6 tbsp/100 g sugar
4 apples or 10 plums, sliced
3½ tbsp Armagnac

Prepare a pastry from the eggs, water, salt, and flour. Shape it into a ball, cover with lightly oiled plastic wrap, and leave in the refrigerator overnight. Place a cloth on a table measuring 6½ feet (2 m), sprinkle with flour, and carefully stretch the pastry over the entire surface. Brush it with butter and sprinkle with sugar. Trim the edges. Fold into three lengthwise, brushing each layer with butter and sprinkling with sugar. Then fold crosswise and cut into four squares. Place some of the fruit on each and cover with a second square. Bake at 430 °F/ 220 °C for about 10 minutes, and then flambé.

1 Stretch the pastry with your hands to cover the cloth on the table.
2 Brush the wafer-thin pastry with melted butter and sprinkle with sugar.
3 Use a knife to straighten the pastry along the edges of the table top.

4 Using the cloth, fold the pastry twice, lengthwise, to make three layers.
5 Spread the top of each folded layer with plenty of butter and sprinkle with sugar.
6 Now fold the pastry in half, and cut into four equal squares.

7 Place a square in a well-buttered round fruit tart pan.
8 Spread finely sliced apple or thin slices of plum over the pastry.
9 Do not forget the Armagnac, which gives this delicate cake its unmistakable flavor.
10 Use a second square to cover the first one, making a star shape.
11 The cake is baked quickly in a very hot oven, brushed with butter again and flambéed with Armagnac.

This dessert trolley contains a distinguished selection. Front center, a plate of *petits fours*, then, continuing in a clockwise direction, *Opéra* chocolate cake, vineyard peaches in Pauillac from Lynch-Bages, *Iles flottants* (whisked egg whites on *crème anglaise* with praliné), a *Mousse au chocolat*, iced melon balls, and a set coffee cream. To the left of the center, light-as-air *Paris-Brest* cake, and, on the right, a *Tarte au chocolat*.

flavored with orange blossom water and rum. This confusion exists solely in the names, since *pastis gascon* is a superfine puff pastry, inherited from the 8ᵗʰ century Moors while en route to Poitiers, but now considered to be a native dish of Gascony, and as such simply must be made with Armagnac.

Growing tobacco

Tobacco, a member of the *nicotiana*, or nightshade, family, needs a mild, moist climate to thrive. Although there are several suitable regions in France, it feels most at home in the southwest, probably because of the alluvial soils in the valleys of the Dordogne, Lot, and some parts of the Garonne. Where this type of soil is not available, the tobacco is planted in fertile, well-draining soils. There are around 10,000 farms in the *départements* of Dordogne, Lot, and Lot-et-Garonne, which are dedicated to this demanding but highly profitable culture.

Tobacco contains tiny little seeds, 10,000–13,000 of which make up 1 gram, which is why it is impossible to sew it directly into the ground and has to be started off in special beds. In the fall, the tobacco grower prepares a well-fertilized and disinfected seed bed, working on about 11 square feet (1 square meter) for every 1100 square feet (100 square meters) of open land. Usually a plastic tunnel is all that is needed to protect the seedlings. The seeds are sewn from March 10 onward, either from a watering can or pulverizer, or perhaps by mixing them with fine sand and scattering them by hand. The seedlings are left in the tunnel for 12–14 weeks, during which time the grower trims the young plants regularly to strengthen them. Nowadays the seeds are often sewn in floating seed trays and fed artificial fertilizers.

Before the seedlings can be planted out, the field has to be prepared. The tobacco crop is rotated; since the plants are susceptible to black root rot, tobacco can only be planted every three to four years in a particular field. Cereals have proved to be particularly satisfactory as a catch crop.

The well-draining soil must contain plenty of organic material, and so cow manure is usually applied in the fall before the tobacco is planted. Green manure is also applied and turned over. Sowing takes place between the beginning of May and the beginning of June, depending on the region, in well-loosened, dry soil, and the tobacco is planted in rows 2–3 feet (60–90 centimeters) apart. Later, carefully measured quantities of artificial fertilizer will be applied to ensure the best possible development of the leaves. The grower has to protect his crop from attack by a number of pests, including snails, aphids, caterpillars, grasshoppers, and anything else that eats leaves, as well as diseases such as mildew and leaf or root rot, and he does this by chemical means. To achieve a good leaf harvest, the buds need to be removed at an early stage, and so the appropriate products are used to prevent them from forming.

Tobacco must be ripe when harvested. About 60 days after planting, the lower leaves show various signs of ripeness, such as a light green marbling; the structure becoming firmer; the midrib vein turning white; the edge of the leaf becoming brittle. If the leaves are being picked by hand (for which in France the plant is divided into four tiers), the individual tiers are brought in by hand. The top, or head, leaves are left to

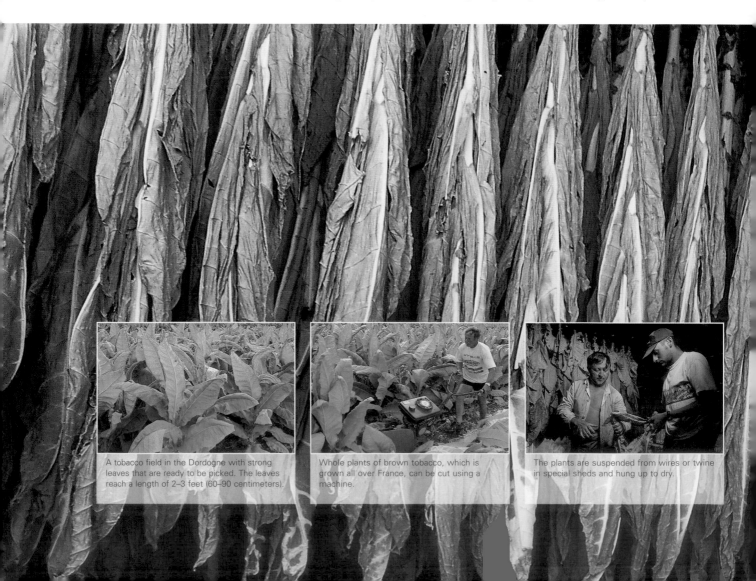

A tobacco field in the Dordogne with strong leaves that are ready to be picked. The leaves reach a length of 2–3 feet (60–90 centimeters).

Whole plants of brown tobacco, which is grown all over France, can be cut using a machine.

The plants are suspended from wires or twine in special sheds and hung up to dry.

ripen for 60 days longer than the lower ones. If the whole plant is being harvested, which is done with a cutting machine, the grower will wait until the upper middle leaves are ready. Each plant consists of 12–14 usable leaves. The tobacco must be hung up to dry as soon as it has been picked, and the grower has special sheds for this purpose.

The drying process (brown tobacco is air-dried) is an important part of the culture. A grower can only plant as much tobacco as he is able to dry under optimum conditions. A standard rule of thumb is 35 plants on 1.2 square yards (1 square meter), and 250–300 leaves per 1.3 cubic yards (1 cubic meter). The drying process consists of three stages.

1 Yellowing. The cells of the leaf should remain alive for as long as possible at an ideal temperature of 68–77 °F (20–25 °C) and relative humidity of 80–90 percent, as this enables the chemical transformation to proceed without hindrance. This stage takes about 12 days.

2 Browning. The moisture in the leaves evaporates slowly at a relative humidity that may exceed 80 percent for a short time only. This stage takes around 23 days.

3 Reducing the ribs. Under the same conditions, moisture finally leaves the ribs of the leaf and moves to the edge, which therefore resumes some flexibility. The third stage takes about 18 days.

Once the tobacco has dried, the leaves are sorted according to color and tier. Quality criteria are good burning ability; full, soft, fine leaves of a uniform light chestnut brown, and well-dried, evenly colored ribs. Packed in bales of no more than 56 pounds (25 kilograms) in weight, the leaves are usually supplied to the cooperatives in December and February, who buy them and carry out fermentation before supplying the tobacco to the manufacturers of tobacco products.

The crucial mark of quality is the color of the leaves: for top quality products it has to be a light chestnut brown.

Types of tobacco

Brown tobacco
This variety has been grown in France for centuries. When dried in fresh air, it provides light brown leaves that are made into smoking tobaccos with a typically French flavor.

Burley
A natural mutation which, due to a lack of chlorophyll, produces pale leaves that turn a warm yellow after drying. The leaf is absorbent, and so is suitable for aromatizing to give the *goût americain*.

Virginia
Meets current requirements better than any other variety. With a pleasant aroma, yellow in color, and packs well in cigarettes. Has to be picked by hand in stages and dried in a special oven.

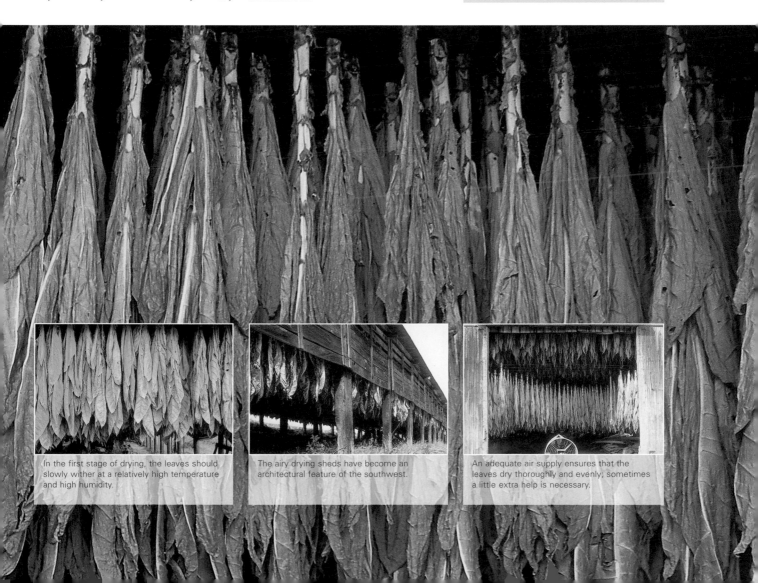

In the first stage of drying, the leaves should slowly wither at a relatively high temperature and high humidity.

The airy drying sheds have become an architectural feature of the southwest.

An adequate air supply ensures that the leaves dry thoroughly and evenly; sometimes a little extra help is necessary.

Blue fog

To Jean Nicot, French envoy to the Portuguese court, tobacco was many things, but most definitely not a poison. He regarded it as a wonder drug, and in 1560 he gave Catherine de' Medici powdered tobacco as a remedy for her migraines. This must have given the sovereign some relief, at least, because tobacco subsequently became extremely popular in France as a medicine. The powder was used as snuff, which, it was believed, both caused and encouraged sneezing, and this was considered beneficial. When its followers went as far as indulging in their habit in church, an interdict was issued in 1624, but this was obviously only of limited success since it had to be renewed in 1650. It would appear that large amounts of tobacco were consumed, since a tobacco tax was levied. In those times, taking snuff was a time-consuming business: first the user had to rub the leaves, which had been bound together in the shape of a carrot, to a fine powder. Ready-to-use snuff did not become available until the end of the 18th century.

Sir Walter Raleigh, the English adventurer, writer, and courtier to Queen Elizabeth I, went down in history in the 16th century as the first European smoker, but it was the Dutch who were the pioneers of puffing — and of the tobacco

Right: Fisherman from the Dombes, smoking a Gitanes Mais.
Below: What were once advertising gifts are now highly desirable collector's items, such as this Celtiques ashtray.

trade. George Sand, the French authoress whose love affairs scandalized 19th-century France, was frequently seen puffing her pipe in public. However, tobacco became more readily and widely available with the invention of the cigarette in 1863. The first branded cigarettes appeared from 1876 onward, and La Hongroise, the precursor of Gauloise, was first smoked in 1878. Twenty years later, the French market boasted 242 different brands, which were sold in bundles, the standard form of cigarette presentation until 1925.

Gauloise were first introduced in 1910, and 101 million of them were sold in the first year. When the familiar blue package with the illustration of the Gaul's helmet and two rows of ten cigarettes first appeared in 1925, 1.7 billion of them went up in smoke. This compared with the more modest figure of 19 million Gitanes, which were also made in 1910. The following year saw the foundation of the S.E.I.T., the *Service d'Exploitation Industrielle des Tabacs*, which became the S.E.I.T.A. in 1935 when matches, the *allumettes*, were included. This organization remains the state association with responsibility for the growing and processing of tobacco allover France.

Tobacco products were an ideal opportunity for the state to settle its debts, and to this end the Régie Française Caisse Autonome d'Amortissement was established. In order to increase income from the monopoly, André Citroën, who was a member of the responsible government commission, suggested that 1 percent of the annual turnover be invested in advertising. Other brands were created to give the consumer a wider choice of variety and flavor. As well as

Balto spreads the idea of the flavor of American cigarettes (design Francis Giletta, 1951).

the typically French flavor of brown tobacco, the S.E.I.T.A. also developed brands with an American flair to compete with foreign cigarettes – which the organization was also responsible for importing. Primrose, Balto, Week-End, Gallia, Naja, Celtique, Anic, High-Life, Congo – these are some of the melodious brand names

which used the idea of wanderlust, leisure, or a fascination for the exotic as an advertising vehicle. Still, Gauloises and Gitanes remained the market leaders. Since the 1930s, the S.E.I.T.A. has been making advertising history with its packages, posters and advertising, and commissioning some of the leading graphic artists in France.

There was something of a boom in the 1950s, when sales of Gauloises (the figures quoted in the following are for the Brunes, so typically French, and the turnover in France) exceeded the 30-million mark, and consumption of Gitanes increased from 1.2 billion in 1951 to 11.5 billion in 1962. In 1975, Gauloises peaked at just 50 billion (Gitanes, 19.2 billion in 1977), but then the figures started to drop, and in 1997 13.7 billion Gauloises were sold, and 5.7 billion Gitanes. The blond versions, which were introduced in 1985 and 1986 respectively, only achieved sales of 5.1 and 0.3 billion, and so are not relevant. While the S.E.I.T.A. has provided only a minimal amount of advertising for Gauloises in France, the advertising for Gitanes has been intense since the 1930s, until the Veil regulations severely restricted tobacco advertising in 1976. As always, though, the success of Gauloises is due to the original concept. "Despite the feminine connotation of the name, the concept is highly virile," points out François Vermeil, professor of graphics. "Smoke a Gauloise, and you are a man, a fighter, a Frenchman."

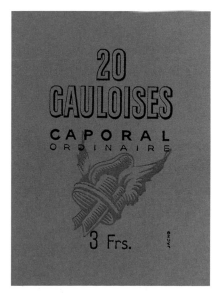

National identity in packets of 20: In 1925, Marcel Jacno designed the world-famous blue packet with the distinctive helmet.

Could the message expressed by a packet of cigarettes be any clearer? Gitanes poster of 1951, designed by René Ravo.

Toulousain
Quercy
Aveyron
Auvergne

André Dominé & Jim Budd

Chasselas de Moissac

Cassoulet de
  Castelnaudary

Millas

Black wine from Cahors

Couscous and the
  Maghreb

Garlic

The best cuts of lamb: souris
  & quasi from Quercy

Wild mushrooms

Laguiole, the knife

Roquefort

The cheeses of the Auvergne

Cheese cookery in the
  Auvergne

Sausages and hams

The green lentils of Puy

Regional baking: the fouace

Mineral water

The fouace from Laguiole is king of the popular crown loaf.

The high meadows of the Cantal produce
excellent, heavyweight cheeses.

Calais
Le Havre
Caen
Brest
Paris
Rennes
Strasbourg
Nantes
Orléans
Tours
Dijon
Limoges
Lyon
Toulousain
Quercy
Bordeaux
Grenoble
Aveyron
Avignon
Auvergne
Nice
Biarritz
Marseille
Toulon
Perpignan

oulouse is the proud capital of the Midi-Pyrénées region, stretching from the barren elevated plains of the Quercy and mountain pastures of the Aubrac to the highest peaks of the Pyrenees. It also includes the Gascon poultry paradise of the Gers, as well as the Montagne Noire or Lacaune area, renowned for its hams and dry sausages. In the past, however, Toulouse was more closely associated with the Languedoc or Tarn than with Gascony and Aquitaine, which is why such specialties as Armagnac and stuffed liver were dealt with in the last chapter. This does not alter the fact that inhabitants of the lively capital of the former Occitanian regions relish ducks, geese – *la grise de Toulouse* – and all sorts of different poultry. It was not without reason that the white corn used for fattening up poultry and preparing *millas*, the loose cornmeal porridge, was planted close by as well as in the nearby countryside of the Lauragais and Albigeois regions. The haricot or navy beans essential to *Cassoulet* also come from here.

Castelnaudary and Carcassonne may lay claim to its origins, but this sumptuous stew is still the favorite gastronomic dish of the Toulousains. Their recipe includes a generous chunk of *saucisse de Toulouse*, probably the finest sausage in France. A Cahors from the banks of the Lot provides a superb accompaniment. Apart from this characterful red wine, which is almost black in color, Cahors is famous for its black truffles. The local cooks are experts on how to prepare these and other wild mushrooms, as well as the delicate milk lamb raised on the barren, elevated plains. Further towards the Massif Central is located one of the most famous cheese regions. It begins in Aveyron with the unparalleled Roquefort, which acquires its uniquely mellow flavor from unpasteurized ewe's milk. The Laguiole is already closely associated with Cantal, one of the most popular cut cheeses. The rustic Salers cattle grazing on the mountain meadows not only produce top-quality milk, but also the best meat, which is processed into highly-valued beef products. The cheeses and lentils produced in the Auvergne owe a lot to the volcanic soil. However, the special geology of this old volcanic region benefits one consumer product which conveys the idea of purity perhaps like no other: mineral water, which bubbles out of countless springs, has replaced wine on an increasing number of tables as an accompaniment for the more substantial regional dishes.

Strawberries

In the Aveyron at Saint-Geniez-d'Olt there is a special variety that has been cultivated by the fruit farmer Antoine Sannié since the end of the 19th century. It produces small, firm, aromatic fruit which are beautifully sweet and very late in ripening, thereby generating a particular market. Today, efforts are being made to encourage their cultivation once more with virus-resistant plants. The major suppliers of strawberries, predominantly the Elsanta (pictured above) and Gariguette varieties, are the Dordogne and Lot-et-Garonne, which together produce over half of the nearly 80,000 tons of French strawberries grown annually. The cost-intensive cultivation is run as an industry beneath plastic sheeting. The season begins in mid-April, reaching its peak in May and June.

Well-tended and carefully trimmed rows of vines characterize the vineyards of Moissac. Any unsuitable grapes are cut off early in the year and all unwanted leaves removed to encourage the healthy fruit.

The winegrowers usually receive 1500 stickers per 2½ acres (1 hectare) of Chasselas for each crate containing 15 pounds (7 kilograms) of grapes. Precise quality and packing checks are run.

The Chasselas is harvested in three cycles, to ensure perfect ripeness each time. The cultivation requires a great deal of manual work, which is why it is based primarily on family businesses.

Chasselas de Moissac

Moissac, a small town close to the confluence of the Tarn and Garonne, is famous for two things – its magnificent Roman abbey, completed in 1100, and its dessert grapes. It was the monks who encouraged the cultivation of vines, but until around 1900 these were used primarily for wine production. The Chasselas grape, regarded as one of the oldest, if not the oldest, grape variety, comes from the Near East and produces a pleasant, often slightly smoky white wine. Known as Fendant, this was particularly prized in Switzerland, while in Germany, under the name of Gutedel, interest in it diminished sharply. At the same time, however, when adequately ripened and with a balanced acidity it produces a fruity, delicate dessert grape which has formed the basis of a thriving trade since the mid-19th century or earlier. Packed in round baskets, the grapes are transported via Bordeaux to London, following the same route as the wines of the Tarn region centuries before. The Parisians, too, acquired a taste for the transparent, golden grapes and in 1845 approximately 40 tons (40,000 kilograms) of Chasselas were transported to the capital by mail coach. When the railways opened up new transport possibilities shortly after, sales in the capital increased fivefold in 1860. Chasselas experienced its golden age. But, like other grape varieties, it proved no match for the *phylloxera*. Yet the success of the dessert grape remained etched on the memories of the winegrowers and when new plants were put in they gave it preference over cask wine. After the First World War, the *chasselatiers de Moissac* had won back their earlier markets and in 1952 it became the first, and hitherto only, fresh fruit to be awarded the *Appellation d'Origine Controlee*.

As with the crus among wines, the area in which the Chasselas is cultivated was precisely defined. Nine-tenths of the cultivation takes place on the elevated plains and south or south-west facing slopes of the Bas-Quercy, as well as on similar rocky sites in the south-west Lot. Only three varieties are permitted – Chasselas de Fontainebleau, Chasselas de Moissac and Chasselas de Montauban. However, the legal requirements extend beyond this. They stipulate that the vines must be trained on a trellis in a fantail. There is a series of regulations on cultivation which are intended to guarantee the growth of perfect grapes. These include thinning out and removing certain leaves to assist ventilation. Harvesting by hand can begin when a minimum of 5½ ounces (160 grams) of sugar per 2 pints (1 liter) of must is achieved, combined with a moderate acidity. The large amount of manual work involved in harvesting the Chasselas has assured the survival of small family businesses. Today, 2360 families cultivate 7400 acres (3000 hectares) of vines, from which they obtain roughly 25,000 tons of grapes annually. This represents 6 percent of France's production of dessert grapes. The season ends around September and October, but thanks to modern refrigeration methods, Chasselas can be supplied up to Christmas. They are graded by weight, with the "extra" category weighing over 5¼ ounces (150 grams) per grape and having a good appearance, while small grapes offer greater sweetness and flavor.

Cassoulet de Castelnaudary

This famous stew from the south-west Languedoc and Toulousain derives its name from the earthenware pot or *cassole* in which it is cooked. It was made in Uxel, a village near Castelnaudary, and is more like a dish, due to its wide open top. It is this design that gives the cassoulet its high proportion of crust and, in turn, characterizes a successful dish. The most important ingredient, the beans, arrived in Italy from Mexico for the first time around 1530 and quickly caught on in Europe. Until then, pulses had been hard to grow and preserve and had produced low yields. In the 17th century their cultivation spread through the south of France. In the Lauragais, between Carcassonne and Toulouse, and also around Revel and Castelnaudary, gravely, alluvial soils provided good conditions for the beans. The beans which prevailed over the many varieties were the white *lingots* with their narrow, elongated kernels. American imports have meant that the once significant production has virtually ceased, although renewed interest has recently been shown in local varieties such as Tarbes, Pamiers and Revel.

Many cooks return their cassoulet to the oven up to eight times.

Cassoulet

14 oz/400 g white Boston (navy) beans
9 oz/250 g pork skins, tied together
1 ham knuckle
2 onions
2 carrots
1 bay leaf
2 sprigs of thyme
12 garlic cloves
25 in/60 cm *saucisse de Toulouse* (fine pork sausage)
2 *confits de canard* with plenty of fat (salt-preserved duck legs)
7 oz/200 g pork ribs
14 oz/400 g neck end of pork
coarse sea salt
coarse pepper

A labor of love

The lengthy preparation of a cassoulet begins with the soaking of the beans in cold water for 12 hours. The water is changed two or three times during this time. The beans are then blanched for 5 minutes before being added to a pan with the pork skins, ham knuckle, onion, carrot, a bay leaf and some thyme. Water is added up to a level two fingers above the beans and the mixture is left to simmer for roughly 1 hour (1). The bones and vegetables are then removed.

Half the pork skins are chopped up with the garlic (2) and ground into a purèe. The sausage is fried in duck fat, while the pork ribs and neck end are browned in lard with the chopped onion and carrot and seasoned with salt and pepper. Water is added and the ingredients are once again left to simmer slowly for 1 hour (3). The vegetables are again removed.

The sausage, pork skins and beans (4) then the leg of preserved duck (5) are placed in the *cassole*. More beans are added along with the garlic purée and bean stock is poured over the top (6). The well-filled bowl is placed in a preheated oven at 375 °F/190 °C. After 1 hour the stock has almost entirely evaporated and is topped up. This process is repeated several times, until the cassoulet has an aromatic crust and the beans have absorbed the flavor of the other ingredients (7).

Millas

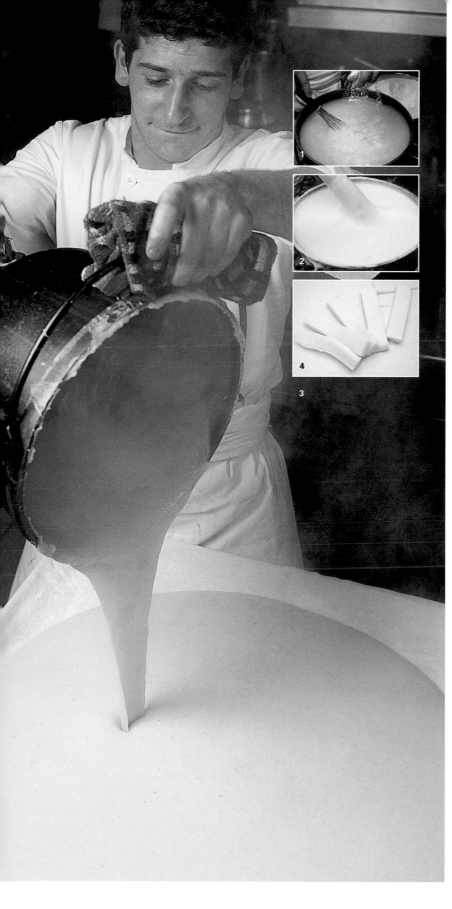

Millas, miques, broyé, are just some of the names used in south-west France for what is called *polenta* in northern Italy – a thick porridge made with cornmeal used as a bread substitute and, in the past, often as the main dish itself. As a result, it became established wherever corn was grown, such as in the Tarn, around Toulouse, in the Pyrenees and the former Gascony. The dried kernels were ground into flour and the bran sieved out. Depending on the region, preference was given to yellow or white corn. In the Pyrenees, where the flour was boiled in milk, yellow was the chosen variety, while on the plains, where corn was used for fattening up poultry, white corn was preferred. Here, the locals chose to prepare *millas* in pots which had previously been used to cook the *confit* and still contained fat. However, because this method of preserving meat in fat diminished during the winter months and cornmeal does not keep for long, *millas* became a food for the cold season.

Making *millas* is easy but time-consuming and requires a good deal of exertion. For every 8 cups (1.2 kilograms) of cornmeal, 20 cups (5 liters) of slightly salted water are brought to the boil. The cornmeal is sprinkled on in handfuls and mixed in continuously with a whisk (1). When all the meal has been added, the mixture is brought to the boil for 15 minutes. The temperature is then lowered and the porridge left to simmer for another 1½ hours. The mixture must be vigorously stirred repeatedly during the cooking time, to prevent it from sticking to the bottom of the pan (2). Next, a floured cloth is placed on a baking sheet and the porridge is poured onto it to cool. The layer should be about ½ inch (15 millimeters) thick (3). Finally, the *millas* is cut into slices 1¼ inches (3 centimeters) wide and 4 inches (10 centimeters) long (4) and fried in a skillet.

Millas can be salted and presented as an accompaniment or sprinkled with sugar and served for dessert.

317

Black wine from Cahors

This deep-red wine from the area around Cahors was once numbered among France's most famous growths. Full-bodied wines have been pressed here since the 7th century, as demonstrated by a letter sent by the bishop of Verdun to his colleagues in Cahors, thanking them for the noble wine they had sent. As with their counterparts from the Bordelais, Quercy wines experienced a significant increase in popularity following the marriage of Eleanor of Aquitaine to Henry II of England. Barrels were shipped to Bordeaux on the Lot, which flows into the Garonne close to Aiguillon, and from there to England. Although the Bordelaise people were constantly contriving to prevent exports from the hinterland, Cahors had influential patrons. The high-living, belligerent monarch François Ier preferred it to Bordeaux and even started his own vineyard at Fontainebleau. Peter the Great swore by Cahors wine, which was said to be the only one his stomach ulcer could tolerate. Priests of the Russian Orthodox church chose it as their sacramental wine and had it planted in the Crimea. Around 1720 Cahors experienced its golden age with vineyards covering 99,000 acres (40,000 hectares). Business letters dated 1779 from Berlin, Danzig and other German towns, in which traders complained about the barrels being too small, demonstrate the wine's popularity in Germany. As in all France's other wine regions, 100 years later the *phylloxera* destroyed all the vines. What was to be the

The carefully tended vineyards of Château Lagrezette, a Renaissance castle renovated at great expense, where the famous Cahors wine is produced.

Gaillac

Gaillac is a melting pot of Mediterranean and Atlantic influences with many grape varieties. Be it a Perlé, Mousseux or still wine, dry or semi-sweet, white, rosé or red, each producer has his own wide range. The most interesting are the whites of Len-de-l'El, Ondenc and Mauzac and the reds of Duras and Braucol. The 3700 acres (1500 hectares) extend along the banks of the Tarn and up hillsides leading to the medieval Cordes.

Marcillac

The best known of the Aveyron wines, planted by monks from the monastery at Conques in the 10th century, enjoys the microclimate of its sheltered valley. Here, 90 percent of the 333 acres (135 hectares) are planted with Fer Servadou, known here as Mansoi, producing a red wine with a bouquet of raspberries and other berries and spicy tannins which was awarded the A.O.C .in 1990. It is usually drunk young at 60 °F (16 °C).

Entraygues et Le Fel

Above the Lot valley, vineyards of these two V.D.Q.S. wines are squeezed onto narrow terraces producing a total area of around 50 acres (20 hectares). The white Entraygues grows in loamy, gravelly soil and granite and is based on the Chenin Blanc, while slate is reserved for the red Le Fel which is produced from Fer Servadou and the Cabernets.

Estaing

Slightly further up the valley, Estaing has since 1965 held its ground as a small V.D.Q.S. wine with fewer than 37 acres (15 hectares) on slatey soils and clayey limestone. Chenin and a small amount of Mauzac go to produce the white, while Gamay, Fer and Cabernets guarantee fruity red and rosé wines.

Côtes de Millau

For over 50 miles (80 km) along the Tarn valley, the 136 acres (55 hectares) of the Chenin and Mauzac, awarded the V.D.Q.S. in 1994, produce fresh whites, rosés and reds, mainly from Gamay, Syrah and Cabernet Sauvignon. They are usually drunk young.

Le Pont Valentré, the 14th century bridge spanning the Lot, is the symbol of the town of Cahors and its most beautiful architectural treasure.

The wine brotherhood of Cahors, which includes such prominent members as A.D. Perrin, head of the Cartier group, and Count André de Monpezat, father-in-law of the Danish queen, defends the reputation of its wines worldwide.

wine's ultimate undoing, however, was the misjudgment of the *phylloxera*-resistant rootstock, which proved to be too early and vigorous for the indigenous Cot, also known as the Malbec or Auxerrois, and has a strong tendency to rot. After World War I, during the time of mass-produced wine, the black Cahors almost sank into obscurity, only to experience a renaissance at the end of the fifties. Now it is back on our tables, the inky colored wine with intensive aromas of berries, licorice and spice, a full-bodied wine with distinct but noble tannins and the right credentials for prolonged aging.

Wines from Lot, Tarn and the Aveyron

Cahors

The Lot winds its way like an artery through the wine area extending from the town of Cahors 25 miles (40 kilometers) to the west, covering an area of 8650 acres (3500 hectares). In addition to the vineyards in the valley and on the hillsides, vines have been planted on the rocky *causse* or high, chalky plateau. The predominant variety is the Cot or Malbec, known here as Auxerrois, which must account for at least 70 percent. It is supplemented by Tannat and Merlot.

Couscous and the Maghreb

The French quite evidently discovered their taste for couscous during the 132 years Algeria spent under French administration, when it was regarded as part of the motherland. Towards the end of the 19ᵗʰ century, when a deep fascination emerged for all things middle eastern and anyone who could afford it furnished at least one room of their home in this style, there was an accompanying increase in taste for Maghreb cuisine, the name used to refer to the countries of north-west Africa including Tunisia, Algeria and Morocco.

However, *couscous*, the national dish of the Maghreb, began its triumphant advance when the French were forced to leave Algeria in 1962. It was not only the *pieds noirs*, the French settlers so named at the time because of their black shoes, who streamed into southern France via Marseille and settled there, but also a large number of Algerians who had worked for them. They opened restaurants in all the larger towns and cities, where customers could enjoy their colorful cuisine and, above all, sample couscous in all its variations.

This couscous comes from Toulouse, where there are several excellent Maghreb restaurants. Nowadays, however, this easily prepared dish is commonly eaten in many households, something which is evident from the number of couscous brands available from grocery stores and supermarkets.

Couscous is precooked semolina made from durum wheat, which is simply soaked in a small amount of water and then steamed. A double pan or *couscoussier* is used for this. Water and stock are added to the bottom section and semolina to the top, which has a perforated base. The same result can be achieved by placing a sieve over a pan and covering it with a lid.

Couscous is a simple, tasty, staple food which can be combined with numerous dishes, provided sufficient liquid is added in the form of stock or sauce. In its native land, couscous is eaten with the fingers, by molding the semolina into small balls.

Mutton stews are a particularly popular accompaniment, but vegetables must always be served as well. In Muslim Algeria they love to eat couscous during Ramadan when it is served with broad beans and raisins. Sauces are often made sharper by adding *harissa*, a spicy paste colored with red pepper with a distinctive flavor of cumin, although many chefs prepare their own seasoning. Meatballs and kebabs are other popular accompaniments, as is *merguez*, the thin, sharp, paprika sausage made from lamb and beef.

Peppermint tea is traditionally served in a glass.

Couscous au mouton à l'algéroise
Mutton couscous Algerian style

Couscous

3 cups/500 g medium couscous, precooked
6½ tbsp/100 g butter

Lamb meatballs

7 oz/200 g minced lamb
3 garlic cloves
2 onions
1 stem of coriander
1 handful of parsley, finely chopped
salt and pepper
1 pinch of ground cumin
1 pinch of grated nutmeg

Mutton

2 lb 3 oz/1 kg shoulder of mutton
1 tbsp oil
3 garlic cloves
2 onions
2 tsp mild red paprika
1 pinch of ras al-hanout
1 pinch of ground cumin
1 pinch of grated nutmeg
1 large pinch of cayenne pepper

Couscous vegetables

7 oz/200 g chick peas (garbanzo beans)
2 tbsp bicarbonate of soda
½ small savoy cabbage
4 carrots
4 white turnips
4 small zucchinis
1 stalk of celery
2 onions
1 tbsp oil

Pour the couscous into a large bowl and add 1 glass of cold water. Carefully fork it through and leave to soak for 10 minutes. Repeat the process once more. Let it stand. If you do not have a *couscoussier*, put the couscous in a metal sieve. Bring some water to the boil in a suitable pan, place the sieve with the couscous over it and cover with a lid. Leave it to steam for around 10 minutes. Melt the butter and mix it into the couscous.

Lamb meatballs: Put the meat in a bowl. Finely chop the garlic, onions and coriander and add them to the meat. Then add the parsley and spices and mix all the ingredients together well. Mold into four balls and leave in a cool place.

Mutton: Cut the meat into cubes and brown them in hot oil in a skillet, then transfer them to a pressure cooker. Chop up the garlic and onions. Pour a little water onto the frying juices and soften them both in the skillet. Reduce the temperature, sprinkle with paprika and mix before adding everything to the pan. Add the spices, pour over plenty of water and cover the pan. Cook the meat in the pressure cooker according to the manufacturer's directions then leave the pan to cool off slowly until all the steam has escaped. Remove the meat from the stock and set it aside.

Left: As well as couscous with additional vegetables (below), the photo shows another classic Maghreb dish: Tajine of chicken with prunes, honey and almonds.

Use the stock for the vegetables.

Couscous vegetables: Soak the chick peas (garbanzo beans) with the bicarbonate of soda in lukewarm water overnight, then pour off the water and cook them in salt water for 30 minutes. Drain. Clean the savoy cabbage and cut it into quarters, remove the stem and slice the cabbage into strips. Clean the remaining vegetables and cut them into bite-size pieces. Add the cabbage, carrots and white turnip to the meat stock and boil for 10 minutes, then add the zucchini and celery and cook for a further 10 minutes.

In the meantime, peel and halve the onions, then slice them thinly. Add the oil to a pan and soften the onions until transparent. Pour on some water, add the chick peas and warm them through. Finally, heat through the meat with the vegetables. Brown the meatballs in a frying pan in hot oil. Transfer everything to separate dishes. For a more lavish version like the one shown in the photograph, add a broiled paprika sausage or *merguez* and a leg of roast chicken.
Timing is crucial with a couscous and all the different accompaniments must be ready at the same time, so they can be served together.

Below: A selection of Maghreb candy including *loukum* (jello candy; top left), *mantécous* (small cinnamon cakes; top right); also (on the server, clockwise from the top): *gabelouz* (semolina cakes with almonds), "gazelle horn" (almond biscuit), *mqckroud* (semolina cakes with dates), *backlava* (puff pastry with almond paste), "almond fingers" (marzipan with dried fruits), *zalabia* (honey doughnut) and *halva* (sesame square; center).

Tajine de poulet aux pruneaux, miel et amandes
Tajine of chicken with prunes, honey and almonds

1 free-range chicken, 2 lb 3 oz/1 kg
2 tbsp oil
1 lb/500 g tomatoes
2 medium-sized onions, grated
1 tsp sugar
1 tsp cinnamon
1 large pinch saffron threads
1 tsp each salt and pepper
2 unwaxed lemons
3 oz/100 g honey
2 tbsp coriander, finely chopped
7 oz/200 g prunes, stoned
3 oz/100 g sugar
2 oz/50 g almonds
1 tbsp groundnut oil
2 tbsp sesame seeds

Cut up the chicken into several pieces and brown them all over in a pan containing the oil. Quarter the tomatoes, remove the seeds and finely chop them. Add them to the meat along with the onions, sugar, cinnamon, saffron, salt and pepper. Squeeze the lemons and pour the juice over the chicken pieces. Add the lemon rind and honey. Cover and leave to simmer gently for about 1 hour, then mix in the coriander, taste and leave to cook for a further 10 minutes. Put the prunes and sugar in a pan of cold water and boil them until the sugar has almost caramelized. Soak the almonds in boiling water, then refresh them in ice cold water and remove the skins. Toast the almonds in the oil in a skillet until golden brown, stirring continuously. Place the chicken pieces on a tajine plate and arrange the prunes around them, then sprinkle with almonds and sesame seeds. Serve immediately.
Tajine is the name given to a stew, and also to a glazed clay dish with the pointed lid used as a cooking utensil.

Dried garlic bulbs with their roots and withered leaves still create an attractive sight.

The loose outer layers are removed from the bulbs by hand, along with the roots.

The rose pink bulb of Lautrec

Garlic

Only a stone's throw from Albi is a sleepy little town called Lautrec, a name it shares with the famous artist. The town and surrounding area have their own local variety of garlic, which stands out from the rest due to its pale or, in some cases, rich pink skin. Apart from the quality of its flavor, this variety has a crucial advantage from which its reputation has been born – it keeps superbly. Garlic, a member of the lily family, is suited to the light but fertile clayey limestone soils in and around Lautrec, combined with the warmth and sun. This bulb plant originating in central Asia was popular even among the Greeks and Romans, who regarded it as a stimulant. In France, too, its therapeutic properties were probably given priority over its culinary attributes to begin with.

When it comes to cultivation, a distinction is drawn between two varieties of garlic. One is planted in autumn then harvested in June and July of the following year when it produces particularly large bulbs. However, its cloves begin to germinate again as early as late autumn, which restricts the length of time it can be kept.

The other variety – and this includes the *ail rose de Lautrec* – is only planted between the start of winter and the New Year. Yet, it is still harvested at the same time. Although its bulbs do not quite reach the size of the varieties planted in autumn, which include the white garlic of Lomagne from the Tarn-et-Garonne and the violet garlic of Cadours from the Haute-Garonne, they are less likely to germinate and can be kept until the next harvest. Garlic is cultivated outdoors and planted by machine. Unlike white garlic, the colored varieties produce scapes which are nipped off at the start of June so that all the plant's energies are channeled toward the bulb. When the leaves dry out at the end of June, the garlic is harvested

Little by little the look of the bulb improves, until it finally reveals a completely white husk which is appealing to the eye.

12 or 24 bulbs on which the stems are trimmed in the required way are plaited to produce the well-known strings or *manouilles*.

mechanically. Although garlic is available commercially both fresh and semi-dried, the majority reaches the customer dried. In Lautrec there is a special garlic market each Friday between July 20 and March 31.

Despite its enormous versatility, there are three methods of preparing the rose-pink variety that are particularly well-rated in the area where it is cultivated. These are bread rubbed with garlic and drizzled with olive oil, garlic soup and a whole bulb of garlic baked in the oven, with its creamy cloves.

The rose-pink garlic dried in well-ventilated sheds and then "cleaned" and meticulously plaited into a string, is the only garlic to have been awarded the Red Label, a guarantee of quality.

France's best sheep

1 **Berrichonne du cher**
A common breed from the center, but also found in the south-west. Mainly barn reared. Good legs. Lambs grow quickly. Weight of lambs at 70 days: 46–59 pounds (21–27 kilograms).
2 **Bleu de Maine**
Large animals with typically blue heads from the west. Good ewes. Meadow reared. Fine, lean meat. Weight of lambs at 70 days: 49–59 pounds (22.5–27 kilograms).
3 **Charmoise**
Very resilient and easily satisfied; makes up the majority of the herds in the center west. Reared outdoors. Weight of lambs at 70 days: 33–40 pounds (15–18.5 kilograms).

4 **Île de France**
Stocky, broad-headed but relatively demanding breed. Rapid weight increase and good quality wool. Reared in barns and outdoors. Weight of lambs at 70 days: 48–59 pounds (22–27 kilograms).
5 **Lacaune**
The most common milk breed, whose milk is used to make Roquefort cheese. Robust, used to meadow rearing. Good meat. Weight of lambs at 70 days: 55–65 pounds (25–30 kilograms).
6 **Mouton charolais**
An old breed from Burgundy and Morwan and to some extent the counterpart of the Charolais cattle. Robust. Predominantly outdoor rearing. Good meat. Weight of lambs at 70 days: 48–59 pounds (22–27 kilograms).

7 **Mouton vendéen**
A robust, adaptable breed well able to tolerate damp winters. Mainly outdoor rearing. Good milk values. Weight of lambs at 70 days: 44–52 pounds (20–24 kilograms).
8 **Rouge de l'est**
A large, adaptable, increasingly common breed. Barn or meadow reared. Good weight increase. Weight of lambs at 70 days: 49–61 pounds (22.5–28 kilograms). Sold as 100-day lambs.
9 **Caussenarde du Lot**
A highly resilient breed, unique in its ability to withstand the harsh conditions of the barren plateaus of the Quercy. Good milk animals, able to lamb throughout the year. Weight of lambs at 3–5 months: 35–42 pounds (16–19 kilograms).

The best cuts of lamb

Souris & quasi from Quercy

The department of the Lot has for some time been renowned for its outstanding lamb and mutton. The secret behind this quality is the *causses*, plateaus from the Jurassic period with their rocky, karst landscape where the grass is meager but there is an abundance of weeds. Only sheep are able to find sufficient nourishment here. An indigenous breed able to cope with the special conditions has developed in this harsh environment – the Caussenarde. The brood ewes are put out to pasture from spring, when the first fresh grass appears, until late autumn, when the weather becomes too hard. They lamb twice a year, in early spring and towards the end of autumn. While they are rearing their lambs, they are given additional grain fodder. The lambs spend their lives in open sheds and are fed by their mothers in the mornings and evenings. This method of rearing means they are sold as *agneau sous la mère*. Their meat is low in fat, bright red and exceptionally fine and delicate. The following three-part dish is based on different leg cuts, as jointed in Quercy. Apart from the full leg, two additional cuts are common – *la souris*, a lean piece of muscle at the knuckle end of the leg, and *le quasi*, a juicy schnitzel from the chump end of the leg.

Quasi d'agneau fermier du Quercy pané aux truffes et persil plat, jus d'ail en chemise
Quasi lamb coated in truffles and parsley with a garlic sauce

Serves 1

1 *quasi*, about 6 oz/180 g
freshly milled pepper and salt
1 tbsp oil
½ oz/15 g truffles
½ oz/10 g flat-leafed parsley
1 egg
½ cep
1 tsp goose fat
1 tbsp *jus d'agneau* (see recipe opposite)

Preheat the oven to 430 °F/220 °C. Season the *quasi* with salt and pepper, quickly brown it in the oil, then roast in the oven for 6 minutes. Remove the lamb and let it rest for 10 minutes.
In the meantime, finely chop the truffles and parsley and mix them together. Beat the egg and coat the lamb with it, then dip the meat in the truffle mixture. Return to the oven for 2 minutes, then remove.
Cut two nice slices of cep and fry them in the goose fat. Use these to garnish the *quasi* and add the *jus d'agneau*.

Souris cloutée
d'ail de Lautrec rôtie
Roasted, garlic-spiked *souris* of lamb

Serves 1

3 garlic cloves
(Lautrec pink garlic)
1 souris
duck fat
1 tbsp jus d'agneau (see recipe opposite)
3 garlic cloves

Preheat the oven to 430 °F/220 °C. Peel 3 cloves of garlic.
Use these to spike the *souris* and brush it with duck fat. Place in a roasting pan and roast in the oven for 20 minutes, then leave the meat to rest for 10 minutes with the oven door half open.
Transter the *souris* to a warmed plate, pour a little *jus d'agneau* around it and garnish with the 3 unpeeled, roasted garlic cloves.
The pink colored garlic is an indigenous variety from the area around Lautrec.

Gigot d'agneau fermier du Quercy
en daube légère
Ragout of Quercy lamb

Serves 8

1 leg of lamb, about 6 lbs/2.7 kg
7 oz/200 g fresh tomatoes
9 oz/250 g onions
salt and coarse pepper
4 garlic cloves
1 bouquet garni
zest and juice of 1 unwaxed orange
3 tbsp hazelnut oil
2 bottles of Cahors wine (3–4 years old)
14 oz/400 g smoked bacon
10 oz/300 g pork skins
garlic croûtons

Trim the leg of lamb, removing all the fat, and cut the meat into cubes weighing about 3 oz/80 g each.
Skin and remove the seeds from the tomatoes and cut them up small. Peel and chop the onions. Put the meat in a casserole and season with salt and pepper. Add the tomatoes, onions, garlic, bouquet garni, orange zest and juice, hazelnut oil and Cahors wine. Stir well and leave to marinate in a cool place for 5 hours. Cut the bacon into small pieces and the pork skins into 1-in/2-cm chunks and add them to the pot. Check that all the ingredients are covered

by the marinade and top up with Cahors if necessary. Ensure the pot is tightly sealed (using a flour and water paste), then cook it in a preheated oven at 400 °F/200 °C for 90 minutes.
Remove the meat and vegetables using a slotted spoon, skim the fat from the stock and reduce it. Adjust the seasoning and serve hot with roasted garlic croûtons.

Jus d'agneau à l'ail en chemise
Lamb stock with garlic in its skin

2 lb 3 oz/1 kg lamb bone
3 tbsp oil
12 unpeeled garlic cloves
9 oz/250 g onions
1 lb/500 g lamb off-cuts
⅞ cup/200 ml white wine
thyme, bay leaf
½ stalk celery
5 tbsp/100 g fresh tomato paste
freshly milled pepper and salt

Place the bone and garlic cloves in a little oil and fry them lightly. Peel the onions and slice them into rings.
Lightly brown them in a pan with the lamb off-cuts then add the bone and garlic and deglaze with the wine. Next pour in 8 cups/2 liters of water. Add the thyme, bay leaf, celery and tomato paste. Simmer for 3 to 4 hours. Skim off the fat and pass the stock through a fine sieve, then reduce as required. Adjust the seasoning and place in the bain-marie.

Souris cloutée d'ail de Lautrec rôtie
Roasted, garlic-spiked *souris* of lamb

Gigot d'agneau fermier du Quercy en daube légère – A light stew of Quercy lamb

...i d'agneau fermier du Quercy pané aux truffes et persil
...jus d'ail en chemise – Quasi lamb coated in truffles and
...ey with a garlic sauce

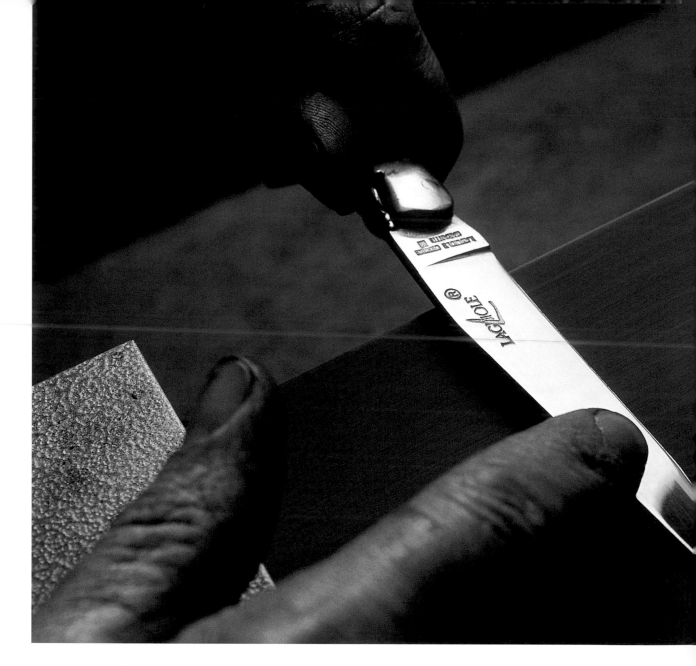

Laguiole, the knife

If you live in France, the chances are you will own a pocket knife from Laguiole (pronounced "layole"), or you may even have traded in an old knife for one from this small town in the north of the Aveyron. Although there are now designer creations, some with inlaid handles, this famous knife came from humble beginnings. At the start of the nineteenth century, local blacksmiths developed a simple knife intended for daily use by the farmers and herders of the Aubrac. It combined a rustic blade from the Basque province of Navarra with the native dagger and a handle turned from the horn of Aubrac cattle, with a pointed implement at the other end. Pierre Jean Calmels was the first to start trading in knives from Laguiole in 1829.

The blade and handle of this genuine Laguiole, with its characteristic "L," were produced entirely in the town of the same name in the Aubrac; only the corkscrew can be better manufactured elsewhere.

Considering the vast range of these knives, which are sold almost all over France and now also in many shops abroad as genuine Laguiole, one might be forgiven for questioning where they actually come from. In fact, only a small proportion of the knives comes from the small town in the Aubrac. Most of them are now produced elsewhere, mainly in Thiers, a town close to Clermont-Ferrand, renowned for its blacksmith's craft.

The revival of knife-making in their home town was led by Calmels' great-great-granddaughters when they took over the family business. This led to the founding of the company Le Couteau de Laguiole, whose owners started by learning the craft in northern France, and eventually to construction of the only true forge, on the edge

The Forge de Laguiole, based on a design by Philippe Starck, and opened in 1987, has become a landmark with its giant blade pointing skyward.

All the individual components and tools a cutler needs in order to assemble the traditional three-part model.

Every knife is hand-crafted and its blade adjusted and ground until it satisfies the criteria for perfection.

The knife's blade, corkscrew, pointed implement, shaft, and handle are joined together at five points by brass pins.

The typical handle is made from the horn of Aubrac cattle and filed and ground until it sits perfectly in the hand.

of the town, the Forge de Laguiole. It was first opened in 1987 and is impossible to miss, thanks to its avant-garde architecture based on a design by Philippe Starck, and its symbol, a 20 yard- (18 meter-)long, high-grade steel blade dramatically pointing skyward.

Ninety craftsmen manufacture 200,000 knives a year in the small factory, undertaking every stage of the production process. This is what distinguishes the real thing from all other supposedly genuine articles (the corkscrew is the only part shipped in). Here the knives are forged, stamped, hardened, ground, and polished, using high-grade 440A or XC75 steel. Each individual knife is crafted by hand and can take from one-and-a-half hours, in the case of the simplest model, to several days to make the

What distinguishes knives made by the Forge de Laguiole from all others that are sold under the name of the town is the blade which is hand-crafted to the highest standards.

most refined knives. Apart from the name stamped on the blade, the trademark of Laguiole knives is the steel fly, the connecting piece between the blade and the handle. The price of the knives varies considerably, depending on whether they are one, two or three-part models, how fine the wood or horn used for the handle is, the time taken to design and craft them, and whether or not they are a one-off item made by a master cutler.

Roquefort

The star among blue cheeses has a primeval disaster to thank for its existence today. The north-eastern edge of the precipitous limestone Massif Combalou, situated between Millau and Saint-Affrique, collapsed, producing a gigantic heap of rubble. The mighty boulders became wedged together during the rock fall, creating caves, some of which were of a considerable size, as well as *fleurines*, long fissures which connected the natural cellars to the outside world and ensured a constant supply of fresh air. This clever ventilation system guarantees low temperatures, while the absorbent limestone provides 95 percent humidity. It soon emerged that these were ideal conditions for a quite unique mold, *Penicillum roqueforti*, which grew on the cave walls. So the cellars are ready, the mold is there, but where does the cheese come from? The Combalou lies on the edge of the barren Causse de Larsac, a windswept limestone plateau where gnarled bushes and wild herbs are the only forms of vegetation to survive – classic sheep country, in other words. Here, herds of thin-coated Lacaune sheep compete for the meager sustenance that gives their fatty milk a fine bouquet. What could be more obvious than to store the cheese made from this milk in the cool caverns? Imagine the surprise of the early New

A perfect cheese marbled with veins of mold.

Unpasteurized ewe milk gives France's most famous blue cheese its unique flavor.

Stone Age herders, who had already moved to this area in droves, when they discovered that what had been laid down as white cheese was now marbled with blue-green mold. They perhaps tried it tentatively, only to find that the taste had improved. If Pliny the Elder is to be believed, the Romans raved over it, as did the table companions of Charlemagne centuries later– or so the story goes.

The 15th century saw the start of a new epoch. The inhabitants of Roquefort-sur-Soulzon, the village lying beneath the Combalou, came up with the profit-making scheme of buying fresh cheeses elsewhere, letting them mature in the caves and them selling them on, in addition to using the caves for their own cheese. Thus, "Roquefort" began to make a name for itself and before long dishonest rivals started to misuse it.

As a result, in 1550 the first complaint was lodged with the local government in Toulouse, but it was to be more than 100 years before trademark protection was finally achieved in 1666 and anyone misrepresenting their cheese as Roquefort could be threatened with severe punishment.

As the infrastructure developed in the mid-19th century, Roquefort experienced an unexpected boom. The cheese cellars obtained sheep cheese from an ever wider area. Around the turn of the century, they had ventured as far as the Pyrenees and a few years later had even gotten as far as Corsica. However, in order to prevent attempts at "diluting" their specialty with cow milk, the producers obtained the *Appellation d'Origine Contrôllée* as early as 1921, the very first to be awarded to a cheese.

Today, Roquefort is produced by the large cooperative company and also by a further ten local cheese companies, which are supplied with fresh sheep cheese from various departments of southern France.

Nowadays, thousands of gallons (liters) of pure, highly nutritious, unpasteurized ewe milk are inoculated with minute quantities of starter bacteria at the dairies, even before the production process begins. This means that the cheeses are already infected when they reach the cellars for maturing.

Before they are laid out on the long, solid oak racks to start their first curing phase uncovered, they are treated with boards of nails. The system of air channels thereby created in the cheese is intended to enable the mold to develop unhindered. This takes at least a month. By this time the mold has taken such a hold that it has to be kept in check. So, the cheese is wrapped in its characteristic thin tin foil jacket and moved to deeper and cooler realms of the Combalou. The mold is given at least a further three months to create its network of arteries. Many qualities are left by producers for up to one year, rare cheeses for even longer.

The dimensions of a Roquefort are rigidly controlled. Its diameter must be 7–8 inches (19–20 centimeters), in other words, twice its height. It weighs between 5½ and 6½ pounds (2.5 and 3 kilograms) and is characterized by a fat content of at least 52 percent, which explains the particular mellowness of the cheese. The younger the Roquefort, the whiter its curds, and the thinner and therefore darker the mold in contrast. With increasing maturity, the cheese turns an ivory color, the mold gains more and more ground and takes on its highly rated greenish blue color with a full flavor. It is delicious when combined with the naturally sweet Muscat wine from the south, particularly the Muscat de Rivesaltes. It is also an essential kitchen ingredient, lending itself to use in salads or soufflés, in cheese toppings or piquant sauces.

To enable the mold to develop in the cheese, it is pierced with needles to produce air ducts at regular intervals.

Penicillium roqueforti, which has germinated on rye bread, guarantees the veining of mold in the sheep cheese.

The first maturing phase of the cheese, stored uncovered on wooden shelves, can last for up to a month.

The cooperative's cheese and cellar master checks the ripeness of each individual cheese.

This unremarkable implement is the cheese master's most important tool, enabling him to take samples.

For the second maturing phase, the cheese is wrapped in tin foil and transferred to cooler caves.

The blue cheese thrives in the caves of the limestone cliffs of Combalou.

The cheeses of the Auvergne

The Auvergne, with its extinct volcanoes and high plateaus, boasts alpine pastures in which a wealth of flora thrives. Even today, gentians and licorice, arnica and saxifrage, aconite and wild anemones can still be found there. But the fertile, volcanic soils containing magnesium and potash, and the abundant supply of water in the Massif Central, bring forth the outstanding meadows with their wealth of different grasses and herbs in the most natural way possible. In this mountainous region with its harsh climate, where there is a very long tradition of alpine dairy farming, the rustic, resilient breeds of Aubrac and Salers cattle have evolved. The cows produce relatively little milk, but what there is has a very high fat content, which induced many farmers to experiment with more productive animals.

From late spring well into autumn, the herders would let their animals graze on the highest alpine pastures – some still do today. During this time, the herders lived in *burons*, sturdy buildings with slate roofs which served as accommodation, dairy and maturing cellar all in one, because the milk was processed on the spot. Because storage was required for long periods of the year and the major markets were remote to the area, techniques and molds were developed which

During the 48-hour procedure, the pressure is gradually increased. The pressing process itself is interrupted several times to turn the cheese and change the cloth wrapped around it.

Resilient cattle breeds evolved in the mountains of the Auvergne, including the Salers with its chestnut hide and splayed horns, which is the most famous.

enabled cheese to be made which kept for months or even years. However, because special bacteria find a breeding ground in many cellars, specialties such as blue cheeses, which do not keep as well, can also be matured here. If the area of Laguiole is included, which juts into Auvergne and is closely related to it, the region can boast six cheeses with the *Appellation d'Origine Contrôlée* classification – a record, even for France.

Cantal

As early as the first century A.D., Pliny the Elder mentions Cantal. This means that it is one of the oldest cheeses in France. Its green land, known as the Pays Vert and covering some 2300 square miles (600,000 hectares), extends around a massif of extinct volcanoes. The most important pasture is to be found on plateaus of over 3000 feet (1000 meters) with an extraordinary wealth of plant life.

The characteristic feature of the cheese production, which uses milk from Salers cows, is that it is put through a press twice. This process means that the curd, which has already been pressed once, is again broken up, then salted and lastly pressed into its final mold. Cantal is sold as *jeune* when it is 30 days old, *entre deux* at between two and six months and *vieux* when it has matured for over six months.

Salers

This cheese comes from the same area as Cantal, but can only be produced during the grazing period between May 1 and October 31, when the fresh alpine herbs lend the milk, and with it the cheese, an unparalleled perfume.

Salers is named after a pretty little town between Aurillac and Mauriac, close to the Cantal mountains. This cheese is also pressed twice, but it has to mature for at least three months. It is often left to develop for 12–18 months, acquiring a thick, dark rind with reddish flecks, an increasingly crumbly texture and a more distinctive, piquant flavor. (Illustrated on page 335.)

Saint-Nectaire

Its home is the volcanic terrain around Monts-Dore at a height of 2500–4000 feet (750–1200 meters). 52 communes of the Puy-du-Dôme and a further 20 in the Cantal are allowed to produce this semisoft cut cheese. Even the dining companions of Louis XIV were able to appreciate its qualities.

The curds are pressed into molds 8 inches (21 centimeters) in diameter and 2 inches (5 centimeters) deep and the finished cheese weighs roughly 3¾ pounds (1.7 kilograms); a smaller version is produced weighing 1 pound 5 ounces (600 grams).

During its three to six week ripening period, it is rinsed off several times with salt water, which encourages the formation of its gray or sandy rind on which yellow or red flecks form. The cheese has a springy, creamy texture and an earthy, occasionally slightly musty flavor. The less common *fermiers* or farm cheeses, which are found mainly around the small town of Besse-en-Chandresse, can be recognized by an oval, green casein symbol. (Illustrated on page 335.)

Fourme d'Ambert

This blue cheese, which was allegedly around when Julius Caesar conquered Gaul, owes its personality to the 2000–5000 feet (600–1600 meters) high region of the Monts du Forez in the Massif Central, where it is produced. The curds are emptied into molds and drained. Once the cheese has dried and the starter bacteria has been added, it is pierced with needles, to enable air to penetrate, thereby promoting the growth of the sought-after blue mold. The cheese, which is 5 inches (13 centimeters) wide, 7½ inches (19 centimeters) deep and weighs 4 pounds 6 ounces (2 kilograms), must mature for at least four weeks before it is sold.

Like its close relative, Fourme de Montbrison, Fourme d'Ambert is mainly produced industrially and has a light, even, blue veining and a mild, creamy taste with a hint of mold. Hand-made cheeses are rare, but occasionally found on the market in Ambert. After a prolonged period of curing, they have developed a highly complex, piquant flavor. (Illustrated on page 335.)

Bleu d'Auvergne

This district takes in all the cheese Appellations of Auvergne, as far as the eastern most area of the Fourme d'Ambert, and extends deep into the Lozère and Lot. At the same time, it is the youngest offspring of this great cheese region, only having been created in the mid-19th century. Based on cow milk, it follows in the blue cheese tradition whereby *Penicillium* is added to the milk. Once it has been turned out of the mold and salted, it is pierced with needles, in order to encourage the mold to grow by providing plenty of air. It matures for at least four weeks in cool, damp cellars, producing a mild, blue cheese. (Illustrated on page 335.)

Laguiole

Laguiole is the most important town in the Aubrac, a mountainous region connecting parts of the Aveyron, Cantal and Lozère, which has been renowned for its cheese since the 16th century. The best cheese is produced according to the old tradition on alpine pastures, generally using milk from the resilient Aubrac cows. This hard, cut cheese made from untreated milk, which is closely related to Salers and Cantal, is pressed into a tall cylindrical mold or *fourme* weighing around 110 pounds (50 kilograms). It is then left to mature for at least four, but also up to twelve months. (Illustrated on page 51.)

The men place 176–220 pounds (80–100 kilograms) of cheese curds in a cloth, which they then fold around them. This package is placed under a flat press typically used for the manufacture of Cantal.

During this first cycle, the bundle of cheese is repeatedly opened, the curds broken up again and turned and then returned to the press, in order to eliminate as much of the whey as possible.

After this, the cheese is transferred to a cold, damp cellar with temperatures of between 50 and 53 °F (10–12 °C), where it is turned and rubbed down two to three times a week. It is cured for 1 to 12 months, depending on the degree of maturity required.

Cheese cookery in the Auvergne

In the remote, mountainous region of the Auvergne, cheese is regarded as one of the staple foods. The enormous cylinders, known as *tomes*, could be kept in the cold, damp cellars for a year or even longer with careful supervision, making them a means of storage for the long winter months. The preferred way, however, was to produce highly nutritious meals from the young, mild, cut cheese, which was less time-consuming and quicker in preparation. Two of these simple, rustic dishes are the *truffade* and, a variation on this, the *aligot*. Both dishes capitalize on the successful combination of potatoes and cheese. The *truffade* is the more rustic of the two, as it is based exclusively on these two ingredients. The *aligot*, which is based on a fine potato purée, also requires some *crème fraîche* and a little milk, both of which are readily available on an alpine or lowland farm. Slightly less rustic, but just as widespread, is the use of cheese in fine soufflés, as a filling for omelettes or crêpes, or cut into chunks in salads. Particularly mild varieties can even be used as an ingredient or filling in sweet dishes. As is so often the case with cookery, the possibilities are virtually boundless.

La Truffade

Serves 6

2 lb 10 oz/1.2 kg potatoes
3 oz/100 g fatty bacon
1 tbsp oil
5 garlic cloves
salt
14 oz/400 g young Cantal

Peel the potatoes and slice them thinly.
Cut the bacon into strips. Heat the oil in a heavy pan, fry the bacon in it and toast the unpeeled garlic cloves (1).
Remove the bacon and garlic from the pan, add the potato (2) and salt. Leave the potatoes on a low heat for 20–30 minutes, turning regularly to prevent them from browning.
In the meantime, cut the young Cantal into thin strips (3).
Once the potatoes are cooked, stir in the cheese (4) and turn continuously until the cheese has melted. Then mash the potatoes (5) and stir the mixture again until it is smooth and stringy. The *truffade* is ready.

La Truffade can be an experience.

Soufflé au Cantal – Cheese soufflé with Cantal

Soufflé au Cantal
Cheese soufflé with Cantal

Serves 5

3 oz/80 g Cantal
2 tbsp butter
2 tbsp flour
½ cup/125 ml milk
freshly milled pepper and salt
3 eggs
1 pinch of grated nutmeg
butter for greasing

Grate the cheese. Melt the butter in a small pan (1). Sprinkle on the flour and whisk well, to prevent lumps from forming. Pour on the hot milk and continue to whisk until it has combined (2). Remove from the heat and season with salt and pepper.

Preheat the oven to 350 °F (180 °C). Separate the eggs. Beat the egg whites with a pinch of salt until very stiff. Add the yolks to the pan and stir (3). Add the cheese and a little grated nutmeg and stir (4).

Now carefully fold the egg whites into the mixture until they are evenly distributed (5).

Grease the soufflé dishes well (6). Transfer the mixture to the dishes and bake in the oven for 15 minutes.

The cheeses of the Auvergne, clockwise from top right:
Salers, Saint-Nectaire, a piece of young Cantal, Fourme d'Ambert, and Bleu d'Auvergne.

Sausages and hams

From Toulouse, the city which lent its name to an excellent sausage, to Clermont-Ferrand, the ancient skill of how to prepare pork correctly hangs like a dense mist over the countryside. In the south are regions such as the Montagne Noire and the Plateau de Lacaune, further north the entire region of the Auvergne, especially Cantal and Puy-de-Dôme, renowned for their outstanding sausages and hams. But also included here are blood sausages such as the *galabar*, the ségala, the white *coudenou* from Mazamet or those containing chestnuts, *fetge*, the salted pig liver prepared in Albi, and the *friton* or coarse mince made from offcuts and cooked in lard, as well as brawn and *fricandoux*, baked meatballs made from the liver and gullet, such as those from the Cévennes.

This culinary wealth has its origins in the natural conditions available to pigs in this expansive territory. In the lowlands and areas of mid-altitude are extensive oak and chestnut forests which provided the animals with their favorite food, giving their meat a particularly fine aroma. In this mountainous area, parts of which were virtually inaccessible and where farmers could be left to their own devices for a large part of the year, survival depended on a reliable means of storage, so farmers were compelled to develop various methods of conserving meat. These sometimes involved heating it in fat, curing, smoking, or air-drying it – a method reserved for the finest cuts.

For many years, industrial production methods have been well-established in Lacaune and the larger towns, yet the present-day reputation of the traditional specialties is based primarily on hand-made products, which are quite frequently prepared by the farmers themselves. This is because the quality of sausage and hams, as well as of roasts and cutlets, is ultimately inseparable from the rigorous demands made on the rearing and keeping of the animals.

It is now no secret – if ever it was one – that the meat from animals which have been reared in the most natural conditions possible is significantly better than that from factory-farmed animals.

°Right: One look is enough to be persuaded of the high quality of these traditional meats and sausages. From front left: A dish of fresh pork chops and roasts; above, a rolled joint of belly pork; the glass jars contain country-cured and liver sausage, pig head brawn, and *rillettes*; alongside are the air-dried country hams, the air-dried sausages, the thin *saucisses* and the thicker *saucissons secs*; in the glass jars are preserved pig trotters, below, side of bacon, and beneath it in the center the oven-baked *pâté de campagne*.

The green lentils of Puy

"Poor man's caviar" was the name given to Puy lentils, emphasizing their combination of excellent flavor and reasonable price. And rightly so, because no other dried vegetable can match them. Their fine characteristics begin with their size. At only ⅛–¼ inch (4–5 millimeters) in diameter, they are exceptionally small and a relatively high proportion of skin explains their powerful aroma. In addition, their skin is finer and their starch content lower than other pulses, resulting in shorter cooking times, easy digestibility and a pleasant consistency. Their green color is produced by the blue pigment anthocyanin which, coupled with the yellow husk, creates the pale green base shade (and serves to strengthen blood vessels). Because the pigment is not evenly distributed throughout the lentil, deeper blue-green flecks emerge. During cooking, however, even green lentils turn brown. Evidence from Gallo-Roman times suggests that lentils have been cultivated in the Velay for almost 2000 years. Different natural factors coming together in this volcanic landscape of the Auvergne favored both their cultivation and their quality in earlier times, as they do today. Almost 750 farmers sow a good 6200 acres (2500 hectares) with the ancient variety Anicia. In March and April, when the soil temperature rises above 41 °F (5 °C), the time is right. The meadows lying at 2000–4000 feet (600–1200 meters) are not fertilized. Cultivated primarily in volcanic soil, which is sufficiently fertile in itself, all the lentils need is nitrogen, which they can absorb from the atmosphere themselves. Something which exerts a greater influence on the quality of the lentils than the volcanic soil is the microclimate. In summer, the Cantal and Margeride mountains in the southwest, as well as the peaks of the Vivarais in the southeast act like protective barriers, usually guaranteeing sun, warmth, and the hot, dry wind. The dryness means that the lentils do not ripen fully. As a result, their starch content remains lower and their skin softer. If harvested between the end of July and mid-September, the lentils will already have dried by natural means. They do not need to be soaked before preparation, as with other pulses, but simply placed in cold water and 25 minutes later they are cooked.

From July lentils are harvested by machine in the Velay, where they are cultivated over an area of 6200 acres (2500 hectares). The lentils, which are dried by the sun out in the fields, contain less than 16 percent moisture. They are simply graded according to size and quality and then packed.

The green Puy lentils contain the blue pigment anthocyanin, which produces a greenish base color when combined with the yellow husk. The pigment is unevenly distributed.

Lentils are traditionally packed in sacks and measured by the hundredweight. Annual harvests in Velay vary between 20,000 and 36,000 hundredweights (1000–1800 tonnes).

Tartare de saumon aux lentilles vertes du Puy – Salmon tartare with green Puy lentils

Croûtes de lentilles vertes et fricassé de grenouilles aux mousserons Lentil crust and frog fricassé with fairy ring mushrooms

Tartare de saumon aux lentilles vertes du Puy
Salmon tartare with green Puy lentils

2 onions
5 oz/150 g Puy lentils
1 bouquet garni
2 tsp vegetable stock granules
3 tbsp olive oil
2 tbsp white wine vinegar
1 tbsp mustard
sea salt, black pepper
10 oz/300 g salmon
3 shallots
3 small pickled cucumbers
1 hard-cooked egg
1 tbsp finely diced parsley
1 tbsp finely diced tarragon
lemon juice
½ an unwaxed orange
2 tbsp orange juice

Chop the onions and rinse the lentils. Put them both in a pan. Add three times as much water, the vegetable stock granules, and bouquet garni. Cook for 20 to 25 minutes then drain the lentils. Prepare a vinaigrette using 2 tbsp oil, the vinegar, mustard, salt and pepper, and add a third of it to the warm lentils.
Cut the salmon into small pieces.
Finely chop the shallots, pickled cucumber, and egg. Add to the salmon with the parsley, tarragon, and remaining vinaigrette, mix well and add lemon juice and salt to taste. Leave in a cool place for 30 minutes.
For each portion fill a small tart mold roughly 4 in/10 cm in diameter two-thirds full with the salmon mixture and press down well. Add a layer of lentils and press down, so that the tart holds together.
Finely peel the zest from the orange avoiding the white pith, then cut the zest into thin strips. Stir together the remaining oil, orange juice, salt and pepper and add the zest.
Turn the salmon tarts onto plates and pour a little orange sauce around each one.

Croûtes de lentilles vertes et fricassé de grenouilles aux mousserons
Lentil crust and frog fricassé with fairy ring mushrooms

Serves 6

Fricassé
15 frogs (roughly 2 lb 3 oz/1 kg)
¼ cup/60 g butter
2 shallots, finely chopped
¾ cup/200 ml white wine
2 tbsp flour
7 oz/200 g fairy ring mushrooms
freshly ground pepper and salt
3½ tbsp/50 ml meat juices

Lentil ragout
3½ oz/100 g smoked bacon
1 small onion
2 carrots
4 tsp/20 g butter
1 tbsp tomato paste
14 oz/400 g lentils
4 cups/1 l chicken stock
1 cup/250 ml cream

Lentil crust
1 cup/150 g wheat flour
1⅓ cups/200 g rice flour
1 tsp salt
14 oz/380 g egg white
2 tbsp/30 g butter

Burnet coulis
3½ oz/100 g flat-leafed parsley
3 oz/100 g burnet
⅓ cup/80 g butter
butter for greasing
milk for brushing

Skin the frogs and set the 30 legs to one side. Heat 2 tsp/20 g butter, add the shallots and soften them until they are transparent, then add the meat and lightly brown. Pour in the white wine and leave to cook on a low heat for 15 minutes. Remove the meat and allow to cool then pull it from the bones and set to one side.

For the lentil ragout, finely chop the bacon, onion, and carrots and leave to sweat in the butter. Mix in the tomato paste and add the lentils. Pour on the chicken stock and simmer for 25 minutes. Drain the lentils and save the stock. Take 3 tbsp cooked lentils and set them to one side. Simmer 2 tbsp lentils with the stock and cream for 15 minutes, purée them and add the remaining lentils.
To make the lentil crust, purée the 3 tbsp lentils and mix with the flour, rice flour, and salt. Fold in the egg white and work in the melted butter. Leave the mixture to stand for 1 hour. Preheat the oven to 355 °F/180 °C. Grease a baking sheet. Divide the mixture into 24 balls about the size of a nut and place them on the baking sheet. Press them flat and brush with milk. Bake in the oven for 8 minutes.
For the coulis, remove the stalks from the parsley and burnet and purée the leaves in a mixer with a small amount of water. Heat carefully and combine with the butter.
For the fricassé, fry the fairy ring mushrooms in 4 tsp/20 g butter, then add the frog meat, heat and season with salt and pepper. Add the lentil ragout and mix well.
Lightly salt the frog legs and coat them with flour. Heat the remaining butter and fry the frog legs until golden brown.
To serve, place a lentil crust on each plate, spread with a thin layer of ragout and cover with another lentil crust. Repeat this, finishing with a fourth lentil crust. Pour some of the burnet coulis around it and garnish with 5 frog legs drizzled with meat juices on each plate.

Le Puy, surrounded by a charming volcanic landscape, lies in the middle of the famous lentil region.

Regional baking:

The fouace

The focal point of every home is the fireplace, which is why the French still refer to their homes as *foyer*. In Roman times, home-baked bread was referred to quite simply as *panis focacius*, from which the French *fouace* or *fougasse* was derived. This began as little more than a sort of flat cake. But as knowledge of ingredients and baking methods grew, the fouace began to develop and take shape and several different forms emerged. It was baked for special occasions, such as Christmas, Easter, or Whitsuntide, and for christenings or weddings. At these times it was prepared using the highest quality, finely ground wheat flour, to which milk and eggs, butter and honey, or later on sugar, were added. However, because people rarely had their own ovens in those days, the fouace was baked in hot ash. In the meantime it had become rich and thick, but its texture was not yet light and open. The addition of yeast would bestow these qualities, resulting in a recipe similar to that of brioche.

So simple and delicious, it continued to spread, with each region adding its own distinctive touch. In the Languedoc and Roussillon, it is prepared as a hearty, flat bread baked on a baking sheet, which is either sweet or marbled with fat, and in some cases shaped like a pretzel. In Provence they are keen on seasoning their fouace with aniseed, or olive oil is occasionally added. In the Auvergne and Aveyron it can be found with candied fruits or prunes. Orange blossom water or grated lemon rind are also used as flavorings.

Laguiole has become a stronghold of fouace. Here you can find especially beautiful, open-textured crown loaves, decorated with *chignons* or small, dough-formed snails, which are not only attractive but informative, as another *chignon* is added to the crown for every pound of dough used. Fouace is eaten at breakfast or as a snack, but it is equally popular as a dessert, served with cream, ice cream, or fruit, or as an aperitive.

Below: Many regions have different variations of the fouace or fougasse. In Laguiole it is decorated with *chignons* or "snails."

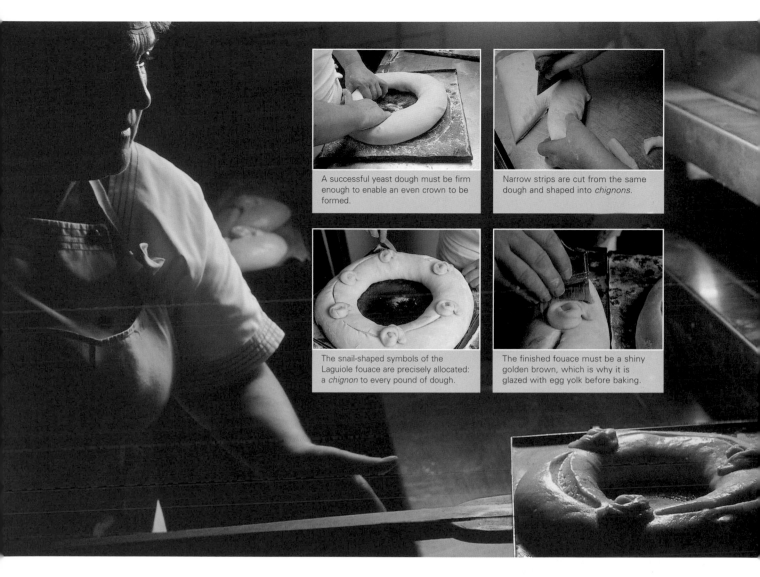

A successful yeast dough must be firm enough to enable an even crown to be formed.

Narrow strips are cut from the same dough and shaped into *chignons*.

The snail-shaped symbols of the Laguiole fouace are precisely allocated: a *chignon* to every pound of dough.

The finished fouace must be a shiny golden brown, which is why it is glazed with egg yolk before baking.

The fouaces emerge from the oven shiny and golden brown. A smaller version is shown here.

Fouace
Crown loaf

Serves 6–8

½ oz/15 g compressed yeast
generous ⅓ cup/100 ml lukewarm water
1⅔ cups/250 g wheat flour
2 eggs, beaten
1 tsp salt
5 tbsp/75 g sugar
2 tbsp orange blossom water
6½ tbsp/100 g butter

The evening before, mix the yeast, water and ⅓ cup/50 g flour, cover and leave for 1 hour. Sieve the remaining flour onto the mixture, add the eggs, and knead vigorously for 10 minutes with the flour. Next knead in the salt, sugar, and orange blossom water. Finally, carefully work in the butter to produce an even dough. Cover the dough and leave it for 3 hours. Knead the dough again and leave it covered overnight in a cool place or in the refrigerator.

Next morning, preheat the oven to 440 °F/225 °C, shape the dough into a crown and bake for roughly 40 minutes until golden brown.

A more luxurious version of this fouace to be eaten at home can be made by adding candied peel and raisins.

Clafoutis

Serves 4–6

17 oz/500 g black cherries
1 tbsp butter
1 cup/150 g wheat flour
5 eggs
5 tbsp/75 g sugar
salt
1 cup/250 ml milk

Preheat the oven to 355 °F/180 °C.
Rinse and dry the cherries and remove the stalks. For a genuine Clafoutis the pits are left in. Grease a soufflé dish with the butter and add the cherries. Sieve the flour into a basin and add the eggs, 3½ tbsp/50 g sugar, a pinch of salt, and a dash of lukewarm milk and stir well. Then gradually add the remaining lukewarm milk, stirring continuously, and work it into a crêpe batter.
Pour the batter onto the cherries and place the dish in a preheated oven for 30 minutes.
Remove from the oven, sprinkle with the remaining sugar, and serve immediately.

Originally a dessert from the Limousin, Clafoutis has a core of support in and around the Massif Central. Pitted cherries are not used in the original version and many cooks add a dash of kirsch, armagnac or rum. Apricots are also an ideal accompaniment but require more sugar to be added.

Mineral water

No other drink can lay claim to such enormous rates of growth as mineral water. And this has been the case for 50 years. But over the last two decades, in particular, consumption has quite simply rocketed.

Countries that barely gave bottled water a second glance in 1980 are today leading the per capita consumption tables. Belgium, Germany, Austria, and Switzerland are among them. The Italians have held the record for several years now, having ousted the French, and they now each consume the equivalent of 28 gallons (130 liters) a year. French bottled waters are the most prominent worldwide. This is to some extent due to the quality of the French springs, but also because they installed efficient bottling plant when everyone else was only servicing a regional customer base. The French are no newcomers to mineral water.

Wherever the Romans discovered a promising springhead in Europe they erected spas, as they not only took pleasure in bathing, but were convinced of the healing properties of the waters. Vicus Calidus, known today as Vichy, was one such spa and also the present day Saint-Galmier, where Badoit is bottled. Later, as the Romans began to lose their power and influence, it was some time before the springs were paid any further attention. It was not until the 16th century, and particularly at the start of the 17th century, that there was renewed interest in their therapeutic properties. Mineral water was regarded as medicine and for the first time it was bottled and sent to the court or wealthy nobility. During this period, Louis XIII had a bath built in Vichy. As a result, members of the royal family and court traveled to Auvergne to take the waters. Madame de Sévigné, for instance, visited both Vichy and Bourbon-L'Archambault on account of her rheumatism. The belief in mineral water as a therapeutic medium grew constantly, producing an ever-increasing trade in bottled water. During the course of the 18th century, various central government decrees sought to control and regulate it. However, the Revolution and troubled times that followed harmed the development of the spa baths as well as mineral water trade.

The golden age of the baths arrived with Napoleon III and his empress Eugenie, as the ruling pair adored the spa towns with their fashionable ambience. Between 1861 and 1865 Vichy became his personal spa, winning the town 300,000 visitors and a momentous upturn in sales of its water. However, the forerunner among modern mineral water bottlers was to be Augustin Badoit who had set up the Saint-Galmier plant in the department of the Loire in 1837. He bottled the water under his own name and built up a widespread distribution network. For Evian, development of the spa bath went hand in hand with the sale of bottled water from 1870. In addition, from 1882 greater emphasis was placed on the importance of advertising, which was regarded as a cost-effective way to increase sales. Starting at 95,000 bottles a year, a figure of over 2 million had been reached by the turn of the 20th century.

Although Vittel, a company built up by the lawyer, Louis Boulomié, was also based on the spa bath and mineral water production, Perrier took a different route. Nobody had been able to turn the source in Vergèze in the Gard, known for its gas emission, into a spa. When Dr Louis Perrier bought it in 1898, he planned primarily to produce lemonade. However, he lacked the capital needed to bottle and market the carbonated water. This was contributed by the Englishman, John Harmsworth, who founded the Compagnie de la Source Perrier in 1906. Only four years later production had already reached 10 million bottles, most of which were exported to the U.S.A. and England. Harmsworth intended the bottle to resemble an Indian club, because until the First World War the therapeutic value of mineral waters had generally been the main focus in marketing. During the twenties and thirties, consumption rose to over a quarter of a billion bottles in France, but the real boom did not come until after 1947.

Various factors are responsible for the popularity of bottled water. Although the purity of tap water is now more closely regulated than ever before, its taste leaves a lot to be desired, particularly in large towns and cities. This produced the need for a substitute. Firstly, consumers wanted to be certain that their drinking water was at least pure, but secondly, the changing circumstances in which people lived and worked led to greater health consciousness and the ideal of slimness. In the aftermath of various drinking water scandals of recent years, there were also some direct environmental considerations at work. And, not least, the exceptional commitment to advertising displayed by the major players in the mineral water business did its bit to bring about this outstanding success.

Auvergne, with its volcanic springs, has become one of the most important mineral water regions. Its success today is based not so much on Vichy and Saint-Yorre as Volvic, situated 6 miles (10 kilometers) to the north of Clermont-Ferrand in the Parc des Volcans. Its water comes from the Chalet des Sources, located in the woody hills above the small town of the same name. It is pumped down to the bottling factory 2½ miles (4 kilometers) away. The factory compound now covers an area of over 17 acres (7 hectares), where each day more than 2.5 million bottles run off six bottling lanes, producing close to a billion

bottles a year. In the fifties, Volvic was filling just 50 million bottles a year. Most of the production, with the exception of the glass bottles destined for the restaurant trade, is put into the plastic containers so popular in France due to their lightness and these are produced on the spot. But they can hardly have a future in a Europe which is increasingly conscious of ecological concerns.

This elaborate drinking pavilion in Vichy dates back to the 19th century, when fashionable spas were still attracting 300,000 visitors a year.

Mineral water consumption in general has now once again reached record levels in France, standing at around 6.5 billion bottles, while the French far and away outstrip all other Europeans when it comes to non-carbonated water.

A distinction must be made, however, between two types of water. Mineral water is what is known as deep water which comes from an underground spring. Over dozens and, in some cases, hundreds of years, the strata of soil and rock lying above it have filtered rain water and enriched it with various minerals and trace elements. Its value in health terms is based on its origin and combination and varies from water to water. Spring water is also a deep water which is protected from any sort of contamination, is microbiologically sound, and suitable for human consumption. It does not require processing or additives, with the exception of the permitted methods of filtration, decanting, and the addition of carbonic acid, which also applies to mineral water. However, spring water need not contain minerals or trace elements and may not be promoted as a product conducive to good health.

First discovered by the Romans, it was not until the 17th century that Vichy became the focus of attention again, thanks largely to Louis XIII.

The great waters of France: Carbonated water

Perrier, Vergèze
Authorized since 1863, spring in the Gard known worldwide, rich in its own carbonic acid.

Vernière,
Large bubbles, little sparkle, slightly mineral, containing magnesium and sulfates, from the Languedoc.

Vals, Vals-les-Bains
Large bubbles, but pleasantly effervescent with a well-balanced composition. From the spa in the Ardèche.

Vichy Célestin
Pleasantly low in carbonic acid, as it is bottled direct from the springs, rich in sodium, calcium and fluorine, dry when swallowed.

Ogeu, Ogeu-les-Bains
Lively, sensitive sparkle, few mineral substances, detoxifying; Pyrenean spring recognized since 1880.

Eau du Boulou, Source Janette
From the Roussillon, rich in mineral salts, particularly sodium, distinctive flavor.

Manon, Vals-les-Bains
A slightly saltier more sparkling water higher in mineral content than that bottled from the main spring.

Saint-Yorre
Faint sparkle, but a high mineral salt content. It comes from two springs, one in the Allier and one in Puy-de-Dôme.

Arvie, Ardes
Rich in calcium, magnesium, potassium, and chlorides; an almost sweet spring water from Auvergne.

Carbonated water

Salvetat, Sources Rieumajou, La Salvetat sur Agout
Finely sparkling, pleasant water with a low mineral content from the national park of the Haut-Languedoc.

Badoit, Source Saint Galmier, Loire
Subdued, medium-sized bubbles, pleasant and well-balanced, light mineral clay, belongs to Evian.

Non-carbonated water

Alet, Source Les Eaux Chaudes
From Alet-les-Bains in the southern French Aude comes a mineralized water suitable for young babies.

Contrex, Source Contrexéville
A water rich in calcium, magnesium, and sulfur from the famous spa town in the Vogesen.

Quézac, Source Diva
A robust water rich in mineral salts from the Cévennes, which was recognized in 1901 and contains fluorine, among other things.

César, Sources de St-Alban
A subtly sparkling, pleasant and very well-balanced water from the Loire to the west of Lyon.

Chateldon
A luxury water from the Puy-de-Dôme, enjoyed by Louis XIV and reserved for the best restaurants and stores.

Thonon, Alpes de Haute Savoie
Like Evian, this water with a low mineral content comes from Lake Geneva and is suitable for young babies.

Cristalline, Source de Sainte-Cécile
The spring is near Cairanne in the Côtes du Rhône region. This water is low in mineral salts and suitable for young babies.

Vauban, Source de Saint-Amand
One of the rare springs in the Nord department supplies this water which contains calcium and sulfates.

Hépar, Vittel
This water from the famous town in the Vosges is characterized by its exceptionally high magnesium content.

Vittel, Grande Source
A famous water from the Vosges with a good calcium and magnesium content which is suitable for a salt-free diet.

La Française, Propiac-les-Bains
With its high calcium and magnesium content, this water from the Drôme is recommended for weight loss cures.

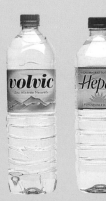

Evian, Source Cachat
This pure, well-balanced spring flows in the Alps, where the water is naturally filtered over 15 years.

Volvic, Sources Clairvic
A popular water from the Auvergne. It only contains a few mineral salts, is very well-balanced and ideal for young babies.

Abatilles, Arcachon
From a depth of 1500 feet (472 meters), this water, which is completely nitrate-free, rises in the pine forests of Arcachon.

Mont Roucous, Gard
From this spring in the Cévennes comes one of the purest waters in France which also has dietetic properties.

Canyon, Source la Souterraine
This water, which is suitable for young babies, is bottled in Alet-les-Bains, to the south of Limoux.

Roussillon
Languedoc
Les Cévennes

André Dominé

Hospitality is the keynote at Domaine Gauby, whose Côtes du Rossillon Villages is known to wine connoisseurs across the world.

Canigou is the holy mountain of the Catalans. It rises out of the Roussillon plain to a height of 9134 feet (2784 meters), and was long considered the highest peak of the eastern Pyrénées..

Calais

Le Havre

Caen Paris

Brest

Rennes Strasbourg

Orléans

Nantes Tours Dijon

Limoges Lyon

Bordeaux Grenoble

Cévennes
Toulouse **Languedoc** Nice
Biarritz **Roussillon**
Marseille Toulon

The *Midi* is the name given to the stretch of land in the south of France that bounds the Golfe du Lion between the river Rhône and the eastern foothills of the Pyrénées. The French name *Midi* is an oblique reference to the midday sun so characteristic of the region. The sunshine and blue skies are indeed elements which have a strong influence on the lifestyle of people in Languedoc and Roussillon, and convey a quality of life which frequently arouses the envy of city-dwellers from the north of France. Eating in restaurants is an extremely popular pastime, especially when the meal can be enjoyed in the open air in one of the charming small squares of the old city center of Montpellier, or in one of the nearby coastal villages. People are not looking for very elaborate and expensive menus; what they want are fresh ingredients, tastily prepared, oysters and mussels.

This is, however, just one aspect of the region. Quite a different aspect is revealed if the traveler ventures beyond the Mediterranean into the larger part of this region. The hilly and often trackless hinterland, gives way to high mountain country in Roussillon. Despite the pervading Mediterranean influence, despite the tangible sense of closeness to nature, life there is and has always been hard and frugal. Nevertheless, the area has its hearty recipes and specialties, especially in the Cévennes region. The ingredients from this vicinity – mushrooms and chestnuts, berries and honey, lamb and game, sausages and pâtés, goat cheese and Roquefort – all these provide a robustness which counterbalances the more easygoing mood down on the plains. The exciting new reputation developing around the largest winegrowing area in the world ultimately rests on the sheer determination, expertise and stubbornness of the viticulturists, laboring to produce quality wines of incomparably Mediterranean character from slopes which are difficult to work. In the same way, the culinary revival of Languedoc-Roussillon is derived from the combination of traditional products and fare with the inspiration of a newly revitalized southern *esprit*. *Mel i mato*, for instance, is a delicious traditional Catalan dish consisting of cream cheese made from goat milk and covered with honey. Here, it is transformed into a mouth watering sorbet. Another local dish in a new guise is the traditional puréed dried cod known otherwise as *brandade*. It is wrapped in the mangold leaves so typical of the region to create an appetizer and specialty. Yet, despite this unexpected combination, there is no loss of the essential character of either ingredient.

Wine-based aperitives

Perhaps better described as aperitives based on the grape, this group of drinks includes some consisting mainly of wine, some of grape must fortified with spirit, and some made up of both. These mixtures became popular in France from the middle of the 19th century onward. They may be flavored with herbally derived additions, especially cinchona, and then spend several months maturing in the barrel, where their flavors harmonize, before being bottled.

Byrrh

Developed in 1873 by the Violet brothers in Thuir and registered under its trade name, this is an aperitive based on unfermented red grape must from the Carignan, Grenache and Alicante varieties, grape spirit and fortified wine. It is flavored with cinchona extract from the bitter cinchona or Peruvian bark, dried orange peel, cocoa and coffee beans. Between the two World Wars, with annual sales of well over 9 million gallons, it was the biggest-selling brand of aperitive in France.

Dubonnet

Joseph Dubonnet, the Parisian maker of liqueurs, was the first to put his mind to the subject of a drink based on *mistelle* and flavored with cinchona, designed to provide a palatable way for colonial troops to take quinine. *Mistelle* is the name given to a grape must in which fermentation has been prevented by the addition of alcohol, so that the entire natural sugar content of the grapes is preserved.

Byrrh is a highly flavored sweet aperitive. Grape must has been stopped from fermenting by adding alcohol.

Today, Dubonnet is sold in a number of countries as a straightforward, unflavored aperitive.

Saint-Raphael

Created by a Lyon doctor called Jupet, this aperitive is made in a white and a red version, and likewise contains cinchona. *Cinchona officinalis*, the bark of a tree which grows in the Peruvian Andes, reduces fever, sharpens appetite and promotes digestion. Its medicinal use was spread through Europe by the Jesuits in the 17th century, and it was highly regarded in the 19th century as possessing general curative and strengthening properties.

Vermouth

Antonio Benedetto Carpano mixed the first vermouth in 1786 in Turin, from wine, absinthe, herbs and spices. In the duchy of Savoy, then part of Piedmont, alpine herbs were used to make the subtler Vermouth de Chambéry. In Lyon, Louis Noilly invented his Noilly-Prat, which is produced in Marseillan near Sète.

At Byrrh, the erstwhile firm in Thuir near Perpignan, the flavorings for the classic aperitive are weighed out as they were a century ago.

Byrrh is mainly flavored with the soothing cinchona bark, and with dried orange rind, coffee and cocoa beans.

The biggest wooden barrel holds a million liters (264,200 gallons). It is one of the sights of Thuir.

When Byrrh was still the most popular aperitive in France, tankers regularly trundled along the factory's own railroad link.

Mussels from the Bassin de Thau

The Bassin de Thau is a 12–16 foot (4–5 meter) deep lagoon covering an area of 29 square miles (7500 hectares), situated between Agdes and Sète. It is separated from the Mediterranean by a narrow strip of land, broken at three points, which allows an exchange of water between the inland lagoon and the sea. Mèze, Marseillan and Loupian all have their share in the harvest of the lagoon, but the most famous of the villages, the one which has lent its name to the oysters produced here, is Bouzigues. Oysters are the main produce of some 650 concerns, which between them farm 1⅓ square miles (352 hectares). The lagoon contains 2600 rectangular frames called *tables*, each 1495 square yards (1250 square meters) in size. From each of these, up to a thousand ropes of oysters hang down into the water. The nutrients are unevenly distributed through the lagoon, making it possible to control the growth of the oysters according to the position of the frames.

Common mussels are also farmed here, and at the end of the 18th century the exceptionally large mussels from this site were considered the best along the entire coast between Aigues Mortes and Cerbère.

The mussels multiply sufficiently on their own; mussel farmers find the young on the backs of the larger mussels or attached to oysters. The small mussels are put into fine-gauge nets and taken out to the frames, where they are attached so as to hang 10–16 feet (3–5 meters) below the surface of the water. As they become larger, the mussels grow out of the nets but remain attached. During the early stage, lasting four to five months, the young mussels remain in the protected waters of the lagoon; they are then taken out into the sea for a further eight to nine months, chained below water on 20–35 foot (6–10 meter) cables which can only be reached by diving. To harvest them, the mussel farmers dive down again to free the nets. These are then hoisted on board the flat-bottomed craft with a winch and put into large basketwork crates. Whereas all sorts of algae, other shellfish, and gelatinous water creatures can adhere to the mussels and the nets in the lagoon, and crabs, shrimps and small fish find them an ideal home, no parasites can settle on the mussels in the sea, on account of the stronger currents. The mussel farmers may sometimes be forced to postpone harvesting when the weather is too

The mussels grow in nets in the lagoon. The nets are hauled out by the mussel farmer and placed in a machine to release the mussels.

stormy. Strong winds can also cause the mussels to become more sandy.

As soon as the craft have tied up by their huts, the nets, together with the mussels attached to them, are put in a machine which thoroughly cleans them and removes anything extraneous. The mussels are then graded by shaking them in stainless steel grids, first in narrow gauge grids and then in wider ones. After this, they are placed in water to let them recover from the stress of transportation and cleaning. Mussels are usually 12–14 months old by the time they are harvested and eaten. The annual mussel harvest from the sea along the coast of Languedoc is 9000–13,000 tons (8000–12,000 tonnes). No precise figures exist for the lagoon, but the amount is estimated at around 2200 tons (2000 tonnes).

Mussels should be eaten as fresh as possible, but certainly within four days. Mussels of medium size, *les moyennes*, around 2 inches (4–5 centimeters) long, are used for *moules marinières*; the larger ones, *les grasses*, are mainly used for *paella* or *moules farcies*, stuffed mussels, or are eaten raw. *Brasucade* is also very popular. For this, the mussels are opened and grilled over vine twigs.

Moules marinières
Mussels mariner style

Serves 2

4½ lbs/2 kg fresh mussels
6½ tbsp/100 g butter
2 large shallots, chopped
4 tbsp chopped parsley
½ bay leaf
1 sprig of thyme
1 tbsp wine vinegar
¾ cup/200 ml white wine
1 tsp cornstarch
Freshly milled salt and pepper

Wash and scrub the mussels thoroughly and remove
all the beards. Discard any open mussels and those
which do not open after pressure is applied.
Melt half the butter in a sufficiently large pan and
sweat the shallots in this until they acquire a transparent sheen. Add half the parsley, the half bay leaf
and the thyme, then add the vinegar and the wine.
Place the cleaned mussels in the pan and bring
quickly to a boil. When (normally after a few minutes) the mussels open, lift them out of the cooking liquid and place into individual dishes.
Mix the cornstarch with a little water until smooth.
Stir the remaining butter into the liquid in which
the mussels were cooked, and combine with the
cornstarch to bind the sauce. Season to taste.
Pour the sauce over the mussels, sprinkle with the
remaining parsley and serve immediately.

Warning: Throw away any mussels which have not
opened during cooking.

1 It is important to clean the mussels thoroughly and in particular to remove all the beards.
2 This fresh, open mussel shows clearly how the beards are attached to the shell at the mouth.
3 Melt a generous quantity of butter in a high-sided pan and sweat the shallots in this before adding the vinegar and wine.

4 Then add the mussels and bring to a boil in the covered pan.
5 After a few minutes, as soon as the mussels have opened, lift them out and place in earthenware dishes ready to serve.
6 Melt some butter in the cooking liquid, bind the sauce with cornstarch mixed to a smooth, thin paste with water, and season.

The ingredients are simple: just a few shallots, thyme, bay, parsley, wine vinegar and white wine together with the mussels. The effect is astonishing.

Fish soup

Whereas *bouillabaisse* has long since become a luxury dish, served in the most elegant restaurants, a simpler version of this fish soup can be found all along the French Mediterranean coast from Cerbère to Menton. Just like their fellow fishermen working on the other coasts, the men bringing in the catches on the Golfe du Lion and Côte d'Azur used to keep back the smaller fish for their own use. To fillet these fish or serve them whole was hardly worth the effort, so instead they were boiled in water with vegetables, tomatoes and garlic, those ubiquitous Mediterranean ingredients. The mixture was then puréed and passed through a sieve, resulting in a thick, reddish soup with an intense flavor. To make it a more satisfying dish, it is served with oven-toasted bread, spread with *rouille*, a piquant paste based on chiles, garlic and olive oil.

If the fishermen had any larger fish left over, they would use these to prepare a *bullinada*. Fish such as scorpion fish, angler fish, sea bass or whiting are first gutted and cut into evenly sized pieces. Alternating layers of thickly sliced potato and pieces of fish are placed in an earthenware pot, fish stock is added, and the whole left to cook slowly on a low heat. Additional flavoring can be given by using a piece of *sagi*, slightly rancid bacon. Eels from the Étang de Leucate are used in the *bullinada d'anguilles*, a version particularly popular in Roussillon.

Soupe de poissons de roche
Fish soup

4 leeks
2 large onions
2 carrots
2 tbsp olive oil
8 tomatoes
6 cloves of garlic
8¾ lbs/4 kg fresh fish (greater weaver fish, gurnard, whiting, conger eel)
½ bunch of flat-leaf parsley, finely chopped
1 tbsp tomato paste
9½ pints/4.5 liters water
1 cup/250 ml dry white wine
1 bouquet garni
Croutons
1 tbsp butter

Clean the leeks, onions and carrots. Cut into small pieces and sweat in the olive oil in a large pot.
Dice the tomatoes and add to the vegetables in the pot, together with 4 crushed garlic cloves.
Cook on a low heat for 15 minutes.
Gut and thoroughly rinse the fish.
Then add the parsley and tomato paste and stir in well.
Place the fish on top of the vegetables. Pour on the water and white wine and add the bouquet garni.

1 First sweat the leeks, onions and carrots in olive oil, followed by the tomatoes and garlic.
2 Cook the vegetables on a low heat for 15 minutes. Then add finely-chopped parsley and tomato paste.

3 Meanwhile gut and wash the fish thoroughly. Then lay them on top of the vegetables in the pot.
4 Add the water, wine and bouquet garni at this stage.

5 Purée all the ingredients to a fairly thick, even consistency.
6 Lastly, pass the soup through a sieve and serve immediately.

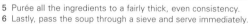

Boil for 20 minutes.
Now purée the soup and pass it through a sieve, pressing the ingredients with a ladle to extract the cooking juices. Keep hot.
Rub the croutons with the remaining garlic and fry them in a pan in a mixture of butter and oil. They can either be placed in the soup dishes with the soup and served immediately, or put on the table separately accompanied by a small bowl of *rouille*.

This simple and popular fish soup is prepared from fresh local ingredients and served with croutons makes a delicious first course.

Rouille
Piquant chili sauce

2 ripe bell peppers
5 cloves of garlic
1 small fresh red chili
1½ tsp/1 g saffron strands
1 tsp sea salt
1 large floury potato, boiled in its skin
¾ cup/200 ml olive oil

Bake the bell peppers in a preheated oven at 390°F/ 200°C until the skin begins to brown in places. Then remove the skin, inner ribs and seeds. Pound in a mortar with the garlic, chili, saffron and salt. Then mix to a thick paste with the boiled potato. Add the olive oil drop by drop, beating constantly, until the sauce has the consistency of a thick, creamy purée.

Recipes from the coast

Gaspacho aux huîtres
Gazpacho with oysters

2 red bell peppers
1 tbsp olive oil
4 tomatoes
Scant ½ cup/100 ml cucumber juice
¾ cup/200 ml tomato juice
¾ cup/200 ml water
1 clove of garlic
2 eggs
Freshly milled salt and pepper
¾ cup/200 ml olive oil
16 oysters (from Bouzigues)
Herbs in season

Lay the bell peppers on the shelf of a preheated oven at 390 °F/200 °C and bake until the skin darkens. Then remove the skin, stalk, ribs and seeds and fry in 1 tbsp of olive oil. Cool.
Peel the tomatoes, remove the centers and dice. Then purée together all the remaining ingredients (except the oysters and herbs) with a hand blender, adding the olive oil drop by drop, until a mayonnaise-like sauce results. Open the oysters, shake off the water or juices, and poach the oyster flesh briefly. Place half a bell pepper, some diced tomato and four oysters in the center of each dish. Top with the sauce and garnish with chopped fresh herbs.

Ollada de petits légumes aux moules et boudin noir
Mixed vegetables with mussels and blood sausage

1 potato
1 small zucchini
1 carrot
3 ½ oz/100 g green beans
1 leek
1 artichoke
salt
1 ¾ oz/50 g *sagi* (slightly rancid bacon)
1 ⅔ cups/400 ml vegetable stock
12 large mussels, cooked in boiling water and removed from their shells
12 thin slices Catalan blood sausage
1 tomato, diced

Clean all the vegetables except the tomato. Cut into small dice, and cook in lightly salted boiling water until tender.
Soak the *sagi* to remove as much salt as possible, then dice finely.
Place the *sagi* in a pan with the vegetable stock and boil for 5 minutes; then leave to stand for another 15 minutes and season to taste.
Heat the cooked vegetables, the cooked and prepared mussels and the slices of blood sausage in a little stock.
Place equal portions of vegetables in four soup dishes, then three slices of blood sausage per dish, a portion of mussels and a few raw tomato dice.
Finally pour the hot stock over the dishes and serve immediately.

Papillotte de moules et filets de sardines aux légumes du soleil
Packages of mussels and fresh sardine fillets with vegetables of the sun

16 sardines
1 green bell pepper
1 red bell pepper
1 zucchini
1 small eggplant
1 small onion
4 cloves of garlic
2 tsp olive oil
Freshly milled salt and pepper
Baking parchment
Generous 2 lb/1 kg mussels, cooked and removed from their shells
1 ¾ cups/200g pitted black olives
½ bunch of flat-leaf parsley, finely chopped

Fillet the sardines. Clean the peppers, zucchini and eggplant and cut into thin strips. Slice the onion and garlic finely and sweat in olive oil. Add salt and pepper and set aside on a plate.
Cut four 18 x 9 inch (50 x 25 centimeter) pieces of baking parchment and brush with olive oil. Divide the vegetables and mussels equally into four portions, placing them in the center of one half of each piece of parchment. Add 4 sardines (8 fillets) and a few olives to each portion. Sprinkle them with olive oil, scatter with parsley and season with salt and pepper. Fold the other half of the parchment over the top and fold the sides firmly together to fasten.
Place the packages in the center of an oven preheated to 390 °F/200 °C and bake until the parchment inflates. Serve immediately.

Baudroie poêlée
aux cèpes des Albères
Fried angler fish with cèpes

1 ¾ lbs/800 g cèpe mushrooms
2 tbsp oil
1 shallot, finely chopped
Freshly milled salt and pepper
1 tbsp chopped parsley
4 slices angler fish, about ¾ inch
(2 centimeters) thick
1 tbsp sunflower oil
3 ½ tbsp water
juice of ½ lemon
6 ½ tbsp/100 g butter
Chervil

Clean and slice the cèpes, and sweat in hot oil in a pan with the finely chopped shallot. Season with salt and pepper, sprinkle with chopped parsley and keep hot.
Preheat the oven to 355 °F/180 °C.
Rinse the fish slices in cold water and pat dry. Fry lightly on both sides in the sunflower oil. Then bake the fried slices of fish for another 6-8 minutes in the preheated oven until they are cooked.
Place the water and lemon juice in a saucepan with a little salt and bring to a boil. Add the butter and stir in well.
Reserve a few cèpes and divide the rest between each plate.
Lay one slice of fish on each, pour over a little butter sauce and finish by garnishing with chervil and the remaining cèpes.

Chapon rôti aux oignons, petit jus
aromatisé au chorizo
Roast ocean perch with onions in chorizo sauce

Generous 2 lbs/1 kg ocean perch
(or brown sea scorpion)
2 tbsp oil
6½ tbsp/100 g butter
Freshly milled pepper
¾ cup/200 ml veal stock
7 oz/200 g chorizo
4 large onions
Fat for frying
Basil leaves

Fillet the fish and cut into four portions. Lightly brown the fillets in oil in a skillet until golden, then bake for 10 minutes in a preheated oven at 355 °F/180 °C.
Soak the bones from the middle of the fish in cold water, then drain and sweat in 3 ½ tbsp/50 g butter. Add freshly milled pepper and deglaze the pan by pouring in the veal stock.
Cut 8 thin slices from the chorizo and set aside. Cut the remaining chorizo into small dice, reserve a few and add the rest to the sauce.
Let boil briefly, then pass through a sieve and add to the concentrated cooking juices in the skillet used to fry the fish. Add the remaining butter and combine.
Slice the onions into rings, fry quickly, then pile in the center of each plate and sprinkle on some chorizo sauce. Place the fillets on top of the onion rings to serve, and garnish each fillet with 2 slices of chorizo and some basil.

Pavé de congre aux supions, beurre
d'arêtes parfumé au vinaigre
Conger eel steak with tiny octopus in vinegar sauce

Vegetables: 1 eggplant, 2 zucchini, ½ red bell
pepper, ½ green bell pepper, 2 tomatoes, 1 onion
5 tbsp olive oil
freshly milled salt and pepper
Herbs of Provence (rosemary, thyme, savory and,
optionally, basil)
4 artichoke hearts, sliced
1¾ lb/800 g conger eel
7 oz/200 g small octopus, ready to cook

Sauce
1 cup/250 g butter
freshly milled pepper
1 ¼ cups/300 ml white wine
1 tbsp tomato paste
½ cup/100 g sugar
¾ cup/200 ml Banyuls vinegar

Cut the vegetables into small pieces and soften them in 2 tbsp olive oil. Season and add the herbs. Cover and cook gently for 20 minutes. Fry the artichoke hearts and keep hot. Debone the eel, roll it up and cut it into 4 slices. Seal in 2 tbsp oil, then bake in a preheated oven at 375 °F/190 °C for 15 minutes. Season the octopus and fry for 2 minutes in the remaining oil. For the sauce, soak the bones in cold water, then pour off and heat them with 3½ tbsp/50 g butter, pepper, white wine and tomato paste. Separately, caramelize the sugar and add the vinegar. Mix the fish butter with the caramel, pass through a sieve and combine with the remaining butter.

Delicately textured *anchois de Collioure* are a specialty and much in demand.

The anchovies are caught in 1300 foot (440 meter) long nets and processed immediately.

Unless they are to be pickled fresh with vinegar, they are simply kept in ice before preparation.

For the traditional *anchois de Collioure*, the fish are mixed with salt as soon as they have been caught.

Anchovies

Collioure is the most famous fishing harbour and resort of the Côte Vermeille and a stone's throw from the Spanish border. Its quayside is lined in summer with the easels of artists both amateur and professional, trying to capture on canvas or in watercolor the sheltered bay with the fortified church and the former summer residence of the kings of Majorca. Collioure seems to have lost nothing of its attraction since the days of the Phoenicians, Greeks and Romans. Quite the contrary: today tourism is its main livelihood. Only its famous anchovies and its wine, Banyuls, a naturally sweet red wine of considerable character, bear witness to a once flourishing economy.

Collioure was for centuries a significant trading port. As early as the Middle Ages, the salted fish produced here – anchovies, sardines, cod and tuna – had won a fine reputation. When Collioure came under French control following the 1659 Treaty of the Pyrénées, the king even relieved it of the burden of the salt tax, the *gabelle*. Whilst Collioure lost all its significance as a trading centre, the golden age of fishing began. The fishermen of Collioure set out to sea with a crew of six in their 30 foot (9 meter) sailing craft, called *catalanes* and cast the *sardinal*, a 1300 foot (400 meter) long net. Anchovies always constituted a large part of their catch. These narrow, elongated herring-type fish are numerous enough in all warm ocean waters, but those of the Mediterranean, especially off Collioure, are considered a particular delicacy. Salting the fish to preserve it was a trade handed down from generation to generation in this small harbor at the foot of the Pyrénées, and one at which many fishermen's wives found employment. At its economic peak, some 30 businesses were engaged in anchovy salting; of these, just four still survive. Of the once proud fishing fleet of 150 vessels,

only about half a dozen remain as a tourist sight. It is some 30 years since the fishermen last set sail from Collioure and headed for the open sea in their *catalanes*. Only Port-Vendres has still kept a small fleet of these old fishing boats.

The freshly caught anchovies are mixed with salt straightaway. They are then gutted, the heads removed, and the fish layered in barrels, each layer being generously scattered with coarse salt. Weighted down with large stones, they then need a period of three months to ripen and develop their pronounced and distinctive aroma. After this, the fish are carefully washed to remove the salt once more and are then graded by size and layered into jars which are finally filled up with brine. Preserved in this way, they will keep for more than a year. Anchovies can be removed from the jar for use in any number, as long as those remaining are left completely covered in brine.

Left: Port-Vendres is the biggest active fishing harbor of Roussillon, where the day's catch is offered for sale on weekdays from 5 p.m.

Buying and using anchovies

Anchois – anchovies
Whole fish preserved in brine, usually sold in jars. They need to be soaked in water for at least 1 hour before use, changing the water frequently, to remove the salt. They are then halved lengthwise, the bones removed, patted well dry and sprinkled with olive oil. A *persillade* of finely chopped parsley and garlic is scattered on top and they are served with hard-cooked eggs.

Filets d'anchois – anchovy fillets
Usually preserved in oil in small jars, these are used as a flavoring ingredient in salads and pizzas.

Crème d'anchois – anchovy paste
A paste made of pieces of anchovy fillet mixed with oil, this is used as flavoring for grilled dishes or as a spread for use on bread or toast. *Anchois de Collioure* give any dish a pronounced Mediterranean flavor.

After salting, the anchovies are gutted and the heads removed, and the fish are layered in barrels.

Coarse salt is scattered between each layer. The anchovies take another three months to mature.

The anchovies are finally marketed as a semi-preserve in jars.

Petit gris, the small gray southern European snail, is largely replacing the Burgundian variety, which has become rare.

The Cargolade

Snails roasted in their shells are regarded as a particular delicacy in many parts of France.

The accomplished masters in the consumption of snails are not the people of Burgundy as one might think, but the Catalans of Roussillon. They hold festive gatherings *en famille* or with friends at certain well-loved barbecue spots to enjoy a *cargolade* together. These gatherings were once celebratory open air meals at Easter or Whitsun, but more recently, any sunny day with not too much wind has become occasion enough. The *cargolade*, whose name comes from *cargol*, the Catalan word for snail, is a sociable occasion at which everyone lends a hand. Quite unlike the elaborate restaurant preparation involved in *escargots à la bourguignonne*, the Catalan procedure is very different: snail enthusiasts in the southernmost province of France hunt out these desirable delicacies themselves. The slightest shower of rain sends them out foraging, armed with plastic bags to carry home their booty. The main places to search are the edges of vineyards and roadside ditches. Large numbers

of *petits gris*, the "little gray ones," as the southern European edible snails are called, tempted out of their shells by the damp, fall victim to the search. Some farming of these snails has now been established, and the cultivated ones do well. The *petits gris* can be recognized by their fairly pointed shells, as opposed to the ones with flatter shells, which are called simply *cargol*, and generally passed over as being less well-flavored. The snails which are caught are made to undergo a radical fast for the following two weeks to cleanse them of any poisonous leaves they may have eaten. If they are kept beyond that, the Catalans feed them a diet of flour, thyme and fennel, which gives the snails a particularly rich flavor. People who do not have the opportunity to go snail-hunting themselves can buy them packed in nets in the weekly markets of the Roussillon plain.

The first stage in preparing the snails is to clean the shells thoroughly, using a sharp knife –

Snail varieties

Escargot de Bourgogne – the Burgundy snail
The central European edible snail has a shell with 1–1½ inches (3–4 centimeters) diameter. These snails are normally preboiled and sold frozen or canned.

Petit gris – common snail
The southern European edible snail has a shell measuring ¾ to 1 inch or so (2–3 centimeters). Various closely related species are found distributed across the region as far as Anatolia, and it is also cultivated. Live snails can be bought in French markets; otherwise they are available in cans.

Escargot achatine – giant African snail
Originally from East Africa, this snail is widespread in Asia, where it is also cultivated. The giant snails weigh up to one pound and are mainly imported from China.
They are increasingly used as a substitute for the Burgundy snail, their flesh being used to fill the shells and sold simply under the name of *escargot*.

The snails produce a seal to prevent themselves from drying out. This layer is removed with a knife.

The snails are seasoned by dipping in a mixture of salt, pepper and thyme.

The cleaned, seasoned snails are placed close together on a special grid with a handle in the middle.

The grid is placed on the glowing embers so that the snails cook in their shells, without any pre-cooking.

The color of the liquid coming out shows how nearly cooked they are. The shell is held in a piece of bread, and the flesh removed with a pin.

Escargots

At the beginning of the 19th century, Antonin Carême (1783-1833), the true founder of fine French cuisine, ensured that *escargots* received due gastronomic honor, served *à la bourguignonne* with butter, garlic and parsley. The cooked and garnished mollusks became so popular that special plates with hollows were made for serving them, and special tongs designed to hold the hot shells while a two-pronged fork was used to pick out the snail. Before they reach this point, however, the snails must pass through many stages of preparation.

Snails have to be subjected to a fast of at least ten days before they can be consumed. They are repeatedly washed, both for reasons of hygiene and to make them palatable. Then they are blanched, cooled, removed from their shells and normally boiled in stock. The shells are meanwhile sterilized, and the cooled snails packed back into the shells. With the addition of herb butter they are ready for the oven.

We can trace the consumption of snails back to our ancient ancestors; we can tell this from looking at prehistoric refuse heaps. The Greeks studied the pseudopods in detail, and the insatiable Romans invented snail culture. They grilled the delicacies in their shells, much as the Catalan and Provençal people do today, without precooking them. In the rest of France (until Carême, at least),

the upper classes were only too content to leave snails to the poorer folk, at most eating them only during set fasts when other foods were forbidden. Since Carême's time, the French have taken their love of snails to extremes. The large Burgundy snail, whose shell reaches a diameter of up to 1½ inches (4 centimeters), has become a victim of gourmets (and of modern agricultural methods), and is now quite rare. Instead, chefs are turning to the *petit gris*, a smaller variety with a spattering of white or yellow markings on its shell. These snails are found in Gascony, Provence, Languedoc and Roussillon. Unlike their larger relatives, they are also suitable for cultivation, *héliculture*. The quantities needed for preserves are provided by Eastern European imports and snails from Turkey; these can be recognized by their darker color and the black edge to the shell. Also, the giant African snail is imported frozen from China; these are at least half a pound in weight.

Opinel or Laguiole are the commonest to remove the seal which the snails form to prevent themselves from drying out. Any secretions are removed too, and dead snails discarded. The snails are then dipped in a mixture of salt and pepper, and sometimes thyme and cayenne pepper. They are arranged on a grid, traditionally a circular one, rather like a cake rack with a handle in the middle.

A fire is made of a bundle of vine twigs, collected as a by-product of the local grape harvest. These produce an even, long-lasting glow. As the snails cook over the fire, they produce a frothy liquid which is at first white, but then begins to color, becoming yellow and then a dark chestnut hue, the sign which tells the experienced snail cook that the meal is ready. Traditionalists put a piece of bacon to melt and drip over the softly sizzling snails so that a little bacon fat runs into each shell. The cooked snails are extracted from their shells with a pin. Slices of bread spread with *aioli*, the piquant garlic mayonnaise, are popularly eaten as an accompaniment. Some experienced Catalan consumers are capable of eating dozens of such snails, but these are nevertheless no more than the appetizer in a full-scale traditional *cargolade*.

Next come pork sausages, black pudding and lamb chops, barbecued over vine twigs. During the meal, the *porró*, a carafe with a pointed spout, constantly circulates and is repeatedly refilled with red wine. They drink *à la regalada*, as freely

as they wish, pouring the wine into their mouths from as great a distance as possible. Practiced drinkers aim the wine into the corner of their mouths, so that it runs in sideways and is easier to swallow.

A *cargolade* worthy of the name includes not only snails but lamb chops and sausages, and a fire of vine twigs.

Wild boar

The mountainous hinterland of the Midi with its extensive Mediterranean forests and the *garrigue* – a wild moorland of heather, rosemary, lavender and other herbs and bushes – is a terrain where wild boar abound.

For some time the boar have had no natural predators, other than huntsmen. In the villages of Languedoc and Roussillon as well as those of Provence, the Cévennes and Ardèche, hunting is the favorite pastime of menfolk in every walk of life. Winegrowers and others with an agricultural background, manual and white collar workers, all share this passion. They hunt on Saturdays and Sundays, and on Wednesdays too, if they can, in a hunting season lasting from September to the middle of January.

The local methods of hunting used involve driving the game towards marksmen using hounds. If a few knowledgeable huntsmen have spotted wild boar, the pack of hounds will be taken up behind the animals and released. They try to drive the boar in such a way that they have to

In the foothills of Canigou, wild boar have adapted extremely well to life in the large free-running enclosure.

cross a clearing or path where huntsmen are posted so as to get a clear shot. The spoil is divided out after the hunt.

Among wild boar, the tuskers usually go their own ways. The packs are made up of matriarchal family units consisting of a sow, younger female offspring and young up to one year old. It is the oldest sow which rules over the family unit. The

sows only separate from the pack when they are in heat. In a year of particular plenty, wild boar produce an unusually large number of young. A fully grown sow normally gives birth to five young, but a strong mother sow can produce up to eleven in the same birth. The main mating period is in November and December, but sows are capable of coming into heat twice in a year. The young in their first year can be recognized by the yellow lengthwise stripes on their bodies. The skin ('rind skin', as it is called in pigs) is covered with short bristles. Its color ranges from ocher to red-brown. The young lose their stripes at five to six months old. In the Mediterranean, wild boar usually have silver gray bristles all year round. In the southern forests they live on acorns, sweet chestnuts, roots and a variety of creatures they find in the ground.

The flesh of wild boar killed in the hunt has a stronger flavor than that of farmed animals, partially as a result of their natural food, and partially because of the stress they are subjected to during the hunt. Occasionally a live youngster will fall into the hands of a huntsman, and not a few hunting farmers have fancied the idea of raising such an animal.

Excellent *charcuterie* such as (left to right) pâté, blood sausage and salami can be prepared from wild boar. Here an air-dried pork ham is also shown.

Farmhouse omelets

The succulent classic omelet of French cuisine is a popular dish served at farms which cater for guests.

Where else can such fresh, delicious eggs be found, producing lightly cooked omelets of a truly golden color? Moreover, flavored – as here – with truffles gathered by hand in the neighboring oak forests, they spell satisfaction for even the most demanding guest.

That was what happened to the Vargas brothers in Roussillon, whose farm is situated in the hills of Aspres to the east of Canigou, an area known for its cork oaks and the large numbers of wild boar that live there. They raised a young tusker, which adapted excellently to its new, more circumscribed surroundings. As a result the brothers bought two young sows as well, enclosed a couple of acres of land and released the trio in it. They soon had a quite respectable pack of wild boar. Ever business-conscious, the family next had the idea of establishing a *ferme-auberge* on their farm, and serving the guests various wild boar recipes. They are able to offer wild roast suckling pig and ragoût of wild boar all year round, unlike restaurants, where game is only on the menu in season. They also turn the meat into pâtés, brawn and sausage, served as appetizers.

Their pack of boar at present numbers a large tusker, eight sows and about 20 young of various ages. The boar have have 42 acres (17 hectares) of enclosed forest at their disposal, and have thoroughly grubbed up the land. Acorns and chestnuts are insufficient to feed the animals, and so they are fed extra raw vegetables and fruit, which Floréal Vargas buys from the nearby wholesale market, and some grain. It matters to him that his cultivated boar should be pure-bred, which he has checked many times with the help of blood tests.

When domestic pigs were still kept in the open on farms some decades ago, a pig might sometimes escape and disappear among the local population of wild boar. Today's descendants with their lean bodies and long snouts may look just like wild boar, but it is quite possible for one to have an extra chromosome in addition to the 36 of a pure wild boar, the extra one having been inherited from some distant ancestor which, as a domestic pig, had 38.

Left: In the kitchen, young animals up to the age of 16 months are referred to by the term *marcassin*; their flesh is still tender and makes a fine roast.

Civet de sanglier
Ragoût of wild boar

1¾ lb/800 g wild boar
Freshly milled salt and pepper
2 cups/500 ml red wine
2 onions
8 cloves of garlic
2 carrots
2 sprigs of thyme
2 bay leaves
2 tbsp pork drippings
4 tsp Cognac
3½ tbsp/50 g butter
2 tbsp flour

Cut the meat into pieces and season with salt and pepper.

Place in a bowl and pour the red wine over it.

Peel and quarter the onions, peel the garlic and clean and cut up the carrots. Add all these to the meat with the herbs, cover and leave the meat to marinate for at least 24 hours.

Lift the meat out of the marinade and pat dry.

Heat the drippings in a skillet, and brown the meat on all sides. Remove with a ladle and transfer to a large, heavy pot.

Pour on the Cognac and flambé.

Strain the marinade onto the meat and braise on a low heat until tender. (For a young animal, this will take about 1–1½ hours. Meat from an older animal may take 2½ hours.)

Before serving, melt the butter, sprinkle on the flour and make a white roux. Stir in a little of the marinade liquid, then add the mixture to the pot and stir in well, allowing to simmer for a few minutes.

Transfer the meat to a suitable dish and pour on the sauce.

Serve with baked or boiled potatoes or white beans.

Civet de sanglier – ragoût of wild boar – is a dish to dream of for those throughout France who love robust food. In the Midi it is traditionally served with white beans, *monjetes*.

Catalan cuisine

Catalan cuisine was the subject of one of the earliest known cookbooks in the world, the Sent Sovi cookbook, written in the 12th century. In the Middle Ages, Catalonia resembled one huge cooking cauldron in which a vast variety of ingredients were mixed: Latin, Arab, Gallic and Germanic influences as well as that of Spain under the Moors all came together. Catalan seafaring flourished, and foreign spices gave local specialities an exotic flair, at least at court. A taste for combinations of the sweet and the savory was already becoming marked at that time and continues to this day; for example, dried fruit, other fruit and even semisweet chocolate are used to delicious effect with poultry, lamb and game.

The charm of Catalan cuisine to the present day lies in the rich variety of ingredients and the uninhibited manner in which they are used, so often creating the association of *mer et montagne*, the Mediterranean and the mountains, illustrated in the recipe given below for spiny lobster and chicken wings.

Supions aux artichauts, vinaigrette à l'orange et crème aux noix
Small octopus with artichokes and savory walnut cream

Vinaigrette

⅔ cup/150 ml oil
Grated zest of 1 unwaxed lemon
Grated zest of 1 unwaxed orange
3½ tbsp Banyuls wine
Freshly milled salt and pepper

Walnut cream

3½ tbsp ground walnuts
3½ oz/100 g fresh goat cheese
1 tbsp wine vinegar
2 tbsp Banyuls wine
2 cloves of garlic, sweated in a little oil
Freshly milled salt and pepper

Octopus

4 purple artichokes from Provence
Mixture of water, flour and lemon juice for poaching
14 oz/400 g small octopus
Olive oil

The day before, heat the oil for the vinaigrette, add the orange and lemon zest and leave to infuse overnight.
Reduce the Banyuls wine to half its volume and add to the flavored oil to make a vinaigrette. Season with salt and pepper.
To make the savory walnut cream, purée together all the ingredients with a hand blender. Chill.
Remove the stalks and leaves from the artichoke and scrape out the choke with a spoon. Poach the hearts gently in a mixture of water, flour and lemon juice for about 15 minutes.
Clean the octopus, rinse in cold water, pat dry and fry briefly in hot olive oil.
Arrange the octopus in the center of four warmed plates to serve. Cut each artichoke heart evenly into slices and arrange in a rosette around the octopus. Sprinkle with a little vinaigrette. Encircle with walnut cream.

Poivrons rouges rôtis et anchois de Collioure
Baked red bell peppers with anchovies

4 red bell peppers
Olive oil
1 oak leaf lettuce
1 orange
7 oz/200 g anchovies (minimum salt)

Preheat the oven to 390 °F/200 °C. Brush the bell peppers with a little olive oil and place in an ovenproof baking dish. Bake, turning occasionally, until the skin begins to blister and brown. Then remove from the oven and peel off the skin. Halve the bell peppers and cut into approximately ½ inch (1 centimeter) strips. Lay the strips in olive oil while still warm and marinate for at least 3 hours.
Wash the lettuce and spin dry. Peel the orange and cut into thin segments.
Arrange the strips of red bell pepper and the anchovies on the plates in a rosette. Garnish the center of each plate with lettuce leaves and orange segments.

Ailes de poulet, langouste au citron et au gingembre
Chicken wings and spiny lobster with lemon and ginger

1 cup/250 ml oil
1 vanilla bean
1 spiny lobster, about generous 2 lbs/1 kg
Selection of soup vegetables (celery, carrot, leek, onion)
½ clove of garlic
1 cup/250 ml white wine
4¼ cups/1 liter water
1 tbsp chopped ginger
Grated zest of ½ unwaxed lemon
8 chicken wings
½ lb/250 g new potatoes
⅓ cup/80 g butter

Heat the oil slightly. Halve and scrape out the seeds from the vanilla bean and infuse in the oil overnight.
Cook the lobster for about 12 minutes in a pressure cooker, then remove the head and set aside. Extract the meat from inside the tail and chill.
Heat a little oil in a large, heavy pot and briefly cook the diced soup vegetables and garlic.
Break the lobster, in its shell, into sections, add to the pot and fry briefly. Pour on the white wine, and cook a little before adding the water, ginger and lemon zest. Boil gently for about 2 hours, until the liquid has reduced to just under ½ cup/ 100 ml. Sieve, pour into a sauce container and keep hot. Meanwhile wash the chicken wings, removing the lower section to use for other purposes.
Peel and dice the potatoes, season with salt and

Left: *Supions aux artichauts, vinaigrette à l'orange et crème aux noix* (small octopus with artichokes and savory walnut cream) – Center: *Poivrons rouges rôtis et anchois de Collioure* (baked red bell peppers with anchovies) – Right: *Ailes de poulet, langouste au citron et au gingembre* (chicken wings and spiny lobster)

Pintade à la catalane (guinea fowl in the Catalan style)

pepper. Heat the vanilla oil and fry the potato dice until crisp.

Fry the chicken wings evenly on all sides in the vanilla oil.

Cut the lobster meat into 16 slices and heat in a pan containing enough butter to coat the bottom. Stir the remaining butter piece by piece into the lobster sauce.

Arrange the potato dice in the center of each plate, surrounded by the chicken wings and the slices of lobster. Lastly, pour the sauce over and around the meat.

In the restaurant "Les Feuillants" in Céret, this dish is often served garnished with sea cucumber, a marine creature of the echinoderm family, as shown in the photograph.

Pintade à la catalane
Guinea fowl in the Catalan style

1 guinea fowl, ready-prepared
8 thin slices smoked fatty bacon
30 cloves of garlic
3 unwaxed lemons
Scant ½ cup/100 ml Rancio wine (or dry Banyuls)
¾ cup/200 ml veal stock
Freshly milled salt and pepper

Wrap the guinea fowl in the bacon and brown all over in a heavy, lidded pot suitable for braising. Add a little water, cover and braise until tender. Meanwhile, peel and halve the garlic, removing the green embryo. Blanch for 1 minute in boiling water and drain.

Peel the lemons, cut two of them into quarters and slice the third. Blanch all three lemons for 1 minute and drain.

When the fowl is tender, remove from the pot and set aside. Deglaze the pot with the wine. Halve the fowl and lift the meat off the carcass. Break the carcass into pieces, adding these to the liquid in the pot. Pour on the veal stock and boil gently for 10 minutes, then pass through a fine sieve. Add the garlic and lemons to the sauce, heat through and season. Cut the guinea fowl into pieces, place in the sauce and continue to heat for 10 minutes.

Serve immediately.

Steamed potatoes or rice make a suitable accompaniment.

Touron

This rich candy has Oriental origins and was brought to Spain by the Moors, whose doctors prescribed it to build up a patient's strength. Its main ingredients, almonds, hazelnuts and honey, were abundant in the area around Alicante and Xixona. Following liberation from Moorish rule, these cities became part of the kingdom of Aragon, and developed into centers of *touron* production, which was made at Christmas and when the great cattle markets were held. Soon *touron* advanced into Barcelona and northern Aragon, whose power extended in the Middle Ages to encompass Roussillon as far as Montpellier and into Provence. At first, *touron* was made at home, but confectioners soon came to specialize in its production and founded craftsmen's guilds. Although a *touron* factory opened its doors as early as 1840 in Perpignan, this specialty did not achieve widespread popularity until Laurent Oriol Ramona arrived on the scene. He was a peripatetic salesman, and founded a shop selling his own homemade *touron* in the capital of Roussillon in 1874. From 1919 he sold them under the trademark L.O.R., the same trademark with which Confiserie du Tech leads the market to this day.

Various types of *touron* are produced in Roussillon, and these fall into two groups. The first is based on marzipan, contains neither honey nor almonds nor hazelnuts, either whole or chopped. This group includes Touron Masapan or Massapà, Touron Toledo and *pannelet*. The second group includes Touron Alicante as well as Xixona and Perpignan. They are closely related to white nougat, and their quality depends above all on the quantity and composition of the honey. The larger manufacturers do not use any honey at all on grounds of cost, using only sugar and glucose. Otherwise, the main difference between the types mentioned is their consistency, which depends on the temperature to which the honey-sugar mixture is heated. Alicante, which is quite hard, is heated highest. Xixona, which is not allowed to exceed 293 °F (145 °C), is softer. The touron with the softest texture is Perpignan, where the maximum temperature is 251 °F (122 °C).

If a traditional *touron* consisting of a great deal of honey and egg white is made for Christmas, the cooler, dry climatic conditions of Roussillon help it to keep for several weeks. For finest quality *touron* three parts of roast almonds, hazelnuts, pine nuts and candied fruits are used, with two parts of honey, just under one part of glucose and one part of sugar.

The temperature of the honey and sugar mixture is important, as it determines the consistency of the finished *touron*.

The egg white is stirred into the honey and sugar until the mixture becomes evenly white in color.

Chopped almonds, hazelnuts, pine nuts and candied fruits are added once the mixture has cooled.

The mixture is stirred, then divided into portions and rolled out. Rice paper is laid on the upper and lower surfaces (below).

Black *touron* is not quite what its name suggests, because it is a caramel, containing hazelnuts and colored sugar nuggets.

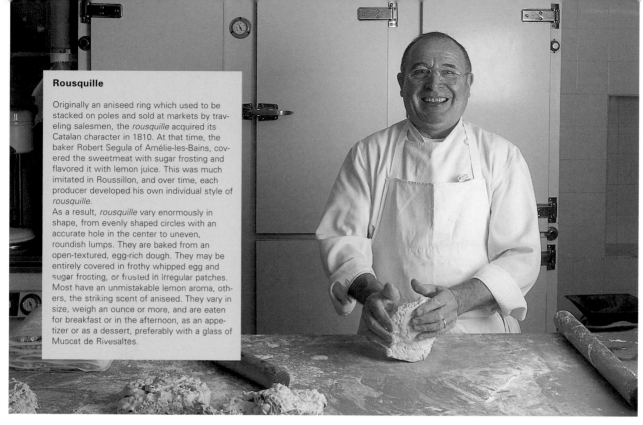

Rousquille

Originally an aniseed ring which used to be stacked on poles and sold at markets by traveling salesmen, the *rousquille* acquired its Catalan character in 1810. At that time, the baker Robert Segula of Amélie-les-Bains, covered the sweetmeat with sugar frosting and flavored it with lemon juice. This was much imitated in Roussillon, and over time, each producer developed his own individual style of *rousquille*.

As a result, *rousquille* vary enormously in shape, from evenly shaped circles with an accurate hole in the center to uneven, roundish lumps. They are baked from an open-textured, egg-rich dough. They may be entirely covered in frothy whipped egg and sugar frosting, or frosted in irregular patches. Most have an unmistakable lemon aroma, others, the striking scent of aniseed. They vary in size, weigh an ounce or more, and are eaten for breakfast or in the afternoon, as an appetizer or as a dessert, preferably with a glass of Muscat de Rivesaltes.

In Perpignan, the *pâtissier* Marcel Begrem prepares slabs of his inimitable *touron*, flavored with various honeys, nuts, candied fruits, herbs and spices.

Types of Touron

Touron Masapan or Massapà
For this variation on marzipan, almonds, and in some cases hazelnuts too, according to the recipe, are ground very finely and mixed with a sugar-glucose syrup which has been heated to no more than 230 °F (110 °C). This type of *touron* is often sold in the form of brightly colored, rectangular sticks or bars, or decorated with candied fruits.

Touron Toledo
Touron Toledo is a roll of marzipan usually weighing a little over 5 ounces (150 grams), containing a mixture of candied fruits and as a finishing touch, rolled in lightly roasted pine nuts.

Pannelet
Pannelet is a walnut-sized ball of flavored marzipan coated in pine nuts. *Pannelets* are usually sold by weight.

Touron Alicante
This hard version of *touron* should consist of equal parts of sugar and honey, mixed with egg white. Peeled, roasted almonds are worked into the white *touron* mixture before it is spread between sheets of rice paper. Touron Alicante is sold as slabs.

Touron Xixona or Jijona
This type of *touron* is likewise made of equal quantities of honey and sugar with egg white and almonds, but the ingredients are finely ground and the mixture is stirred as it is heated to a less high temperature. It has an even texture and an appetizing light brown color, and comes in slab form.

Touron de Perpignan or Catalan
Soft, white *touron* with a high honey content, containing a mixture of almonds, hazelnuts, pine nuts and pieces of candied fruit, enclosed in two sheets of rice paper. It is sold as a slab or triangle, or by weight.

Touron noir
A clear, dark caramel made of sugar and glucose, containing whole, peeled, roasted hazelnuts and colored sugar nuggets. It is sold in slab form or in pieces by weight.

Coffee and nuts

Candied cherries and pistachios

Candied oranges

Candied oranges and apricots

Thyme and candied fruits

Aniseed and candied fruits

Lavender and candied fruits

Cinnamon and prunes

Vanilla and figs

The sweet legacy of the Knights Templar

Vins Doux Naturels

The birth of the *vin doux naturel* came in 1285 when the Knight Templar, doctor of medicine and scholar Arnaldus of Villanova, later to become rector of the university of Montpellier, succeeded in distilling alcohol from wine according to an Arab recipe. As Arnaldus experimented with the alcohol, grape spirit, he discovered that he could use it to interrupt the fermentation process, preserve some of the natural sugar of the wine and prevent it from turning to vinegar. This method, the so-called *mutage* (silencing) enabled him to achieve impressive success for these long-lived, naturally sweet wines in the Middle Ages and far beyond.

The *vins doux naturels* received their *Appellation d'Origine Contrôlée* status as long ago as 1936. The *Appellation* lays down the exact vineyard location, the grape varieties, vinification and minimum maturation for each. Since that time the driest and hottest slopes and terraces of Roussillon, which have 2600 hours of sunshine per year, have been reserved for their cultivation. The grapes have to reach a specified minimum sugar concentration before they are allowed to be har-

vested. The minimum for these is set at 252 grams per liter, equivalent to a "potential alcohol" of 14.4 percent. Sunshine alone is not enough to enable the grapes to ripen to this degree; a maximum yield of 30 hectoliters per hectare (approximate equivalent 1.7 tons/acre) is also laid down. Once fermentation has begun, the winegrower or winemaker keeps a precise watch on the fermentation process of transforming sugar into alcohol, and selects the moment when he will add the grape spirit to the fermenting must. In this way, he decides the character of his wine. The earlier the *mutage*, the higher the residual sugar content will be, and the longer he waits, the drier the wine will become. It is not permitted for the residual sugar content to be below 50 grams per liter (5 percent), or above 125 grams per liter (15 percent).

Roussillon produces 90 percent of France's *vins doux naturels*. Of the four main grape varieties permitted for this wine, Muscat, Macabeu, Malvoisie and Grenache, the Grenache Noir from the last category occupies a special place. This traditional variety, which originates from the Iberian peninsula and also lends character to southern European red wines (think of Châteauneuf-du-Pape) produces the best quality Banyuls, Maury and Rivesaltes. This is founded, apart from a fine-quality harvest, on the special method of *mutage sur les grains* or *sur marc*, in which the grape spirit is added not to the must but to the partly fermented grapes, which are then macerated for anything from several days to four weeks. During this period, the increased alcohol content releases coloring and

Right-hand page: At Mas Amiel, the first stage in the maturation of Maury wines in carboys occurs in the open air, the containers exposed to heat and cold alike for a year.

aromatic substances as well as tannins from the grape skins, before pressing takes place and some of the alcohol is lost.

Traditional Banyuls, Maury and Rivesaltes are aged in large wooden vats, in which they are deliberately allowed to undergo some oxidation. To speed up the development of the aromas, the wines can be exposed to the large variations in temperature between day and night, summer and winter in 600-liter *demi-muids*, wooden vats able to hold the equivalent of 158½ gallons, or even in carboys in the open air. The bouquet and flavor of the wine in the first stage of maturation resembles stewed fruit and fresh figs and also peaches and candied cherries. Then comes a stage in which dried fruits such as prunes, raisins, figs and apricots predominate. From about the seventh year, roasted aromas such as biscuit, roasted nuts and caramel too emerge. Then follow the aromas of cocoa, coffee and, later on, tobacco, until after 15 to 20 years *rancio* notes develop. These can also be found in very old Cognacs, old dry sherries and *vins jaunes* from the Jura. They are characterized by the aroma of green walnut shells, which appear in combination with other nut aromas and roasted notes.

Since 1975 a new type has been in existence, and has become established above all in Banyuls and Maury. This is the *vintage*, often called *rimage* in Banyuls. For this, the wines are bottled early, giving them a very thick, succulent quality. Their color at that point is often inky red. The intense aroma is mainly characterized by fresh and ripe notes of cherry and of berries, and the sweetness of the grape sugar conceals the mostly very pronounced tannins. In the bottle, laid down in the cellar, they age like great red wines, and their sweetness becomes ever more subtle.

Appellations

Banyuls and Banyuls Grand Cru
Almost 3000 acres in the coastal regions of Collioure, Port-Vendres, Banyuls and Cerbère. Slato soils predominate. A minimum of 50 percent Grenache Noir, for *Grand Cru* 75 percent, plus Grenache Blanc or Gris, Macabeu, Malvoisie and Muscat varieties, and 10 percent of other varieties. Production around 3.5 million bottles. Maturation: 1 year for Banyuls, 30 months for Grand Cru. There is also a small quantity of Banyuls Blanc.

Maury
Approximately 1700 hectares (4200 acres), extending from Maury itself into the area belonging to the communes of Saint-Paul de Fenouillet, Lesquerde, Tautavel and Rasiguères. Predominantly slate soils. Minimum 70 percent Grenache Noir, plus the other VDN (vin doux naturel) varieties and 10 percent additional red grape varieties. Production approximately 4.6 million bottles. Maturation: minimum 1 year.

Rivesaltes
Approximately 7000 hectares (17,290 acres), scattered over 86 communes of the Pyrénées Orientales and nine of the Aude region, currently being reduced. Great variation in soil character, but dry and hot in low-lying, very sunny locations. Grenaches Noir, Gris and Blanc, plus Macabeu and a little Malvoisie, and 10 percent other varieties. Yield: maximum of 30 hecto

liters/hectare (approximate equivalent 1.7 tons/acre). Production: about 17 million bottles. Maturation according to category: Vintage – 12 months, of which three in the bottle; Ambré – only white varieties, minimum 24 months; Tuilé – mainly red grapes, minimum 24 months; Hors d'âge – Rivesaltes ambré or tuilé, aged beyond five years.

Muscat de Rivesaltes
Approximately 5700 hectares (14,079 acres) in 90 communes in the Pyrénées Orientales and nine in the Aude. Great variation in soil character, but lime-rich soils especially suited. Exclusively the varieties Muscat à Petits Grains and Muscat d'Alexandrie. Minimum of 100 grams (10 percent) residual sugar content. Production: around 20 million bottles. Bottled early. Since 1997 there has been a Muscat de Noël, bottled specially for the festive season.

Muscats und Rasteau
The other *vins doux naturels* are mainly found in Languedoc, where Muscat de Frontignan, Muscat de Lunel, Muscat de Mireval and Muscat de Saint-Jean de Minervois are produced on a total of 1500 hectares (3703 acres). In the Vaucluse, Muscat de Beaumes de Venise is grown on 450 hectares (1112 acres) and Rasteau, produced from Grenache varieties, on 50 hectares (124 acres).

The *porró* is the traditional drinking vessel of the Catalans. The wine is poured into the mouth from the greatest possible distance.

Quéribus, the castle of the Cathars, stands above the slopes of Maury with their rows of Grenache Noir.

White varieties too can be used to produce *vins doux naturels*, using white varieties alone or in a mixture with Grenache Noir; they age magnificently. After ten years or more they often develop aromas of dried apricots and orange peel and a note of pine resin. When young, the sweet wines from Macabeu and Grenache Blanc tend to remain reticent. They are exceeded by Muscat de Rivesaltes in both popularity and quality. This wine, which, being white, is vinified at low temperature, bears the delicate but intense aroma of the Muscat grape. In Roussillon it can exhibit very fresh aromas of lemon or peach and sometimes notes of gorse, fennel and aniseed. It is delicious with Roquefort, but is more often served well chilled as an aperitive, or alternatively with a dessert. A young Muscat should always have a very pale color.

Banyuls, Maury and Rivesaltes too are pleasant apéritifs cooled to 53–59 °F (12–15 °C), and do not detract from subsequent wines, despite their intense aroma. They accompany *foie gras* and duck prepared with fruit; they also go well with goat's milk and blue-veined cheeses. At dessert, they are served with cakes, and have a unique ability to complement chocolate desserts which overwhelm other wines. Young Vintages or dry Banyuls succeed especially well here. If they have developed ripe aromas, the choice of the connoisseur is to drink them after dinner as a *digestif*, marveling at their incomparable complexity.

Categories

Blanc: Mainly from Grenache Blanc, Macabeu and very occasionally from the rare Malvoisie. Pale in color, with aromas of gorse, fennel and aniseed, and later acquiring notes of honey. Primarily in the form of Rivesaltes, especially from the villages of the Aude, but also Banyuls Blanc. Accompanies liver pâtés or marinated fish.

Rosé: Obtained, as with dry rosé, by the *saignée* method which uses the juice run-off from Grenache Noir or Grenache Gris, drawn off from the must at an early stage. Pale in color with light, fruity aromas; served very cold as an apéritif or with sorbet.

Ambré: A type of Rivesaltes made from white grape varieties and aged for only a few years, this initially develops a rich golden color, in which case it is also called Doré. It is usually drunk at a later stage, however, by which time it has an amber color and aromas of nuts, candied orange peel, dried fruit and honey. Best to accompany desserts.

Rubis: Describes a young, ruby-colored or garnet-red *vin doux naturel* (VDN), usually made from Grenache Noir. Bouquet and flavor characterized by cherry as well as berry notes. Slightly chilled, it makes a pleasant apéritif. It also goes with melon and with desserts made of red fruits.

Tuilé: VDNs mainly based on red grapes, allowed to develop oxidatively for a few years, have a brick red color.

3, 6, 8, 10, 15 ans d'age: Declarations of age give the minimum age of the wine. It will often have been improved by blending with older wines.

Hors d'age: This denotes older wines. It is not defined for Banyuls or Maury, but for Rivesaltes it guarantees a minimum age of five years. Oxidative development gives the wines not only aromas of dried fruit but also marked roasted notes.

Rancio: Describes a particular aroma which emerges after long oxidative development and is reminiscent above all of green walnuts. It is a mark of particularly fine old VDNs.

Vintage: Also called Rimage (a Catalan word for the age of the grapes), this is a style of wine developed after the pattern of port, for which the vintage is bottled early.

Rimage Mise Tardive: Vintage wines which are allowed to age and develop in wooden barrels, usually *barriques*, for a few months before bottling, and have a more mature bouquet than Vintages.

Sec, Demi-sec, Demi-doux, Doux: These terms which designate the sweetness or dryness of Banyuls indicate how and when it should be served. Dry Banyuls, with a sugar content around 60 grams (6 percent), but greater alcohol content, is suitable to serve as an apéritif, with *hors d'oeuvre* and postprandially. *Demi-sec*, still more *demi-doux* and *doux*, accompany desserts, and the latter goes excellently with cheese.

From excess to finesse

The wines of Languedoc

Only very recently has the stretch of land between the Rhône and Narbonne had any success in shaking off the bad reputation which it earned through the production of bulk wines. Yet its poor soils and its dry and sun-drenched *terroirs* offer excellent conditions for viticulture. The first vines were planted there by the Phoenicians, and in their footsteps came the Romans. They founded the province of Gallia Narbonensis. Its wines enjoyed a good reputation even in Rome itself, and were exported to territories as far off as Germania. With the fall of the Roman empire, viticulture ceased to have significance outside local boundaries. It was pursued by the many monasteries being founded from the 9th century onward, but in the Middle Ages wine was used only for local consumption within the region. It was not until the end of the 17th century that there was a marked revival of winegrowing in Languedoc, when the infrastructure improved following the building of the harbor at Sète, the Canal du Midi and a number of long-distance roads. There was great demand at that time for

eau-de-vie to strengthen and extend the life of wines. The result was a change to distillation of large portions of the wine produced. While on the one hand robust, high-yield vines such as Aramon and Carignan were planted on the plains, the winegrowers in villages situated at higher elevations with their stony slopes opted for Grenache or Mourvèdre in order to achieve better quality. The renown of individual communes and locations dates from this time.

The rapid advance of industrialization in the cities of northern France during the 19th century brought a decisive change in the market. It created a new social class and new habits of consumption. Wine acquired its established place in the workers' hard daily routine as a source of sustenance and enjoyment. The increasing network of railroads ensured the supply. The business became so lucrative that in the Midi, expanses of vineyard supplanted all other forms of cultivation. The Languedoc with over 460,000 hectares (1,136,700 acres) became the largest winegrowing region in the world. The fate of the better growths was sealed. Instead of being sold on their own merits, stronger, more deeply colored qualities of wine were simply used to ameliorate thin brews and were marketed as medicinal wines. Despite repeated crises, the phylloxera catastro-

These pebbles belong to one of the 12 special *terroirs* of the Coteaux du Languedoc, La Méjanelle, which lies on the northeastern outskirts of Montpellier.

A Mourvèdre vine stands before the Falaise de l'Hortus. This area is currently the most sought-after *terroir* of the Coteaux du Languedoc.

phe, World Wars I and II, the winegrowers of Languedoc continued to opt for quantity. It took the drastic consequences of overproduction to bring understanding, late, but fortunately not too late. As a result, restructuring began to take place in 1970, and in the process hill locations such as Faugères and Saint-Chinian regained their esteem, more aromatic varieties were planted and 100,000 hectares (247,110 acres) of bulk vines were decommissioned. It took until 1985 for the Coteaux du Languedoc, Corbières and Minervois to achieve the acknowledgement of an *Appellation d'Origine Contrôlée*. Since then, great shifts in quality have taken place. For the first time in the viticultural history of the region, there has emerged a group of top winegrowers producing deep, dark, concentrated, skillfully matured Mediterranean wines full of character, which achieve international recognition

Simultaneously another, quite different development came about. As a new crisis hit the winegrowing industry in the mid-1980s, a few pioneers formed an alliance of winegrowers in 1987, and the Vin de Pays d'Oc was born. This was a country wine with regional character and a guarantee of quality. They opted above all for internationally popular grape varieties and the fertile locations classed as Vin de Pays, on which higher yields

This device enables perfect labeling of a single bottle, as needed. It is useful for winegrowers who keep their stock in pallets, *tiré-bouché*, simply filled and corked.

are permitted. Using modern winemaking technology, especially temperature control, they began to produce varietal wines. This was a product type that corresponded to market and consumer demand, a fact which is still more true today than it was then. At the outset, their syndicate numbered 200 members with a production of 200,000 hectoliters (the approximate equivalent of 26.7 million bottles) of country wine. Ten

years later it included over a thousand businesses which between them marketed 2.6 million hectoliters (346.7 million bottles), of which 80 percent were exported. Languedoc-Roussillon is once more proud of being the largest undivided wine region in the world, as well as the one with the greatest potential for varietal wines. Today it is one of the most desirable wine producing regions in France.

The Appellations

Faugères
This forested area begins 9 miles (15 kilometers) north of Béziers. Faugères is the only *Appellation d'Origine Contrôlée* of the Languedoc to have soils of a single type throughout. These are slaty, and produce high-quality red wines. Today production is mostly of wines with a high proportion of Syrah, which are much desired for their complexity, concentration and elegance.

St-Chinian
This area lies between Minervois and Faugères, and achieved *Appellation* status at the same time, 1982. Its center is the small town of the same name. The southern part of the production area has clay and calcareous soils on which full-bodied, tannin-rich varieties grow. Those of the northern part, occupying the foothills of the Monts de l'Espinouse, are of slate. The *Appellation d'Origine Contrôlée* has recently been experiencing a renaissance, demonstrated by complex, full reds. As in Faugères, only

In Saint-Chinian, winegrowers invite visitors to taste their wine with notices like this.

the rosé shares in the classification. The whites come under the Coteaux du Languedoc *Appellation*.

Clairette du Languedoc
This *Appellation*, granted back in 1948, was given in acknowledgment of the grape variety of the same name. It has been grown for centuries in 11 villages between Pézenas and Clermont-l'Hérault, initially for the production of sherry-like wines, then to provide the basic material for the vermouth industry. Only recently have modern winemaking techniques revealed another aspect of this variety, its freshness and fruitiness.

Coteaux-du-Languedoc
The production area of Coteaux du Languedoc begins at Nîmes and ends in Narbonne. It runs along the Mediterranean for more than 80 miles (130 kilometers), stretching inland for some 30 miles (50 kilometers). The area includes the *Appellation d'Origine Contrôlée* mentioned above, which are also entitled to use the general *Appellation*. It has 157 winegrowing communes, and has great geological diversity. Red wines predominate by far, with the Carignan grape continuing to represent the common denominator. The proportion of Carignan is not allowed to exceed 40 percent. Grenache and Syrah or Mourvèdre must be included in the blend of grapes. Cinsault is used for rosés in particular. Winegrowers distinguish two groups as regards the varieties for white wines. Up to a maximum of 60 percent use Clairette, Picpoul, Ugni Blanc, Carignan Blanc and Terret Blanc, and at least 40 percent are designated to use Macabeu, Grenache Blanc, Bourboulenc, Marsanne and Vermentino. Half the communes classified have only the general *Appellation*; the other half is divided into 12 *terroirs* whose name may be stated in addi-

tion. These (from north to south) are: Coteaux de Vérargues, Saint-Christol, Saint-Drézery, Pic Saint-Loup, Montpeyroux, Saint-Saturnin, La Méjanelle, Saint-Georges d'Orques, Cabrières, Picpoul de Pinet, La Clape and Quatourze. Around 350,000 hectoliters are produced in all, equivalent to 46.6 million bottles.

Costières de Nîmes
The *département* of Gard, capital Nîmes, is part of Languedoc-Roussillon, though its winegrowers feel that they belong more to the Rhône valley. So while the area's Côtes du Rhône continue to be listed with the other Rhône wines, the former Costières du Gard are grouped with the Languedoc. The region has 12,000 hectares (29,700 acres) of vineyards in production in 24 communes, and extends southeast from Nîmes toward the Camargue. The hills are strewn with river pebbles. Its reds are round and often very fruity. These and the area's balanced rosés are vinified from Grenache, Syrah, Mourvèdre, Cinsault and Carignan. The whites account for only 3 percent of the volume of wine produced, 150,000 hectoliters (20 million bottles). For these, the varieties available are Grenache Blanc, Bourboulenc, Clairette, Marsanne, Roussanne, Rolle and Ugni Blanc.

Clairette de Bellegarde
Southeast of Nîmes, on the plateau des Costières, where the typical round river pebbles form a layer some 30 feet (10 meters) thick, lies the home of this Clairette. Today, 500 hectoliters (about 67,000 bottles) are produced. This white wine received its *Appellation* in 1949. It is a full wine with floral and fruity aromas which carry conviction.

Hearty traditional fare

Manoul & moche

Historically, no animal has been of greater significance for the Lozère than the sheep. Cutlets and saddle, sweetbreads and kidneys, gigot and shoulder may be variously roast or braised, but a particular use was found for the organ meat and the foot; that was for *manoul*. This is the stuffed stomach of the sheep. Sections of the rumen are sewn to form small pouches, and these stuffed with chopped lamb and mutton organ meat and tripe, the meat from the foot, and raw, smoked ham or bacon. Other stuffing ingredients are carrots, onions, garlic, parsley, bay and thyme, with salt and pepper. Every butcher has his own, slightly different recipe.

The most popular size of lamb for the dish is the *broutard*. These are lambs which are already weaned. They have left the ewe and have begun to graze independently. *Manouls* weighing a little over half a pound (300 grams) used to be taken to the baker's on the way to market, to be slowly casseroled in his oven. Returning later from the cattle market, the weary owner would find them nicely cooked to provide him with a nutritious light lunch. The same dish is called *tripoux* in the Hérault.

"The quality of *tripes* is all a matter of cleanliness," emphasizes Patrick Pagès in Vialas, a champion of traditional regional recipes from Languedoc and the Cévennes. "*Tripier* is a declining profession nowadays. Mad cow disease will unfortunately only hasten its demise. These are

the people who go to the abattoirs and clean up the organ meat, feet and heads. It is a science in itself. Mediocrity will not do when you are dealing with organ meat. A region like the Cévennes and Lozère is going to enable the survival of such professions. Ours is a region where traditions last longer than reality."

Pork has an honored place in the culinary tradition of Lozère. It was a mark of prosperity to be able to keep one or even two pigs. An important reason for the usefulness of pork in the kitchen was that, unlike lamb, mutton or goat, the meat could be preserved by drying and salting, or boiling and potting it.

On the day the pig was slaughtered, the meal would begin as usual with *crudités*, grated raw vegetables with vinaigrette, and this would be followed by *carbonnade*. The main ingredient of this is blood sausage; in the Cévennes, this contains not only blood but herbs, onions and a small amount of *pastis*. Roast fillet of pork is served with it, with potatoes fried from raw, braised onions and apples such as *reinette grise*. In Lozère, when the pig is boned, some meat is left on the bones to be cured and either made into *petits salés* or potted in its own drippings. They round off the combination of flavors in a hearty casserole or stew.

Sausages containing cabbage, other leafy vegetables and herbs, such as the ones called *moche* or *maôche*, are also popular. They are about 12

Above: In areas such as Lozère, where diners can rely on the meat having come from animals bred and cared for by natural methods within the local region, calf's head and other organ meats are increasingly popular specialties.

inches (30 centimeters) long and up to 2½ inches (6 centimeters) thick. The recipe contains ground pork, shoulder and breast, and (in the original version) lungs, together of course with cabbage. Chopped herbs, dandelion and mangold can be added as available and as liked. Some butchers swear by a recipe with one-third vegetables; others prefer one-third meat as the maximum. Some add potatoes to the sausagemeat while others, allow them only as an accompaniment. The tiny *saucisses d'herbes* are one simple variation on the theme. In the south of Lozère, mangold alone is used for these; in the north, cabbage is the only vegetable added.

Another specialty more widely found in the Montagne Noire and Rhône valley, as well as Provence (where they are called *caillettes*) are *fricandeaux*. These are small pâtés of liver and neck, flavored with bay and thyme and wrapped in a fine inner membrane from the animal. They are baked in the oven in earthenware or glass baking dishes or pans. *Fricandeaux* are sold by the slice and served either as an appetizer or additional course, or as a main dish.

Tête de veau en estouffade, condiments et aromates en ravigote

Ragoût of calf's head with herb sauce

Serves 10

1 calf's head, 5½ lb/2.5 kg
8 oz/250 g carrots
8 oz/250 g celery
8 oz/250 g celeriac
8 oz/250 g leeks
½ cup/80 g chopped onions
Bay leaves, cloves, peppercorns
Coarse sea salt
1½ cup/200 g flour
2 cups/500 ml vinegar
1¾ lbs/800 g puff pastry
1 egg yolk

Sauce
5 eggs
⅓ cup/80 g capers
⅓ cup/80 g gherkins
½ bunch of parsley
3½ tbsp red wine vinegar
⅔ cup/150 ml grapeseed oil
1 tsp mustard
Freshly milled salt and pepper

Bone the calf's head and tie it together with culinary thread. Plunge it into boiling water and precook it. Remove from the cooking liquid and place in cold water with the vegetables, herbs and spices, and salt. Bring to a boil and cook for 2½ hours, skimming frequently. At the end of the cooking time, blend the flour with the vinegar and add to the cooking liquid, stirring constantly. Remove the vegetables and calf's head. Untie the thread, drain and leave to cool. Cut the vegetables and calf's head into small pieces.

To make the sauce, hard boil the eggs, peel and sieve them. Chop the capers, gherkins and parsley finely. Mix the vinegar, oil and mustard thoroughly and stir in the capers, gherkins, parsley and eggs. Season with salt and pepper. Preheat the oven to 465 °F/240 °C.

Roll out the pastry thinly and cut out either 1 large or 10 small pieces. Layer the meat and vegetables in 1 large or 10 small ovenproof dishes. Cover with the pastry lids and trim, brush with egg yolk and bake in the pre-heated oven until the pastry is risen and golden.

Serve immediately, with the herb sauce presented separately.

Manouls lozérien

Stuffed lambs' stomachs

Serves 10

10 stuffed lambs' stomachs
4 carrots
1 leek
1 turnip
3 onions
6 cups/1.5 liters stock
1 lb/500 g celery
2½ lbs/1.2 kg potatoes
⅓ cup/80 g butter
1½ cups/250 g finely chopped onions
20 bay leaves
Freshly milled salt and pepper
20 thin slices raw smoked ham
1 bunch of parsley, finely chopped

The lambs' stomachs can usually be bought ready prepared from the butcher. Otherwise, the lambs' rumen can be stuffed with chopped meat from the foot, raw smoked ham, garlic and parsley.

Place the lambs' stomachs in boiling water and blanch.

Drain, rinse under cold water and boil for 3 hours in the stock with the cleaned carrots, leek, turnip, onions and a little salt. Leave to cool.

Fry the celery in a little butter until transparent. Peel, rinse and dice the potatoes.

Melt the remaining butter in a pan and fry the potato dice lightly.

Place the potatoes, onions, celery and meat in a heavy, lidded casserole. Add the bay leaves, salt and pepper and braise in an oven preheated to 410 °F/210 °C for 30 minutes. This dish can be served on individual plates, but looks more impressive taken to the table in the casserole in which it was cooked.

Moche et saucisse d'herbes

Moche and herb sausage

Serves 10

4 *moche* sausages
5 herb sausages
Generous 2 lbs/1 kg potatoes (Roseval)
¾ cup/200 ml oil
14 oz/400 g sweet onions (from Saint-André)
Bay leaf, cloves, salt
3½ tbsp/50 ml olive oil
Flat-leaf parsley
Butter

Precook the sausages in boiling water, rinse in cold water and drain.

Boil the potatoes in their skins until they are cooked but still whole; cut into cubes.

Cook the onions, sausages and potatoes with the spices and salt in oil for 25 minutes in a covered saucepan. Drain off and reserve the cooking juices.

Cut the sausages into pieces and arrange on a plate with the potatoes. Keep hot.

Add the olive oil to the cooking juices, scatter with chopped parsley and freshly milled pepper. Pour the hot sauce over the dish, and garnish with a few stewed cranberries.

Serve immediately.

Carbonnade languedocienne

Pork fillets Languedoc-style

Serves 10

3½ lbs/1.5 kg fillet of pork
1½ lbs/700 g apples
¾ cup/100 g butter
1½ lbs/700 g onions
1 cup/250 ml oil
1¾ lbs/800 g potatoes
Generous 2 lbs/1 kg blood sausage
Sherry vinegar
2 cups/500 ml veal stock
Freshly milled salt and pepper
Chopped parsley

Divide the meat into portions, trim and set aside. Quarter the apples and fry in the butter. Peel the onions, slice into thin rings and fry lightly in oil. Peel and rinse the potatoes, slice evenly and fry in hot oil.

Preheat the oven to 390 °F/200 °C.

Brown the pieces of pork fillet well on both sides in a casserole; cover and finish cooking in the preheated oven for 10 minutes. Set aside. Fry the blood sausage in one piece and then remove the skin.

Add a few drops of sherry vinegar to the cooking juices from the pork to deglaze; also add the veal stock, reduce and season.

To serve, warm the plates and place a portion of the fried apple in the center of each. Top and surround with the onions and potatoes. Arrange three portions of pork fillet and three pieces of blood sausage around each plate.

Pour the sauce round the meat and sausage and sprinkle with parsley.

Serve immediately.

Left: *Manoul*, stuffed lambs' stomach, is a dish which sums up the spirit and history of the Cévennes. – Center: The high proportion of vegetables in *moche* and herb sausages gives them their characteristic texture and incomparable flavor. – Right: *Carbonnade* is the traditional dish served to celebrate the slaughter of the pig. It is a treat for connoisseurs of the Cévennes.

Cévennes honey

How could it be otherwise? The favorite honey of the inhabitants of the Cévennes is the one made from chestnut blossom. There is a still closer connection between the tree which so represents this region and the art of bee-keeping; hives were traditionally made from chestnut trunks. These ancient, rustic, almost gnome-like presences have long since disappeared from other areas, but here in the Cevennes they are often to be seen, even if their use as hives has almost been abandoned. Bees do quite often still inhabit them, and they make a secure home; this

Some interesting facts about honey

Many plants need to have their flowers fertilized by the pollen from others of the species. They produce sweet nectar containing a host of substances to attract bees and other pollinating insects. Enticed by this, the bees force their way into the flower, brush off the pollen and carry it with them to the next flower. They suck up the nectar with a proboscis, and enzymes in their honey sacs convert it into what we call honey.

Whether bees collect nectar from flowers or honeydew from leaves, they keep to the same variety of plant. This is what makes single-variety honey possible. The significance of such honeys is increasing with the advance of monocultures. Honeys from regions of varied flora, on the other hand, have an amazing complexity of flavor and variety of components.

Honey consists of 80 percent sugar, but this is in many cases made up of about 20 different types, mainly glucose and fructose. As a foodstuff, honey constitutes the most quickly effective source of energy there is, because these sugars are instantly absorbed by the body. Apart from a water content of 17 percent, honey contains over 180 other substances, including almost the whole range of minerals and trace elements, various organic acids and amino-acids. The enzymes, hormones, pollen and lysozymes (which are natural antibiotics) in honey make it a valuable aid to health.

Bees store the honey in "combs," sealed with wax. The natural method of bee-keeping involves gathering only the mature honey, which is extracted using a centrifuge. It is then filtered and put into jars. In this way, it retains its valuable constituents. Heating would reduce these considerably. Honey should be stored in a cool, dark place, away from strong odors, since heat, light and moisture impair its quality. The description "pure honey" is illegal in France, because honey must always be pure as a matter of course.

A typical old farmhouse in the Cévennes with rows of occupied hives.

Hives used to be made out of hollow chestnut tree trunks, covered with a stone slab. This type of hive was called a *buc*.

type of hive was never ideal for the bee-keeper. Collecting the honey was difficult, and done with a ladle or knife. It involved being stung repeatedly. Nevertheless, bee-keeping continues to flourish in Lozère.

The two most important honeys gathered there are the *miel de châtaignier*, the clear, fairly thick, mellow brown chestnut honey, whose season happens in June, and *miel de toutes fleurs*, a blossom honey usually called *miel des Cévennes*. Unlike the honey of the plains, which comes mainly from the fields of sunflowers and oilseed rape, the honey of this region is from wild flowers, giving it a darker color and richer aroma. It is collected at the end of July and beginning of August Other honeys are the *miel de montagne*, from mountainsides up around 4,600 feet (1400 meters), and *miel de causse*, which is gathered in mid July, strongly perfumed but mild in flavor, since it comes from the many tiny, insignificant-looking herbs and flowers of the lime-rich high plateaus. *Miel de bruyère* is an outstanding heather honey, whose turn comes in mid-September, when the other honeys have all been gathered. *Miel à la brèche* is comb honey, just as it comes from the hive: unextracted and in its richest and most natural state. Extracting honey introduces air, and however slight the effect, there is some consequent change. *Miel d'arbre* or *miellat* are the names used to describe propolis, the resin collected and converted by the bees to use as a glue in the hive. In the Cévennes it is very dark, as it is based on the secretions of insects living on oak and chestnut trees. It is the varied natural flora of the region, which provides such pure, healthy and aromatic nectar, that makes the Cévennes such a distinctive source of honey. This means that single-variety honeys are rare. The blossom determines the color, flavor and consistency of the honey. Thus, for example, single-variety acacia honey never hardens. Honey from rape and orange blossom, on the other hand, crystallizes quickly. In the winter, some bee-keepers take their colonies of bees down to the valleys of the Gard or Hérault, where it is warmer and the season for blossom arrives earlier. Bees need to be fed for a shorter period there, which avoids gastric problems.

Bee-keepers who work in a style that accords respect to the bees allow the colony sufficient freedom to develop along natural lines and build the comb themselves. In the south, people like to compare its shape with the oval of a rugby ball. Bees instinctively produce more honey than they need. This is what makes it possible to gather honey. The modern hive has a lower and an upper section. The colony occupies the lower box, and when the bees have filled this, they continue storing honey by filling the frames suspended in the smaller boxes on top. These are the ones that the bee-keeper removes to gather the honey. Any conscientious bee-keeper leaves the honey in the breeding section completely

untouched. The combs from the honey collection area are extracted. The honey flows out easily, because the temperature in the hive remains constantly around 95°F (35 (C). There is often insufficient time to extract all the combs immediately after they are gathered, so they are stored temporarily in stainless steel drums. In southern France, the honey in these remains liquid until October or even November, but hardens and 'crystallizes' as the temperature falls. When that happens, the bee-keeper has to bring the temperature back to 95°F (35 (C) before extracting, so that it regains the consistency at which extraction is possible. This is not regarded as constituting heating. Bee-keepers look askance at the idea of heating honey beyond 104-113°F (40-45°C), and practically none of them would do such a thing.

There are differences of approach regarding propagation. The one which is gaining support in most European countries is to work in harmony with the species. Following this approach, the bee-keeper does not intervene until the bees would naturally have swarmed. Just as the old queen is about to leave the hive, the bee-keeper anticipates the event and removes her, leading to a division of the colony. By this method, the emergence of new queens happens naturally. Most bee-keepers opt for a targeted approach. They do not wait for moment when the bees

leave the hive, but divide the swarms in spring, breeding queens from the best colonies and assigning them to hives deprived of a queen. Humanity has an interest in other products from the hive, apart from honey (and wax). Pollen is one. Bees bring in pollen on their legs, where it adheres when the bee visits a flower. They brush it off and mix it with honey from secretory glands. Bee-keepers harvest the clumps of pollen by setting up a mesh in front of the hive. As the bees squeeze through the mesh, about 15 percent of the pollen falls off and is collected. This needs to be dried at 104°F (40°C) for 24 hours. It contains proteins and glycerides, and is highly nutritious. Bees use it in the form of a sort of soup called *bouillie* to feed their normal offspring, as opposed to the queen. Pollen is regarded as fortifying and natural. It is also recognized as a treatment for prostate problems. It gives off a remarkable scent of dried flowers and yeast. *Gelée royale* is the substance used to feed the queens. The production of royal jelly is not something most bee-keepers practice, because the queens have to be bred artificially and killed after they have fulfilled their purpose.

From left: *Miel des Cévennes* – blossom honey; *Miel de bruyère* – heather honey; *Miel des Fenouillèdes* – Roussillon honey; *Miel de châtaignier* – chestnut honey

Provence
Côte d'Azur

André Dominé

Paul Fouque, born in 1921, working on a *santon* called
"coup de mistral," or "blast of the mistral," the first and most
famous of these clay figures to capture movement.
It is composed of 14 molded sections.

On the outskirts of Nyons in the *département* of Drôme lies the most northerly olive-growing region in France, one of the oldest and most famous in the country.

Calais

Le Havre

Caen
Paris

Brest

Strasbourg

Rennes

Orléans

Nantes
Tours
Dijon

Limoges
Lyon

Bordeaux
Grenoble

Toulouse
Provence
Côte d'Azur

Biarritz

Perpignan

Year after year the charm of Provence draws painters and poets, photographers and filmmakers, just as surely as it attracts tourists from all over France and indeed the world. No other province of France offers such a wealth of impressions to appeal to all the senses. There is the light, which casts a spell over its countryside and villages, in which textures constantly take on a different quality; there is the sound of the wind, the incredible scents borne upon it, and the extraordinary intensity of the experience as they mingle, as they do at times, with the impact of flavors. Characterless residential developments and monstrous commercial centers seem ever calculated to shatter the idyll. Provence, in answer to such monotonous architecture, spreads out its treasury of contrasting landscapes.

There is the Camargue, where the land merges imperceptibly into the sea, land of the black bulls, the white horses, the cowboys and the gypsies; the Côte d'Azur with its luxury residences, palm trees and citrus groves; the Comtat, around Avignon, rich in fruit and vegetables; there is the bare Haute Provence, with its breathtaking fields of lavender, delightful Lubéron with its picturesque villages, surrounded by a gentle sort of wildness, and the bustling, fiery, contradictory, populous Marseille, where exceptionally good *bouillabaisse* is to be had.

The extreme variety brings an almost inexhaustible culinary wealth, which unfolds as a tangible reality in the wonderful markets of the region's larger towns. That is where it becomes clear that Provence is the biggest supplier of fruit, vegetables and herbs in France. It produces the most olives, the best olive oil, and excellent honey. It also makes goat cheese, air-dried sausages, produces meat from lamb and steer, creates sweet and dry wines and is home to a whole range of sweet temptations.

The people of Provence know how to handle this natural abundance, and do so with true Mediterranean respect for each item of local produce, always demanding freshness. No wonder the resulting cuisine is rich in color, crispness and vitamins, and spicy aromas envelop the food. The locals like to emphasize these aromas with garlic and anchovy stirred into their various sauces. All that is required now is a shady spot before the walls of the country retreat, the *cabanon*, or on a sheltered terrace where the fragrances of the countryside waft in, and the play of the senses begins anew.

Real bouillabaisse

"If you maintain your integrity as a cook, a proper *bouillabaisse* these days is inevitably expensive. Every day during the summer, guests sit down at a table on our terrace, look at the price of our *bouillabaisse Miramar*, then get up and leave. They think our price is excessive, but our profit margin is less than that of others who charge less, but do not use quality ingredients. There are certain ground rules that must be adhered to:

- The freshness of the fish is the prime rule.
- The variety and quantity of fish contributes decisively to the quality of the stock on which the soup is based. All the fish are cooked fresh to order.
- Pure, genuine saffron is essential (strictly speaking, neither paprika nor herbs of Provence add anything of benefit to a *bouillabaisse*).
- The fish should be cut and served in the presence of the guest, rather than being brought ready prepared from the kitchen, unless the number of guests is too high.

It is worth pointing out that spiny lobster can never be seen as an essential ingredient of *bouillabaisse*, because it was originally a very simple dish to use up the fish that were either damaged or had not been sold. It might be stretched to feed all the family by adding potatoes.

It helps for people to know that *bouillabaisse du pêcheur* was originally prepared using sea water, which was boiled up on the beach while the fishermen were untangling their nets. When the water boiled, in went the fish that were destined for the soup, along with fennel, tomatoes and so on, to cook. Once the work of untangling the nets was done, the *bouillabaisse* would be ready and the fishermen and their families could sit down and eat. It was only later that the original *bouillabaisse* underwent the various refinements that we use today.

Instead of starting with sea water, a base was prepared using small rock fish, cooked with tomatoes, onions, garlic, fennel and saffron. Today, this base, which already has a great deal of flavor in its own right, is boiled to create the stock in which to cook the fish. This type is called rich *bouillabaisse* or *Bouillabaisse Marseillaise*.

Our belief is that if you have gone to the effort and expense of a long journey to experience a different region and its culinary specialties, you should do your best to find out about it, and search out a product prepared to the highest standards in the authentic way, even if the price does seem startling.

Fish has an indispensable place in Provençal cuisine. The classic cookbooks like 'Reboul' include a multitude of recipes based on fish. *Bouillabaisse* is the best known, but some of the other great classics, and still very much in vogue, are *aïoli*, *anchoïade*, *bourride*, *oursinade*, *la soupe de poissons à la Marseillaise*, and there are many more. The cuisine we have here in Provence creates a perfect blend of fish and the great variety of herbs from the wild moorlands. This combination tastes magnificent in partnership with our incomparable olive oil.

All this awaits you in Provence, along with a smile and a glass of pastis."

Pierre and Jean-Michel Minguella
Restaurant Miramar, Marseille

Bouillabaisse
Rich Provençal fish soup

Serves 6

17 ½ lb/8 kg fresh Mediterranean fish (scorpion fish and a variety of at least 6 other types: greater weaver fish, angler fish, gurnard, whiting, sea bass, John Dory and, optionally, crab and spiny lobster)
2 large onions
12 tbsp olive oil
4 tomatoes
1 bouquet garni
1 strip of untreated orange zest
4 cloves of garlic, crushed
1 ½ tsp/1 g saffron threads
Freshly milled salt and pepper
½ in /1.5 cm thick slices rustic bread, lightly toasted in the oven
Generous 1 ½ lbs/750 g potatoes (optional)

Prepare the fish and crabs. Separate the fish with firm flesh (scorpion fish, greater weaver fish, angler fish, gurnard, crabs, and spiny lobster) from the ones with light-textured flesh (whiting, sea bass and John Dory).

Peel the onions and chop finely, and cook gently in 8 tbsp of olive oil, without letting them brown. Peel and dice the tomatoes and add to the onions, followed by the bouquet garni, orange zest, garlic and saffron.

Season with salt and pepper. Lay the firm-fleshed fish, starting with the crabs, on top of the vegetables, and pour over the remaining olive oil. Leave to infuse for 10 minutes, then carefully add enough boiling water to cover the fish. Bring quickly to a boil, and simmer strongly for 5 minutes. Then add the light-textured fish and boil vigorously for another 5 to 7 minutes. A good *bouillabaisse* needs to boil vigorously for 10 to 15 minutes in order to combine the oil and the soup. Place a slice of bread in each soup plate and pour on the liquid soup. Serve the crabs, fish and piquant sauce separately. If liked, potatoes can be cooked with the fish for this soup. They are quartered and layered on top of the vegetables.

Rouille
Piquant sauce to accompany fish soup

2 cloves of garlic, peeled
2 red chiles, cleaned
Cayenne pepper
A pinch of saffron
2 tbsp breadcrumbs, soaked in chicken stock
2\3 cup/150 ml olive oil

Peel the garlic and pound in a mortar with the chiles. Season with cayenne and saffron. Squeeze out the breadcrumbs, and mix with the seasonings. Beat in the oil, a drop at a time, until the sauce has a similar consistency to mustard.

For an authentic *bouillabaisse*, the fish are brought to the table whole, to be served there. The soup is served separately.

1 For *bouillabaisse*, the vegetables are first cooked in olive oil with the herbs; then the firmer-fleshed fish are added.
2 The basic recipe allows all sorts of variations, since it originated as a way of using left-overs. One such is to add potatoes.
3 After about 5 minutes' cooking time, the tender-fleshed fish are added to the boiling stock, and cooked together with the rest for another 5-7 minutes.

Fish and shellfish of the Mediterranean

Anchois – Anchovy
Small, inexpensive herring.
Mediterranean ones have particular
flavor; best served fresh in summer,
uncooked but briefly marinated.

Sardine
The fleshy relative of the herring.
Sardines have a strong flavor which
appeals to the southern French palate;
they are often arranged in a sunburst
pattern on a grid and grilled over vine
twigs for a *sardinade*.

Congre, fiélas – Conger eel
Almost black, and up to 10 feet
(3 meters) long. It is found on all
coasts and is available all year
round. It has many bones, so is
best used for soups and sauces.

Daurade royale – Gilt head bream
Not only a Mediterranean fish, but
especially highly regarded in Provence.
Served whole or filleted, baked or
broiled. Available all year round; now
often farmed.

Grondin – Gurnard
The gurnard has firm, aromatic flesh, but
its spiny scales and large head make for
a lot of waste, so it is best used for
soups.

Baudroie, lotte – Angler fish
Its ugly head means that this fish is
always served without the head and
skinned. It lives in deep water in the
Mediterranean and Atlantic. It has
firm flesh, and is often rolled and
cooked in the oven as a *rôti*.

Rouget-barbet – Red mullet
These belong mainly to the
Mediterranean, though they are fished
along the Atlantic coast of France. They
are prepared using herbs and olive oil,
never poached.

Merlan – Whiting
Delicate food fish with fine-textured
flesh, which should be cooked very fresh.
Mostly caught in the Atlantic; it has
become rare in the Mediterranean.

Saint-Pierre – John Dory
In demand and expensive, on account of
its fine, aromatic flesh. It is rare, though
it occurs in a number of seas and oceans.
Usually poached or fried in the form of
fillets, or included in *bouillabaisse*, since
there is a good deal of waste with this
fish.

Loup de mer – Sea bass
Called *loup de mer* in the Mediterranea
where it has become rare in the wild, b
is being successfully bred. Its flesh is
fine and delicate, but highly expensive.
Usually grilled whole, fried or baked in
salt crust. The season is from August t
March.

Anguille – Eel
Caught in the Camargue and Étang de Berry, where it is one of
the traditional fishermen's dishes

Thon rouge – Tuna
The tuna caught in the Mediterranean is sold as steaks in the
markets, and is grilled or fried with Mediterranean herbs and
vegetables. Best season: early summer.

Morue – Dried cod
Popular in France too, where the best-known recipe is *brandade
de morue*, a purée of dried cod from Nîmes. The love of the dried
variety is increasing the popularity of fresh cod, which is very
versatile in the kitchen.

**Rascasse, chapon
Brown sea scorpion**
Spines and armour plating are not
enough to protect this fish from use
as a valuable ingredient in
bouillabaisse. Its white flesh has a
lovely aroma.

Mulet, muge – Mullet
In Provence it is the roe, the *poutargue*,
rather than the fish itself, which is
valued. In Martigues, this is salted.
Otherwise, the fish is prepared in the
same way as sea bass, often as fillets.

Araignée de mer – Sea spider
Also called the spiny spider crab, these often measure 8 inches (20 centimeters) across, and have fine, highly aromatic flesh. It is eaten boiled. The stuffed shells are also a popular dish.

Favouille – Shore crab
A small crab caught along the coast and in the lagoons. Rich aroma. Popular in soups or with rice.

Langoustine – Scampi, Dublin bay prawn
Slim-bodied, graceful relative of the lobster, with a splayed end to its tail and long, thin claws. Best when obtained from colder waters, but also found in the Mediterranean.

Encornet – Squid
These have an elongated body. Very small ones are often eaten fried. With larger ones, the body is stuffed.

Poulpe – Octopus
Can grow to an enormous size. Only the small ones, less than a hand's breadth, have tender flesh. The others have to be beaten and stewed for a long time, ideally in wine.

Oursin violet – Sea urchin
A delicacy, and common along the coast of Provence. The ovaries, which have a strong iodine smell, are swallowed raw, or used to give their characteristic flavor to a soup called *oursinade*.

The edible parts of a lobster

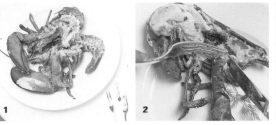
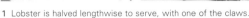

1 Lobster is halved lengthwise to serve, with one of the claws.
2 The excellent tail meat is almost completely exposed, and easy to extract with a knife and fork. The greenish liver in the head section of the lobster is a sought-after means of flavoring.
3 Access to the claw begins at the lower part of the limb. The lobster crackers are used.

4 Using the slim lobster pick, it is easy to reach the meat and draw it out. The thin legs are accessed in the same way: twist to pull them off, then open them up with the lobster crackers and extract the meat with the pick. The lobster crackers have hinged jaws of two different sizes.
5 Grasping the claw with the lobster crackers can be awkward.
6 Once the claw is open, the delicious meat can be reached.

Lobster crackers and lobster pick are used alongside the usual cutlery. They are useful and effective implements for dealing with a lobster.

The edible parts of a sea urchin

1 Hold the top of the urchin in the palm of the hand. Strong cutters are used to pierce the underside.
2 Cut around the mouth opening, removing a sufficiently large circle to provide access.
3 Remove the inedible mouth parts and innards. Only the ovaries, the "gonads" or "tongues," are spooned out to be eaten. The liquid inside the urchin is valued as flavoring.

Handling crabs and other crustaceans

Langouste, the spiny lobster, has fine meat, though it is less aromatic than true lobster.

Tourteau, the common crab, has aromatic, fibrous meat

True crabs are distinguished by having four pairs of legs, rather than three, behind their claws. All these are removed from the body to extract the meat. Here, too, the claws are the best portion. The shell is opened on the underside. The liver is considered a delicacy.

Boil the spiny lobster in water. Halve it lengthwise when cooked, and remove the roe with a spoon. The roe is a delicacy, used for sauces.

The tail contains most meat, as with many crustaceans. Use a knife to loosen it for removal.

Grande cigale, the slipper lobster, has excellent meat.

Its meat will prove its downfall. It is already heavily overfished in the Mediterranean, where it used to be common. Once cooked, it can be cut in half lengthwise, and the meat easily removed.

With care, it is possible to remove the meat from the shell in one piece.

Hold the cooked shrimp between thumb and forefinger, and remove the head with the hard top part of the shell.

Press the body gently between the fingers to loosen the segments of the shell.

The upper segments of shell sometimes have to be taken off the meat individually.

Once the first segments of the body are free of the shell, the tapering tail can usually be pulled out with it.

Crevette, shrimp and prawns, can be pulled apart between the front and the segmented body section of the shell. All the meat is edible, apart from a small piece in the head section.

Place the sea spider top shell uppermost, underside down. Press down onto it.

The shell breaks apart under the pressure, and the meat inside can be reached.

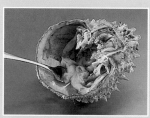

The best way to release the meat clinging to the inside of the shell is with a fork.

Once loosened, lift the meat out with the fork, piece by piece.

Araignée de mer, the sea spider. Its meat is very aromatic. It should certainly have a place in a seafood platter.

393

Olives

The silvery, shimmering leaves of the olive tree, its lightness and evergreen foliage are a familiar sight in regions of France where the climate is sunny and dry.

The trees can attain an age of 100 years, and their growth is leisurely. They reach a height of 10–33 feet (3–10 meters), their trunks becoming ever more gnarled with time. The custom used to be to plant them far apart and use the space in between for other crops, but today, they are planted more closely.

Olive trees bear fruit after four to ten years and reach their prime at 30 to 35 years, with decline setting in at 75 years. In spring, buds form in the leaf axils, producing inconspicuous white flowers at the beginning of June. Pollination is done by the wind, and can be very irregular. An attempt to achieve more even pollination is being made by planting various different varieties in new orchards. Not every branch will bear fruit, because the tree has a two-year cycle of growth. The pattern is for the young wood to bear fruit in its first year, and to devote itself entirely to growth in the second year. Both phases will be present at the same time on a single tree, though some varieties have a marked tendency to fruit and put on growth in alternate years. One such variety is the Tanche, which would, if left to itself, crop heavily in the first year and put all its strength into growth in the subsequent year. To counter this, olive farmers prune in the spring.

The first olives for eating can be picked from the end of August. However, the proper olive harvest in Provence begins in October. Riper fruits are picked at the end of November or beginning of December, and fully ripe, black olives in December and January.

Whatever their degree of ripeness, olives are too bitter to eat straight from the tree, and need some form of preparation. Green olives may need no more than light crushing, and a few days' soaking in several changes of water, before being preserved in brine, with herbs. They will nevertheless retain a slightly bitter taste. Green olives such as *picholines* or *salonenques* infuse for 6 to 12 hours in a 10 percent solution of sodium carbonate, are then steeped in water for six days, and finally preserved in 10 percent salt solution by boiling up with fennel, coriander and bay, then cooling. They are ready to eat after about two weeks.

Black olives such as *Tanches* in Nyons or the Nice variety *Cailletiers* simply need a few months' preservation in brine. At home, *Grossane* from the Bouches-du-Rhône can be preserved by pricking with a fork, layering in a barrel with coarse salt, and leaving out for five days to be exposed to the night frosts.

Picholines
Traditional variety of Provence

Olives cassées à la provençale
Piquant olives

Olives dénoyautées
Pitted olives

Olives farcies à l'…
Olives stuffed with …

Petites olives façon niçoise
Small olives, Nice style

Picholines au fenouil
Olives with fennel

Panaché d'olives pimentées
Olives with chiles

Olives niçoi…
Large purple Nice …

Olives cassées paysanes
Crushed piquant olives

Olives cassées en escabèche
Large marinated olives

Olives vertes goût piment
Olives stuffed with pimento

Olives noires prov…
Black Provençal …

Close of day during the olive harvest

Tapenade
Olive paste

6 cloves of garlic
⅓ cup/50 g capers
10 anchovy fillets in oil
1 ¾ cups/200 g pitted black olives
1 level tsp finely chopped fresh thyme
1 level tsp finely chopped fresh summer savory
Juice of ½ lemon
Freshly milled pepper
Olive oil

Peel the garlic cloves, remove the shoots and chop the garlic finely. Rinse the capers thoroughly and dry them. Pat the anchovy fillets dry and chop small. Place these ingredients in a food processor with the thyme, savory, and lemon juice, and purée. Season with pepper, then add olive oil in a thin stream and mix, adding just enough to achieve the consistency of a thick, spreadable paste.

Tapenade is spread on slices of bread which have been lightly toasted in the oven, and served as an appetizer. It also makes an excellent seasoning for other dishes, used in small quantities.

Everything is ready for the starter: toasted baguette with *tapenade*, different kinds of olives, garlic bread with olive oil and air-dried sausage.
Olives, olive oil and red wine are increasingly recognized the world over for promoting a healthy, long life. In Provence, that goes without question.

Olive Oil

The cuisine of Provence, like that of the Mediterranean as a whole, is unimaginable without olive oil.

The olive tree, *Olea europea*, is a native of the Mediterranean, and existed in the wild in Provence. It was cultivated by the Greeks, if not even earlier, and its fruits pressed to obtain and use the oil. For a long time the oil was considered too precious for cooking, and was used to anoint the skin and fuel lamps. It acquired great religious and medical significance. The Phoenicians, founders of the city we know as Marseille back in 600 BC, promoted the planting and cultivation of olive trees in Provence. Later, under the Romans, olive oil became an important product of the region, and essential in its cooking. Abundant archeological evidence of olive cultivation exists.

As the most important source of fat, olive oil became the basis of the Mediterranean diet, a role underlined in the fasting regulations of the Christian church. For centuries, the cultivation of the olive was carried on by the many monasteries of Provence.

The olive is exposed to major risks, the most devastating being frost. Despite its mild climate, Provence does suffer occasional severe frosts from time to time, and olive trees cannot withstand this. (The last was in 1956.) Competition from other producer countries has given the growers of Provence cause for concern over the centuries. The problem in the 20th century has revolved around the cheap production of oilseed and a preference among consumers for lighter oils with a more neutral flavor, which have reduced demand for olive oil. Now, more and more people are acquiring a taste for olive oil, not least because of certain highly positive qualities. It is easy to digest, has a beneficial effect on the stomach and digestive tract, provides some protection against tumors and prevents gallstones. It contains a high proportion of mono-unsaturated fatty acids, 75 percent. This is not only far greater than that of animal fats, but well in excess of most vegetable oils. Its mono-unsaturate content reduces the risk of heart disease and circulatory problems by keeping the blood vessels more elastic. Lastly, it contains high levels of antioxidants, and so is able to withstand being heated to temperatures over 395 °F (200 °C) without breaking down into substances harmful to health, as happens with animal and other vegetable fats. The antioxidants probably also protect the body against cancers. All this means that Mediterranean cooking with olive oil is gaining many friends, in France as elsewhere. Consumption of olive oil climbed slowly but steadily for 20 years, reaching 33,069 tons (30,000 tonnes) in 1993. Then the curve altered and took off; five years later, sales reached 55,115 tons (50,000 tonnes), and continue to climb steeply.

Since France produces only 5 percent of its own needs, a breeze of optimism wafts through the olive groves of Provence and of the Midi. The 120 local mills and cooperatives are often already sold out by the beginning of the summer. A mark of the high esteem which olive oil has newly achieved, and the self-confidence of the producers, is the fact that the traditional production areas have been recognized and awarded an *Appellation d'Origine Contrôlée*. The first, recognized in 1994, was awarded to Nyons in the Drôme, the most northerly olive producing region in France.

Below: The mill shop in Nyons sells not only olive oil, but all sorts of olive products, such as soap.

The bottle proudly displays the A.O.C. symbol showing the origin of the oil, molded into the glass. Nyons was the first region to receive this status.

The paste is spread on mats before placing under the hydraulic press. The oil runs through the mats, but the solids are retained.

The color of the olives indicates their degree of ripeness.

Heavy granite millstones first grind the olive fruits into an even, moist paste.

Paradise comes cold pressed

November is the month when the olives on the trees darken and reach the stage of ripeness required by the Provençal mills. Black olives yield a good quantity of oil with smooth, mild characteristics.

The olives are either picked by hand or they are shaken down into nets by machine. The harvest from each mature tree is about 22–66 pounds (10–30 kilograms).

The first day at the mill is spent washing and picking over the olives. Milling then follows. An edge mill is used, with huge circular granite millstones rolling over a thin layer of fruits, crushing them to an even, moist paste. The millstones are motor-driven today, but otherwise, nothing else about the ancient method has changed.

The paste is spread thinly on round mats called *scroutins*, which are nowadays made of nylon instead of coconut matting. These are stacked beneath a hydraulic press, and the pressure increased slowly. The yield is usually a generous 2 pints (1 liter) of oil from around 11 pounds (5 kilograms) of olives. The juice is an emulsion of oil and water. The method of separating them used to rely on the fact that oil is not as heavy as water, and would settle out, but that exposes the oil longer to the air, so today, a centrifuge is used. The product is a golden green, unfiltered oil with a slight cloudiness, an oil from the first cold pressing, as intense and as genuine as can possibly be.

Olive oils of Provence

Nyons
The olives and olive oil from this production area in southern Drôme and the north of Vaucluse obtained the first *Appellation d'Origine Contrôlée* for these products in 1994. The only variety grown (apart from 5 percent pollinating varieties) is the highly productive *Tanche*. The minimum space for a tree is 24 square meters (28.7 square yards), the maximum yield is 6 tonnes per hectare (2.7 tons per acre). The ripe olives must be cold pressed within seven days of harvesting.

Vallée des Baux
The area of this olive oil *Appellation*, recognized in 1997, lies in the département of Bouches-du-Rhône. The main varieties recognized are *Salonenque, Berguette, Grossane and Verdale*, which must now make up 50 percent. Picholine and local varieties are permitted in addition. Maximum yield is 8 tonnes (3.6 tons/acre), the other specifications being as for Nyons.

Also possessing Appellation status
Nice: the area around Nice, with its small *Cailletiers* variety. Application has also been made to register the fruits for eating purposes.
Aix-en-Provence: the area around Aix-en-Provence, where the dominant variety is Picholine.
Haute-Provence: *Aglandau* is the main variety grown in the hinterland of the Côte d'Azur. It produces a particularly complex oil.

Qualities
Huile d'olive vierge extra: The best quality of cold-pressed natural olive oil from the first pressing, which contains less than 1 percent (often 0.5 per cent or less) free fatty acids, which diminish the quality of the oil for consumption. It has an untainted, excellent, above average flavor.
Huile d'olive vierge: Good quality cold pressed natural olive oil from the first pressing, containing a maximum of 2 percent free fatty acids, and having an untainted, good flavor.
Huile d'olive vierge courante: Sound quality cold-pressed natural olive oil, usually from the second pressing, with a maximum of 3.3 percent free fatty acids.
Huile d'olive: A mixture of cold-pressed and refined oil, i.e. olive oil extracted by chemical means.

Storage
Stored in dark, dry, cool conditions, olive oil keeps for 2 years. Once opened, it is best to keep it in the refrigerator.

The people of Provence, Catalonia and Spain today contest the honor of being the first to invent *aïoli*. To make it, separate the garlic bulb into cloves, which are then peeled and chopped.

When making traditional *aïoli*, there is no substitute for using the traditional utensils. A stone mortar and turned olivewood pestle are ideal.

Grind the chopped garlic thoroughly to a paste. Then add the only other ingredient, cold-pressed olive oil from the first pressing, drop by drop to begin with and then in a thin stream. Rotate the pestle quickly.

Authentic *aïoli* differs from ordinary garlic mayonnaise in three respects: it has a thinner consistency, a paler color and a fiery sharpness of flavor.

Aïoli & pistou

Any native of Provence, whether from the Camargue, the Côte d'Azur, Haute-Provence or Vaucluse, would surely take *aïoli* to be a Provençal invention. If it were then proved to him that *aïoli* has had its place on the dinner plates of Roussillon, Catalonia and the rest of Spain for centuries, he might turn to a different argument. Without doubt, *grand aïoli* is exclusively Provençal.

Once a meal for times of fasting, *grand aïoli* has become more of a feast. The centerpiece is a generous supply of *aïoli*, surrounded by a variety of ingredients. Traditionally, dating back to the times of fast, one of these is *morue*, dried cod. The large-shelled periwinkles, or *bulots*, are popular accompaniments, but the meal does often also include meat in the form of boiled lamb or beef. Hard-cooked eggs are always part of the menu in any version. Above all, though, *grand aïoli* is a feast of vegetables. Artichokes and zucchini, celery and carrots, snap beans, fava beans, small turnips and fennel, broccoli, potatoes, and anything else in season will be there. They are simply boiled in salted water, each type separately, and eaten still crisp. They are served warm with fish or meat, eggs and olives, arranged around the *aïoli*. Each person helps themselves, and the rich variety of foods provides the perfect excuse to enjoy copious quantities of the garlic mayonnaise.

In Provence, garlic is mainly grown in Vaucluse. About 2470 acres (1000 hectares) are given over to its cultivation. As in the neighboring *département* of Drôme, it is mainly the white varieties that are grown, because they keep better. In the hinterland of the Côte d'Azur, it is the local pink garlic, which often has much smaller cloves.

The fresh garlic harvest appears in June, just in time for the summer visitors.

Aïoli
Traditional version

1 bulb of garlic
1–1¼ cups/250–300 ml olive oil

Separate the cloves from the bulb of garlic, peel and chop them. Then either pound them in a mortar or purée them in a food processor.
Add the olive oil drop by drop, stirring the mixture constantly. When the mixture begins to thicken, pour the oil a little more freely until a paste is obtained.
The garlic paste can be seasoned with a pinch of salt and a few drops of lemon juice.
Beware: this version has an extremely sharp flavor. It tastes even better the next day.

Aïoli
Adapted version

10 cloves of garlic
¼ tsp fine sea salt
2 egg yolks
1 cup/250 ml olive oil
2 tsp lemon juice
Black pepper

Bring all the ingredients to room temperature. Peel the garlic, pound together with the salt and then mix thoroughly with the egg yolks.
Add the olive oil in a thin stream, stirring constantly. The paste will already have emulsified when half the oil has been added. The rest of the oil can then be added a little more quickly.
Finally stir in the lemon juice and season the mayonnaise with pepper.

Pistou
Basil paste

6 cloves of garlic
Sea salt
2 bunches of basil
Scant 1 cup/100 g freshly grated Parmesan
Freshly milled pepper
3½ tbsp olive oil

Peel the garlic cloves and chop finely.
Place in a mortar, sprinkle with a pinch of salt and pound.
Cut the basil into thin strips, add to the garlic and mix to an even paste.
Add the Parmesan, season lightly with pepper, and stir together well.
Begin adding the olive oil drop by drop, stirring constantly, then continue to add in a thin stream, still stirring, until an even paste is formed.
Pistou is twin to the Italian *pesto*. In Provence, it is used to flavor not only fish and lamb, but above all it is an ingredient in a vegetable soup based on white beans.

The Romans were probably the first to make a paste of garlic and olive oil, and so to invent *aïoli*. The quality of the *aïoli* depends very much on that of the garlic. It should be as fresh as possible, and on no account dried up.

Herbes de Provence

The magic of herbs

Thyme, rosemary, sage, summer savory, fennel, lavender and other herbs have formed part of the natural flora of Provence ever since the Romans felled the extensive forests 2000 years ago. Heather and herbs took over the land, covering the limestone karst which was left behind. The people of Provence of course made use of this natural bounty from what was otherwise an agricultural no man's land. Collectors took a wealth of different herbs to apothecaries, *parfumiers* and spice merchants in Marseille, Nice, Grasse and Apt. Lavender became the undisputed star among the aromatic herbs; *farigoule* (the Provençal word for *Thymus vulgaris*) the foremost of the culinary ones. No other herb combines so readily with so many different ingredients. Sausages, hams, figs and prunes are all enhanced by thyme. Medically speaking, its effect is on the stomach, the digestion and the lungs; romantically it does wonders for the emotions. Girls in Provence would know that someone loved them if they found a bunch of thyme at the door.

The demand for herbs, especially thyme, has risen since World War II, but cultivation has remained modest for most of this time because it is labor-intensive, especially at harvest. That changed in the early 1980s, with the invention of a harvesting machine. Thyme is grown in closely set rows, and forms small clumps. From late April to June, it bears its pinkish red blossoms. Early in spring, the space between the rows is plowed and weeded; if weeding waits until harvest, separating the wheat from the tares becomes impossible. Harvesting is done just before the thyme blooms. The harvest is brought into drying rooms and where it forms huge mats 12 square yards (10 square meters) in size, 4 feet 6 inches (1.5 meters) thick, and weighing 2¼ tons (2 tonnes). Warm air is blown through these from below. The leaves are then separated, graded, packed and distributed. Herbes de Provence is a mixture generally consisting of three or four herbs, the blend varying slightly from producer to producer. Thyme and rosemary are always included, often marjoram and summer savory, and sometimes sage and bay. They are usually dried, rubbed and packed ready mixed, but are sometimes sold individually, and these days increasingly packed fresh, either individually or in mixed bunches. Essences and pastes are also available.

Haute-Provence is the biggest supplier of lavender. Its use in the kitchen is mainly in the form of exquisite lavender honey, usually in desserts. Used as a herb, it requires great care.

The most important herbs of Provence

Thyme
The king of Provençal herbs. Thyme is very versatile; its almost sweet yet intense flavor goes with vegetables, fish, meat and a variety of sauces.

Sage
Has an intense and insistent aroma, so needs care. Lends a delightful flavor to pork and mutton, also poultry, when used sensitively.

Rosemary
Has an intense, resinous aroma which goes well with lamb and Mediterranean fish dishes. Also an excellent flavoring for roast potatoes and *ratatouille*.

Basil
Originally from Asia; reached Provence via Italy. *Pesto* became the well-loved Provençal *pistou*, but basil is also widely used apart from this.

Savory
It goes well with recipes based on beans, grilled meat and ragouts. It also has the Provençal name *pebre d'ase*, donkey's pepper.

Fennel
Increasingly rare in the wild, but a native herb and vegetable nonetheless. Used with olives and fish, and also for *pastis*. The foliage and flowers resemble dill.

Marjoram
Has a similar intense aroma to thyme, but finer and sweeter. Especially suited to ground meat dishes and poultry, as well as meat and tomato sauces.

Tarragon
Came from Russia to the Mediterranean in the Middle Ages. Not a typical Provençal herb, but grows well there. Often used for fish, salads and *sauce Béarnaise*.

Oregano
Wild marjoram is a more powerful flavoring ingredient than its cultivated relative. Only the dried oregano fully develops this quality of flavoring, especially in tomato sauces and vegetable dishes.

Bay
This is not a herb, but a tree, which can grow to a considerable height. Its leaves are important for flavoring, especially for marinades and sauces.

Pastis

A familiar sight in the bistros of Marseille in the 1920s was a young salesman seeking customers for his wine. The label, painted by himself, showed vines, olive trees and the bright sun of Provence, his homeland. Paul Ricard dreamed of commercial success and the freedom it would bring him to do what he really wanted. His ambition had in fact been to study painting, but his father would not allow it, so he started work in his father's business, selling wine. He dealt with deliveries, learned bookkeeping and racked his brains to find a way forward. *Vin ordinaire* was not the answer. Neither his wine nor his own brand brought him that sort of success, but he did notice on his frequent visits what people most liked to drink: *pastis*.

Following the ban on absinthe in 1915, the government in 1922 had recognized that anise was in fact harmless, but had only permitted a liqueur with a minimum sugar content of 150 grams (about 5¼ ounces). The people of Provence had long appreciated the refreshing flavor of anise, and were little troubled by such regulations. Every winemaker and bartender could conjure up a recipe of his own. The forbidden drinks were poured "under the counter" in bistros and cafés. The ingredients were common knowledge: alcohol and water, anise, licorice, and a little sugar, with various herbs and spices added according to taste and whim. The *pastis* tasted different from one place to the next, some better, some not so good. Paul Ricard saw his chance.

He set tirelessly to work every evening, blending his own version of *pastis* from alcohol, essence of anise and herbs. He writes in his autobiography, *La passion de créer*, "I adopted the habit of taking a sample with me on my rounds the morning after my distillations, macerations and filtrations. Encouraged by the comments and wishes of my tasters, I honed my product, enabling me to continue my enquiry the following morning in another bar." At the end of a few months, he felt totally sure of himself.

One obstacle remained: the ban. When that was eventually lifted in 1932, he began production of his Ricard in the back yard of his parents' house in the Marseille suburb of Sainte-Marthe. He deliberately gave a Mediterranean flair to his *vrai pastis de Marseille*, as an advertising ploy. This was personified in the figure of the singer Dargelys, a roguish Provençal with an open shirt and impudent charm.

Soon, no large event was without Ricard; it exceeded all its competitors in popularity. The new aniseed liqueur was an instant success, as its typically spicy flavor with the added note of licorice recalled the notorious absinthe, and was mixed in just the same way with water to the

Pastis is never drunk undiluted. Ice cold water alone is used to dilute it, not ice cubes. The characteristic cloudy appearance is caused when the oil of mint in *pastis* crystallizes.

individual's own personal taste. *Pastis* became the most popular aperitive of the whole French nation.

From 1951 onward, many former makers of absinthe began to make *pastis*, with labels reminiscent of their illegal predecessors. They were based on essence of anise, which has a soothing effect on the stomach. It is usually made from star anise, the fruit of an evergreen Chinese tree a little like a cypress, though anethol can also be obtained from aniseed, fennel and tarragon. Other ingredients are licorice and herbs of Provence, prepared by mixing with water and alcohol. These ingredients flavor a 45 percent volume alcohol,

further colored and flavored with sugar and caramel. A new generation of *pastis* represents a further refinement, based on old Provençal recipes. They combine up to 72 different plants and spices. These aperitives are bottled unfiltered, uncolored and often unsweetened, and offer a higher degree of finesse and aromatic complexity.

All types of *pastis*, however, have one thing in common. They are diluted before drinking. The connoisseur will simply add ice cold water, never ice cubes, because they would cause the anethol to separate out. Even bottles of *pastis* are never chilled, because this would cause the liqueur to turn cloudy.

Bitters

The ingredients in *pastis* put it in the herb liqueur category, along with another group of apéritifs, bitters. The name "bitters" came to be used for apéritifs whose slightly bitter taste was produced by cinchona bark and bitter orange peel, occasionally gentian or pine extract. The main ingredients are alcohol, water, sugar, caramel and flavorings of plant origin. The two best known examples in France are:

Amer Picon
The first bitters were the invention of the Provençal Gaëton Picon in Algiers, in the mid-19th century. He transferred production to Marseille in 1872. Amer Picon is flavored with cinchona, gentian roots and distillate of orange. It became the most popular French apéritif following the absinthe ban. Today, demand is mainly for Picon Bière, which is drunk mixed with beer.

Suze
Suze was invented around the turn of the 19th–20th century by a banker's son called Henri Porté. It was acquired by Pernod in 1965. This apéritif is based mainly on gentian roots, macerated in alcohol for some months. The gentians mainly come from the *Massif Central*. It is the best known of the gentian liqueurs; it stimulates the appetite, and is served as a long drink with ice cubes and soda.

There were once hundreds of small brands of *pastis* in Provence, and they were thought to have died out. Now a new generation of individual types is appearing.

Ingredients used for *pastis*
1 Mint – 2 Birch leaves – 3 Maize – 4 Vervain 5 Sapwood – 6 Licorice – 7 Camomile – 8 Blackcurrant leaves – 9 Poppy seeds 10 Thyme – 11 Coriander – 12 Parsley – 13 Cinnamon – 14 Star anise – 15 Fennel – 16 Summer savory 17 Cumin – 18 Aniseed

Vegetables of the south

Unlike other regions of France, Provence is a paradise for those who love vegetables. The colorful markets in every town are instant proof of this; there, the vegetable stalls display an overwhelming variety. The richness of the local vegetable produce is reflected in the cuisine, including, exceptionally, that of the restaurants. Provençal cooks devote much care and attention to salads and vegetable dishes; preparing vegetables always takes time. Varieties and eating habits owe a great deal to the nearness of Italy. The sociable *bagna cauda*, a vegetable fondue at which guests dip strips of almost raw vegetables into a hot anchovy and garlic sauce, originated in Piedmont, and is starting to gain ground beyond Provence, but only slowly. The love of vegetables can be seen at every stage of the meal from appetizer to dessert. The famous *soupe au pistou* is entirely a vegetable soup, and other soups are based on tomatoes or pumpkins. Stuffed tomatoes in their original form came from Provence, where artichokes were being plucked long before French diners in other regions knew what to do with them. Provence is the home of *pan bagnat*, white bread luscious with some olive oil and piled with onions, tomato,

green bell pepper, black olives, hard-cooked egg and anchovies.

Cooks here know how to bake hearty cakes, popularly made with mangold or spinach, and here they bake *tians*, a range of vegetable gratins named after the red-brown earthenware dishes in which they are made.

Olive oil is always used, of course; practically no recipe forgets the garlic, almost none will omit a pinch of ground chili, and the temptation to add a couple of anchovies (whole, or as the purée *pissalat*) is seldom resisted. Many take the trouble to stuff vegetables or zucchini flowers, or prepare *ratatouille*, a Mediterranean dish of stewed vegetables, in accordance with some old and laborious recipe. This dish comes originally from Nice, but must by now have conquered the whole of Europe. *Grand aïoli* would lose its entire character without the vegetables.

There is even a recipe for a sweet raisin cake, *tourte de bléa*, which uses mangold; pumpkin too is used to make a sweet cake which is a traditional dessert. As these examples show, vegetables are as much part of Provence as the sun, the pines and the cicadas.

This view of the market at Aix-en-Provence gives just a glimpse of the rich array of produce on sale in a typical provençal town. Vegetables and salads are an important part of the local cuisine.

Beet is normally sold ready cooked in Provence.

Vegetable stallholders take time to arrange their wares attractively.

Bell peppers, eggplants and zucchini, once the pillars of Mediterranean cuisine.

The great variety of different types of bean is astonishing in itself.

409

Vegetable cuisine

Ratatouille is perhaps the most successful combination of the four most typical Mediterranean vegetables. Whatever the individual variation as to quantities, agreement is universal that it should contain tomatoes, bell peppers, eggplants and zucchini, along with garlic, a bouquet garni and a sufficient amount of olive oil. Controversy arises over whether basil adds the final touch or ruins the dish. Opinion is equally hotly divided over methods of preparation. Purists insist on frying each type of vegetable separately in olive oil until they are cooked to just the right degree. The tomatoes, garlic and bouquet garni for the sauce are also simmered separately. Some even layer the different types of vegetable individually, each perfectly cooked, in a serving dish of Provençal pottery, serving the tomato sauce separately. Surely this raises *ratatouille* to a culinary work of art. The second method combines the vegetables in one pan, pouring over the tomato sauce and leaving the whole to cook long and slowly. This is less complicated, and so more popular. Cooking the vegetables separately certainly preserves the integrity of each, but lose the full combination of flavors.

Les petits farcis de légumes provençaux, salade de mesclun au pistou et parmesan

Small stuffed Provençal vegetables, *mesclun* with *pistou* and Parmesan

4 new, round potatoes, firm-textured when boiled
4 medium sized tomatoes
Salt
4 purple artichokes
Scant 1 cup/100 g freshly grated Parmesan
Olive oil
Juice of 1 lemon
1 tbsp *pistou* (see page 401)
Freshly milled pepper
5½ oz/150 g *mesclun* (mixed young salad leaves)
1 piece of Parmesan

Filling
14 oz/400 g leftover ragout of beef or 3½ cups/400g ground beef
7 oz/200 g potatoes
Olive oil
1 large onion
4 cloves of garlic
1 bunch parsley
1 bunch basil
2 tbsp freshly grated Parmesan
Freshly milled salt and pepper

Boil the new potatoes in their skins in salted water. Cool, cut off the top third and scoop out the bottom section.
Cut the lid off the tomatoes, and scoop out the rest. Sprinkle the hollowed-out section with salt and place upside down on a grid to drain.
Cut at least two thirds off the top of the artichokes and remove the stem and hard outside leaves. Boil in salted water. Do not let them become too soft. Cool, and remove the choke with a teaspoon.
To make the filling, chop the beef ragout very small.
Peel the potatoes, cut into pieces and fry them in olive oil over a medium heat.
Crush the cooked potatoes with a fork.
Peel the onion, cut into rings and fry lightly in olive oil in a saucepan.
If raw ground beef is used, brown and fry briefly in a little oil.
Peel the garlic, and chop finely along with the parsley and basil.
Mix the cooked potatoes, chopped ragout (or fried ground beef), garlic, parsley and basil, and add 2 tbsp Parmesan. Stir together and season, adding plenty of pepper. Preheat the oven to 355 °F/180 °C.
Place the prepared vegetables in an ovenproof dish and stuff with the filling. Sprinkle with grated Parmesan and heat through in the oven.
Mix a dressing of olive oil, lemon juice and *pistou* in a large bowl.
Tear apart the salad leaves, mix and toss in the dressing. Place the salad in the middle of each plate and grate Parmesan over it. Arrange the warm stuffed vegetables on top. Drizzle with olive oil and serve.

Fleurs de courgettes frites

Deep-fried zucchini flowers

2 eggs
Scant½ cup/100 ml mineral water
3½ tbsp/50 ml white wine
1 tbsp oil
Sea salt
Freshly milled black pepper
1½ cups/200 g wheat flour
16 zucchini flowers with embryo zucchini at base
Oil for frying

Separate the eggs. Mix the egg yolks, mineral water, wine, oil, salt and pepper, then add the flour gradually.
Leave the mixture to rest for about 20 minutes. Then beat the egg whites until very stiff and fold into the yolk mixture.
Heat plenty of oil in a pan suitable for deep frying. Clean the zucchini flowers carefully, but do not wash. Dip the flowers into the batter to coat, and fry them in batches. Drain on paper towels before serving.

Bagna cauda

Vegetable fondue

Vegetables
Celery
Fennel
Bell peppers
Carrots
Endive hearts
Broccoli
Radishes

Sauce
3 oz/75 g anchovy fillets in oil
5 cloves of garlic
1¼ cups/300 ml olive oil

Prepare a selection of vegetables in season by washing and drying, then cutting or dividing them into strips. Separate the celery stalks; cut the fennel into eight; cut the peppers into strips; quarter the

Les petits farcis de légumes provençaux, Salade de mesclun – Stuffed vegetables with *mesclun*

Fresh Mediterranean vegetables such as zucchini and eggplants are the basis of *Ratatouille*.

Red and green bell peppers, halved, cored and cut into pieces, provide color.

Olive oil helps provide important additional flavor, as do lightly browned onions.

The eggplants and bell peppers also taste better for their initial sweating in oil.

Add the tomatoes after the zucchini. They should be as ripe as possible.

chicory hearts and divide the broccoli into florets. The radishes can be halved or left whole. Arrange the vegetables attractively on a platter, so that they are all within reach of every guest.

To make the sauce, crush the anchovy fillets in a mortar.

Peel and chop the garlic, crush this too and mix with the anchovy.

Add the olive oil gradually, stirring constantly. Transfer the sauce to a small saucepan and place over a low heat, stirring constantly until hot and creamy.

Place the sauce on a heated stand in the middle of the table.

Guests each dip a piece of vegetable into the sauce as wished, and eat it still crisp, almost raw. The sauce must not be allowed to become so hot that it smokes or boils. White bread is served to accompany the fondue, and a pétillant rosé from the Côtes de Provence.

Ratatouille
Provençal stewed vegetables
(illustration above)

4 small zucchini
2 eggplants
2 red and 2 green bell peppers
4 fleshy tomatoes
2 onions
3 cloves of garlic
8 tbsp olive oil
Freshly milled salt and pepper
1 bouquet garni: parsley, rosemary, marjoram, thyme, tarragon, summer savory

Slice the zucchini ½ inch (1 centimeter) thick and dice the eggplants. Halve the bell peppers, core and cut into pieces. Peel the tomatoes by first carefully pouring boiling water over them, then pulling away the peel. Quarter them. Cut the onions up small and chop the garlic finely.

Preheat the oven to 355 °F/180 °C.
Heat the olive oil in a large, heavy, lidded pan (ideally, one capable of being used as a casserole in the oven). Lightly brown the onions in this. Add and sweat the eggplants and bell peppers. Soon afterwards add the zucchini and tomatoes.
Season with salt and pepper and sprinkle on the chopped garlic.
Mix all the ingredients thoroughly but carefully.
Place the bouquet garni on top and cover.
Place the covered pan or casserole in the oven and cook for 1 hour. Alternatively, allow to cook gently on the stove top over a low heat for 50 to 60 minutes.
Remove the bouquet garni and serve.

Whether the vegetables are cooked together in one pot or separately, *ratatouille* can be served warm or hot with fish and meat, or as a main dish. On a hot day, it should be tried chilled. This makes a refreshing first course.

411

Truffle time in Provence

Provence in winter: what can it possibly have to offer? The days are short, the weather prone to disappoint. Many of the best addresses on the culinary scene are closed. Yet there are lovers of good food who beat a path to Provence at this unlikely time of year. They seem drawn by the scent of truffles. Provence, more precisely the *département* of Vaucluse, is the most important supplier of truffles in the world. The days of overwhelming abundance are long gone, though truffles do still grow in the oak forests of Mont Ventoux. Today, 90 percent of the truffles produced in Provence come from cultivated groves, planted with oak trees infected with the spores. It takes ten years for a *truffière* to yield its first modest harvest. It will continue to produce black diamonds for another 40 winters before dwindling away.

Truffles are formed in April and May. There need to be thunderstorms in April, May should not be too cold, June and July not too dry, then slightly damp around the time of wine harvest. December will then bring excellent, ripe *Tuber melanosporum*, the botanical name for these edible fungi. Some early truffles appear as early as November, late ones until mid-March, but the main season is from January 15 to February 15. Conditions are not equally favorable every year, so the harvest varies. Around 1900, it amounted to several thousand tons, but it now ranges from about 22 tons (20 tonnes) in a very poor year to

38 tons (35 tonnes) in a very good one. World production is 88 tons (80 tonnes). The truffles come from plantations with spore-infected oaks; they have a symbiotic relationship with the trees, and prefer oaks. Harvests from these are irregular and unpredictable. Only when the truffles are ripe do they develop their intense aroma. Dogs or pigs can then scent out these unremarkable-looking clumps of what seem to be earth.

The truffle market in Carpentras happens on Friday morning in front of the "Univers" bar near the Hôpital. The crowd jostles. There are many older people, many peaked caps; plastic bags in profusion. The atmosphere is conspiratorial; whispering, surreptitious glances into baskets and plastic bags; people sniff and feel the wares. Then the overseer blows the whistle to start, and chaos miraculously gives way to order. Those with truffles to sell line up, and the work of the *courtiers*, the brokers, begins. A steely blue sky lies over all, and the *mistral* blows cold around the ears and noses of the participants. A vigorous, short-haired man with a basket half full of some 8 pounds (nearly 4 kilograms) of truffles is attracting attention. He has gathered them on his leasehold land of about 2500 acres (1000 hectares) on Mont Ventoux in a period of six days. He had three dogs working simultaneously. Pigs are a thing of the past. The brokers have opened up their "offices" in the heated vestibule of the "Univers." There, they weigh the goods in a practiced way, quietly hand over money or hastily write a check. All this happens opposite the gaily colored weekly market of Carpentras, with its olives, sausages, goat cheese, vegetables and household tools. It is considered one of the best markets in Provence, with Nice and Toulon.

Types of truffle

- *Tuber aestivum* is collected in the summer. It looks outwardly like a black truffle, but the inside is light colored and the flavor dull.
- *Tuber brumale* appears at the same time as *Tuber melanosporum* and looks outwardly similar, but it is rare. The network of veins is less dense, and both scent and flavor are less strong.
- *Tuber magnatum*, the white truffle of Piedmont, retains its aromatic power only when fresh. It is not found in France.
- *Tuber melanosporum*, the true truffle of Périgord (and of Provence) is black, with a network of pale, fine veins running through it. Its intense, captivating perfume is reminiscent of musk and bay. The aroma develops fully only when cooked.

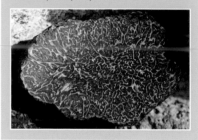

When midday arrives, truffle hunters and farmers will be toasting their commercial success, but for the brokers, the afternoon's work is just beginning. At their pitches, they are now sorting the morning's acquisitions into two size groups and two qualities. The coating of earth is left on the truffles, because it keeps them in top condition for three to four days. They lose their aroma within a day if they are washed and

Baskets like this one are used to carry 15 pounds (7 kilograms) of truffles apiece from the brokers to the dealers.

brushed clean. The baskets contain over 15 pounds (7 kilograms), mainly ordered by the famous producers of preserves from Périgord, though local firms too buy supplies, and mainly use local brokers (*courtiers*). Profit margins are less generous than one might imagine, at least according to the brokers. Two thirds of the price go in broker's expenses. Only top quality truffles earn top prices – the consumer had to pay up to $240 for 3 1/2 ounces of best black truffel during the winter of 2003/2004 – and about 30 percent of the truffles they buy in will not make the grade. They will be sold on to the food processing industry at a much lower price. About 10–15 percent of soil is allowed for in the weight, because it helps preserve the freshness of the truffles in the short term.

Fortunately, truffles are lightweight enough to go a long way, and a quantity of under a quarter of a pound (100 grams) is enough to flavor a number of foods and put into pâtés. Bearing in mind the pleasure they give, they might even be called a bargain.

Around 11 on a Saturday morning, the village street in Richeranches, in the heart of the most famous truffle growing region of Provence, is impassable. More and more people are standing around in groups, talking. There is an occasional laugh. The subject of every conversation is nowhere to be seen: truffles, at the most famous truffle market of all. A dealer says that the prices are still too high, so no deals are being done. The real business of the day, when it happens, is unspectacular. To see it involves watching the small delivery vans, parked surrounded by knots of people at the side of the road. Peering over someone's shoulder might provide a glimpse of bags and baskets of truffles, and the *courtiers'* weighing scales. About 15 brokers have gathered. The quantity of truffles here is four or five times that in Carpentras, roughly 900 pounds (400 kilograms) of truffles have been sold, and many thousands of Euros have changed hands in one single morning.

Even a professional seldom sees such a magnificent example of *Tuber melanosporum*. It takes exceptional growing conditions to produce one this size.

Truffle-hunting dogs have long since replaced the traditional pigs. No farmer could operate without them.

When matters reach the interesting stage, the *courtiers* produce a set of hanging scales. Generally a conclusion is quickly arrived at.

An ordinary person acquiring a few truffles will find that the best way to keep them is to clean them and put them in sunflower oil in the freezer.

Vegetables are not all

Meat and poultry

The people of Provence have an especial liking for sheep. The passage of flocks up to the mountain pastures, the traditional *transhumance*, has become rare. They used to travel great distances across this large province, for instance from the meadows of Crau, southeast of Arles, to the mountain pastures of Haute-Provence, in search of grazing and more bearable summer temperatures. Most sheep farmers today use large transporters which carry a couple of hundred sheep at a time, though a minority still adheres to the old tradition of taking the flocks to the Provençal Alps on foot. Progress is mainly made at night, resting during the day and giving the sheep some time to feed and recover in meadows that have been reserved in advance *en route*. Some flocks have a three-week journey to reach the summer pastures where they will spend three months.

In times gone by, when many thousands of animals headed for the mountains in the middle of June, returning in the middle of September, the twice-yearly procession also acted as a sort of travelling market. Some sheep and lambs would be sold directly for the table, to be braised or grilled over vine twigs, still the most popular barbecue method for lamb in the region today.

In this way, Avignon received its sheep delivered fresh to the door, and this was the meat used for its famous *daube*, a slow pot roast made with beef elsewhere. The traveling flocks of sheep may also have been the reason behind another popular Provençal lamb recipe, *pieds et paquets*, which means "feet and packets." This hearty dish was originally one made at the Marseilles restaurant "La Pomme," but has long since spread to the whole of Provence. It is a combination of sheep's feet and tripe, with a stuffing of lamb brawn, ham, garlic and parsley. The ingredients are stewed together for several hours at very low temperature in a good meat stock until they melt in the mouth.

Apart from such hearty recipes and the general love of braised dishes, the character of meat cookery from Montélimar to Menton is typified by the inspired use of seasonings. At its simplest, this consists of herbs, garlic and chili powder, but examples of more daring approaches include the use of *tapenade* or *anchoïade*, anchovy paste. Elegant seasoning alternatives are offered by lavender honey or *pastis*. Whatever the approach, Provençal meat cookery is unmistakably true to its roots.

Râble de lapin farci à la tapenade – Saddle of rabbit stuffed with *tapenade*

Râble de lapin farci à la tapenade
Saddle of rabbit stuffed with *tapenade*

1 saddle of rabbit
1 carrot
1 onion
1 stalk of celery
1 bouquet garni: bay, thyme, rosemary
¾ cup/200 ml white wine
2 tbsp olive oil
freshly milled salt and pepper

Tapenade
Scant 1 cup/100 g black olives
1 oz/25 g anchovies
1 clove of garlic

Bone the rabbit, chop up the bones and brown them lightly in a saucepan. Clean the carrot, onion and celery and cut into pieces. Add the vegetables and herbs to the bones, pour on the wine and reduce. Then add a little water and cook for another 20 minutes. Pass the sauce through a sieve. Make the *tapenade* by blending the olives, anchovies and garlic using a hand blender.
Preheat the oven to 355 °F/180 °C. Take the fillets obtained from the rabbit when boned, along with the thin layer of meat from the ribs, season the inside with salt and pepper, and spread with *tapenade*. Roll the thin layer of meat around the fillets, enclosing the stuffing. Tie with thread. Brown on all sides in 1 tbsp of olive oil, and then cook in the oven for 15 minutes, basting frequently with the juices.
Leave to rest for 10 minutes, then take out the meat and deglaze the roasting pan by pouring in the sauce. Stir the remaining olive oil into the sauce and check the seasoning. Warm the rabbit through in the oven, then slice into *médaillons* and pour over the sauce.
Serve immediately.

Daube avignonnaise
Ragout of lamb Avignon

1 lb 5 oz/600 g boned shoulder of lamb
2 carrots
2 onions
2 cups/500 ml dry white wine
2 cloves of garlic
2 stems of parsley
2 bay leaves
1 sprig of rosemary
1 clove
A pinch of nutmeg
Freshly milled salt and pepper
Scant ½ cup/100 ml olive oil
2 medium slices/20 g fat bacon

Cut the meat into cubes.
Clean the vegetables and cut into pieces. Marinate the meat in the white wine for 4 hours along with the carrots, one of the onions, the garlic, herbs, spices and olive oil.
Heat the bacon in a heavy, lidded saucepan until the fat runs, chop the remaining onion and sweat this in the bacon fat, then add and brown the meat. Pour on the marinade, cover, and cook for 3 hours. Remove the meat and keep hot while reducing the sauce to the desired consistency.
Serve with steamed potatoes.

Daube de bœuf à la provençale
Beef in the style of Provence

Serves 6

Generous 3 lb/1½ kg top rib of beef (or eye of round)
1 calf's foot
2 tbsp olive oil
Freshly milled salt and pepper
About 2 pints/ 1 liter dry white wine
2 carrots
5 oz/150 g onions
10½ oz/300 g champignon mushrooms
2 tomatoes, blanched and peeled
5 oz/150 g smoked bacon
Scant 1 cup/100 g black olives
1 bouquet garni
Zest of 1 unwaxed orange
2 cups/500 ml veal stock
Flour

Cube the beef and marinate with the calf's foot, olive oil, salt, pepper and white wine for 24 hours.
Clean the vegetables. Cut the carrots, onions and mushrooms into strips and dice the tomatoes.
Remove the meat from the marinade and brown it.
Add the vegetables, bacon, olives, bouquet garni and orange zest, and pour on equal quantities of the marinade and veal stock, just sufficient to cover.
Preheat the oven to 355 °F/180 °C. Make a flour and water paste, and use this to make an airtight seal around the lid of the casserole.
Cook in the oven for 6 hours.

Poulettes au pastis
Small chickens in pastis

Serves 6

2 young chickens, quartered
2½ tbsp/40 ml pastis
A pinch of saffron
1 cup/250 ml olive oil
Freshly milled salt and pepper
2 onions
6 cloves of garlic
4 tomatoes, blanched and skinned
1 stem of fennel
2 stems of parsley
4 potatoes

Marinate the chicken pieces overnight in the pastis, saffron, generous ⅓ cup olive oil, salt and pepper.
Peel the onions and garlic, and chop finely. Sweat these in olive oil and add the tomatoes and stems of fennel and parsley.
Place the chicken pieces on top.
Pour over the marinade and top up with boiling water. Cover and let boil for 10 minutes.
Peel and slice the potatoes. Add them to the pan, replace the lid and simmer for another 20 minutes.
Shortly before serving, boil strongly for a few moments to bind the olive oil and the remaining cooking liquids.
Serve accompanied by slices of rustic bread, spread with *rouille*.

Canette laquée au miel de lavande
Breast of duck in lavender honey

2 young duck
lavender honey
1 carrot
1 onion
1 stalk of celery
1 bouquet garni: thyme, bay, rosemary
Freshly milled salt and pepper
1 tsp butter

Bone the duck, extracting the breast fillets.
Brush the skin side of the breast of duck with honey.
Make a stock from the duck bones, vegetables and herbs.
Simmer this for 1½ hours, then season with salt and pepper.
Preheat the oven to 375 °F/190 °C.
Brown the skin side of the duck fillets in a skillet, without fat or oil, until they are golden and caramelized. Roast for 5 minutes in the hot oven, then leave to rest for 10 minutes.
Remove the fillets and keep warm in the oven.
Deglaze the pan with the stock, reduce and then stir in the butter. Arrange the duck on warmed plates, pour over the sauce, and serve immediately.
Potatoes or braised tomatoes and bell peppers make a good accompaniment.

Canette laquée au miel de lavande – Breast of duck in lavender honey

Camargue rice

The land known for its bulls and wild horses is home to another, simpler specialty, though no less important: rice. The Camargue is the most northerly rice-growing area in Europe. This has a long tradition behind it, rice having been introduced first to Spain by the Moors, from there to Italy, and to France in the 13th century. It was not until the swampy region of the Rhône delta was enclosed by dykes in 1870 that rice growing became at all widespread. The dykes caused salinization, and farmers planted rice as an interim crop to prepare for vine planting. Serious interest in rice as a crop developed as a consequence of World War II, when imports stopped, and of the move toward independence in the French colony of Indochina, which meant that projected supplies would be inadequate. Under the Marshall Plan, irrigation canals and pumping stations were built in the Camargue after 1945. In the ensuing 15 years, this developed into one of the most important rice-growing areas in Europe, covering some 74,000 acres (30,000 hectares).

Rice is a plant cultivated in water, and so requires completely level fields. This used to be highly labor-intensive, with stakes every 10 yards (10 meters) to check the ground level. Any unevenness was rectified by hand. Since the middle of the 1980s, levelling has been done using computer-controlled bulldozers equipped with lasers. They operate to within a tolerance of less than an inch (within 2 centimeters) over an area the size of a football pitch, and the depth of the water need nowhere be more than 2-4 inches (5-10 centimeters) as a result. This has a direct effect on yields. Rice needs warmth to grow, something which cannot adequately be guaranteed here. The shallower the water, the more quickly it warms up.

Sowing is done from mid-April onward. The rice farmers flood their fields with water from the Rhône for four or five days. Rice needs a temperature of 59–63 °F (15–17° C) to germinate, so there needs to be enough sunshine at this time of the year. After about a month, the water is gradually drained away so that the young rice plants can sink low enough to strike root. When this has happened, the fields are flooded again. The rice flowers in the second half of August, but only for 1½ hours. It is a difficult moment. If conditions are unfavorable at that time, the seed will not fill. It takes 130–150 days from the time the rice germinates to the harvest. It cannot tolerate temperatures below 54 °F (12 °C), which can cause difficulties in some years. The 25–27 percent moisture on harvesting needs to be reduced to 14 percent before the rice can be husked and polished. This is usually done artificially using special ovens. This and all subsequent tasks are carried out by commercial firms, since the rice farmers are prevented by law from taking part in the distribution of their own harvest.

Untreated rice, paddy, is surrounded by a hard husk. If this inedible outer coat is removed, the result is brown rice. This has a silvery skin and contains the germ, with most of the nutritional value, especially the important B vitamins. Brown rice keeps less well (and is better stored in the refrigerator). It is therefore usually polished by machine; this has the effect of removing most of the nutrients and vitamins, including vitamin B1, which the body needs to digest the starch contained in the grain. This is how white rice came to cause the neuropathic disease beriberi in Asia.

The ricefields are laid out in such a way that water polluted by conventional agricultural methods can run off into the Etang de Vacarès. It would benefit the conservation area of the Camargue if rice production became organic.

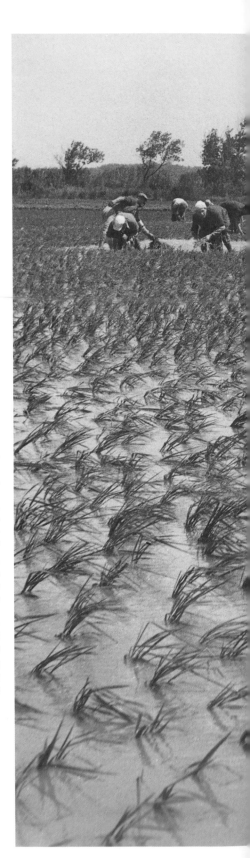

Left: Red rice is a specialty of the Camargue.
Right: In the 1950s, rice was often planted by hand. Today state of the art machines are used.

Rice – stages of processing

Paddy: Freshly harvested rice is surrounded by a protective husk. It cannot be eaten like this, however, and must be husked.

Brown, cargo: The outer layers of the grain remain after the husk has been removed. These contain the germ with its important nutrients.

Polished rice: The outer layers are removed to give the rice its white appearance. This removes the germ, and with it two thirds of the nutrients.

Parboiled rice: Steaming the rice prior to polishing enables the grain to absorb some of the nutrients, so that they are not removed by polishing.

As long as weather conditions are favorable during the short flowering period, the stems droop to the ground, heavy with panicles of ripe grain.

A group of *manardiers* and their friends mounted on the agile white horses of the Camargue, have rounded up a small group of bulls from the herd. They are now leading them to the arena, pinned between the horses.

The entertainment is nearing its end. The bulls and cows are released once more and chased back to their natural pastures in the wetlands, where they live almost wild in the open all year round.

The bulls of the Camargue

Small, jet black bulls with upright horns have been bred from medieval times in the wetlands of the Camargue, in the delta at the mouth of the Rhône. Recently they were given an *Appellation d'Origine Contrôlée* for their flavorsome, tender meat. For the breeders of these bulls, however, the *manadiers*, owners of a *manade* or herd, the meat is by no means the only thing which interests them. The *toros* of the Camargue have a quite different fate from Spanish bulls, which are taunted by elegant *toreros* at the *corrida*, and pay with their lives for the ignominy; a Camargue bull simply needs to have sufficient cunning and malice to have a great career before it. They first enter an arena at the age of about three to four years; the largest of these are in Arles, Nîmes, Lunel, Beaucaire and Châteaurenard. A *cocarde* consisting of a cord with two tassels is tied between the horns of the young bull, which is then called a *cocardier*, a fighting bull. Next, it is sent into the arena, usually a circle enclosed with a high barrier, and approached by men called *razeteurs*, usually dressed in white, who try to snatch the cockade from the bull using a special short hook. There is a money prize. If the bull, *lo biou*, resists with enough fury and cunning to frustrate the *razeteurs* and keep its cockade throughout the 15 minutes that the contest lasts, it returns in triumph to its breeder's truck. The breeder releases it back into its field until the next contest. July and August are the main season for bulls and cows. From November until March, they can graze undisturbed beneath the wide skies of the Camargue, nourishing their hatred for enclosed arenas, yelling crowds and irritating *razeteurs*. If one of these black cattle, which live almost wild on the pastures, feeding only on the grasses that grow there, is more peaceably disposed, it takes the route to the pot. It is likely to end its career in a *gardiane*, a ragoût of Camargue steer meat simmered in red wine (a Costières de Nîmes is preferred), a dish whose quality is measured by the thickness of the gravy.

A *course camarguaise* is often a wedding entertainment. The men try to snatch the cockade from the head of a young cow, in the expectation that she will defend her honor with suitably auspicious fury.

AOC Vallée du Rhône
AOC Côtes du Rhône
Crus des Côtes du Rhône

N

0   20 km

Crest

Die

Crémant de Die
Clairette de Die

Montélimar

Ardèche

Rhône

Coteaux
du Tricastin

Rousset-les-Vignes

Côtes du Rhône/
Côtes du Rhône Villages

Rochegude

Pont-St-Esprit

Rasteau

Vaison-la-Romaine

Cairanne

St-Gervais

Gigondas

Orange

Vacqueyras

Alès

Côtes du Rhône/
Côtes du Rhône Villages

Laudun

Beaumes-de-Venise

Sault

Lirac

Châteauneuf-
du-Pape

Carpentras

Gard

Tavel

L'Isle-sur-la-Sorgue

Rhône

Avignon

Côtes du Ventoux

Nîmes

Apt

Costières de Nîmes

Cavaillon

Côtes du Lubéron

Durance

Lunel

Arles

Petit Rhône

Salon-de-Provence

Grand Rhône

Aix-en-Provence

Étang de Vaccarès

Étang de Berre

The wines of the southern Rhône

Between Montélimar and Avignon, city of the Popes, extensive vineyards cover the low hills on either side of the Rhône. These mostly belong to the *Appellation* Côtes du Rhône, which was recognized in 1937. It comprises 43,500 hectares (107,493 acres) and accounts for four out of every five bottles of Rhône wine. In this large region there is a variety of different soils and microclimates, in which the most important common factors are the Mediterranean sun, the dryness and the cold *mistral*. From the outset these factors dictate the production of red wines. They have also resulted in the greater success of certain varieties along the southern Rhône and

to the consequent spread of these varieties. The clear leader is Grenache Noir, which achieves high levels of alcohol and great fruitiness. It is usually blended with other varieties, however, to increase color, tannins and complexity. In wines of fairly modest quality this is done using Carignan vinified by the carbonic maceration method; in those of more demanding quality, Syrah and Mourvèdre are used. It is Grenache which brings the warmth of the sun into the Côtes du Rhône, and this is precisely what has made it so popular in cooler countries and at colder times of year. Whites and rosés account for only 2 percent each of the production figure, around 2.1 million hectoliters (280 million bottles) a year.

The uncontested star of Côtes du Rhône wines is Châteauneuf-du-Pape, both in its red and its rarer white forms. It accounts for 7 percent of the *Appellation*. A total of 13 varieties are permitted for this wine, although no single winegrower is likely to use them all at once. In recent years, the main varieties included in many *cuvées* have been Syrah and Mourvèdre, to provide an elegant structure

without reducing body. In other communes, too, winegrowers have endowed their wines with greater depth. In the *Appellation* Côtes du Rhône Villages, granted in 1966, many communes have earned themselves a name in their own right on account of the rise in quality. Gigondas, which received its own *Appellation* as long ago as 1971, led the way. Vacqueyras at last achieved recognition as an independent *cru* in 1990, and Cairanne soon will. In Gard, on the right bank (which is in fact over the border in Languedoc-Roussillon), the winegrowers regard themselves from the wine point of view as belonging to the Rhône. There, Lirac, Tavel rosé and the Costières de Nîmes have their own *Appellations*. To round off the list from this production area, there are the sparkling wines of Die, the naturally sweet wines of Muscat de Beaumes de Venise and Rasteau, Côteaux de Tricastin, south of Montélimar, and the Côtes du Lubéron.

Séguret, built by the Knights Templar, is one of the most picturesque villages of the Côtes du Rhône. It is known for powerful red wines with a long finish.

Appellations of the southern Rhône

Côtes du Rhône
The regional *Appellation*, which covers all the villages and *crus*, includes classed *terroirs* in 163 communes. Within this area, 1720 estates and 75 winegrowing cooperatives produce predominantly red wines. Some are bottled at the end of November as fruity, quaffable Primeur, and the main wine type is pleasant, round and fruity. The stony soils and the best winegrowers produce dark, spicy, powerful reds. Rosés and whites play a minor role.

Côtes du Rhône Villages
This *Appellation*, given in 1966, comprises 77 communes with 5700 hectares (14,085 acres) of vineyards in the departments of Drôme, Vaucluse, Gard and Ardèche. Sixteen have the right to add their own name: in Drôme, these are Rochegude, Rousset-les-Vignes, Saint-Maurice, Saint-Pantaléon-les-Vignes and Vinsobres; in Vaucluse, they are Beaumes-de-Venise, Cairanne, Rasteau, Roaix, Sablet, Séguret, Valréas and Visan; and in Gard, they are Chusclan, Laudun and Saint-Gervais. The *Appellation* applies to all three colors.

Châteauneuf-du-Pape
The most famous *cru* of the southern Rhône. From the 14th century, it was promoted under the anti-popes. Special *terroir*, very hot and sunny with sandy loam soils strewn with large river pebbles. The total area is 3200 hectares (7908 acres) with a maximum yield of 35 hectoliters/hectares (about 2 tons/acre). Strong red wines with great volume, mostly from Grenache, Syrah, Mourvèdre and Cinsault, with aromas of cherry, leather, licorice and spices. Very southern, full whites with a long finish from Clairette, Bourboulenc and Roussanne.

Gigondas
East of Orange, 1200 hectares (2965 acres) in the commune of the same name. Weighty red and

rosé wines from very hot, stony alluvial soil where a renaissance of this great *terroir* has taken place since the 1960s. Grenache predominates; at least 15 percent of this variety must be present, blended with Syrah and Mourvèdre. The reds are initially very fruity and mostly matured in old oak vats. With long aging they develop pronounced notes of musk and game.

Vacqueyras
At the foot of the Dentelles de Montmirail, the winegrowers have increased their quality step by step to progress from the simple Côtes du Rhône to their own *cru*. Vineyards occupy about 800 hectares (1977 acres). Red, rosé and white are all recognized, though the red accounts for 95 percent of the volume produced. When young, the nose of these robust red wines is reminiscent of ripe berries and licorice.

Lirac
The 450 hectares (1112 acres) of the *Appellation*, situated on the right bank of the Rhône, encompass the four communes of Lirac, Roquemaure, Saint-Laurent-les-Arbres and Saint-Géniès-de-Comolas in Gard. For centuries the wines were exported to the north from the port of Roquemaure. Four-fifths are fruity, herby red wines, one eighth sturdy rosés and the rest, round white wines.

Châteauneuf-du-Pape

Tavel
The king of the rosés is the only *terroir* in France reserved exclusively for rosé production. It is blended from red varieties such as Grenache, Syrah, Mourvèdre, Cinsault, Carignan and the rustic Calitor, as well as white grapes such as Clairette, Picpoul and Bourboulenc. Its aroma is characterized by red fruits and roasted almonds. It is aromatic, spicy and well structured, and is served not too cold, around 55°F (13°C).

Coteaux du Tricastin
Situated south of Montélimar and extending as far as Grignan, this *Appellation* comprises 2500 hectares (6178 acres) of vineyards. Some 92 percent of their production is of red wines, with the accent often very much on fruit.

Clairette de Die & Crémant de Die
The sparkling wines of the central Rhône have been known since times long past. The Clairette is based on at least three quarters Muscat and has a characteristic bouquet. The Crémant on the other hand is vinified from the Clairette grape alone.

Côtes du Ventoux
This is an enormous region, extending from Vaison-la-Romaine in the north, westward and southward around the huge limestone massif of Mont Ventoux and on as far as Apt. Close to 7000 hectares (17,300 acres) are planted with vineyards. Due to the temperate climate, they produce mainly fairly light, pleasant red wines and fresh rosés.

Côtes du Lubéron
This *Appellation*, like the Côtes du Ventoux, is managed from Avignon, and administratively it belongs to the Rhône valley. Despite this, the Lubéron region, in its situation north of the Durance, is deepest Provence. It produces fruity, harmonious red wines, elegant rosés and delightful, balanced whites which account for one quarter of the production from about 3000 hectares (7400 acres).

The wines of Provence

The charm of their color is a delight, glowing in every shade of pink from rose blossoms to palest salmon and through to a fresh, raspberry hue. This rosé conjures images of the Mediterranean, of brightly decked tables on shady terraces, of olives and pistachios, *bagna cauda* and *aïoli*, grilled fish and cutlets of lamb. The agreeable rosé wine which can be served with such ease, well chilled, with any dish, is a blessing to winegrowers and cooperatives. It fills their coffers just as quickly as it is quaffed. It is made mainly from Grenache and Cinsault, but the art of raising it above mediocrity is all too rare.

The best winegrowers of the region concentrate with far greater enthusiasm on the red wines, for which a wide spectrum of varieties is available. Syrah and Mourvèdre set the tone, along with

Cabernet Sauvignon, which has been established in Provence for over a century. To these are added Grenache Noir and sometimes old Carignan or the indigenous Counoise. Modern developments such as stainless steel tanks, controlled fermentation temperatures and *barrique* aging have all made their entry on the scene here; this wine region has attracted more well-to-do newcomers than any other in France. Nevertheless, the predominant character of the red wines has remained agreeably traditional. A few years' aging is required for the wines to develop a pronounced bouquet in which mingle aromas of game, leather, wild herbs, berries and oriental spices.

The most fascinating are the red wines of Bandol, the best of which consist mainly of Mourvèdre. In the Bandol region, the vineyards lie facing the Mediterranean, able to benefit from the moisture coming in off the sea. On the *restanques*, the typical broad terraces of Provençal vineyards, the demanding, late-ripening Mourvèdre finds ideal growing conditions. It is

distinguished for its color, structure and fine tannins, and is esteemed as an ingredient in the blend of grapes for many *Appellations* of the Midi. One should not be misled, however, by the foreground aromas of black berries which the Mourvèdre displays in its youth. As a general rule, a red Bandol needs at least eight years to reveal its true nature, a scent of leather and spices and a rare finesse in the mouth. In great vintages, which are by no means the same as those of Bordeaux, Bandol has sufficient strength and firmness to gain in dimension over 15 years and more. The generally high standard of the *Appellation* is remarkable, and disappointment with its red wines is very rare. On the other hand, the banality of the rosés, the predominant type in terms of quantity, is a frequent source of regret. White wines, which often reflect their Mediterranean homeland in their fruity, floral aromas, usually represent in contrast less than a tenth of production in the whole of Provence.

In the cellars of Château Simone, close to Aix-en-Provence, the excellent wines of the tiny *Appellation* Palette are maturing.

Grenache Noir plays a significant role in Provence, as it does in the southern Rhône and in the Midi.

Appellations of Provence

Bandol
Promoted to become an independent *Appellation* in 1941, this occupies an area of just 1300 hectares (3212 acres) in the hinterland of the coastal resort of Bandol. The winegrowers both then and now have shown their ability to foster the special nature of their wine. Both red and rosé owe their character to the Mourvèdre. One tenth of the 5 million bottles produced annually is accounted for by dry white wines.

Les Baux-de-Provence
Previously grouped under Coteaux d'Aix, this delightful small region situated on the southern and northern slopes of the picturesque Alpilles achieved its own independent *Appellation* for red and rosé wines in 1995. The red wines, which predominate, are blended from Grenache, Syrah and/or Mourvèdre. These must represent at least 60 percent. The most famous of the 14 *domaines* cultivate their vineyards organically.

Bellet
Nice's own *cru* is grown on the heights overlooking the town and produces just 75,000 bottles per year. The white wines, made from Rolle and Vermentino, are very aromatic; the reds are vinified from Braquet and Fuella, two indigenous varieties full of charm and finesse.

Cassis
Cassis owes its special place to its white wine, which has great fullness and character. It makes up three quarters of production from the 170 hectares (420 acres) of vineyards comprising this area, and is based on Ugni Blanc, Clairette, Sémillon and Marsanne. The grapes grow on terraces facing the sea, where vines have been cultivated since ancient times. The winegrowers' desire for quality earned them the first in A.O.C. Provence, back in 1936. The remaining quarter of production is accounted for by very pale rosés, produced from Grenache, Cinsault and Carignan. Their pale color derives from the predominantly used method of using juice pressed without maceration.

Coteaux d'Aix-en-Provence
Bounded on the east by Montagne Sainte-Victoire and on the southwest by the Alpilles, the 3600 hectares (8900 acres) of vineyards south of the Durance cover 49 communes. Rosé now accounts for most of the annual production of almost 20 million bottles. This is followed by red, which has gained in quality thanks to Syrah and Cabernet Sauvignon. The pleasant whites are comparatively rare.

Coteaux Varois
Situated in the center of Provence and surrounded by Côtes de Provence, the numerous wine cooperatives were not initially interested in an *Appellation*. A late change of heart eventually led to recognition in 1993. About 1800 hectares (4450 acres) are in production, yielding mostly rosé, 70 percent of which comes from Cinsault and Grenache, as well as red and some white wine.

Côtes de Provence
Its 18,000 hectares (44,500 acres) make this the largest *Appellation* in the southeast. It has existed since 1977, comprising 83 communes in Var, Bouches-du-Rhône and Vaucluse. It is subdivided into five areas: the slopes descending from the Massif des Maures to the sea between Hyères and St.-Tropez, the broad inner valley to the north of this massif, the hills of the Haut-Pays which rise northward, the depression of Beausset and the lands lying at the foot of Montagne Saint-Victoire. Four-fifths are rosé wine, the rest mainly red. The spicy, aromatic white wines are rare.

Palette
One of the wines of Provence with the greatest character and rarity grows near Aix, on north and northeast-facing slopes occupying only 32 hectares (79 acres). Both the red wines, which consist mainly of Grenache Noir, Mourvèdre and Cinsault, and the whites, mainly Clairette, age magnificently, gaining great complexity.

Calissons d'Aix

Each year on the first Sunday in September in Aix-en-Provence, the blessing of the almond boats takes place. This custom, revived in 1996, dates back to 1630. At that time, the plague had struck the town, and a great Mass was held. A lay judge called Martelly swore to have a service of thanksgiving held every year in September, and this was done; all the church bells of the town would ring out in remembrance, until the French Revolution. During these Masses, the congregation was called forward with the Latin words *venite ad calicem* to receive blessing. The almond cakes were being blessed at the same time, so the locals adapted the pious exhortation with a cheeky grin to *venes toui i calissoum*, meaning "all come to the *calisson*."

Calissons are inseparably linked with almonds. Evidence that an almond cake called *calisone* was being made in Padua comes from a Latin text of 1170. One hundred years later, *calissons* were being distributed at the feast of St. Mark in Venice. The word itself goes back to the Greek verb *kalikos* meaning 'to surround,' from the almond-shaped glory of light, the *mandorla*, which surrounds Christ or the Virgin Mary in Christian art. Perhaps this is the reason that the princes of the church were so fond of *calizioni di marzapane*, especially Pope Pius V in the 16th century, who is supposed to have had a secret passion for them.

Almond trees originated in West Asia, and were cultivated as long ago as Roman times in Italy. They were spreading through Provence as early as the Middle Ages. Their cultivation received a boost at the end of the 16th century when the agronomist Olivier de Serres brought almond and mulberry trees to the south of France from Asia. They encountered excellent growing conditions in Provence. The extent of the almond groves there meant that the world market price for almonds was for a long time decided in Aix.

Confiseurs in Aix each have their own version of the basic recipe, but every *calisson* has three parts: a rice paper base, a paste of almonds and candied fruits, and frosting on top. For the paste, the almonds are peeled and ground and mixed with candied melon from Apt, and a lesser quantity of candied oranges. All three ingredients are worked into a thick paste, which is cooked in a double boiler for 1½ hours. During this time, sugar syrup is stirred in, the only preservative, and by the end of it the paste has become moist and even-textured. It then has to rest for 72 hours, after which the *calissons* are formed, using an automatic process. The paste is put into molds with one tube, while another spreads on the frosting and rollers position the rice paper base underneath. A deft turn deposits the freshly prepared *calisson* on a conveyor belt which carries it through a drying oven. Once they are cool, the lozenge-shaped goodies are ready for packing. Only genuine *calissons* made in Aix have the right to carry the name "Calissons d'Aix-en-Provence." They make their appearance as one of the 13 Christmas desserts on Christmas Eve in Provence.

Right: While the paste of candied melons, oranges and almonds is heating in the double boiler, the syrup is added to just the right consistency.
Below: The paste is pressed into a boat shape, receives its base and its frosting, and is automatically carried into the oven.

Candied melons from Apt are one of the most important ingredients of Calissons d'Aix.

They are mixed with candied oranges, a further flavor, and chopped.

The other basic ingredient is blanched almonds. The best come from Provence.

The candied fruits and almonds are chopped and mixed.

The fruits and almonds remain in the processor until a firm paste is formed.

Sugar syrup is the only preservative used; a thoroughly natural recipe.

The crowd at the crib

Santons

The brightly colored clay figurines called *santons* can be seen in Provence even in the summer months. They depict all kinds of traditional activities and professions, providing a varied picture of this delightful province. Many of the figures show rural activities, others the *métiers de bouche*, which are concerned with food and gastronomic pleasures. The fishwife, the miller and the country woman carrying pumpkins are there; the huntsman, the fisherman and the garlic growers, the goose-breeder, cheese merchant, baker, cook and truffle hunter, the olive picker, the wine merchant, the seller of chestnuts and many more. A close look will reveal a Provençal woman making *aïoli*, and another setting out the ingredients for the *pompe*, the Christmas cake. These figures all surround the crib with its centerpiece, the baby Jesus, the Virgin Mary and Joseph, and add so much to the scene.

Cribs had been set up in the churches since the 16th century. It was at the time of the French Revolution that *santons* (the word comes from the Provençal *santoum*, meaning "little saint") first appeared. At that time the churches were closed, but the tradition of the crib was carried on at home in the family. People simply made smaller figures, using whatever materials came to hand: wood, plaster, clay and bread dough. They painted them or dressed them in fabric. Jean-Louis Lagnel was the first to make plaster casts based on models, from which he went on to mold a series of clay figures. Other *santonniers* continued to dress the figures they made. The first *santon* Mass took place in Marseille in December 1803. The role of the crib received a boost as a result of the pastoral play "Maurel," which shows Jesus being born into a small village in Provence in the 19th century. It opened the way for the people of Provence themselves to be involved with the group around the crib, alongside the biblical characters, and it came to mirror family life. Each member of the family has a particular figure representing him or her, and other figures represent friends and relatives. The whole family helps to build and decorate the crib with moss, dried plants, pieces of wood and pretty stones, and goes out together to collect them on the first Sunday in Advent. The earliest date allowed for opening the boxes containing the figures is December 4, but the Christ child is not added until December 24, before the great Christmas Eve supper. The three kings do not appear until Epiphany. The family's crib is added to each year, so it grows over the generations, and no Christmas would be complete without it. A crib scene should depict an entire stretch of country with several houses, stables, mills and

How a *santon* is made

Preparation of the clay
This is extracted from the clay pit, washed and filtered. The slurry is run into settling pits where it lies for about two months. The excess water evaporates in the sun over the summer months, and as soon as the mass left behind no longer sticks to the fingers, it is brought to store-rooms to lie for a year in cool, damp conditions. The *santons* are made from this pure clay.

Making the santons
Paul or Mireille Fouque will always make the first figure themselves by hand. It serves as a model for the succeeding figures, and is used to produce a two-part press mold or matrix. This is first left to dry. It leads on to the copy mold, and from here, ultimately whole runs of *santons* can be made. A few figures need molds made up of several sections, so as to create figures whose postures have more movement in them. In this case, the parts need to be cast separately – arms, hands, head, hat and items they are carrying, for example – and attached with slurry (liquid clay).

Drying
When the figure is taken out of the mold, the next step is to work over it, smoothing and burring it to remove attached pieces of surplus clay. The figures must be left to dry out slowly in drying chambers to avoid the risk of cracking. This can take between a week and two months, depending on the size of the figure.

Firing
Once fully dry, the *santons* are placed in the kiln, carefully positioned so as not to break. The temperature inside the kiln is brought gradually up to 1760 °F (960 °C) over a period of 9 hours. The kiln must be kept closed for 24 to 48 hours, after which it will have cooled once more and the *santons*, now brick-hard, can be taken out.

Decoration
This is slow, exacting work and involves applying oil paint with slim brushes. One color at a time is applied, working over a figure several times until all the details and items of clothing have been painted on. The matt paint preserves the condition of the figures for a long time, and the oil paints used result in the high quality for which they are recognized. New *santons* are produced every year, using the same method that has been employed for two centuries.

bridges. It is kept on display to be admired for two months. Not until February 2 is it carefully packed away for the following Christmas, though there are other celebrations and events during the year, like the olive or grape harvest, when certain *santons* may be fetched out of their summer repose. *Santons* do also serve as regular decorations in a number of Provençal houses and gardens.

1   In the Aix workshop, the figures are handmade using methods that date back 200 years. Assembling the more complex ones is a fine art.
2, 3 When the figures are taken out of the mold, the clay is still soft, but the edges and contours are rough. The surface needs retouching before they are dried and fired.

La Corse

Sharon Sutcliffe

Dried chestnuts are ground into flour in age-old mills such as this one. Corsicans used to make bread from this flour, and it is still a key ingredient in many traditional recipes today.

The simple church of Sainte Michelle de Murato is situated on the only patch of green grass in the midst of the rugged hinterlands of Bastia.

Calais
Le Havre
Caen
Paris
Brest
Rennes
Strasbourg
Orléans
Nantes
Tours
Dijon
Limoges
Lyon
St-Étienne
Bordeaux
Grenoble
Avignon
Toulouse
Nice
Biarritz
Marseille
Toulon
Perpignan
Corsica

Tourists send picture postcards of its golden beaches and the flatlands with their citrus and olive groves, and it is no surprise that the French refer to Corsica as the island of beauty. But anyone who wants to see and experience the real Corsica must leave the coast and look for it in the thick woods of Castagniccia, on winding mountain roads, and in tiny villages. And they must taste it. Napoleon, who was born in Ajaccio, is quoted as saying, "I'd know my island with my eyes closed, just from the scent of the maquis [thick scrubby underbrush] as it wafts over the waves." He was referring to the island's brushwood, apparently inaccessible to strangers, but a veritable "larder" for the natives. Corsica is scented by the herbs of the maquis, and these aromas are transferred to its cooking.

Despite the impressiveness of the island's coastal regions, Corsicans are more attached to the interior of the island. In former times, power-hungry predators landed repeatedly on its shores, forcing the Corsicans deeper and deeper into the woods and mountainous parts of the island. There they had to learn to survive on whatever food they could find, and authentic Corsican cooking is a true representation of just how successfully they adapted. Inland, the countryside is ideal for rearing goats and sheep. Lambs and kids provide *stufato*, aromatic ragouts, and sumptuous roasts. Milk is made into piquant cheeses, and also into the famous brocciu, without which no Corsican dish would be complete.

Once upon a time, the Castagniccia, the dense chestnut forest which is interspersed with tiny hamlets, was the heart of the island. It not only offered protection, but also provided chestnuts, the flour of which was, for centuries, a staple – the basic ingredient of bread, cakes, and polenta – and which was mixed with acorns too for pig fodder to ensure that the islanders' meat requirements were met. Although traditionally the Corsicans are hunters rather than fishermen, proof of the generous bounty of the sea is often evident in the native cuisine, and the freshness of the fish and seafood is legendary.

A Corsican meal is generally rounded off simply and without great ceremony. Quiet pleasure is derived from a juicy nectarine or a fresh fig. Candied citrons lend their bitter sweetness to nougats and cakes, and chestnuts and brocciu are also used in the desserts. Needless to say, there is also a wine to go with each of the island's dishes.

Fish

Barbarians, Greeks, Romans, Iberians, Saracens, Pisans, Genoese – all were, at one time or another, tempted by the beautiful island of Corsica. All tried, sometimes repeatedly, to draw it into their sphere of influence, and this drove the Corsicans ever deeper into the heart of the island. They became hunters, and learned to live off the bounty of the land. To them, the coast spelt danger. There, the ground was mainly marshy, and infested with malaria-carrying mosquitoes. As a 19th-century visitor to the island recorded in his diary: "Many of them [the Corsicans] have never even seen the sea, and one of the peculiarities of their character is the revulsion these mountain-dwellers have for the element that surrounds their island." The term "Go to hell!" translated into Corsican is, "Che tu vaga in mare!" – "Go to the sea!"

In view of this negative attitude, it is hardly surprising that fish does not play the part in Corsican cooking that one would expect of a Mediterranean island. And yet, the fish is of excellent quality. It has the sort of freshness only found in fish that is caught in daily forays, made in little wooden fishing boats that travel no farther than 6 miles (9.5 kilometers) out to sea. The catches consist of small amounts of different types of fish, of which about 50 are at home in Corsican waters. These include red mullet, John Dory, conger eel, sea robin, scorpion fish, gray mullet, dogfish, squid, octopus, and many other Mediterranean varieties, such as *sar*, white bream, *denté*, and the rainbow-hued *girelle*, or rainbow wrasse. This wonderful variety is often combined with olive oil, garlic, fennel, saffron, thyme, bay leaves, and orange peel in a steaming pot of *Aziminu*, the Corsican fish stew. However, attitudes have now changed somewhat, and today more than 200 little fishing boats set forth from the countless tiny harbors that are dotted along the island's shores, to catch the wonderfully fresh delicacies for the island's local markets. There is also a small fleet of fishing trawlers that go farther out into the Mediterranean to catch perch, swordfish, tuna, and sardines. They also bring back John Dory and sea bass, which are bred in cages in the open sea. Nor is there any lack of shellfish. The sea urchin, which is caught only in winter, is greatly prized by the locals. Spring is the best time for the sea spider, which is just as much at home on the rock beds around Corsica as the spiny lobster, although stocks of the latter have been seriously decimated. Lakes Diane and Urbino, where flat-bottomed barques were traditionally used for fishing, provide oysters and mussels.

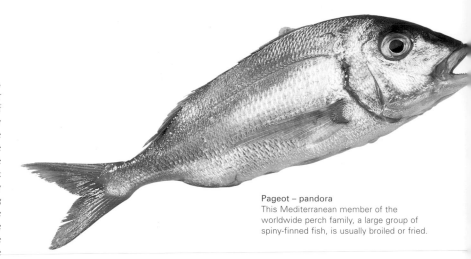

Pageot – pandora
This Mediterranean member of the worldwide perch family, a large group of spiny-finned fish, is usually broiled or fried.

Loup de mer – sea bass
Extremely fine, delicate fish, preferably broiled whole, now bred successfully in Corsican lakes.

Liche – jack mackerel
Also known as the "bastard mackerel." There are numerous types and varieties. Although the flesh is quite dry, it is popular in fish stews.

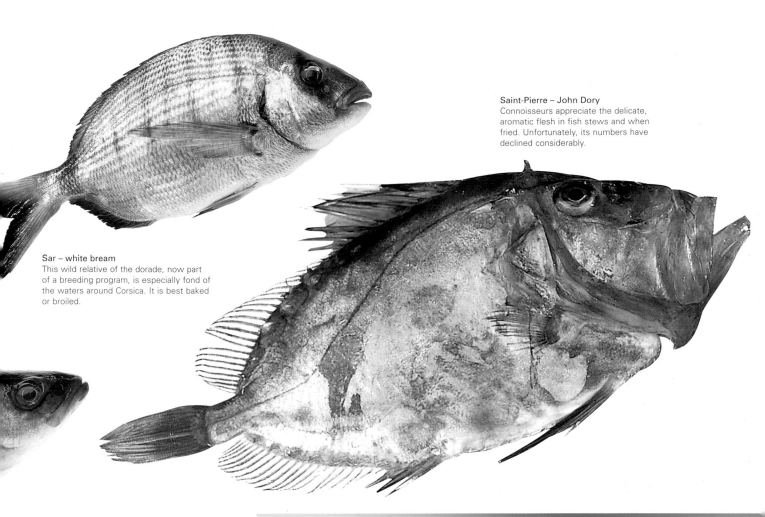

Sar – white bream
This wild relative of the dorade, now part of a breeding program, is especially fond of the waters around Corsica. It is best baked or broiled.

Saint-Pierre – John Dory
Connoisseurs appreciate the delicate, aromatic flesh in fish stews and when fried. Unfortunately, its numbers have declined considerably.

Rouget – red mullet
The red mullet has become a symbol of the Mediterranean kitchen. It is only broiled or fried, and is delicious with olive oil and herbs from the maquis.

In Bastia, as in the countless tiny harbors that are dotted along the shores of the island, fishing has become an increasingly important economic factor. The freshness of the catches is exemplary.

437

Corsican fish recipes

The quality of the available fish is so high that it requires the minimum of attention before cooking, and it is delicious simply broiled or baked, then sprinkled with olive oil or lemon juice. Stuffings are also extremely popular, such as with the ubiquitous *Sardines farcies au brocciu*, and in various squid recipes, and usually consist of tomato, onions and garlic. Small red mullet and common dentex are broiled with fennel, or baked in a tomato and anchovy sauce. Eel is usually fried with garlic and parsley. Crab with rice is a specialty of Bastia, and the sea spider, which is usually caught off the coast, is served with a spaghetti sauce. For centuries, Catholic households have served a dried cod dish at Easter, since cod was the only fish that was available in the heart of the island. While the island was under Genoese rule, Corsicans remained faithful to cod fish even when the only ones they caught were of inferior quality. This bit of history lives on in the expression "baccalà per Corsica," which refers to anything that is regarded with disdain or ridicule.

The sea provides the Corsican kitchen with some particularly delicious specialties. As well as *boutargue*, Corsican caviar, *bianchetti*, which are caught in the Gulf of Ajaccio, are regarded as culinary supremacy. *Bianchetti* are primarily the spawn of sardines, and move through the waters of the gulf in great swarms in February and March, when the water is churned up and murky after storms. What the *friture* is to the mainland French, the *bianchetti* – tiny, transparent mini-fish that measure no more than 1 inch (2.5 centimeters) – are to the Corsicans. Whether dipped in batter and baked, served in a fish stew, or dressed with vinaigrette, they have been a culinary delight for centuries – but one to which ecological common sense will soon be putting a stop. Spiny lobsters are the most expensive specialty. Up to the middle of the 20th century, they were so abundant that the Corsicans caught 330 tons (300 tonnes) per year. Today, as the result of indiscriminate overfishing, numbers have been decimated to such an extent that they are offered only to more affluent visitors. Native coastal residents will, however, indulge themselves for a special occasion, such as the Assumption of the Virgin Mary on August 15. Inland, veal is the preferred choice for celebrations.

Left: *Sardines farcies au brocciu* – sardines stuffed with brocciu
Right: *Pavé de loup vigneronne à la myrte* – sea bass in a wine and myrtle sauce.

Boutargue

Fishermen are especially pleased if they catch a *mulet cabot*, a gray mullet, which grows to between 20 and 40 inches (50 and 100 centimeters) in length, in June. Although they enjoy it grilled or fried, their primary interest is in the female's roe, known locally as *boutargue, poutargue*, or Corsican caviar. This delicacy was already popular – and expensive – in the Middle Ages, and it is believed that Corsica was one of the main suppliers. The east coast, with its natural lakes, exudes a peculiar attraction to the gray mullet, and offers it plenty of food and ideal conditions for breeding. Long ago, the Corsicans worked out means of catching them before the females spawned. One method was blocking the passages from the lakes to which the fish gained access when they traveled from the sea through natural channels. This endeavor had to be timed precisely in June. Another method starts offshore. Once several gray mullet have been spotted in a bay, a number of fishing boats will surround them with the *battida*, a high net. Great care is exercised when removing the roe so that the fine membrane that surrounds the tiny eggs is not damaged. The roe is salted immediately, placed under a weight, and left in the sun to dry for several days. Corsicans like *boutargue* cut into thin slices, over which they drizzle a little olive oil and lemon juice, and grind some pepper. Another popular recipe is as an extremely delicious sauce for spaghetti.

Sardines farcies au brocciu
Sardines stuffed with brocciu

12 fresh sardines
1 tbsp oil
1 bunch of fresh mint
8 oz/250 g brocciu
3 eggs
Salt and freshly milled pepper
2 cups/500 ml tomato sauce

Slit open the sardines along the abdomen, then remove the innards and the bones. Open the fish out and place, skin-side down, in a well-oiled dish. Wash and dry the mint. Pluck off the leaves and chop finely. Mix together the brocciu cheese, eggs and mint, and season to taste. Spread 1 tbsp of this mixture over each of the sardines and broil for about 7 minutes. Serve with a hot tomato sauce.

Pavé de loup vigneronne à la myrte
Sea bass in a wine and myrtle sauce

Per person

1 shallot
¼ cup/60 g soft butter
1 cup/250 ml red wine
1 handful of myrtle leaves
Thyme flowers or leaves
Salt and freshly milled pepper
1 sea bass steak
1 tbsp olive oil

Peel and finely chop the shallot and sauté gently in 2 tsp butter. Pour in the red wine and reduce to half the original quantity. Add the myrtle leaves and continue to reduce; then add the thyme and season with salt and pepper.
Fry the sea bass steak in hot oil, turning once, and season with salt and pepper.
Meanwhile, reduce the sauce to about 2 tbsp, and then whisk in the remaining butter. Pour the sauce onto a plate, and place the fish in the center of it.

Aziminu de bianchetti
Fish soup made from small fry

3 mangel-wurzel leaves
1 tomato
2 potatoes
1 onion
3 cloves garlic
2 tbsp olive oil
Generous 1 lb/500 g *bianchetti*
Salt and freshly milled pepper
Thinly sliced white toast

Remove the center vein from the mangel-wurzel leaves, and finely chop the green. Peel the tomato, remove the seeds, and dice the flesh. Peel the potatoes and cut into thin slices. Peel and finely chop the onion, and crush the garlic. Heat the oil, then gently sauté the onion, followed by the garlic. Add the mangel-wurzel, tomato, potatoes, and a third of the *bianchetti*. Stir well, season to taste, and add 4 cups/1 liter of water. Simmer for about 20 minutes. When the potatoes

Left: *Aziminu de bianchetti* (fish soup made from small fry) – center: *Salade de poulpe* (squid salad) – right: *Méli mélo de roches* (basic recipe for rockfish salad)

are cooked, add the remaining *bianchetti*, and cook for another minute.
Place the toast in soup bowls, and pour the soup over the toast.

Spaghetti à la boutargue
Spaghetti with Corsican caviar

3 cloves garlic
4 tbsp oil
3 stems dried fennel
1 chili
⅔ cup/150 ml white wine
Salt
Generous 1 lb/500 g spaghetti
3½ oz/100 g *boutargue*
1 bunch of parsley

Peel and finely chop the garlic. In a heavy saucepan, slowly heat the olive oil, garlic, fennel and chili. Add the wine and some salt, and reduce to a half.
At the same time, bring a generous amount of salt water to a boil and cook the spaghetti. Drain well and place in a warmed dish; drizzle over a little olive oil.
Grate the *boutargue* and finely chop the parsley; add both to the hot sauce (do not let it boil). Pour the sauce over the spaghetti. Serve immediately while still very hot.

Salade de poulpe
Squid salad

1 squid, about 2¼ lbs/1 kg
1 cup/250 ml white wine
2 slices of an unwaxed lemon
1 carrot
1 small leek
1 bay leaf
2 stems of dried fennel
3 tbsp olive oil
1 tbsp mature red wine vinegar
Sea salt from Guérande, freshly milled pepper
Broiled fish fillets or red bell pepper (optional)

Clean the squid.
Pour 6 cups/1.5 liters water into a pressure cooker. Add the wine, lemon, chopped carrot, leek, bay leaf and fennel, and cook for 15 minutes.
Add the squid and cook for another 30 minutes in the pressure cooker. Leave to cool.
Lift out the squid, remove the skin, and chop the flesh into small pieces.
Make a vinaigrette from the oil, vinegar, salt and pepper.
Arrange the squid on a bed of mixed salad leaves. Sprinkle over the vinaigrette and serve.
If you like, this dish can be garnished with broiled, skinned fish fillets or with strips of broiled, skinned red bell pepper.

Méli mélo de roches
Basic fish salad recipe

1 unwaxed lemon
3 tbsp olive oil
Salt and freshly milled pepper
2¼ lbs/1kg fresh rockfish (such as sea bass, red mullet, ocean perch, scorpion fish)

Rinse the lemon in hot water and peel thinly. Place the lemon strips in boiling water and boil for 5 minutes, then drain. Bring some more water to a boil, boil the lemon peel for another 5 minutes, drain and finely chop.
Squeeze ½ a lemon, and mix the juice with the olive oil. Add the chopped lemon peel, and season the vinaigrette with salt and pepper.
Prepare the fish for cooking, rinse, and fillet. Remove the bones from the fish fillets and pat the fish dry with paper towels. Flash-fry on both sides in hot oil.
Pour the vinaigrette onto a plate, and arrange the fish fillets (see illustration). Mashed potatoes, made with a few drops of high-quality olive oil, go well with this dish.

Spaghetti à la boutargue – Spaghetti with Corsican caviar

Fruit wines, liqueurs etc.

Corsica is a veritable paradise of distillers, macerators, mixers and blenders. Nature has bestowed an abundance of lemons, seedless tangerines, oranges, cherries, figs and myrtle berries, and then added grapes, which provide the island's strong, robust wines. The tradition once followed throughout the continent of Europe of aromatizing and fortifying wine to make it more full-bodied and improve its "shelf life," still flourishes in Corsica.

In the 16th century, when Corsican Muscadets were causing a furore in Italy, the islanders began to macerate the local fruit in brandy. Production was unexpectedly and dramatically increased at the beginning of the 19th century, when the island received its first stills. And since the *haut monde* of France (which acquired Corsica from Genoa in 1768) simply adored liqueurs of all kinds, especially lemon-flavored ones, the islanders were quick to capitalize on this. Soon, every village had its stills, and each family developed its own recipes for a variety of apéritifs and "soothing potions." Fruit farmers and vintners were especially inventive, creating a variety of elixirs and developing increasingly complicated production methods as they gained in experience and confidence. For example, they macerated the fruit in wine spirits, and then distilled the extract to obtain a colorless aromatic concentrate. Rosé wines were used as a base for many of these drinks, the most famous of which was Vin du Cap Corse from Quinquina, created in 1872 by Louis Napoléon Mattei. As with Dubonnet and Byrrh, its close relatives on the French mainland, this *apéritif à base de vin* was aimed primarily at soldiers who were sent on duty overseas. It was intended as a pleasant way for them to take cinchona (or Peruvian) bark, the "miracle product," for medicinal purposes, and to offer them protection against fevers and stomach upsets. Furthermore, the apéritif, which was known simply as Cap Corse, was also used as a remedy by Corsicans all over the world who were suffering from homesickness.

The Mattei company grew to become one of the island's leading providers of alcoholic drinks. It understood perfectly how to improve the recipes for a variety of traditional drinks, and how to master the manufacturing processes for numerous drinks and sell them under its own name. However, in reality the roots of these drinks reached back through the generations, and so similar drinks are also produced by a number of smaller companies. One of these is Domaine Orsini, a company that has made a name for itself as the producer of a variety of irresistible specialties, made from fruit the company grows itself, which otherwise are usually only available from private producers.

Cédratine is a fine digestive which is based on an old Corsican recipe. It is made from the citron, the island's symbol; shown below is a candied whole fruit.

Corsican elixirs

Cap Corse

This most famous Corsican apéritif is made from grape must, only from the *Appellation Cap Corse*, which has been "silenced" by the addition of wine spirit. It is flavored with 17 different plant essences, including gentian, cocoa bean, Seville oranges, vanilla extract and cinchona bark. It was extremely popular both in France and overseas at the time of the Belle Epoque. Best drunk chilled but without ice, or as a Marseillaise, which is made from two parts Cap Corse and one part lemonade.

Cédratine
Liqueur de cédrat

In 1880, Mattei marketed a liqueur under the name of Cédratine, which owed its intense aroma of lemon and cedar to the citron, thereby continuing a centuries-old tradition. The peel is left to macerate in wine spirits for a year, after which time the extract is distilled. The basic liqueur – syrup and alcohol – is then flavored with the distillate. Best drunk well chilled.

Bonapartine
Liqueur d'orange

In 1920, Mattei registered another product, a liqueur made from oranges and mandarins, which is 22 percent proof and whose sister, Impératrice, is 30 percent proof.
Other producers on the island make a simple Liqueur d'Orange, which is made from orange peel macerated in wine spirits, then distilled, after which the distillate is mixed with syrup, and possibly with other plant and spice extracts.

Liqueur de myrte

The berries, which are picked on the maquis, are left to dry for three weeks and then steeped in alcohol (ratio: 4 cups/1 liter alcohol to 2¼ lbs/1 kilogram berries). A concentrated syrup is added after a 40-day maceration period, and the resulting liqueur is purple in color. It is filtered, bottled, and stored for a period of time. If the berries are distilled, the liqueur is colorless. These basic recipes are frequently varied by other manufacturers – and private individuals as

well – using old family recipes, many of which have been in the families for generations.

Vins de fruit

As a rule, fruit wine can be made from just about any type of fruit. On Corsica, though, citrus fruit, wild cherries, vineyard peaches and wild arbutus (fruit from the strawberry tree) are the preferred choices, as are myrtle berries which are gathered on the maquis. The fruit is usually steeped in wine spirits and left to macerate for three months or longer. The highly aromatic alcohol is then filtered, mixed with rosé, and finally sweetened with sugar.

Rappu

Rappu, which is made mainly in Patrimonio, is a blend of Grenache, Aleatico, and Alicante. The grapes are left on the vine until well after they are ripe to increase the sugar content, and then are mashed together with the stalks, which is what gives Rappu its typical flavor. The vintners then leave the must to ferment. When about 6 tbsp (100 grams) of residual sugar are left, they stop the fermentation process by adding young brandy. Left in a barrel to age, the liqueur turns the color of mahogany, and takes on the aroma of stewed fruit, toast and caramel.

Eau-de-vie de châtaigne

Edible chestnuts are not just used for flour, bread, cakes and pastes. The Corsicans also make a delicious, highly unusual schnapps from them. First, they grind the chestnuts, then steep them. They leave them to ferment, and then distill them. Each distiller has his own version of the recipe, to suit whichever of the 50 or so different types of chestnut he has.

Old labels, ashtrays, and other forms of advertising bear witness to the many decades for which Corsican apéritifs and liqueurs have been giving pleasure.

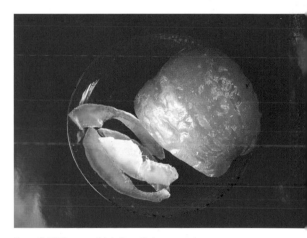

Up until 1950, every third citron that was used anywhere in the world (the candied version was extremely popular and in wide use) came from Corsica. It is now comparatively rare.

Citron – promising fragrance

The "first lemon," which came to the Mediterranean from the distant Far East in ancient times, soon spread throughout Italy and the Provence. Brought to Corsica by sailors in the Middle Ages, where a mutant variety with sweet flesh, known as *cédrat de Corse*, thrived. However, it cannot be eaten fresh. It is a yellow, thick-skinned (only one-third of it is juicy flesh) fruit that resembles a lemon, but is less acid. It grows on a bush-like, prickly tree that reaches a height of 10-13 feet (3-4 meters) on Corsica, and is quite demanding. It does not like wind or great variations in temperature, and will not tolerate frost. It does, however, like well-fed soil. Under these conditions, an adult tree will produce up to 220 pounds (100 kilograms) of fruit, up to 10 inches (25 centimeters) long, and weighing up to 9 pounds (4 kilograms).

The fact that the citron has become as popular and well-known as it is, is due in part to its intense, fascinating fragrance, which is similar to cedar, and in part to the Jews. The Jewish religion considers the citron to be the banned fruit that imparts knowledge, the very one that Adam was unable to resist in the Garden of Eden. So, during the time that Corsica was occupied by the Genoese (1300-1768), Italian Jews ordered vast quantities of citrons, which were shipped in barrels of sea water, and which they ate as candied fruit, especially at the Feast of Tabernacles (Booths).
The French continued to export the fruit, fresh or candied, and which was also turned into a liqueur, when the island was under their rule. The cultivation of the citron tree peaked in the second half of the 19th century. At that time, the fruit was considered to be the symbol of the

island. Once other fruits and early vegetables promised quicker, and especially easier, profits, the popularity of the citron rapidly declined, but since 1970 interest has again been on the increase.
Candied citrons are comparatively expensive as they are rare, and quite difficult to produce. First, the fruit, either whole, halved or cut into pieces, is placed in a barrel containing salt water. It is left there to ferment, as this helps to reduce its bitterness. Depending on the size of the pieces, this stage takes from a few days to several weeks. Thoroughly rinsed, the fruit is then boiled several times in hot sugar syrup. Small pieces of the fragrant citron are ideal for flavoring many different types of cake. The fruit can also be used for jellies, or used to make an extract that is used as the base for citron liqueur.

Prisuttu, figatellu & co.

All about salt and smoke

If ever the Corsicans wanted to entice a gourmet to the most remote spot, one that could only be reached via the most breathtaking and perilous mountain roads, they would whisper: *salumu, coppa, lonzu, figatellu, prisuttu, sangui.* To discover these real treasures of Corsican gastronomy, you have to experience its hams, sausages and other meat products. In bygone days, the pig and its fat played a leading part in the lives of the Corsicans. And it wasn't just any old pink pig, either, but the Corsican pig, which today is still what other pigs used to be: a fleet-of-foot forest-dweller that is left to roam freely. In summer, swineherds guide the black or black-and-pink animals up into the coolness of the hills, and in October, when the acorns and chestnuts ripen, they bring them back down again so that the pigs can enjoy this bounty, and acquire a generous layer of fat. This truly traditional style of pig-rearing is still continued today, simply because it remains in the hands of the farmers, who originally had the well-being of their own families at heart before that of the pigs. Although there are now several specialists among the 900 pig-breeders, they have never supplied commercial markets. Their products are offered only to private customers, although some of them also run *fermes-auberges*, farmhouse "bed-and-breakfasts," where guests can sample the farmer's own products "on site," as it were.

The piglets are born in July and January. When, after an idyllic porcine life, they depart this mortal coil, this happens on or after the Feast of Santa Lucia on December 13, when they will be at least 15 months of age, and weigh something in the region of 290 pounds (130 kilograms). It is estimated that around 25,000 pigs are slaughtered on Corsica every year, although no one is absolutely sure of the number. Only as many pigs are slaughtered on the farms and in the small slaughterhouses (which are under permanent veterinary supervision) as each family can process with the help of its workforce. The back is then made into *coppa*, and the fillet into *lonzu*. Blood, brains and fat are made into blood pudding, *sangui*, and liver and the innards into *figatellu*. The best meat and fat pieces are air-dried to make *salumu*, and the rest is made into fresh sausage, *salcietta. Panzetta*, bacon, and *prisuttu*, ham, are salted. The latter is the showpiece of the Corsican home butchery. Making ham is an art, and not every ham survives the experience. The less fatty, lower quality ones are made into *salumu*. The following rule of thumb now applies for determining the duration of the salting period: 1 day for every 2¼ pounds (1 kilogram), plus 5 days. Once the salt has done its job, the ham is taken into mountain huts to dry, where it spends the hot summer in a cool basement. The best hams mature for 12, 18 or 24 months. The quality of the ham is tested before it is offered for sale. To do this, the meat is pierced in three places, using a specially shaped horse's bone – nothing absorbs fragrance (or odors) like this material does. The expert can tell, simply from the smell, whether the ham has reached the best degree of maturity.

Right: Smoke soon surrounds the *fucone*, completely enveloping the sausages.
Below (clockwise, starting from the top): *figarettu*, smoked and dried liverwurst; *salumu*, a fine, dried, long-keeping sausage; *prisuttu*, farmer's ham; *coppa*, dried rib cut; *lonzu*, delicate, dried pork fillet.

The valuable hams are left in the smoke chamber for between one and two years, waiting to reach the required degree of maturity.

A master ham-maker can judge the degree of maturity and depth of flavor just by inserting a piece of horse's bone in the meat and sniffing it.

The thickest part of the ham resists the smoke for the longest, and offers the finest flavor and culinary pleasure.

Give us this day our daily chestnut

Bread from a tree

The chestnut was so important to the Corsicans that they named an entire region after it. "La Castagniccia" is a dense forest of chestnut trees in the heart of the island, between 1640 and 3280 feet (500 and 1000 meters) above sea level. The soil there is not at all suitable for agricultural purposes, but the trees thrive on the thin, acid, chalky ground – so much so that some of them grow to a height of 100 feet (30 meters), and can reach an age of 500 years. The tree that provides the bread (and of which there are some 50 varieties) has always played a fundamental role, both in the island's economy and in its history. For centuries, its fruit was a basic source of food, and was traded for olive oil, cheese and wine. People trusted in the chestnut when times were hard, and it was highly valued by rich and poor alike.

Not only are chestnuts full of energy, vitamins, and minerals, they also contain twice as much starch as potatoes, as well as large amounts of essential minerals, B vitamins, and, uncooked, almost as much vitamin C as lemons. They are good for the stomach and an aid to digestion, generally relaxing, and an excellent source of iron. Because of their dense consistency, they satisfy quickly and effectively, and their sugar is released slowly. They are the perfect food for people whose work involves physical labor, as well as being warming fare in the winter.

From the 16th century onward, clerics and the better-off built their houses under the chestnut trees farther inland on the island; people judged their wealth by the number of trees on their properties. Ordinary people always made sure there was a drying loft above the living area of their dwellings, where they would spread out the chestnuts to benefit from the warmth of the *fucone*, the stove. The chestnut became the island's main export product. However, the chestnut forests that covered almost one-sixth of the island in the 18th century were also an ideal hideaway for bandits and rebels. The governor at the time, who was appointed by the French

Chestnut flour is slightly yellow in color, and is suitable for bread, cookies, cakes, and also for a type of polenta.

In hot air, chestnuts dry within a week, and lose two-thirds of their original weight.

Before the chestnuts can be ground to make flour, the hard skin and furry layer have to be removed.

government, would have liked to destroy all the forests, but as they were so important economically, this simply could not even be a consideration!

Although the forests were unspoilt and appeared to be wild, they were in fact well tended. Every tree had an owner. Caring for the trees and grinding the flour was the men's work; the women were responsible for gathering the chestnuts. In September, the men removed the undergrowth and fern from beneath the trees, which made it easier to gather the ripe chestnuts in October and November. All the women then had to do was rake the chestnuts together. Today, it is common practice to hang nets from the lowest branches of the trees and catch the chestnuts in them. After the harvest, it is the pigs' turn to enjoy what is left of the chestnuts.

At the beginning of the 20th century, the chestnut forests on Corsica (as elsewhere in France) began to decline. At first they fell victim to the rural exodus, as the result of which four-fifth of the trees were abandoned, and the untended trees slowly died. The decline was hastened by two infestations, although the government counteracted the damage with subsidies. Now, however, a project has been initiated on Corsica with the aim of planting high-quality edible chestnuts on 1976 acres (800 hectares) of land. Some 14,825 acres (6000 hectares) are currently being farmed, although the total area of overgrown chestnut forests is estimated to be at least four times that figure. In a good year, some 2204 tons (2000 tonnes) of chestnuts are harvested on Corsica, which is about 15 percent of the entire French chestnut production.

The chestnuts have to be dried before they can be ground to make flour. The traditional method, which is still practiced in certain regions on the island today, involves smoke-drying them for 30-40 days, and this gives the flour a delicate, smoky flavor. More usually, though, they are dried in warm air. Although this takes no longer than a week, it does mean they lose two-thirds of their weight. The peel is removed from the dried chestnuts by machine, and any rotten or burnt fruit is disposed of. The chestnuts are then usually taken straight to the mill for grinding. However, the cream-colored flour does not have quite the same full-bodied aroma as that from chestnuts that have been dried in the village oven. In this case, the oven is filled with wood and heather, and lit. The glowing embers are removed, and two hours later, when it is possible to place a hand on the oven door without being burnt, the chestnuts are put in the oven for two days. After that time, they are left overnight to cool, and the next day they are placed in a sack and beaten repeatedly against a tree. This removes the furry skin that surrounds the fruit, as it contains bitter substances that would taint the flavor of the flour. The light cream-colored chestnuts are again sorted before being ground. Traditional mills contain one fixed and one rotating millstone, powered by water in the past, but now more likely to run on electricity. This process produces flour that is slightly reddish color, and has a delicate caramel flavor.

Chestnut flour still plays a very important part in traditional Corsican cooking. For example, 22 different dishes containing chestnut flour were, until recently, served at wedding celebrations in the Alesani region (Haute-Corse), and many traditional Corsican recipes are still based on ground chestnuts, such as *pisticcin*, a flat bread roll; *frascajoli*, soft bread; *nicci*, crispy pancakes; *fritelli*, deep-fried pastries; *brilluli*, cookies; *castagnacciu*, a moist chestnut cake, and *pulenta*, a firm-textured mush that is similar to cornmeal polenta.

Pietra is the latest creation made from chestnuts. First brewed in Furiani in 1996, it is made from malt, coarsely ground chestnuts, and the Acqua Bianca spring water. Left to ferment at a low temperature, it provides a 6 percent proof specialty that is reminiscent of the Christmas ales brewed in other countries.

Pure Corsica

The reason why most of the Corsican recipes that have been handed down through the generations have remained free from foreign influences and superficial refinements (apart from the occasional Italian touch, of course, such as the slightly cavalier attitude toward *pasta*) is because the fearless conquerors were not actually interested in the maquis or the mountain regions. Fortunately for those who enjoy the good things in life, the heart of the island was always able to resist European influence. Farmhouse "bed-and-breakfasts" and small, family-run mountain hotels provide the best opportunities for sampling the local cuisine, for these are owned by the people who know how to make, or obtain, the unique sausages and hams; who have 1001 recipes for brocciu; who roast the excellent lambs and kids in the oven, simply and deliciously; who braise rabbit and boar in the way that other people seem to have forgotten.

Fricassée de lapereau aux citrons
Fricassee of rabbit with lemon
(illustration below)

1 rabbit, dressed
3½ tbsp olive oil
2 onions
3 carrots
3 cloves of garlic
4 sprigs of thyme
2 bay leaves
5 sage leaves
1 tbsp honey
Salt and freshly milled pepper
2 cups/500 ml white wine
2 unwaxed lemons, cut into quarters

Cut the rabbit into pieces. Heat the olive oil in a cast-iron pot and brown the meat on all sides. Peel the onions and cut into thin slices. Peel and slice the carrots. Add the onions, carrot, and peeled garlic to the rabbit, and brown slightly. Drain off the fat. Add the herbs and honey, and season to taste. Pour on the wine and add the lemon quarters. Cover with a lid and braise in a preheated oven at 375 °F/190 °C for about an hour. Remove the rabbit and arrange on a serving dish. Taste the sauce, season if required, and then pour over the rabbit. Serve immediately.

Terrine à la châtaigne
Chestnut pâté

Serves 10
(no illustration)

6 large onions
2¼ lb/1 kg rabbit pieces
2¼ lb/1 kg veal bones
4 sprigs of thyme
2 bay leaves
2 tbsp olive oil
10 oz/300 g beef
10 oz/300 g pork
7 oz/200 g veal
7 oz/200 g calf's liver
2½ cups/300 g dry white breadcrumbs
8 cloves of garlic
Salt and freshly milled pepper
¾ cup/200 ml fig brandy
7 oz /200 g chestnuts
2 cups/500 ml meat stock, stiffened with gelatin (prepare a day ahead)

A day ahead, peel and slice the onions and brown in hot oil, together with the rabbit pieces. Wash the veal bones and herbs and add to the onions. Pour in 12 cups/3 liters of water. Cook for 3 hours, adding more hot water if necessary. Reduce until 4 cups/1 liter of stock is left. Strain, leave overnight, and next day skim off the fat.

Fricassée de lapereau aux citrons
Rabbit fricassée with lemon

Put the meat through a meat grinder and mix it well. Heat half the stock and soak the breadcrumbs in it. Purée with the peeled garlic, then add to the meat, and pour in the fig brandy. Layer the chestnuts and the meat in a heatproof dish. Place the terrine in a roasting pan half-filled with water and cook in a preheated oven at 250-300 °F/120-150 °C, for 2 hours.

Heat the remaining stock and pour over the warm terrine. Leave in a cool place for about 12 hours before slicing.

Agneau de lait
Suckling lamb

2¼ lb/1 kg sucking lamb
3 tbsp oil
Salt and freshly milled pepper
2 sprigs of thyme
1 small sprig of rosemary
2 onions
3 bay leaves
¾ cup/200 ml rosé wine

Cut the lamb into large pieces. Heat the olive oil in a large cast-iron pot. Add the meat, season with salt and pepper, and sprinkle over the herbs. Turn the lamb over after 15 minutes. Peel and quarter the onions and put, with the bay leaves, in the pot. Simmer for another 15 minutes, then turn the meat over again. Add the wine and cook until it has evaporated. Place portions on warm plates, or arrange on a warm serving dish.

Sautéed potatoes and *Tomates confites* – baked tomatoes (see recipe below) – go well with this dish. A dry rosé wine is a suitable accompaniment.

For a lamb to qualify as a sucking lamb, it should be no more than six months old, and have been fed only on milk. The meat is normally very pale, but quickly absorbs the colors of certain ingredients during the cooking process.

Tomates confites
Baked tomatoes

10 ripe beefsteak tomatoes
Salt and freshly milled pepper
1 bunch of flat-leafed parsley, chopped
4 cloves of garlic, chopped
Olive oil

Heat the oven to 390 °F/200 °C.

Wash and dry the tomatoes. Cut them in half and remove the seeds. Place the halves, side by side, in a well-oiled dish and season to taste. Sprinkle with the chopped parsley and garlic, and drizzle over a generous quantity of olive oil.

Bake the tomatoes in the preheated oven for 30 minutes. Then reduce the heat to 300 °F/150 °C, and bake for another 30 minutes. Make sure the tomatoes do not burn.

Baked tomatoes are an ideal accompaniment for summery meat dishes. When served with fresh, white bread and a green salad, they make a delicious snack.

So that they could enjoy tomatoes all year round, the Corsicans used to dry them in the sun, and preserve them, with some dried herbs, in olive oil.

Above: *Agneau de lait* – suckling lamb
Below: *Tomates confites* – baked tomatoes

Brocciu

Some culinary specialties are happy for zealous gourmets to take them hundreds, or even thousands, of miles from their home, and still be at their best, to rekindle happy memories. Others, however, stubbornly refuse to travel, will absolutely not leave home, and therefore can only be enjoyed in situ. Brocciu belongs to this second group. It remains faithful to its Corsican roots, only revealing itself to the more adventurous traveler who is prepared to make the effort to discover the culinary delights this wild landscape has to offer. It is unusual to find brocciu away from the island, and then it will never be at its best. Brocciu, which has been awarded the *Appellation*, is eaten fresh, ideally in the first three days after production. After that time, it is used in the preparation of wonderful dishes, ranging from appetizers to desserts. No Corsican meal is complete without it. In bygone days, whenever a young couple announced its intention to marry, the two families would meet to celebrate the impending event in the correct manner – with brocciu "doughnuts." The engagement was "sealed" with the first bite.

But what is brocciu? Well, Corsica has cheese, and it has brocciu, and they are two completely different things. Cheese is made when milk curdles, and brocciu is made from the whey that is left over from the cheesemaking process. The herdsman pours the whey into a vast container and adds rennet when it has reached the right temperature. The milk curdles, and the broken curds sink to the bottom, while the whey rises to the top. The whey is poured into a copper kettle and heated to 149 °F (65 °C) to eliminate the remaining rennet. Then a little salt and between a quarter and a third (relative to the whey) of the previous evening's milk (*u purricciu*) is added. This apparently straightforward process actually requires years of experience, as the quality of the brocciu is determined at the moment the milk is added. The whey solidifies somewhat while it continues to heat. At 176 °F (80 °C), the proteins in the lactoserum flocculate. The particles that will become brocciu rise to the surface, swirling upward like snowflakes. The cheesemaker removes the foam, and scoops the brocciu up in a large wooden ladle (*u coppulu*). Each ladleful of brocciu is placed in a perforated mold (*fattoghje*). When the molds are all full, each one is tipped over onto another one to double the quantity.

The brocci weigh between 8½ ounces (250 grams) and 6½ pounds (3 kilograms). It can be eaten as soon as it has drained, when it is fresh and smooth, glossy, and flavored with mountain herbs. It can be sprinkled with sugar or Schnapps. It can also be used fresh in desserts, or in *fiadone*, a baked cheesecake mixture, which is made from brocciu, eggs, sugar, and flavorings such as lemon zest, orange flower water, or liqueur. Otherwise, brocciu goes in the cellar, ideally a natural rock cellar (*le casgile*), where the surface is salted on the first day, and the cheese is left to ripen for 21 days. After that time, it is offered for sale as *brocciu passu*. If it has been covered with salt, it is known as *salitu*. This variety is dry, or semi-dry, and needs to be soaked in water for 24 hours to remove the salt; the water is changed frequently.

Corsican cheeses

D'Alesani
A round, mild goat cheese that is available all year round; weighs about 14 ounces (400 grams).

Bastelicaccia
A creamy, soft cheese made by hand from unpasteurized sheep milk; round, uneven cylinders of different weights; only available in winter.

Calenzana
A soft cheese, made from goat or sheep milk; piquant, square in shape, and weighing between 10½ and 14 ounces (300 and 400 grams); only available in winter.

Corte
A mild, round, soft cheese, made from sheep milk from the Corte region; weighs 14 ounces (400 grams); eaten when soft or semi-dry.

Galéria
A soft, square cheese, made from goat milk; highly piquant, since it is covered with salt, and left to mature for a long period of time.

Niolo
A very creamy soft cheese, made from unpasteurized sheep or goat cheese; mild to sharp in flavor; square in shape; pieces weigh between 1 and 1½ pounds (500 and 700 grams); only available in summer.

Sarteno
A soft, firm cheese, made from goat or sheep cheese (or both); strong to sharp in flavor; flattened ball; weighs between 2¼ and 3⅓ pounds (1 and 1.5 kilograms).

Venaco
A soft, red cheese spread, made only by hand from goat and sheep milk; available either as roundels or squares weighing between 14 ounces and 1 pound (400 and 500 grams); left to ripen for 2 to 3 months.

1 Galéria – **2** Calenzana – **3** Brocciu – **4** Venaco **5** Brocciu poivré – **6** Niolo at various stages of ripeners

Once the goat and sheep cheeses are ready, and the residues have been dealt with elsewhere, it's time for Brocciu.

Sheep and goats

Corsica is home to 130,000 sheep and 48,000 goats. They belong to some 900 shepherds and goatherds. For almost a century, a large proportion of the sheep milk has been made into Roquefort, but for some time now the production of Corsican cheeses has been increasing. This is thanks to the efforts of a large number of shepherds and goatherds, since genuine Corsican cheeses are made on the farms, especially in the mountains, where the animals always spend the summer months. They spend the winters grazing on the lower and coastal levels.

The cheeses that are made by hand in the mountains are left to ripen for a time. This gives soft cheese and red cheese spread a certain piquancy, and strength of flavor, and it is said that they are like the Corsicans themselves: they appear to be rough, and slightly coarse at first, but behind this hard exterior beats a soft heart.

The most prolific breeds on Corsica have adapted beautifully to the natural conditions of extensive rearing. The Corsican milk sheep is small in stature, robust, undemanding, and perfectly happy in the mountains.

The Corsican goat, however, is even more of an original, and still bears a strong resemblance to its Asian forefathers. It is even less demanding than the Corsican sheep, and finds plenty of food in the maquis. Most kids are born in November and are a welcome sight on the Christmas table as the Corsicans' favorite roast.

The Brocciu, which is made from whey, is placed in perforated plastic molds to drain; extra cheese is added from a ladle.

The shepherd places one mold on top of another to double the weight of the Brocciu.

Brocciu is rubbed with salt as a preservative. The brocciu becomes drier as it absorbs the salt (right).

449

Brocciu à la carte

Storzapretti

2 cups/500 g brocciu
1 egg
Marjoram
Scant 1 cup/100 g freshly grated sheep cheese
Flour
1¼ cups/300 ml sauce (see below)

Mix the brocciu, egg, marjoram, and a generous ¼ cup of the grated cheese together, combining the ingredients thoroughly. Use your hands to shape the mixture into small dumplings. Roll the dumplings in the flour and cook them in boiling salted water for 5 minutes. Remove from the water and place in a heatproof dish. Pour over the sauce and sprinkle over the remaining grated cheese. Place under a preheated broiler to brown.

Best served with roasts, so the meat juices can be used for the sauce. Otherwise make a white sauce.

Raviolis au brocciu
Brocciu-filled ravioli

7 oz/200 g mangel-wurzel leaves or spinach
5¼ cups/600 g flour
7 eggs
Salt and freshly milled pepper
2 tbsp olive oil
2 cups/500 g brocciu
Scant 1 cup /100 g grated sheep cheese
2 cups/500 ml tomato coulis

Wash the mangel-wurzel leaves or spinach, and blanch half of them in boiling salted water for about 8 minutes. Drain in a sieve (or squeeze the spinach) and chop.

Place the flour in a bowl and make a well in the center. Place the vegetables, 5 eggs, salt, pepper, and olive oil in the well, and knead together to make a smooth dough. Cover with a damp cloth and place in the refrigerator for 1 hour to rest. Meanwhile, chop the remaining mangel-wurzel leaves or spinach. Drain the cheese, mix it with the remaining eggs, and season to taste. Divide the dough into four equal pieces, and roll out thinly on a floured surface.

Cut out rounds of a diameter to suit yourself, place some of the mixture in the center of a round. Cover with a second round of dough and press the edges together firmly. Place on a floured baking sheet to rest. Cook in boiling salted water for about 10 minutes (depending on the size). Remove with a slotted spoon and drain well. Sprinkle with grated cheese, serve with the tomato coulis.

Beignets de brocciu
Brocciu "doughnuts"

2¾ cups/700 g brocciu (drained weight)
4½ cups/500 g wheat flour
1½ tsp/7 g active dry yeast
Pinch of salt
1 egg
Oil for deep-frying

Crumble the cheese and combine with the flour, yeast, and salt. Add the egg and a little water; the dough should remain firm in consistency. Leave to rest for 30 minutes. Shape the dough into small balls, and deep-fry until an appetizing shade of gold.

Storzapretti, oven-baked brocciu dumplings, are delicious with any sauce. They can also be sprinkled with a little olive oil and grated cheese, and browned under the broiler as a complete meal.

Raviolis au brocciu – brocciu-filled ravioli

Beignets de brocciu – brocciu "doughnuts"

Place on paper towels to dry. Serve warm (the flavor is impaired if the "doughnuts" are served too hot).

Gâteau de crêpes aux pommes
Apple crêpes cake

Serves 6

1¾ cups/200 g chestnut flour
Scant 1cup /100 g wheat flour
2 cups/500 ml milk
4 eggs
6½ tbsp/100 g melted butter
8 average-sized apples
6½ tbsp/100 g butter
½ cup/100 g sugar
2 tbsp chestnut honey

To make the crêpes, combine the flours, milk, eggs and melted butter to a smooth dough, and leave to stand for about 30 minutes. Peel and thinly slice the apples.
Melt the butter in a pan. Add the apples and sugar, and allow to caramelize.
Make the crêpes and stack them and the apples, in alternating layers, to make a cake, ending with a crêpe. Warm the honey and pour over the top.

Flan de brocciu, coulis d'orange
Brocciu custard with orange coulis

Serves 6-8

8 eggs
⅔ cup/150 g sugar
2 cups/500 g brocciu
Grated zest of 1 unwaxed lemon
1¼ cups/300 ml whipping cream
Juice of 10 oranges
⅔ cup/150 g sugar
Clementines to decorate

Preheat the oven to 300 °F/150 °C.
Beat together the eggs and sugar until light and creamy. Drain the brocciu, and add to the egg mixture with the lemon zest and cream. Pour into small, heatproof dishes, place in a roasting pan half-filled with water, and bake for about 1 hour.
To make the orange coulis, melt the sugar in the orange juice over a low heat, and leave to cool.

Fiadone
Brocciu cheesecake

1⅔ cups/400 g brocciu
5 eggs, separated
¾ cup/180 g sugar
2 tbsp Aquavita di baghi (Schnapps made from the fruit of the strawberry tree)
Salt
2 tbsp/30 g butter

Drain the brocciu well. Beat together the egg yolks and sugar until fluffy, add the brocciu and Schnapps. Beat the egg whites and the salt until stiff, and carefully combine with the egg yolk mixture. Preheat the oven to 355 °F/180 °C. Butter a nonstick, high-sided, square baking pan, and pour in the brocciu mixture. Level it off with a knife and bake for 40 minutes. Remove the cake from the oven. Take it out of the pan after 15 minutes, and leave it to cool completely. Cut the cake into small squares, and serve with Aquavita.

Gâteau de crêpes aux pommes – apple crêpes cake; shown here with the brocciu recipes, since a fresh cheese filling makes a delicious substitute for the apple filling.

Flan de brocciu, coulis d'orange

Fiadone – brocciu cheesecake

Corsican wine

It is not often that a wine connoisseur will have the opportunity to sample Corsica's wines anywhere else: 80 percent of the island's wine production is actually drunk on the island – and that mainly by summer visitors. Vin de Pays de l'Ile de Beauté is the lyrical name for the ordinary table wines that make up four-fifths of the production; the remaining fifth has been awarded the *Appellation*. Anyone who wants to see the island's vineyards will have to contend with winding roads and dusty paths, many of which often seem to lead to nowhere. But then suddenly, out of nowhere, an estate will appear, belonging to a member of the new generation of vintners, who make excellent, highly individual wines from traditional grape varieties.

In 565 BC, the Phoenicians founded Alalia (now known as Aléria) on the east coast, and were the first to recognize Corsica's potential for high-quality wines. As usual, the ball started rolling in Rome, when a number of centurions were sent to Corsica in 100 BC on their retirement. The wine industry blossomed in the 16th century, when the island was under Genoese rule. In 1850, Corsica boasted some 49,400 acres (20,000 hectares) of vines, which provided three-quarters of its population with a living. Less than fifty years later, *phylloxera* devastated the vineyards, and, like the chestnut forests, they continued to decline after World War I. Rural exodus was almost the last straw, but in the 1960s many islanders who had emigrated to Algeria returned to Corsica, and began to plant new vineyards. Unfortunately, they based their choice of grapes on yield. A decade later, however, a new generation of winegrowers decided to make the quality of the wine their prime concern, and instead opted for native varieties and improved techniques.

At the moment, Corsica boasts something in the region of 20,000 acres (8100 hectares) of vines, 5435 acres (2200 hectares) of which have been classified as *Appellation d'Origine Contrôlée*. Sugar and water may not be added. Red wines account for 50 percent, whites 10 percent, and rosés 10 percent of the production.

The island's geography is as important for winegrowing as its climate and soils are. The vine parcels on this "mountain in the sea" benefit from the protection of the slopes; during the day, the Mediterranean obligingly absorbs most of the sun's heat, and radiates it back at night. The sirocco, which blows throughout the year, especially in the Patrimonio region, tempers the summer heat. Geologically, the island is a mosaic of slate, gneiss, sandy marl, clay, chalk and granite, which also make up most of the vineyard soils. Some 20 varieties are grown, including Cinsault, Ugni Blanc, Syrah, Carignan, Grenache, Merlot, and Alicante, but the three main types stand supreme, since they are of Italian origin:

The white Vermentino, also known as Malvoisie on Corsica, is known in Provence as Rolle. Often with a high alcohol content, it has a floral bouquet, and gives an impression of fullness, combined with almonds and apples, on the palate. Its best wines come from the northern part of the island.

The red Nielluccio is identical to Sangiovese, the well-known Chianti variety. Grown mainly in Patrimonio and on the eastern part of Corsica, it produces a deep red, full-bodied wine with hints of licorice and spices.

The red Sciacarello is the main variety in Ajaccio, where it grows on granite, and produces light red wines with a fragrance of the maquis, and a slightly peppery flavor. It is usually assembled with other varieties to add body.

Sciacarello feels most at home in the area around Ajaccio. Somewhat brittle at first, the carefully vinified wines develop a fascinating bouquet after a few years, and it is well worth leaving them to mature.

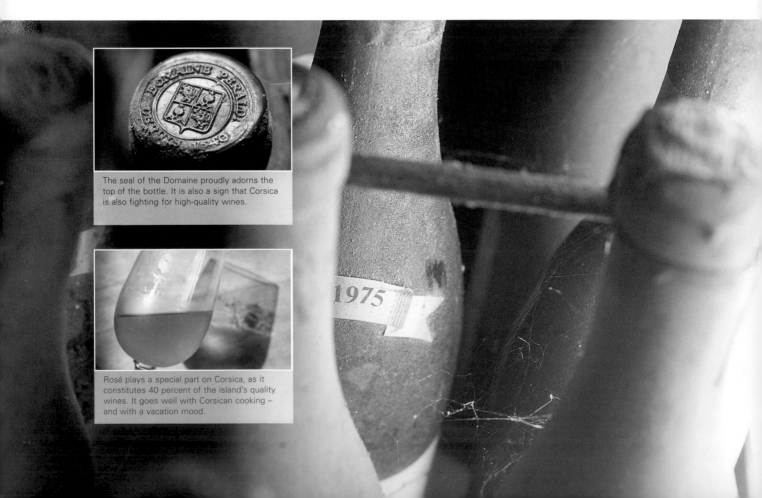

The seal of the Domaine proudly adorns the top of the bottle. It is also a sign that Corsica is also fighting for high-quality wines.

Rosé plays a special part on Corsica, as it constitutes 40 percent of the island's quality wines. It goes well with Corsican cooking – and with a vacation mood.

1975

The estates of the new generation of winegrowers are usually miles from the island's main roads, in the heart of wild, beautiful countryside – like the ascending Domaine Leccia, shown here.

The new wine regions

Patrimonio
The oldest *appellation*, awarded in 1968. Situated at the north of the wine island, on rare argillaceous soil. The estates are mainly small ones, and produce highly individual wines. The red wines, which are based on Nielluccio, are meaty, with plenty of tannin, and age well. The rosés are edgy. The whites, made from Vermentino, are fruity and enduring, thanks to the chalky soil.

Ajaccio
The second *cru* after Patrimonio; was awarded the *Appellation* in 1984. It is a testimony to the native Sciacarello grape, which thrives on the granite soil, and which, from the year 2000, must make up at least 60 percent of the production. The rosé often contains a large proportion of Vermentino, which gives it lots of body.

Vin de Corse
This is the most comprehensive *Appellation*. It applies for all of the classified locations on the island. However, the accessible, easily "quaffable" wines come mainly from the eastern plain. Nielluccio and Sciacarello are often used for reds and rosés, and the white calls for 75 percent Vermentino.

Vin de Corse Calvi
Seneca is known to have praised these wines, which now are no longer grown at Calvi, but in the northwestern region of Balagne, the Corsican equivalent of Tuscany.

Vin de Corse Coteaux du Cap Corse
Just 75 acres (30 hectares) are left of what was once an important wine region in the 19th century, with vineyards covering 5683 acres (2300 hectares). The main variety pressed here is good, round Vermentino.

Vin de Corse Figari
This Villages *Appellation* covers the southern tip of Corsica, one of the island's oldest winegrowing regions, where the granite soils produce strong, rustic wines.

Vin de Corse Porto-Vecchio
Founded in 383 BC, the mountainous hinterland of the former Portus Syracusanus provides well-aging reds, grainy whites and pleasant rosés.

Vin de Corse Sartène
The red wines that come from around the southern capital often possess the aroma of red berries and a robust structure; the whites tend to be fine and aromatic.

Muscat du Cap Corse
The Vin Doux Naturel, which has been famous since the 16th century, finally received the *Appellation* in 1993. It is based on Muscat à petit grain, which often has a citrus fragrance, and is drunk chilled as an apéritif or as an accompaniment to desserts.

Above: Putting wine in new oak barrels to age is still something of the exception on Corsica (and the company of *putti* certainly is).

Clementines

The clementine is the only Corsican fruit to be awarded an *Appellation*, and it has long since replaced the citron as the island's symbol. The evergreen clementine trees, which grow to between 10 and 16 feet (3 to 5 meters) in height, cover a good 4940 acres (2000 hectares) of a narrow strip of land, just 6¼ miles (10 kilometers) wide and 50 miles (80 kilometers) long, between the coast and the mountains, and reaching from Bastia to Solenzara. Visitors to this part of the Haute-Corse between November and February will be greeted by the sight of countless tiny,

orange-colored fruit hanging from the trees. The packaging and marketing of the fruit is subject to very strict quality controls. A particular attraction of the Corsican clementine, which is now being copied by fruit farmers in other countries, is the practice of leaving a pair of leaves attached to every single fruit. Not only do they provide a delightful contrast to the jewel-like color of the fruit, but they are also an indisputable guarantee of freshness, since the leaves shrivel and fall off only a few days after the fruit is picked. The rules of *Appellation* insist on the presence of these leaves, and fruit farmers have to work hard to meet this requirement. It means that the fruit has to be picked by hand; if it were to be shaken from the tree mechanically, it is unlikely that the leaves

Clémentines confites
Preserved clementines

| 2¼ lb/1 kg small, slightly tart clementines |
| 5 cups/1 kg sugar |

Remove the stalk area from the clementines and halve the fruit. Do not peel it. Cook with a little sugar, in a pot over a low heat. As soon as the clementines become soft, add some more sugar until it has all been absorbed. Then leave to cool.

Clementines confites is made with slightly sour fruit that is picked in November and December.

The clementines are cut from the branch with scissors, which is why the pickers wear a glove on the hand that holds the fruit.

The clementine harvest is a highly labor-intensive process that calls for a large number of seasonal workers over four winter months.

would still be attached when it fell. It also has a further important advantage for the consumer: Corsican clementines are dispatched as soon as they are picked, since they do not ripen in storage. This means that any parts of the fruit that do not get the sun remain green, even though the fruit is beautifully ripe. The annual yield amounts to 27,500 tons (25,000 tonnes), most of which is sold in France.

Citrus fruit has been cultivated on Corsica since Roman times, but clementines are still comparatively new. The majority of orchards were planted between 30 and 40 years ago. The clementine is a cross between a tangerine and a Seville orange. It was first created in 1902, in an orchard belonging to an orphanage near Oran in Algeria that was run by a French missionary, Father Clement Dozier. Corsican clementines, which grow to between 2 and 2½ inches (5 to 6 cm), are usually easy to peel and segment. One of the main reasons for their popularity is the fact that they are virtually seedless (no more than two). They are high in vitamin C, sweeter than tangerines, and extremely juicy. Their wonderful fragrance, due to essential oils, is another attraction. They are usually eaten fresh, but on Corsica they are also made into aromatic liqueurs and fruit wines, candied, and preserved in syrup.

Corsicans love to serve preserves with their cheese, such as the fig preserve shown above (front), and green tomato preserve (top).

Glossary

Affinage Cheese: the ripening process by which the cheese reaches optimum condition and is ready to eat. Wine: Maturation in the bottle.

Affineur Cheese dealer who purchases young cheeses and matures them to perfect condition in his own cellars.

Aïoli A mayonnaise made from garlic, sometimes with the addition of egg yolk. Eaten with fish soups, cold meats, vegetables or first courses.

Amuse-bouche An appetizer to "entertain the palate," to accompany an aperitive or before the first course. More often (and more substantial) *amuse-gueule.*

Anatto Reddish golden natural food coloring bixin (E160b) obtained from the anatto tree (*Bixa orellana*), a native of the Amazon region.

Andoulllette Sausage made of organ meat.

Aperitive A small drink enjoyed before a meal, to awaken the appetite. Also, a category of alcoholic drink.

Appellation d'Origine Contrôlée, A.O.C. The highest category of French wine. There is official control of the declaration of origin.

Assemblage The blending of different grape varieties or grapes grown in different locations.

Bain-marie Double boiler. A small bowl or saucepan held in place inside a larger pot (or a special double-skinned pot); the outer pot contains boiling water. The ingredients to be cooked are placed in the inner one. Enables gentle cooking without the risk of burning underneath.

Bavarois Cold dessert consisting of fruit purée set with gelatin, or crème anglaise.

Blanch To place an ingredient (usually vegetables) briefly in boiling water to pre-cook it and destroy micro-organisms and enzymes. The cooking process is halted by plunging the item in iced water immediately after blanching.

Botrytis cinerea Noble rot; a fungus which draws moisture out of ripe grapes, producing a higher sugar content. It also lends a subtle aroma.

Bouquet garni A small bunch of herbs added to cooking. Always includes thyme and bay, and usually parsley. May also contain rosemary, marjoram, lovage or celery, varying according to recipe and region. Usually but not always tied together.

Bouquet The aroma of a wine once it has had time to develop; the "nose."

Cargolade Catalan barbecue in which snails are the main food grilled.

Charlotte A creamy dessert edged with an outer ring of sponge fingers; made using a straight-sided mold.

Confit French "preserve." Term often used to describe candied fruits. Also (as a noun) potted fish or poultry; often goose or duck, occasionally pork. The portions of meat are usually potted in their own fat.

Coulis A thick sauce of puréed fruit or vegetables.

Court-bouillon A cooking liquid made by boiling onion, carrot, leek and sometimes celery, plus herbs and spices, in water.

Crème anglaise French name meaning "English cream." A thick, sweet sauce made of sugar, egg yolk, cream and vanilla.

Crème fraîche (épaisse) Type of cream with a thick consistency and mildly sharp flavor. Used to enrich and bind sauces and other dishes, sweet or savory.

Crème pâtissière Confectioner's custard; a versatile, creamy filling or sauce made of egg yolk, sugar, flour and milk for use in or on pastries and desserts. Often vanilla flavored.

Crêpes Very thin pancakes served with a wide range of fillings. Originally from Brittany.

Croûtons Crispy cubes of bread.

Cru Good vineyard or winegrowing location ("growth"); Grand Cru has superior status. The adjective cru means "raw;" used of butter and cheese, it means "unpasteurized."

Cuvée Term used of a champagne or wine, where the creation of the finished product has been done by blending wine from different barrels or tanks.

Daube Meat cooked very slowly with vegetables.

Decant To transfer wine out of its bottle into a carafe. Done either to aerate the wine or to separate it from sediment in the bottle.

Deglaze To pour on liquid and stir, so as to loosen and take up juices that have collected on the bottom of a pot or pan during cooking.

Dégustation Tasting, especially of wines, to discover their aroma and character.

Destem To remove the stems of grapes in winemaking.

Disgorgement Procedure in the making of sparkling wine; yeast sediment that has been shaken down into the bottle neck is removed, usually by freezing the sediment.

Eau-de-vie Meaning "water of life;" refers to any spirit made by distillation.

Farce Stuffing. Meat or fish with herbs, spices and sometimes other ingredients which have been minced and mixed together to fill pies, poultry, fish, vegetables, etc. Also used as a spread.

Foie gras Delicacy consisting of the enlarged liver of a goose (*d'oie*) or duck (*de canard*).

Fond Juices or natural gravy remaining after meat or fish have been cooked. Used as a sauce base.

Fricassée In France, usually a meat stew giving each person a small number of fairly large pieces of meat or poultry.

Frost To cover a cake with a sugar coating. Also called "to ice" (especially in UK).

Fumet French "scent." Concentrated cooking liquor (usually derived from fish, seafood or mushrooms) obtained by boiling, reducing and straining. Used as a base for soups and sauces.

Glaze To cover cold savory dishes with gelatin.

Gratin A dish which has been browned on top, usually after sprinkling with cheese or breadcrumbs.

Gribiche Dressing flavored with capers, gherkins, herbs and finely chopped hard-boiled eggs.

Hors d'oeuvre Collective term for first course items, hot or cold.

Julienne Ingredients, usually vegetables, cut into fine strips.

Jus French "juice." Also: meat juices remaining after roasting, from which the fat has been removed.

Langoustine Also known under its Italian name *scampi*. No relation of the lobster.

Lees The sediment forming in wine during the winemaking process. See "racking."

Macerate Term mainly from winemaking or other drink production: to leave alcohol, wine or grape must in contact with fruit or other ingredients to dissolve and infuse.

Malolactic fermentation ("malo") A biological process which reduces acidity and breaks down malic acid into the softer-tasting lactic (milk) acid. Usually occurs as a second fermentation, though sometimes during the main fermentation process. Often steps are taken to prevent or reduce it in the making of white wines, to preserve their fresh character.

Marinate To steep ingredients in a mixture of oil and vinegar, lemon juice, or sometimes wine, with herbs and spices, to tenderize or flavor them.

Mash Mixture of mashed solids and liquid during the beer brewing process.

Mirepoix Mixture of finely diced, browned vegetables (carrots, onions, scallions etc.), herbs and smoked ham, used to enrich the flavor of sauces, soups and other dishes.

Must Pulpy mixture of grapes and juice in winemaking. May also contain skins, which are sometimes allowed to steep in the mixture as fermentation progresses.

Mutage Word meaning "to silence." To add alcohol to fermenting must in order to halt the fermentation process. Used to produce wine apéritifs and Vins Doux Naturels.

Noble rot see Botrytis.

Parfait Semi-frozen or whipped mousse prepared from luxury ingredients such as *foie gras* or lobster.

Persillade A mixture of finely chopped parsley and garlic.

Phylloxera A louse which destroys vines. Word mainly associated with the devastation of vines by this louse during the latter half of the 19th century.

Poach To cook gently (without boiling) in liquid.

Potage Puréed and thickened vegetable soup.

Praliné A candy of caramelized almonds.

Racking To transfer wine from one barrel or tank to another in order to separate it from the lees.

Rancio Wine term. Describes a note that develops in the bouquet and flavor of old brandies and sweet wines; reminiscent of fresh walnuts. Also: type of old sweet wine.

Ras al-hanout Moroccan spice mixture. The exact list of individual spices varies, but includes pepper, all spice, mace, cloves, dill seeds, bay leaves, turmeric, caraway, galangal, rose blossom and many more, ground as needed.

Reduce To boil a liquid strongly so that some of the water in it evaporates, and the remainder becomes thicker and more concentrated, and smaller in quantity.

Sabayon Whipped, creamy wine sauce.

Sauce béchamel Sauce based on a roux mixed with milk and seasoned with nutmeg and salt.

Soufflé Light, baked, egg-based dish which involves stiffly whipping the whites; cooked in a special, deep, china soufflé dish. May be sweet or savory.

Source Spring (of water).

Spike To insert slivers of bacon, truffle or garlic under the skin (beneath the surface) of meat or poultry. A special tool is often used for this.

Tannins Substances contained in wine. They come from the grape skins and stems and act as a natural preservative, giving red wines longevity. They offer protection against vascular diseases.

Terroir Winegrowing term: A defined vineyard location with its own soil characteristics and climate.

Tian Food item from Provence, consisting of baked and browned vegetables or fish (or other). Named after the shallow earthenware baking dish in which the food is cooked.

Tournedos Thick, tender piece of tenderloin steak.

Trou normand, trou gascon A young Calvados or Armagnac served between the courses of a meal, to create an appetite for the coming culinary delight. The word literally means "hole."

Velouté Meaning "velvety." Roux-based soup enriched with egg yolk, butter and cream; similar sauce for meat or fish.

Vin Doux Naturel (VDN) Naturally sweet wine: a special category of southern French sweet and dessert wines. They include Banyuls, Maury, Rasteau, Rivesaltes and various Muscats.

Vin de Pays Literally, "country wine." In France, these wines are subject to precise controls. These relate mainly to origin and yield.

Vinaigrette Cold salad dressing based on vinegar (*vinaigre*) and oil, often flavored with mustard.

Vinification The whole winemaking process.

Vivier Sea water aquarium in restaurants or at the fishmonger, used mainly for lobsters and spiny lobsters (*langoustes*).

Bibliography

Androuet, Pierre: Un fromage pour chaque jour, Paris 1981

ANITTA–Association Nationale Interprofessionnelle Technique du Tabac:
Burley – Du semis à la livraison, Bergerac 1997
Tabac Brun – Du semis à la livraison, Bergerac 1997
Virginie – Du semis à la livraison, Bergerac 1996

Assire, Jérôme: Le Livre du Pain, Paris 1996

Auby, Jean-François: Les Eaux Minérales, Paris 1994

Aurières, Albert / Antonietti, Armand: Le Service du Restaurant des Étages, du Salon de Thé, du Bar, Paris 1974

Bonneton, Christine (Ed.): Champagne Ardenne, Cahors 1987

Bourgeat, Jacques: Les Plaisirs de la Table en France gaulois à nos jours, Paris 1963

Brochier, Jean-Jacques: La Cuisine des Gibiers, Paris 1993

Brunet, Pierre: Histoire et Géographie des Fromages, Caen 1987

Buren, Raymond: Le Jambon, Grenoble 1990

Cantin, Christian: Les Fromages, Paris 1978

Centre d'Études et de Documentation du Sucre – Le Sucre: Richesse agro-alimentaire française, Paris 1992

Collection de l'Université du Vin: Le Vin des Historiens (Suze-la-Rousse), 1990

Courtine, Robert: Le Ventre de Paris – La Vie Parisienne – De la Bastille à l'Étoile des siècles d'appétit, Paris 1985

Cousteaux/Casamayor: Le Guide de l'Amateur de l'Armagnac, Toulouse 1985

Cuisine et Gastronomie de Bretagne (Éditions Quest-France), Rennes n.d.

Davidson, Alan / Knox, Charlotte: Seafood, London 1998

Dominé, André (ed.): Culinaria – Europäische Spezialitäten, Vol II, Cologne 1995

Dominé, André: Die Kunst des Aperitif, Weingarten 1989

Dominé, André: Roussillon und die Côte Vermeille, Badenweiler 1992

Dovaz / Lecouty / Martini / Spurrier: Encyclopédie des Vins de Corse, Paris 1990

Drischel / Poulain / Tuchelut: Histoire et Recettes de l'Alsace Gourmande, Toulouse 1994

Dumont, Cédric: Sprachführer für Gourmets, Französisch – Deutsch, Bern 1992

Encyclopédie des Aliments, Paris 1997

Fuchs, Claude: L'Âme des Winstubs (Éditions du Rhin)

Gay, Lisa: Éloge de l'huître, Paris 1990

Gerbelle, Antoine / Couvreur, Dominique: Vins et Vignobles en France, Paris 1996/1997

Green, Maureen and Timothy: The Good Water Guide, London 1985

Hubatschek, Irmtraud: L'Île des Bergers, Innsbruck 1997

I.N.A.O.: L'atlas des Vins de France, Paris 1989

L'inventaire du patrimoine culinaire de la France: Aquitaine, Paris 1997

L'inventaire du patrimoine culinaire de la France: Bourgogne, Paris 1993

L'inventaire du patrimoine culinaire de la France: Bretagne, Paris 1994

L'inventaire du patrimoine culinaire de la France: Corse, Paris 1996

L'inventaire du patrimoine culinaire de la France: Île-de-France, Paris 1993

L'inventaire du patrimoine culinaire de la France: Languedoc-Roussillon, Paris 1998

L'inventaire du patrimoine culinaire de la France: Midi-Pyrénées, Paris 1996

L'inventaire du patrimoine culinaire de la France: Nord-Pas-de-Calais, Paris 1993

L'inventaire du patrimoine culinaire de la France: Pays-de-la-Loire, Paris 1992

L'inventaire du patrimoine culinaire de la France: Provence-Alpes-Côte d'Azur, Paris 1995

L'inventaire du patrimoine culinaire de la France: Rhônes-Alpes, Paris 1995

Johnson, Hugh: Der neue Weinaltas, Bern 1994

Joly, Nicolas: Le vin – du ciel à la terre, Paris 1997

Koffmann, Pierre: Memories of Gascony, London 1993

Larousse des Vins, Paris 1995

Larousse gastronomique, Paris 1997

Le Divellec, Jacques: Les Poissons, Paris 1990

Maestracci, Marie-Louise and Fabienne: Corses Gourmandes, 1997

Malaval, Catherine / Oberlé, Roland: L'Histoire des Pâtes d'Alsace, Strasbourg n.d.

Meiller, Daniel / Vannier, Paul: Limousines – L'aventure de la race bovine limousine, n.p., n.d. (La Manufacture)

Meurville, Elisabeth de / Creignou, Michel: La France Gourmande, Paris 1997

Meurville, Elisabeth de / Girard, Sylvie: L'Atlas de la France Gourmande, Paris 1990

Morand, Simone: Bretagne, Châteaulin 1996

Musset, Danielle: Lavandes et plantes aromatiques, Marseilles 1989

Olivier, Jean-François: Huiles et matières grasses, Paris 1992

Pebeyre, Pierre-Jean and Jacques: Le Grand Livre de la Truffe, Paris 1987

Pitiot, Sylvain / Servant, Jean-Charles: Les Vins de Bourgogne, Paris 1997

Poussier, Jean-Luc: Bretagne, Paris 1995

Quand les Bretons passent à Table (Éditions Apogée), Rennes 1994

Renaud, Guy: Histories de moutarde, cassis et pain d'épice, Dijon 1987

Rio, Bernard / Buytaert, Jean-Luc: Terroirs de Bretagne, Rennes 1996

Robinson, Jancis: The Oxford Companion to Wine, Oxford 1994

Robinson, Jancis: Vines, Grapes and Wines, London 1986

Sharman, Fay / Chadwick, Brian: The A–Z Gastronomique, London 1990

Terrasson, Laurence: Atlas des desserts de France, Paris 1995

Traité de l'alimentation et du corps (Flammarion), Paris 1994

Willan, Anne: French Regional Cooking, London 1989

Periodicals:
Bourgogne aujourd'hui
Cuisine et Vins de France
Essen & Trinken
Der Feinschmecker
Gault-Millau
Revue du Vin de France
Saveurs

Picture Credits

Acknowledgements

Paris & Ile-de-France
Semmaris, Rungis
Compagnie des Courtiers Jurés, Piqueurs de Vins de Paris
Boulangerie Jean-Luc Poujauran, 7. Arrondissement
Rémie Romieu, Brûlerie des Ternes, 16. Arrondissement
Spécialités yiddish, Sacha and Florence Finkelsztajn, 4. Arrondissement
Pâtisserie Dalloyau, Pascal Niaü and Jean-Luc Matyjasik, 8. Arrondissement
Brasserie Mollard, Joël Renty, 8. Arrondissement
Brasserie La Coupole, Mme Nadine Gros, 14. Arrondissement
Hôtel Ritz and its staff, 1. Arrondissement
Historical recipes, Hôtel du Louvre, Jean Michel Mougard, 1. Arrondissement
Traiteur Potel et Chabot, Jean-Pierre Biffi, Chef des cuisines, 16. Arrondissement
Pneu Michelin, M. Alain Arnaud, 75341 Paris
Jacques Valet de Reganhac, École Hôtelière Ferrandi, Paris, 6. Arrondissement
Les Maîtres d'Hôtel de France, Clichy
Cooking utensils: Ets Michel Lejeune, Asnières
Fromagerie Roland Barthélémy, 7. Arrondissement
Fil o'Fromage, Sylvie and Chérif Boubrit

Champagne, Lorraine & Alsace
Comité Interprofessionnel du Vin de Champagne, Epernay
CIVC, Jacques Lechat, Brussels
Champagne Moët et Chandon, Epernay
Hôtel Ritz, Paris, 1. Arrondissement
Biscuiterie Rémoise, Charles de Fougeroux, Rheims
Clotilde Frenneaux, Crepac, Chalons-sur-Marne
Pig's trotters: Le Soleil d'Or, Yvan de Singly, Sainte-Menehould
Le Saint-Hubert, Haybes
Charcuterie Roffidal, Haybes
Game recipes: Restaurant Les Echevins, Pascal Oudea, Mouzon
Confitures Dutriez, André Dutriez, Bar-le-Duc
Philippe Thomé, Charleville-Mézières
Restaurant La Marmite, Gérard Silvestre, Rouvray
Comité Régional de Tourisme, Michèle Wagner, Nancy
Pâtisserie Palet d'Or, André Cordel, Bar-le-Duc
Baba au rhum: Pâtisserie Begrem, Perpignan
Biscuits Saint-Michel Grellier, St-Michel
Boulangerie Daniel Helmstetter, Colmar
Choucroute: Restaurant Chez Philippe, Philippe Schadt, Blaesheim
Brasserie Schutzenberger, Rina Muller-Walter, Schiltigheim, Strasbourg
Association de Gestion et de Promotion de la Route de Bière d'Alsace, Strasbourg
Monique Dognin, ABDOCOM
Foie gras: Charcuterie La Ferme, Bernard Voinot, Colmar
Winstub: Chez Yvonne S'Burjestuwel, Yvonne Haller, Strasbourg
Munster: Fromagerie Jacques Haxaire, Lapoutroie
Syndicat Interprofessionnel du Fromage Munster-Géromé
Comité Interprofessionnel des Vins d'Alsace, Pierre Bouard, Colmar
Distillerie Jean-Paul Metté, M. Traber, Ribeauvillé
Fédération Nationale des Distillateurs d'Eaux-de-Vie, Paris

Nord – Pas de Calais, Picardy, Normandy & Brittany
Brasserie La Coupole, Paris, 14. Arrondissement
Association des producteurs d'Agneaux de pré-salés de la baie du Mont-St-Michel, St-Senier-sous-Avranches
Crié de Boulogne, Chambre de Commerce et d'Industrie, M. Wyts, Boulogne
Fournier et Fils fish smokers, Christophe and Stéphane Fournier, Calais
Comité d'Expansion Agro-Alimentaire de Normandie, Caen
Pascal Copin, REC Communication, Cesson Sévigné
Restaurant Le Chalut, Jean-Philippe Foucat, St-Malo
Restaurant Tiré-Guérin, Roger Tirel, La Gouesnière
Le Germinal, David Etcheverry, Cesson Sévigné
Moulin de la Charbonnière, M. R. Schmitt, St-Grégoire
Lecoq Gadby, Véronique Bregeon, Rennes
Auberge Grand Maison, J. Guillo, Mûr de Bretagne
Jean-Bernard Bourdier, St. Coulomb
Marc Brisset, Cherbourg
Genièvre: Distillerie Persyn, M. Hugues Persyn, Houlle
Louis Peugniez, Les Amis de la Bière, Aire-sur-la-Lys
Pierrot Coucke, Le Bistrot de Pierrot, Lille
Jean-Paul Belot, Fontaine-Notre-Dame
Office de Tourisme de Lille
Le Succès Berckois, Micheline Matifas, Berck-Plage
Confiserie Afchain, Cambrai
Fromagerie Leduc-Frouhin, Sommeron
Syndicat Normand des Fabricants de Camembert, Caen
Sopexa, Paris
Comité Départemental du Tourisme du Calvados, Armelle Le Goff, Chantal Ollivier, Caen
Andouillerie Artisanale Bernard Boscher, St-Denis-Le-Gast
Lobster and tripe: Restaurant La Bourride, Michel Bruneau, Caen
Cidrerie Château d'Hauteville, Eric Bordelet, Charchigné
Bureau National Interprofessionnel du Calvados, Michèle Frêné, Caen
Comité Départemental du Tourisme du Finistère, J. L. Jourdain
Conseil Régional de Tourisme de Bretagne, Chantal Fournier
Apple puddings: Restaurant La Bourride, Michel Bruneau, Caen
Galettes and crêpes: Crêperie Ti Nevez, St-Malo

Pays de Loire & Central France
Jean-Roland Barret, C.D.D.M., Angers
Champignonnière du Saut aux Loups, Jannick Neveux, Montsoreau
Fish dishes: Restaurant Villa Mon Rêve, Gérald Ryngel, Basse-Goulaine
Charcuterie Hardouin, André and Jacques Hardouin, Vouvray
Centre d'Information de Viande, Paris
Château de la Preuille, Philippe Dumortier, St-Hilaire de Loulay
Domaine L'Echansonne, Gaston Huet and Noël Pinguet, Vouvray
Château de la Roche aux Moines, Nicolas Joly, Savennières
Vinaigres Martin-Pouret, Jean-François Martin, Fleury-Orléans
Pralines: Mazet de Montargis, B. Digeon, Montargis
Confiserie Edé, Thierry Edé, Nougatines, Nevers
Crottin: Fromagerie Dubois, Gilles Dubois, Chavignol

Burgundy & Franche-Comté
Abbaye de Citeaux and its monks
Anis de Flavigny, Cathérine Troubat, Flavigny-sur-Ozerain
Jean-Baptiste Joannet, Liquoriste, Arcenat
Gabriel Boudier, Dijon
Traditional Burgundian recipes: Auberge la Beursaudière, Gérald Carpentier, Nitry
Paul Fénéon, Charolais-Züchter, St-Julien-de-Civry
Jacques Despierres, Chevillard, St-Christophe-en-Brionnais
Sopexa, Paris

Moutarde Edmond Fallot, Beaune
Huilerie Artisanale Leblanc, Famille Leblanc, Iguérande
Hostellerie de l'Ecusson, Jean-Pierre Senelet, Beaune
Comité Interprofessionnel des Vins de Bourgogne, Beaune und Chablis
Château de Monthélie, Eric de Suremain, Monthélie
Distillerie Joseph Cartron, Nuits-St-Georges
Jean-Claude Gros, Destillateur, Vosne-Romanée
Comité de Promotion des Produits Régionaux Franche-Comté, Besançon
Boulangerie Le Belflore, Dominique Fiorone, Belfort
Charcuterie Salaisons Pierre Faivre, Grand Combe Châteleu
Jambon persillé: Hostellerie de l'Ecusson, Beaune
Comté: Fromagerie Rieme, Jean-François Rieme, Pont de la Roche
Groupement Interprofessionnel Gruyère de Comté
Distillerie Pierre Guy, François Guy, Pontarlier
Domaine Hubert Clavelin, Voiteur
Institut des Vins du Jura, Nicolas Visier, Château Pécaud, Arbois

Lyons & Rhône-Alpes
Bistro dishes: Bistrot de Lyon, Jean-Paul Lacombe, Guy Gâteau, Frédéric Gros, Lyons
Charcuterie Reynon, Georges and Michel Reynon, Lyons
Chocolatiers Maurice and Jean-Jacques Bernachon, Lyons
Mousse au chocolat: Restaurant La Littorine, Jean-Marie Patroueix, Banyuls
Coulis art: Restaurant Claude Lutz, Jean-Philippe Monnot, Méximieux
Domaine du Moulin Blanc, Alain and Danièle Germain, Charnay en Beaujolais
Union Interprofessionnelle des Vins du Beaujolais, Michel Deflache, Villefranche-sur-Saône
Coopérative agricole de producteurs de poisson des Dombes, Meximieux
Comité Interprofessionnel des Volailles de Bresse, Louhans
Robert Maugard, La Ferme du Canardier, Anneville-Ambourville
Volaillerie Saint-Antoine, Familie Colls, Porpignan
Houdan Distribution, Houdan
Poultry dishes: Restaurant Claude Lutz, Claude Lutz, Chalan Chabane, Meximieux
Maison Alpes Dauphiné Isère, Claude Lauzière, Paris
Comité Départementale de la Drôme, Christophe Bonin
Drôme dishes: Restaurant Le Caveau, Christian and Muriel Cormont, Nyons
Bioobst: Domaine Combier, Laurent Combier, Pont de l'Isère
Sopexa, Anja von Treskow, Dusseldorf
Office National Interprofessionnel des Fruits, des Légumes et de l'Horticulture, Paris
Direction Régionale de l'Agriculture et de la Forêt Rhône-Alpes, Patrick Landrot, Lyons
Direction de l'Agriculture et du Tourisme, Marie-Rose Narce, Charbonnières-les-Bains
Comité Interprofessionnel des Vins d'AOC Côtes du Rhône et de la Vallée du Rhône, Avignon
Comité Interprofessionnel des Vins de Savoie, Chambéry
Chartreuse Diffusion, Mme Moscatoba, Voiron

Poitou-Charentes & Limousin
Jim Budd, London
Philippe Huvé, Chambre d'Agriculture Poitou-Charente, Poitiers
Fish dishes: Restaurant Les Jardins du Lac, Michel Suire and Alain Orillac, Trizay
Beurre d'Echiré, M. Chartier, Echiré
Candied angelica: Angeli Cado, Bernard Albert, Niort
Sopexa, Paris
Pork and rabbit dishes: Charlou Reynal, Brive-la-Gaillarde

Index

References to recipes and more detailed entries are in
semibold.

APPENDIX